How to Design and Evaluate Research in Education

FIFTH EDITION

How to Design and Evaluate Research in Education

FIFTH EDITION

Jack R. Fraenkel
San Francisco State University

Norman E. Wallen
San Francisco State University

Boston   Burr Ridge, IL   Dubuque, IA   Madison, WI   New York   San Francisco   St. Louis
Bangkok   Bogotá   Caracas   Kuala Lumpur   Lisbon   London   Madrid   Mexico City
Milan   Montreal   New Delhi   Santiago   Seoul   Singapore   Sydney   Taipei   Toronto

McGraw-Hill Higher Education

A Division of The **McGraw-Hill** *Companies*

HOW TO DESIGN AND EVALUATE RESEARCH IN EDUCATION
Published by McGraw-Hill, a business unit of The McGraw-Hill Companies, Inc., 1221 Avenue of the Americas, New York, NY, 10020. Copyright © 2003, 2000, 1996, 1993, 1990 by The McGraw-Hill Companies, Inc. All rights reserved. No part of this publication may be reproduced or distributed in any form or by any means, or stored in a database or retrieval system, without the prior written consent of The McGraw-Hill Companies, Inc., including, but not limited to, in any network or other electronic storage or transmission, or broadcast for distance learning. Some ancillaries, including electronic and print components, may not be available to customers outside the United States.

This book is printed on acid-free paper.

4 5 6 7 8 9 0 DOW/DOW 0 9 8 7 6 5 4 3

ISBN 0-07-248560-4

Publisher: *Jane Karpacz*
Sponsoring editor: *Beth Kaufman*
Developmental editor: *Cara Harvey*
Project manager: *Rebecca Nordbrock*
Production supervisor: *Susanne Riedell*
Coordinator of freelance design: *Mary E. Kazak*
Supplement producer: *Betty Hadala*
Media producer: *Lance Gerhart*
Photo research coordinator: *David A. Tietz*
Cover design: *Asylum Studios*
Interior design: *Ellen Pettengell Design*
Typeface: *10/12 Times Roman*
Compositor: *ElectraGraphics, Inc.*
Printer: *R. R. Donnelley & Sons Company*

Library of Congress Control Number: 2002100206

www.mhhe.com

About the Authors

 **Jack R. Fraenkel** is currently Professor of Interdisciplinary Studies in Education and Director of the Research and Development Center, College of Education, San Francisco State University. He received his Ph.D. from Stanford University and has taught courses in research methodology for more than 20 years. In 1997, he received the James A. Michener prize in writing for his writings about the social studies and the social sciences. His current work centers around advising and assisting faculty and students in generating and developing research endeavors.

 **Norman E. Wallen** is Professor Emeritus of Interdisciplinary Studies in Education at San Francisco State University, where he taught from 1966 to 1992. An experienced researcher, he received his Ph.D. from Syracuse University and taught courses in statistics and research design to master's and doctoral students for many years. He is a recent member of the City Council of Flagstaff, Arizona, and the Executive Committee, Grand Canyon Chapter of the Sierra Club.

To Marge and Lina for all their support

List of Features

Controversies in Research

List of Tables and Figures

Tables

Figures

Contents in Brief

Contents

PART 3 Data Analysis 197

PART 4 Quantitative Research Methodologies 265

PART 5 Introduction to Qualitative Research 427

PART 6 Qualitative Research Methodologies 509

PART 7 Research by Practitioners 569

PART **8** Writing Research Proposals and Reports 599

Preface

How to Design and Evaluate Research in Education is directed to students taking their first course in educational research. Because this field continues to grow so rapidly with regard to both the knowledge it contains and the methodologies it employs, the authors of any introductory text are forced to carefully define their goals as a first step in deciding what to include in their book. In our case, we continually kept three main goals in mind. We wanted to produce a text that would:

1. Provide students with the basic information needed to understand the research process, from idea formulation through data analysis and interpretation.
2. Enable students to use this knowledge to design their own research investigation on a topic of personal interest.
3. Permit students to read and understand the literature of educational research.

The first two goals are intended to satisfy the needs of those students who must plan and carry out a research project as part of their course requirements. The third goal is aimed at students whose course requirements include learning how to read and understand the research of others. Many instructors, ourselves included, build all three goals into their courses, since each one seems to reinforce the others. It is hard to read and fully comprehend the research of others if you have not yourself gone through the process of designing and evaluating a research project. Similarly, the more you read and evaluate the research of others, the better equipped you will be to design your own meaningful and creative research. In order to achieve the above goals, we have developed a book with the following characteristics.

CONTENT COVERAGE

Goal one, to provide students with the basic information needed to understand the research process, has resulted in an eight-part book plan. Part One (Chapter One) introduces students to the nature of educational research, briefly overviews each of the seven methodologies discussed later in the text, and presents an overview of the research process as well as criticisms of it.

Part Two (Chapters Two through Nine) discusses the basic concepts and procedures that must be understood before one can engage in research intelligently or critique it meaningfully. These chapters explain variables, definitions, ethics, sampling, instrumentation, validity, reliability, and internal validity. These and other concepts are covered thoroughly, clearly, and relatively simply. Our emphasis throughout is to show students, by means of clear and appropriate examples, how to set up a research study in an educational setting on a question of interest and importance.

Part Three (Chapters Ten through Twelve) describes in some detail the processes involved in collecting and analyzing data.

Parts Four (Chapters Thirteen through Seventeen) describes and illustrates the methodologies most commonly used in quantitative educational research. Many key concepts presented in Part Two are considered again in these chapters in order to illustrate their application to each methodology. Finally, each methodology chapter concludes with a carefully chosen study from the published research literature. Each study is analyzed by the authors with regard to both its strengths and weaknesses. Students are shown how to read and critically analyze a study they might find in the literature.

Part Five (Chapters Eighteen through Twenty) and Six (Chapters Twenty-One through Twenty-Three) discuss qualitative research. Part Five begins the coverage by describing qualitative research, its philosophy, and essential features. It has been expanded to include various types of qualitative research as well as combinations of quantitative and qualitative methods. This is followed by an expanded treatment of both data collection and analysis methods. Part Six presents the qualitative methodologies of ethnography and historical research. As with the quantitative methodology chapters, these are followed by a carefully chosen research report from the published research literature, along with our analysis and critique.

Part Seven (Chapter 23) describes the assumptions characteristics, and steps of action research. Classroom examples of action research questions bring the subject to life, as does the addition of a critique of a published study.

Part Eight (Chapter 24) shows how to prepare a research proposal or report (involving a methodology of choice) that builds on the concepts and examples developed and illustrated in previous chapters.

RESEARCH EXERCISES

In order to achieve our second goal of helping students learn to apply their knowledge of basic processes and methodologies, we organized the first 12 chapters in the same order that students normally follow in developing a research proposal or conducting a research project. Then we concluded each of these chapters with a research exercise that includes a fill-in problem sheet. These exercises allow students to apply their understanding of the major concepts of each chapter. When completed, these accumulated problem sheets will have led students through the step-by-step processes involved in designing their own research projects. Although this step-by-step development requires some revision of their work as they learn more about the research process, the gain in understanding that results as they slowly see their proposal develop "before their eyes" justifies the extra time and effort involved.

Problem Sheet templates are located in the Student Workbook, and electronically on the Interactive Student CD-ROM and the Online Learning Center.

ACTUAL RESEARCH STUDIES

Our third goal, to enable students to read and understand the literature of educational research, has led us to conclude each of the methodology chapters in Parts Four, Five, and Six with an annotated study that illustrates a particular research method. At the end of each study we analyze its strengths and weaknesses and offer suggestions as to how it might be improved. Similarly, at the end of our chapter on writing research proposals and reports, we include a student research proposal that we have critiqued with marginal comments. This annotated proposal has proved an effective means of helping students understand both good and questionable research practices.

STYLE OF PRESENTATION

Because students are typically anxious regarding the content of research courses, we have taken extraordinary care not to overwhelm them with dry, abstract discussions. More than any text to date, our presentations are laced with clarifying examples and with summarizing charts, tables, and diagrams. Our experience in teaching research courses for more than 30 years has convinced us that there is no such thing as having "too many" examples in a basic text.

In addition to the many examples and illustrations that are embedded in our (we hope) informal writing style, we have built the following pedagogical features into the book: (1) a graphic organizer for each chapter, (2) chapter objectives, (3) chapter-opening examples, (4) end-of-chapter summaries, (5) key terms with page references, (6) discussion questions, and (7) an extensive end-of-book glossary.

CHANGES IN THE FIFTH EDITION

All chapters have been revised and updated. The book has been reorganized into eight parts. Parts One through Four (Chapters One through Seventeen), dealing with quantitative research, remain as they were in previous editions, although much of the material in each has been revised and updated. Part Five has been expanded and reorganized into two new parts: Introduction to Qualitative Research (Part Five, consisting of three chapters), and Qualitative Research Methodologies (Part Six, consisting of two chapters). We have added a chapter that discusses recent developments in Action Research (Part Seven). Part Eight continues to deal with the writing of research proposals and reports.

Much new material has been added to many chapters, including a comparison of the philosophic assumptions underlying qualitative and quantitative research, techniques and procedures involved in interview research, mixed-method models, action research, an expanded discussion of power in quantitative research, and the coding of qualitative data.

Several new examples of published research, along with our analysis and annotation of each, have been added. In addition, more than 50 new illustrations and figures have been included.

SPECIAL FEATURES

The fifth edition has retained the popular *More About Research* feature and introduces two new features: *Research Tips* and *Controversies in Research*. *More About Research* continues to take a closer look at important topics in educational research and application to other fields. *Research Tips* provides practical suggestions for doing research. *Controversies in Research* focuses on controversial issues in educational research. A complete listing of these features is located on pages vii and viii.

INTERACTIVE AND APPLIED LEARNING

The existing theme of interactive and applied learning has been highlighted and expanded in the fifth edition. At the start of each chapter, the *Interactive and Applied Learning Tools* feature lists the different activities and resources available for the student while studying the chapter. At the end of each chapter, students are reminded of the student study guide resources available on the Interactive Student CD-ROM and the Online Learning Center.

STUDENT SUPPLEMENTS

Three supplements were developed for students using *How to Design and Evaluate Research in Education*.

The Interactive Student CD-ROM includes a student study guide (with quizzes and key term practice activities), interactive activities, a statistics program, electronic versions of the problem sheets, and numerous other resources valuable as study, practice, and research tools. Of particular interest is the Learn More About feature, which contains a number of short audio excerpts in which the authors discuss various aspects of research that go beyond what they present in the text, often with interesting and amusing examples.

The Online Learning Center at *www.mhhe.com/ fraenkel5e* houses the student study guide, Web links, and other Internet resources.

The Student Workbook contains several practice exercises per chapter, as well as hard copies of the problem sheets.

INSTRUCTOR SUPPLEMENTS

The Instructor's Manual and Test Bank has been revised. A dual platform CD-ROM test bank is available for test construction. New to this edition is an Instructor's Resource CD-ROM that includes the Instructor's Manual and Test Bank, and PowerPoint slides developed for the text. The Instructor's Online Learning Center houses a wealth of resources for the instructor.

ACKNOWLEDGMENTS

Directly and indirectly, many people have contributed to the preparation of this book. We will begin by acknowledging the students in our research classes who, over the years, have taught us much. Also, we wish to thank the reviewers of this edition, whose generous comments have guided the preparation of this text. They include:

Mike Auer, California State University, Northridge

Dennis Badaczewski, Northern Michigan University

Robert Barcikowski, Ohio University

Jeff Beaudry, University of Southern Maine

David N. Boote, University of Central Florida

Stan Carpenter, Texas A&M University

Libby G. Cohen, University of Southern Maine

James Cooper, California State University, Dominiguez Hills

Duane M. Covrig, University of Akron

Gail Delicio, Clemson University

Beverly Edmondson, Buena Vista University

Virgil L. Franklin, Virginia State University

Patricia K. Freitag, George Washington University

Malinda H. Green, University of Central Oklahoma

Patricia Hageman, Rivier College

H. D. Hill, South Carolina State University

John D. Hoge, University of Georgia

Seock-Ho Kim, University of Georgia

Marguerite G. Lodico, College of Saint Rose

Craig A. Mertler, Bowling Green State University

Gregory P. Montalvo, Western Illinois University

Anastasia S. Monroe, Indiana University-Purdue University Indianapolis

Ron Oliver, California State University, Fullerton

Susan Kaye Pepper, University of Mississippi

Darryl A. Pifer, Illinois State University

Doris L. Prater, University of Houston

Dianne Richardson, University of West Alabama

Roger Shouse, Pennsylvania State University

Sandra Stein, Rider University

Charles L. Thomas, George Mason University

Paul Vogt, Indiana University

Charles A. Weiner, Henderson State University

Carol Winkle, Aquinas College

Denise K. Wood, Southeast Tennessee University

Nancy Zeller, Eastern Carolina University

We wish to extend a special word of thanks to our colleague, Enoch Sawin, San Francisco State University, whose unusually thorough reviews of the manuscript in various preliminary forms led to innumerable improvements.

We would also like to thank the editors and staff at McGraw-Hill, Inc., for their efforts in turning the manuscript into the finished book before you: Becky Nordbrock for shepherding the manuscript through editing and production, and Clair James, the copyeditor who called our attention to those places in the manuscript that needed clarification.

Finally, we would like to thank our wives for their unflagging support during the highs and lows that inevitably accompany the preparation of a text of this magnitude.

Jack R. Fraenkel
Norman E. Wallen

A Guided Tour of *How to Design and Evaluate Research in Education*

Welcome to *How to Design and Evaluate Research in Education.*

This comprehensive introduction to research methods was designed to present the basics of educational research in as interesting and understandable a way as possible. To accomplish this, we've created the following features for each chapter.

Opening Illustration

Each chapter opens with an illustrative depiction of a key concept that will be covered in the chapter.

Graphic Organizer

Next, a graphic outline lists the chapter topics to follow.

Interactive and Applied Learning Tools

This special feature lists the practice activities and resources related to the chapter that are available in the student supplements.

Objectives

Chapter objectives prepare the student for the chapter ahead.

Marge Jenkins and Jenna Rodriguez are having coffee following the meeting of their graduate seminar in educational research. Both are puzzled by some of the ideas that came up in today's meeting of the class.

"I'm not sure I agree with Ms. Naser (their instructor)," says Jenna. "She said that there are a lot of advantages to predicting how you think a study will come out."

"Yeah, I know," replies Marge. "But formulating a hypothesis seems like a good idea to me."

"Well, perhaps, but there are some disadvantages, too."

"Really? I can't think of any."

"Well, what about . . . ?"

Actually, both Jenna and Marge are correct. There are *both* advantages and disadvantages to stating a hypothesis in addition to one's research question. Examples of both are one of the things we'll discuss in this chapter.

Chapter-Opening Example

The chapter text begins with a practical example—a dialogue between researchers or a peek into a classroom—related to the content to follow.

More About Research

These boxes take a closer look at important topics in educational research. See a full listing of these boxes, starting on page vii.

More about Research
The Difficulty in Generalizing from a Sample

In 1936, the *Literary Digest*, a popular magazine of the time, selected a sample of voters in the United States and asked the individuals in the sample for whom they would vote in the upcoming presidential election—Alf Landon (Republican) or Franklin Roosevelt (Democrat). The magazine editors obtained a sample of 2,375,000 individuals from lists of automobile and telephone owners in the United States (about 20 percent returned the mailed postcards). On the basis of their findings, the editors predicted that Landon would win by a landslide. In fact, it was Roosevelt who won the landslide victory. What was wrong with the study?

Certainly not the size of the sample. The most frequent explanations have been that the data were collected too far ahead of the election and that *a lot of* people changed their minds, and/or that the sample of voters was heavily biased in favor of the more affluent, and/or that the 20 percent return rate introduced a major bias. What do you think?

A misconception that is common among beginning researchers is illustrated by the following statement: "Although I obtained a random sample only from schools in San Francisco, I am entitled to generalize my findings to the entire state of California because the San Francisco schools (and hence my sample) reflect a wide variety of socioeconomic levels, ethnic groups, and teaching styles." The statement is incorrect because variety is not the same thing as representativeness. In order for the San Francisco schools to be representative of all the schools in California, they must be very similar (ideally, identical) with respect to characteristics such as the ones mentioned. Ask yourself: "Are the San Francisco schools representative of the entire state with regard to ethnic composition of students?" The answer, of course, is that they are not.

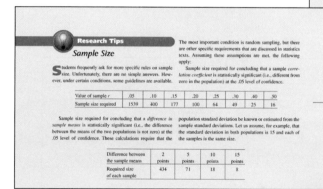

Research Tips
Sample Size

Students frequently ask for more specific rules on sample size. Unfortunately, there are no simple answers. However, under certain conditions, some guidelines are available.

The most important condition is random sampling, but there are other specific requirements that are discussed in statistics texts. Assuming these assumptions are met, the following apply:

Sample size required for concluding that a sample *correlation coefficient* is statistically significant (i.e., different from zero in the population) at the .05 level of confidence.

Value of sample r	.05	.10	.15	.20	.25	.30	.40	.50
Sample size required	1539	400	177	100	64	49	25	16

Sample size required for concluding that *a difference in sample means* is statistically significant (i.e., the difference between the means of the two populations is not zero) at the .05 level of confidence. These calculations require that the population standard deviation be known or estimated from the sample standard deviations. Let us assume, for example, that the standard deviation in both populations is 15 and each of the samples is the same size.

Difference between the sample means	2 points	5 points	10 points	15 points
Required size of each sample	434	71	18	8

Research Tips

These boxes provide practical pointers for doing research. See a full listing of these boxes on page vii.

Controversies in Research
High-Stakes Testing

High-stakes testing" refers to the use of tests (often only a single achievement test) as the primary, or only basis for decisions having major consequences. For students, such consequences include retention in grade and/or the denial of diplomas and awards. For schools, they include public praise or condemnation, sanctions, and financial rewards or punishments. "In state after state, legislatures, governors, and state boards, supported by business leaders, have imposed tougher requirements in mathematics, English, science, and other fields, together with new tests by which the performance of both students and schools is to be judged."*

For years, tests had been used as one indicator of performance, what was new was exclusive reliance on them. "The backlash, touching virtually every state that has instituted high-stakes testing, arises from a spectrum of complaints. A major complaint is that the focus on testing and obsessive test preparation, sometimes beginning in kindergarten, is killing innovative teaching and curricula and driving out good teachers. Other complaints are that (conversely) the standards on which the tests are based are too vague and that students have not been taught the material on which the tests are based. Or that the tests are unfair to poor and minority students; or to those who lack test-taking skills; or that the tests put too much stress on young children. And some argue that they are too long (in Massachusetts they can take up to 13 hours!) or too tough or simply not good enough."†

In response, the American Educational Research Association developed a position statement of "conditions essential to sound implementation of high-stakes educational testing programs."‡ It contained 14 specific points, 4 of the most important being that such decisions about students should not be based on test score alone; tests should be made fairer to all students; tests should match the curriculum; and that the reliability and validity of tests should continually be evaluated.

Two examples of responses to the guidelines were the following:

- "In the face of too much testing with far too severe consequences, the AERA positions, if implemented, would be a step forward relative to current practice."§

- "The statement reflects what is desired for all state tests and assessments. But, just as all students have not yet met the standards, not all state tests and assessments will immediately meet the goals contained in this statement."‖

What do you think? Are the complaints about high-stakes tests warranted?

*P. Schrag (2000). High stakes are for tomatoes. *Atlantic Monthly*, 286:(August): 19.
†Ibid.
‡American Educational Research Association (2000). Position statement of the American Educational Research Association concerning high-stakes testing in pre-12 education. (2000). *Educational Researcher*, 29, (11): 24–35.
§M. Neill (2000). Quoted in Initial responses to AERA's position statement concerning high-stakes testing. *Educational Researcher*, 29:(11): 28.
‖W. Martin (2000). Quoted in Ibid., p. 27.

Controversies in Research

These boxes highlight a controversy in research to provide you with a greater understanding of the issue. See a full listing of these boxes on page viii.

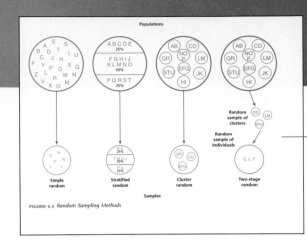

FIGURE 6.3 *Random Sampling Methods*

Figures and Tables

Numerous figures and tables explain or extend concepts presented in the text.

Research Reports

Published research reports are included at the conclusion of methodology chapters. The reports have been annotated to provide excellent and practical examples.

Analysis of the Study

PURPOSE/JUSTIFICATION

The purpose of this study is partly clear at the outset: To study the effects of cooperative learning with Hispanic students in elementary social studies. Under "Purpose," we learn that the students are economically disadvantaged fourth-graders. It is clear in the introduction that the effects studied are social studies achievement (later clarified as unit tests) and self-esteem. The introduction (actually a summary of prior research) reviews several empirical and theoretical justifications for studying cooperative learning and for the position that it improves achievement and self-esteem. We think the case could be made more forcefully and that it is especially weakened by the frequent use of the words "can" and "may," since the question is not whether these effects *can* occur, but whether they *do*. The major justification for this study is that there appears to have been few studies focused on elementary social studies and none focused on the effects relative to gender with fourth-grade, low-income Hispanic students. While this kind of justification is common—that is, using a group that hasn't been studied yet—it is nevertheless weak. Why is it important to study this method and these outcomes with this group?

Probably little justification is needed for studying achievement since this is presumably what schools are primarily about. Self-esteem is more controversial, being viewed by some as a fuzzy-minded frill. Citations in the introduction provide a beginning justification for looking at gender and ethnicity in relation to self-esteem that could be connected to the prior arguments that were made for cooperative learning. It may have seemed obvious to the authors why it is important to find out whether cooperative learning improves achievement and self-esteem, and particularly for girls, but their report would be greatly strengthened by spelling it out. The assertion in the abstract that "there is a close affinity between the goals of citizenship education and social skills promoted by cooperative learning" is not obvious and requires explanation. There appear to be no ethical issues involving confidentiality, risk, or deception.

DEFINITIONS

Specific definitions, as such, are not provided; we believe they should be. Cooperative learning is "defined" by descriptions of what occurred during the study

("Brown Book Training," Jigsaw II, Group Investigation) that are not likely to be familiar to the general readership of the *Journal of Educational Research*. Further description provides a pretty good idea of what occurred and is consistent with most definitions of cooperative learning. Description of the traditional classrooms serves to clarify further the differences between the two methods.

Social studies achievement is operationally defined (by implication) as the score on criterion-referenced unit tests based on two specified units on Texas history published by Scott, Foresman ("Settling Our State" and "A Changing Texas"). The reader is provided with little help in assessing what is considered achievement in this context. Self-esteem is also defined operationally as a score on the Coopersmith Self-Esteem Inventory. Once again, a reader unfamiliar with this scale is given little help in defining self-esteem. Inclusion of the definition that accompanies the manual for this scale would be helpful.

PRIOR RESEARCH

As mentioned under "Purpose," the review of general literature on cooperative learning appears to be adequate, and a justification for studying cooperative learning as a means of enhancing the self-esteem of Hispanic girls can be inferred. We object to the description of higher self-esteem reported by Hispanic males as "interesting" without discussion of its meaning or importance.

HYPOTHESES

Although not stated—and we think they should be—two directional hypotheses seem clearly implied in the two questions that are stated. They are:

* When compared to traditional instruction, cooperative learning will result in greater gains in achievement and self-esteem.
* The gains under cooperative learning, as compared to traditional instruction, will be greater for girls than for boys.

SAMPLE

As is common (unfortunately), a convenience sample was used. Description of students is limited to gender breakdown and income level (free and reduced-cost lunches). It is unclear whether income applies to all stu-

---

Each research report is critiqued by the authors, with both its strengths and weaknesses discussed.

Chapter Review

The chapter ends with a listing of the review resources available for the student in the student study guide located on the Online Learning Center and on the Interactive Student CD-ROM.

Main Points

Bulleted main points highlight the key concepts of the chapter.

Go back to the **Interactive and Applied Learning Tools** feature at the beginning of the chapter for a listing of interactive and applied activities. Go to the **Online Learning Center** at www.mhhe.com/fraenkel5e or your **Interactive Student CD-ROM** to take practice quizzes and receive immediate feedback, practice with key terms, review chapter content and main ideas, and find annotated Web links.

THE VALUE OF A LITERATURE REVIEW

Main Points

* A literature review helps researchers learn what others have written about a topic. It also lets researchers see what have been the results of other, related studies.
* A detailed literature review is often required of master's and doctoral students when they design a thesis.

TYPE OF SOURCES FOR A LITERATURE REVIEW

* Researchers need to be familiar with three basic types of sources (general references, primary sources, and secondary sources) in doing a literature review.
* General references are sources a researcher consults to locate other sources.
* Primary sources are publications in which researchers report the results of their investigations. Most primary source material is located in journal articles.
* Secondary sources refer to publications in which authors describe the work of others.
* *Education Index* and CIJE are two of the most frequently used general references in educational research.
* Search terms, or "descriptors" are key words researchers use to help locate relevant primary sources.

STEPS INVOLVED IN A LITERATURE SEARCH

* The essential steps involved in a review of the literature include: (1) defining the research problem as precisely as possible; (2) perusing the secondary sources; (3) selecting and perusing an appropriate general reference; (4) formulating search terms; (5) searching the general references for relevant primary sources; (6) obtaining and reading the primary sources, and noting and summarizing key points in the sources.

WAYS TO DO A LITERATURE SEARCH

* Today, there are two main ways to do a literature search—manually, using the traditional paper approach, and electronically, by means of a computer.
* There are five essential points (problem, hypotheses, procedures, findings, and conclusions) that researchers should record when taking notes on a study.

DOING A COMPUTER SEARCH

* Computer searches of the literature have a number of advantages—they are fast, are fairly inexpensive, provide printouts, and enable researchers to search using more than one descriptor at a time.
* The steps in a computer search are similar to those in a manual search, except much of the work is done by a computer.
* Researching the World Wide Web (WWW) should be considered, in addition to ERIC and PsycINFO, in doing a literature search.

Key Terms

For Discussion

1. Why might it be unwise for a researcher not to do a review of the literature before planning a study?
2. Many published research articles include only a few references to related studies. How would you explain this? Is this justified?
3. Which do you think are more important to emphasize in a literature review—the opinions of experts in the field or related studies? Why?
4. Which of the secondary sources described in this chapter would be most appropriate to consult on the following topics?
   a. Recent research on social studies education.
   b. A brief overview on new developments in science teaching.
   c. An extensive review of recent and past research on a particular research question.
   d. A survey of recent research on homogeneous grouping.
5. One rarely finds books referred to in literature reviews. Why do you suppose this is so? Is it a good idea to refer to books?

Key Terms

Key terms are listed with page references.

For Discussion

End-of-chapter questions are designed for in-class discussion.

Research Exercise Three: **The Research Hypothesis**

Try to formulate one testable hypothesis involving a relationship. It should be related to the research question you developed in Research Exercise Two. Using Problem Sheet 3, state the hypothesis in a sentence or two. Check to see if it suggests a relationship between at least two variables. If it does not, revise it so that it does. Now name these variables, and then indicate which is the independent variable and which is the dependent variable. Last, list as many extraneous variables as you can think of that might affect the results of your study.

An electronic version of this Problem Sheet that you can fill in and print, save, or e-mail is available on the Online Learning Center at www.mhhe.com/fraenkel5e and on your Interactive Student CD-ROM.

A full-sized version of this Problem Sheet that you can fill in or photocopy is in your Student Workbook.

PROBLEM SHEET 3

The Research Hypothesis

1. My research question is: _____
2. I intend to use a hypothesis to investigate this question.   Yes _____   No _____
3. If no, my reasons are as follows: _____
   _____
   _____
4. If yes, my hypothesis is: _____
   _____
5. This hypothesis suggests a relationship between at least two variables.
   They are _____ and _____
6. More specifically, the variables in my study are:
   a. Dependent _____
   b. Independent _____
7. The dependent variable is (check one) categorical _____ quantitative _____
   The independent variable is (check one) categorical _____ quantitative _____
8. Possible extraneous variables that might affect my results include:
   a. _____
   b. _____
   c. _____
   d. _____
   e. _____

Research Exercises

The research exercise explains how to fill in the Problem Sheet that follows.

Problem Sheets

Individually, the problem sheets allow the student to apply their understanding of the major concepts of each chapter. As a whole, they walk the student through each step of the research process.

Introduction to Research

Research takes many forms. In Part One, we introduce you to the subject of educational research and explain why knowledge of the various types of research is of value to educators. Because research is but one way to obtain knowledge, we also describe several other ways and compare the strengths and weaknesses of each. We give a brief overview of the research methodologies that are used in education to set the stage for a more extensive discussion of them in later chapters. Lastly, we discuss criticisms of the research process.

The Nature of Research

CHAPTER 1

The Nature of Research

Some Examples of Educational Concerns

A Brief Overview of the Research Process

Why Research Is of Value

Critical Analysis of Research

Ways of Knowing

Sensory Experience
Agreement with Others
Expert Opinion
Logic
The Scientific Method

General Research Types

Quantitative Versus Qualitative Research
Meta-analysis

Types of Research

Experimental Research
Correlational Research
Causal-Comparative
Research
Survey Research
Ethnographic Research
Historical Research
Action Research
All Have Value

Objectives

Studying this chapter should enable you to:

- Explain *what is meant by the term "educational research" and* give two examples *of the kinds of topics educational researchers might investigate.*
- Explain *why a knowledge of scientific research methodology can be of value to educators.*
- Name *and* give an example of *four ways of knowing other than the method used by scientists.*
- Explain *what is meant by the term "scientific method."*
- Give an example of *six different types of research methodologies used by educational researchers.*
- Describe *briefly what is meant by critical research.*
- Describe *the differences among descriptive, associational, and intervention-type studies.*
- Describe *briefly the difference between quantitative and qualitative research.*
- Describe *briefly the basic components involved in the research process.*

Interactive and Applied Learning

After, or while, reading this chapter:

●● Go to the Study Guide on the Online Learning Center at www.mhhe.com/fraenkel5e or Interactive Student CD-ROM to:

- Take a Learning Styles Assessment
- Read the Study Skills Primer
- Read the Internet Primer

● Go to your Interactive Student CD-ROM to:

- Learn More About Why Research Is of Value

●● Go to your Interactive Student CD-ROM or Student Workbook to do the following activities:

- Activity 1.1: Empirical Versus Nonempirical Research
- Activity 1.2: Basic Versus Applied Research
- Activity 1.3: Types of Research
- Activity 1.4: Assumptions

Dr. Hunter? I'm Molly Levine. I called you about getting some advice about the master's degree program in your department."

"Hello, Molly. Pleased to meet you. Come on in. How can I be of help?"

"Well, I'm thinking about enrolling in the master's degree program in marriage and family counseling, but first I want to know what the requirements are."

"I don't blame you. It's always wise to know what you are getting into. To obtain the degree, you'll need to take a number of courses, and there is also an oral exam once you have completed them. You also will have to complete a small-scale study."

"What do you mean?"

"You actually will have to do some research."

"Wow! What does that involve? What do you mean by 'research,' anyway? And how does one 'do' it? What kinds of research are there?"

To find out the answers to Molly's questions, as well as a few others, read this chapter.

Some Examples of Educational Concerns

- A high school principal in San Francisco wants to improve the morale of her faculty.
- The director of the gifted student program in Denver would like to know what happens during a typical week in an English class for advanced placement students.
- An elementary school counselor in Boise wishes he could get more students to "open up" to him about their worries and problems.
- A tenth-grade biology teacher in Atlanta wonders if discussions are more effective than lectures in motivating students to learn biological concepts.
- A physical education teacher in Tulsa wonders if ability in one sport correlates with ability in other sports.
- A seventh-grade student in Philadelphia asks her counselor what she can do to improve her study habits.
- The president of the local PTA in Little Rock, parent of a sixth-grader at Cabrillo School, wonders how he can get more parents involved in school-related activities.

Each of the above examples, although fictional, represents a typical sort of question or concern facing many of us in education today. Together, these examples suggest that teachers, counselors, administrators, parents, and students continually need information to do their jobs. Teachers need to know what kinds of materials, strategies, and activities best help students learn. Counselors need to know what problems hinder or prevent students from learning and how to help them with these problems. Administrators need to know how to provide an environment for happy and productive learning. Parents need to know how to help their children succeed in school. Students need to know how to study to learn as much as they can.

Why Research Is of Value

How can educators, parents, and students obtain the information they need? Many ways of obtaining information, of course, exist. One can consult experts, review books and articles, question or observe colleagues with relevant experience, examine one's own experience in the past, or even rely on intuition. All these approaches suggest possible ways to proceed, but the answers they provide are not always reliable. Experts may be mistaken; source documents may contain no insights of value; colleagues may have no experience in the matter; one's own experience or intuition may be irrelevant or misunderstood.

This is why a knowledge of scientific research methodology can be of value. The scientific method provides us with another way of obtaining information—information that is as accurate and reliable as we can get. Let us compare it, therefore, with some of the other ways of knowing that exist.

Ways of Knowing

SENSORY EXPERIENCE

We see, we hear, we smell, we taste, we touch. Most of us have seen the fireworks on the Fourth of July, heard the whine of a jet airplane's engines overhead, smelled a rose, tasted chocolate ice cream, and felt the wetness of a rainy day. The information we take in from the world through our senses is the most immediate way we have of knowing something. Using sensory experience as a means of obtaining information, the director of the gifted student program mentioned above, for example, might visit an advanced placement English class to see and hear what happens during a week or two of the semester.

Sensory data, to be sure, can be refined. Seeing the temperature on an outdoor thermometer can refine our knowledge of how cold it is; a top-quality stereo system can help us hear Beethoven's Fifth Symphony with greater clarity; smell, taste, touch—all can be enhanced, and usually need to be. Many experiments in sensory perception have revealed that we are not always wise to trust our senses too completely. Our senses can (and often do) deceive us: The gunshot we hear becomes a car backfiring; the water we see in the road ahead is but a mirage; the chicken we thought we tasted turns out to be rabbit.

Sensory knowledge is undependable; it is also incomplete. The data we take in through our senses do not account for all (or even most) of what we seem to feel is the range of human knowing. To obtain reliable knowledge, therefore, we cannot rely on our senses alone, but must check what we think we know with other sources.

AGREEMENT WITH OTHERS

One such source is the opinions of others. Not only can we share our sensations with others, we can also check on the accuracy and authenticity of these sensations: Does this soup taste salty to you? Isn't that John over there? Did you hear someone cry for help? Smells like mustard, doesn't it?

Obviously this is a great advantage. Checking with others on whether they see or hear what we do can help us discard what is untrue and manage our lives more intelligently by focusing on what is true. If, while hiking in the country, I do not hear the sound of an approaching automobile but several of my companions do, I am likely to proceed with caution. All of us frequently discount our own sensations when others report that we are missing something or "seeing" things incorrectly. Using agreement with others as a means of obtaining information, the tenth-grade biology teacher in Atlanta, for example, might check with her colleagues to see if they find discussions more effective than lectures in motivating their students to learn.

The problem with such common knowledge is that it, too, can be wrong. A majority vote of a committee is no guarantee of the truth. My friends might be wrong about the presence of an approaching automobile, or the automobile they hear may be moving away from rather than toward us. Two groups of eyewitnesses to an accident may disagree as to which driver was at fault. Hence, we need to consider some additional ways to obtain reliable knowledge.

EXPERT OPINION

Perhaps there are particular individuals we should consult—experts in their field, people who know a great deal about what we are interested in finding out. We are likely to believe a noted heart specialist, for example, if he says that Uncle Charlie has a bad heart. Surely, a person with a Ph.D. in economics knows more than most of us do about what makes the economy tick. And shouldn't we believe our family dentist if she tells us that back molar has to be pulled? To use expert opinion as a means of obtaining information, perhaps the physical education teacher in Tulsa we mentioned should inquire of a noted authority in the physical education field whether or not ability in one sport correlates with ability in another.

Well, maybe. It depends on the credentials of the experts and the nature of the question about which they are being consulted. Experts, like all of us, can be mistaken. For all their study and training, what experts know is still based primarily on what they have learned from reading and thinking, from listening to and observing others, and from their own experience. No expert, however, has studied or experienced all there is to know in a given field, and thus even an expert can never be totally sure. All any expert can do is give us an opinion based on what he or she knows, and no matter how much this is, it is never all there is to know. Let us consider, then, another way of knowing: logic.

LOGIC

We also know things logically. Our intellect—the capability we have to reason things out—allows us to use sensory data to develop a new kind of knowledge. Consider the famous syllogism:

All human beings are mortal.
Sally is a human being.
Therefore, Sally is mortal.

To assert the first statement (called the major premise), we need only generalize from our experience about the mortality of individuals. We have never experienced anyone who was not mortal, so we state that all human beings are. The second statement (called the minor premise) is based entirely on sensory experience. We come in contact with Sally and classify her as a human being. We don't have to rely on our senses, then, to know that the third statement (called the conclusion) must be true. Logic tells us it is. As long as the first two statements arc true the third statement must be true.

Take the case of the counselor in Philadelphia who is asked to advise her counselee on how to improve her study habits. Using logic, she might present the following argument: Students who take notes on a regular basis in class find that their grades improve; if you will take notes on a regular basis, then your grades should improve as well.

This is not all there is to logical reasoning, of course, but it is enough to give you an idea of another way of knowing. There is a fundamental danger in logical reasoning of which we need to be aware, however: It is only when the major and minor premises of a syllogism are *both* true that the conclusion is guaranteed to be true. If either of the premises is false, the conclusion may or may not be true.*

There is still another way of knowing to consider: the method of science. We turn to it next.

THE SCIENTIFIC METHOD

When many people hear the word "science," they think of things like white lab coats, laboratories, test tubes, or space exploration. Scientists are people who know a lot and the term "science" suggests a tremendous body of knowledge. What we are interested in here, however, is science as a method of knowing. It is the **scientific method** that is important to researchers.

What is this method? Essentially it involves the testing of ideas in the public arena. Almost all of us humans are capable of making connections—of seeing relationships and associations—among the sensory information we experience. Most of us then identify these connections as "facts"—items of knowledge about the world in which we live. We may speculate, for example, that our students may be less attentive in class when we lecture than when we engage them in discussion. A physician

may guess that people who sleep between six to eight hours each night will be less anxious than those who sleep more or less than that amount. A counselor may feel that students read less than they used to because they spend most of their free time watching television. But in each of these cases, we do not really know if what we think is true. What we are dealing with are only guesses or hunches, or as scientists would say, hypotheses.

What we must do now is put each of these guesses or hunches to a rigorous test to see if they hold up under more controlled conditions. To investigate our speculation on attentiveness scientifically, we can observe carefully and systematically how attentive our students are when we lecture and when we hold a class discussion. The physician can count the number of hours individuals sleep, then measure and compare their anxiety levels. The counselor can compare the reading habits of students who watch different amounts of television.

Such investigations, however, do not constitute science unless they are made public. This means that all aspects of the investigation are described in sufficient detail so that the study can be repeated by any who question the results—provided, of course, that those interested possess the necessary competence and resources. Private procedures, speculations, and conclusions are not scientific until they are made public.

There is nothing very mysterious, then, about how scientists work in their quest for reliable knowledge. In reality, many of us proceed this way when we try to reach an intelligent decision about a problem that is bothering us. These procedures can be boiled down to five distinct steps.

- First, there is a problem of some sort—some disturbance in our lives that disrupts the normal or desirable state of affairs. Something is bothering us. For most of us who are not scientists, it may be a tension of some sort, a disruption in our normal routine. Examples would be if our students are not as attentive as we wish or if we have difficulty making friends. To the professional scientist, it may be an unexplained discrepancy in one's field of knowledge, a gap to be closed. Or it could be that we want to understand the practice of human sacrifice in terms of its historical significance.
- Second, steps are taken to define more precisely the problem or the questions to be answered, to become clearer about exactly what the purpose of the study is. For example, we must think through what we mean by student attentiveness and why we consider

---

*In the note-taking example, the major premise (all students who take notes on a regular basis in class improve their grades) is probably *not* true.

it insufficient. The scientist must clarify what is meant by human sacrifice (e.g., how does it differ from murder?).

• Third, we attempt to determine what kinds of information would solve the problem. Generally speaking, there are two possibilities: study what is already known or carry out a piece of research. As you will see, the first is a prerequisite for the second; the second is a major focus of this text. In preparation, we must be familiar with a wide range of possibilities for obtaining information, so as to get first-hand information on the problem. For example, the teacher might consider giving a questionnaire to students or having someone observe during class. The scientist might decide to examine historical accounts or spend time in societies where the practice of human sacrifice exists (or has until recently). Spelling out the details of information gathering is a major aspect of planning a research study.

• Fourth, we must decide, as far as it is possible, how we will organize the information that we obtain. It is not uncommon, in both daily life and research, to discover that we cannot make sense of all the information we possess (sometimes referred to as *information overload*). Anyone attempting to understand another society while living in it has probably experienced this phenomenon. Our scientist will surely encounter this problem, but so will our teacher unless she has figured out how to handle the questionnaire and/or observational information that is obtained.

• Fifth, after the information has been collected and analyzed, it must be interpreted. While this step may seem straightforward at first, this is seldom the case. As you will see, one of the most important parts of research is to avoid kidding ourselves. The teacher may conclude that her students are inattentive because they dislike lectures, but she may be misinterpreting the information. The scientist may conclude that human sacrifice is or was a means of trying to control nature, but this also may be incorrect.

In many studies, there are several possible explanations for a problem or phenomenon. These are called *hypotheses* and may occur at any stage of an investigation. Some researchers state a hypothesis (e.g., "Students are less attentive during lectures than during discussions") right at the beginning of a study. In other cases, hypotheses emerge as a study progresses, sometimes even when the information that has been collected is being analyzed and interpreted. The scientist might find that instances of sacrifice seemed to

be more common after such societies made contact with other cultures, suggesting a hypothesis such as: "Sacrifice is more likely when traditional practices are threatened."

We want to stress two crucial features of scientific research: freedom of thought and public procedures. At every step, it is crucial that the researcher be as open as humanly possible to alternatives—in focusing and clarifying the problem, in collecting and analyzing information, and in interpreting results. Further, the process must be as public as possible. It is not a private game to be played by a group of insiders. The value of scientific research is that it can be *replicated* (i.e., repeated) by anyone interested in doing so.*

The general order of the scientific method, then, is as follows:

Identifying a problem or question
Clarifying the problem
Determining the information needed and how to obtain it
Organizing the information
Interpreting the results

In short, the essence of all research originates in curiosity—a desire to find out how and why things happen, including why people do the things they do, as well as whether or not certain ways of doing things work better than other ways.

A common misperception of science fosters the idea that there are fixed, once-and-for-all answers to particular questions. This contributes to a common, but unfortunate tendency to accept, and rigidly adhere to, oversimplified solutions to very complex problems. While certainty is appealing, it is contradictory to a fundamental premise of science: All conclusions are to be viewed as tentative and subject to change, should new ideas and new evidence warrant such. It is particularly important for educational researchers to keep this in mind, since the demand for final answers from parents, administrators, teachers, and politicians can often be intense. An example of how science changes is shown in the following More About Research box.

So, as you see there are many methods we use to collect information about the world around us. Figure 1.1 illustrates some of these "ways of knowing."

---

*This is not to imply that replicating a study is a simple matter. It may require resources and training—and it may be impossible to repeat any study in exactly the same way it was done originally. The important principle, however, is that *public* evidence (as opposed to private experience) is the criterion for belief.

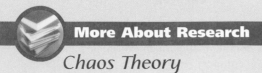

Chaos Theory

The origins of what has come to be known as **chaos theory** are usually placed in the 1970s. Since then, it has come to occupy a prominent place in mathematics and the natural sciences and, to a lesser extent, in the social sciences.

Although the physical sciences have primarily been known for their basic laws or "first principles," it has long been known by scientists that most of these laws only hold precisely under ideal conditions that are not found in the "real" world. Many phenomena, such as cloud formations, waterfall patterns, and even the weather, elude precise prediction. Chaos theorists argue that the natural laws that are so useful in science may, in themselves, be the exception rather than the rule.

A major principle of chaos theory is that, whereas precise prediction of such phenomena as the swing of a pendulum or what the weather will be at a particular time is in most cases impossible, repeated patterns can be discovered and used, even when the content of the phenomena is chaotic. Developments in computer technology, for example, have made it possible to translate an extremely long sequence of "data points," such as the test scores of a large group of individuals, into colored visual pictures of fascinating complexity and beauty. Surprisingly, these pictures show distinct patterns that are often quite similar across different content areas, such as physics, biology, economics, astronomy, and geography. Even more surprising is the finding that certain patterns recur as these pictures are enlarged. The most famous example is the "Mandlebrot Bug," shown in Photographs 1.1 and 1.2. Note that Photograph 1.2 is simply a magnification of a portion of Photograph 1.1. The tiny box in the lower left corner of Photograph 1.1 is magnified to produce the box in the upper left-hand corner of Photograph 1.2. The tiny box within this box is then, in turn, magnified to produce the larger portion of Photograph 1.2, including the reappearance of the "Bug" in the lower right corner. The conclusion is that, even with highly complex data (think of trying to predict the changes that might occur in a cloud formation), predictability exists if patterns can be found across time or when the scale of a phenomenon is increased.

IMPLICATIONS FOR EDUCATIONAL RESEARCH

We hope that this brief introduction has not only stimulated your interest in what has been called, by some, the third revolution in science during the twentieth century (the theory of relativity and the discovery of quantum mechanics being the first two), but that it helps to make sense out of what we view as some implications for educational research. What are these implications?*

If chaos theory is correct, the difficulty in discovering widely generalizable rules or laws in education, let alone the social sciences in general, may not be due to inadequate concepts and theories or to insufficiently precise measurement and methodology, but may simply be an unavoidable fact about the world. Another implication is that whatever "laws" we do discover may be seriously limited in their applicability—across geography, across individual and/or group differences, and across time. If this is so, chaos theory provides support for researchers to concentrate on studying topics at the local level—classroom, school, agency—and for repeated studies over time to see if such laws hold up.

Another implication is that educators should pay more attention to the intensive study of the exceptional or the unusual, rather than treating such instances as trivial, incidental, or "errors." Yet another implication is that researchers should focus on predictability on a larger scale—that is, looking for patterns in individuals or groups over larger units of time. This would suggest a greater emphasis on long-term studies rather than the easier-to-conduct (and cheaper) short-time investigations that are so currently the norm.

Not surprisingly, chaos theory has its critics. In education, the criticism is not of the theory itself, but more with misinterpretations and/or misapplications of it.† Chaos theorists do not say that all is chaos; quite the contrary, they say that we must pay more attention to chaotic phenomena and revise our conceptions of predictability. At the same time, the laws of gravity still hold, as, with less certainty, do many generalizations in education.

*For more extensive implications in the field of psychology, see M. P. Duke (1994). Chaos theory and psychology: Seven propositions. *Genetic, Social and General Psychology Monographs, 120:*267–286.
†See W. Hunter, J. Benson, and D. Garth (1997). Arrows in Time: The misapplication of chaos theory to education. *Journal of Curriculum Studies, 29:*87–100.

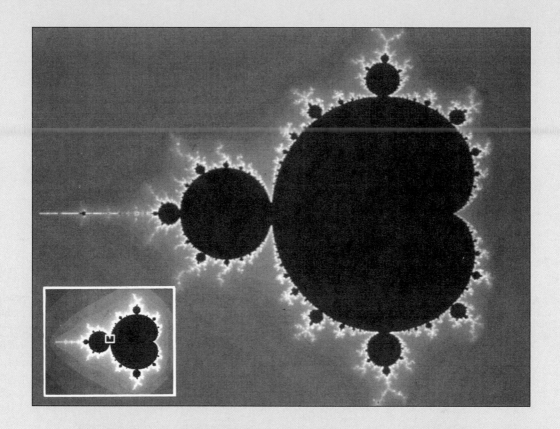

Photograph 1.1 and 1.2 The Mandlebrot bug. Heinz-Otto Peitgen and Peter H. Richter (1986). *The beauty of fractals.* Berlin: Springer-Verlag.

Figure 1.1 *Ways of Knowing*

Types of Research

All of us engage in actions that have some of the characteristics of formal research, although perhaps we do not realize this at the time. We try out new methods of teaching, new materials, new textbooks. We compare what we did this year with what we did last year. Teachers frequently ask students and colleagues their opinions about school and classroom activities. Counselors interview students, faculty, and parents about school activities. Administrators hold regular meetings to gauge how the faculty feels about various issues. School boards query administrators, administrators query teachers, teachers query students and each other.

We observe, we analyze, we question, we hypothesize, we evaluate. But rarely do we do these things systematically. Rarely do we observe under controlled conditions. Rarely are our instruments as accurate and reliable as they might be. Rarely do we use the variety of research techniques and methodologies at our disposal.

The term "research" can mean any sort of "careful, systematic, patient study and investigation in some field of knowledge, undertaken to discover or establish facts and principles."[1] In scientific research, however, the emphasis is on obtaining evidence to support or refute proposed facts or principles. There are many methodologies that fit this definition. If we learn how to use more of these methodologies where they are appropriate and if we can become more scientific in our research efforts, we can obtain more reliable information upon which to base our educational decisions. Let us look, therefore, at some of the research methodologies we might use. We shall return to each of them in greater detail in Parts Four and Five.

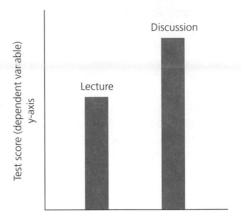

Figure 1.2 *Example of Results of Experimental Research: Effect of Method of Instruction on History Test Scores*[a]

[a]Many of the examples of data presented throughout this text, including that shown in Figure 1.2, are hypothetical. When actual data are shown, the source is indicated.

EXPERIMENTAL RESEARCH

Experimental research is the most conclusive of scientific methods. Because the researcher actually establishes different treatments and then studies their effects, results of this type of research are likely to lead to the most clear-cut interpretations.

Suppose a history teacher is interested in the following question: How can I most effectively teach important concepts (such as democracy or colonialism) to my students? The teacher might compare the effectiveness of two or more methods of instruction (usually called the *independent variable*) in promoting the learning of historical concepts. After systematically assigning students to contrasting forms of history instruction (such as inquiry versus programmed units), the teacher could compare the effects of these contrasting methods by testing students' conceptual knowledge. Student learning in each group could be assessed by an objective test or some other measuring device. The average scores on the test (usually called the *dependent variable*), if they differ, would give some idea of the effectiveness of the various methods. A simple graph could be plotted to show the results, as illustrated in Figure 1.2.

In the simplest sort of experiment, there are two contrasting methods to be compared and an attempt is made to control for all other **(extraneous) variables**—such as student ability level, age, grade level, time, materials, and teacher characteristics—that might affect the outcome under investigation. Methods of such control could include holding the classes during the same or closely related periods of time, using the same materials in both groups, comparing students of the same age and grade level, and so on.

Of course, we want to have as much control as possible over the assignment of individuals to the various treatment groups, to ensure that the groups are similar. But in most schools, systematic assignment of students to treatment groups is difficult, if not impossible, to achieve. Nevertheless, useful comparisons are still possible. You might wish to compare the effect of different teaching methods (lectures versus discussion, for example) on student achievement or attitudes in two or more *intact* history classes in the same school. If a difference exists between the classes in terms of what is being measured, this result can suggest how the two methods compare, even though the exact causes of the difference would be somewhat in doubt. We discuss this type of experimental research in Chapter Thirteen.

Another form of experimental research, **single-subject research,** involves the intensive study of a single individual (or sometimes a single group) over time. These designs are particularly appropriate when individuals with special characteristics are studied by means of direct observation. We discuss this type of research in Chapter Fourteen.

CORRELATIONAL RESEARCH

Another type of research is done to determine relationships among two or more variables, and to explore their implications for cause and effect; this is called **correlational research.** This type of research can help us make more intelligent predictions.

For instance, could a math teacher predict which sorts of individuals are likely to have trouble learning the subject matter of algebra? If we could make fairly accurate predictions in this regard, then perhaps we could suggest some corrective measures for teachers to use to help such individuals so that large numbers of "algebra-haters" are not produced.

How do we do this? First, we need to collect various kinds of information on students that we think are related to their achievement in algebra. Such information might include their performance on a number of tasks logically related to the learning of algebra (such as computational skills, ability to solve word problems, and understanding of math concepts), their verbal abilities, their study habits, aspects of their backgrounds, their early experiences with math courses and math teachers, the number and kinds of math courses they've taken, and anything else that might conceivably point to how those students who do well in math differ from those who do poorly.

We then examine the data to see if any relationships exist between some or all of these characteristics and subsequent success in algebra. Perhaps those who perform better in algebra have better computational skills or higher self-esteem or receive more attention from the teacher. Such information can help us to predict more accurately the likelihood of learning difficulties for certain types of students in algebra courses. It may even suggest some things to try out with students to help them learn better.

In short, correlational research seeks to investigate the extent to which one or more relationships of some type exist. The approach requires no manipulation or intervention on the part of the researcher other than that required to administer the instrument(s) necessary to collect the data desired. In general, this type of research would be undertaken when one wants to look for and describe relationships that may exist among naturally occurring phenomena, without trying in any way to alter these phenomena. We talk more about correlational research in Chapter Fifteen.

CAUSAL-COMPARATIVE RESEARCH

Another type of research is intended to determine the cause for or the consequences of differences between groups of people; this is called **causal-comparative research.** Suppose a teacher wants to determine whether students from single-parent families do more poorly in her course than students from two-parent families. To investigate this question experimentally, the teacher would systematically select two groups of students and then assign each to a single- or two-parent family—which is clearly impossible (not to mention unethical!).

To test this question using a causal-comparative design, the teacher might compare two groups of students who already belong to one or the other type of family to see if they differ in their achievement. Suppose the groups do differ. Can the teacher definitely conclude that the difference in family situation produced the difference in achievement? Alas, no. The teacher can conclude that a difference does exist but cannot say for sure what caused the difference.

Interpretations of causal-comparative research are limited, therefore, because the researcher cannot say conclusively whether a particular factor is a cause or a result of the behavior(s) observed. In the example presented here, the teacher could not be certain whether (1) any perceived difference in achievement between the two groups was due to the difference in home situation, (2) the parent status was due to the difference in achievement between the two groups (although this seems unlikely), or (3) some unidentified factor was at work. Nevertheless, despite problems of interpretation, causal-comparative studies are of value in identifying *possible* causes of observed variations in the behavior patterns of students. In this respect, they are very similar to correlational studies. We discuss causal-comparative research in Chapter Sixteen.

SURVEY RESEARCH

Another type of research obtains data to determine specific characteristics of a group. This is called **survey research.** Take the case of a high school principal who wants to find out how his faculty feels about his administrative policies. What do they like about his policies? What do they dislike? Why? Which policies do they like the best or least?

These sorts of questions can best be answered through a variety of survey techniques that measure faculty attitudes toward the policies of the administration. A *descriptive survey* involves asking the same set of questions (often prepared in the form of a written questionnaire or ability test) of a large number of individuals either by mail, by telephone, or in person. When answers to a set of questions are solicited in person, the research is called an *interview.* Responses are then tabulated and reported, usually in the form of frequencies or percentages of those who answer in a particular way to each of the questions.

The difficulties involved in survey research are mainly threefold: (1) ensuring that the questions to be answered are clear and not misleading; (2) getting respondents to answer questions thoughtfully and honestly; and (3) getting a sufficient number of the questionnaires completed and returned so that meaningful analyses can be made. The big advantage of survey research is that it has the potential to provide us with a lot of information obtained from quite a large sample of individuals.

If more details about particular questions in a survey are desired, the principal (or someone else) can conduct personal interviews with faculty. The advantages of an interview (over a questionnaire) are that open-ended questions (those requiring a response of some length) can be used with greater confidence, particular questions of special interest or value can be pursued in depth, follow-up questions can be asked, and items that are unclear can be explained. We discuss survey research in Chapter Seventeen.

ETHNOGRAPHIC RESEARCH

In all the examples presented so far, the questions being asked involve *how well, how much,* or *how efficiently* knowledge, attitudes, or opinions and the like exist or are being developed. Sometimes, however, researchers may wish to obtain a more complete picture of the educational process than answers to the above questions provide. When they do, some form of *qualitative research* is called for. Qualitative research differs from the previous (quantitative) methodologies in both its methods and its underlying philosophy. In Chapter Eighteen, we discuss these differences along with recent efforts to reconcile the two approaches.

Consider the subject of physical education. Just how do physical education teachers teach their subject? What kinds of things do they do as they go about their daily routine? What sorts of things do students do? In what kinds of activities do they engage? What are the explicit and implicit rules of the game that exist in PE classes that seem to help or hinder the process of learning?

To gain some insight into such concerns, an **ethnographic study** can be conducted. The emphasis in this type of research is on documenting or portraying the everyday experiences of individuals by observing and interviewing them and relevant others. An elementary classroom, for example, might be observed on as regular a basis as possible, and the students and teacher involved might be interviewed in an attempt to describe, as fully and as richly as possible, what goes on in that classroom. Descriptions (a better word might be "portrayals") might depict the social atmosphere of the classroom; the intellectual and emotional experiences of students; the manner in which the teacher acts toward and reacts to students of different ethnicities, sexes, or abilities; how the "rules" of the class are learned, modified, and enforced; the kinds of questions asked by the teacher and students; and so forth. The data could include detailed prose descriptions by students of classroom activities, audiotapes of teacher-student conferences, videotapes of classroom discussions, examples of teacher lesson plans and student work, sociograms depicting "power" relationships in the classroom, and flowcharts illustrating the direction and frequency of certain types of comments (for example, the kinds of questions asked by teacher and students of one another and the responses that different kinds produce).

In addition to ethnographic research, qualitative research includes **historical research** (see Chapter Twenty-Two) and several other, less commonly used, approaches. Casey,[2] for example, has identified 18 types of "narrative" methods. In Chapter Eighteen, we discuss four of the most distinctive of these. These include *biography*—where the researcher focuses on important experiences in the life of an individual and interacts with the person to clarify meanings and interpretations (e.g., a study of the career of a high school principal)—and *phenomenology*—in which the researcher focuses on a particular phenomenon (such as school board conflict), collects data through in-depth interviews with participants, and then identifies what is common to their perceptions. A third approach is the *case study,* in which a single individual, group, or important example is studied extensively and varied data are collected and used to formulate interpretations applicable to the specific case (e.g., a particular school board) or in an effort to provide useful generalizations. Lastly, *grounded theory* emphasizes continual interplay between raw data and the researcher's interpretations that emerge from the data. Its central purpose is the development of theory inductively from data (e.g., a study of teacher morale in a particular school beginning with interviews and other types of data).

HISTORICAL RESEARCH

You are probably already familiar with historical research. In this type of research, some aspect of the past is studied, either by perusing documents of the period or by interviewing individuals who lived during the time. An attempt is then made to reconstruct as accurately as possible what happened during that time and to explain why it did.

For example, a curriculum coordinator in a large urban school district might want to know what sorts of arguments have been made in the past as to what should be included in the social studies curriculum for grades K–12. She could read what various social studies and other curriculum theorists have written on the topic and then compare the positions they espoused. The major problems in historical research are making sure that the documents or individuals really did come from (or live during) the period under study, and once this is established, ascertaining that what the documents or individuals say is true. We discuss historical research in more detail in Chapter Twenty-Two.

ACTION RESEARCH

Action research differs from all the preceding methodologies in two fundamental ways. The first is that generalization to other persons, settings, or situations is of minimal importance. Instead of searching for powerful generalizations, action researchers (often teachers or other education professionals rather than professional researchers) focus on getting information that will enable them to change conditions in a particular situation in which they are personally involved. Examples would include improving the reading capabilities of students in a specific classroom, reducing tensions between ethnic groups in the lunchroom at a particular middle school, or identifying better ways to serve special education students in a specified school district. Accordingly, any of the methodologies discussed earlier may be appropriate.

The second difference centers around the attention paid to the active involvement of the subjects in a study (i.e., those on whom data is collected), as well as those likely to be affected by the study's outcomes. Commonly used terms in action research, therefore, are "participants" or "stakeholders," reflecting an intent to involve them directly in the research process as part of "the research team." The extent of participation varies from just helping to select instruments and/or collect data to helping to formulate the research purpose and question to actually participating in all aspects of the research investigation from start to finish. We discuss action research in some detail in Chapter Twenty-Three.

ALL HAVE VALUE

It must be stressed that each of the research methodologies described so briefly above has value for us in education. Each constitutes a different way of inquiring into the realities that exist within our classrooms and schools and into the minds and emotions of teachers, counselors, administrators, parents, and students. Each represents a different tool for use in trying to understand what goes on, and what works, in schools. It is inappropriate to consider any one or two of these approaches as superior to any of the others. The effectiveness of a particular methodology depends in large part on the nature of the research question one wants to ask and the specific context within which the particular investigation is to take place. We need to gain insights into what goes on in education from as many perspectives as possible, and hence we need to construe research in broad rather than narrow terms.

As far as we are concerned, research in education should ask a variety of questions, move in a variety of directions, encompass a variety of methodologies, and use a variety of tools. Different research orientations, perspectives, and goals should be not only allowed, but encouraged. The intent of this book is to help you learn how and when to use several of these methodologies.

General Research Types

It is useful to consider the various research methodologies we have described as falling within one or more general research categories—descriptive, associational, or intervention-type studies.

Descriptive Studies. **Descriptive studies** describe a given state of affairs as fully and carefully as possible. One of the best examples of descriptive research is found in biology, where each variety of plant and animal species is meticulously described and information is organized into useful taxonomic categories, as is done so thoroughly in botany and zoology.

In educational research, the most common descriptive methodology is the survey, as when researchers summarize the characteristics (abilities, preferences, behaviors, and so on) of individuals or groups, or (sometimes) physical environments (such as schools). Qualitative approaches, such as ethnographic and historical methodologies are also primarily descriptive in nature. Examples of descriptive studies in education include identifying the achievements of various groups of students; describing the behaviors of teachers, administrators, or counselors; describing the attitudes of parents; and describing the physical capabilities of schools. The description of phenomena is the starting point for all research endeavors.

Descriptive research, in and of itself, however, is not very satisfying, since most researchers want to have a more complete understanding of people and things. This requires a more detailed analysis of the various aspects of phenomena and their interrelationships. Advances in biology, for example, have come about, in large part, as a result of the categorization of descriptions and the subsequent determination of relationships among these categories.

Associational Research. Educational researchers also want to do more than simply describe situations or events. They want to know how (or if), for example, differences in achievement are related to such things as teacher behavior, student diet, student interests, or parental attitudes. By investigating such possible relationships, researchers are able to understand phenomena more completely. Furthermore, the identification of relationships enables one to make predictions. If researchers know that student interest is related to achievement, for example, they can predict that students who are more interested in a subject will demonstrate higher achievement in that subject than students who are less interested. Research that investigates relationships is often referred to as **associational research.** Correlational and causal-comparative methodologies are the principal examples of associational research. Examples of associational studies include studying relationships (a) between achievement and attitude, between childhood experiences and adult characteristics, or between teacher characteristics and student achievement—all of which are correlational studies; and (b) between methods of instruction and achievement (comparing students who have been taught by each method), or between gender and attitude (comparing attitudes of males and females)—both of which are causal-comparative studies.

As useful as associational studies are, they too are ultimately unsatisfying because they do not permit researchers to "do something" to influence or change outcomes. Simply determining that student interest is predictive of achievement does not tell us how to change or improve either interest or achievement, although it does suggest that increasing interest would increase achievement. To find out whether one thing will have an effect on something else, researchers need to conduct some form of intervention study.

Intervention Studies. In **intervention studies,** a particular method or treatment is expected to influence one or more outcomes. Such studies enable researchers to assess, for example, the effectiveness of various teaching methods, curriculum models, classroom arrangements, and other efforts to influence the characteristics of individuals or groups. Intervention studies can also contribute to general knowledge by confirming (or failing to confirm) theoretical predictions (for instance, that abstract concepts can be taught to young children). The primary methodology used in intervention research is the experiment.

Some types of educational research may combine these three general approaches. Although historical, ethnographic, and other qualitative research methodologies are primarily descriptive in nature, at times they may be associational if the investigator examines relationships. A descriptive historical study of college entrance requirements over time that examines the relationship between those requirements and achievement in mathematics is also associational. An ethnographic study that describes in detail the daily activities of an inner-city high school and also finds a relationship between media attention and teacher morale in the school is both descriptive and associational. An investigation of the effects of different teaching methods on concept learning that also reports the relationship between concept learning and gender is an example of a study that is both an intervention and an associational-type study.

QUANTITATIVE VERSUS QUALITATIVE RESEARCH

Another distinction involves the difference between **quantitative** and **qualitative research.** Although we shall discuss the basic differences between these two types of research more fully in Chapter Eighteen, we want to give you a brief overview here. In the simplest sense, quantitative data deal primarily with numbers, whereas qualitative data primarily involve words. But this is too simple and too brief. Quantitative and qualitative methods are based on different assumptions and differ about the purpose of research itself, the methods utilized by researchers, the kinds of studies undertaken, the role of the researcher, and the degree to which generalization is possible.

Quantitative researchers usually base their work on the belief that facts and feelings can be separated, that the world is a *single reality* made up of facts that can be discovered. Qualitative researchers, on the other hand, assume that the world is made up of *multiple realities,* socially constructed by different individual views of the same situation.

When it comes to the purpose of research, quantitative researchers seek to establish relationships between variables and look for and sometimes explain the *causes* of such relationships. Qualitative researchers, on the other hand, are more concerned with understanding situations and events from the viewpoint of the participants. Accordingly, the participants often tend to be directly involved in the research process itself.

Quantitative research has established widely agreed-on general formulations of steps that guide researchers in their work. Quantitative research designs tend to be *preestablished* ahead of time. Qualitative researchers have a much greater flexibility in both the strategies and techniques they use and the overall research process itself. Their designs tend to *emerge* during the course of the research.

The ideal researcher role in quantitative research is that of a *detached* observer, whereas qualitative researchers tend to become *immersed* in the situations in which they do their research. The prototypical study in the quantitative tradition is the *experiment;* for qualitative researchers, it is an *ethnography.*

Lastly, most quantitative researchers want to establish generalizations that transcend the immediate situation or particular setting. Qualitative researchers, on the other hand, often do not even try to generalize beyond the particular situation, but may leave it to the reader to assess applicability. When they do generalize, their generalizations are usually very limited in scope.

Many of these distinctions, of course, are not absolute. One sometimes finds, for example, the use of both quantitative and qualitative methods in experimental studies. Combinations of these approaches are becoming more common, but combining the two is often difficult to do.

META-ANALYSIS

Meta-analysis is an attempt to reduce the limitations of individual studies by trying to locate all of the studies on a particular topic and then using statistical means to synthesize the results of these studies. In Chapter Five, we discuss meta-analysis in more detail. In subsequent chapters, we examine in detail the limitations that are likely to be found in various types of research. Some apply to all types; some are more likely to apply to particular types.

Critical Analysis of Research

There are some who feel that researchers who engage in the kinds of research we have just described take a bit too much for granted—indeed, that they make a number of unwarranted (and usually unstated) assumptions about the nature of the world in which we live. These critics (usually referred to as "critical" researchers) raise a number of philosophical, linguistic, ethical, and political questions not only about educational research as it is usually conducted but also about all fields of inquiry, ranging from the physical sciences to literature.

In an introductory text, we cannot hope to do justice to the many arguments and concerns these critics have raised over the years. What we can do is provide an introduction to some of the major questions they have repeatedly asked.

The first issue is *the question of reality:* As any beginning student of philosophy is well aware, there is no way to demonstrate whether anything "really exists." There is, for example, no way to prove conclusively to others that I am looking at what I call a "pencil" (e.g., others may not be able to see it; they may not be able to tell where I am looking; I may be dreaming). Further, it is easily demonstrated that different individuals may describe the same individual, action, or event quite differently—leading some critics to the conclusion that there is no such thing as reality, only individual (and different) perceptions of it. One implication of this view is that any search for knowledge about the "real" world is doomed to failure.

We would acknowledge that what the critics say is correct: We cannot, once and for all, "prove" anything, and there is no denying that perceptions differ. We would argue, however, that our commonsense notion of reality (that what most knowledgeable persons agree exists is what is real) has enabled humankind to solve many problems—even the question of how to put a man on the moon.

The second issue is *the question of communication.* Let us assume that we can agree that some things are "real." Even so, the critics argue that it is virtually impossible to show that we use the same terms to identify these things. For example, it is well known that the Inuit have many different words (and meanings) for the English word "snow." To put it differently, no matter how carefully we define even a simple term such as "shoe," the possibility always remains that one person's shoe is not another's. (Is a slipper a shoe? Is a shower clog a shoe?) If so much of language is imprecise, how then can relationships or laws—which try to indicate how various terms, things, or ideas are connected—be precise?

Again, we would agree. People often do not agree on the meaning of a word or phrase. We would argue, however (as we think would most researchers), that we can define terms clearly enough to enable different people to agree sufficiently about what words mean that they *can* communicate and thus get on with the acquisition of useful knowledge.

The third issue is *the question of values.* Historically, scientists have often claimed to be value-free, that is "objective," in their conduct of research. Critics have argued, however, that what is studied in the social sciences, including the topics and questions with which educational researchers are concerned, is never objective, but rather socially constructed. Such things as teacher-student interaction in classrooms, the performance of students on examinations, the questions teachers ask, and a host of other issues and topics of concern to educators do not exist in a vacuum. They are influenced by the society and times in which people live. As a result, such topics and concerns, as well as how they are defined, inevitably reflect the *values* of that society. Further, even in the physical sciences, the choice of problems to study and the means of doing so reflect the values of the researchers involved.

Here, too, we would agree. We think that most researchers in education would acknowledge the validity of the critics' position. Many critical researchers charge, however, that such agreement is not sufficiently reflected in research reports. They say that many researchers fail to admit or identify "where they are coming from," especially in their discussions of the findings of their research.

The fourth issue is *the question of unstated assumptions.* An **assumption** is anything that is taken for granted rather than tested or checked. Although this issue is similar to issue number three, it is not limited to values but applies to both general and specific assumptions that researchers make with regard to a particular study. Some assumptions are so generally accepted that they are taken for granted by practically all social researchers (e.g., the sun will come out; the earth will continue to rotate). Other assumptions are more questionable. An example given by Krathwohl[3] clarifies this. He points out that if researchers change the assumptions under which they operate, this may lead to different consequences. If we assume, for example, that mentally limited students learn in the same way as other students, but more slowly, then it follows that given sufficient time and motivation, they can achieve as well as other students. The consequences of this view are to give these individuals more time, to place them in classes where the competition is less intense, and to motivate them to achieve. If, on the other hand, we assume that they use different conceptual structures into which they fit what they learn, this assumption leads to a search for simplified conceptual structures they can learn that will result in learning that approximates that of other students. Frequently authors do not make such assumptions clear.

In many studies, researchers implicitly assume that the terms they use are clear, that their samples are appropriate, and that their measurements are accurate. Designing a good study can be seen as trying to reduce these kinds of assumptions to a minimum. Readers should always be given enough information so that they do not have to make such assumptions. Figure 1.3 illustrates how an assumption can often be incorrect.

The fifth issue is *the question of societal consequences.* Critical theorists argue that traditional research efforts (including those in education) predominantly serve political interests that are, at best, conservative or, at worst, oppressive. They point out that such research is almost always focused on improving existing practices rather than raising questions

Figure 1.3 *Is This Assumption Correct?*

about the practices themselves. They argue that, intentional or not, the efforts of most educational researchers have served essentially to reinforce the status quo. A more extreme position alleges that educational institutions (including research), rather than enlightening the citizenry, have served instead to prepare them to be uncritical functionaries in an industrialized society.

We would agree with this general criticism, but note that there have been a number of investigations of the status quo itself, followed by suggestions for improvement, that have been conducted and offered by researchers of a variety of political persuasions.

Let us look at how each of these issues might relate to a hypothetical example.* Suppose a researcher decides to study the effectiveness of a course in formal logic in improving the ability of high school students to analyze arguments and arrive at defensible conclusions from data. The researcher accordingly designs a study that is sound enough in terms of design to provide at least a partial answer as to effectiveness of the course. Let us address the five issues presented above as they impinge on this study.

1. *The question of reality:* The abilities in question (analyzing arguments and concluding correctly) clearly are abstractions. They have no physical reality per se. But does this mean that such abilities do not "exist" in any way whatsoever? Are they nothing more than artificial by-products of our conceptual-

*For a real-life example, see L. Kamin (1974), *The science and politics of IQ* in the list of suggested readings for Chapter One.

language system? Clearly, this is not the case. Such abilities do indeed exist in a somewhat limited sense, as when we talk about the "ability" of a person to do well on tests. But is test performance indicative of how well a student can perform in real life? If it is not, is the performance of students on such tests important? A critic might allege that the ability to analyze, for example, is situation-specific: some people are good analyzers on tests, others in public forums, others of written materials, and so forth. If this is so, then the concept of a general ability to "analyze arguments" would be an illusion. We think a good argument can be made that this is not the case—based on commonsense experience and on some research findings. We must admit, however, that the critic has a point (we don't know for sure how general this ability is), and one that should not be overlooked.

2. *The question of communication:* Assuming that these abilities do exist, can we define them well enough so that meaningful communication can result? We think so, but it is true that even the clearest of definitions does not always guarantee meaningful communication. This is often revealed when we discover that the way *we use* a term differs from how *someone else uses* the same term, despite previous agreement on a definition. We may agree, for example, that a "defensible conclusion" is one that does not contradict the data and that follows logically from the data, yet still find ourselves disagreeing as to whether or not a particular conclusion is a defensible one. Debates among scientists often boil down to differences as to

what constitutes a "defensible conclusion" from data.

3. *The question of values:* Researchers who decide to investigate outcomes such as the ones in this study make the assumption that the outcomes are either desirable (and thus to be enhanced) or undesirable (and thus to be diminished), and they usually point out why this is so. Seldom, however, are the values (of the researchers) that led to the study of a particular outcome discussed. Are these outcomes studied because they are considered of highest priority? Because they are traditional? Socially acceptable? Easier to study? Financially rewarding?

The researcher's decision to study whether a course in logic will affect the ability of students to analyze arguments reflects his or her values. Both the outcomes and the method studied reflect Eurocentric ideas of value; the Aristotelian notion of the "rational man" (or woman) is not dominant in all cultures. Might some not claim, in fact, that we need people in our society who will question basic assumptions more than we need people who can argue well from these assumptions? While researchers probably cannot be expected to discuss such complex issues in every study, these critics render a service by urging all of us interested in research to think about how our values may affect our research endeavors.

4. *The question of unstated assumptions:* In carrying out such a study, the researcher is assuming not only that the outcome is desirable but that the findings of the study will have some influence on educational practice. Otherwise, the study is nothing more than an academic exercise. Educational methods research has been often criticized for leading to suggested practices that, for various reasons, are unlikely to be implemented. While we believe that such studies should still be done, researchers have an obligation to make such assumptions clear and to discuss their reasonableness.

5. *The question of societal consequences:* Finally, let us consider the societal implications of a study such as this. Critics might allege that this study, while perhaps defensible as a scientific endeavor, will have a negative overall impact. How so? First by fostering the idea that the outcome being studied (the ability to analyze arguments) is more important than other outcomes (e.g., the ability to see novel or unusual relationships). This allegation has, in fact, been made for many years in education—that researchers have

overemphasized the study of some outcomes at the expense of others.

A second allegation might be that such research serves to perpetuate discrimination against the less privileged segments of society. If it is true, as some contend, that some cultures are more "linear" and others more "global," then a course in formal logic (being primarily linear) may increase the advantage already held by students from the dominant linear culture.[4] It can be argued that a fairer approach would teach a variety of argumentative methods, thereby capitalizing on the strengths of all cultural groups.

To summarize, we have attempted to present the major issues raised by an increasingly vocal part of the research community. These issues involve the nature of reality, the difficulty of communication, the recognition that values always affect research, unstated assumptions, and the consequences of research for society as a whole. Further treatment of these issues can be found in the list of suggested readings for this chapter. While we do not agree with some of the specific criticisms raised by these writers, we believe the research enterprise is the better for their efforts.

A Brief Overview of the Research Process

Regardless of methodology, all researchers engage in a number of similar activities. Almost all research plans include, for example, a problem statement, a hypothesis, definitions, a literature review, a sample of subjects, tests or other measuring instruments, a description of procedures to be followed, including a time schedule, and a description of intended data analyses. We deal with each of these components in some detail throughout this book, but we want to give you a brief overview of them before we proceed.

Figure 1.4 presents a schematic of the research components. The solid-line arrows indicate the sequence in which the components are usually presented and described in research proposals and reports. They also indicate a useful sequence for planning a study (that is, thinking about the research problem, followed by the hypothesis, followed by the definitions, and so forth). The broken-line arrows indicate the most likely departures from this sequence (for example, consideration of instrumentation sometimes results in changes in the

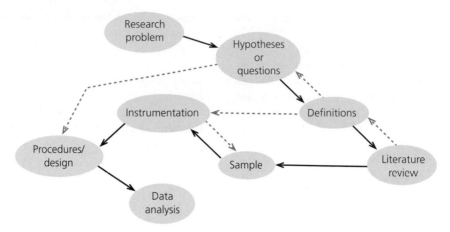

Figure 1.4 *The Research Process*

sample; clarifying the question may suggest which type of design is most appropriate). The nonlinear pattern is intended to point out that, in practice, the process does not necessarily follow this precise sequence. In fact, experienced researchers often consider many of these components simultaneously as they develop their research plan.

Statement of the research problem: The problem of a study sets the stage for everything else. The **problem statement** should be accompanied by a description of the background of the problem (what factors caused it to be a problem in the first place) and a rationale or justification for studying it. Any legal or ethical ramifications related to the problem should be discussed and resolved.

Formulation of an exploratory question or a hypothesis: Research problems are usually stated as questions, and often as hypotheses. A **hypothesis** is a prediction, a statement of what specific results or outcomes are expected to occur. The hypotheses of a study should clearly indicate any relationships expected between the **variables** (the factors, characteristics, or conditions) being investigated and be so stated that they can be tested within a reasonable period of time. Not all studies are hypothesis-testing studies, but many are.

Definitions: All key terms in the problem statement and hypothesis should be defined as clearly as possible.

Review of the related literature: Other studies related to the research problem should be located and their results briefly summarized. The **literature review** (of appropriate journals, reports, mono-

graphs, etc.) should shed light on what is already known about the problem and should indicate logically why the proposed study would result in an extension of this prior knowledge.

Sample: The subjects* (the **sample**) of the study should be identified, and the larger group, or **population** (to whom results are to be generalized) should be clearly identified. The sampling plan (the procedures by which the subjects will be selected) should be described.

Instrumentation: Each of the measuring **instruments** that will be used to collect data from the subjects should be described in detail and a rationale should be given for their use.

Procedures: The actual **procedures** of the study—what the researcher will do (what, when, where, how, and with whom) from beginning to end, in the order in which they will occur—should be spelled out in detail (although this is not written in stone). This, of course, is much less feasible and appropriate in a qualitative study. A realistic time schedule outlining when various tasks are to be started, along with expected completion dates, should also be provided. All materials (e.g., textbooks) and/or equipment (e.g., computers) that will be used in the study should also be described. The general design or methodology (e.g., an experiment or a survey) to be used should be stated. In addition, possible sources of bias should be

*The term "subjects" is offensive to some because it can imply that those being studied are deprived of dignity. We use it because we know of no other term of comparable clarity in this context.

identified and how they will be controlled should be explained.

Data analysis: Any statistical techniques, both descriptive and inferential, to be used to analyze the data should be described. The comparisons to be made to answer the research question should be made clear.

Go back to the **Interactive and Applied Learning Tools** feature at the beginning of the chapter for a listing of interactive and applied activities. Go to the **Online Learning Center** at www.mhhe.com/fraenkel5e or your **Interactive Student CD-ROM** to take practice quizzes and receive immediate feedback, practice with key terms, review chapter content and main ideas, and find annotated Web links.

WHY SCIENTIFIC RESEARCH METHODOLOGY IS OF VALUE

Main Points

- The scientific method provides an important way to obtain accurate and reliable information.

WAYS OF KNOWING

- There are many ways to obtain information, including sensory experience, agreement with others, expert opinion, logic, and the scientific method.
- The scientific method is considered by researchers the most likely way to produce reliable and accurate knowledge.
- The scientific method involves answering questions through systematic and public data collection and analysis.

TYPES OF RESEARCH

- Some of the most commonly used scientific research methodologies in education are experimental research, correlational research, causal-comparative research, survey research, ethnographic research, historical research, and action research.
- Experimental research involves manipulating conditions and studying effects.
- Correlational research involves studying relationships among variables within a single group, and frequently suggests the possibility of cause and effect.
- Causal-comparative research involves comparing known groups who have had different experiences to determine possible causes or consequences of group membership.
- Survey research involves describing the characteristics of a group by means of such instruments as interview schedules, questionnaires, and tests.
- Ethnographic research concentrates on documenting or portraying the everyday experiences of people using observation and interviews.
- Ethnographic research is one form of qualitative research. Another common form of qualitative research involves case studies.
- A case study is a detailed analysis of one or a few individuals.
- Historical research involves studying some aspect of the past.
- Action research is a type of research by practitioners designed to help improve their practice.

- Each of the research methodologies described constitutes a different way of inquiring into reality and is thus a different tool to use in understanding what goes on in education.

GENERAL RESEARCH TIPS

- Individual research methodologies can be classified into general research types. Descriptive studies describe a given state of affairs. Associational studies investigate relationships. Intervention studies assess the effects of a treatment or method on outcomes.
- Quantitative and qualitative research methodologies are based on different assumptions; they also differ on the purpose of research, the methods used by researchers, the kinds of studies undertaken, the researcher's role, and the degree to which generalization is possible.
- Meta-analysis attempts to synthesize the results of all the individual studies on a given topic by statistical means.

CRITICAL ANALYSIS OF RESEARCH

- Critical analysis of research raises basic questions about the assumptions and implications of educational research.

THE RESEARCH PROCESS

- Almost all research plans include a problem statement, an exploratory question or hypothesis, definitions, a literature review, a sample of subjects, instrumentation, a description of procedures to be followed, a time schedule, and a description of intended data analyses.

Key Terms

Action research 14	Experimental research 11	Problem statement 20
Associational research 15	Expert opinion 5	Procedure 20
Assumption 17	Extraneous variable 11	Qualitative research 16
Case study 13	Historical research 13	Quantitative research 16
Causal-comparative research 12	Hypothesis 20	Sample 20
Chaos theory 8	Instruments 20	Scientific method 6
Correlational research 12	Intervention studies 15	Sensory data 4
Critical analysis 16	Literature review 20	Single-subject research 11
Data analysis 21	Logic 5	Societal consequences 17
Descriptive studies 15	Meta-analysis 16	Survey research 12
Ethnographic research 13	Participant 14	Values 17
	Population 20	Variables 11

1. Listed below are several research questions. What methodology do you think would be the most appropriate to investigate each?
   a. What do students think are the least popular courses in the high school curriculum, and why?
   b. How do parents feel about the elementary school counseling program?
   c. How can Tom Adams be helped to learn to read?
   d. Do students who have high scores on reading tests also have high scores on writing tests?
   e. Does team teaching help or hinder student learning?
   f. What sorts of activities are of most interest to slow learners?
   g. What effect does the gender of a counselor have on how he or she is received by counselees?
   h. In what ways were the kinds of bills passed into law during the administrations of Richard Nixon and Ronald Reagan similar and different?
2. Can any of the above questions be investigated by means other than the scientific method? If so, which ones? How?
3. Can you think of some other ways of knowing besides those mentioned in this chapter? What are they? What, if any, are the limitations of these methods?
4. What other questions, besides those mentioned in the text, can you suggest that would not lend themselves to scientific research?
5. Many people seem to be uneasy about the idea of research, particularly research in schools. How would you explain this?
6. To what extent do you agree with the allegations raised by critical researchers? Can you suggest any examples that might be used to support their position? To refute it?

Notes

1. *Webster's new world dictionary of the American language,* second college edition (1984). New York: Simon and Schuster, p. 1208.

2. K. Casey (1995, 1996). The new narrative research in education. *Review of Research in Education, 21:*211–253.

3. D. R. Krathwohl (1998). *Methods of educational and social science research,* 2nd ed. New York: Longman, p. 88.

4. M. Ramirez and A. Casteneda (1974). *Cultural democracy, biocognitive development and education.* New York: Academic Press.

Research Exercise One: What Kind of Research?

Think of a research idea or problem you would like to investigate. Using Problem Sheet 1, briefly describe the problem in a sentence or two. Then indicate the type of research methodology you would use to investigate this problem.

An electronic version of this Problem Sheet that you can fill in and print, save, or e-mail is available on the Online Learning Center at www.mhhe.com/fraenkel5e and on your Interactive Student CD-ROM.

A full-sized version of this Problem Sheet that you can fill in or photocopy is in your Student Workbook.

PROBLEM SHEET 1

Type of Research

1. A possible topic or problem I am thinking of researching is: _____
   _____
   _____

2. The type of research that seems most appropriate to this topic or problem is: *(circle one)*

   a. An experiment

   b. A correlational study

   c. A causal-comparative study

   d. A survey using a written questionnaire

   e. A survey using interviews of several individuals

   f. An ethnographic study

   g. A case study

   h. A content analysis

   i. A historical study

3. What questions (if any) might a critical researcher raise with regard to your study? ____
   _____
   _____
   _____

The Basics
of Educational Research

In Part Two, we introduce or expand on many of the basic ideas

involved in educational research. These include concepts such as

hypotheses, variables, sampling, measurement, validity, reliability, and

many others. We also begin to supply you with certain skills that will

enhance your ability to understand and master the research process.

These include such things as how to select a research problem, for-

mulate a hypothesis, conduct a literature search, choose a sample,

define words and phrases clearly, develop a valid instrument, plus

many others. Regardless of the methodology a researcher uses, all of

these skills are important to master. We also discuss the ethical

implications involved in the conduct of research itself.

The Research Problem

CHAPTER 2

The Research Problem

- What Is a Research Problem?
- Research Questions
- Research Questions Often Investigate Relationships
- Characteristics of Good Research Questions
  - Research Questions Should Be Feasible
  - Research Questions Should Be Clear
  - Research Questions Should Be Significant

Objectives

Studying this chapter should enable you to:

- Give some examples of *potential research problems in education.*
- Formulate *a research question.*
- Distinguish *between researchable and nonresearchable questions.*
- Name *five characteristics that good research questions possess.*
- Describe *three ways to clarify unclear research questions.*
- Give an example *of an operational definition and explain how such definitions differ from other kinds of definitions.*
- Explain *what is meant, in research, by the term "relationship" and give an example of a research question that involves a relationship.*

Interactive and Applied Learning

After, or while, reading this chapter:

Go to your Interactive Student CD-ROM to:
- Learn More About What Makes a Question Researchable

Go to your Interactive Student CD-ROM or Student Workbook to do the following activities:
- Activity 2.1: Research Questions and Related Designs
- Activity 2.2: Changing General Topics into Research Questions
- Activity 2.3: Operational Definitions
- Activity 2.4: Justification

Robert Adams, a high school teacher in Omaha, Nebraska, wants to investigate whether the inquiry method will increase the interest of his eleventh grade students in history. Phyllis Gomez, a physical education teacher in an elementary school in Phoenix, Arizona, wants to find out how her sixth-grade students feel about the new exercise program recently mandated by the school district. Tami Mendoza, a counselor in a large inner-city high school in San Francisco, wonders whether a client-centered approach might help ease the hostility that many of her students display during counseling sessions. Each of these examples presents a problem that could serve as a basis for research. Research problems—the focus of a research investigation—are what this chapter is about.

What is a Research Problem?

A research problem is exactly that—a problem that someone would like to research. A problem can be anything that a person finds unsatisfactory or unsettling, a difficulty of some sort, a state of affairs that needs to be changed, anything that is not working as well as it might. Problems involve areas of concern to researchers, conditions they want to improve, difficulties they want to eliminate, questions for which they seek answers.

Research Questions

Usually a research problem is initially posed as a question, which serves as the focus of the researcher's investigation. The following list of examples of possible research questions in education are not sufficiently developed for actual use in a research project, but would be suitable for an early stage of formulating a research question. An appropriate methodology is provided for each question, in parentheses. Although there are other possible methodologies that might be used, we consider those given here as particularly suitable.

- Does client-centered therapy produce more satisfaction in clients than traditional therapy? (traditional experimental research)
- Does behavior modification reduce aggression in autistic children? (single-subject experimental research)
- Are the descriptions of people in social studies discussions biased? (grounded theory research)
- What goes on in an elementary school classroom during an average week? (ethnographic research)
- Do teachers behave differently toward students of different genders? (causal-comparative research)
- How can we predict which students might have trouble learning certain kinds of subject matter? (correlational research)

- How do parents feel about the school counseling program? (survey research)
- How can a principal improve faculty morale? (interview research)

What all these questions have in common is that we can collect data of some sort to answer them (at least in part). That's what makes them researchable. For example, a researcher can measure the satisfaction levels of clients who receive different methods of therapy. Or researchers can observe and interview in order to describe the functioning of an elementary school classroom. To repeat, then, what makes these questions researchable is that some sort of information *can* be collected to answer them.

There are other kinds of questions, however, that *cannot* be answered by collecting and analyzing data. Here are two examples:

- Should philosophy be included in the high school curriculum?
- What is the meaning of life?

Why can't these questions be researched? What about them prevents us from collecting information to answer them? The answer is both simple and straightforward: There is no way to collect information to answer either question. Both questions are, in the final analysis, not researchable.

The first question is a question of *value*—it implies notions of right and wrong, proper and improper—and therefore does not have any **empirical** (or observable) **referents.** There is no way to deal, empirically, with the verb "should." How can we empirically determine whether or not something "should" be done? What data could we collect? There is no way for us to proceed. However, if the question is changed to "Do people *think* philosophy should be included in the high school curriculum?" it becomes researchable. Why? Because now we can collect data to help us answer the question.

The second question is *metaphysical* in nature—that is, beyond the physical, transcendental. Answers to this sort of question lie beyond the accumulation of information.

Here are more ideas for research questions. Which ones (if any) do you think are researchable?

1. Is God good?
2. Are children happier when taught by a teacher of the same gender?
3. Does high school achievement influence the academic achievement of university students?
4. What is the best way to teach grammar?
5. What would schools be like today if World War II had not occurred?

We hope you identified questions 2 and 3 as the two that are researchable. Questions 1, 4, and 5, as stated, cannot be researched. Question 1 is another metaphysical question, and, as such, does not lend itself to empirical research (we could ask people if they *believe* God is good, but that would be another question). Question 4 asks for the "best" way to do something. Think about this one for a moment. Is there any way we can determine the *best* way to do anything? To be able to determine this, we must examine *every* possible alternative, and a moment's reflection brings us to the realization that this can never be accomplished. How would we ever be sure that all possible alternatives have been examined? Question 5 requires the creation of impossible conditions. We can, of course, investigate what people

think schools would be like. Figure 2.1 illustrates the difference between researchable and nonresearchable questions.

Characteristics of Good Research Questions

Once a research question has been formulated, researchers want to turn it into as good a question as possible. Good research questions possess four essential characteristics.

1. The question is *feasible* (i.e., it can be investigated without an undue amount of time, energy, or money).
2. The question is *clear* (i.e., most people would agree as to what the key words in the question mean).
3. The question is *significant* (i.e., it is worth investigating because it will contribute important knowledge about the human condition).
4. The question is *ethical* (i.e., it will not involve physical or psychological harm or damage to human beings, or to the natural or social environment of which they are a part). We will discuss the subject of ethics in detail in Chapter Four.

Let us discuss some of these characteristics in a bit more detail.

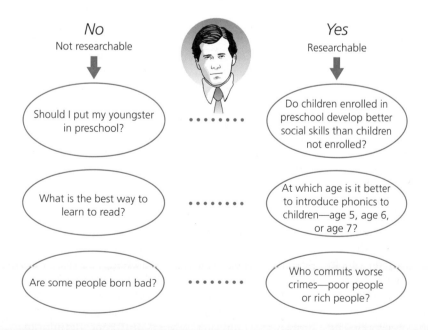

Figure 2.1
Researchable Versus Nonresearchable Questions

No
Not researchable

Yes
Researchable

Should I put my youngster in preschool? ········ Do children enrolled in preschool develop better social skills than children not enrolled?

What is the best way to learn to read? ········ At which age is it better to introduce phonics to children—age 5, age 6, or age 7?

Are some people born bad? ········ Who commits worse crimes—poor people or rich people?

RESEARCH QUESTIONS
SHOULD BE FEASIBLE

An important issue in designing research studies is that of feasibility. A feasible question is one that can be investigated with available resources. Some questions (such as those involving space exploration, for example, or the study of the long-term effects of special programs, like Head Start) require a great deal of time and money; others require much less. Unfortunately, the field of education, unlike medicine, business, law, agriculture, pharmacology, or the military, has never established an ongoing research effort tied closely to practice. Most of the research that is done in schools or other educational institutions is likely to be done by "outsiders"—often university professors and their students—and usually is funded by temporary grants. Thus, lack of feasibility often seriously limits research efforts. Following are two examples of research questions, one feasible and one not so feasible.

> *Feasible:* How do the students at Oceana High School feel about the new guidance program recently instituted in the district?
>
> *Not so feasible:* How would giving each student his or her own laptop computer to use for a semester affect achievement?

RESEARCH QUESTIONS
SHOULD BE CLEAR

Because the research question is the focus of a research investigation, it is particularly important that the question is clear. What exactly is being investigated? Let us consider two examples of research questions that are not clear enough.

Example 1. *"Is a humanistically oriented classroom effective?"* Although the phrase "humanistically oriented classroom" may seem quite clear, many people may not be sure exactly what it means. If we ask, "What *is* a humanistically oriented classroom?" we begin to discover that it is not as easy as we might have thought to describe its essential characteristics. What happens in such classrooms that is different from what happens in other classrooms? Do teachers use certain kinds of strategies? Do they lecture? In what sorts of activities do students participate? What do such classrooms look like—how is the seating arranged, for example? What kinds of materials are used? Is there much variation to be found from classroom to classroom in the strategies employed by the teacher or in the sorts of activities in which students engage? Do the kinds of materials available and/or used vary?

Another term in this question is also ambiguous. What does the term "effective" mean? Does it mean "results in increased academic proficiency," "results in happier children," "makes life easier for teachers," or "costs less money"? Maybe it means all these things and more.

Example 2. *"How do teachers feel about special classes for the educationally handicapped?"* The first term that needs clarification is "teachers." What age group does this involve? What level of experience (i.e., are probationary teachers, for example, included)? Are teachers in both public and private schools included? Are teachers throughout the nation included, or only those in a specific locality? Does the term refer to teachers who do not teach special classes as well as those who do?

The phrase "feel about" is also ambiguous. Does it mean opinions? Emotional reactions? Does it suggest actions? Or what? The terms "special classes" and "educationally handicapped" also need to be clarified. An example of a legal definition of an educationally handicapped student is:

> A minor who, by reason of marked learning or behavioral disorders, is unable to adapt to a normal classroom situation. The disorder must be associated with a neurological handicap or an emotional disturbance and must not be due to mental retardation, cultural deprivation, or foreign language problems.

Note that this definition itself contains some ambiguous words, such as "marked learning disorders," which lend themselves to a wide variety of interpretations. This is equally true of the term "cultural deprivation," which is not only ambiguous but also often offensive to members of ethnic groups to whom the term is frequently applied.

As we begin to think about these (or other) questions, it appears that terms which seemed at first glance to be words or phrases that everyone would easily understand are really quite complex and far more difficult to define than we might originally have thought.

This is true of many current educational concepts and methodologies. Consider such terms as "core curriculum," "client-centered counseling," "active learning," and "quality management." What do such terms mean? If you were to ask a sample of five or six teachers, counselors, or administrators that you know, you probably would get several different definitions.

Although such ambiguity is valuable in some circumstances and for certain purposes, it represents a problem to investigators of a research question. Researchers have no choice but to be specific about the terms used in a research question, to define precisely what is to be studied. In making this effort, researchers gain a clearer picture of how to proceed with an investigation, and, in fact, sometimes decide to change the very nature of the research. How, then, might the clarity of a research question be improved?

Defining Terms. There are essentially three ways to clarify important terms in a research question. The first is to use a **constitutive definition**—that is, to use what is often referred to as the *dictionary approach*. Researchers simply use other words to say more clearly what is meant. Thus, the term "humanistic classroom" might be defined as:

> A classroom in which: (1) the needs and interests of students have the highest priority; (2) students work on their own for a considerable amount of time in each class period; and (3) the teacher acts as a guide and a resource person rather than an informant.

Notice, however, that this definition is still somewhat unclear, since the words being used to explain the term "humanistic" are themselves ambiguous. What does it mean to say that the "needs and interests of students have the highest priority" or that "students work on their own"? What is a "considerable amount" of each class period? What does a teacher do when acting as a "guide" or a "resource person"? Further clarification is needed.

Students of communication have demonstrated just how difficult it is to be sure that the message sent is the message received. It is probably true that no one ever completely understands the meaning of terms that are used to communicate. That is, we can never be certain that the message we receive is the one the sender intended. Some years ago, one of the leaders in our field was said to have become so depressed by this idea that he quit talking to his colleagues for several weeks. A more constructive approach is simply to do the best we can. We must try to explain our terms to others. While most researchers try to be clear, there is no question that some do a much better job than others.

Another important point to remember is that often it is a term or phrase that needs to be defined rather than only a single word. For example, the term "nondirective therapy" will surely not be clarified by precise definitions of "nondirective" and "therapy," since it has a more specific meaning than the two words defined sep-

arately would convey. Similarly, such terms as "learning disability," "bilingual education," "interactive video," and "home-centered health care" need to be defined as linguistic wholes.

Here are three definitions of the term "motivated to learn." Which do you think is the clearest?

1. Works hard
2. Is eager and enthusiastic
3. Sustains attention to a task*

As you have seen, the dictionary approach to clarifying terms has its limitations. A second possibility is to clarify *by example*. Researchers might think of a few humanistic classrooms with which they are familiar and then try to describe as fully as possible what happens in these classrooms. Usually we suggest that people observe such classrooms to see for themselves how they differ from other classrooms. This approach also has its problems, however, since our descriptions may still not be as clear to others as they would like.

Thus, a third method of clarification is to define important terms operationally. **Operational definitions** require that researchers specify the actions or operations necessary to measure or identify the term. For example, here are two possible operational definitions of the term "humanistic classroom."

1. Any classroom *identified* by specified experts as constituting an example of a humanistic classroom
2. Any classroom *judged* (by an observer spending at least one day per week for four to five weeks) to possess all the following characteristics:
   a. No more than three children working with the same materials at the same time.
   b. The teacher never spending more than twenty minutes per day addressing the class as a group.
   c. At least half of every class period open for students to work on projects of their own choosing at their own pace.
   d. Several (more than three) sets of different kinds of educational materials available for every student in the class to use.
   e. Nontraditional seating—students sit in circles, small groupings of seats, or even on the floor to work on their projects.
   f. Frequent (at least two per week) discussions in which students are encouraged to give their opinions and ideas on topics being read about in their textbooks.

*We judge 3 to be the clearest, followed by 1 and then 2.

Key Terms to Define in a Research Study

- Terms necessary to ensure that the research question is sharply focused
- Terms that individuals outside the field of study may not understand
- Terms that have multiple meanings
- Terms that are essential to understanding what the study is about
- Terms to provide precision in specifications for instruments to be developed or located

"It all depends on how you define 'chop.'"

© The New Yorker Collection 1998 Tom Cheney from cartoonbank.com. All Rights Reserved.

The above listing of characteristics and behaviors may be a quite unsatisfactory definition of a humanistic classroom to many people (and perhaps to you). But it is considerably more specific (and thus clearer) than the definition with which we began.* Armed with this definition (and the necessary facilities), researchers could decide quickly whether or not a particular classroom qualifies as an example of a humanistic classroom.

Defining terms operationally is a helpful way to clarify their meaning. Operational definitions are useful tools and should be mastered by all students of research. Remember that the operations or activities necessary to measure or identify the term must be specified. Which of the following possible definitions of the term "motivated to learn mathematics" do you think are operational?

1. As shown by enthusiasm in class.
2. As judged by the student's math teacher using a rating scale she developed.
3. As measured by the "Math Interest" questionnaire.
4. As shown by attention to math tasks in class.
5. As reflected by achievement in mathematics.
6. As indicated by records showing enrollment in mathematics electives.
7. As shown by effort expended in class.
8. As demonstrated by number of optional assignments completed.
9. As demonstrated by reading math books outside class.
10. As observed by teacher aides using the "Mathematics Interest" observation record.[†]

In addition to their value in helping readers understand how researchers actually obtain the information they need, specifying operational definitions is often helpful in clarifying terms. Thinking about how to measure "job satisfaction," for example, is likely to force a researcher to clarify, in his or her own mind, what he or she means by the term. (For everyday examples of times when operational definitions are needed, see Figure 2.2)

Despite their virtues, however, operational definitions in and of themselves are often not illuminating. Reading that "language proficiency is (operationally) defined as the student's score on the TOLD test" is not very helpful unless the reader is familiar with this particular test. Even when this is the case, it is more satisfactory to be informed of what the researcher means by the term. For these reasons we believe that an operational definition should always be accompanied by a constitutive one.

---

*This is not to say that this list would not be improved by making the guidelines even more specific. These characteristics, however, do meet the criterion for an operational definition—they specify the actions researchers need to take to measure or identify the variable being defined.

[†]The operational definitions are 2, 3, 6, 8, and 10. The nonoperational definitions are 1, 4, 5, 7, and 9, because the activities or operations necessary for identifying the behavior have not been specified.

Figure 2.2 *Some Times When Operational Definitions Would Be Helpful*

The importance of researchers being clear about the terms in their research questions cannot be overstated. It is difficult to proceed with plans for the collection and analysis of data if researchers do not know exactly what kind of data to look for. And researchers will not know what data to look for if they are unclear about the meaning of the key terms in the research question.

RESEARCH QUESTIONS SHOULD BE SIGNIFICANT

Research questions also should be *worth* investigating. In essence, we need to consider whether a question is worth spending time and energy (and often money) on to get an answer. What, we might ask, is the value of in-

vestigating a particular question? In what ways will it contribute to our knowledge about education? To our knowledge of human beings? Is such knowledge important in some way? If so, how? These questions ask researchers to think about why a research question is worthwhile, that is, important or significant.

It probably goes without saying that a research question is of interest to the person who asks it. But is interest alone sufficient justification for an investigation? For some people, the answer is a clear "yes!" They say that any question that someone sincerely wants an answer to is worth investigating. Others, however, say that personal interest, in and of itself, is insufficient as a reason for investigating a question. Too often, they point out, personal interest can result in the pursuit of trivial

The Importance of a Rationale

Research in education, as in all of social science, has sometimes been criticized as trivial. Some years ago, Senator William Proxmire gained considerable publicity for his "golden fleece" awards, which he bestowed on government-funded studies that he considered particularly worthless or trivial. Some recipients complained of "cheap shots," arguing that their research had not received a complete or fair hearing. While it is doubtless true that research is often specialized in nature and not easily communicated to persons outside the field, we believe more attention should be paid to:

- Avoiding esoteric terminology
- Defining key terms clearly and, when feasible, both constitutively and operationally
- Making a clear and persuasive case for the importance of the study

or insignificant questions. Because most research efforts require some (and often a considerable) expenditure of time, energy, materials, money, and/or other resources, it is easy to appreciate the point of view that some useful outcome or payoff should be forthcoming as a result of the research. The investment of oneself and others in a research enterprise should contribute some knowledge of value to the field of education.

Generally speaking, most researchers do not believe that research efforts based primarily on personal interest alone warrant investigation. Furthermore, there is some reason to question a "purely curious" motive on psychological grounds. Most questions probably have some degree of hidden motivation behind them, and, for the sake of credibility, these reasons should be made explicit.

One of the most important tasks for any researcher, therefore, is to think through the value of the intended research before too much preliminary work is done. There are three important questions to ask about a research question.

1. How might answers to this question advance knowledge in my field?
2. How might answers to this question improve educational practice?
3. How might answers to this question improve the human condition?

As you think about possible questions that might be researched, therefore, ask yourself: Why would it be important to answer this question? Does the question have implications for the improvement of practice? For administrative decision making? For program planning? Is there an important issue that can be illuminated to some degree by a study of this question? Is it related to a current theory that I have doubts about or would like to substantiate? Thinking through possible answers to these questions can help us judge the significance of a potential research question.

In our experience, student justifications for a proposed study are likely to have two weaknesses. The first is that they assume too much, for example, that everyone would agree with them (i.e., it is self-evident) that it is important to study something like "self-esteem" or "ability to read." In point of fact, not everyone does agree that these are important topics to study; in any case, it is still the researcher's job to make the case that they *are* important rather than merely assuming that this is the case.

The second weakness is that students often overstate the implications of a study. Evidence of the effectiveness of a particular teaching method does *not,* for example, imply that the method will be generally adopted or that improvement in student achievement will automatically result. It *would* imply, for example, that more attention should be given to the method in teacher-training programs.

Research Questions Often Investigate Relationships

There is an additional characteristic that good research questions often possess. They frequently (but not always) suggest a relationship of some sort to be investigated. (We discuss the reasons for this in Chapter Three.) A suggested relationship means that two qualities or characteristics are tied together or connected in some way. Are motivation and learning related? If so, how?

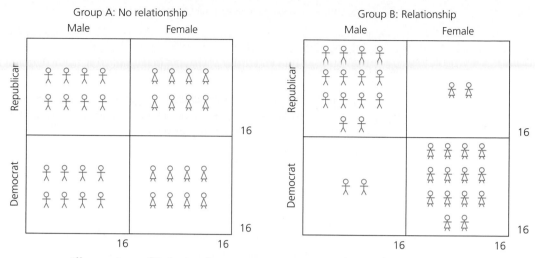

Figure 2.3 *Illustration of Relationship Between Voter Gender and Party Affiliation*

What about age and attractiveness? Speed and weight? Height and strength? A principal's administrative policies and faculty morale?

It is important to understand how the term "relationship" is used in research, since the term has other meanings in everyday life. When researchers use the term "relationship," they are not referring to the nature or quality of an association between people, for example. What we and other researchers mean is perhaps best clarified visually. Look, for example, at the data for groups A and B in Figure 2.3. What do you notice?

The hypothetical data for group A show that out of a total of 32 individuals, 16 were Republicans and 16 were Democrats. It also shows that half were male and half were female. Group B shows the same breakdown by party affiliation. What is different in the two figures is that there is no association or relationship between gender and political party shown in group A, whereas there is a very strong relationship between these two factors shown in group B. We can express the relationship in group B by saying that males tend to be Republicans while females tend to be Democrats. We can also express this relationship in terms of a prediction. Should another female join group B, we would predict she would be a Democrat since 14 of the previous 16 females are Democrats.

Go back to the **Interactive and Applied Learning Tools** feature at the beginning of the chapter for a listing of interactive and applied activities. Go to the **Online Learning Center** at www.mhhe.com/fraenkel5e or your **Interactive Student CD-ROM** to take practice quizzes and receive immediate feedback, practice with key terms, review chapter content and main ideas, and find annotated Web links.

RESEARCH PROBLEM

Main Points

- A research problem is the focus of a research investigation.

RESEARCH QUESTIONS

- Many research problems are stated as questions.
- The essential characteristic of a researchable question is that there is some sort of information that can be collected in an attempt to answer the question.

CHARACTERISTICS OF GOOD RESEARCH QUESTIONS

- Research questions should be feasible—that is, capable of being investigated with available resources.
- Research questions should be clear—that is, unambiguous.
- Research questions should be significant—that is, worthy of investigation.
- Research questions often (although not always) suggest a relationship to be investigated. The term "relationship," as used in research, refers to a connection or association between two or more characteristics or qualities.

DEFINING TERMS IN RESEARCH

- Three commonly used ways to clarify ambiguous or unclear terms in a research question involve the use of constitutive (dictionary-type) definitions, definition by example, and operational definitions.
- A constitutive definition uses additional terms to clarify meaning.
- An operational definition describes how examples of a term are to be measured or identified.

Key Terms

Clarity (of research question) 30

Constitutive definition 31

Empirical referent 28

Ethical research question 29

Feasibility (of research question) 30

Operational definition 31

Rationale 34

Relationship 34

Research problem 28

Research question 28

Significance (of research question) 33

For Discussion

1. Listed below are a series of questions. Think how a researcher could collect information (from friends, colleagues, students, or others) to help answer each question, at least in part. Could data be collected on all of these questions? If so, how? If not, why not?
   a. Does client-centered or traditional therapy produce more satisfaction in clients?
   b. How might staff morale be improved?
   c. Should psychology be required of all students in graduate school?
   d. Do students learn more from a teacher of the same gender?
2. What relationship (if there is one) is suggested in each of the above questions?
3. Here are three examples of research questions. How would you rank them (1 = highest) for clarity? For significance? Why?
   a. How many students in the sophomore class signed up for a course in driver training this semester?
   b. Why do so many students in the district say they dislike English?
   c. Is inquiry or lecture more effective in teaching social studies?

Research Exercise Two: The Research Question

Using Problem Sheet 2, restate the research problem you listed in Research Exercise One in a sentence or two, and then formulate a research question that relates to this problem. Now list all the key terms in the question that you think are not clear and need to be defined. Define each of these terms both constitutively and operationally, and then state why you think your question is an important one to study.

Problem Sheet 2

The Research Question

1. My (restated) research problem is: _____

   _____

2. My research question is: _____

   _____

3. The following are the key terms in the problem or question that are not clear and thus need to be defined:

   a. _____   *d.* _____

   b. _____   *e.* _____

   c. _____   *f.* _____

4. Here are my constitutive definitions of these terms: _____

   _____

   _____

   _____

5. Here are my operational definitions of these terms: _____

   _____

   _____

   _____

6. My justification for investigating this question/problem (why I would argue that it

   is an important question to investigate) is as follows: _____

   _____

   _____

An electronic version of this Problem Sheet that you can fill in and print, save, or e-mail is available on the Online Learning Center at www.mhhe.com/ fraenkel5e and on your Interactive Student CD-ROM.

A full-sized version of this Problem Sheet that you can fill in or photocopy is in your Student Workbook.

Variables and Hypotheses

CHAPTER 3

How many variables can you identify?

Variables and Hypotheses

The Importance of Studying Relationships

Hypotheses

What Is a Hypothesis?
Advantages of Stating Hypotheses in Addition
to Research Questions
Disadvantages of Stating Hypotheses
Significant Hypotheses
Directional Versus Nondirectional Hypotheses

Variables

What Is a Variable?
Quantitative Versus Categorical Variables
Independent Versus Dependent Variables
Extraneous Variables

Objectives

Studying this chapter should enable you to:

- Explain *what is meant by the term "variable" and* name *five variables that might be investigated by educational researchers.*
- Explain *how a variable differs from a constant.*
- Distinguish *between a quantitative and a categorical variable.*
- Explain *how independent and dependent variables are related.*
- Explain *what a hypothesis is and* formulate *two hypotheses that might be investigated in education.*
- Name *two advantages and two disadvantages of stating research questions as hypotheses.*
- Distinguish *between directional and nondirectional hypotheses and* give *an example of each.*

Interactive and Applied Learning

After, or while, reading this chapter:

Go to your Interactive Student CD-ROM to:
- Learn More About Hypothesis: To State or Not to State

Go to your Interactive Student CD-ROM or Student Workbook to do the following activities:
- Activity 3.1: Directional Versus Nondirectional Hypotheses
- Activity 3.2: Testing Hypotheses
- Activity 3.3: Categorical Versus Qualitative Variables
- Activity 3.4: Independent and Dependent Variables

Marge Jenkins and Jenna Rodriguez are having coffee following the meeting of their graduate seminar in educational research. Both are puzzled by some of the ideas that came up in today's meeting of the class.

"I'm not sure I agree with Ms. Naser (their instructor)," says Jenna. "She said that there are a lot of advantages to predicting how you think a study will come out."

"Yeah, I know," replies Marge. "But formulating a hypothesis seems like a good idea to me."

"Well, perhaps, but there are some disadvantages, too."

"Really? I can't think of any."

"Well, what about . . . ?"

Actually, both Jenna and Marge are correct. There are *both* advantages and disadvantages to stating a hypothesis in addition to one's research question. Examples of both are one of the things we'll discuss in this chapter.

The Importance of Studying Relationships

We mentioned in Chapter Two that an important characteristic of many research questions is that they suggest a relationship of some sort to be investigated. Not all research questions, however, suggest relationships. Sometimes researchers are interested only in obtaining descriptive information to find out how people think or feel or to describe how they behave in a particular situation. Other times the intent is to describe a particular program or activity. Such questions also are worthy of investigation. As a result, researchers may ask questions like the following:

- How do the parents of the sophomore class feel about the counseling program?
- What changes would the staff like to see instituted in the curriculum?
- Has the number of students enrolling in college preparatory as compared to noncollege preparatory courses changed over the last four years?
- How does the new reading program differ from the one used in this district in the past?
- What does an inquiry-oriented social studies teacher do?

Notice that no relationship is suggested in these questions. The researcher simply wants to identify characteristics, behaviors, feelings, or thoughts. It is often necessary to obtain such information as a first step in designing other research or making educational decisions of some sort.

The problem with purely descriptive research questions is that answers to them do not help us understand why people feel or think or behave a certain way, why programs possess certain characteristics, why a particular strategy is to be used at a certain time, and so forth. We may learn what happened, or where or when (and even how) something happened, but not why it happened. As a result, our understanding of a situation, group, or phenomenon is limited. For this reason scientists consider research questions that suggest relationships to be investigated extremely important, because the answers to them help explain the nature of the world in which we live. We learn to understand the world by learning to explain how parts of it are related. We begin to detect *patterns* or connections between the parts.

We believe that understanding is generally enhanced by the demonstration of relationships or connections. It is for this reason that we favor the formation of a hypothesis that predicts the existence of a relationship. There may be times, however, when a researcher wants to hypothesize that a relationship does *not* exist. Why so? The only persuasive argument we know of is that of contradicting an existing widespread (but perhaps erroneous) belief. For example, if it can be shown that a great many people believe, in the absence of adequate evidence, that young boys are less sympathetic than young girls, a study in which a researcher finds no difference between boys and girls (i.e., *no* relationship between gender and sympathy) might be of value (such a study may have been done, although we are not aware of one). Unfortunately, most (but by no means all) of the methodological mistakes made in research (such as using inadequate instruments or too small a sample of participants) increase the chance of finding no relationship between variables. (We shall discuss several such mistakes in later chapters.)

Variables

WHAT IS A VARIABLE?

At this point, it is important to introduce the idea of variables, since a relationship is a statement about variables. What is a variable? A **variable** is a concept—a noun that stands for variation within a class of objects, such as chair, gender, eye color, achievement, motivation, or running speed. Even "spunk," "style," and "lust for life" are variables. Notice that the individual members in the class of objects, however, must differ—or vary—to qualify the class as a variable. If all members of a class are identical, we do not have a variable. Such characteristics are called **constants,** since the individual members of the class are not allowed to vary, but rather are held constant. In any study, some characteristics will be variables, while others will be constants.

An example may make this distinction clearer. Suppose a researcher is interested in studying the effects of reinforcement on student achievement. The researcher systematically divides a large group of students, all of whom are ninth-graders, into three smaller subgroups. She then trains the teachers of these subgroups to reinforce their students in different ways (one gives verbal praise, the second gives monetary rewards, the third gives extra points) for various tasks the students perform. In this study, "reinforcement" would be a variable (it contains three variations), while the grade level of the students would be a constant.

Notice that it is easier to see what some of these concepts stand for than others. The concept of "chair," for example, stands for the many different objects that we sit on that possess legs, a seat, and a back. Furthermore, different observers would probably agree as to how particular chairs differ. It is not so easy, however, to see what a concept like "motivation" stands for, or to reach agreement as to what it means. The researchers must be specific here—they must define "motivation" as clearly as possible. They must do this so that it can be measured or manipulated. We cannot meaningfully measure or manipulate a variable if we cannot define it. As we mentioned above, much educational research involves looking for a relationship among variables. But what variables?

There are many variables "out there" in the world that can be investigated. Obviously, we can't investigate them all, so we must choose. Researchers choose certain variables to investigate because they have a suspicion that these variables are somehow related and that, if they can discover the nature of this relationship, it can help us make more sense out of the world in which we live.

QUANTITATIVE VERSUS CATEGORICAL VARIABLES

Variables can be classified in several ways. One way is to distinguish between quantitative and categorical variables. **Quantitative variables** exist in some degree (rather than all or none) along a continuum from "less" to "more," and we can assign numbers to different individuals or objects to indicate how much of the variable they possess. An obvious example is height (John is 6 feet tall and Sally is 5 feet 4 inches) or weight (Mr. Adams weighs only 150 pounds and his wife 140 pounds, but their son tips the scales at an even 200 pounds). We can also assign numbers to various individuals to indicate how much "interest" they have in a subject, with a 5 indicating very much interest, a 4 much interest, a 3 some interest, a 2 little interest, a 1 very little interest, down to a 0 indicating no interest in the subject. If we can assign numbers in this way, we have the variable "interest."

Quantitative variables can often (but not always) be subdivided into smaller and smaller units. "Length," for example, can be measured in miles, yards, feet, inches, or in whatever subdivision of an inch is needed. By way of contrast, **categorical variables** do not vary in degree, amount, or quantity but are qualitatively different. Examples include eye color, gender, religious preference, occupation, position on a baseball team, and most kinds of research "treatments" or "methods." For example, suppose a researcher wished to compare certain attitudes in two different groups of voters, one in which each individual was registered as a member of one political party and the other in which individuals were members of another party. The variable involved would be *political party.* This is a categorical variable—a person is either in one or the other category, not somewhere in between being a registered member of one party and being a registered member of another party. All members within each category of this variable are considered the same as far as party membership is concerned (see Figure 3.1).

Can "teaching method" be considered a variable? Yes, it can. Suppose a researcher is interested in studying teachers who use different methods in teaching. The researcher locates one teacher who lectures exclusively, another who buttresses her lectures with slides and filmstrips, and a third who uses the case-study method and lectures not at all. Does the teaching method

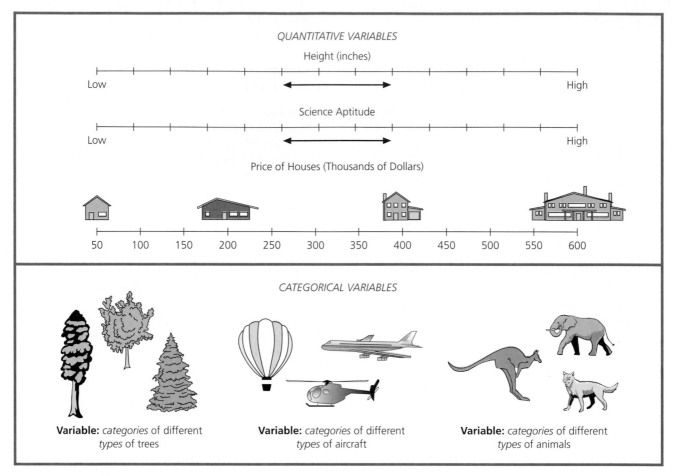

Figure 3.1 *Illustration of Quantitative Compared with Categorical Variables*

"vary"? It does. You may need to practice thinking of differences in methods, or in groups of people (teachers compared to administrators, for example) as variables, but mastering this idea is extremely useful in learning about research.

Now, here are several variables. Which ones are quantitative variables and which ones are categorical variables?

1. Make of automobile
2. Learning ability
3. Ethnicity
4. Cohesiveness
5. Heartbeat rate
6. Gender*

*1, 3, and 6 represent categorical variables; 2, 4, and 5 represent quantitative variables.

Researchers in education often study the relationship between (or among) either (*a*) two (or more) quantitative variables; (*b*) one categorical and one quantitative variable; or (*c*) two or more categorical variables. Here are some examples of each:

a. *Two quantitative variables*
   * Age and amount of interest in school.
   * Reading achievement and mathematics achievement.
   * Classroom humanism and student motivation.
   * Amount of time watching television and aggressiveness of behavior.
b. *One categorical and one quantitative variable*
   * Method used to teach reading and reading achievement.
   * Counseling approach and level of anxiety.
   * Nationality and liking for school.
   * Student gender and amount of praise given by teachers.

Some Important Relationships That Have Been Clarified by Educational Research

1. The more time beginning readers spend on phonics, the better readers they become. (Despite a great deal of research on the topic, this statement can neither be clearly supported nor refuted. It is clear that phonic instruction is an important ingredient; what is not clear is how much time should be devoted to it.)*

2. The use of manipulatives in elementary grades results in better math performance. (The evidence is quite supportive of this method of teaching mathematics.)†

*R. Calfee and P. Drum (1986). Research on teaching reading. In M. C. Wittrock (Ed.), *Handbook of research on teaching,* 3rd ed. New York: Macmillan, pp. 804–849.
†M. N. Suydam (1986). Research report: Manipulative materials and achievement. *Arithmetic Teacher, 10:* (February): 32.

3. Behavior modification is an effective way to teach simple skills to very slow learners. (There is a great deal of evidence to support this statement.)††

4. The more teachers know about specific subject matter, the better they teach it. (The evidence is inconclusive despite the seemingly obvious fact that teachers must know more than their students.)§

5. Among children who become deaf before language has developed, those with hearing parents become better readers than those with deaf parents. (The findings of many studies *refute* this statement.)∥

††S. L. Deno (1982). Behavioral treatment methods. In H. E. Mitzel (Ed.), *Encyclopedia of educational research,* 5th ed. New York: Macmillan, pp. 199–202.
§L. Shulman (1986). Paradigms and research programs in the study of teaching. In M. C. Wittrock, (Ed.), *Handbook of research on teaching,* 3rd ed. New York: Macmillan, pp. 3–36.
∥C. M. Kampfe and A. G. Turecheck (1987). Reading achievement of prelingually deaf students and its relationship to parental method of communication: A review of the literature. *American Annals of the Deaf, 10:* (March): 11–15.

---

c. *Two categorical variables*
- Ethnicity and father's occupation.
- Gender of teacher and subject taught.
- Administrative style and college major.
- Religious affiliation and political party membership.

Sometimes researchers have a choice of whether to treat a variable as quantitative or categorical. It is not uncommon, for example, to find studies in which a variable such as "anxiety" is studied by comparing a group of "high-anxiety" students to a group of "low-anxiety" students. This treats anxiety as though it were a categorical variable. While there is nothing really wrong with doing this, there are three reasons why it is preferable in such situations to treat the variable as quantitative.

1. Conceptually, we consider variables such as anxiety in people to be a matter of degree, not a matter of either-or.

2. Collapsing the variable into two (or even several) categories eliminates the possibility of using more detailed information about the variable, since differences among individuals within a category are ignored.

3. The dividing line between groups (for example, between individuals of high, middle, and low anxiety) is almost always arbitrary (that is, lacking in any defensible rationale).

INDEPENDENT VERSUS DEPENDENT VARIABLES

A common and useful way to think about variables is to classify them as *independent* or *dependent.* **Independent variables** are those that the researcher chooses to study in order to assess their possible effect(s) on one or more other variables. An independent variable is presumed to affect (at least partly cause), or somehow influence, at least one other variable. The variable that the independent variable is presumed to affect is called a **dependent variable.** In commonsense terms, the dependent variable "depends on" what the independent variable does to it, how it affects it. For example, a researcher studying the relationship between childhood success in mathematics and adult career choice is likely to refer to the former as the independent variable and subsequent career choice as the dependent variables.

It is possible to investigate more than one independent (and also more than one dependent) variable in a study. For simplicity's sake, however, we present examples in which only one independent and one dependent variable are involved.

The relationship between independent and dependent variables can be portrayed graphically as follows:

At this point, let's check your understanding. Suppose a researcher plans to investigate the following question: Will students who are taught by a team of three teachers learn more science than students taught by one individual teacher? What are the independent and dependent variables in this question?*

Notice that there are two conditions (sometimes called levels) in the independent variable—"three teachers" and "one teacher." Also notice that the dependent variable is not "science learning" but "*amount of science learning.*" Can you see why?

At this point, things begin to get a bit complicated. Independent variables may be either *manipulated* or *selected.* A **manipulated variable** is one that the researcher *creates.* Such variables are typically found in experimental studies (see Chapter Thirteen). Suppose, for example, that a researcher decides to investigate the effect of different amounts of reinforcement on reading achievement and systematically assigns students to three different groups. One group is praised continuously every day during their reading session; the second group is told simply to "keep up the good work"; the third group is told nothing at all. The researcher, in effect, manipulates the conditions in this experiment, thereby creating the variable "amount of reinforcement." Whenever a researcher sets up experimental conditions, one or more variables are created. Such variables are called manipulated variables, **experimental variables,** or **treatment variables.**

Sometimes, researchers *select* an independent variable that already exists. In this case, the researcher must locate and select examples of it, rather than creating it. In our earlier example of reading methods, the researcher would have to locate and select existing examples of each reading method, rather than arranging for

them to happen. Selected independent variables are not limited to studies that compare different treatments; they are found in both causal-comparative and correlational studies (see Chapters Fifteen and Sixteen). They can be either categorical or quantitative. The key idea here, however, is that the independent variable (either created or selected) is thought to affect the dependent variable. Here are a few examples of some possible relationships between a selected independent variable and a dependent variable:

Independent Variable	Dependent Variable
Gender (categorical)	Musical aptitude (quantitative)
Mathematical ability (quantitative)	Career choice (categorical)
Gang membership (categorical)	Subsequent marital status (categorical)
Test anxiety (quantitative)	Test performance (quantitative)

Notice that none of the independent variables in the above pairs could be directly manipulated by the researcher. Notice also that, in some instances, the independent/dependent relationship might be reversed, depending which one the researcher thought might be the cause of the other. For example, he or she might think that test performance causes anxiety, not the reverse.

Generally speaking, most studies in education that have one quantitative and one categorical variable are studies comparing different methods or treatments. As we indicated above, the independent variable in such studies (the different methods or treatments) represents a categorical variable. Often the other (dependent) variable is quantitative and is referred to as an **outcome variable.**[†] The reason is rather clear-cut. The investigator, after all, is interested in the effect(s) of the differences in method on one or more outcomes (student achievement, their motivation, interest, and so on).

Again, let's check your understanding. Suppose a researcher plans to investigate the following question: "Will students like history more if taught by the inquiry method than if taught by the case-study method?" What is the outcome variable in this question?[‡]

---

*The independent (categorical) variable is the "number of teachers," and the dependent (quantitative) variable is the "amount of science learning."

[†]It is also possible for an outcome variable to be categorical. For example, the variable "college completion" could be divided into the categories of "dropouts" and "college graduates."
[‡]Liking for history.

EXTRANEOUS VARIABLES

A basic problem in research is that there are many possible independent variables that could have an effect on the dependent variables. Once researchers have decided which variables to study, they must be concerned about the influence or effect of other variables that exist. Such variables are usually called "extraneous variables." The task is to control these extraneous variables somehow to eliminate or minimize their effect.

Extraneous variables are independent variables that have not been controlled. Look again at the research question about team teaching presented above. What might be some other variables that could have an effect on the learning of students in a classroom situation?

There are many possible extraneous variables that might have an effect on student learning here. The personality of the teachers involved is one possibility. The experience level of the students is another. Time of day the classes are taught, nature of the subject taught, textbooks used, type of learning activities the teachers employ, and teaching methods—all are possible other variables that could affect learning. Such variables would probably be extraneous variables in this study. Figure 3.2 illustrates the importance of identifying extraneous variables.

One way to control extraneous variables is to hold them constant. For example, if a researcher were to include only boys as the subjects of a study, she would be controlling the variable of gender. We would say that the gender of the subjects does not vary; it would be a constant in this study.

Researchers must continually think about how they might control the possible effect(s) of extraneous variables. We will discuss how to do this in some detail in Chapter Nine, but for now you need to make sure you understand the difference between independent and dependent variables and to be aware of extraneous variables. Try your hand at the following question: "Will female students who are taught history by a teacher of the same gender like the subject more than female students taught by a teacher of a different gender?" What are the variables?*

---

*The dependent variable is *liking for history,* the independent variable is the *gender of the teacher.* Possible extraneous variables include the *personality* and *ability* of the teacher(s) involved; the *personality* and *ability level* of the students; the *materials used,* such as textbooks, etc.; the *style of teaching; ethnicity* and/or *age* of the teacher and students; and others. The researcher would want to control as many of these variables as possible.

Hypotheses

WHAT IS A HYPOTHESIS?

A **hypothesis** is, simply put, a prediction of some sort regarding the possible outcomes of a study. For example, here is a research question followed by its restatement in the form of a possible hypothesis:

Question: Will students who are taught history by a teacher of the same gender like the subject more than students taught by a teacher of a different gender?

Hypothesis: Students taught history by a teacher of the same gender will like the subject more than students taught history by a teacher of a different gender.

Here are two more examples of research questions followed by the restatement of each as a possible hypothesis:

Question: Is rapport with clients different with counselors using client-centered therapy than with those using behavior modification therapy?

Hypothesis: Counselors who use a client-centered therapy approach will have a greater rapport with their clients than counselors who use a behavior-modification approach.

Question: How do teachers feel about special classes for the educationally handicapped?

Hypothesis: Teachers in XYZ School District believe that students attending special classes for the educationally handicapped are thereby stigmatized.

or

Teachers in XYZ School District believe that special classes for the educationally handicapped will help such students improve their academic skills.

Many different hypotheses can come from a single question. As an illustration of this, see Figure 3.3.

ADVANTAGES OF STATING HYPOTHESES IN ADDITION TO RESEARCH QUESTIONS

Stating hypotheses has both advantages and disadvantages. What are some of the advantages? First, a hypothesis forces us to think more deeply and specifically about the possible outcomes of a study. Elaborating on

The principal of a high school compares the final examination scores of two history classes taught by teachers who use different methods, not realizing that they are also different in many other ways because of <u>extraneous</u> <u>variables</u>. The classes differ in:

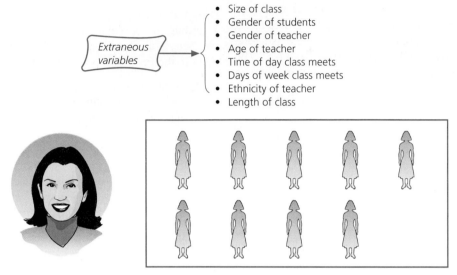

- Size of class
- Gender of students
- Gender of teacher
- Age of teacher
- Time of day class meets
- Days of week class meets
- Ethnicity of teacher
- Length of class

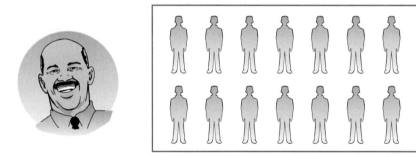

Ms. Brown's (age 31) history class meets from 9:00 to 9:50 A.M., Tuesdays and Thursdays. The class contains nine students, all girls.

Mr. Thompson's (age 54) history class meets from 2:00 to 3:00 P.M. Mondays and Wednesdays. The class contains 16 students, all boys.

Figure 3.2 *Examples of Extraneous Variables*

a question by formulating a hypothesis can lead to a more sophisticated understanding of what the question implies and exactly what variables are involved. Often, as in the case of the third example above, when more than one hypothesis seems to suggest itself, we are forced to think more carefully about what we really want to investigate.

A second advantage of restating questions as hypotheses involves a philosophy of science. The rationale underlying this philosophy is as follows: If one is attempting to build a body of knowledge in addition to answering a specific question, then stating hypotheses is a

good strategy because it enables one to make specific predictions based on prior evidence or theoretical argument. If these predictions are borne out by subsequent research, the entire procedure gains both in persuasiveness and efficiency. A classic example is Albert Einstein's theory of relativity. Many hypotheses were formulated as a result of Einstein's theory, which were later verified through research. As more and more of these predictions were shown to be fact, not only did they become useful in their own right, they also provided increasing support for the original ideas in Einstein's theory, which generated the hypotheses in the first place.

Figure 3.3 *A Single Research Question Can Suggest Several Hypotheses*

Lastly, stating a hypothesis helps us to see if we are, or are not, investigating a relationship. If not, we may possibly see a need to formulate one.

DISADVANTAGES OF STATING HYPOTHESES

Essentially, the disadvantages of stating hypotheses are threefold. First, stating a hypothesis may lead to a **bias,** either conscious or unconscious, on the part of the researcher. Once investigators state a hypothesis, they may be tempted to arrange the procedures or manipulate the data in such a way as to bring about a desired outcome.

This is probably more the exception than the rule. Researchers are assumed to be intellectually honest—although there are some famous exceptions. All studies should be subject to peer review; in the past, a review of suspect research has, on occasion, revealed such inadequacies of method that the reported results were cast into doubt. Furthermore, any particular study can be replicated to verify the findings of the study. Unfortunately, few educational research studies are repeated, so

this "protection" is somewhat of an illusion. A dishonest investigator stands a fair chance of getting away with falsifying results. Why would a person deliberately distort his or her findings? Probably because professional recognition and financial reward accrue to those who publish important results.

Even for the great majority of researchers who are honest, however, commitment to a hypothesis may lead to distortions that are unintentional and unconscious. But it is probably unlikely that any researcher in the field of education is ever totally disinterested in the outcomes of a study; therefore, his or her attitudes and/or knowledge may favor a particular result. For this reason, we think it is desirable for researchers to make known their predilections regarding a hypothesis so that they are clear to others interested in their research. This also allows investigators to take steps to guard (as much as possible) against their personal biases.

The second disadvantage of stating hypotheses at the outset is that it may sometimes be unnecessary, or even inappropriate, in research projects of certain types, such as descriptive surveys and ethnographic studies. In many such studies, it would be unduly presumptuous, as well as futile, to predict what the findings of the inquiry will be.

The third disadvantage of stating hypotheses is that focusing attention on a hypothesis may prevent researchers from noticing other phenomena that might be important to study. For example, deciding to study the effect of a "humanistic" classroom on student motivation might lead a researcher to overlook its effect on such characteristics as sex-typing or decision making, which would be quite noticeable to another researcher who was not focusing solely on motivation. This seems to be a good argument for ensuring that not all research be directed toward hypothesis testing.

Consider the example of a research question presented earlier in this chapter. The question was, "How do teachers feel about special classes for the educationally handicapped?" We offered two (of many possible) hypotheses that might arise out of this question: (1) "Teachers believe that students attending special classes for the educationally handicapped are thereby stigmatized" and (2) "Teachers believe that special classes for the educationally handicapped will help such students improve their academic skills." Both of these hypotheses implicitly suggest a comparison between special classes for the educationally handicapped and some other kind of arrangement. Thus, the relationship to be investigated is between teacher beliefs and type of class. Notice that it is important to compare what teachers think about special classes with their beliefs about other kinds of arrangements. If researchers looked only at teacher opinions about special classes without also identifying their views about other kinds of arrangements, they would not know if their beliefs about special classes were in any way unique or different.

SIGNIFICANT HYPOTHESES

As we begin to think about possible hypotheses suggested by a research question, we begin to see that some of them are more significant than others. What do we mean by "significant"? Simply that some may lead to more useful knowledge. Compare, for example, the following pairs of hypotheses. Which hypothesis in each pair would you say is more significant?

PAIR 1

a. Second-graders like school less than they like watching television.
b. Second-graders like school less than first-graders but more than third-graders.

PAIR 2

a. Most students with academic disabilities prefer being in regular classes rather than in special classes.
b. Students with academic disabilities will have more negative attitudes about themselves if they are placed in special classes than if they are placed in regular classes.

PAIR 3

a. Counselors who use client-centered therapy procedures get different reactions from counselees than do counselors who use traditional therapy procedures.
b. Counselees who receive client-centered therapy express more satisfaction with the counseling process than do counselees who receive traditional therapy.

In each of the three pairs, we think that the second hypothesis is more significant than the first since in each case (in our judgment) not only is the relationship to be investigated clearer and more specific but also investigation of the hypothesis seems more likely to lead to a greater amount of knowledge. It also seems to us that the information to be obtained will be of more use to people interested in the research question.

DIRECTIONAL VERSUS NONDIRECTIONAL HYPOTHESES

Let us make a distinction between directional and nondirectional hypotheses. A **directional hypothesis** is one in which the specific direction (such as higher, lower, more, or less) that a researcher expects to emerge in a relationship is indicated. The particular direction expected is based on what the researcher has found in the literature, from personal experience, or from the experience of others. The second hypothesis in each of the three pairs above is a directional hypothesis.

Sometimes it is difficult to make specific predictions. If a researcher suspects that a relationship exists, but has no basis for predicting the direction of the relationship, she cannot make a directional hypothesis. A **nondirectional hypothesis** does not make a specific prediction about what direction the outcome of a study will take. The above three hypotheses, in nondirectional form, would be stated as follows:

Nondirectional hypothesis for 1b: First-, second-, and third-graders will feel differently toward school.

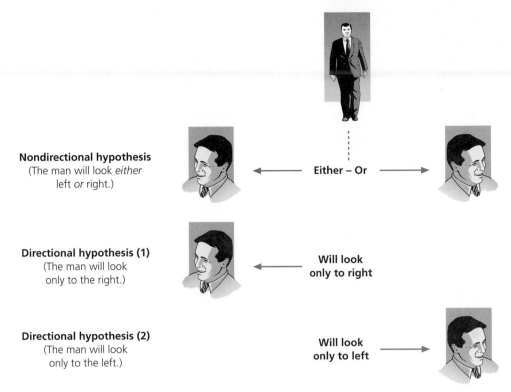

Nondirectional hypothesis
(The man will look *either*
left *or* right.)

Either – Or

Directional hypothesis (1)
(The man will look
only to the right.)

**Will look
only to right**

Directional hypothesis (2)
(The man will look
only to the left.)

**Will look
only to left**

Figure 3.4 *Directional Versus Nondirectional Hypotheses*

Nondirectional hypothesis for 2b: There will be a difference between the scores on an attitude measure of students with academic disabilities placed in special classes and such students placed in regular classes.

Nondirectional hypothesis for 3b: There will be a difference in expression of satisfaction with the counseling process between students who receive client-centered therapy and students who receive traditional therapy.

Figure 3.4 illustrates the difference between a directional and a nondirectional hypothesis. If the person pictured is approaching a street corner, three possibilities exist when he reaches the corner:

- He will continue to look straight ahead.
- He will look to his right.
- He will look to his left.

A nondirectional hypothesis would predict that he will look one way *or* the other. A directional hypothesis would predict that he will look in a particular direction (for example, to his right). Since a directional hypothesis is more risky (because it is less likely to occur), it is more convincing when confirmed.*

Both directional and nondirectional hypotheses appear in the literature of research, and you should learn to recognize each.

*If he looks straight ahead, neither a directional nor a nondirectional hypothesis is confirmed.

Go back to the **Interactive and Applied Learning Tools** feature at the beginning of the chapter for a listing of interactive and applied activities. Go to the **Online Learning Center** at www.mhhe.com/fraenkel5e or your **Interactive Student CD-ROM** to take practice quizzes and receive immediate feedback, practice with key terms, review chapter content and main ideas, and find annotated Web links.

Main Points

THE IMPORTANCE OF STUDYING RELATIONSHIPS

- Identifying relationships among variables enhances understanding.
- Understanding relationships helps us to explain the nature of the world in which we live.

VARIABLES

- A variable is any characteristic or quality that varies among the members of a particular group.
- A constant is any characteristic or quality that is the same for all members of a particular group.
- Several kinds of variables are studied in educational research, the most common being independent and dependent variables.
- An independent variable is a variable presumed to affect or influence other variables.
- A dependent (or outcome) variable is a variable presumed to be affected by one or more independent variables.
- A quantitative variable is a variable that varies in amount or degree, but not in kind.
- A categorical variable is a variable that varies only in kind, not in degree or amount.
- An extraneous variable is an independent variable that may have unintended effects on a dependent variable in a particular study.

HYPOTHESES

- The term "hypothesis," as used in research, refers to a prediction of results usually made before a study commences.
- A significant hypothesis is one that is likely to lead, if it is supported, to a greater amount of important knowledge than a nonsignificant hypothesis.
- Stating a research question as a hypothesis has both advantages and disadvantages.
- A directional hypothesis is a prediction about the specific nature of a relationship—for example, method A is more effective than method B.
- A nondirectional hypothesis is a prediction that a relationship exists without specifying its exact nature—for example, there will be a difference between method A and method B (without saying which will be more effective).

Key Terms

Bias 47	Extraneous variable 45	Outcome variable 44
Categorical variable 41	Hypothesis 45	Quantitative variable 41
Constant 41	Independent variable 43	Relationship 40
Dependent variable 43	Manipulated variable 44	Significant hypothesis 48
Directional hypothesis 48	Nondirectional	Treatment variable 44
Experimental variable 44	hypothesis 48	Variable 41

For Discussion

1. Here are several research questions. Which ones suggest relationships?
   a. How many students are enrolled in the sophomore class this year?
   b. As the reading level of a text passage increases, does the number of errors students make in pronouncing words in the passage increase?
   c. Do individuals who see themselves as socially "attractive" expect their romantic partners also to be (as judged by others) socially attractive?
   d. What does the faculty dislike about the new English curriculum?
   e. Who is the brightest student in the senior class?
   f. Will students who score above the 90th percentile on a standardized reading test also score above the 90th percentile on a standardized writing test?
   g. Which political party contains the most Protestants—Democratic or Republican?
2. What kinds of variables can you identify in each of the above questions?
3. See if you can restate each of the questions in item 1 as (a) a directional hypothesis and (b) a nondirectional hypothesis.
4. How would you rank the questions in item 1 in terms of significance? Why?
5. Listed below are a number of variables. Which ones are quantitative and which ones are categorical?
   a. Religious preference
   b. Neatness
   c. Eye color
   d. Curiosity
   e. Writing ability
   f. Jumping ability
   g. Fluency in Spanish
   h. Test anxiety
   i. Grade level
   j. Appreciation of classical music
   k. Mathematics ability
   l. Judged essay quality
6. What might cause a researcher to state a directional hypothesis rather than a nondirectional hypothesis? What about the reverse?
7. Are there any variables that researchers should *not* study? Explain.

Research Exercise Three: The Research Hypothesis

Try to formulate one testable hypothesis involving a relationship. It should be related to the research question you developed in Research Exercise Two. Using Problem Sheet 3, state the hypothesis in a sentence or two. Check to see if it suggests a relationship between at least two variables. If it does not, revise it so that it does. Now name these variables, and then indicate which is the independent variable and which is the dependent variable. Last, list as many extraneous variables as you can think of that might affect the results of your study.

An electronic version of this Problem Sheet that you can fill in and print, save, or e-mail is available on the Online Learning Center at www.mhhe.com/ fraenkel5e and on your Interactive Student CD-ROM.

A full-sized version of this Problem Sheet that you can fill in or photocopy is in your Student Workbook.

PROBLEM SHEET 3

The Research Hypothesis

1. My research question is: _____

2. I intend to use a hypothesis to investigate this question.   Yes _____   No _____

3. If no, my reasons are as follows: _____

    _____

    _____

4. If yes, my hypothesis is: _____

    _____

5. This hypothesis suggests a relationship between at least two variables.

    They are _____ and _____

6. More specifically, the variables in my study are:

    a. Dependent _____

    b. Independent _____

7. The dependent variable is (check one) categorical _____   quantitative _____

    The independent variable is (check one) categorical _____   quantitative _____

8. Possible extraneous variables that might affect my results include:

    a. _____

    b. _____

    c. _____

    d. _____

    e. _____

Ethics and Research

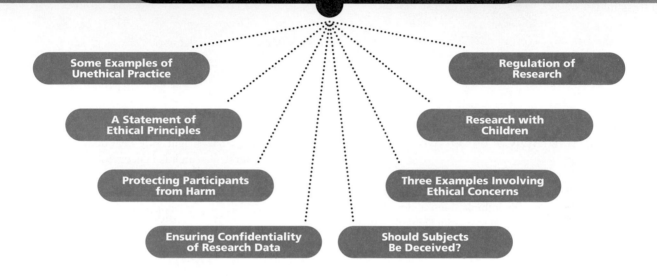

CHAPTER 4

Ethics and Research

- Some Examples of Unethical Practice
- A Statement of Ethical Principles
- Protecting Participants from Harm
- Ensuring Confidentiality of Research Data
- Should Subjects Be Deceived?
- Three Examples Involving Ethical Concerns
- Research with Children
- Regulation of Research

Mary Abrams and Lamar Harris, both juniors at a large Midwestern university, meet weekly for lunch. "I can't believe it," she says.

"What's the matter?" replies Lamar.

"Professor Thomas says that we have to participate in one of his research projects if we want to pass his course. He says it is a course 'requirement.' I don't think that's right, and I'm pretty upset about it. Can you believe it?"

"Wow. Can he do that?" "I mean, is that ethical?"

No, it's not! Mary has a legitimate (and ethical) complaint here. This issue—whether professors can require students to participate in research projects in order to pass a course—is one example of an unethical practice that sometimes occurs.

The whole question of what is—and what isn't—ethical, is what you will read about in this chapter.

Some Examples of Unethical Practice

The term "ethics" refers to questions of right and wrong. When researchers think about ethics, they must ask themselves if it is *right* to conduct a particular study or carry out certain procedures. Are there some kinds of studies that should *not* be conducted? You bet! Here are some examples of unethical practice:

A researcher:

- requires a group of high school sophomores to sign a form in which they agree to participate in a research study;
- asks first-graders sensitive questions without obtaining the consent of their parents to question them;
- deletes data he collects that do not support his hypothesis;
- requires university students to fill out a questionnaire about their sexual practices;
- involves a group of eighth-graders in a research study that may harm them psychologically without informing them of this fact.

Each of the above examples involves one or more violations of ethical practice. When researchers think about ethics, the basic question to ask in this regard is, "Will any physical or psychological harm come to anyone as a result of my research?" Naturally, no researcher wants this to happen to any of the subjects in a research study. Because this is such an important (and often overlooked) issue, we need to discuss it in some detail.

In a somewhat larger sense, ethics also refers to questions of right and wrong. By behaving ethically, a person is doing what is right. But what does it mean to be "right" as far as research is concerned?

A Statement of Ethical Principles

Webster's New World Dictionary defines ethical (behavior) as "conforming to the standards of conduct of a given profession or group." What researchers consider to be ethical, therefore, is largely a matter of agreement among them. Some years ago, the Committee on Scientific and Professional Ethics of the American Psychological Association published a list of ethical principles for the conduct of research with human subjects. We have adapted many of these principles so they apply to educational research. Please read carefully the statement that follows below and think carefully about what it means.

The decision to undertake research rests upon a considered judgment by the individual educator about how best to contribute to science and human welfare. Once one decides to conduct research, the educator considers various ways by which he might invest his talents and resources. Keeping this in mind, the educator carries out the research with respect and concern for the dignity and welfare of the people who participate and with cognizance of federal and state regulations and professional standards governing the conduct of research with human participants.

a. In planning a study, researchers have the responsibility to evaluate carefully any ethical concerns. Should any of the ethical principles listed below be compromised, the educator has a correspondingly serious obligation to observe stringent safeguards to protect the rights of human participants.

b. Considering whether a participant in a planned study will be a "subject at risk" or a "subject at minimal risk," according to recognized standards, is of primary ethical concern to the researcher.

c. The researcher always retains the responsibility for ensuring that a study is conducted ethically. The researcher is also responsible for the ethical treatment of research participants by collaborators, assistants, students, and employees, all of whom, however, incur similar obligations.

d. Except in minimal-risk research, the researcher establishes a clear and fair agreement with research participants, before they participate, that clarifies the obligations and responsibilities of each. The researcher has the obligation to honor all promises and commitments included in that agreement. The researcher informs the participants of all aspects of the research that might reasonably be expected to influence their willingness to participate in the study and answers honestly any questions they may have about the research. Failure by the researcher to make full disclosure prior to obtaining informed consent requires additional safeguards to protect the welfare and dignity of the research participants. Furthermore, research with children or with participants who have impairments that would limit understanding and/or communication requires special safeguarding procedures.

e. Sometimes the design of a study makes necessary the use of concealment or deception. When this is the case, the researcher has a special responsibility to: (i) determine whether the use of such techniques is justified by the study's prospective scientific or educational value; (ii) determine whether alternative procedures are available that do not use concealment or deception; and (iii) ensure that the participants are provided with sufficient explanation as soon as possible.

f. The researcher respects the right of any individual to refuse to participate in the study or to withdraw from participating at any time. The researcher's obligation in this regard is especially important when he or she is in a position of authority or influence over the participants in a study. Such positions of authority include, but are not limited to, situations in which research participation is required as part of employment or in which the participant is a student, client, or employee of the investigator.

g. The researcher protects all participants from physical and mental discomfort, harm, and danger that may arise from participating in a study. If risks of such consequences exist, the investigator informs the participant of that fact. Research procedures likely to cause serious or lasting harm to a participant are not used unless the failure to use these procedures might expose the participant to risk of greater harm, or unless the research has great potential benefit and fully informed and voluntary consent is obtained from each participant. All participants must be informed as to how they can contact the researcher within a reasonable time period following their participation should stress or potential harm arise.

h. After the data are collected, the researcher provides all participants with information about the nature of the study and does his or her best to clear up any misconceptions that may have developed. Where scientific or humane values justify delaying or withholding this information, the researcher has a special responsibility to carefully supervise the research and to ensure that there are no damaging consequences for the participant.

i. Where the procedures of a study result in undesirable consequences for any participant, the researcher has the responsibility to detect and remove or correct these consequences, including long-term effects.

j. Information obtained about a research participant during the course of an investigation is confidential unless otherwise agreed upon in advance. When the possibility exists that others may obtain access to such information, this possibility, together with the plans for protecting confidentiality, is explained to the participant as part of the procedure for obtaining informed consent.[1]

The above statement of ethical principles suggests three very important issues that every researcher should address: the protection of participants from harm, the ensuring of confidentiality of research data, and the question of deception of subjects. How can these issues be addressed, and how can the interests of the subjects involved in research be protected?

Protecting Participants from Harm

Perhaps the most important ethical consideration of all, it is a fundamental responsibility of every researcher to

Clinical Trials— Desirable or Not?

Clinical trials are the final test of a new drug. They offer an opportunity for drug companies to prove that new and previously unused medicines are safe and effective to use by giving such medicines to volunteers. Recently, however, there has been an increase in the number of complaints against such trials as well as a growing concern that some scientists may have a financial stake in the outcome of such trials. The most flagrant example of this was recently cited in the *San Francisco Chronicle.** A scientist gave a volunteer participant in one such trial what turned out to be a lethal dose of an experimental drug.

*Tom Abate (2001). Maybe conflicts of interest are scaring clinical trial patients. *San Francisco Chronicle,* May 28.

There has been an increase in the number of clinical trials as well as a corresponding increase in the number of volunteers involved in such trials. In 1995 about 500,000 volunteers participated; by 1999 it was reported that the number had jumped to 700,000.† The second concern is that some of the physicians who conduct such trials may have a financial stake in the outcome. No uniform policy currently exists on the disclosure of investigator's financial interest to patients who participate in such trials.

Arguments in favor of clinical trials are that, when properly conducted, they have paved the way for new medicines and procedures that have saved many lives. Volunteers can gain access to promising drugs long before they are available to the general public. And patients usually get excellent care from physicians and nurses while they are undergoing such trials. Last, but not least, such care often is free.

What do you think? Are clinical trials justified?

†Report issued at the Association of Clinical Research Professionals Convention, San Francisco, California, May 20, 2001.

do all in his or her power to ensure that participants in a research study are protected from physical or psychological harm, discomfort, or danger that may arise due to research procedures. Any sort of study that is likely to cause lasting, or even serious, harm or discomfort to any participant should not be conducted, unless the research has the potential to provide information of extreme benefit to human beings. Even when this may be the case, participants should be fully informed of the dangers involved and in no way required to participate.

A further responsibility in protecting individuals from harm is obtaining the consent of individuals who may be exposed to any risk. (See Figure 4.1 for an example of a consent form.) Fortunately, almost all educational research involves activities that are within the customary, usual procedures of schools or other agencies and as such involve little or no risk. Legislation recognizes this by specifically exempting most categories of educational research from formal review processes.[2] Nevertheless, researchers should carefully consider whether there is any likelihood of risk involved and, if there is, provide full information followed by formal consent by participants (or their guardians). Three important ethical questions to ask about harm in any study are:

1. Could people be harmed (physically or psychologically) during the study?
2. If so, could the study be conducted in another way to find out what the researcher wants to know?
3. Is the information that may be obtained from this study so important that it warrants possible harm to the participants?

These are difficult questions, and they deserve discussion and consideration by all researchers.

Ensuring Confidentiality of Research Data

Once the data in a study have been collected, researchers should make sure that no one else (other than perhaps a few key research assistants) has access to the data. Whenever possible, the names of the subjects should be removed from all data collection forms. This can be done by assigning a number or letter to each form, or subjects can be asked to furnish information anonymously. When this is done, not even the researcher can link the data to a particular subject. Sometimes, however, it is important in a study to identify in-

> *CONSENT TO SERVE AS A SUBJECT IN RESEARCH*
>
> I consent to serve as a subject in the research investigation entitled: _____
> _____
> _____
>
> The nature and general purpose of the research procedure and the known risks involved have been explained to me by _____.
> The investigator is authorized to proceed on the understanding that I may terminate my service as a subject at any time I so desire.
>
> I understand the known risks are: _____
> _____
> _____
>
> I understand also that it is not possible to identify all potential risks in an experimental procedure, and I believe that reasonable safeguards have been taken to minimize both the known and the potentially unknown risks.
>
> Witness _____   Signed _____
>   (subject)
>
>   Date _____
>
> To be retained by the principal investigator.

Figure 4.1 *Example of a Consent Form*

dividual subjects. When this is the case, the linkage system should be carefully guarded.

All subjects should be assured that any data collected from or about them will be held in confidence. The names of individual subjects should never be used in any publications that describe the research. And all participants in a study should always have the right to withdraw from the study or to request that data collected about them not be used.

Should Subjects Be Deceived?

The issue of deception is particularly troublesome. Many studies cannot be carried out unless some deception of subjects takes place. It is often difficult to find naturalistic situations in which certain behaviors occur frequently. For example, a researcher may have to wait a long time for a teacher to reinforce students in a certain way. It may be much easier for the researcher to ob-

serve the effects of such reinforcement by employing the teacher as a confederate.

Sometimes it is better to deceive subjects than to cause them pain or trauma, as investigating a particular research question might require. The famous Milgram study of obedience is a good example.[3] In this study, subjects were ordered to give increasingly severe electric shocks to another subject whom they could not see sitting behind a screen. What they did not know was that the individual to whom they thought they were administering the shocks was a confederate of the experimenter, and no shocks were actually being administered. The dependent variable was the level of shock subjects administered before they refused to administer any more. Out of a total of 40 subjects who participated in the study, 26 followed the "orders" of the experimenter and (so they thought) administered the maximum shock possible of 450 volts! Even though no shocks were actually administered, publication of the results of the study produced widespread controversy. Many people felt the study was unethical. Others argued

"We are required to ask you to sign this consent form. You needn't read it; it's just routine."

"A few cases seemed quite different from the rest, so we deleted them."

"Yes, as a student at this university you are required to participate in this study."

"There is no need to tell any of the parents that we are modifying the school lunch diet for this study."

"Requiring students to participate in class discussions might be harmful to some, but it is necessary for our research."

Figure 4.2 *Examples of Unethical Research Practices*

that the importance of the study and its results justified the deception. Notice that the study raises questions about not only deception but also harm, since some participants could have suffered emotionally from later consideration of their actions.

Current professional guidelines are as follows:

- Whenever possible, a researcher should conduct the study using methods that do not require deception.
- If alternative methods cannot be devised, the researcher must determine whether the use of deception is justified by the prospective study's scientific, educational, or applied value.

- If the participants are deceived, the researcher must ensure that the participants are provided with sufficient explanation as soon as possible.

Perhaps the most serious problem involving deception is what it may ultimately do to the reputation of the scientific community. If people in general begin to think of scientists and researchers as liars, or as individuals who misrepresent what they are about, the overall image of science may suffer. Fewer and fewer people will be willing to participate in research investigations. As a result, the search for reliable knowledge about our world may be impeded.

Three Examples Involving Ethical Concerns

Here are brief descriptions of three research studies. Let us consider each in terms of (1) presenting possible harm to the participants; (2) ensuring the confidentiality of the research data; and (3) knowingly practicing deception. (See Figure 4.2 for some examples of unethical research practices.)

Study 1

The researcher plans to observe (unobtrusively) students in each of 40 classrooms—eight visits each of 40 minutes' duration. The purpose of these observations is to look for relationships between the behavior of students and certain teacher behavior patterns.

Possible Harm to the Participants. This study would fall within the exempt category regarding the possibility of harm to the participants. Neither teachers nor students are placed under any risk, and observation is an accepted part of school practice.

Confidentiality of the Research Data. The only issue that is likely to arise in this regard is the possible but unlikely observation of a teacher behaving in an illegal or unethical way (e.g., physically or verbally abusing a student). In the former case, the researcher is legally required to report the incident. In the latter case, the researcher must weigh the ethical dilemma involved in not reporting the incident against that of violating assurances of confidentiality.

Patients Given Fake Blood Without Their Knowledge*

Failed Study Used Change in FDA Rules

ASSOCIATED PRESS

CHICAGO—A company conducted an ill-fated blood substitute trial without the informed consent of patients in the study—some of whom died, federal officials say.

Baxter International Inc. was able to test the substitute, known as HemAssist, without consent because of a 1996 change in federal Food and Drug Administration regulations.

The changes, which broke a 50-year standard to get consent for nearly all experiments on humans, were designed to help research in emergency medicine that could not happen if doctors took the time to get consent.

But the problems with the HemAssist trial are prompting some medical ethicists to question the rule change.

San Francisco Chronicle, January 18, 1999

"People get involved in something to their detriment without any knowledge of it," George Annas, a professor of health law at the Boston University School of Public Health, told the *Chicago Tribune.* "We use people. What's the justification for that?"

No other company has conducted a no-consent experiment under the rule, FDA officials said.

Baxter officials halted their clinical trial of HemAssist last spring after reviewing data on the first 100 trauma patients placed in the nationwide study.

Of the 52 critically ill patients given the substitute, 24 died, representing a 46.2 percent mortality rate. The Deerfield, Ill.-based company had projected 42.6 percent mortality for critically ill patients seeking emergency treatment.

There has been an intense push to find a blood substitute to ease the effects of whole-blood shortages.

Researchers say artificial blood lasts longer than conventional blood, eliminates the time-consuming need to match blood types and wipes out the risk of contamination from such viruses as HIV and hepatitis.

The 1996 regulations require a level of community notification that is not used in most scientific studies, including community meetings, news releases and post-study follow-up.

No lawsuits have arisen from the blood substitute trial, Baxter officials said.

Deception. Although no outright deception is involved, the researcher is going to have to give the teachers a rationale for observing them. If the specific teacher characteristic being observed (e.g., need to control) is given, the behavior in question is likely to be affected. To avoid this, the researcher might explain that the purpose of the study is to investigate different teaching styles—without divulging the specifics. To us, this does not seem to be unethical. An alternative is to tell the teachers that specific details cannot be divulged until after data have been collected for fear of changing their behavior. If this alternative is pursued, some teachers might refuse to participate.

STUDY 2

The researcher wishes to study the value of a workshop on suicide prevention for high school students. The workshop is to consist of three two-hour meetings in which danger signals, causes of suicide, and community resources that provide counseling will be discussed. Students will volunteer, and half will be assigned to a comparison group that will not participate in the workshop. Outcomes will be assessed by comparing the information learned and attitudes of those attending with those who do not attend.

Possibility of Harm to the Participants. Whether this study fits the exempt category with regard to any possibility of risk for the participants depends on the extent to which it is atypical for the school in question. We think that in most schools, this study would probably be considered atypical. In addition, it is conceivable that the material presented could place a student at risk by stirring up emotional reactions. In any case, the researcher should inform parents as to the nature of the study and the possible risks involved and obtain their consent for their children to participate.

Confidentiality of the Research Data. No problems are foreseen in this regard, although confidentiality as to what will occur during the workshop cannot, of course, be guaranteed.

Deception. No problems are foreseen.

Figure 4.3 *Example of a Consent Form for a Minor to Participate in a Research Study*

*AUTHORIZATION FOR A MINOR TO SERVE
AS A SUBJECT IN RESEARCH*

I authorize the service of _____ as a subject in the research investigation entitled: _____ _____ _____

The nature and general purpose of the research procedure and the known risks have been explained to me. I understand that _____
(name of minor)
will be given a preservice explanation of the research and that he/she may decline to serve. Further, I understand that he/she may terminate his/her service in this research at any time he/she so desires.

I understand the known risks are: _____ _____ _____

I understand also that it is not possible to identify all potential risks in an experimental procedure, and I believe that reasonable safeguards have been taken to minimize both the known and the potential but unknown risks.

I agree further to indemnify and hold harmless S. F. State University and its agents and employees from any and all liability, actions, or causes of actions that may accrue to the subject minor as a result of his/her activities for which this consent is granted.

Witness _____   Signed _____
(parent or guardian)

Date _____

To be retained by researcher.

STUDY 3

The researcher wishes to study the effects of "failure" versus "success" by teaching junior high students a motor skill during a series of six 10-minute instructional periods. After each training period, the students will be given feedback on their performance as compared with that of other students. In order to control extraneous variables (such as coordination), the researcher plans to randomly divide the students into two groups—half will be told their performance was "relatively poor" and the other half will be told that they are "doing well." Their actual performance will be ignored.

Possibility of Harm to the Participants. This study presents several problems. Some students in the "failure" group may well suffer emotional distress. Although students are normally given similar feedback on their performance in most schools, feedback in this study (being arbitrary) may conflict dramatically with their prior experience. The researcher cannot properly inform students, or their parents, about the deceptive nature of the study, since to do so would in effect destroy the study.

Confidentiality of the Research Data. Confidentiality does not appear to be an issue in this study.

More About Research

An Example of Unethical Research

A series of studies reported in the 1950s and 1960s received widespread attention in psychology and education and earned their author much fame, including a knighthood. They addressed the question of how much of one's performance on IQ tests was likely to be hereditary and how much was due to environmental factors.

Several groups of children were studied over time, including identical twins raised together and apart, fraternal twins raised together and apart, and same-family siblings. The results were widely cited to support the conclusion that IQ is about 80 percent hereditary and 20 percent environmental.

Some initial questions were raised when another researcher found a considerably lower hereditary percentage. Subsequent detailed investigation of the initial studies* revealed highly suspicious statistical treatment of data, inadequate specification of procedures, and questionable adjustment of scores, all suggesting unethical massaging of data. Such instances, which are reported occasionally, underscore the importance of repeating studies as well as the essential requirement that all procedures and data be available for public scrutiny.

*L. Kamin (1974). *The science and politics of I.Q.* New York: John Wiley.

Deception. The deception of participants is clearly an issue. One alternative is to base feedback on actual performance. The difficulty here is that each student's extensive prior history will affect both individual performance and interpretation of feedback, thus confounding the results. Some, but not all, of these extraneous variables can be controlled (perhaps by examining school records for data on past history or by pretesting students). Another alternative is to weaken the experimental treatment by trying to lessen the possibility of emotional distress (e.g., by saying to participants in the failure group: "You did not do quite as well as most") and confining the training to one time period. Both of these alternatives, however, would lessen the chances of any relationship emerging.

Research with Children

Studies using children as participants present some special issues for researchers. The young are more vulnerable in some respects, have fewer legal rights, and may not understand the language of informed consent. Therefore, the following specific guidelines need to be considered.

- Informed consent of parents or of those legally designated as caretakers is required for participants defined as minors. Signers must be provided all necessary information in appropriate language and must have the opportunity to refuse. (See Figure 4.3 for an example of a consent form for a minor.)

- Researchers do not present themselves as diagnosticians or counselors in reporting results to parents, nor do they report information given by a child in confidence.
- Children may never be coerced into participation in a study.
- Any form of remuneration for the child's services does not affect the application of these (and other) ethical principles.

Regulation of Research

Research that involves human subjects is often difficult to conduct. Before any research involving human beings can be conducted at a university or other institution that receives federal funds (e.g., funds from the federal government for research or scholarships), the research must be approved by an institutional review board (IRB) at the institution. Such a review must take place whether the research is done by a single researcher or a group of researchers and whether it is financed by private or government funds. In the case of federally funded investigations, failure to comply can mean that the entire institution (e.g., a university) will lose all its federal support (e.g., veterans' benefits, scholarship money). Needless to say, this is a severe penalty. The federal agency that has the major responsibility for establishing the guidelines for research involving human subjects is the Department of Health and Human Services (HHS).

The IRB at a particular institution is charged with weighing the risk involved for subjects, determining

63

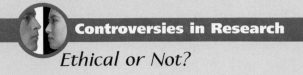
Ethical or Not?

In September 1998, a U.S. District Court judge halted a study begun in 1994 to evaluate the effectiveness of the U.S. Job Corps program. For two years, the researchers had randomly assigned 1 out of every 12 eligible applicants to a control group that was denied service for three years—a total of 6000 applicants. If applicants refused to sign a waiver agreeing to participate in the study, they were told to reapply two years later. The class action lawsuit alleged psychological, emotional, and economic harm to the control subjects. The basis for the judge's decision was a failure to follow the federal law that required the methodology to be subject to public review. A preliminary settlement pledged to locate all of the control subjects by the year 2000, invite them into the Job Corps (if still eligible), and pay each person $1000.*

In a letter to the editor† of *Mother Jones,* in April, 1999, however, Judith M. Gueron, the President of Manpower Demonstration Research Corporation (*not* the company awarded the evaluation grant) defended the study on two grounds:

(*a*) since there were only limited available openings for the program, random selection of qualified applicants "is arguably fairer" than first-come, first-served; and (*b*) the alleged harm to those rejected is unknown, since they were free to seek other employment or training.

What do you think?

*John Price (1999). Job Corps lottery. *Mother Jones,* January/February, pp. 21–22.
†Backtalk (1999). *Mother Jones,* April, p. 13.

whether informed consent has been planned for, and whether plans have been made to debrief the participants (i.e., informing subjects once the experiment is completed). If a researcher intends to request federal funds, then his or her research proposal is evaluated by a national review panel composed of other researchers with some experience in the area of research being proposed. Once the proposed research has been approved by the appropriate review board or boards, then the researcher must obtain a group of subjects who are willing to participate in the study. In some instances, informed consent forms are used to ensure that all the participants have been fully informed.

Some researchers were unhappy with some of the regulations that were issued in 1974 because they felt that the rules interfered unnecessarily with risk-free projects. Their opposition resulted in a 1981 set of revised guidelines, as shown in the More About Research box on page 65. These guidelines apply to all research funded by HHS. IRBs decide which studies qualify to be exempt from the guidelines.

One further legal matter should be mentioned. Attorneys, physicians, and members of the clergy are protected by laws concerning privileged communications (i.e., they are protected by law from having to reveal information given to them in confidence). Researchers do not have this protection. It is possible, therefore, that any subjects who admit, on a questionnaire, to having committed a crime could be arrested and prosecuted. As you can see, it would be a risk therefore for the participants in a research study to admit to a researcher that they had participated in a crime. If such information is required to attain the goals of a study, a researcher can avoid the problem by omitting all forms of identification from the questionnaire. When mailed questionnaires are used, the researcher can keep track of nonrespondents by having each participant mail in a separate card indicating that they completed the questionnaire.

Department of Health and Human Services Revised Regulations for Research with Human Subjects

The revised guidelines exempt many projects from regulation by HHS. Below is a list of projects now free of the guidelines.

1. Research conducted in educational settings, such as instructional strategy research or studies on the effectiveness of educational techniques, curricula, or classroom management methods.
2. Research using educational tests (cognitive, diagnostic, aptitude, and achievement) provided that subjects remain anonymous.

3. Survey or interview procedures, except where all of the following conditions prevail:
   (*a*) Participants could be identified.
   (*b*) Participants' responses, if they become public, could place the subject at risk on criminal or civil charges, or could affect the subjects' financial or occupational standing.
   (*c*) Research involves "sensitive aspects" of the participant's behavior, such as illegal conduct, drug use, sexual behavior, or alcohol use.
4. Observation of public behavior (including observation by participants), except where all three of the conditions listed in item 3 above are applicable.
5. The collection or study of documents, records, existing data, pathological specimens, or diagnostic specimens if these sources are available to the public or if the information obtained from the sources remains anonymous.

Go back to the **Interactive and Applied Learning Tools** feature at the beginning of the chapter for a listing of interactive and applied activities. Go to the **Online Learning Center** at www.mhhe.com/fraenkel5e or your **Interactive Student CD-ROM** to take practice quizzes and receive immediate feedback, practice with key terms, review chapter content and main ideas, and find annotated Web links.

Main Points

BASIC ETHICAL PRINCIPLES

- "Ethics" refers to questions of right and wrong.
- There are a number of ethical principles that all researchers should be aware of and apply to their investigations.
- The basic ethical question for all researchers to consider is, "Will any physical or psychological harm come to anyone as a result of my research?"
- All subjects in a research study should be assured that any data collected from or about them will be held in confidence.
- The term "deception," as used in research, refers to intentionally misinforming the subjects of a study as to some or all aspects of the research topic.

RESEARCH WITH CHILDREN

- Children as research subjects present problems for researchers that are different from those of adult subjects. Children are more vulnerable, have fewer legal rights, and often do not understand the meaning of "informed consent."

THE REGULATION OF RESEARCH

- Before any research involving human beings can be conducted at an institution that receives federal funds, it must be reviewed by an institutional review board (IRB) at the institution.
- The federal agency that has the major responsibility for establishing the guidelines for research studies that involve human subjects is the Department of Health and Human Services.

Key Terms

Ethics 56

Ethical principles 56

Protecting participants from harm 60

Confidentiality of research data 60

Deception 59

Research with children 62

Regulation of research 63

Unethical research 60

For Discussion

1. Here are three descriptions of ideas for research. Which (if any) might have some ethical problems? Why?
   a. A researcher is interested in investigating the effects of diet on physical development. He designs a study in which two groups are to be compared. Both groups are composed of 11-year-olds. One group is to be given an enriched diet, high in vitamins, that has been shown to have a strengthening effect on laboratory animals. A second group is not to be given this diet. The groups are to be selected from all the 11-year-olds in an elementary school near the university where the researcher teaches.
   b. A researcher is interested in the effects of music on attention span. She designs an experimental study in which two similar high school government classes are to be compared. For a five-week period, one class has classical music played softly in the background as the teacher lectures and holds class discussions on the Civil War (the period of history the class is studying during this time). The other class studies the same material and participates in the same activities as the first class, but does not have any music played during the five weeks.
   c. A researcher is interested in the effects of drugs on human beings. He asks the warden of the local penitentiary for subjects to participate in an experiment. The warden assigns several prisoners to participate in the experiment but does not tell them what it is about. The prisoners are injected with a number of drugs whose effects are unknown. Their reactions to the drugs are then described in detail by the researcher.
2. Which, if any, of the above studies would be exempt under the revised guidelines shown in the More About Research box on p. 65?
3. Can you suggest a research study that would present ethical problems if done with children, but not if done with adults?
4. Are there any research questions that should *not* be investigated in schools? If so, why not?

Notes

1. Adapted from the Committee on Scientific and Professional Ethics and Conduct (1981). Ethical principles of psychologists. *American Psychologist, 36:*633–638. Copyright 1981 by the American Psychological Association. Reprinted by permission.

2. Family Educational Rights and Privacy Act (also known as the Buckley Amendment) of 1974.

3. S. Milgram (1967). Behavioral study of obedience. *Journal of Abnormal and Social Psychology,* 67:371–378.

Research Exercise Four: Ethics and Research

Using Problem Sheet 4, restate the research question you developed in Problem Sheet 3. Identify any possible ethical problems in carrying out such a study. How might such problems be remedied?

Problem Sheet 4

Ethics and Research

1. My research question is: _____
   _____

2. The possibilities for harm to participants (if any) are as follows: _____
   _____
   _____
   _____

   I would handle these problems as follows: _____
   _____

3. The possibilities of problems of confidentiality (if any) are as follows: _____
   _____
   _____
   _____

   I would handle these problems as follows: _____
   _____

4. The possibilities of problems of deception (if any) are as follows: _____
   _____
   _____
   _____

   I would handle these problems as follows: _____
   _____

5. If you think your proposed study would fit the guidelines for exempt status, state why here.
   _____
   _____
   _____
   _____

An electronic version of this Problem Sheet that you can fill in and print, save, or e-mail is available on the Online Learning Center at www.mhhe.com/ fraenkel5e and on your Interactive Student CD-ROM.

A full-sized version of this Problem Sheet that you can fill in or photocopy is in your Student Workbook.

Review of the Literature

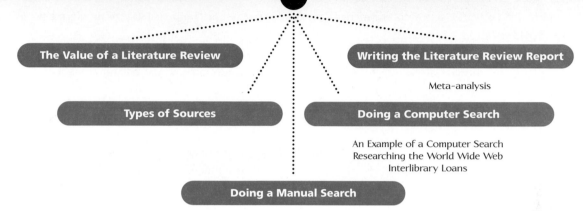

CHAPTER 5

Review of the Literature

- **The Value of a Literature Review**
- **Types of Sources**
- **Writing the Literature Review Report**
  - Meta-analysis
- **Doing a Computer Search**
  - An Example of a Computer Search
  - Researching the World Wide Web
  - Interlibrary Loans
- **Doing a Manual Search**
  - Steps Involved in a Literature Search

Objectives

Studying this chapter should enable you to:

- Describe *briefly why a literature review is of value.*
- Name *the steps a researcher goes through in conducting a review of the literature.*
- Describe *briefly the kinds of information contained in a general reference and* give an example *of such a source.*
- Explain *the difference between a primary and a secondary source and* give an example *of each type.*
- Explain *what is meant by the phrase "search term" and how such terms are used in literature searches.*
- Conduct *both a manual and a computer search of the literature on a topic of interest to you after a small amount of "hands-on" computer time and a little help from a librarian.*
- Write *a summary of your literature review.*
- Explain *what a meta-analysis is.*

Interactive and Applied Learning

After, or while, reading this chapter:

🔵 🔵 Go to the Study Guide on the Online Learning Center at www.mhhe.com/fraenkel5e or Interactive Student CD-ROM to:
- Read the Guide to Electronic Research

🔵 📖 Go to your Interactive Student CD-ROM or Student Workbook to do the following activities:
- Activity 5.1: Library Worksheet
- Activity 5.2: Where Would You Look?
- Activity 5.3: Do a Computer Search of the Literature

After a career in the military, Phil Gomez is in his first year as a teacher at an adult school in Logan, Utah. He teaches United States history to students who did not graduate from high school but now are trying to obtain a diploma. He has learned the hard way, through trial and error, that there are a number of techniques that simply put students to sleep. He sincerely wants to be a good teacher, but he is sort of at his wit's end in thinking up how to interest his students in the subject. As he is the only history teacher in the school, the other teachers are not of much help.

He wants to get some ideas, therefore, about other approaches, strategies, and techniques that he might use. He decides to do a search of the literature on teaching to see what he can find out. But he has no idea where to begin. Should he look at books? Journal articles? Reports or papers? Are there references particularly geared to the teaching of American history? What about the possibility of an electronic search? Where should he look?

In this chapter, you will learn some answers to these (and other, related) questions. When you have finished reading, you should have a number of ideas about how to do both a manual and an electronic search of the educational literature.

The Value of a Literature Review

A **literature review** is helpful in two ways. It not only helps researchers glean the ideas of others interested in a particular research question, but it also lets them see what the results of other (similar, or related) studies of the question have been. A detailed literature review, in fact, is usually required of master's and doctoral students when they design a thesis. Researchers then weigh information from a literature review in the light of their own concerns and situation. Thus, there are two important points here. Researchers need to be able not only to locate other work dealing with their intended area of study but also to be able to evaluate this work in terms of its relevance to the research question of interest.

Types of Sources

Researchers need to be familiar with three basic types of sources as they begin to search for information related to the research question.

1. **General references** are the sources researchers often refer to first. In effect, they tell where to look to locate other sources—such as articles, monographs, books, and other documents—that deal directly with the research question. Most general references are either *indexes,* which list the author, title, and place of publication of articles and other materials, or **abstracts,** which give a brief summary of various publications, as well as their author, title, and place of publication. An index frequently used by researchers in education is *Current Index to Journals in Education.* A commonly used abstract is *Psychological Abstracts.*

2. **Primary sources** are publications in which researchers report the results of their studies. Authors communicate their findings directly to readers. Most primary sources in education are journals, such as the *Journal of Educational Research* or the *Journal of Research in Science Teaching.* These journals are usually published monthly or quarterly, and the articles in them typically report on a particular research study.

3. **Secondary sources** refer to publications in which authors describe the work of others. The most common secondary sources in education are textbooks. A textbook in educational psychology, for example, may describe several studies that have been done in psychology as a way to illustrate various ideas and concepts. Other commonly used secondary sources include educational encyclopedias, research reviews, and yearbooks.

Researchers who seek information on a given topic would refer first to one or more general references to locate primary and secondary sources of value. For a quick overview of the problem at hand, secondary sources are probably the best bet. For detailed information about the research that others have done, primary sources should be consulted.

Today, there are two main ways to do a literature search—manually, using the traditional paper approach, and electronically, by means of a computer. Let's first examine the traditional approach, and then consider how to do a computer search. (These days, researchers usually do a computer search first, going to a manual search only if they do not come up with very much electronically.)

Doing a Manual Search

STEPS INVOLVED IN A LITERATURE SEARCH

Several steps are involved in a literature review.

1. Define the research problem as precisely as possible.
2. Look at relevant secondary sources.
3. Select and peruse one or two appropriate general reference works.
4. Formulate search terms (key words or phrases) pertinent to the problem or question of interest.
5. Search the general references for relevant primary sources.
6. Obtain and read relevant primary sources; note and summarize key points in the sources.

Let us consider each of these steps in some detail.

Define the Problem as Precisely as Possible.
The first thing a researcher needs to do is to state the research question as specifically as possible. General questions like "What sorts of teaching methods work well in the classroom?" or "How can a principal be a more effective leader?" are too fuzzy to be of much help when one starts to look through a general reference. The question of interest should be narrowed down to a specific area of concern. More specific questions, therefore, might be "Is discussion more effective than slide-tape presentations in motivating students to learn social studies concepts?" or "What sorts of strategies do principals judged to be effective by their staffs use to improve faculty and staff morale?" A serious effort should be made to state the question so that it focuses on the specific issue for investigation.

Look Through One or Two Secondary Sources.
Once the research question has been stated in specific terms, it is a good idea to look through one or two secondary sources to get an overview of previous work that has been done on the problem. This needn't be a monumental chore nor take an overly long time. The main intent is to get some idea of what is already known about the problem of which the question is a part and of

some of the other questions that are being asked. Researchers may also get an idea or two about how to revise or improve the research question. Here are some of the most commonly used secondary sources in educational research:

Encyclopedia of Educational Research (current edition): Contains brief summaries of over 300 topics in education. Excellent source for getting a brief overview of the problem.

Handbook of Research on Teaching: Contains longer articles on various aspects of teaching. Most are written by educational researchers who specialize in the topic on which they are writing. Includes extensive bibliographies.

National Society for the Study of Education (NSSE) Yearbooks: Published every year, these yearbooks deal with recent research on various topics. Each book usually contains from 10 to 12 chapters dealing with various aspects of the topic. The society also publishes a number of volumes on contemporary educational issues that deal in part with research on various topics. A list of these volumes can be found in the back of the most recent yearbook.

Review of Educational Research: Published four times a year, this is a journal that contains reviews of research on various topics in education. Includes extensive bibliographies.

Review of Research in Education: Published yearly, each volume contains surveys of research on important topics written by leading educational researchers.

Subject Guide to Books in Print (most recent edition): Each of the above sources contains reviews of research on various topics of importance in education. There are many topics, however, that have not been the subjects of a recent review. If a research question deals with such a topic, the best chance for locating information discussing research on the topic lies in recent books or monographs on the subject. The best source for identifying books that might discuss research on a topic is the current edition of *Books in Print.*

In addition, many professional associations and organizations have published handbooks of research in their fields. These include the:

- *Handbook of Reading Research*
- *Handbook of Research on Curriculum*

- *Handbook of Research on Educational Administration*
- *Handbook of Research on Mathematics Teaching and Learning*
- *Handbook of Research on School Supervision*
- *Handbook of Research on Multicultural Education*
- *Handbook of Research on Music Teaching and Learning*
- *Handbook of Research on Social Studies Teaching and Learning*
- *Handbook of Research on Teacher Education*
- *Handbook of Research on the Teaching of English*
- *Handbook of Research on the Education of Young Children*

Each of these handbooks includes a current summary of research dealing with important topics related to their particular field of study. Other places to look for books on a topic of interest are the card catalog* and the curriculum department (for textbooks) in the library. *Education Index* and *Psychological Abstracts* also list newly published professional books in their fields.

Select the Appropriate General References. After reviewing a secondary source to get a more informed overview of the problem, researchers should have a clearer idea of exactly what to investigate. At this point it is a good idea to look again at the research question to see if it needs to be rewritten in any way to make it more focused. Once satisfied, researchers can select one or two general references to help identify particular journals or other primary sources related to the question.

There are many general references a researcher can consult. Here is a list of the ones most commonly used.

> *Education Index:* Published monthly. Indexes articles from over 300 educational publications, but gives only bibliographical data (author, title, and place of publication). For this reason, *Current Index to Journals in Education,* or CIJE, is preferred by most educational researchers doing a literature search on a topic in education. Figure 5.1 illustrates part of a page listing under the topic of "Thought and thinking" in *Education Index.*

---

*More and more, card catalogs are a thing of the past. Most universities have converted much of the information in their card catalogs into a computer database. Rather than scanning through a number of cards, most researchers now simply ask a computer to call up on screen the bibliographic data of the particular sources in which they are interested.

Reader's Guide to Periodical Literature: The *Reader's Guide* is similar to *Education Index* in that it does not contain any abstracts, only bibliographic data. It is worth considering if one's topic extends beyond the field of education, but otherwise it is not usually a profitable source for educational researchers. It does not cover the field in depth as does *Education Index,* but it includes a much wider range of material. It also focuses on magazines that appeal to a more general readership. An article on education that appears in *Time* magazine, for example, would be indexed in the *Reader's Guide* but not in CIJE or *Psychological Abstracts.* It is published monthly, with an annual cumulative index, and can be searched by computer. A page from the *Reader's Guide* looks similar to the page from *Education Index* that is shown in Figure 5.1.

Social Science Citation Index (SSCI): Another type of citation and indexing service, SSCI offers the forward search, a unique feature that can be helpful to researchers. When a researcher has found an article that contains information of interest, he or she can locate the author's name in the SSCI (or enter it into a computer search if the library has SSCI online) to find out the names of other authors who have cited this same article and the journals in which their articles appeared. These additional articles may also be of interest to the researcher. He or she can look to see what additional books and articles were cited by these other authors, and thus conceivably obtain information that otherwise might be missed (a summary of the major indexes and abstracts is shown in Table 5.1).

Psychological Abstracts: Published monthly by the American Psychological Association. Covers over 1300 journals, reports, monographs, and other documents (including books and other secondary sources). Abstracts (brief summaries of articles) are presented in addition to bibliographical data. Although there is considerable overlap with CIJE, *Psych Abstracts* (as it is often called) usually gives a more thorough coverage of psychological than educational topics. It should definitely be consulted for any topic dealing with some aspect of psychology.

PsycINFO: Corresponding to the printed *Psychological Abstracts* is its online version, *PsycINFO.* In a manner similar to *Psych Abstracts, PsycINFO* includes citations to journal articles, books, and book chapters in psychology and the behavioral

Thought and thinking
See also
Abstraction
Children's conceptions
Cognition
Creative thinking
Critical thinking
Meditation
Memory
Problem solving
Questioning
Reasoning
Van Hiele levels of geometric thought
Visualization
Audiovisual aids
Richard Konieczka teaches the 59 second mind map [vido review]
Libr J v123 no10 p177-8 Je 1 '98 L. Lampert
Curriculum
Evaluation
Inductive reasoning in third grade: intervention promises and constraints. J. H. M. Hamers and others. bibl
Contemp Educ Psychol v23 no2 p132-48 Ap '98
Teaching
See also
Cognitive strategy instruction
Learning to think abstractly S. J. Greenspan and S. Wieder por *Sch Early Child Today* v12 no8 p22-3 My/Je '98
Moving beyond "I feel good". M. Mooney. *Teach PreK-8* v28 no8 p48-9 My '98
An old friend of the social studies teacher. J. R. Freese. *Can Soc Stud* v32 no4 p124-5+ Summ '98
Word class: using thinking skills to enhance spelling instruction. A. P. Johnson. bibl *Read Horiz* v38 no4 p257-65 Mr/Ap '98
Spain
The improvement of moral development through an increase in reflection. A training programme. B. G. López and R. G. López. bibl *J Moral Educ* v27 no2 p225-41 Je '98
Teaching Methods
See also
Mediated learning experience approach
Encouraging thinking in high school and middle school: constraints and possibilities. E. F. Sparapani. *Clearing House* v71 no5 p274-6 My/Je '98
An examination of the CATM blocks and block pattern intervention. R. P. Unruh and M. Dupree. *J Instr Psychol* v25 no2 p134-8 Je '98
Intuition in nursing practice: sharing graduate students' exemplars with undergraduate students. C. T. Beck. bibl *J Nurs Educ* v37 no4 p169-72 Ap '98
Penetrating the barriers to teaching higher thinking. V. Supon. bibl *Clearing House* v71 no5 p274-6 My/Je '98
Teaching students to think reasonably: some findings of the Philosophy for Children Program. M. Lipman. *Clearing House* v71 no5 p277-80 My/Je '98
Teaching thinking in the secondary school [symposium]; ed. by T. R. McDaniel. bibl *Clearing House* v71 no5 p260-301 My/Je '98

Figure 5.1 *Part of a Page from* Education Index

Source: Education Index, September 1998, p. 468. Reprinted by permission of H. W. Wilson Co., Bronx, New York.

sciences, such as anthropology, medicine, psychiatry, and sociology. There is a separate file for books and book chapters. Coverage is from January 1987 to the present. There are three files for journal articles, covering the years 1967–1983, 1984–1993, and 1993 to the present.

Resources in Education (RIE): Published monthly by the Educational Resources Information Center (ERIC), these volumes report on all sorts of documents researchers could not find elsewhere. The monthly issues of RIE review speeches given at professional meetings, documents published by state departments of education, final reports of federally funded research projects, reports from school districts, commissioned papers written for government agencies, and other published and unpublished documents. Bibliographic data and also an abstract (usually) are provided on all documents. Many reports that would otherwise never be published are reported in RIE, which makes this an especially valuable resource. RIE should always be consulted, regardless of the nature of a research topic (see Figure 5.2).

Current Index to Journals in Education (CIJE): Also published monthly by ERIC, this index covers what RIE does not—journal articles. Complete citations and abstracts of articles from almost 800 publications, including many from foreign countries, are provided, and a cumulative index is included at the end of each year. The abstract tells what the article is about; the citation gives the exact page number in a specific journal where one can read the entire article (see Figure 5.3).

ERIC online: ERIC can also be searched via computer online. As in the printed version, it includes citations to the literature of education, counseling, and related social science disciplines, and it includes both CIJE and RIE. Citations to articles from over 750 journals and unpublished curriculum guides, conference papers, and research reports are included. There are three files, covering the years 1966–1981, 1982–1991, and 1992 to the present. Because the coverage is so thorough, a search of RIE and CIJE should be sufficient, for most research problems in education, to locate most of the relevant references, and this can now be done quite easily via a computer search online. We'll show you how to do an ERIC search of the literature later in this chapter.

Two additional general references that sometimes provide information about education to researchers are the following:

Sociological Abstracts: Published five times a year, this source is similar in format to *Psych Abstracts.* It provides bibliographic data plus abstracts. It is

Table 5.1 *Some of the Major Indexing and Abstracting Services Used in Educational Research*

	Education Index	ERIC	Psychology Abstracts	Reader's Guide	SSCI
Focus	Education	Education	Education	General interest	Social sciences
Include abstracts?	No	Yes	Yes	No	No
Search via computer?	Yes	Yes	Yes	Yes	Yes
Author index provided?	With main entries	Monthly	Monthly	With main entries	Three times per year
First year published	1929	CIJE—1969 RIE—1966	1927	1890	1973
Include unpublished documents?	No	Yes (in RIE)	No	No	No
Chief advantage	Includes some material not in CIJE	Very comprehensive	Very comprehensive	Includes popular material on education not in CIJE or *Ed Index*	Forward search to see where related articles of interest may be located
Chief disadvantage	No abstracts	Uneven quality of entries in RIE	Much that is not related to education	Very little information from scholarly journals	A bit difficult to learn how to use at first

ED 417 080   **SE 061 198**
Cabot, Kathy L.
The Effects of Relaxation and Visualization on Infor-
   mation Retention in Fifth Grade Science Students.
Pub Date—1997-05-00
Note—16p
Pub Type— Reports - Research (143)
EDRS Price - MF01/PC02 Plus Postage.
Descriptors—Academic Achievement. Concept Formation. Educational Strategies. Grade 5. Intermediate Grades. *Learning Strategies. *Relaxation
   Training. *Science Education. *Study Skills. *Visualization
   This paper examines the effectiveness and feasibility
of introducing relaxation and visualization techniques
as study skills. Fifth grade science students from Char-
lottesville, Virginia (N=43) received six 20-minute
classes using relaxation to study information on
famous scientists. Results of this study indicate that
relaxation and visualization can be used as a regular
classroom activity and will enhance student achievement by reducing stress. increasing attention span.
and helping students learn more effectively. Findings
also suggest that relaxation and visualization are effective study techniques and should be incorporated into
teacher training programs. Transcript exerpts of lesson plans are provided in Appendix A. Appendix B
contains relaxation exercises. Appendix C contains
several biographies of important scientists. Appendix
D provides the actual Creative Study skills assessment
test. Appendix E calculates the number of correct
responses for each question. Appendix F lists several
comments by the students on their response to the
program. (Contains 18 references.) (DDR)

Figure 5.2 *Excerpt from RIE*

Source: RIE. U.S. Department of Education: Washington, D.C. July, 1998,
p. 148.

worth consulting if the topic involves some aspect
of sociology or social psychology.

Exceptional Child Education Resources (ECER):
   Published quarterly by The Council for Exceptional Children. It provides information about exceptional children from over 200 journals. Using
   a format similar to CIJE, it provides author, subject, and title indexes. It is worth consulting if a
   research topic deals with exceptional children,
   since it covers several journals not searched for in
   CIJE.

Most doctoral dissertations and many master's theses in education report on original research and hence
are valuable sources for literature reviews.

Dissertation Abstracts International (DAI): The major reference for dissertations, published monthly.
   DAI contains the abstracts of doctoral dissertations submitted by almost 500 universities in the
   United States and Canada. There are two sections: Section A contains dissertations in the humanities and the social sciences and includes education (see Figure 5.4). Section B contains
   dissertations in the physical sciences and engineering and includes psychology.

Keyword Index: Comes with each monthly issue of
   DAI. It is just what its title implies—an alphabet-

```
┌─────────────────────────────────────────────┐
│ EJ 558 112                    EA 534-148      │
│ The Making of a World-Class Elementary School.│
│ Haynes, Richard M.; Chalker, Donald M.        │
│ Principal, v77 n3 p5-6,8-9 Jan 1998           │
│ Descriptors: *Academic Standards; *Comparative│
│   Education; Educational Finance; Elementary Edu- │
│   cation; *Excellence in Education; Foreign Coun- │
│   tries; Homework; *International Education; Parent │
│   Student Relationship; Principals; Student Evalua- │
│   tion; Teacher Responsibility                 │
│ Identifiers: *World Class Standards            │
│ After spending six years studying elementary schools of 10 coun- │
│ tries noted for educational excellence (Britain, Canada, France, │
│ Germany, Israel, Japan, New Zealand, South Korea, Taiwan, and │
│ the United States), the authors reveal world-class standards they │
│ have identified for time-on-task curriculum, assessment, parent- │
│ ing, and student behavior. Being world-class begins with strong │
│ leadership, teachers who foster high expectations, and a symbiotic │
│ parent/school relationship. (MLH)              │
├─────────────────────────────────────────────┤
│ EJ 557 814                    CE 532 115      │
│ A Primer in Survey Research. Watson, Suzanne C. │
│ Journal of Continuing Higher Education: v46 n1 p31- │
│ 40 Win 1998                                    │
│ Descriptors: Adult Education; Interviews; *Question- │
│   naires; Research Methodology; *Response Rates │
│   (Questionnaires); *Surveys                   │
│ Compares types and methods of survey research, including mail, │
│ telephone, face-to-face, drop-off, and electronic surveys. Explains │
│ steps for conducting survey research and suggests how to improve │
│ response rate. (SK)                            │
├─────────────────────────────────────────────┤
│ EJ 558 952                    SP 526 539      │
│ Character Development. Can Character be Mea- │
│ sured? Stoll, Sharon Kay; Beller, Jennifer M. Journal │
│ of Physcial Education, Recreation and Dance; v69 n1 │
│ p19-24 Jan 1998                                │
│ Descriptors: Athletics; Elementary School Students; │
│   Elementary Secondary Education; *Ethical │
│   Instruction; *Moral Development; *Moral Values; │
│   Physical Education; Research Methodology; Sec- │
│   ondary School Students; Student Behavior     │
│ Identifiers: *Character Development            │
│ Discusses whether character can be measured, describing moral │
│ development research, and noting how moral educators may use │
│ many tools, types of research designs, and qualitative and quanti- │
│ tative methods in trying to understand moral education. The │
│ paper examines the role of moral education in the development of │
│ personal character, discussing moral education within American │
│ sport. (SM)                                    │
└─────────────────────────────────────────────┘
```

Figure 5.3 *Sample Entries from* Current Index to Journals in Education (*CIJE*)

Source: Reprinted from *Current Index to Journals in Education,* July 1998, pp. 3, 25, 92.

ical listing of key words contained in the titles of the dissertations included in that issue. In looking for dissertations dealing with a specific topic, researchers identify key terms (see the discussion below) in the research question and then see if there are any relevant abstracts listed under these terms in the *Keyword Index* (see Figure 5.5).

Dissertation Abstracts Ondisc: Many universities now have this computer database with search software that allows an individual to do a computer search (by keyword, subject, author, even school!) of the *Dissertation Abstracts* database. It includes information on over 900,000 doctoral dissertations and master's theses in hundreds of subject areas, with some 30,000 new titles being added each year.

Formulate Search Terms. Once a general reference work has been selected, researchers need to formulate some **search terms**—words or phrases they can use to locate primary sources. Such words or phrases are also called **descriptors.** They are the most important words in the problem statement. Take, for example, the research question "Do students taught by a teaching team learn more than students taught by an individual teacher?" What are the most important words—the key terms—in this question? Remember that a researcher conducts a literature search to find out what other research has been done with regard to, and what others think about, the research question of interest. The key term in this question, therefore, is "teaching team." This term, plus other terms that are similar to it, or synonyms for it, should be listed. Possibilities here, therefore, might include "team teaching," "joint teaching," "cooperative teaching," and the like. The researcher would list these key words alphabetically, and then consult the general reference work to see what articles are listed under these descriptors. He or she would then select the articles that seem to bear on the research topic.

Search the General References. What is a useful way to search through a general reference work? Although there is no magic formula to follow, the following is one that is used by many researchers in education. Let us use *Education Index* as an example.

1. Find the most recent issue and work backward. Each of the monthly issues is combined every quarter, and the quarterly issues in turn are combined into a yearly volume. Researchers would need to search through each of the monthly issues for the current quarter, therefore, then the quarterly issues for the current year, and then the yearly volumes for as far back as they wish to go.
2. Look to see if there are any articles listed under each of the descriptors (the search terms) in the current issue.
3. List the bibliographical data of pertinent articles on bibliographic cards. If any articles are found that deal with some aspect of the researcher's topic, the

The evolution of writing in kindergarten: The role of student-teacher conferencing. Tobin, Thomas L., Ed.D. *University of Pennsylvania,* 1998. 189pp. Supervisor: Charles Dwyer

Order Number DA 9830679

This case study of two kindergarten classes during the 1996–97 school year examined the evolution of children's writing and focused on the role of the student-teacher writing conference. These two kindergarten classes had a daily journal writing program and held student-teacher conferences every day, or every other day.

Research questions included: (1) What can be learned by tracing the evolution of kindergarten children's writing when there is a program of daily writing and conferencing? (2) What can be learned by the examination of kindergarten teachers' responses to the drawing and writing of young children in a conference? (3) What can be learned by investigating and observing the effects of daily writing and conferencing on kindergartners' attitudes about themselves as writers?

The methodology used was that of participant observer using ethnographic methods. Data was collected from September 1996 through June 1997. Data sources included field notes and audiotapes from classroom observations, interviews with teachers and students, and documents including students' written products.

Significant findings include: (1) In these two classrooms daily journal writing and conferencing were an integral part of the kindergarten program. Routine procedures and processes that promoted writing were in place. Students progressed in their writing skill level and grew in their confidence as writers. (2) The individualized nature of writing and conferencing within these classrooms allowed each child to progress at an individual rate of comfort, while providing opportunities for teachers to stretch students to higher levels. (3) Ten distinct categories of responses that teachers used in writing conferences with their students were found. (4) Student-teacher conferences added to the teachers' knowledge of each indiviudal student's language development and to their personal understanding of each child. (5) The encouragement and acceptance of inventive spelling helped students to apply their knowledge of sounds and letters and to rely on themselves as writers. (6) An unexpected outcome was the positive influence that a writing journal can have upon a student's ability to be reflective.

Figure 5.4 *Excerpt from* Dissertation Abstracts International

Source: From *Dissertation Abstracts International—A: Humanities and Social Sciences, 59,* no. 4 (October 1998): 1074. Reprinted by permission of University Microfilms International.

Dropout

A comparative analysis of school satisfaction and dropout risk of middle school students attending programs for students with emotional handicaps, severe emotional disturbance and general education students attending center schools and satellite schools. *Lockwood, Hope D. Jacobson,* p.1121A

A comparison of the undergraduates in good academic standing who persist and who depart the City College of New York. *Morales, Thomas David,* p.1093A

A longitudinal study of graduation, retention, and school dropout for students in regular and special education. *Smith, Karen S.,* p. 1036A

An examination of the effects of parental influence on secondary school completion. *Stambler, Benita Jamie,* p.1116A

The impact on the relationship between type of school and droput rate in Urhobo rural areas of Nigeria. *Aganbi, Isaac Ataphiaminyo,* p.1013A

Dropouts

An integrative review of research on characteristics of students who drop out of school. *McHenry, Nancy Lynn,* p.1115A

Credentials, skills, and dropouts: The GED as labor market signal and as a measure of skills. *Tyler, John Harold,* p.1284A

Figure 5.5 *Excerpt from* Keyword Index *of DAI*

Source: Key Word Index, Dissertation Abstracts International— A: Humanities and Social Sciences, 59, no. 4 (October 1998). Reprinted by permission of University Microfilms International.

author, title, page, publication date, and publication source should be listed on a 3×5 (or perhaps larger) card (see Figure 5.6).* A separate card should be used for each reference listed. The important thing is to take care to record the bibliographic data completely and accurately. Nothing is more annoying than finding that a reference is listed incorrectly on a bibliographic card and thus cannot be located.

4. Continue looking through other issues. When enough articles have been gathered to obtain an adequate idea as to what else has been written about the topic, the search can be stopped. How many articles is enough? Again, there is no magic number. It depends on the purpose of the search. To obtain a fairly

complete listing of what has been written on a topic, a researcher would need to extend the search over several years. To simply obtain a few articles to get a "feeling" for the kinds of articles that have been written on a topic, it may be necessary to search only a few issues.

Searching Psychological Abstracts. If a researcher decides to search through *Psychological Abstracts* manually (this might be necessary if a researcher is looking for articles published earlier than 1970, for example), he or she would first turn to the index volume for a particular year to check for search terms. The subjects of the articles (e.g., motivation) will be listed there, followed by a number (e.g., 23150). The number is the number of the abstract, which can then be looked up in the appropriate volume of abstracts.

Searching RIE and CIJE. A manual search through RIE and CIJE is similar to a search in *Psychological*

---

*Some researchers prefer 4×6 (or 5×8) cards so they can later make notes pertaining to the contents of the reference on the same card.

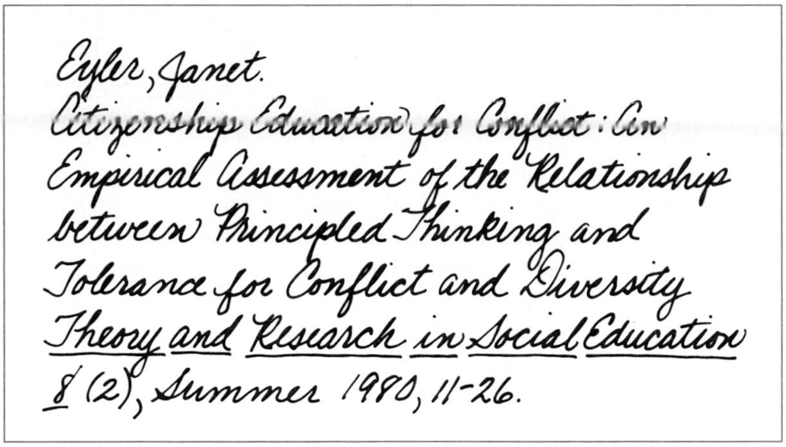

Figure 5.6 *Sample Bibliographic Card*

Eyler, Janet.
Citizenship Education for Conflict: An Empirical Assessment of the Relationship between Principled Thinking and Tolerance for Conflict and Diversity
Theory and Research in Social Education
8 (2), Summer 1980, 11-26.

Abstracts. Researchers first go to the *Thesaurus of ERIC Descriptors* (a separate volume) and locate the descriptors. Today, most researchers find it easier and quicker, however, to do a search of *Psychological Abstracts, RIE,* and *CIJE* (as well as most other references) online (unless, as mentioned, they need to find articles that were published some time ago). We will discuss how to do an online search of these references a bit later in the chapter.

Any document abstracted in RIE or CIJE can be ordered from ERIC—the latest issue of RIE tells how to order an ERIC document. Most university libraries, however, maintain a collection of ERIC documents on microfiche (small sheets of microfilm), which are read in a special microfiche viewer.

Clearly, the abstracts provided in *Psychological Abstracts,* RIE, and CIJE are more informative than just the bibliographic data provided in *Education Index.* Thus it is perhaps somewhat easier to determine if an article is pertinent to a particular topic. If a topic pertains directly to education, little is to be gained by searching through *Psychological Abstracts.* If a topic involves some aspect of psychology, however (such as educational psychology), it often is useful to check *Psych Abstracts* as well as *Education Index,* RIE, and CIJE.

In sum, the abstracts in RIE and *Psychological Abstracts* are presented in more detail than those in CIJE. *Education Index* is less comprehensive than CIJE and gives only bibliographic information, not abstracts. CIJE also covers more journals.

The best strategy for a thorough search is probably as follows.

1. Before 1965: search *Education Index.*
2. From 1966 to 1968: search RIE and *Education Index.*
3. From 1969 to the present: search RIE and CIJE, preferably online.

Obtain Primary Sources. After searching the general references, researchers will have a pile of bibliographic cards. The next step is to locate each of the sources listed on the cards and then read and take notes on those relevant to the research problem. There are two major types of primary sources to be familiar with in this regard—journals and reports.

Professional Journals. Many journals in education publish reports of research. Some publish articles on a wide range of educational topics, while others limit what they print to a particular specialization, such as social studies education. Most researchers become familiar with the journals in their field of interest and look them over from time to time. Examples of such journals include the *American Educational Research Journal, Child Development, Educational Administration Quarterly, Journal of Educational Research, Journal of Research in Science Teaching, Reading Research Quarterly,* and *Theory and Research in Social Education.*

Reports. Many important research findings are first published as reports. Almost all funded research projects produce a final report of their activities and findings when research is completed. In addition, each year many reports on research activities are published by the United States government, by state departments of education, by private organizations and agencies, by local school districts, and by professional associations. Furthermore, many individual researchers give a report on their recent work at professional meetings and conferences.

Most reports are abstracted in the Documents Résumé section of RIE, and ERIC distributes microfiche copies of them to most college and university libraries. Many papers, such as the reports of presidential task forces, national conferences, or specially called professional meetings, are published only as reports. They are usually far more detailed than journal articles and much more up to date. Also, they are not copyrighted. Reports are a very valuable source of up-to-date information that could not be obtained anywhere else.

Locating Primary Sources. Most primary source material is located in journal articles and reports, since that is where most of the research findings in education are published. Although the layout of libraries varies, one often is able to go right to the stacks where journals are shelved alphabetically. In some libraries, however, the stacks are closed and one must ask the librarian to get the journals.

As is almost always the case, some of the references desired will be missing, at the bindery, or checked out by someone else. If an article is particularly important for a researcher to acquire, it often can be obtained directly from the author. Addresses of authors are listed in *Psychological Abstracts* or RIE, but not in *Education Index* or CIJE. Sometimes an author's address can be found in the directory of a professional association, such as the *American Educational Research Association Biographical Membership Directory*, or in *Who's Who in American Education*. If a reprint cannot be obtained directly from the author, it may be possible to obtain it from another library in the area or through an interlibrary loan, a service that nearly all libraries provide.

Reading Primary Sources. When all the desired journal articles are gathered together, the review can begin. It is a good idea to begin with the most recent articles and work backward. The reason for this is that most of the more recent articles will cite the earlier articles and thus can give a quicker understanding of previous work.

How should an article be read? While there is no one perfect way to do this, here are some ideas:

- Read the abstract or the summary first. This will tell whether the article is worth reading in its entirety.
- Record the bibliographic data at the top of a 5 × 8 note card.

- Take notes on the article or photocopy the abstract or summary. Almost all research articles follow approximately the same format. They usually include an abstract; an introductory section that presents the research problem or question and reviews other related studies; the objectives of the study or the hypotheses to be tested; a description of the research procedures, including the subjects studied, the research design, and the measuring instruments used; the results or findings of the study; a summary (if there is no abstract); and the researcher's conclusions.
- Be as brief as possible in taking notes, yet do not exclude anything that might be important to describe later in the full review.

Some researchers copy off on note cards the essential steps mentioned above (problem, hypothesis, procedures, findings, conclusions) ahead of time, leaving space to take notes after each step. For each of these steps, the following should be noted.

1. *Problem.* State it clearly.
2. *Hypotheses or objectives.* List them exactly as stated in the article.
3. *Procedures.* List the research methodology used (experiment, case study, and so on), the number of subjects and how they were selected, and the kind of instrument (questionnaire, tally sheet, and so on) used. Make note of any unusual techniques employed.
4. *Findings.* List the major findings. Indicate whether the objectives of the study were attained and whether the hypotheses were supported. Often the findings are summarized in a table, which might be photocopied and pasted to the back of the note card.
5. *Conclusions.* Record or summarize the author's conclusions. Note your disagreements with the author and the reasons for such disagreement. Note strengths or weaknesses of the study that make the results particularly applicable or limited with regard to your research question.

Figure 5.7 gives an example of a completed note card based on the bibliographic card shown in Figure 5.6.

Doing a Computer Search

A computer search of the literature can be performed in almost all university libraries and most public libraries. Many state departments of education also conduct com-

What a Good Summary of a Journal Article Should Contain

- The problem being addressed.
- The purpose of the study.
- The hypotheses of the study (if there are any).
- The methodology the researcher used.
- A description of the subjects involved.
- The results.
- The conclusions.
- Particular strengths, weaknesses, and limitations of the study.

puter searches, as do some county offices of education and some large school systems. Online computer terminals are linked to one or more information retrieval systems (such as the Lockheed DIALOG system) that retrieve information from a number of databases. The database most commonly used by educational researchers is ERIC, which can be searched by computer back to 1966. Other databases include *Psychological Abstracts, Exceptional Child Education Resources,* and the *Comprehensive Dissertation Index,* all of which are available in the Lockheed retrieval system. Over 200 databases exist that can be computer-searched. Information about them can be obtained from most librarians.

A computer search has a number of advantages over a manual search. First, it is much faster than a manual search. Second, at most universities it is free, and even when it is not, it is inexpensive. A typical search of the ERIC database should take less than an hour. Third, a printout of the search, including abstracts of sources, can be obtained. Fourth, but perhaps most important, more than one descriptor can be searched at the same time.

Suppose a researcher was interested in finding information on the use of questioning in teaching science. A search of the ERIC database using the descriptors "questioning techniques" and "science" would reveal the abstracts and citations of several articles, two of which

Problem: Is there a relationship btwn. principled polit. thinking & tendency to be polit. tolerant?

Hypotheses: Principl. thinkers more likely to: (1) apply principl. of democ. to specific cases than non-principl. thinkers; (2) accept polit. conflict as desirable & legitimate; (3) endorse an active citizenship role; (4) show more polit. involvement than citizens who reason predom. at conventional level.

Procedures: Sample = 135 college fr. & soph. median age 18/19. 2/3 fem. Sampled by classes in requir. gen'l ed. curricul. of small pvt. tchr's. college. Questionnaire study. Rest's Defining Issues Test (DIT) used to identify principled and non-principled thinkers. Of the 135, 15 Questionnaires discarded due to incomplete. 25 S_s indentif. as P thinkers; 34 as low in such thinking. sex ratio each group was same. Subjects asked respond various items on Q.

Findings: All hypotheses except #4 supported.

Conclusions: Civic tolerance & cognitive moral dvlpmnt. are associated. This intellectual growth is crucial for dvlpmnt. of citizen competence & must be fostered in schools. Tchrs should focus & promote discussions of kinds of conflict which generate controversy in the community. S_s also should be involved in polit. participation experiences in school involving decisions they make, and also in their community outside of school.

Figure 5.7 *Sample Note Card*

```
       ERIC NO: EJ556131
        AUTHOR: Watts, Mike; Barber, Brenda; Alsop, Steve
         TITLE: Children's Questions in the Classroom.
          YEAR: 1997
        SOURCE: Primary Science Review (n49 p6-8 Sep-Oct 1997)
      PUB TYPE: Journal article; Research/technical report
      LANGUAGE: English
      ABSTRACT: Presents accounts from primary teachers as they worked toward
                fostering questioning. Techniques included providing good
                stimuli for questions, having students share thoughts in
                groups of increasing size, and modeling good questions and
                question-asking. (PVD)
    MAJOR DESC: Group Discussion; Grouping (Instructional Purposes);
                Inquiry; Modeling (Psychology); Questioning Techniques
    MINOR DESC: Curiosity; Early Childhood Education;
                Elementary School Science; Foreign Countries;
                Informal Assessment; Learning Strategies; Role Models;
                Science Instruction; Teaching Methods
   IDENTIFIERS: United Kingdom
CLEARINGHOUSE NUMBER: SE558781
```

```
       ERIC NO: EJ557526
        AUTHOR: Ward, Charlotte
         TITLE: Never Give 'Em a Straight Answer.
          YEAR: 1997
        SOURCE: Science and Children (v35 n3 p46-49 Nov-Dec 1997)
      PUB TYPE: Classroom teaching guide; Journal article
      LANGUAGE: English
      ABSTRACT: Shares some strategies for encouraging students to notice
                their environment in the broadest sense through using the
                Socratic method. Focuses on specific examples with historical
                significance such as exploring the period of a pendulum. (DDR)
    MAJOR DESC: Concept Formation; Hands on Science; Physics;
                Questioning Techniques; Science Activities
    MINOR DESC: Elementary Education; Inquiry; Learning Strategies;
                Science Process Skills
   IDENTIFIERS: Socratic Method
CLEARINGHOUSE NUMBER: SE558989
```

Figure 5.8 *Example of Abstracts Obtained Using the Descriptors "Questioning Techniques" and "Science"*

are shown in Figure 5.8. Notice that the word "source" indicates where to find the articles if the researcher wants to read all or part of them—one is in the journal *Science and Children,* and one is in *Primary Science Review.*

Searching *PsycINFO*. Searching through *PsycINFO* is similar to searching through RIE and CIJE. One first pulls up the PsychInfo database. Similar to a search in ERIC, descriptors can be used singularly or in various combinations to locate references. We used the terms "democracy" and "schools" as shown in Figure 5.9, and came up with a list of 15 possible references, one of which is shown in Figure 5.10.

All articles of interest can then be located in the identified journals. As you can see, the article mentioned in the record shown in Figure 5.10 can be found in the Spring 1998 issue of the journal *Theory and Research in Social Education.*

AN EXAMPLE OF A COMPUTER SEARCH

The steps involved in a computer search are similar to those involved in a manual search, except that much of the work is done by the computer. To illustrate the steps involved, we can describe an actual search conducted using the ERIC database.

Define the Problem as Precisely as Possible. As for a manual search, the research problem should be stated as specifically as possible so that relevant descriptors can be identified. A broad statement of a problem such as "How effective are questioning techniques?" is much too general. It is liable to produce an extremely large number of references, many of which probably will be irrelevant to the researcher's question of interest. For the purposes of our search, therefore, we posed the following research question: What sorts of questioning techniques help students understand historical concepts most effectively?

Decide on the Extent of the Search. The researcher must now decide on the desired number of references to obtain. For a review for a journal article, a researcher might decide to review only 20 to 25 fairly recent references. For a more detailed review, such as a master's thesis, perhaps 30 or 40 might be reviewed. For a very exhaustive review, as for a doctoral dissertation, as many as 100 or more references might be searched.

Figure 5.9
*Using the
Descriptors
"Democracy"
and "Schools"
to Search
PsychINFO*

Search

Type a word or phrase, then click Search.

Hint: Use **swim*** to match **swim, swims, swimming**, etc. <u>Help</u> is available.

☐ **Words Anywhere** ☑ **Title** ☐ **Author** ☐ **Subject**

`democracy and schools` [Search] [Clear]

Language: ☐ Any Language ☑ English ☐ French ☐ Spanish ☐ German ☐ Other `_____`

Publication Year: ● Any Year ○ 1999 Only ○ From: `1990` To `1999`

Search History

#1 **'Democracy-'** in DE (*216 records*)

Figure 5.10 *Abstract
Obtained in a
PsychINFOSearch*

ACCESSION NUMBER
    1998-10544-001
DOCUMENT TYPE
    Journal-Article
TITLE
    Practicing democracy at school: A qualitative analysis of an elementary class council.
AUTHOR
    Angell,-Ann-V.
SOURCE
    Theory-and-Research-in-Social-Education. 1998 Spr; Vol 26(2): 149-172
ISSN
    0093-3104
PUBLICATION YEAR
    1998
ABSTRACT
    Advocates of democratic education argue that regular class meetings are essential to the school curriculum, offering students practice in democratic process as they deliberate issues that affect them. This article describes an experiment with regular class meetings over 3 yrs in a mixed-age upper elementary class. Students readily adopted the rudiments of parliamentary order and also invented democratic procedures to achieve their goals. Analysis of the minutes of 216 meetings suggested students' implicit goals were self-definition and consensus-building; explicitly they defended respect, fairness, and the right to work undisturbed. Negotiating standards for conduct, sharing information, and planning events provided opportunities for students to improve deliberation skills, develop empathy, and build community. The mixed ages in the class appeared to facilitate the development of moral reasoning. Students' inclination to imitate peers, however, suggests their need for help developing tolerance for minority positions and practice defending unpopular points of view. ((c) 1998 APA/PsycINFO, all rights reserved)

[Back to Record Display]

Decide on the Database. As we mentioned earlier, many databases are available, but the one most commonly used is ERIC. Descriptors must fit a particular database; some descriptors may not be applicable to different databases, although many do overlap. We used the ERIC database in this example, as it is still the best for searches involving educational topics.

Select Descriptors. Descriptors are the words the researcher uses to tell the computer what to search for. The selection of descriptors is somewhat of an art. If the descriptor is too general, too many references may be located, many of which are likely to be irrelevant. If the descriptor is too narrow, too few references will be located, and many that might be applicable to the research question may be missed.

Because we used the ERIC database, we selected our descriptors from the *Thesaurus of ERIC Descriptors.* Descriptors can be used singly or in various combinations to locate references. Certain key words, called **boolean operators,** enable the retrieval of terms in various combinations. The most commonly used boolean operators are "and" and "or." For example, by asking a computer to search for a single descriptor such as "inquiry," all references containing this term would be selected. By connecting two descriptors with the word "and," however, researchers can narrow the search to locate only the references that contain *both* of the descriptors. Asking the computer to search for "questioning techniques" *and* "history instruction" would narrow the search because only references containing both descriptors would be located. On the other hand, by using the word "or," a search can be broadened, since any references with *either* one of the descriptors would be located. Thus, asking the computer to search for "questioning techniques" *or* "history instruction" would broaden the search because references containing either one of these terms would be located. Figure 5.11 illustrates the results of using these boolean operators.

All sorts of combinations are possible. For example, a researcher might ask the computer to search for "(questioning techniques or inquiry) and (history instruction or civics instruction)." For a reference to be selected, it would have to contain *either* the descriptor term "questioning techniques" *or* the descriptor term "inquiry," *as well as either* the descriptor term "history instruction" or the descriptor term "civics instruction."

For our search, we chose the following descriptors: questioning techniques, concept teaching, and history instruction.

We also decided there were a number of related terms to our descriptors that we felt should also be

Figure 5.11 *Venn Diagrams Showing the Boolean Operators "and" and "or"*

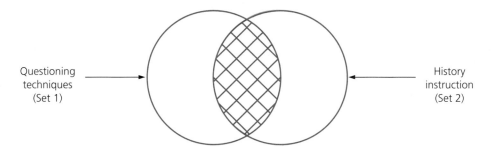

Select questioning techniques *and* history instruction (Combine 1 *and* 2)
Decreases output

Broader search

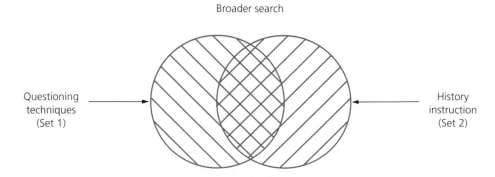

Select questioning techniques *or* history instruction (Combine 1 *or* 2)
Increases output

Figure 5.12 *Printout of Search Results*

[**Database**= ERIC]

Use this screen to enter a new search command, combine previous search results, or both. (1) Enter a new search term and/or select a connector to combine selected search results.
(2) Click on **Search/Combine**. *Note* : Click on a previous search to redo the search.

Command (<u>Help</u>) *Example:*   (#8 not au:smith not su:(boring or dated))

Search for [   ]

[Search/Combine]   [Expand]   [Return]

Connector ● AND ○ OR ○ NOT

Select	#	Previous Search (20 maintained)	Results
☐	#1	su:(questioning techniques)	4123
☐	#2	su:(history instruction)	12948
☐	#3	(#1 and #2)	76
☐	#4	(concept teaching)	12268
☐	#5	(#3 and #4)	6
☐	#6	inquiry	8577
☐	#7	(concept formation)	9497
☐	#8	((#7 or #6 or #4) and #3)	30

<u>Databases</u>   <u>Search</u>   <u>Results</u>   Record   <u>News</u>   <u>Exit</u>   <u>Help</u>

[<u>TOP</u>]   **English**   <u>Français</u>   <u>Español</u>   <u>Text Only</u>

considered. These included "inquiry," "teaching methods," and "learning processes" under "questioning techniques"; and "concept formation" and "cognitive development" under "concept teaching." Upon reflection, however, we decided not to include "teaching methods" or "learning processes" in our search, as we felt these terms were too broad to apply specifically to our research question. We also decided not to include "cognitive development" in our search for the same reason.

Conduct the Search. After determining which descriptors to use, the next step is to enter them into the computer and let it do its work. Figure 5.12 presents a computer printout of the search results. As you can see, we asked the computer first to search for "questioning techniques" (search #1), followed by "history instruction" (search #2), followed by a combination (search #3) of these two descriptors (note the use of the boolean operator "and"). This resulted in a total of 4123 references for questioning techniques, 12,948 references for history instruction, and 76 for a combination of these two descriptors. We then asked the computer to search just for the descriptor "concept teaching" (search #4). This produced a total of 12,268 references. Because we were particularly interested in concept teaching as applied to questioning techniques and history instruction, however, we

asked the computer to search for a combination (search #5) of these three descriptors (again note the use of the operator "and"). This produced only six references. This was much too limited a harvest, so we decided to broaden our approach by asking the computer to look for references that included the following combination (search #8) of descriptors: "(concept teaching *or* concept formation *or* inquiry) *and* (questioning techniques *and* history instruction)." This produced a total of 30 references (see Figure 5.12). At this point, we called for a printout of these 30 references and ended our search.

If the initial effort of a search produces too few references, the search can be broadened by using more general descriptors. Thus, we might have used the term "social studies instruction" rather than "history instruction" had we not obtained enough references in our search. Similarly, a search can be narrowed by using more specific descriptors. For example, we might have used the specific descriptor "North American history" rather than the inclusive term "history."

Obtain a Printout of Desired References. Several printout options are available. Just the title of the reference and its accession number in ERIC (or whatever database is being searched) is acceptable. In ERIC, this is either the EJ or ED number. Here is an example:

EJ556131

Children's Questions in the Classroom

As you can see, however, this option is not very useful, in that titles in and of themselves are often misleading or not very informative. Hence most researchers choose to obtain more complete information, including bibliographic data, the accession number, the document type, the publication year, and an abstract of the article if one has been prepared. Figures 5.2, 5.3 and 5.10 are examples of more complete printout options.

RESEARCHING THE WORLD WIDE WEB

The **World Wide Web** (WWW) is part of the Internet, a vast reservoir of information on all sorts of topics in a wide variety of areas. Prior to 1993, the Internet was barely mentioned in the research literature. Today, it cannot be ignored. Despite the fact that ERIC and (on occasion) *PsycINFO* remain the databases of choice when it comes to research involving most educational topics, re-

searching the Web should also be considered. Space prevents us from describing the Internet in detail, but we do wish to point out some of its important features.

Using a **Web browser** (the computer program that lets you gain access to the WWW), a researcher can find information on almost any topic with just a few clicks of the mouse button. Some of the information on the Web has been classified into **directories,** which can be easily searched by going from one category to another. In addition, several **search engines** are available that are similar in many respects to those we used in our search of the ERIC database. Let us consider both directories and search engines in a bit more detail.

Directories. Directories group websites together under similar *categories,* such as Australian universities, London art galleries, and science laboratories. This is similar to what libraries do when they group similar kinds of information resources together. The results of a directory search will be a list of websites related to the topic being searched. Figure 5.13 shows some of the

Figure 5.13 *The Yahoo! Web Page*

Table 5.2 *Major Directories on the World Wide Web*

Directory	HRL
Galaxy	http://galaxy.einet.net
Go Network	http://www.go.com
Hotbot Directory	http://www.hotbot.com
LookSmart	http://www.looksmart.com
Magellan Web Guide	http://magellan.excite.com
Open Directory Project	http://dmoz.org
Web Crawler Channels	http://webcrawler.com
Yahoo!	http://www.yahoo.com

categories used by Yahoo!, a particularly good example of a directory. If a researcher is interested in finding the site for a particular university in Australia, for example, he or she should try using a directory. Table 5.2 presents a list of the most well-known directories on the World Wide Web.

Directories often provide an excellent starting point for a review of the literature. This is especially true when a researcher does not have a clear idea for a research question or topic to investigate. Browsing through a directory can be a profitable source of ideas. Felden and Garrido offer an illustration:

> For a real-world comparison, suppose I need some household hardware of some sort to perform a repair; I may not always know exactly what is necessary to do the job. I may have a broken part, which I can diligently carry to a hardware store to try to match. Luckily, most hardware stores are fairly well organized and have an assortment of

aisles, some with plumbing supplies, others with nails and other fasteners, and others with rope, twine, and other materials for tying things together. Proceeding by general category (i.e., electrical, plumbing, woodworking, etc.), I can go to approximately the right place and browse the shelves for items that may fit my repair need. I can examine the materials, think over their potential utility, and make my choice.[1]

Search Engines. If one wants more specific information, such as biographical information about George Orwell, however, one should use a search engine, because it will search *all* of the contents of a website. Table 5.3 presents brief descriptions of the leading Internet search engines. Indexes such as AltaVista (see Figure 5.14) use software programs (sometimes called *spiders* or *webcrawlers*) that search the entire Internet, looking at millions of Web pages and then indexing all of the words on them. The search results obtained are usually ranked in order of relevancy (i.e., the number of times the researcher's search terms appear in a document, or how closely the document appears to match one of the *key words* submitted as query terms by the researcher.

A search engine like AltaVista will search for and find the individual pages of a website that match a researcher's search, even if the site itself has nothing to do with what the researcher is looking for. As a result, one usually has to wade through an awful lot of irrelevant information. Felden and Garrido give us an example:

> Returning to the hardware store analogy, if I went to the store in search of some screws for my household project and employed an automatic robot instead of using my native cunning to browse the (well-arranged) aisles, the

Table 5.3 *Leading Search Engines*

AltaVista	http://www.altavista.com	Fast, powerful, and comprehensive. It is extremely good in locating obscure facts and offers the best field-search capabilities.
Excite	http://www.excite.com	Particularly strong on locating current news articles and information about travel.
Google	http://www.google.com	Increasingly popular. A very detailed directory. Good place to go to first when doing a search on the Internet.
HotBot	http://www.hotbot.com	Very easy to use when searching for multimedia files or to locate websites by geography.
Lycos	http://www.lycos.com	Offers very good website reviews. Has a very good multimedia search feature.
Northern Light	http://www.northernlight.com	Indexes Web documents, but also includes a fee-based database containing about one million articles from over 5000 sources. Search results are organized in folders, a unique feature.

Figure 5.14 *AltaVista Web Page*

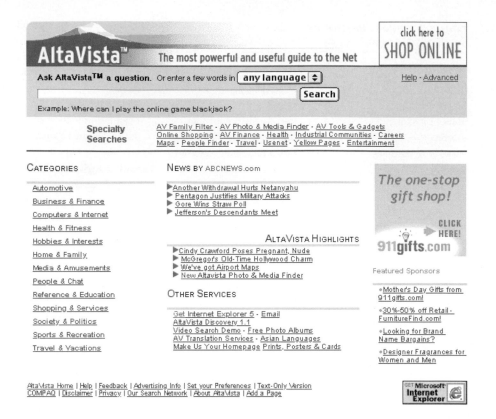

robot could conceivably return (after perusing the entire store) with everything that had a screw in it somewhere. The set of things would be a wildly disparate collection. It would include all sorts of boxes of screws, some of them maybe even the kind I was looking for, but also a wide array of other material, much of it of no use for my project. There might be birdhouses of wood held together with screws, tools assembled with screws, a rake with a screw fastening its handle to its prongs. The robot would have done its job properly. It had been given something to match, in this case a screw, and it went out and did its work efficiently and thoroughly, although without much intelligence.[2]

In order to be satisfied with the results of a search, therefore, one needs to know what to ask for and how to phrase the request to increase the chances of getting what is desired. If a researcher wants to find out information about universities, but not English universities, for example, he or she should ask specifically in that way.

Thus, although it would be a mistake to search only the Web when doing a literature search (thereby ignoring a plethora of other material that often is so much better organized), it has some definite advantages for some kinds of research. Unfortunately, it also has some disadvantages. Here are some of each:

Advantages of Searching the World Wide Web

- *Currency.* Many resources on the Internet are updated very rapidly; often they represent the very latest information about a given topic.
- *Access to a wide variety of materials.* Many resources, including works of art, manuscripts, even entire library collections, can be reviewed at leisure using a personal computer.
- *Varied formats.* Material can be sent over the Internet in different formats, including text, video, sound, or animation.
- *Immediacy.* The Internet is "open" 24 hours a day. Information can be viewed on one's own computer and can be examined as desired or saved to a hard drive or disk for later examination and study.

Disadvantages of Searching the World Wide Web

- *Disorganization.* Unfortunately, much of the information on the Web is not well organized. Few of the well-developed classification systems used by libraries and archives are currently being used. This disorganization makes it an absolute necessity for researchers to have good online searching skills.

- *Time-consuming.* Searching the literature has always been very time consuming. There is always a need to search continually for new and more complete information. Doing a search on the WWW often (if not usually) can be quite time-consuming and (regretfully) sometimes less productive than doing a search using more traditional sources.
- *Lack (sometimes) of credibility.* Anyone can publish something on the Internet. As a result, much of the material one finds there may have little, if any, credibility.
- *Uncertain reliability.* It is so easy to publish information on the Internet that it often is difficult to judge its worth. One of the most valuable aspects of a library collection is that most of its material has been collected carefully. Librarians make it a point to identify and select important works that will stand the test of time. Much of the information one finds on the WWW is ill-conceived or trivial in nature.
- *Ethical violations.* Because material on the Internet is so easy to obtain, there is a greater temptation for researchers to use the material without citation or permission. Violation of copyright is much more likely than with traditional material.
- *Undue reliance.* The amount of information available on the Internet has grown so rapidly in the last few years that some researchers may be misled to think they can find everything they need on the Internet, thereby causing them to ignore other, more traditional sources of information that might not be on the Internet.

In searching the WWW, then, here are a few tips to get the best search results:[3] Many of these would apply to searching ERIC or *PsycINFO* as well.

- *Use the most unique key word you can think of.* Take some time to list several of the words that are likely to appear on the kind of Web page you have in mind. Then pick the most unique or unusual word from your list. For example, "if you're looking for information about efforts to save tiger populations in Asia, don't use *tigers* as your search term. You'll be swamped with Web pages about the Detroit *Tigers,* the Princeton *Tigers,* and every other sports team that uses the word tigers in its name. Instead, try searching for a particular tiger species that you know to be on the endangered list—*Bengal tiger* or *Sumatran tiger* or *Siberian tiger.*"[4]

- *Make it a multistep process.* Don't assume that you will find what you want on the first try. Review the first couple of pages of your results. Look particularly at the sites that contain the kind of information you want. What unique words appear on those pages? Now do another search using just those words.
- *Narrow the field by using just your previous results.* If the key words you choose return too much information, try a second search of just the results you obtained in your first search. This is sometimes referred to as *set searching.* Here's a tip we think you'll find extremely helpful: Simply add another key word to your search request and submit it again.
- *Look for your key word in the Web page title.* Frequently, the best strategy is to look for your unique key word in the title of Web pages (both AltaVista and Infoseek offer this type of search). If you are looking for information about inquiry teaching in secondary school history classes, for example, begin with a search of Web pages that have "inquiry teaching" in the title. Then do a second search of just those results, looking for "secondary school history classes."
- *Find out if case counts.* Check to find out if the search engine you are using pays any attention to upper- and lowercase letters in your key words. "Will a search for java, a microsystems program, for example, also find sites that refer to the program as JAVA?"[5]
- *Check your spelling.* If you have used the best key words that you can think of, and the search engine reports "No results found" (or something similar), check your spelling before you do anything else. Usually, the fact that a search engine does not come up with any results is due to a spelling or typing error.

INTERLIBRARY LOANS

A problem that every researcher faces at one time or another is that a needed book or journal is not available in the library. With the coming of computers, however, it is now very easy to borrow books from distant libraries. In many libraries, librarians can enter information into a computer terminal and find out within seconds which libraries within a designated area have a particular book or journal that a researcher desires. The librarian can then arrange to borrow the material by means of interlibrary loan, usually for only a minimal fee.

Writing the Literature Review Report

After reading and taking notes on the various sources collected, researchers can prepare the final review. Literature reviews differ in format, but typically they consist of the following five parts.

1. The *introduction* briefly describes the nature of the research problem and states the research question. The researcher also explains in this section what led him or her to investigate the question, and why it is an important question to investigate.
2. The *body* of the review briefly reports what others have found or thought about the research problem. Related studies are usually discussed together, grouped under subheads (to make the review easier to read). Major studies are described in more detail, while less important work can be referred to in just a line or two. Often this is done by referring to several studies that reported similar results in a single sentence, somewhat like this: "Several other small-scale studies reported similar results (Adams, 1976; Brown, 1980; Cartright, 1981; Davis, 1985; Frost, 1987)."
3. The *summary* of the review ties together the main threads revealed in the literature reviewed and presents a composite picture of what is known or thought to date. Findings may be tabulated to give readers some idea of how many other researchers have reported identical or similar findings or have similar recommendations.
4. Any *conclusions* the researcher feels are justified based on the state of knowledge revealed in the literature should be included. What does the literature suggest are appropriate courses of action to take to try to solve the problem?
5. A *bibliography* with full bibliographic data for all sources mentioned in the review is essential. There are many formats that can be used to list references, but the format used by the Publication Manual of the American Psychological Association (1994) is easy to use.

META-ANALYSIS

Literature reviews accompanying research reports in journals are usually required to be brief. Unfortunately, this largely prevents much in the way of critical analysis of individual studies. Furthermore, traditional literature reviews basically depend on the judgment of the reviewer and hence are open to the criticism of subjectivity.

In an effort to augment (or replace) the subjectivity and time required in reviewing many studies on the same topic, therefore, the concept of meta-analysis has been developed.[6] In the simplest terms, when a researcher does a meta-analysis, he or she averages the results of the selected studies to get an overall index of outcome or relationship. The first requirement is that results be described statistically; most commonly through the calculation of **effect sizes** and **correlation coefficients** (we explain both later in the text). In one of the earliest studies using meta-analysis (Smith et al.), 375 studies on the effectiveness of psychotherapy were analyzed, leading to the conclusion that the average client was, after therapy, appreciably better off than the average person not in therapy.

As you might expect, this methodology has had widespread appeal in many disciplines—to date, hundreds of meta-analyses have been done. Critics raise a number of objections, some of which have been at least partly remedied by statistical adjustments. We think the most serious criticisms are that a poorly designed study counts as much as one that has been carefully designed and executed, and that the evaluation of the meaning of the final index remains a judgment call, although an informed one. The former objection can be remedied by deleting "poor" studies, but this brings back the subjectivity meta-analysis was designed to replace. It is clear that meta-analysis is here to stay; we agree with those who argue that it cannot replace an informed, careful review of individual studies, however. In any event, the literature review should include a search for relevant meta-analysis reports, as well as individual studies.

Go back to the **Interactive and Applied Learning Tools** feature at the beginning of the chapter for a listing of interactive and applied activities. Go to the **Online Learning Center** at www.mhhe.com/fraenkel5e or your **Interactive Student CD-ROM** to take practice quizzes and receive immediate feedback, practice with key terms, review chapter content and main ideas, and find annotated Web links.

Main Points

THE VALUE OF A LITERATURE REVIEW

- A literature review helps researchers learn what others have written about a topic. It also lets researchers see what have been the results of other, related studies.
- A detailed literature review is often required of master's and doctoral students when they design a thesis.

TYPE OF SOURCES FOR A LITERATURE REVIEW

- Researchers need to be familiar with three basic types of sources (general references, primary sources, and secondary sources) in doing a literature review.
- General references are sources a researcher consults to locate other sources.
- Primary sources are publications in which researchers report the results of their investigations. Most primary source material is located in journal articles.
- Secondary sources refer to publications in which authors describe the work of others.
- *Education Index* and CIJE are two of the most frequently used general references in educational research.
- Search terms, or "descriptors" are key words researchers use to help locate relevant primary sources.

STEPS INVOLVED IN A LITERATURE SEARCH

- The essential steps involved in a review of the literature include: (1) defining the research problem as precisely as possible; (2) perusing the secondary sources; (3) selecting and perusing an appropriate general reference; (4) formulating search terms; (5) searching the general references for relevant primary sources; (6) obtaining and reading the primary sources, and noting and summarizing key points in the sources.

WAYS TO DO A LITERATURE SEARCH

- Today, there are two main ways to do a literature search—manually, using the traditional paper approach, and electronically, by means of a computer.
- There are five essential points (problem, hypotheses, procedures, findings, and conclusions) that researchers should record when taking notes on a study.

DOING A COMPUTER SEARCH

- Computer searches of the literature have a number of advantages—they are fast, are fairly inexpensive, provide printouts, and enable researchers to search using more than one descriptor at a time.
- The steps in a computer search are similar to those in a manual search, except much of the work is done by a computer.
- Researching the World Wide Web (WWW) should be considered, in addition to ERIC and PsycINFO, in doing a literature search.

- Some of the information on the Web is classified into directories, which group web-sites together under similar categories. Yahoo! is an example of a directory.
- To obtain more specific information, search engines should be used, because they search all of the contents of a website.

THE LITERATURE REVIEW REPORT

- The literature review report consists of an introduction, the body of the review, a summary, the researcher's conclusions, and a bibliography.
- When a researcher does a meta-analysis, he or she averages the results of a group of selected studies to get an overall index of outcome or relationship.
- A literature review should include a search for relevant meta-analysis reports, as well as individual studies.

Key Terms

Abstract 70

Bibliography 88

Boolean operators 82

Computer search of the
literature 78

*Current Index to Journals
in Education* (CIJE) 73

Descriptors 75

Directory 84

*Dissertation Abstracts
International*
(DAI) 74

Education Index 72

Educational Resources
Information Center
(ERIC) 73

*Exceptional Child
Education Resources*
(ECER) 74

General reference 70

Interlibrary loan 78

Keyword Index 74

Literature review 70

Manual search of the
literature 71

Meta-analysis 88

Primary source 70

Professional journal 77

PsychINFO 72

Psychological Abstracts 72

*Reader's Guide to
Periodical Literature* 72

Resources in Education
(RIE) 73

Search engine 84

Search terms 75

Secondary source 70

*Social Science Citation
Index* (SSCI) 72

Sociological Abstracts 73

Spider 85

The World Wide Web
(WWW) 84

*Thesaurus of ERIC
Descriptors* 82

Web browser 84

Webcrawler 85

For Discussion

1. Why might it be unwise for a researcher not to do a review of the literature before planning a study?
2. Many published research articles include only a few references to related studies. How would you explain this? Is this justified?
3. Which do you think are more important to emphasize in a literature review—the opinions of experts in the field or related studies? Why?
4. Which of the secondary sources described in this chapter would be most appropriate to consult on the following topics?
   a. Recent research on social studies education.
   b. A brief overview on new developments in science teaching.
   c. An extensive review of recent and past research on a particular research question.
   d. A survey of recent research on homogeneous grouping.
5. One rarely finds books referred to in literature reviews. Why do you suppose this is so? Is it a good idea to refer to books?

6. Which of the general references listed in this chapter would you consult on each of the following?
   a. Marriage and family counseling.
   b. Elementary school administration.
   c. Small group discussions.
   d. Deaf children.
   e. A master's thesis on client-centered therapy.
   f. Archery instruction.

1. N. Felden and M. Garrido (1998). *Internet research: Theory and practice.* Jefferson, NC: McFarland & Co., Inc., p. 116.

2. Ibid., p. 118.

3. A. Glossbrenner and E. Glossbrenner (1998). *Search engines.* San Francisco: San Francisco State University Press, pp. 11–13.

4. Ibid., p. 12

5. Ibid.

6. M. L. Smith, G. V. Glass, and T. I. Miller (1980). Primary, secondary, and meta-analysis research. *Educational Researcher, 5:* (10): 3–8.

Notes

Research Exercise Five: Review of the Literature

Using Problem Sheet 5, again state either your research question or the hypothesis of your study. Then consult an appropriate general reference and list at least three search terms relevant to your problem. Next do a computer search to locate three studies related to your question. Read the studies, taking notes as you read similar to those shown on the sample note card in Figure 5.7. Attach each of your note cards (one per journal article) to Problem Sheet 5.

An electronic version of this Problem Sheet that you can fill in and print, save, or e-mail is available on the Online Learning Center at www.mhhe.com/fraenkel5e and on your Interactive Student CD-ROM.

A full-sized version of this Problem Sheet that you can fill in or photocopy is in your Student Workbook.

Problem Sheet 5

Review of the Literature

1. The question or hypothesis in my study is: _____
   _____

2. The general reference(s) I consulted was (were): _____
   _____

3. The database I used in my search was: _____

4. The descriptors (search terms) I used were (list single descriptors and combinations in the order in which you did your search):

   _____   _____

   _____   _____

5. The results of my search using these descriptors were as follows:

Search #	Descriptor(s)	Results

6. Attached is a printout of my search (Attach to the back of this sheet.)

7. The title of one of the abstracts located using the descriptors identified above is: _____
   _____ (Attach a copy of the abstract.)

8. The titles of the studies I read (note cards are attached) were:

   a. _____

   b. _____

   c. _____

Sampling

CHAPTER 6

Cities of 100,000 people are identified by researchers.

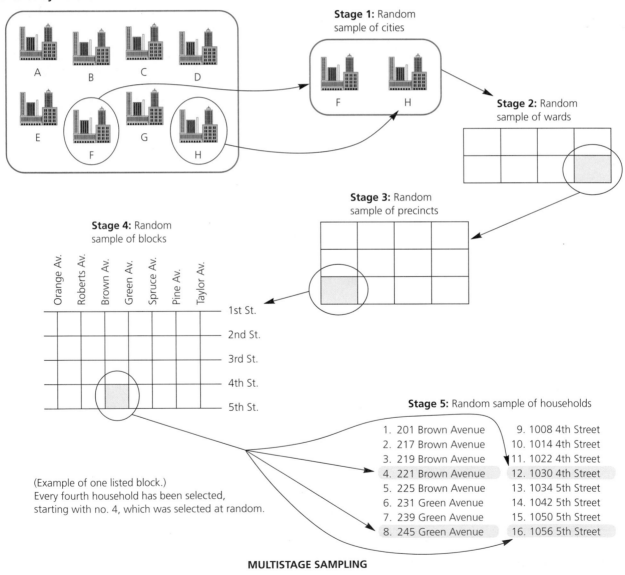

Stage 1: Random sample of cities

Stage 2: Random sample of wards

Stage 3: Random sample of precincts

Stage 4: Random sample of blocks

Orange Av. Roberts Av. Brown Av. Green Av. Spruce Av. Pine Av. Taylor Av.

1st St.
2nd St.
3rd St.
4th St.
5th St.

Stage 5: Random sample of households

1. 201 Brown Avenue
2. 217 Brown Avenue
3. 219 Brown Avenue
4. 221 Brown Avenue
5. 225 Brown Avenue
6. 231 Green Avenue
7. 239 Green Avenue
8. 245 Green Avenue

9. 1008 4th Street
10. 1014 4th Street
11. 1022 4th Street
12. 1030 4th Street
13. 1034 5th Street
14. 1042 5th Street
15. 1050 5th Street
16. 1056 5th Street

(Example of one listed block.)
Every fourth household has been selected,
starting with no. 4, which was selected at random.

MULTISTAGE SAMPLING

Sampling

What Is a Sample?

Samples and Populations
Defining the Population
Target Versus Accessible Populations
Random Versus Nonrandom Sampling

Random Sampling Methods

Simple Random Sampling
Stratified Random Sampling
Cluster Random Sampling
Two-Stage Random Sampling

Nonrandom Sampling Methods

Systematic Sampling
Convenience Sampling
Purposive Sampling

External Validity: Generalizing from a Sample

Population Generalizability
When Random Sampling Is Not Feasible
Ecological Generalizability

Sample Size

A Review of Sampling Methods

Objectives

Studying this chapter should enable you to:

- Distinguish *between a sample and a population.*
- Explain *what is meant by the term "representative sample."*
- Explain *how a target population differs from an accessible population.*
- Explain *what is meant by "random" sampling and* describe briefly *three ways of obtaining a random sample.*
- Use *a table of random numbers to select a random sample from a population.*
- Explain *what is meant by systematic sampling, convenience sampling, and purposive sampling.*
- Explain *how the size of a sample can make a difference in terms of representativeness of the sample.*
- Explain *what is meant by the term "external validity."*
- Distinguish *between population generalizability and ecological generalizability and* discuss *when it is (and when it is not) appropriate to generalize the results of a study.*

Interactive and Applied Learning

After, or while, reading this chapter:

🔵 Go to your Interactive Student CD-ROM to:
- Learn More About Sampling and Representativeness

🔵 📖 Go to your Interactive Student CD-ROM or Student Workbook to do the following activities:
- Activity 6.1: Identifying Types of Sampling
- Activity 6.2: Drawing a Random Sample
- Activity 6.3: When Is It Appropriate to Generalize?

elen Hyun, a research professor at a large eastern university, wishes to study the effect of a new mathematics program on the mathematics achievement of students who are performing poorly in math in elementary schools throughout the United States. Because of a number of factors, of which time and money are only two, it is impossible for Helen and her colleagues to try out the new program with the entire population of such students. They must select a *sample*. What is a sample anyway? Are there different kinds of samples? Are some kinds better than other kinds to study? And just how does one go about obtaining a sample in the first place? Answers to questions like these are some of the things you will learn about in this chapter.

When we want to know something about a certain group of people, we usually find a few members of the group who we know—or don't know—and study them. After we have finished "studying" these individuals, we usually come to some conclusions about the larger group of which they are a part. Many "commonsense" observations, in fact, are based on observations of relatively few people. It is not uncommon, for example, to hear statements such as: "Most female students don't like math"; "You won't find very many teachers voting Republican"; and "Most school superintendents are men."

What Is a Sample?

Most people, we think, base their conclusions about a group of people (students, Republicans, football players, actors, and so on) on the experiences they have with a fairly small number, or **sample,** of individual members. Sometimes such conclusions are an accurate representation of how the larger group of people acts, or what they believe, but often they are not. It all depends on how representative (i.e., how similar) the sample is of the larger group.

One of the most important steps in the research process is to select the sample of individuals who will participate (be observed or questioned) as a part of the study. **Sampling** refers to the process of selecting these individuals.

SAMPLES AND POPULATIONS

A "sample" in a research study refers to any group on which information is obtained. The larger group to which one hopes to apply the results is called the **population.*** All 700 (or whatever total number of) stu-

*In some instances the sample and population may be identical.

dents at State University who are majoring in mathematics, for example, constitute a population; 50 of those students constitute a sample. Students who own automobiles make up another population, as do students who live in the campus dormitories. Notice that a group may be both a sample in one context and a population in another context. All State University students who own automobiles constitute the population of automobile owners at State, yet they also constitute a sample of all automobile owners at state universities in the United States.

When it is possible, researchers would prefer to study the entire population in which they are interested. Usually, however, this is difficult to do. Most populations of interest are large, diverse, and scattered over a large geographic area. Finding, let alone contacting, all the members can be time-consuming and expensive. For that reason, of necessity, researchers often select a sample to study. Some examples of samples selected from populations follow.

- A researcher is interested in studying the effects of diet on the attention span of third-grade students in a large city. There are 1500 third-graders attending the elementary schools in the city. The researcher selects 150 of these third-graders, 30 each in five different schools, as a sample for study.
- An administrator in a large urban high school is interested in determining the opinions of students about a new counseling program that has recently been instituted in the district. There are six high schools and some 14,000 students in the district. From a master list of all students enrolled in the district schools, the administrator selects a sample of 1400 students (350 from each of the four grades, 9–12) to whom he plans to mail a questionnaire asking their opinion of the program.
- The principal of an elementary school wants to investigate the effectiveness of a new U.S. history textbook used by some of the teachers in the district. Out

of a total of 22 teachers who are using the text, she selects a sample of 6. She plans to compare the achievement of the students in these teachers' classes with those of another six teachers who are not using the text.

DEFINING THE POPULATION

The first task in selecting a sample is to define the population of interest. In what group, exactly, is the researcher interested? To whom does he or she want the results of the study to apply? The population, in other words, is the group of interest to the researcher, the group to whom the researcher would like to generalize the results of the study. Here are some examples of populations:

- All high school principals in the United States.
- All elementary school counselors in the state of California.
- All students attending Central High School in Omaha, Nebraska, during the academic year 1987–1988.
- All students in Ms. Brown's third-grade class at Wharton Elementary School.

The above examples reveal that a population can be any size and that it will have at least one (and sometimes several) characteristic(s) that sets it off from any other population. Notice that a population is always *all* of the individuals who possess a certain characteristic (or set of characteristics).

In educational research, the population of interest is usually a group of persons (students, teachers, or other individuals) who possess certain characteristics. In some cases, however, the population may be defined as a group of classrooms, schools, or even facilities. For example,

- All fifth-grade classrooms in Delaware (the hypothesis might be that classrooms in which teachers display a greater number and variety of student products have higher achievement)
- All high school gymnasiums in Nevada (the hypothesis might be that schools with "better" physical facilities produce more winning teams)

TARGET VERSUS ACCESSIBLE POPULATIONS

Unfortunately, the actual population (called the **target population**) to which a researcher would really like to generalize is rarely available. The population to which a researcher is *able* to generalize, therefore, is the **accessible population.** The former is the researcher's ideal choice; the latter, his or her realistic choice. Consider these examples:

Research problem to be investigated: The effects of computer-assisted instruction on the reading achievement of first- and second-graders in California.

Target population: All first- and second-grade children in California.

Accessible population: All first- and second-grade children in the Laguna Salada elementary school district of Pacifica, California.

Sample: Ten percent of the first- and second-grade children in the Laguna Salada district in Pacifica, California.

Research problem to be investigated: The attitudes of fifth-year teachers-in-training toward their student teaching experience.

Target population: All fifth-year students enrolled in teacher-training programs in the United States.

Accessible population: All fifth-year students enrolled in teacher-training programs in the State University of New York.

Sample: Two hundred fifth-year students selected from those enrolled in the teacher-training programs in the State University of New York.

The more narrowly researchers define the population, the more they save on time, effort, and (probably) money, but the more they limit generalizability. It is essential that researchers describe the population and the sample in sufficient detail so that interested individuals can determine the applicability of the findings to their own situations. Failure to define in detail the population of interest, and the sample studied, is one of the most common weaknesses of published research reports. It is important to note that the actual sample may be different from the sample originally selected because of refusal on the part of some subjects to participate, some subjects dropping out, data being lost, and the like. We repeat, therefore, that it is very important to describe the characteristics of the actual sample studied in some detail.

RANDOM VERSUS NONRANDOM SAMPLING

Following is an example of each of the two main types of sampling.

Figure 6.1
Representative Versus Nonrepresentative Samples

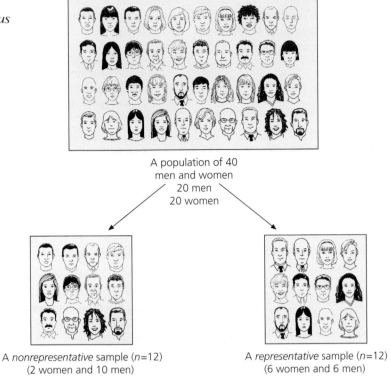

A population of 40
men and women
20 men
20 women

A *nonrepresentative* sample (*n*=12)
(2 women and 10 men)

A *representative* sample (*n*=12)
(6 women and 6 men)

Random sampling: The dean of a school of education in a large midwestern university wishes to find out how her faculty feel about the sabbatical leave requirements currently in operation at the university. She places all 150 names of the school faculty in a hat, mixes them thoroughly, and then draws out the names of 25 individuals to interview.*

Nonrandom sampling: The president of the same university wants to know how his junior faculty feel about a new promotion policy that he has recently introduced (with the advice of a faculty committee). He selects a sample of 30 from the total faculty of 1000 to talk with. Five faculty members from each of the six schools that make up the university are chosen on the basis of the following criteria: They have taught at the university for less than five years, they are nontenured, they belong to one of the faculty associations on campus, and they have not been a member of the committee that helped the president draft the new policy.

*A better way to do this will be discussed shortly, but this gives you the idea.

In the first example, 25 names were selected from a hat after all the names had been mixed thoroughly. This is called random sampling because every member of the population (the 150 faculty in the school) presumably had an equal chance of being selected. There are more sophisticated ways of drawing a **random sample,** but they all have the same intent—to select a *representative* sample from the population (see Figure 6.1). The basic idea is that the group of individuals selected are very much like the entire population. One can never be sure of this, of course, but if the sample is selected randomly, and is sufficiently large, a researcher should get an accurate view of the larger group. The best way to ensure this is to make sure that no bias enters the selection process—that the researcher (or other factors) cannot consciously or unconsciously influence who gets chosen to be in the sample. We explain more about how to minimize bias later in this chapter.

In the second example, the president wants representativeness, but not as much as he wants to make sure there are certain kinds of faculty in his sample. Thus, he has made sure that each of the individuals selected possesses all the criteria mentioned. Each member of the population (the entire faculty of the university) does *not* have an equal chance of being selected; some, in fact, have *no* chance. Hence, this is an example of **nonrandom sampling,** sometimes called "purposive sampling" (see pp. 103–105). Here is another example of a random sample contrasted with a nonrandom sample.

Random: A researcher wishes to conduct a survey of all social studies teachers in a midwestern state to determine their attitudes toward the new state guidelines for teaching history in the secondary schools. There are a total of 725 social studies teachers in the state. The names of these teachers are obtained and listed alphabetically. The researcher then numbers the names on the list from 001 to 725. Using a table of random numbers, which he finds in a statistics textbook, he selects 100 teachers for the sample.

Nonrandom: The manager of the campus bookstore at a local university wants to find out how students feel about the services the bookstore provides. Every day for two weeks during her lunch hour, she asks every person who enters the bookstore to fill out a short questionnaire she has prepared and drop it in a box near the entrance before leaving. At the end of the two-week period, she has a total of 235 completed questionnaires.

In the second example, notice that all bookstore users did not have an equal chance of being included in the sample, only those who visited during the lunch hour. That is why the sample is not random. Notice also that some may not complete the questionnaire.

Random Sampling Methods

After making a decision to sample, researchers try hard, in most instances, to obtain a sample that is representative of the population of interest—that means they prefer random sampling. The three most common ways of obtaining this type of sample are simple random sampling, stratified random sampling, and cluster sampling. A less common method is two-stage sampling.

SIMPLE RANDOM SAMPLING

A **simple random sample** is one in which each and every member of the population has an equal and independent chance of being selected. If the sample is large, it is the best way yet devised by human beings to obtain a sample representative of the population from which it has been selected. Let's take an example: Define a population as all eighth-grade students in school district Y.

Table 6.1 *Part of a Table of Random Numbers*

011723	223456	222167	032762	062281	565451
912334	379156	233989	109238	934128	987678
086401	016265	411148	251287	602345	659080
059397	022334	080675	454555	011563	237873
666278	106590	879809	899030	909876	198905
051965	004571	036900	037700	500098	046660
063045	786326	098000	510379	024358	145678
560132	345678	356789	033460	050521	342021
727009	344870	889567	324588	400567	989657
000037	121191	258700	088909	015460	223350
667899	234345	076567	090076	345121	121348
042397	045645	030032	657112	675897	079326
987650	568799	070070	143188	198789	097451
091126	021557	102322	209312	909036	342045

Imagine there are 500 such students. If you were one of these students, your chance of being selected would be 1 in 500, if the sampling procedure were indeed random. Everyone would have the same chance of being selected.

The larger a random sample is in size, the more likely it is to represent the population. Although there is no guarantee of representativeness, of course, the likelihood of it is greater when researchers use large random samples than with any other method. Any differences that exist between the sample and the population should be small and unsystematic. Any differences that do occur are the result of chance rather than bias on the part of the researcher.

The key to obtaining a random sample is to ensure that each and every member of the population has an equal and independent chance of being selected. This can be done by using what is known as a **table of random numbers**—an extremely large list of numbers that has no order or pattern. Such lists can be found in the back of most statistics books. Table 6.1 illustrates what a typical table of random numbers might look like.

For example, to obtain a sample of 200 from a population of 2000 individuals, using such a table, select a column of numbers, start anywhere in the column, and begin reading four-digit numbers. (Why four digits? Because the final number, 2000, consists of four digits, and we must always use the same number of digits for each person. Person 1 would be identified as 0001; person 2 as 0002; person 635 as 0635; and so forth.) The researcher would then proceed to write down the first 200 numbers in the column that have a value of 2000 or less.

Let us take the first column of four numbers in Table 6.1 as an example. Look at the first number in the column: It is 0117, so number 117 in the list of individuals in the population would be selected for the sample. Look at the second number: It is 9123. There is no 9123 in the population (because there are only 2000 individuals in the entire population). So the researcher goes on to the third number: It is 0864, hence number 864 in the list of individuals in the population would be chosen. The fourth number in the table of random numbers is 0593, so number 593 gets selected. The fifth number is 6662. There is no 6662 in the population, so the researcher goes on to the next number, and so on, until he or she has selected a total of 200 numbers, each representing an individual in the population who will be selected for the sample.

The advantage of random sampling is that, if large enough, it is very likely to produce a representative sample. Its biggest disadvantage is that it is not easy to do. Each and every member of the population must be identified. In most cases, we must be able to contact the individuals selected. In all cases, we must know *who* 117 (for example) is.

Furthermore, simple random sampling is not used if researchers wish to *ensure* that certain subgroups are present in the sample in the same proportion as they are in the population. To do this, researchers must engage in what is known as stratified sampling.

STRATIFIED RANDOM SAMPLING

Stratified random sampling is a process in which certain subgroups, or *strata,* are selected for the sample in the same proportion as they exist in the population. Suppose the director of research for a large school district wants to find out student response to a new twelfth-grade American government textbook the district is considering adopting. She intends to compare the achievement of students using the new book with that of students using the more traditional text the district has purchased in the past. Since she has reason to believe that gender is an important variable that may affect the outcomes of her study, she decides to ensure that the proportion of males and females in the study is the same as in the population. The steps in the sampling process would be as follows:

1. She identifies the target (and accessible) population: all 365 twelfth-grade students enrolled in American government courses in the district.

2. She finds that there are 219 females (60 percent) and 146 males (40 percent) in the population. She decides to have a sample made up of 30 percent of the target population.

3. Using a table of random numbers, she then randomly selects 30 percent *from each strata* of the population, which results in 66 female (30 percent of 219) and 44 male (30 percent of 146) students being selected from these subgroups. The proportion of males and females is the same in both the population and sample—40 and 60 percent (Figure 6.2).

The advantage of stratified random sampling is that it increases the likelihood of representativeness, especially if one's sample is not very large. It virtually ensures that any key characteristics of individuals in the population are included in the same proportions in the sample. The disadvantage is that it requires still more effort on the part of the researcher.

CLUSTER RANDOM SAMPLING

In both random and stratified random sampling, researchers want to make sure that certain kinds of individuals are included in the sample. But there are times when it is not possible to select a sample of individuals from a population. Sometimes, for example, a list of all members of the population of interest is not available. Obviously, then, simple random or stratified sampling cannot be used. Frequently, researchers cannot select a sample of individuals due to administrative or other restrictions. This is especially true in schools. For example, if a target population was all eleventh-grade students within a district enrolled in U.S. history courses, it would be unlikely that the researcher could pull out randomly selected students to participate in an experimental curriculum. Even if they could, the time and effort required would make such selection difficult. About the best the researcher could hope for would be to study a number of intact classes, that is, classes already in existence. The selection of groups, or clusters, of subjects rather than individuals is known as **cluster sampling.** Just as simple random sampling is more effective with larger numbers of individuals, cluster random sampling is more effective with larger numbers of clusters.

Let us consider another example of cluster sampling. The superintendent of a large unified school district in a city on the East Coast wants to obtain some idea of how teachers in the district feel about merit pay. There are 10,000 teachers in all the elementary and secondary

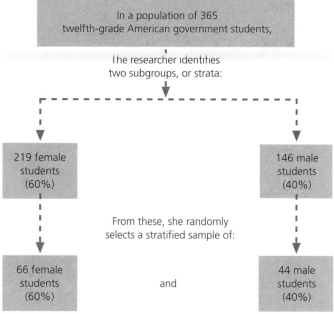

Figure 6.2 *Selecting a Stratified Sample*

In a population of 365 twelfth-grade American government students,

The researcher identifies two subgroups, or strata:

| 219 female students (60%) | 146 male students (40%) |

From these, she randomly selects a stratified sample of:

| 66 female students (60%) | and | 44 male students (40%) |

schools of the district, and there are 50 schools distributed over a large area. The superintendent does not have the funds to survey all teachers in the district, and he needs the information about merit pay quickly. Instead of randomly selecting a sample of teachers from every school, therefore, he decides to interview all the teachers in selected schools. The teachers in each school, then, constitute a cluster. The superintendent assigns a number to each school and then uses a table of random numbers to select 10 schools (20 percent of the population). All the teachers in the selected schools then constitute the sample. The interviewer questions the teachers at each of these 10 schools rather than having to travel to all the schools in the district. If these teachers do represent the remaining teachers in the district, then the superintendent is justified in drawing conclusions about the feelings of the entire population of teachers in his district about merit pay. It is possible that this sample is not representative, of course. Because the teachers to be interviewed all come from a small number of schools in the district, it might be the case that these schools differ in some ways from the other schools in the district, thereby influencing the views of the teachers in those schools with regard to merit pay. The more schools selected, the more likely the findings will be applicable to the population of teachers.

Cluster sampling is similar to simple random sampling except that groups rather than individuals are randomly selected (that is, the sampling unit is a group rather than the individual). The advantages of cluster sampling are that it can be used when it is difficult or impossible to select a random sample of individuals, it is often far easier to implement in schools, and it is frequently less time-consuming. Its disadvantage is that there is a far greater chance of selecting a sample that is not representative of the population.

There is a common error with regard to cluster sampling that many beginning researchers make. This is the mistake of randomly selecting only *one* cluster as a sample, and then observing or interviewing all individuals within that cluster. Even if there is a large number of individuals within the cluster, it is the cluster that has been randomly selected, rather than individuals, and hence the researcher is not entitled to draw conclusions about a target population of such individuals. Yet, some researchers do draw such conclusions. We repeat, they should not.

TWO-STAGE RANDOM SAMPLING

It is often useful to combine cluster random sampling with individual random sampling. Rather than randomly selecting 100 students from a population of 3000 ninth-graders located in 100 classes, the researcher might decide to select 25 classes randomly from the population of 100 classes and then randomly select four students from each class. This is much less time-consuming than

Populations

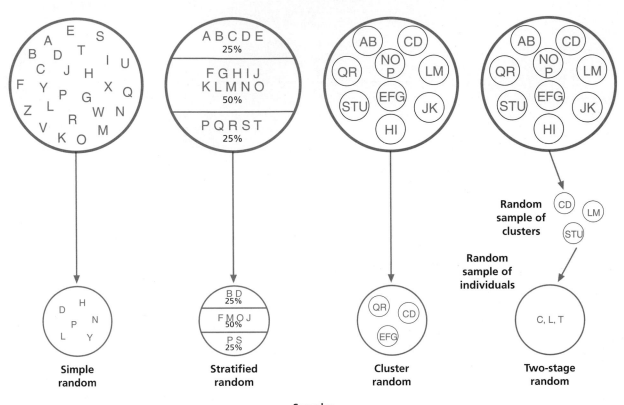

Samples

FIGURE 6.3 *Random Sampling Methods*

visiting most of the 100 classes. Why would this be better than using all the students in four randomly selected classes? Because four classes are too few to ensure representativeness, even though they were selected randomly.

Figure 6.3 illustrates the different random sampling methods we have discussed.

Nonrandom Sampling Methods

SYSTEMATIC SAMPLING

In a systematic sample, every *n*th individual in the population list is selected for inclusion in the sample. For example, in a population list of 5000 names, to select a sample of 500, a researcher would select every tenth name on the list until a total of 500 names was chosen. Here is an example of this type of sampling:

The principal of a large middle school (grades 6–8) with 1000 students wants to know how students feel about the new menu in the school cafeteria. She obtains an alpha-betical list of all students in the school and selects every tenth student on the list to be in the sample. To guard against bias, she puts the numbers 1 to 10 into a hat, and draws one out. It is a 3. So she selects the students numbered 3, 13, 23, 33, 43, and so on until she has a sample of 100 students to be interviewed.

The above method is technically known as **systematic sampling** *with a* **random start**. In addition, there are two terms that are frequently used when referring to systematic sampling. The *sampling interval* is the distance in the list between each of the individuals selected for the sample. In the example given above, it was 10. A simple formula to determine it is:

Population size
_____
Desired sample size

The **sampling ratio** is the proportion of individuals in the population that is selected for the sample. In the example above, it was .10, or 10 percent. A simple way to determine the sampling ratio is:

$$\frac{\text{Sample size}}{\text{Population size}}$$

There is a danger in systematic sampling that is sometimes overlooked. If the population has been ordered systematically—that is, if the arrangement of individuals on the list is in some sort of pattern that accidentally coincides with the sampling interval—a markedly biased sample can result. This is sometimes called **periodicity.** Suppose that the middle school students in the preceding example had not been listed alphabetically, but rather by homeroom, and the homeroom teachers had previously listed the students in their rooms by grade point average, high to low. That would mean that the better students would be at the top of each homeroom list. Suppose also that each homeroom has 30 students. If the principal began her selection of every tenth student with the first or second or third student on the list, her sample would consist of the better students in the school rather than a representation of the entire student body. (Do you see why? Because in each homeroom, the poorest students would be those who were numbered between 24 and 30, and they would never get chosen.)

When planning to select a sample from a list of some sort, therefore, researchers should carefully examine the list to make sure there is no cyclical pattern present. If the list has been arranged in a particular order, researchers should make sure the arrangement will not bias the sample in some way that could distort the results. If such seems to be the case, steps should be taken to ensure representativeness—for example, by randomly selecting individuals from each of the cyclical portions. In fact, if a population list is randomly ordered, a systematic sample drawn from the list is a random sample.

CONVENIENCE SAMPLING

Many times it is extremely difficult (sometimes even impossible) to select either a random or a systematic nonrandom sample. At such times, a researcher may select a convenience sample. A **convenience sample** is a group of individuals who (conveniently) are available for study (see Figure 6.4). Thus, a researcher might decide to study two third-grade classes at a nearby elementary school because the principal asks for help in evaluating the effectiveness of a new spelling textbook. Here are some examples of convenience samples:

- To find out how students feel about food service in the student union at an East Coast university, the manager stands outside the main door of the cafeteria one Monday morning and interviews the first 50 students who walk out of the cafeteria.
- A high school counselor interviews all the students who come to him for counseling about their career plans.
- A news reporter for a local television station asks passersby on a downtown street corner their opinions about plans to build a new baseball stadium in a nearby suburb.
- A university professor compares student reactions to two different textbooks in her statistics classes.

In each of the above examples, a certain group of people was chosen for study because they were available. The obvious advantage of this type of sampling is that it is convenient. But just as obviously, it has a major disadvantage in that the sample will quite likely be biased. Take the case of the TV reporter who is interviewing passersby on the downtown street corner. Many possible sources of bias exist. First of all, of course, anyone who is not downtown that day has no chance to be interviewed. Second, those individuals who are unwilling to give their views would not be interviewed. Third, those who agree to be interviewed would probably be individuals who hold strong opinions one way or the other about the stadium. Fourth, depending on the time of day, those who are interviewed quite possibly would be unemployed or have jobs that do not require them to be indoors. And so forth.

In general, convenience samples cannot be considered representative of any population and should be avoided if at all possible. Unfortunately, sometimes they are the only choice a researcher has. When such is the case, the researcher should be especially careful to include information on demographic and other characteristics of the sample that was actually studied. The study should also be *replicated,* that is, repeated, with a number of similar samples to decrease the likelihood that the results obtained were simply a one-time occurrence. We will discuss replication in more depth later in the chapter.

PURPOSIVE SAMPLING

On occasion, based on previous knowledge of a population and the specific purpose of the research, investigators use personal judgment to select a sample. Researchers assume they can use their knowledge of the

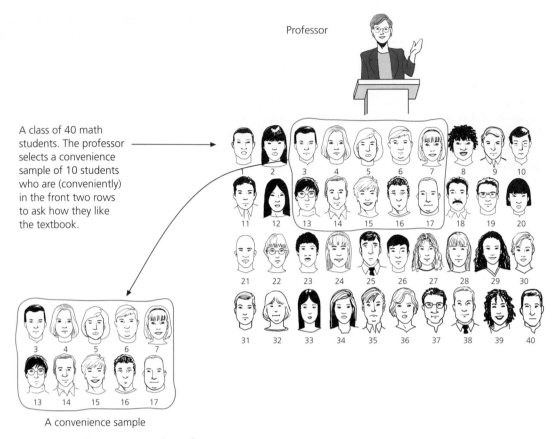

Professor

A class of 40 math students. The professor selects a convenience sample of 10 students who are (conveniently) in the front two rows to ask how they like the textbook.

A convenience sample

Figure 6.4 *Convenience Sampling*

population to judge whether or not a particular sample will be representative. Here are some examples:

- An eighth-grade social studies teacher chooses the two students with the highest grade point averages in her class, the two whose grade point averages fall in the middle of the class, and the two with the lowest grade point averages to find out how her class feels about including a discussion of current events as a regular part of classroom activity. Similar samples in the past have represented the viewpoints of the total class quite accurately.
- A graduate student wants to know how retired people age 65 and over feel about their "golden years." He has been told by one of his professors, an expert on aging and the aged population, that the local Association of Retired Workers is a representative cross section of retired people age 65 and over. He decides to interview a sample of 50 people who are members of the association to get their views.

In both of these examples, previous information led the researcher to believe that the sample selected would

be representative of the population. There is a second form of purposive sampling in which it is not expected that the persons chosen are themselves representative of the population, but rather that they possess the necessary information *about* the population. For example,

- A researcher is asked to identify the unofficial power hierarchy in a particular high school. She decides to interview the principal, the union representative, the principal's secretary, and the school custodian because she has prior information that leads her to believe they are the people who possess the information she needs.
- For the past five years, the leaders of the teachers' association in a midwestern school district have represented the views of three-fourths of the teachers in the district on most major issues. This year, therefore, the district administration decides to interview just the leaders of the association rather than to select a sample from all the district's teachers.

Purposive sampling is different from convenience sampling in that researchers do not simply study who-

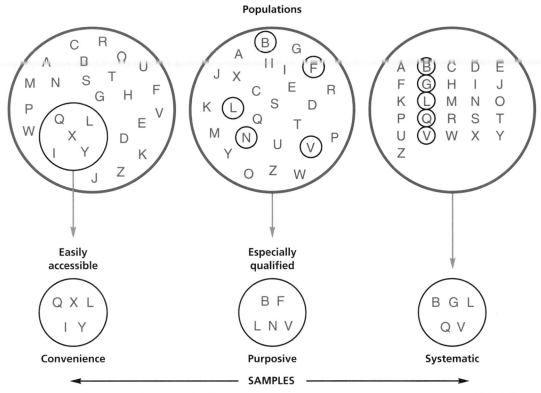

Figure 6.5 *Nonrandom Sampling Methods*

ever is available, but use their judgment to select a sample that they believe, based on prior information, will provide the data they need. The major disadvantage of purposive sampling is that the researcher's judgment may be in error—he or she may not be correct in estimating the representativeness of a sample or their expertise regarding the information needed. In the second example above, this year's leaders of the teacher's association may hold views markedly different from those of their members. Figure 6.5 illustrates the methods of convenience, purposive, and systematic sampling.

A Review of Sampling Methods

Let us illustrate each of the previous sampling methods using the same hypothesis: "Students with low self-esteem demonstrate lower achievement in school subjects."

> *Target population:* All eighth-graders in California.
> *Accessible population:* All eighth-graders in the San Francisco Bay Area (seven counties).
> *Feasible sample size: n* = 200–250.

Simple random sampling: Identify all eighth-graders in all public and private schools in the seven counties (estimated number of eighth-grade students = 9000). Assign each student a number and then use a table of random numbers to select a sample of 200. The difficulty here is that it is time-consuming to identify every eighth-grader in the Bay Area and to contact (probably) about 200 different schools in order to administer instruments to one or two students in those schools.

Cluster random sampling: Identify all public and private schools having an eighth grade in the seven counties. Assign each of the schools a number, and then randomly select four schools and include all eighth-grade classes in each school. (We would estimate 2 classes per school × 30 students per class × 4 schools = a total of 240 students.) Cluster random sampling is much more feasible than simple random sampling to implement, but it is limited because of the use of only four schools, even though they are to be selected randomly. For example, the selection of only four schools may exclude the selection of private-school students.

Stratified random sampling: Obtain data on the number of eighth-grade students in public versus private schools and determine the proportion of each type (e.g., 80 percent public, 20 percent private). Determine the number from each type to be sampled: public = 80 percent of 200 = 160; private = 20 percent of 200 = 40. Randomly select samples of 160 and 40 students from respective subpopulations of public and private students. Stratification may be used to ensure that the sample is representative on other variables as well. The difficulty with this method is that stratification requires that the researcher know the proportions in each strata of the population, and it also becomes increasingly difficult as more variables are added. Imagine trying to stratify not only on the public-private variable but also (for example) on student ethnicity, gender, and socioeconomic status, and on teacher gender and experience.

Two-stage random sampling: Randomly select 25 schools from the accessible population of schools, and then randomly select eight eighth-grade students from each school ($n = 8 \times 25 = 200$). This method is much more feasible than simple random sampling and more representative than cluster sampling. It may well be the best choice in this example, but it still requires permission from 25 schools and the resources to collect data from each.

Convenience sampling: Select all eighth-graders in four schools to which the researcher has access (again, we estimate two classes of 30 students per school, so $n = 30 \times 4 \times 2 = 240$). This method precludes generalizing beyond these four schools, unless a strong argument with supporting data can be made for their similarity to the entire group of accessible schools.

Purposive sampling: Select eight classes from throughout the seven counties on the basis of demographic data showing that they are representative of all eighth-graders. Particular attention must be paid to self-esteem and achievement scores. The problem is that such data are unlikely to be available and, in any case, cannot eliminate possible differences between the sample and the population on other variables—such as teacher attitude and available resources.

Systematic sampling: Select every forty-fifth student from an alphabetical list for each school.

$$\frac{200 \text{ students in sample}}{9000 \text{ students in population}} = \frac{1}{45}$$

This method is almost as inconvenient as simple random sampling and is likely to result in a biased sample, since the forty-fifth name in each school is apt to be in the last third of the alphabet (remember there are an estimated 60 eighth-graders in each school), introducing probable ethnic or cultural bias.

Sample Size

Drawing conclusions about a population after studying a sample is never totally satisfactory, since researchers can never be sure that their sample is perfectly representative of the population. Some differences between the sample and the population are bound to exist, but if the sample is randomly selected and of sufficient size, these differences are likely to be relatively insignificant and incidental. The question remains, therefore, as to what constitutes an adequate, or sufficient, size for a sample.

Unfortunately, there is no clear-cut answer to this question. Suppose a target population consists of 1000 eighth-graders in a given school district. Some sample sizes, of course, are obviously too small. Samples with one or two or three individuals, for example, are so small that they cannot possibly be representative. Probably any sample that has less than 20 to 30 individuals within it is too small, since that would only be 2 or 3 percent of the population. On the other hand, a sample can be too large, given the amount of time and effort the researcher must put into obtaining it. In this example, a sample of 250 or more individuals would probably be needlessly large, as that would constitute a quarter of the population. But what about samples of 50 or 100? Would these be sufficiently large? Would a sample of 200 be too large? At what point, exactly, does a sample stop being too small and become sufficiently large? The best answer is that a sample should be as large as the researcher can obtain with a reasonable expenditure of time and energy. This, of course, is not as much help as one would like, but it suggests that researchers should try to obtain as large a sample as they reasonably can.

To illustrate how the size of a sample can make a difference, let us refer to Table 6.2. The data in the table represent information about a population of 99 students (numbered 01 to 99) in three schools, Adams, Beals, and Cortez. In each school, students have been listed in order by their IQ scores from high to low and identified

Table 6.2 *A Hypothetical Population of 99 Students*

Student Number	Sex	School	IQ	Student Number	Sex	School	IQ
01	F	Adams	134	51	M	Beals	110
02	F	Adams	133	52	M	Beals	110
03	F	Adams	130	53	M	Beals	109
04	F	Adams	127	54	M	Beals	108
05	F	Adams	123	55	M	Beals	107
06	M	Adams	123	56	M	Beals	106
07	M	Adams	121	57	M	Beals	101
08	M	Adams	120	58	M	Beals	101
09	F	Adams	119	59	M	Beals	98
10	M	Adams	118	60	M	Beals	97
11	F	Adams	117	61	F	Beals	91
12	F	Adams	117	62	F	Beals	86
13	M	Adams	115	63	F	Beals	83
14	M	Adams	111	64	F	Cortez	137
15	M	Adams	109	65	M	Cortez	136
16	M	Adams	108	66	F	Cortez	133
17	M	Adams	108	67	F	Cortez	130
18	F	Adams	106	68	F	Cortez	128
19	F	Adams	105	69	F	Cortez	125
20	F	Adams	104	70	F	Cortez	125
21	F	Adams	103	71	M	Cortez	122
22	F	Adams	101	72	F	Cortez	121
23	F	Adams	101	73	M	Cortez	118
24	M	Adams	101	74	F	Cortez	118
25	M	Adams	100	75	M	Cortez	113
26	M	Adams	98	76	F	Cortez	113
27	M	Adams	97	77	M	Cortez	111
28	M	Adams	97	78	F	Cortez	111
29	M	Adams	96	79	F	Cortez	107
30	F	Adams	95	80	F	Cortez	106
31	F	Adams	89	81	F	Cortez	106
32	F	Adams	88	82	F	Cortez	105
33	F	Adams	85	83	F	Cortez	104
34	F	Beals	133	84	F	Cortez	103
35	F	Beals	129	85	F	Cortez	102
36	F	Beals	129	86	M	Cortez	102
37	F	Beals	128	87	M	Cortez	100
38	F	Beals	127	88	M	Cortez	100
39	F	Beals	127	89	M	Cortez	99
40	F	Beals	126	90	M	Cortez	99
41	M	Beals	125	91	M	Cortez	99
42	M	Beals	124	92	F	Cortez	98
43	M	Beals	117	93	M	Cortez	97
44	M	Beals	116	94	F	Cortez	96
45	M	Beals	115	95	F	Cortez	95
46	M	Beals	114	96	F	Cortez	93
47	M	Beals	114	97	F	Cortez	85
48	M	Beals	113	98	M	Cortez	83
49	M	Beals	111	99	M	Cortez	83
50	M	Beals	111				

Parameters: Average IQ = 109.8; Proportions: sex: M = .49, F = .51; schools: A = .33, B = .31, C = .36

by gender. The **parameters** (summary characteristics) of this population are shown at the bottom of the table.

Let us select a sample of 10 from this population. Using the table of random numbers in Appendix A, and starting with the first two digits of the first row under column (b), we select the following student numbers: 52, 63, 82, 75, 92, 36, 03, 11, 43, and 08. We record the data for each of these students, as shown in Table 6.3. Summarizing the statistics of this sample, we find that there are four males (.40) and six females (.60); three students attending Adams (.30), four students attending Beals (.40), and three students attending Cortez (.30); and an average IQ score of 112.2. Table 6.4 compares these statistics to the population parameters.

Table 6.3 *Sample 1, Selected from the Population in Table 6.2*

Student Number	Sex	School	IQ
52	M	Beals	110
63	F	Beals	83
82	F	Cortez	105
75	M	Cortez	113
92	F	Cortez	98
36	F	Beals	129
03	F	Adams	130
11	F	Adams	117
43	M	Beals	117
08	M	Adams	120

As you can see, our sample is not very representative of the population. Where the population is almost evenly divided between males and females, our sample has a proportion of .40 males (40 percent) to .60 females (60 percent). In our sample, only .30 students (30 percent) attend Cortez, as compared to .36 (36 percent) of the population. The average IQ of our sample, 112.2, is 2.4 points above the average IQ of the population.

Table 6.4 *Statistics of Sample 1 Compared to Population Parameters from Table 6.2*

	Proportions by Sex		Proportions by School			Average IQ
	Males	Females	A	B	C	
Population	.49	.51	.33	.31	.36	109.8
Sample	.40	.60	.30	.40	.30	112.2

Let us select another sample and see how it compares, both to the first sample we selected and to the

population as a whole. Once again, we use the table of random numbers in Appendix A. This time, we begin with column (c), reading the *last* two digits—72, 64, 94, 49, 41, 20, 05, 93, 14, and 99—and record the data for each number, as shown in Table 6.5.

Table 6.5 *Sample 2, Selected from the Population in Table 6.2*

Student Number	Sex	School	IQ
72	F	Cortez	121
64	F	Cortez	137
94	F	Cortez	96
49	M	Beals	111
41	M	Beals	125
20	F	Adams	104
05	F	Adams	123
93	M	Cortez	97
14	M	Adams	111
99	M	Cortez	83

In Table 6.6 these data are compared with the data from sample 1 and from the population. This sample differs considerably from both sample 1 and the population.

What happens if we combine the statistics of samples 1 and 2? Not only is the sample size increased from 10 to 20, but the sample statistics change, as shown in Table 6.7. The statistics of the enlarged sample are more similar to the parameters of the population.

Table 6.6 *Statistics of Samples 1 and 2 Compared to Population Parameters from Table 6.2*

	Sex		School			Average IQ
	Males	Females	A	B	C	
Population	.49	.51	.33	.31	.36	109.8
Sample 1	.40	.60	.30	.40	.30	112.2
Sample 2	.50	.50	.30	.20	.50	110.8

Table 6.7 *Combined Sample Statistics Compared to Population Parameters from Table 6.2*

	Sex		School			Average IQ
	Males	Females	A	B	C	
Population	.49	.51	.33	.31	.36	109.8
Both samples	.45	.55	.30	.30	.40	111.5

Table 6.8 *Samples 3 and 4, Selected from the Population in Table 6.2*

	Student Number	Sex	School	IQ
Sample 3	83	F	Cortez	104
	37	F	Beals	128
	69	F	Cortez	125
	22	F	Adams	101
	06	M	Adams	123
	36	F	Beals	129
	32	F	Adams	88
	48	M	Beals	113
	14	M	Adams	111
	23	F	Adams	101
Sample 4	52	M	Beals	110
	25	M	Adams	100
	24	M	Adams	101
	11	F	Adams	117
	59	M	Beals	98
	54	M	Beals	108
	84	F	Cortez	103
	31	F	Adams	89
	92	F	Cortez	98
	71	M	Cortez	122

Table 6.9 *Combined Statistics for All Four Samples Compared to Population Parameters*

	Sex		School			Average IQ
	Males	Females	A	B	C	
Population	.49	.51	.33	.31	.36	109.8
All four samples	.45	.55	.37	.30	.32	110.0

group can be defended if they are very tightly controlled; studies using only 15 subjects per group should probably be replicated, however, before too much is made of any findings that occur.*

External Validity: Generalizing from a Sample

As indicated earlier in this chapter, researchers generalize when they apply the findings of a particular study to people or settings that go beyond the particular people or settings used in the study. The whole notion of science is built on the idea of **generalizing.** Every science seeks to find basic principles or laws that can be applied to a great variety of situations and, in the case of the social sciences, to a great many people. Most researchers wish to generalize their findings to appropriate populations. But when is generalizing warranted? When can researchers say with confidence that what they have learned about a sample is also true of the population? Both the nature of the sample and the environmental conditions—the setting—within which a study takes place must be considered in thinking about generalizability. The extent to which the results of a study can be generalized determines the **external validity** of the study.

POPULATION GENERALIZABILITY

Population generalizability refers to the degree to which a sample represents the population of interest. If the results of a study only apply to the group being studied, and if that group is fairly small or is narrowly defined, the usefulness of any findings is seriously limited. This is why trying to obtain a **representative sample** is so important. Because conducting a study takes a

Let us see what happens if we draw two more samples, again using the table of random numbers in Appendix A. This time we begin at the top of column (h) and then column (l) and read the first two digits. Our samples are composed of the numbers shown in Table 6.8. Now let us combine the statistics of all four samples. The sample size is now increased to 40, and the sample statistics change, as shown in Table 6.9. This time the average IQ of our combined sample is almost identical to the average IQ of the population. The lesson of the above, we hope, is clear. The larger the sample, the more likely it is to represent the population from which it comes, provided it is randomly selected.

There are a few guidelines that we would suggest with regard to the *minimum* number of subjects needed. For descriptive studies, we think a sample with a minimum number of 100 is essential. For correlational studies, a sample of at least 50 is deemed necessary to establish the existence of a relationship. For experimental and causal-comparative studies, we recommend a minimum of 30 individuals per group, although sometimes experimental studies with only 15 individuals in each

*More specific guidelines are provided in the More About Research box on p. 262 in Chapter Twelve.

considerable amount of time, energy, and (frequently) money, researchers usually want the results of an investigation to be as widely applicable as possible.

When we speak of representativeness, however, we are referring only to the essential, or *relevant,* characteristics of a population. What do we mean by relevant? Only that the characteristics referred to might possibly be a contributing factor to any results that are obtained. For example, if a researcher wished to select a sample of first- and second-graders to study the effect of reading method on pupil achievement, such characteristics as height, eye color, or jumping ability would be judged to be irrelevant—that is, we would not expect any variation in them to have an effect on how easily a child learns to read, and hence we would not be overly concerned if those characteristics were not adequately represented in the sample. Other characteristics, such as age, gender, or visual acuity, on the other hand, might (logically) have an effect, and hence should be appropriately represented in the sample.

Whenever purposive or convenience samples are used, generalization is made more plausible if data are presented to show that the sample is representative of the intended population on at least some relevant variables. This procedure, however, can never guarantee representativeness on all relevant variables.

One aspect of generalizability that is often overlooked in "methods" or "treatment" studies is that which pertains to the teachers, counselors, administrators, or others who administer the various treatments. We must remember that such studies involve not only a sample of students, clients, or other recipients of the treatments but also a sample of those who implement the various treatments. Thus, a study that randomly selects students but not teachers is only entitled to generalize the outcomes to the population of students—*if* taught by the same teachers. To generalize to other teachers, the sample of teachers must also be selected randomly and must be sufficiently large.

Finally, we must remember that the sample in any study is the group about whom data are actually obtained. The best sampling plan is of no value if information is missing on a sizable portion of the initial sample. Once the sample has been selected, every effort must be made to ensure that the necessary data are obtained on each person in the sample. This is often difficult to do, particularly with questionnaire-type survey studies, but the results are well worth the time and energy expended. Unfortunately, there are no clear guidelines as to how many subjects can be lost before repre-

sentativeness is seriously impaired. Any researchers who lose over 10 percent of the originally selected sample would be well advised to acknowledge this limitation and qualify their conclusions accordingly.

Do researchers always want to generalize? The only time researchers are not interested in generalizing beyond the confines of a particular study is when the results of an investigation are of interest only as applied to a particular group of people at a particular time, and where all of the members of the group are included in the study. An example might be the opinions of an elementary school faculty on a specific issue such as whether or not to implement a new math program. This might be of value to that faculty for decision making or program planning, but not to anyone else.

WHEN RANDOM SAMPLING IS NOT FEASIBLE

As we have shown, sometimes it is not feasible or even possible to obtain a random sample. When this is the case, researchers should describe the sample as thoroughly as possible (using, for example, age, gender, ethnicity, and socioeconomic status) so that interested others can judge for themselves the degree to which any findings apply, and to whom and where. This is clearly an inferior procedure compared to random sampling, but sometimes it is the only alternative one has.

There is another possibility when a random sample is impossible to obtain: It is called **replication.** The researcher (or other researchers) repeats the study using different groups of subjects and in different situations. If a study is repeated several times, using different groups of subjects and under different conditions of geography, socioeconomic level, ability, and so on, and if the results obtained are essentially the same in each case, a researcher may have additional confidence about generalizing the findings.

In the vast majority of studies that have been done in education, random samples have not been used. There seem to be two reasons for this. First, there may be insufficient awareness on the part of educational researchers of the hazards involved in generalizing when one does not have a random sample. Second, in many studies it is simply not feasible for a researcher to invest the time, money, or other resources necessary to obtain a random sample. For the results of a particular study to be applicable to a larger group, then, the researcher must argue convincingly that the sample employed, even though not chosen randomly, is in fact representa-

The Difficulty in Generalizing from a Sample

In 1936, the *Literary Digest,* a popular magazine of the time, selected a sample of voters in the United States and asked the individuals in the sample for whom they would vote in the upcoming presidential election—Alf Landon (Republican) or Franklin Roosevelt (Democrat). The magazine editors obtained a sample of 2,375,000 individuals from lists of automobile and telephone owners in the United States (about 20 percent returned the mailed postcards). On the basis of their findings, the editors predicted that Landon would win by a landslide. In fact, it was Roosevelt who won the landslide victory. What was wrong with the study?

Certainly not the size of the sample. The most frequent explanations have been that the data were collected too far ahead of the election and that *a lot* of people changed their minds, and/or that the sample of voters was heavily biased in favor of the more affluent, and/or that the 20 percent return rate introduced a major bias. What do you think?

A misconception that is common among beginning researchers is illustrated by the following statement: "Although I obtained a random sample only from schools in San Francisco, I am entitled to generalize my findings to the entire state of California because the San Francisco schools (and hence my sample) reflect a wide variety of socioeconomic levels, ethnic groups, and teaching styles." The statement is incorrect because variety is not the same thing as representativeness. In order for the San Francisco schools to be representative of all the schools in California, they must be very similar (ideally, identical) with respect to characteristics such as the ones mentioned. Ask yourself: "Are the San Francisco schools representative of the entire state with regard to ethnic composition of students?" The answer, of course, is that they are not.

tive of the target population. This is difficult, however, and always subject to contrary arguments.

ECOLOGICAL GENERALIZABILITY

Ecological generalizability refers to the degree to which results of a study can be extended to other settings or conditions. Researchers must make clear the nature of the environmental conditions—the setting—under which a study takes place. These conditions must be the same in all important respects in any new situation in which researchers wish to assert that their findings apply. For example, it is not justifiable to generalize from studies on the effects of a new reading program on third-graders in a large urban school system to teaching mathematics, even to those students in that system. Research results from urban school environments may not apply to suburban or rural school environments; results obtained with transparencies may not apply to textbooks. What holds true for one subject, or with certain materials, or under certain conditions, or at certain times may not generalize to other subjects, materials, conditions, or times.

An example of inappropriate ecological generalizing occurred in a study that found that a particular method of instruction applied to map reading resulted in greater transfer to general map interpretation on the part of fifth-graders in several schools. The researcher accordingly recommended that the method of instruction be used in other content areas, such as mathematics and science, overlooking differences in content, materials, and skills involved, in addition to probable differences in resources, teacher experience, and the like. Improper ecological generalizing such as this remains the bane of much educational research.

Unfortunately, application of the powerful technique of random sampling is virtually never possible with respect to ecological generalizing. While it is conceivable that a researcher could identify "populations" of organization patterns, materials, classroom conditions, and so on and then randomly select a sizable number of combinations from all possible combinations, the logistics of doing so boggle the mind. Therefore, researchers must be cautious about generalizing the results from any one study. Only when outcomes have been shown to be similar through replication across specific environmental conditions can we generalize across those conditions. Figure 6.6 illustrates the difference between population and ecological generalizing.

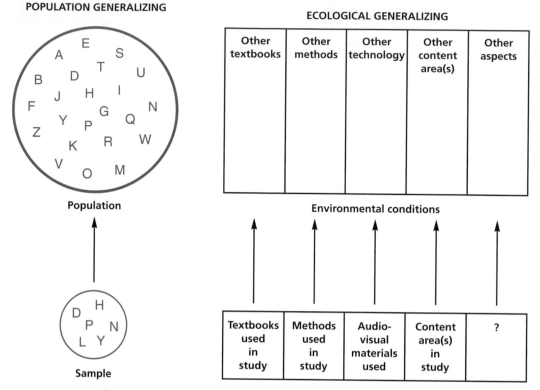

Figure 6.6 *Population as Opposed to Ecological Generalizing*

Go back to the **Interactive and Applied Learning Tools** feature at the beginning of the chapter for a listing of interactive and applied activities. Go to the **Online Learning Center** at www.mhhe.com/fraenkel5e or your **Interactive Student CD-ROM** to take practice quizzes and receive immediate feedback, practice with key terms, review chapter content and main ideas, and find annotated Web links.

Main Points

SAMPLES AND SAMPLING

- The term "sampling," as used in research, refers to the process of selecting the individuals who will participate (e.g., be observed or questioned) in a research study.
- A sample is any part of a population of individuals on whom information is obtained. It may, for a variety of reasons, be different from the sample originally selected.

SAMPLES AND POPULATIONS

- The term "population," as used in research, refers to all the members of a particular group. It is the group of interest to the researcher, the group to whom the researcher would like to generalize the results of a study.
- A target population is the actual population to whom the researcher would like to generalize; the accessible population is the population to whom the researcher is entitled to generalize.

- A representative sample is a sample that is similar to the population on all characteristics.

RANDOM VERSUS NONRANDOM SAMPLING

- Sampling may be either random or nonrandom. Random sampling methods include simple random sampling, stratified random sampling, and cluster random sampling. Nonrandom sampling methods include systematic sampling, convenience sampling, and purposive sampling.

RANDOM SAMPLING METHODS

- A simple random sample is a sample selected from a population in such a manner that all members of the population have an equal chance of being selected.
- A stratified random sample is a sample selected so that certain characteristics are represented in the sample in the same proportion as they occur in the population.
- A cluster random sample is one obtained by using groups as the sampling unit rather than individuals.
- A two-stage random sample selects groups randomly and then chooses individuals randomly from these groups.
- A table of random numbers is a table of numbers, listed and arranged in no particular order, that is used to select a random sample.

NONRANDOM SAMPLING METHODS

- A systematic sample is a sample obtained by selecting every nth name in a population.
- A convenience sample is any group of individuals that is conveniently available to be studied.
- A purposive sample is a sample selected because the individuals have special qualifications of some sort, or because of prior evidence of representativeness.

SAMPLE SIZE

- Samples should be as large as a researcher can obtain with a reasonable expenditure of time and energy. A recommended minimum number of subjects is 100 for a descriptive study, 50 for a correlational study, and 30 in each group for experimental and causal-comparative studies.

EXTERNAL VALIDITY (GENERALIZABILITY)

- The term "external validity," as used in research, refers to the extent that the results of a study can be generalized from a sample to a population.
- The term "population generalizability" refers to the extent to which the results of a study can be generalized to the intended population.
- The term "ecological generalizability" refers to the extent to which the results of a study can be generalized to conditions or settings other than those that prevailed in a particular study.

REPLICATION

- When a study is replicated, it is repeated with a new sample and sometimes under new conditions.

Key Terms

Accessible population 97

Biased sample 103

Cluster sampling 100

Convenience sampling 103

Ecological
generalizability 111

External validity 109

Generalizing 109

Nonrandom sampling 98

Parameter 108

Periodicity 103

Population 96

Population
generalizability 109

Purposive sampling 104

Random sampling 98

Random start 102

Replication 110

Representative sample 98

Sample 96

Sample size 106

Sampling 96

Sampling ratio 102

Simple random sample 99

Stratified random
sampling 100

Systematic sampling 102

Table of random
numbers 99

Target population 97

Two-stage random
sampling 101

For Discussion

1. Listed below are three examples of sampling. One involves simple random sampling, one stratified sampling, and one cluster sampling. Which example involves which method?
   a. Forty pennies are randomly selected from a large jar containing $4.00 in pennies.
   b. A random sample of 10 airports is surveyed by sending trained interviewers to solicit reactions about air safety from passengers disembarking from arriving airplanes.
   c. A community is found in which the total population consists of individuals with the following religious affiliations: Catholic, 25 percent; Protestant, 50 percent; Jewish, 15 percent; nonaffiliated, 10 percent. The researcher selects a random sample of 100 individuals, made up of 25 Catholics, 50 Protestants, 15 Jews, and 10 nonaffiliated.

2. A team of researchers wants to determine the attitudes of students about the recreational services available in the student union on campus. The team stops the first 100 students it meets on a street in the middle of the campus and asks each of these students questions about the union. What are some possible ways that this sample might be biased?

3. Suppose a researcher is interested in studying the effects of music on learning. He obtains permission from a nearby elementary school principal to use the two third-grade classes in the school. The ability level of the two classes, as shown by standardized tests, grade point averages, and faculty opinion, is quite similar. In one class, the researcher plays classical music softly every day for a semester. In the other class, no music is played. At the end of the semester, he finds that the class in which the music was played has a markedly higher average in arithmetic than the other class, although they do not differ in any other respect. To what population (if any) might the results of this study be generalized? What, exactly, could the researcher say about the effects of music on learning?

4. When, if ever, might a researcher *not* be interested in generalizing the results of a study? Explain.

5. "The larger a sample, the more justified a researcher is in generalizing from it to a population." Is this statement true? Why or why not?

6. Some people have argued that no population can *ever* be studied in its entirety. Would you agree? Why or why not?

Research Exercise Six: Sampling Plan

Use Problem Sheet 6 to describe, as fully as you can, your sample—that is, the subjects you will include in your study. Describe the type of sample you plan to use and how you will obtain the sample. Indicate whether or not you expect your study to have population generalizability: if so, to what population; if not, why it would not. Then indicate whether the study would have ecological generalizability: if so, to what settings; if not, why it would not.

PROBLEM SHEET 6

Sampling Plan

1. My intended sample (subjects who would participate in my study) consists of (tell who and how many): _____

    _____

2. Demographics (characteristics of the sample) are as follows:

    a. Age range _____

    b. Sex distribution _____

    c. Ethnic breakdown _____

    d. Location (where are these subjects?) _____

    e. Other characteristics not mentioned above that you deem important (use a sheet of paper if you need more space) _____

    _____

3. Type of sample: simple random _____ stratified random _____

    cluster random _____ two-stage random _____ convenience _____ purposive _____

4. I will obtain my sample by: _____

    _____

    _____

5. External validity (I will generalize to the following population):

    a. To what accessible population? _____

    b. To what target population? _____

    c. If not generalizable, why not? _____

6. Ecological validity (I will generalize to the following settings/conditions):

    a. Generalizable to what setting(s)? _____

    b. Generalizable to what condition(s)? _____

    c. If not generalizable, why not? _____

An electronic version of this Problem Sheet that you can fill in and print, save, or e-mail is available on the Online Learning Center at www.mhhe.com/fraenkel5e and on your Interactive Student CD-ROM.

A full-sized version of this Problem Sheet that you can fill in or photocopy is in your Student Workbook.

Instrumentation

Instructions: Circle the choice after each statement that indicates your opinion.

1. Teachers' unions should be abolished.

Strongly agree	Agree	Undecided	Disagree	Strongly disagree
(5)	(4)	(3)	(2)	(1)

2. School administrators should be required to teach at least one class in a public school every year.

Strongly agree	Agree	Undecided	Disagree	Strongly disagree
(5)	(4)	(3)	(2)	(1)

3. Classroom teachers should choose who the administrators will be in their school.

Strongly agree	Agree	Undecided	Disagree	Strongly disagree
(5)	(4)	(3)	(2)	(1)

Instrumentation

What Are Data?

Key Questions
Validity, Reliability, and Objectivity
Usability

Means of Classifying
Data-Collection Instruments

Who Provides the Information?
Where Did the Instrument Come from?
Written Response Versus Performance

Examples of
Data-Collection Instruments

Researcher-Completed Instruments
Subject-Completed Instruments
Unobtrusive Measures

Types of Scores

Raw Scores
Derived Scores
Which Scores to Use?

Preparing Data for Analysis

Scoring the Data
Tabulating and Coding the Data

Measurement Scales

Nominal Scales   Ratio Scales
Ordinal Scales   Measurement Scales
Interval Scales   Reconsidered

Norm-Referenced Versus
Criterion-Referenced Instruments

Norm-Referenced Instruments
Criterion-Referenced Instruments

Objectives

Studying this chapter should enable you to:

- Explain *what is meant by the term "data."*
- Explain *what is meant by the term "instrumentation."*
- Name *three ways in which data can be collected by researchers.*
- Explain *what is meant by the term "data-collection instrument."*
- Describe *five types of researcher-completed instruments used in educational research.*
- Describe *five types of subject-completed instruments used in educational research.*
- Explain *what is meant by the term "unobtrusive measures" and* give *two examples of such measures.*
- Name *four types of measurement scales and* give *an example of each.*
- Name *three different types of scores used in educational research and give an example of each.*
- Describe *briefly the difference between norm-referenced and criterion-referenced instruments.*
- Describe *briefly how to score, tabulate, and code data for analysis.*

Interactive and Applied Learning

After, or while, reading this chapter:

Go to your Interactive Student CD-ROM to:
- Learn More About Developing Instruments

Go to your Interactive Student CD-ROM or Student Workbook to do the following activities:
- Activity 7.1: Major Categories of Instruments and Their Uses
- Activity 7.2: Which Type of Instrument Is Most Appropriate?
- Activity 7.3: Types of Scales
- Activity 7.4: Norm-Referenced Versus Criterion-Referenced Instruments
- Activity 7.5: Design an Instrument

Monica Stuart and Ben Colen are discussing last night's lecture in their educational research class.

"I must admit that I was pretty impressed," says Monica.

"How come?"

"That list of measuring instruments Professor Mendoza described last night. Questionnaires, rating scales, true-false tests, sociograms, logs, anecdotal records, tally sheets, . . . It just went on and on. I never knew there were so many ways to measure something—so many measuring devices. And what he said about measurement—that really impressed me! Remember? He said that if something exists, you can measure it!"

"Yeah, it was quite a feat. I have to admit that. I don't know about the idea that everything can be measured, though. What about something that is very abstract?"

"Like what?"

"Well, how about, say, 'alienation'? Or 'motivation'? How would you measure them? I'm not sure they even *can* be measured!"

"Well, here's what I'd do," says Monica. "I would . . ."

How would *you* measure motivation? Do instruments exist that one could use to measure something this abstract? To get some ideas, read this chapter.

What Are Data?

The term **"data"** refers to the kinds of information researchers obtain on the subjects of their research. Demographic information, such as age, gender, ethnicity, religion, and so on, is one kind of data; scores from a commercially available or researcher-prepared test are another. Responses to the researcher's questions in an oral interview or written replies to a survey questionnaire are other kinds. Essays written by students, grade point averages obtained from school records, performance logs kept by coaches, anecdotal records maintained by teachers or counselors—all constitute various kinds of data that researchers might want to collect as part of a research investigation. An important decision for every researcher to make during the planning phase of an investigation, therefore, is what kind(s) of data he or she intends to collect. The device (such as a pencil-and-paper test, a questionnaire, or a rating scale) the researcher uses to collect data is called an instrument.*

KEY QUESTIONS

Generally, the whole process of preparing to collect data is called **instrumentation.** It involves not only the selection or design of the instruments but also the *pro-*

cedures and the conditions under which the instruments will be administered. Several questions arise.

1. *Where* will the data be collected? This question refers to the *location* of the data collection. Where will it be? In a classroom? A schoolyard? A private home? On the street?
2. *When* will the data be collected? This question refers to the *time* of collection. When is it to take place? In the morning? Afternoon? Evening? Over a weekend?
3. *How often* are the data to be collected? This question refers to the *frequency* of collection. How many times are the data to be collected? Only once? Twice? More than twice?
4. *Who* is to collect the data? This question refers to the *administration* of the instruments. Who is to do this? The researcher? Someone selected and trained by the researcher?

These questions are important because how researchers answer them may affect the data obtained. It is a mistake to think that researchers need only locate or develop a "good" instrument. The data provided by any instrument may be affected by any or all of the preceding considerations. The most highly regarded of instruments will provide useless data, for instance, if administered incorrectly, by someone disliked by respondents, under noisy, inhospitable conditions, or when subjects are exhausted.

---

*Most, but not all, research requires use of an instrument. In studies where data are obtained exclusively from existing records (grades, attendance, etc.), no instrument is needed.

All the above questions are important for researchers to answer, therefore, *before* they begin to collect the data they need. A researcher's decisions about location, time, frequency, and administration are always affected by the kind(s) of instrument to be used. And every instrument, no matter what kind, if it is to be of any value, must allow researchers to draw accurate conclusions about the capabilities or other characteristics of the people being studied.

VALIDITY, RELIABILITY, AND OBJECTIVITY

A frequently used (but somewhat old-fashioned) definition of a valid instrument is that it measures what it is supposed to measure. A more accurate definition of **validity** revolves around the defensibility of the inferences researchers make from the data collected through the use of an instrument. An instrument, after all, is a device used to gather data. Researchers then use these data to make inferences about the characteristics of certain individuals.* But to be of any use, these inferences must be correct. All researchers, therefore, want instruments that permit them to draw warranted, or valid, conclusions about the characteristics (ability, achievement, attitudes, and so on) of the individuals they study.

To measure math achievement, for example, a researcher needs to have some assurance that the instrument she intends to use actually does measure such achievement. Another researcher, who wants to know what people think or how they feel about a particular topic, needs assurance that the instrument used will allow him to make accurate inferences. There are various ways to obtain such assurance, and we discuss them in Chapter Eight.

A second consideration is **reliability.** A reliable instrument is one that gives consistent results. If a researcher tested the math achievement of a group of individuals at two or more different times, for example, he or she should expect to obtain close to the same results each time. This consistency would give the researcher confidence that the results actually represented the achievement of the individuals involved. As with validity, there are a number of procedures that can be used

---

*Sometimes instruments are used to collect data on something other than individuals (such as groups, programs, and environments), but since most of the time we are concerned with individuals in educational research, we use this terminology throughout our discussion.

to determine the reliability of an instrument. We discuss several of them in Chapter Eight.

A final consideration is objectivity. **Objectivity** refers to the absence of subjective judgments. Whenever possible, researchers should try to eliminate subjectivity from the judgments they make about the achievement, performance, or characteristics of subjects. Unfortunately, complete objectivity is probably never attained.

We discuss each of these concepts in much more detail in Chapter Eight; in this chapter we look at some of the various kinds of instruments that can be (and often are) used in research and discuss how to find and select them.

USABILITY

There are a number of practical considerations every researcher needs to think about. One of these is how easy it will be to use any instrument he or she designs or selects. How long will it take to administer? Are the directions clear? Is it appropriate for the ethnic or other groups to whom it will be administered? How easy is it to score? To interpret the results? How much does it cost? Do equivalent forms exist? Have any problems been reported by others who used it? Does evidence of its reliability and validity exist? Getting satisfactory answers to such questions can save a researcher a lot of time and energy and can prevent a lot of headaches.

Means of Classifying Data-Collection Instruments

Instruments can be classified in a number of ways. Here are some of the most useful.

WHO PROVIDES THE INFORMATION?

In educational research there are three general methods available for obtaining information. Researchers can get the information (1) themselves, with little or no involvement of other people; (2) directly from the subjects of the study; or (3) from others, frequently referred to as **informants,** who are knowledgeable about the subjects. Let us follow a specific example. A researcher wishes to test the hypothesis that inquiry teaching in history classes results in higher-level thinking than when such classes are taught by the lecture method. The researcher may elect option 1, in which case she may observe students in the classroom, noting the frequency of oral statements indicative of higher-level thinking. Or, she may examine existing student records that may include test results and/or anecdotal material she considers indicative of higher-level thinking. If she elects option 2, the researcher is likely to administer tests or request student products (essays, problem sheets) for evidence. She may also decide to interview students using questions designed to reveal their thinking about history (or other topics). Finally, if the researcher chooses option 3, she is likely to interview persons (teachers, other students) or ask them to fill out rating scales in which the interviewees assess each student's thinking skills based on their prior experience with the student. Here are examples of each type of method:

1. *Researcher instruments*
   - A researcher interested in learning and memory development counts the number of times it takes different nursery school children to learn to navigate their way correctly through a maze located in a corner of their school playground. He records his findings on a **tally sheet.**
   - A researcher interested in the concept of "mutual attraction" describes in ongoing *field notes* how the behaviors of people who work together in various settings have been observed to differ on this variable.
2. *Subject instruments*
   - A researcher in an elementary school administers a *weekly spelling test* that requires students to spell correctly the new words learned in class during the week.
   - At a researcher's request, an administrator passes out a **questionnaire** during a faculty meeting that asks the faculty's opinions about the new mathematics curriculum recently instituted in the district.
   - High school English teachers are asked by a researcher to ask their students to keep a *daily log* in which they record their reactions to the plays they read each week.
3. *Informant instruments*
   - Teachers are asked by a researcher to use a *rating scale* to rate each of their students on their phonic reading skills.
   - Parents are asked by a researcher to keep *anecdotal records* describing the TV characters spontaneously role-played by their preschoolers.

- The president of the student council is interviewed regarding student views on the school's disciplinary code. Her responses are recorded on an *interview schedule.*

WHERE DID THE INSTRUMENT COME FROM?

There are essentially two basic ways for a researcher to acquire an instrument: (1) find and administer a previously existing instrument of some sort, or (2) administer an instrument the researcher personally developed or had developed by someone else.

Development of an instrument by the researcher has its problems. Primarily, it is not easy to do. Development of a "good" instrument usually takes a fair amount of time and effort, not to mention a considerable amount of skill.

Selecting an already developed instrument when appropriate, therefore, is preferred. Such instruments are usually developed by experts who possess the necessary skills. Choosing an instrument that has already been developed takes far less time than it does to develop a new instrument to measure the same thing.

Designing one's own instrument is time-consuming, and we do not recommend it for those without a considerable amount of time, energy, and money to invest in the endeavor. Fortunately, a number of already developed, useful, instruments exist, and they can be located quite easily by means of a computer. The most comprehensive listing of testing resources currently available can be found by accessing the *ERIC Clearinghouse on Assessment and Evaluation* at the following website: http://www.ericae.net/ (see Figure 7.1).

Clicking on Test Locator brings up the *ERIC/AE Test Locator-Search* form, which contains the ETS Test File, as shown in Figure 7.2.

We typed the word "shyness" in the box labeled "Find" in the ETS Test File. This produced the list of matching documents shown in Figure 7.3. We clicked on #4, "Social Phobia and Anxiety Inventory," to obtain the description of this instrument (see Figure 7.4).

Almost any topic can be searched in this way to obtain a list of instruments that measure some aspect of the topic. Notice that a printed copy of the instrument can be obtained by contacting the source listed under "Contact Information."

ERIC Clearinghouses change their location from time to time, and hence the assessment clearinghouse may be at a different address than the one we have cited here. An alternative, therefore, is to use the search

ERIC Clearinghouse on Assessment and Evaluation

Educational Resources Information Center

Search
ERIC

Test
Locator

Assessment
FAQ's

Bookstore

Full-text
Library

The ERIC ® Clearinghouse on Assessment and Evaluation seeks to provide 1) balanced information concerning educational assessment and 2) resources to encourage responsible test use.

Feature Article: Grading the Nation's Report Card National Academy of Science (be sure to read Chapter 5 on the NAEP scales). **NEW!**

Assessment, Evaluation, Statistics, & Educational Research

Test Locator
Assessment & Evaluation on the Internet
Search and explore all assessment & eval sites
ERIC & the American Educational Research Association
K12ASSESS-L Listserv

ERIC/AE On-Line Assessment Library
Recent ERIC/AE briefing papers (Digests)
How-to series
Assessment and Testing in newspapers and magazines

An Online, Interactive Computer Adaptive Testing Tutorial

Educational Resources Information Center (ERIC®)

Track papers submitted to ERIC/AE
Search ERIC (RIE & CIJE)
ERIC System Home page
ERIC/AE Staff (& pictures)
ERIC/AE Education Partners Program

Directory of ERIC Resource Collections
ERIC/AE Web page usage statistics
Submitting documents to ERIC and our Reproduction Release Form

Key numbers:

- ACCESS ERIC-- (800) 538-3742 (800 LET-ERIC), (301) 519-5789 -General number for ERIC resources and questions
- ERIC Document Reproduction Service -- (800) 443-3742, (703) 440-1400 -To obtain hard copy and microfiche

Figure 7.1 *The ERIC Clearinghouse on Assessment and Evaluation Home Page*

engines that we described in Chapter Five to locate ERIC. What you want to find is ERIC's test collection of more than 9000 instruments of various types, as well as *The Mental Measurements Yearbooks.* Now produced by the Buros Institute at the University of Nebraska,* the yearbooks are published about every other year, with supplements produced between each issue. Each yearbook provides reviews of the standardized tests that have been published since the last issue. The Institute's *Tests in Print* is a comprehensive bibliography of commercial tests. Unfortunately, only the references to the instruments and reviews of them are available online; the actual instruments themselves are available only in print form.

Here are some other references you can consult that list various types of instruments:

- T. E. Backer (1977). *A directory of information on tests.* ERIC TM Report 62-1977. Princeton, NJ: ERIC Clearinghouse on Assessment and Evaluation, Educational Testing Service.

*So named for Oscar Buros, who started the yearbooks back in 1938.

- K. Corcoran and J. Fischer (Eds.) (1994). *Measures for clinical practice* (2 volumes). New York: Free Press.
- *ETS test collection catalog: Volume 1, Achievement tests* (1992); *Volume 2, Vocational tests* (1988); *Volume 3, Tests for special populations* (1989); *Volume 4, Cognitive, aptitude, and intelligence tests* (1990); *Volume 5, Attitude measures* (1991); *Volume 6, Affective measures and personality tests* (1992). Phoenix, AZ: Oryx Press.
- E. Fabiano and N. O'Brien (1987). *Testing information sources for educators.* TME Report 94. Princeton, NJ: ERIC Clearinghouse on Assessment and Evaluation, Educational Testing Service. This source updates Backer to 1987, but it is not as comprehensive.
- B. A. Goldman and D. F. Mitchell (1974–1995). *Directory of unpublished experimental mental measures.* Volumes 1–6. Washington, DC: American Psychological Association.
- M. Hersen and A. S. Bellack (1988). *Dictionary of behavioral assessment techniques.* New York: Pergamon.

Figure 7.2 *The ERIC/AE Test Locator*

ERIC/AE Test Locator

The *Test Locator* is a joint project of the ERIC Clearinghouse on Assessment and Evaluation at the Catholic University of America, the Library and Reference Services Division of the Educational Testing Service, the Buros Institute of Mental Measurements at the University of Nebraska in Lincoln, the Region III Comprehensive Center at GW University, and Pro-Ed test publishers.

Announcement: We have teamed with several publishers and amazon.com to bring you our assessment and evaluation bookstore. Please come and browse.

- ❑ ETS/ERIC Test File
- ❑ Test Review Locator
- ❑ Buros/ERIC Test Publisher Locator
- ❑ CEEE/ERIC Test Database (tests commonly used with LEP students)
- ❑ Code of Fair Testing Practices.
- ❑ Test Selection Tips

ETS Test File

The Educational Testing Service (ETS) Test Collection database contains records on over 10,000 tests and research instruments. These records describe the instruments and provide availability information.

Via webinator search engine

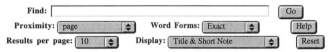

We have a FAQ (frequently asked questions) sheet on the ETS Test Collection, and information about the ETS Tests on Microfiche collection.

The Test Collection encompasses virtually all fields from vocational interest inventories for adults to instruments that measure shyness or predict recidivism in released criminal offenders, to assessment of managerial style, as well as education-related achievement and aptitude tests. The test descriptions are indexed with ERIC Thesaurus terms for subject accessibility. ETS Library and Reference Services Division prepares the descriptions. ERIC_AE maintains the database and hosts the Search System.

| Page top | ETS Test Collection | Test Review Locator | Buros Test Publisher Locator |

- S. E. Krug (published biannually). *Psychware sourcebook.* Austin, TX: Pro-Ed, Inc. A directory of computer-based assessment tools, such as tests, scoring, and interpretation systems.
- H. I. McCubbin and A. I. Thompson (Eds.) (1987). *Family assessment inventories for research and practice.* Madison, WI: University of Wisconsin–Madison.
- R. C. Sweetland and D. J. Keyser (Eds.) (1991). *Tests: A comprehensive reference for assessments in psychology, education, and business,* 3rd ed. Kansas City, MO: Test Corporation of America.

With so many instruments now available to the research community, we recommend that, except in unusual cases, researchers devote their energies to adapting (and/or improving) those that now exist rather than trying to start from scratch to develop an entirely new measure.

WRITTEN RESPONSE VERSUS PERFORMANCE

Another way to classify instruments is in terms of whether they require a written or marked response or a more general evaluation of performance on the part of the subjects of the study. **Written-response instruments** include objective (e.g., multiple-choice, true-false, matching, or short-answer) tests, short essay examinations, questionnaires, interview schedules, rating scales, and checklists. **Performance instruments** include any device designed to measure either a procedure or a product. **Procedures** are ways of doing things, such as mixing a chemical solution, diagnosing a problem in an automobile, writing a letter, solving a puzzle, or setting the margins on a typewriter. **Products** are the end results of procedures, such as the correct chemical solution, the correct diagnosis of auto malfunction, or a properly typed letter. Performance instruments are designed to see whether and how well procedures can be followed and to assess the quality of products.

Written-response instruments are generally preferred over performance instruments, since the use of the latter is frequently quite time-consuming and often requires equipment or other resources that are not readily available. A fairly long period of time would have to be provided to have even a fairly small sample of students (imagine 35!) complete the steps involved in a high school science experiment.

ERIC/AE l Test Locator l Test File l Review Locator l Publisher Locator l LEP

Matching documents

Find: shyness   [Help] [Go]

Search type: | Exact match   ⬍ | Word Forms: | Exact   ⬍ | Results per page: | 10 ⬍ | Display:
| Title & Short Note   ⬍ |

☐ 1: **Cheek and Buss Shyness Scale**
Cheek and Buss Shyness Scale Cheek, Jonathan M. Table of Contents Descriptive information Contact   Find Similar
information Suggestions to extend your search Descriptive Information Title: Cheek and Buss Shyness Scale   Match Info
Author: ...   Translate
http://ericae.net/tc2/TC018446.htm (1K)

☐ 2: **Communicative Adaptability Scale (CAS).**
Communicative Adaptability Scale (CAS). Duran, Robert L. Table of Contents Descriptive information Contact   Find Similar
information Suggestions to extend your search Descriptive Information Title: Communicative Adaptability Scale   Match Info
...   Translate
http://ericae.net/tc2/TC019340.htm (2K)

☐ 3: **Assertiveness, Aggressiveness, and Complaining Behavior.**
The last item did not load highly on any factor. The scores to the items within each factor are summed to form   Find Similar
factor indices. (JL) Materials: 1. Descriptive material 2. Test Publication Date: 1979 Most recent update ...   Match Info
http://ericae.net/tc2/TC014745.htm (2K)   Translate

☐ 4: **Social Phobia and Anxiety Inventory (SPAI).**
Social Phobia and Anxiety Inventory (SPAI). Turner, Samuel M.; and Others Table of Contents Descriptive   Find Similar
information Contact information Suggestions to extend your search Descriptive Information Title: Social Phobia   Match Info
...   Translate
http://ericae.net/tc2/TC019874.htm (2K)

☐ 5: **Differential Emotions Scale.**
Number of Test Items: 30. Testing Time: 10; approx minutes. Age Range: Adults. Publication Date: 1971 Most   Find Similar
recent update to the database: Jun 1982 ETS Tracking Number: TC008926 Contact Information This measure is   Match Info
...   Translate
http://ericae.net/tc2/TC008926.htm (2K)

Figure 7.3 *The ERIC/AE Matching Document Page*

Examples of Data-Collection Instruments

When it comes to *administering* the instruments to be used in a study, either the researchers (or their assistants or other informants) must do it themselves or they must ask the subjects of the study to provide the information desired. Therefore, we group the instruments in the following discussion according to whether they are completed by researchers or by subjects. Examples of these instruments include the following:

Researcher completes	Subject completes
Rating scales	Questionnaires
Interview schedules	Self-checklists
Tally sheets	Attitude Scales
Flowcharts	Personality (or character)
Performance	inventories
checklists	Achievement/aptitude tests
Anecdotal records	Performance tests
Time-and-motion	Projective devices
logs	Sociometric devices

This distinction, of course, is by no means absolute. Many of the instruments we list might, on a given occasion, be completed by either the researcher(s) or subjects in a particular study.

RESEARCHER-COMPLETED INSTRUMENTS

Rating Scales. A rating is a measured judgment of some sort. When we rate people, we make a judgment about their behavior or something they have produced. Thus, both behaviors (such as how well a person gives an oral report) and products (such as a written copy of a report) of individuals can be rated.

Notice that the terms "observations" and "ratings" are not synonymous. A rating is intended to convey the rater's judgment about an individual's behavior or product. An observation is intended merely to indicate whether a particular behavior is present or absent (see the time-and-motion log in Figure 7.12). Sometimes, of course, researchers may do both. The activities of a small group engaging in a discussion, for example, can be both observed and rated.

Social Phobia and Anxiety Inventory (SPAI).
Turner, Samuel M.; and Others

Table of Contents

Descriptive Information

Title: Social Phobia and Anxiety Inventory (SPAI).
Author: Turner, Samuel M.; and Others
Abstract: The Social Phobia and Anxiety Inventory (SPAI) is a self-report inventory which assesses the somatic, cognitive and behavioral symptoms of social phobia across a wide range of social situations and settings. It consists of 45 statements to be rated on a 7-point Likert scale. The SPAI has two subscales: Social Phobia (SP) and Agoraphobia (Ag). Subscales are scored separately by summing across all items for each scale. The maximum score for the SP subscale is 192, and for the Ag subscale, 78. A Difference score is derived by subtracting the Ag score from the SP score, yielding a purer measure of social phobia. In addition to its quantitative scores, the scale can be used to examine the pattern of responses of a specific individual to plan a specific plan of treatment. The SPAI can be used with people 14 years old and older. (JL)

Materials:
    1. Manual
    2. Inventory

Publication Date: 1996
Most recent update to the database: Jun 1996
ETS Tracking Number: TC019874

Contact Information

For more detailed information about this measure and its related materials, please contact or consult:

Multi-Health Systems, Inc., 908 Falls Blvd., North Tonawanda, NY 14120-2060.

Suggestions to extend your search

To search for similar measures in the ERIC/ETS Test Locator, you can either:

    1. Click the back button to return to your list of search results and then click the More Like This icon ⊜ that is next to this test title; or
    2. Reconstruct your query using one or more of the following descriptive words/phrases:

Descriptors: *Anxiety; Interpersonal Competence; Shyness; Social Isolation; Likert Scales; Adults; Adolescents
Identifiers: Social Phobia and Anxiety Inventory (SPAI)

Figure 7.4 *The Social Phobia and Anxiety Inventory Page*

Behavior Rating Scales. Behavior rating scales appear in several forms, but those most commonly used ask the observer to circle or mark a point on a continuum to indicate the rating. The simplest of these to construct is a *numerical rating scale,* which provides a series of numbers, with each number representing a particular rating.

Figure 7.5 presents an example of such a scale designed to rate teachers. The problem with this rating scale is that different observers are quite likely to have different ideas about the meaning of the terms that the numbers represent ("excellent," "average," etc.). In other words, the different rating points on the scale are not described fully enough. The same individual, therefore, might be rated quite differently by two different observers. One way to address this problem is to give additional meaning to each number by describing it more fully. For example, in Figure 7.5, the number "5" could be defined as "among the top 5 percent of all teachers you have had." In the absence of such definitions, the researcher must either rely on the training of respondents or treat the ratings as subjective opinions.

The *graphic rating scale* is an attempt to improve on the vagueness of numerical rating scales. A graphic rating scale describes each of the characteristics to be rated and places them on a horizontal line on which the observer is to place a check. Figure 7.6 presents an example of a graphic rating scale. Here again, this scale would be improved by adding definitions, such as defining "always" as "95 to 100 percent of the time," and "frequently" as "70 to 94 percent of the time."

Product Rating Scales. As we mentioned earlier, researchers may wish to rate products. Examples of prod-

Some Tips About Developing Your Own Instrument

1. Be sure you are clear as to what variables are to be assessed. Much time and effort can be wasted by definitions that are too ambiguous. If more than one variable is involved, be sure that both the meaning and the items for each variable are kept distinct. In general, a particular item or question should be used for only one variable.

2. Review existing instruments that measure similar variables in order to decide upon a format and to obtain ideas on specific items.

3. Decide on a format for each variable. Although it is sometimes appropriate to mix multiple-choice, true-false, matching, rating, and open-ended items, doing so complicates scoring and is usually undesirable. Remember: Different variables often require different formats.

4. Begin compiling and/or writing items. Be sure that, in your judgment, each is logically valid—that is, that the item is consistent with the definition of the variable. Try to ensure that the vocabulary is appropriate for the intended respondents.

5. Have colleagues review the items for logical validity. Supply colleagues with a copy of your definitions and a description of the intended respondents. Be sure to have them evaluate format as well as content.

6. Revise items based on colleague feedback. At this point, try to have about twice as many items as you intend to use in the final form (generally at least 20). Remember that more items generally means higher reliability.

7. Locate a group of people with experience appropriate to your study. Have them review your items for logical validity. Make any revisions needed and complete your items. You should have half again as many items as intended in the final form.

8. Try out your instrument with a group of respondents who are as similar as possible to your study respondents. Have them complete the instrument and then discuss it with them, to the extent that this is feasible, given their age, sophistication, and so forth.

9. If feasible, conduct a statistical item analysis with your tryout data (at least 20 respondents are necessary). Such analyses are not difficult to carry out, especially if you have a computer. The information provided on each item indicates how effective it is and, sometimes, even suggests how to improve it. See, for example, K. R. Murphy and C. O. Davidshofer (1991). *Psychological testing: Principles and applications.* Englewood Cliffs, NJ: Prentice Hall.

10. Select and revise items as necessary until you have the number you want.

---

ucts that are frequently rated in education are book reports, maps and charts, diagrams, drawings, notebooks, essays, and creative endeavors of all sorts. Whereas the rating of behaviors must be done at a particular time (when the researcher can observe the behavior), a big advantage of product ratings is that they can be done at any time.* Figure 7.7 presents an example of a scale rating the product "handwriting." To use this scale, an actual sample of the student's handwriting is obtained. It is then moved along the scale until the quality of the handwriting in the sample is most similar to the example shown on the scale. Although more than 40 years old, it remains a classic example of this type of instrument.

Interview Schedules. Interview schedules and questionnaires are basically the same kind of instrument—a

*Some behavior rating scales are designed to assess behavior over a period of time; for example, how frequently a teacher asks high-level thought questions.

Instructions: For each of the behaviors listed below, circle the appropriate number, using the following key: 5 = Excellent, 4 = Above Average, 3 = Average, 2 = Below Average, 1 = Poor.

A. Explains course material clearly

    1   2   3   4   5

B. Establishes rapport with students

    1   2   3   4   5

C. Asks high-level questions

    1   2   3   4   5

D. Varies class activities

    1   2   3   4   5

Figure 7.5 *Excerpt from a Behavior Rating Scale for Teachers*

Figure 7.6 *Excerpt from a Graphic Rating Scale*

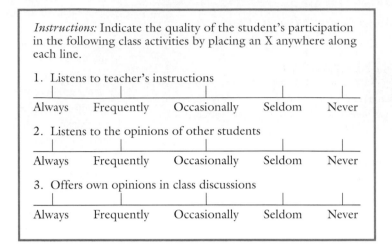

Instructions: Indicate the quality of the student's participation in the following class activities by placing an X anywhere along each line.

1. Listens to teacher's instructions

Always	Frequently	Occasionally	Seldom	Never

2. Listens to the opinions of other students

Always	Frequently	Occasionally	Seldom	Never

3. Offers own opinions in class discussions

Always	Frequently	Occasionally	Seldom	Never

set of questions to be answered by the subjects of the study. There are some important differences in how they are administered, however. Interviews are conducted orally, and the answers to the questions are recorded by the researcher (or someone he or she has trained). The advantages of this are that the interviewer can clarify any questions that are obscure and also can ask the respondent to expand on answers that are particularly important or revealing. A big disadvantage, on the other hand, is that it takes much longer than the questionnaire to complete. Furthermore, the presence of the researcher may inhibit respondents from saying what they really think.

Figure 7.8 presents an example of a structured interview schedule. Notice in this interview schedule that the interviewers have to do considerable writing, unless the interview is taped. Some interview schedules phrase questions so that the responses are likely to fall in certain categories. This is sometimes call *precoding*. Precoding enables the interviewer to check appropriate items rather than transcribe responses, thus preventing the respondent from having to wait while the interviewer records a response.

Tally Sheets. A tally sheet is a device often used by researchers to record the frequency of student behaviors, activities, or remarks. How many high school students follow instructions during fire drills, for example? How many instances of aggression or helpfulness are observed for elementary students on the playground? How often do students in Mr. Jordan's fifth-period U.S. history class ask questions? How often do they ask inferential questions? Tally sheets can help researchers record answers to these kinds of questions efficiently.

A tally sheet is simply a listing of various categories of activities or behaviors on a piece of paper. Every time a subject is observed engaging in one of these activities or behaviors, the researcher places a tally in the appropriate category. The kinds of statements that students make in class, for example, often indicate the degree to which they understand various concepts and ideas. The possible category systems that might be devised are probably endless, but Figure 7.9 presents one example.

Flowcharts. A particular type of tally sheet is the participation flowchart. Flowcharts are particularly helpful in analyzing class discussions. Both the number and direction of student remarks can be charted to gain some idea of the quantity and focus of students' verbal participation in class.

One of the easiest ways to do this is to prepare a seating chart on which a box is drawn for each student in the class being observed. A tally mark is then placed in the box of a particular student each time he or she makes a verbal comment. To indicate the direction of individual student comments, arrows can be drawn from the box of a student making a comment to the box of the student to whom the comment is directed. Figure 7.10 illustrates what such a flowchart might look like. This chart suggests that Robert, Felix, and Mercedes dominated the discussion, with contributions from Al, Gail, Jack, and Sam. Joe and Nancy said nothing. Note that a subsequent discussion, or a different topic, however, might reveal a quite different pattern.

Performance Checklists. One of the most frequently used of all measuring instruments is the *check-*

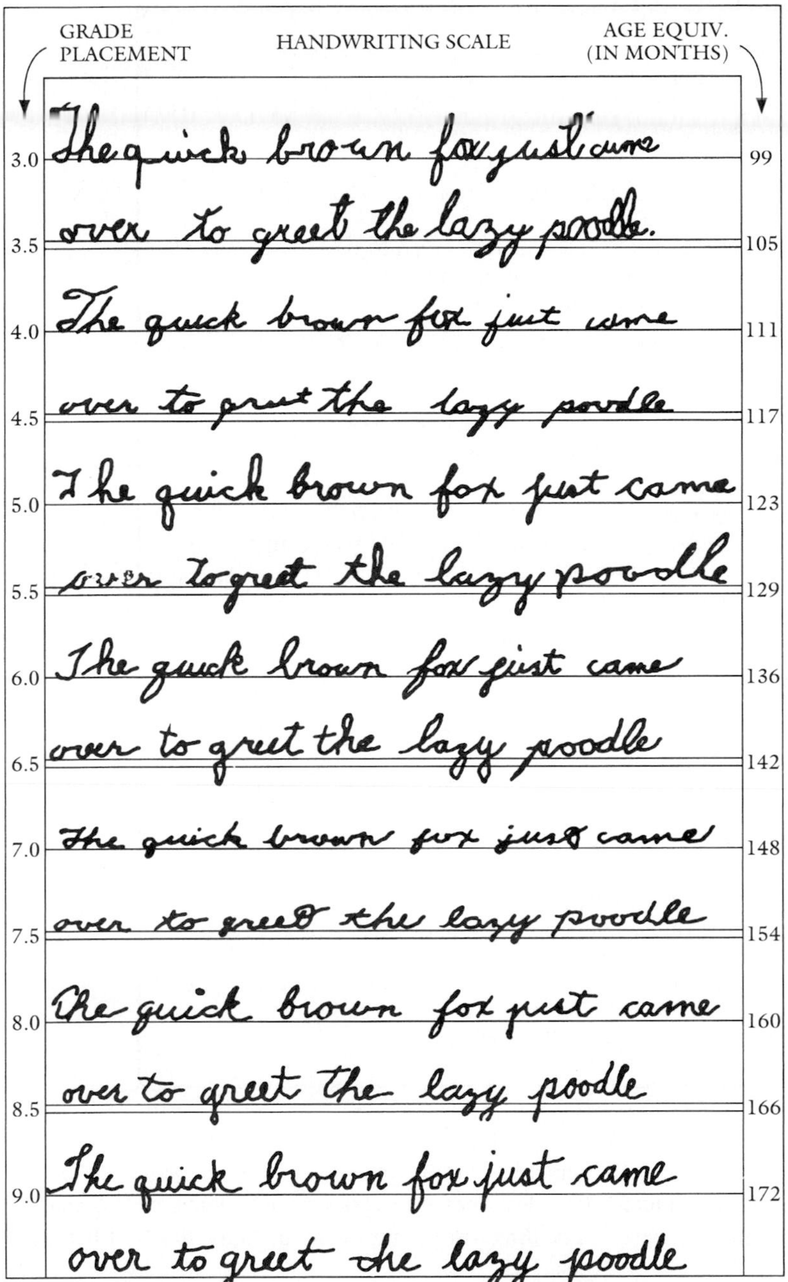

Source: Handwriting scale used in the California Achievement Tests, Form W (1957). TB/McGraw-Hill, Del Monte Research Park, Monterey, CA 93940. Copyright 1957 by McGraw-Hill.

Figure 7.7 *Example of a Product Rating Scale*

list. A performance checklist consists of a list of behaviors that make up a certain type of performance (using a microscope, typing a letter, solving a mathematics problem, and so on). It is used to determine whether or not an individual behaves in a certain (usually desired) way when asked to complete a particular task. If a particular behavior is present when an individual is observed, the researcher places a check opposite it on the list.

Figure 7.11 presents part of a performance checklist developed over 50 years ago to assess a student's skill in using a microscope. Note that the items on this checklist (as any well-constructed checklist should) ask the observer to indicate only *if* the desired behaviors

Figure 7.8 *Interview Schedule (for Teachers) Designed to Assess the Effects of a Competency-Based Curriculum in Inner-City Schools*

1. Would you rate *pupil academic learning* as excellent, good, fair, or poor?
   a. If you were here last year, how would you compare *pupil academic learning* to previous years?
   b. Please give specific examples.

2. Would you rate *pupil attitude toward school generally* as excellent, good, fair, or poor?
   a. If you were here last year, how would you compare *pupil attitude toward school generally* to previous years?
   b. Please give specific examples.

3. Would you rate *pupil attitude toward learning* as excellent, good, fair, or poor?
   a. If you were here last year, how would you compare *attitude toward learning* to previous years?
   b. Please give specific examples.

4. Would you rate *pupil attitude toward self* as excellent, good, fair, or poor?
   a. If you were here last year, how would you compare *pupil attitude toward self* to previous years?
   b. Please give specific examples.

5. Would you rate *pupil attitude toward other students* as excellent, good, fair, or poor?
   a. If you were here last year, how would you compare *attitude toward other students* to previous years?
   b. Please give specific examples.

6. Would you rate *pupil attitude toward you* as excellent, good, fair, or poor?
   a. If you were here last year, how would you compare *pupil attitude toward you* to previous years?
   b. Please give specific examples.

7. Would you rate *pupil creativity–self-expression* as excellent, good, fair, or poor?
   a. If you were here last year, how would you compare *pupil creativity–self-expression* to previous years?
   b. Please give specific examples.

take place. No subjective judgments are called for on the part of the observer as to how well the individual performs. Items that call for such judgments are best left to rating scales.

Anecdotal Records. Another way of recording the behavior of individuals is the anecdotal record. It is just what its name implies—a record of observed behaviors written down in the form of anecdotes. There is no set format; rather, observers are free to record any behavior they think is important and need not focus on the same behavior for all subjects. To be most useful, however, observers should try to be as specific and as factual as possible and to avoid evaluative, interpretive, or overly

generalized remarks. The American Council on Education describes four types of anecdotes, stating that the first three are to be avoided. Only the fourth type is desired.

1. Anecdotes that evaluate or judge the behavior of the child as good or bad, desirable or undesirable, acceptable or unacceptable . . . *evaluative statements* (to be avoided).
2. Anecdotes that account for or explain the child's behavior, usually on the basis of a single fact or thesis . . . *interpretive statements* (to be avoided).
3. Anecdotes that describe certain behavior in general terms, as happening frequently, or as character-

Type of Remark		
1. Asks question calling for factual information	Related to lesson	ᚻᚻ
	Not related to lesson	|
2. Asks question calling for clarification	Related to lesson	ᚻᚻ ||
	Not related to lesson	
3. Asks question calling for explanation	Related to lesson	ᚻᚻ |||
	Not related to lesson	
4. Asks question calling for speculation	Related to lesson	|
	Not related to lesson	
5. Asks question of another student	Related to lesson	|
	Not related to lesson	||
6. Gives own opinion on issue	Related to lesson	|
	Not related to lesson	|||
7. Responds to another student	Related to lesson	
	Not related to lesson	||||
8. Summarizes remarks of another student	Related to lesson	
	Not related to lesson	
9. Does not respond when addressed by teacher	Related to lesson	
	Not related to lesson	||
10. Does not respond when addressed by another student	Related to lesson	|
	Not related to lesson	

Figure 7.9 *Discussion Analysis Tally Sheet*

izing the child . . . *generalized statements* (to be avoided).

4. Anecdotes that tell exactly what the child did or said, that describe concretely the situation in which the action or comment occurred, and that tell clearly what other persons also did or said . . . *specific or concrete descriptive statements* (the type desired).[1]

Here are examples of each of the four types.

Evaluative: Julius talked loud and much during poetry; wanted to do and say just what he wanted and didn't consider the right working out of things. Had to ask him to sit by me. Showed a bad attitude about it.

Interpretive: For the last week Sammy has been a perfect wiggle-tail. He is growing so fast he cannot be settled. . . . Of course the inward change that is taking place causes the restlessness.

Generalized: Sammy is awfully restless these days. He is whispering most of the time he is not kept busy. In the circle, during various discussions, even though he is interested, his arms are moving or he is punching the one sitting next to him. He smiles when I speak to him.

Specific (the type desired): The weather was so bitterly cold that we did not go on the playground today. The children played games in the room during the regular recess period. Andrew and Larry chose sides for a game which is known as stealing the bacon. I was talking to a group of children in the front of the room while the choosing was in process and in a moment I heard a loud altercation. Larry said that all the children wanted to be on Andrew's side rather than on his. Andrew remarked, "I can't help it if they all want to be on my side."[2]

Time-and-Motion Logs. There are occasions when researchers want to make a very detailed observation of an individual or a group. This is often the case, for example, when trying to identify the reasons underlying a particular problem or difficulty that an individual or class is having (working very slowly,

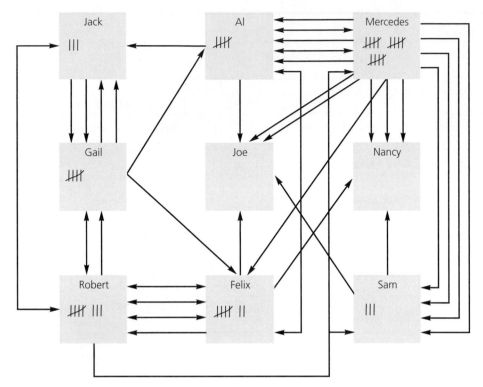

Figure 7.10 *Participation Flowchart*

Source: Adapted from E. I. Sawin (1969). *Evaluation and the work of the teacher.* Belmont, CA: Wadsworth, p. 179.

failing to complete assigned tasks, inattentiveness, and so on).

When a detailed observation is desired, a time-and-motion study can be performed. A time-and-motion study is the observation and detailed recording over a given period of time of the activities of one or more individuals (for example, during a 15-minute laboratory demonstration). Observers try to record everything an individual does as objectively as possible and at brief, regular intervals (such as every three minutes, with a one-minute break interspersed between intervals).

The late Hilda Taba, a pioneer in educational evaluation, once cited an example of a fourth-grade teacher who believed that her class's considerable slowness was due to the fact that they were extremely meticulous in their work. To check this out, she decided to conduct a detailed time-and-motion study of one typical student. The results of her study indicated that this student, rather than being overly meticulous, was actually unable to focus his attention on a particular task for any concerted period of time. Figure 7.12 illustrates what she observed.

SUBJECT-COMPLETED INSTRUMENTS

Questionnaires. The interview schedule shown in Figure 7.8 could be used as a questionnaire. In a questionnaire, the subjects respond to the questions by writing, or, more commonly, by marking an answer sheet. Advantages of questionnaires are that they can be mailed or can be given to large numbers of people at the same time. The disadvantages are that unclear or seemingly ambiguous questions cannot be clarified and the respondent has no chance to expand on, or react verbally to, a question of particular interest or importance.

Selection items on questionnaires include multiple-choice, true-false, matching, or interpretive-exercise questions. Supply items include short-answer or essay questions. We'll give some examples of each of these types of items when we deal with achievement tests later in the chapter.

Self-Checklists. A self-checklist is a list of several characteristics or activities presented to the subjects of a study. The individuals are asked to study the list and then to place a mark opposite the characteristics they

1. Takes slide _____
2. Wipes slide with lens paper _____
3. Wipes slide with cloth _____
4. Wipes slide with finger _____
5. Moves bottle of culture along the table _____
6. Places drop or two of culture on slide _____
7. Adds more culture _____
8. Adds few drops of water _____
9. Hunts for cover glasses _____
10. Wipes cover glass with lens paper _____
11. Wipes cover glass with cloth _____
12. Wipes cover with finger _____
13. Adjusts cover with finger _____
14. Wipes off surplus fluid _____
15. Places slide on stage _____
16. Looks through eyepiece with right eye _____
17. Looks through eyepiece with left eye _____
18. Turns to objective of lowest power _____
19. Turns to low-power objective _____
20. Turns to high-power objective _____
21. Holds one eye closed _____
22. Looks for light _____
23. Adjusts concave mirror _____
24. Adjusts plane mirror _____
25. Adjusts diaphragm _____
26. Does not touch diaphragm _____
27. With eye at eyepiece, turns down coarse adjustment screw _____
28. Breaks cover glass _____
29. Breaks slide _____
30. With eye away from eyepiece, turns down coarse adjustment screw _____

31. Turns up coarse adjustment screw a great distance _____
32. With eye at eyepiece, turns down fine adjustment screw a great distance _____
33. With eye away from eyepiece, turns down fine adjustment screw a great distance _____
34. Turns up fine adjustment screw a great distance _____
35. Turns fine adjustment screw a few turns _____
36. Removes slide from stage _____
37. Wipes objective with lens paper _____
38. Wipes objective with cloth _____
39. Wipes objective with finger _____
40. Wipes eyepiece with lens paper _____
41. Wipes eyepiece with cloth _____
42. Wipes eyepiece with finger _____
43. Makes another mount _____
44. Takes another microscope _____
45. Finds object _____
46. Pauses for an interval _____
47. Asks, "What do you want me to do?" _____
48. Asks whether to use high power _____
49. Says, "I'm satisfied." _____
50. Says that the mount is all right for his or her eye _____
51. Says, "I cannot do it." _____
52. Told to start a new mount _____
53. Directed to find object under low power _____
54. Directed to find object under high power _____

Figure 7.11 *Performance Checklist Noting Student Actions*

Source: Adapted from R. W. Tyler (1930). A test of skill in using a microscope. *Educational Research Bulletin, 9:* (11):493–496.

possess or the activities in which they have engaged for a particular length of time. Self-checklists are often used when researchers want students to diagnose or to appraise their own performance. One example of a self-checklist for use with elementary school students is shown in Figure 7.13.

Attitude Scales. The basic assumption that underlies all attitude scales is that it is possible to discover attitudes by asking individuals to respond to a series of statements of preference. Thus, if individuals agree with the statement "A course in philosophy should be required of all candidates for a teaching credential," researchers infer that these students have a positive attitude toward such a course (assuming students understand the meaning of the statement and are sincere in their responses). An attitude scale, therefore, consists of a set of statements in which an individual is asked to respond. The pattern of responses is then viewed as evidence of one or more underlying attitudes.

Attitude scales are often similar to rating scales in form, with words and numbers placed on a continuum. Subjects are asked to circle the word or number that best represents how they feel about the topics included in the questions or statements in the scale. A commonly used attitude scale in educational research is the **Likert scale,** named after the man who designed it.[3] Figure 7.14 presents a few examples from a Likert scale. On some items, a 5 (strongly agree) will indicate a positive attitude, and be scored 5. On other items, a 1 (strongly

Time	Activity	Time	Activity
11:32	Stacked paper		Watched L.
	Picked up pencil		Laughed at her
	Wrote name		Erased
	Moved paper closer		Hand up
	Continued with reading		Laughed. Watched D.
	Rubbed nose		Got help
	Looked at Art's paper	11:50	Looked at Lorrie
	Started to work . . .		Tapped fingers on desk
11:45	Worked and watched		Wrote
	Made funny faces		Slid down in desk
	Giggled. Looked at Lorrie and smiled		Hand to head, listened to D. helping
	Borrowed Art's paper		Lorrie
	Erased		Blew breath out hard
	Stacked paper		Fidgeted with paper
	Read		Looked at other group
	Slid paper around		Held chin
	Worked briefly		Watched Charles
	Picked up paper and read		Read, hands holding head
	Thumb in mouth, watched Miss D		Erased
11:47	Worked and watched		Watched other group, chin on hand
	Made funny face		Made faces—yawned—fidgeted
	Giggled. Looked and smiled at Lorrie		Held head
	Paper up—read		Read, pointing to words
	Picked eye		Wrote
	Studied bulletin board		Put head on arm on desk
	Paper down—read again		Held chin
	Fidgeted with paper		Read
	Played with pencil and fingers		Rubbed eye
	Watched me	11:55	Wrote

Figure 7.12 *Time-and-Motion Log*

Source: Hilda Taba (1957). Problem identification. In *Research for Curriculum Improvement, 1957 Yearbook*, pp. 60–61. Reprinted with permission of the Association for Supervision and Curriculum Development and Hilda Taba. Copyright © 1957 by the Association for Supervision and Curriculum Development. All rights reserved.

disagree) will indicate a positive attitude and be scored 5 (thus, the ends of the scale are reversed when scoring), as shown in item 2 in Figure 7.14.

A unique sort of attitude scale that is especially useful for classroom research is the **semantic differential.**[4] It allows a researcher to measure a subject's attitude toward a particular concept. Subjects are presented with a continuum of several pairs of adjectives ("good-bad," "cold-hot," "priceless-worthless," and so on) and asked to place a check mark between each pair to indicate their attitudes. Figure 7.15 presents an example.

A suggestion that has particular value for determining the attitudes of young children is to use simply drawn faces. When the subjects of an attitude study are primary-age children or younger, they can be asked to place an *X* under a face, such as the ones shown in Figure 7.16, to indicate how they feel about a topic.

The subject of attitude scales is discussed rather extensively in the literature on evaluation and test development, and students interested in a more extended treatment should consult a standard textbook on these subjects.[5]

Personality (or Character) Inventories. Personality inventories are designed to measure certain traits of individuals or to assess their feelings about themselves. Examples of such inventories include the Minnesota Multiphasic Personality Inventory, the IPAT Anxiety Scale, the Piers-Harris Children's Self-Concept Scale (How I Feel About Myself), and the Kuder Preference

Date _____   Name _____

Instructions: Place a check (✓) in the space provided for those days, during the past week, when you have participated in the activity listed. Circle the activity if you feel you need to participate in it more frequently in the weeks to come.

	Mon	Tues	Wed	Thurs	Fri
1. I participated in class discussions.	✓	✓	✓		
2. I did not interrupt others while they were speaking.	✓	✓	✓	✓	✓
3. I encouraged others to offer their opinions.		✓			✓
4. I listened to what others had to say.	✓	✓	✓		✓
5. I helped others when asked.				✓	
6. I asked questions when I was unclear about what had been said.		✓		✓	
7. I looked up words in the dictionary that I did not know how to spell.					✓
8. I considered the suggestions of others.	✓	✓	✓		
9. I tried to be helpful in my remarks.	✓	✓		✓	
10. I praised others when I thought they did a good job.					✓

Figure 7.13 *Example of a Self-Checklist*

Figure 7.14 *Examples of Items from a Likert Scale Measuring Attitude Toward Teacher Empowerment*

Instructions: Circle the choice after each statement that indicates your opinion.

1. All professors of education should be required to spend at least six months teaching at the elementary or secondary level every five years.

Strongly agree	Agree	Undecided	Disagree	Strongly disagree
(5)	(4)	(3)	(2)	(1)

2. Teachers' unions should be abolished.

Strongly agree	Agree	Undecided	Disagree	Strongly disagree
(1)	(2)	(3)	(4)	(5)

3. All school administrators should be required by law to teach at least one class in a public school classroom every year.

Strongly agree	Agree	Undecided	Disagree	Strongly disagree
(5)	(4)	(3)	(2)	(1)

Figure 7.15 *Example of the Semantic Differential*

Instructions: Listed below are several pairs of adjectives. Place a checkmark (✓) on the line between each pair to indicate how you feel. Example: Hockey:

exciting :___:___:___:___:___:___:___: dull

If you feel that hockey is very exciting, you would place a check in the first space next to the word "exciting." If you feel that hockey is very dull, you would place a checkmark in the space nearest the word "dull." If you are sort of undecided, you would place a checkmark in the middle space between the two words. Now rate each of the activities that follow [*only one is listed*]:

Working with other students in small groups

friendly :___:___:___:___:___:___:___: unfriendly

happy :___:___:___:___:___:___:___: sad

easy :___:___:___:___:___:___:___: hard

fun :___:___:___:___:___:___:___: work

hot :___:___:___:___:___:___:___: cold

good :___:___:___:___:___:___:___: bad

laugh :___:___:___:___:___:___:___: cry

beautiful :___:___:___:___:___:___:___: ugly

Record. Figure 7.17 presents an example of some typical items from this type of test. The specific items, of course, reflect the variable(s) the inventory addresses.

Achievement Tests. **Achievement,** or ability, tests measure an individual's knowledge or skill in a given area or subject. They are mostly used in schools to measure learning or the effectiveness of instruction. The California Achievement Test, for example, measures achievement in reading, language, and arithmetic. The Stanford Achievement Test measures a variety of areas, such as language usage, word meaning, spelling, arithmetic computation, social studies, and science. Other commonly used achievement tests include the Comprehensive Tests of Basic Skills, the Iowa Tests of Basic Skills, the Metropolitan Achievement Test, and the Sequential Tests of Educational Progress (STEP). In research that involves comparing instructional methods, achievement is frequently the dependent variable.

Figure 7.16 *Pictorial Attitude Scale for Use with Young Children*

Instructions: Check the option that most correctly describes you.

	Quite often	Sometimes	Almost never
SELF-ESTEEM			
1. Do you think your friends are smarter than you?	____	____	____
2. Do you feel good about your appearance?	____	____	____
3. Do you avoid meeting new people?	____	____	____
	Quite often	Sometimes	Almost never
STRESS			
1. Do you have trouble sleeping?	____	____	____
2. Do you feel on top of things?	____	____	____
3. Do you feel you have too much to do?	____	____	____

Figure 7.17 *Sample Items from a Personality Inventory*

Achievement tests can be classified in several ways. General achievement tests are usually batteries of tests (such as the STEP tests) that measure such things as vocabulary, reading ability, language usage, math, and social studies. One of the most common general achievement tests is the Graduate Record Examination, which students must pass before they can be admitted to most graduate programs. Specific achievement tests, on the other hand, are tests that measure an individual's ability in a specific subject, such as English, world history, or biology. Figure 7.18 presents some examples of the kinds of items found on an achievement test.

Aptitude Tests. Another well-known type of ability test is the so-called general **aptitude,** or intelligence, **test,** which assesses intellectual abilities that are not, in

Instructions: Use the map to answer questions 1 and 2. Circle the correct answer.

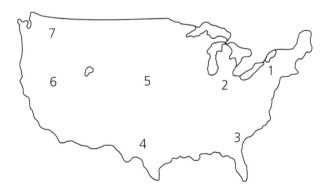

Figure 7.18 *Sample Items from an Achievement Test*

1. Which number shows an area declining in population?

    A   1
    B   3
    C   5
    D   7

2. Which number shows an area that once belonged to Mexico?

    A   3
    B   5
    C   6
    D   None of the above

Look at the foldout on the left. Which object on the right can be made from it?

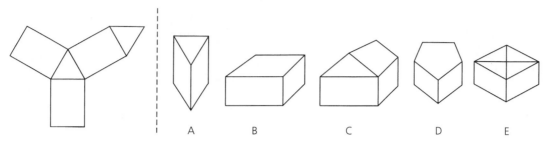

Figure 7.19 *Sample Item from an Aptitude Test*

most cases, specifically taught in school. Some measure of general ability is frequently used as either an independent or a dependent variable in research. In attempting to assess the effects of different instructional programs, for example, it is often necessary (and very important) to control this variable so that groups exposed to the different programs are not markedly different in general ability.

Aptitude tests are intended to measure an individual's potential to achieve; in actuality, they measure present skills or abilities. They differ from achievement tests in their purpose and often in content, usually including a wider variety of skills or knowledge. The same test may be either an aptitude or an achievement test, depending on the purpose for which it is used. A mathematics achievement test, for example, may also measure aptitude for additional mathematics. Although such tests are used primarily by counselors to help individuals identify areas in which they may have potential, they also can be used in research. In this regard, they are particularly useful for purposes of control. For example, to measure the effectiveness of an instructional program designed to increase problem-solving ability in mathematics, a researcher might decide to use an aptitude test to adjust for initial differences in ability. Figure 7.19 presents an example of one kind of item found on an aptitude test.

Aptitude tests may be individually administered or group tests. Each method has both advantages and disadvantages. The big advantage of group tests is that they are more convenient to administer and hence save considerable time. Their disadvantages are that they require a great deal of reading, and students who are low in reading ability are thus at a disadvantage. Furthermore, it is difficult for those taking the test to have test instructions clarified or to have any interaction with the examiner (which sometimes can raise scores). Lastly, the range of possible tasks on which the student can be examined is much less with a group-administered test than with an individually-administered test.

The California Test of Mental Maturity (CTMM) and the Otis-Lennon are examples of group tests. The best-known of the individual aptitude tests is the Stanford-Binet Intelligence Scale, although the Wechsler scales are being used more and more frequently. Whereas the Stanford-Binet gives only one IQ score, the Wechsler scales also yield a number of subscores. The two Wechsler scales are the Wechsler Intelligence Scale for Children (WISC-III) for ages 5 to 15 and the Wechsler Adult Intelligence Scale (WAIS-III) for older adolescents and adults.

Many intelligence tests provide reliable and valid evidence when used with certain kinds of individuals and for certain purposes (for example, predicting the college grades of middle-class Caucasians). On the other hand, they have increasingly come under attack when used with other persons or for other purposes (such as identifying members of certain minority groups to be placed in special classes). Furthermore, there is increasing recognition that most intelligence tests fail to measure many important abilities, including the ability to identify or conceptualize unusual sorts of relationships. As a result, researchers must be especially careful in evaluating any such test before using it and must determine whether it is appropriate for the purpose of the study. (We discuss some ways to do this when we consider validity in Chapter Eight.) Figure 7.20 presents examples of the kinds of items on an intelligence test.

Performance Tests. As we have mentioned, a performance test measures an individual's performance on a particular task. An example would be a typing test, in

1. How are *frog* and *toy* alike and how are they different?

2. Here is a sequence of pictures.

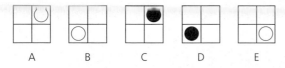

Which of the following would come next in the sequence?

Figure 7.20 *Sample Items from an Intelligence Test*

which individual scores are determined by how accurately and how rapidly people type.

As Sawin has suggested, it is not always easy to determine whether a particular instrument should be called a performance test, a performance checklist, or a performance rating scale.[6] A performance test is the most objective of the three. When a considerable amount of judgment is required to determine if the various aspects of a performance were done correctly, the device is likely to be classified as either a checklist or rating scale. Figure 7.21 presents an example of a performance test developed over 60 years ago to measure sewing ability. In this test, the individual is requested to sew *on* the line in part A of the test, and *between* the lines on part B of the test.[7]

Projective Devices. A projective device is any sort of instrument with a vague stimulus that allows individuals to project their interests, preferences, anxieties, prejudices, needs, and so on through their responses to it. This kind of device has no "right" answers (or any clear-cut answers of any sort), and its format allows an individual to express something of his or her own personality. There is room for a wide variety of possible responses.

Perhaps the best-known example of a projective device is the Rorschach Ink Blot Test, in which individuals are presented with a series of ambiguously-shaped ink blots and asked to describe what the blots look like. Another well-known projective test is the Thematic Apperception Test (TAT), in which pictures of events are presented and individuals are asked to make up a story about each picture. One application of the projective approach to a classroom setting is the Picture Situation Inventory, one of the few examples especially adapted to classroom situations. This instrument consists of a series of cartoonlike drawings, each portraying a classroom situation in which a child is saying something. Students taking the test are to enter the response of the

Directions: Sew on the line in part A and between the lines in part B.

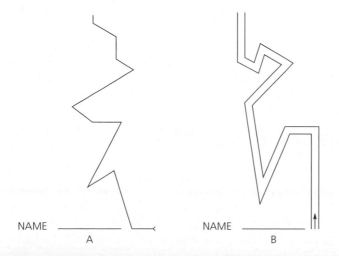

NAME ⎯⎯⎯⎯⎯⎯⎯

A

NAME ⎯⎯⎯⎯⎯⎯⎯

B

Figure 7.21 *Example from the Blum Sewing Machine Test*
Source: M. L. Blum (1943). Selection of sewing machine operators. *Journal of Applied Psychology, 27:* (2): 36.

Figure 7.22 *Sample Items from the Picture Situation Inventory*

Source: N. T. Rowan (1967). The relationship of teacher interaction in classroom situations to teacher personality variables. Unpublished doctoral dissertation. Salt Lake City: University of Utah, p. 68.

teacher, thereby presumably indicating something of their own tendencies in the situation. Two of the pictures in this test are reproduced in Figure 7.22.

Sociometric Devices. Sociometric devices ask individuals to rate their peers in some way. Two examples include the sociogram and the "group play." A *sociogram* is a visual representation, usually by means of arrows, of the choices people make about other individuals with whom they interact. It is frequently used to assess the climate and structure of interpersonal relationships within a classroom, but it is by no means limited to such an environment. Each student is usually represented by a circle (if female) or a triangle (if male), and arrows are then drawn to indicate different student choices with regard to a particular question that has been asked. Students may be asked, for example, to list three students whom they think are leaders of the class; admire the most; find especially helpful; would like to have for a friend; would like to have as a partner in a research project; and so forth. The responses students give are then used to construct the sociogram. Figure 7.23 is an illustration of a sociogram.

Another version of a sociometric device is the assigning of different individuals, on paper, to various

parts in a *group play.* Students can be asked to cast different members of their group in various roles in a play to illustrate their interpersonal relationships. The roles are listed on a piece of paper, and then the members of the group are asked to write in the name of the student they think each role best describes. Almost any type of role can be suggested. The casting choices that individuals make often shed considerable light on how some individuals are viewed by others. Figure 7.24 presents an example of this device.

Item Formats. Although the types of items or questions used in different instruments can take many forms, they all can be classified as either a selection item or a supply item. A *selection item* presents a set of possible responses from which respondents are to select the most appropriate answer. A *supply item,* on the other hand, asks respondents to formulate and then supply their own answers. Here are some examples of each type.

Selection Items. *True-false items:* True-false items present either a true or a false statement, and the respondent has to mark either true (T) or false (F). Frequently used variations of the words "true" and "false" are "yes-no" or "right-wrong," which often are more

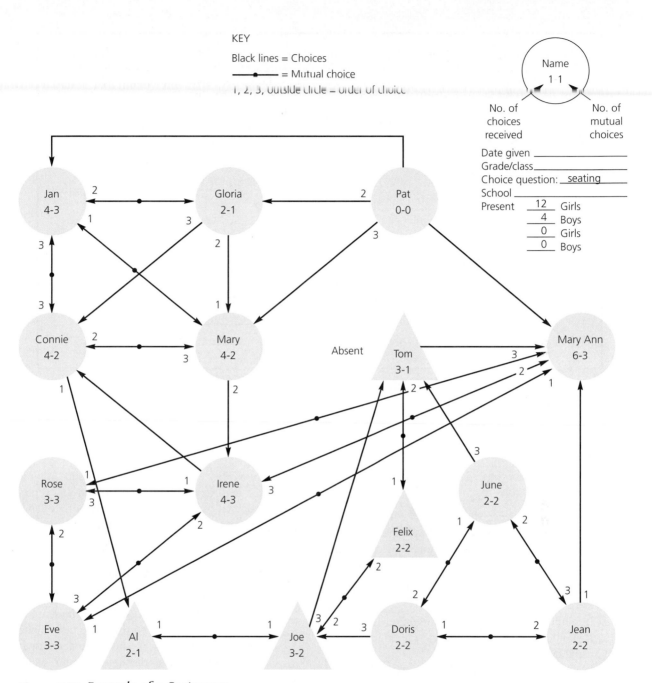

Figure 7.23 *Example of a Sociogram*

Directions: Imagine you are the casting director for a large play. Your job is to choose the individuals who will take the various parts (listed below) in the play. Since some of the parts are rather small, you may select the same individual to play more than one part. Choose individuals you think would be the most *natural* for the part, that is, those who are most like the role in real life.

1. The parts

Part 1—someone who is well-liked by all members of the group _____

Part 2—someone who is disliked by many people _____

Part 3—someone who always gets angry about things of little consequence _____

Part 4—someone who has wit and a good sense of humor _____

Part 5—someone who is very quiet and rarely says anything _____

Part 6—someone who does not contribute much to the group _____

Part 7—someone who is angry a lot of the time _____

Part 8—etc. _____

2. Your role

Which part do you think you could play best? _____

Which part would other members of the group ask you to play? _____

Figure 7.24 *Example of a Group Play*

useful when attempting to question or interview young children. Here is an example of a true-false item.

> T F I get very nervous whenever I have to speak in public.

Multiple-choice items: Multiple-choice items consist of two parts: the stem, which contains the question, and several (usually four) possible choices. Here is an example:

> Which of the following expresses your opinion on abortion?
> *a.* It is immoral and should be prohibited.
> *b.* It should be discouraged but permitted under unusual circumstances.
> *c.* It should be available under a wide range of conditions.
> *d.* It is entirely a matter of individual choice.

Matching items: Matching items are variations of the multiple-choice format. They consist of two groups listed in columns—the first, or leftmost, column containing the questions or items to be thought about, and the second, or rightmost, column containing the possible responses to the questions. The respondent is asked to pair the choice from the second column with the question or item in the first column to which it corresponds. Here is an example:

> Instructions: For each item in the left-hand column, select the item in the right-hand column that represents your first reaction. Place the appropriate letter in the blank. Each lettered item may be used more than once or not at all.

Column A	Column B
Special classes for the:	
___ 1. severely retarded	a. should be increased
___ 2. mildly retarded	b. should be maintained
___ 3. hard of hearing	c. should be decreased
___ 4. visually impaired	d. should be eliminated
___ 5. learning handicapped	
___ 6. emotionally disturbed	

Interpretive Exercises. One difficulty with using true-false, multiple-choice, and matching items to measure achievement is that these items often do not measure complex learning outcomes. One way to get at more complex learning outcomes is to use what is called an *interpretive exercise.* An interpretive exercise consists of a selection of introductory material (this may be a paragraph, map, diagram, picture, chart) followed by one or more selection items that ask a respondent to interpret this material. Two examples of interpretive exercises follow.

Example 1

Directions: Read the following comments a teacher made about testing. Then answer the question that follows the comments by circling the letter of the best answer.

"Students go to school to learn, not to take tests. In addition, tests cannot be used to indicate a student's absolute level of learning. All tests can do is rank students in order of achievement, and this relative ranking is influenced by guessing, bluffing, and the subjective opinions of the teacher doing the scoring. The teaching-learning process would benefit if we did away with tests and depended on student self-evaluation."

1. Which one of the following unstated assumptions is this teacher making?
   a. Students go to school to learn.
   b. Teachers use essay tests primarily.
   c. Tests make no contribution to learning.
   d. Tests do not indicate a student's absolute level of learning.

Example 2

Directions: Paragraph A contains a description of the testing practices of Mr. Smith, a high school teacher. Read the description and each of the statements that follow it. Mark each statement to indicate the type of *inference* that can be drawn about it from the material in the paragraph. Place the appropriate letter in front of each statement using the following *key:*

T—if the statement may be *inferred* as *true.*
F—if the statement may be *inferred* as *untrue.*
N—if *no inference* may be drawn about it from the paragraph.

Paragraph A

Approximately one week before a test is to be given, Mr. Smith carefully goes through the textbook and constructs multiple-choice items based on the material in the book. He always uses the exact wording of the textbook for the correct answer so that there will be no question concerning its correctness. He is careful to include some test items from each chapter. After the test is given, he lists the scores from high to low on the blackboard and tells each student his or her score. He does not return the test papers to the students, but he offers to answer any questions they might have about the test. He puts the items from each test into a test file, which he is building for future use.

Statements on Paragraph A

(T) 1. Mr. Smith's tests measure a limited range of learning outcomes.
(F) 2. Some of Mr. Smith's test items measure at the understanding level.
(N) 3. Mr. Smith's tests measure a balanced sample of subject matter.
(N) 4. Mr. Smith uses the type of test item that is best for his purpose.
(T) 5. Students can determine where they rank in the distribution of scores on Mr. Smith's tests.
(F) 6. Mr. Smith's testing practices are likely to motivate students to overcome their weaknesses.[8]

Supply Items. *Short-answer items:* A short-answer item requires the respondent to supply a word, phrase, number, or symbol that is necessary to complete a statement or answer a question. Here is an example:

Directions: In the space provided, write the word that best completes the sentence.

When the number of items in a test is increased, the _____ of the scores on the test is likely to increase. (Answer: reliability.)

Short-answer items have one major disadvantage: It is usually difficult to write a short-answer item so only one word completes it correctly. In the question above, for example, many students might argue that the word "range" would also be correct.

Essay questions: An essay question is one that respondents are asked to write about at length. As with short-answer questions, subjects must produce their own answers. Generally, however, they are free to determine how to answer the question, what facts to present, which to emphasize, what interpretations to make, and the like. For these reasons, the essay question is a particularly useful device for assessing an individual's ability to organize, integrate, analyze, and synthesize information. It is especially useful in measuring the so-called "higher-level" learning outcomes, such as analysis, synthesis, and evaluation. Here are two examples of essay questions:

Example 1

Mr. Rogers, a ninth-grade science teacher, wants to measure his students' "ability to interpret scientific data" with a paper-and-pencil test.

1. Describe the steps that Mr. Rogers should follow.
2. Give reasons to justify each step.

Example 2

For a course that you are teaching or expect to teach, prepare a complete plan for evaluating student achievement. Be sure to include the procedures you would follow, the instruments you would use, and the reasons for your choices.[9]

UNOBTRUSIVE MEASURES

Many instruments require the cooperation of the respondent in one way or another and involve some kind of intrusion into ongoing activities. On occasion, respondents will dislike or even resent being tested, observed, or interviewed. Furthermore, the reaction of respondents to the instrumentation process—that is, to being tested, observed, or interviewed—often will, to some degree, affect the nature of the information researchers obtain.

To eliminate this reactive effect, researchers at times attempt to use what are called **unobtrusive measures,**[10] which are data-collection procedures that involve *no* intrusion into the naturally occurring course of events. In most instances, no instrument is required; only some form of recordkeeping. Here are some examples of such procedures:

- The degree of fear induced by a ghost-story-telling session can be measured by noting the shrinking diameter of a circle of seated children.
- Library withdrawals could be used to demonstrate the effect of the introduction of a new unit on Chinese history in a social studies curriculum.
- The interest of children in Christmas or other holidays might be demonstrated by the amount of distortion in the size of their drawings of Santa Claus or other holiday figures.

- Racial attitudes in two elementary schools might be compared by noting the degree of clustering of members of different ethnic groups in the lunchroom and on the playground.
- The values held by people of different countries might be compared through analyzing different types of published materials, such as textbooks, plays, handbooks for youth organizations, magazine advertisements, and newspaper headlines.
- Some idea of the attention paid to patients in a hospital might be determined by observing the frequency of notes, both informal and required, made by attending nurses to patients' bedside records.
- The degree of stress felt by college students might be assessed by noting the nature and frequency of sick-call visits to the college health center.
- Student attitudes toward, and interest in, various topics can be noted by observing the amount of graffiti about those topics written on school walls.

Many variables of interest can be assessed, at least to some degree, through the use of unobtrusive measures. The reliability and validity of inferences based on such measures will vary depending on the procedure used. Nevertheless, unobtrusive measures add an important and useful dimension to the array of possible data sources available to researchers. They are particularly valuable as supplements to the use of interviews and questionnaires, often providing a useful way to corroborate (or contradict) what these more traditional data sources reveal.[11]

Types of Scores

Quantitative data are usually reported in the form of scores. Scores can be reported in many ways, but an important distinction to understand is the difference between raw scores and derived scores.

RAW SCORES

Almost all measurement begins with what is called a **raw score,** which is the initial score obtained. It may be the total number of items an individual gets correct or answers in a certain way on a test, the number of times a certain behavior is tallied, the rating given by a teacher, and so forth. Examples include the number of questions answered correctly on a science test, the number of questions answered "positively" on an attitude scale, the number of times "aggressive" behavior is observed, a teacher's rating on a "self-esteem" measure, or the number of choices received on a sociogram.

Taken by itself, an individual raw score is difficult to interpret, since it has little meaning. What, for example, does it mean to say a student received a score of 62 on a test if that is all the information you have? Even if you know that there were 100 questions on the test, you don't know whether 62 is an extremely high (or extremely low) score, since the test may be easy or difficult.

We often want to know how one individual's raw score compares to those of other individuals taking the same test, and (perhaps) how he or she has scored on similar tests taken at other times. This is true whenever we want to interpret an individual score. Because raw scores by themselves are difficult to interpret, they often are converted to what are called "derived scores."

DERIVED SCORES

Derived scores are scores that have been derived from raw scores into more useful scores on some type of standardized basis. They indicate where a particular individual's raw score falls in relation to all other raw scores in the same distribution. They enable a researcher to say how well the individual has performed compared to all others taking the same test. Examples of derived scores are age- and grade-level equivalents, percentile ranks, and standard scores.

Age and Grade-level Equivalents. **Age-equivalent scores** and **grade-equivalent scores** tell us of what age or grade an individual score is typical. Suppose, for example, that the average score on a beginning-of-the-year arithmetic test for all eighth-graders in a certain state is 62 out of a possible 100. Students who score 62 will have a grade equivalent of 8.0 on the test regardless of their actual grade placement—whether in sixth, seventh, eighth, ninth, or tenth grade, the student's performance is typical of beginning eighth-graders. Similarly, a student who is 10 years, 6 months old may have an age-equivalent score of 12-2, meaning that his or her test performance is typical of students who are 12 years, 2 months old.

Percentile Ranks. A **percentile rank** refers to the percentage of individuals scoring at or below a given raw score. Percentile ranks are sometimes referred to as

percentiles, although this term is not quite correct as a synonym.*

Percentile ranks are easy to calculate. A simple formula for converting raw scores to percentile ranks (Pr) is as follows:

$$Pr = \frac{\text{number of students} \atop \text{below score} + \text{all students} \atop \text{at score}}{\text{total number in group}} \times 100$$

Suppose a total of 100 students took an examination, and 18 of them received a raw score above 85, while two students received a score of 85. Eighty students, then, scored somewhere below 85. What is the percentile rank of the two students who received the score of 85? Using the formula:

$$Pr = \frac{80 + 2}{100} \times 100 = 82$$

the percentile rank of these two students is 82.

Often percentile ranks are calculated for each of the scores in a group. Table 7.1 presents a group of scores with the percentile rank of each score indicated.

Standard Scores. Standard scores provide another means of indicating how one individual compares to other individuals in a group. **Standard scores** indicate how far a given raw score is from a reference point. They are particularly helpful in comparing an individual's relative achievement on different types of instruments (such as comparing a person's performance on a chemistry achievement test with an instructor's rating of his work in a laboratory). Many different systems of standard scores exist, but the two most commonly used and reported in educational research are z scores and T scores. Understanding them requires some knowledge of descriptive statistics, however, and hence we will postpone a discussion of them until Chapter Ten.

WHICH SCORES TO USE?

Given these various types of scores, how do researchers decide which to use? Recall that the usefulness of

---

*A percentile is the *point* below which a certain percentage of scores fall. The 70th percentile, for example, is the *point* below which 70 percent of the scores in a distribution fall. The 99th percentile is the *point* below which 99 percent of the scores fall, and so forth. Thus, if 20 percent of the students in a sample score below 40 on a test, then the 20th percentile is a score of 40. A person who obtains a score of 40 has a percentile rank of 20.

Table 7.1 *Hypothetical Examples of Raw Scores and Accompanying Percentile Ranks*

Raw Score	Cumulative Frequency	Percentile Frequency	Rank
95	1	25	100
93	1	24	96
88	2	23	92
85	3	21	84
79	1	18	72
75	4	17	68
70	6	13	52
65	2	7	28
62	1	5	20
58	1	4	16
54	2	3	12
50	1	1	4
	N = 25		

derived scores is primarily in making individual raw scores meaningful to students, parents, teachers, and others. Despite their value in this respect, some derived scores should *not* be used in research. This is the case if the researcher is assuming an interval scale, as often is done. Interval scales are discussed on pages 145–146. Percentile ranks, for example, should never be used because they, almost certainly, do not constitute an interval scale. Age- and grade-equivalent scores likewise have serious limitations because of the way in which they are obtained. Usually the best scores to use are standard scores, which are sometimes provided in instrument manuals and, if not, can easily be calculated. (We discuss and show how to calculate standard scores in Chapter Ten.) If standard scores are not used, it is far preferable to use raw scores—converting derived scores, for example, back to the original raw scores, if necessary—rather than use percentile ranks or age/grade equivalents.

Norm-Referenced Versus Criterion-Referenced Instruments

NORM-REFERENCED INSTRUMENTS

All derived scores give meaning to individual scores by comparing them to the scores of a group. This means that the nature of the group is extremely important.

Whenever such scores are used, researchers must be sure that the reference group makes sense. Comparing a boy's score on a grammar test to a group of girls' scores on that test, for example, may be quite misleading since girls usually score higher in grammar. The group used to determine derived scores is called the **norm group,** and instruments that provide such scores are referred to as **norm-referenced instruments.**

CRITERION-REFERENCED INSTRUMENTS

An alternative to the use of customary achievement or performance instruments, most of which are norm-referenced, is to use a **criterion-referenced instrument**—usually a test.

The intent of such tests is somewhat different from that of norm-referenced tests, in that criterion-referenced tests focus more directly on instruction. Rather than evaluating learner progress through gain in scores (for example, from 40 to 70 on an achievement test), a criterion-referenced test is based on a specific goal, or target (called a **criterion**), for each learner to achieve. This criterion for mastery or "pass" is usually stated as a fairly high percentage of questions (such as 80 or 90 percent) to be answered correctly. Examples of criterion-referenced and norm-referenced evaluation statements are as follows:

Criterion-referenced: A student . . .

- spelled every word in the weekly spelling list correctly.
- solved at least 75 percent of the assigned problems.
- achieved a score of at least 80 out of 100 on the final exam.
- did at least 25 push-ups within a five-minute period.
- read a minimum of one nonfiction book a week.

Norm-referenced: A student . . .

- scored at the 50th percentile in his group.
- scored above 90 percent of all the students in the class.
- received a higher grade point average in English literature than any other student in the school.
- ran faster than all but one other student on the team.
- and one other in the class were the only ones to receive A's on the midterm.

The advantage of a criterion-referenced instrument is that it gives both teacher and students a clear-cut goal to work toward. As a result, it has considerable appeal as a means of improving instruction. In practice, however, several problems arise. First, teachers seldom set or reach the ideal of individualized student goals. Rather, class goals are more the rule, the idea being that all students will reach the criterion—though, of course, some may not and many will exceed it. The second problem is that it is difficult to establish even class criteria that are meaningful. What, precisely, should a class of fifth-graders be able to do in mathematics? Solve story problems, many would say. We would agree, but of what complexity? and requiring which mathematics subskills? In the absence of independent criteria, we have little choice but to fall back on existing expectations, and this is typically (though not necessarily) done by examining existing texts and tests. As a result, the specific items in a criterion-referenced test often turn out to be indistinguishable from those in the usual norm-referenced test, with one important difference: A criterion-referenced test at any grade level will almost certainly be easier than a norm-referenced test. It *must* be easier if most students are to get 80 or 90 percent of the items correct. In preparing such tests, researchers must try to write items that will be answered correctly by 80 percent of the students—after all, they don't want 50 percent of their students to fail. The desired difficulty level for norm-referenced items, however, *is* at or about 50 percent, in order to provide the maximum opportunity for the scores to distinguish the ability of one student from another.

While a criterion-referenced test *may* be more useful at times and in certain circumstances than the more customary norm-referenced test (this issue is still being debated), it is often inferior for research purposes. Why? Because, in general, a criterion-referenced test will provide much less variability of scores, because it is easier. Whereas the usual norm-referenced test will provide a range of scores somewhat less than the possible range (that is, from zero to the total number of items in the test), a criterion-referenced test, if it is true to its rationale, will have most of the students (surely at least half) getting a high score. Because, in research, we usually want maximum variability in order to have any hope of finding relationships with other variables, the use of criterion-referenced tests is often self-defeating.*

*An exception is in program evaluation, where some researchers advocate the use of criterion-referenced tests because they want to determine how many students reach a predetermined standard (criterion).

Measurement Scales

You will recall from Chapter Three that there are two basic types of variables—quantitative and categorical. Each uses a different type of analysis and measurement, requiring the use of different measurement scales. There are four types of measurement scales: nominal, ordinal, interval, and ratio (see Figure 7.25).

NOMINAL SCALES

A **nominal scale** is the simplest form of measurement researchers can use. When using a nominal scale, researchers simply assign numbers to different categories in order to show differences (see Figure 7.26). For example, a researcher concerned with the variable of gender might group data into two categories, male and female, and assign the number "1" to females and the number "2" to males. Another researcher, interested in studying methods of teaching reading, might assign the number "1" to the whole word method, the number "2" to the phonics method, and the number "3" to the "mixed" method. In most cases, the advantage to assigning numbers to the categories is to facilitate computer analysis. There is no implication that the phonics method (assigned number "2") is "more" of anything than the whole word method (assigned number "1").

ORDINAL SCALES

An **ordinal scale** is one in which data may be ordered in some way—high to low or least to most. For example, a researcher might rank-order student scores on a biology test from high to low. Notice, however, that the difference in scores or in actual ability between the first- and second-ranked students and between the fifth- and sixth-ranked students would not necessarily be the same. Ordinal scales indicate relative standing among individuals, as Figure 7.27 demonstrates.

INTERVAL SCALES

An **interval scale** possesses all the characteristics of an ordinal scale with one additional feature: The distances between the points on the scale are equal. For example, the distances between scores on most commercially available mathematics achievement tests are usually considered equal. Thus, the distance between

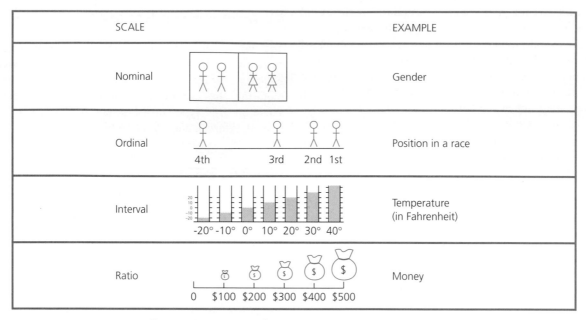

SCALE		EXAMPLE
Nominal		Gender
Ordinal	4th 3rd 2nd 1st	Position in a race
Interval	-20° -10° 0° 10° 20° 30° 40°	Temperature (in Fahrenheit)
Ratio	0 $100 $200 $300 $400 $500	Money

Figure 7.25 *Four Types of Measurement Scales*

scores of 70 and 80 is considered to be the same as the distance between scores of 80 and 90. Notice that the zero point on an interval scale does not indicate a total absence of what is being measured, however. Thus, 0° (zero degrees) on the Fahrenheit scale, which measures temperature, does not indicate *no* temperature.

Figure 7.26 *A Nominal Scale of Measurement*

To illustrate further, consider the commonly used IQ score. Is the difference between an IQ of 90 and one of 100 (10 points) the same as the difference between an IQ of 40 and one of 50 (also 10 points)? Or between an IQ of 120 and one of 130? If we believe that the scores constitute an interval scale, we *must* assume that 10 points has the same meaning at different points on the scale. Do we know whether this is true? No, we do not, as we shall now explain.

With respect to some measurements, we can demonstrate equal intervals. We do so by having an agreed upon standard unit. This is one reason why we have a Bureau of Standards, located in Washington, DC. You could, if you wished to do so, go to the bureau and actually "see" a standard "inch," "foot," "ounce," and so on, that defines these units. While it might not be easy, you could conceivably check your carpenter's rule using the "standard inch" to see if an inch is an inch all along your rule. You literally could place the "standard inch" at various points along your rule.

There is no such standard unit for IQ or for virtually any variable commonly used in educational research. Over the years, sophisticated and clever techniques have been developed to create interval scales for use by researchers. The details are beyond the scope of this text, but you should know that they all are based on highly questionable assumptions.

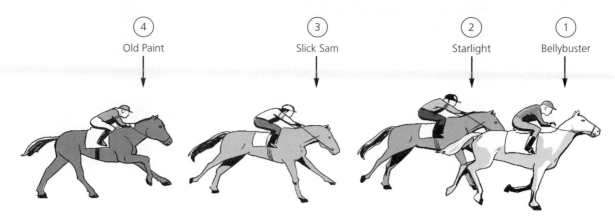

Figure 7.27 *An Ordinal Scale: The Outcome of a Horse Race*

In actual practice, most researchers prefer to "act as if" they have an interval scale, because it permits the use of more sensitive data analysis procedures and because, over the years, the results of doing so make sense. Nevertheless, acting as if we have interval scales requires an assumption that (at least to date) cannot be proved.

RATIO SCALES

An interval scale that does possess an actual, or true, zero point is called a **ratio scale.** For example, a scale designed to measure height would be a ratio scale, because the zero point on the scale represents the absence of height (that is, *no* height). Similarly, the zero on a bathroom weight scale represents zero, or no, weight. Ratio scales are almost never encountered in educational research, since rarely do researchers engage in measurement involving a true zero point (even on those rare occasions when a student receives a zero on a test of some sort, this does not mean that whatever is being measured is totally absent in the student). Some other variables that *do* have ratio scales are income, time on task, and age.

MEASUREMENT SCALES RECONSIDERED

At this point, you may be saying, "Well, okay, but so what? Why are these distinctions important?" There are two reasons why you should have at least a rudimentary understanding of the differences between these four types of scales. First, they convey different amounts of information. Ratio scales provide more information than do interval scales, interval more than ordinal, and ordinal more than nominal. Hence, if possible, researchers should use the type of measurement that will provide them with the maximum amount of information needed to answer the research question being investigated. Second, some types of statistical procedures are inappropriate for the different scales. The way in which the data in a research study are organized dictates the use of certain types of statistical analyses, but not others (we shall discuss this point in more detail in Chapter Eleven). Table 7.2 presents a summary of the four types of measurement scales.

Often researchers have a choice to make. They must decide whether to consider data as ordinal or interval. For example, suppose a researcher uses a self-report questionnaire to measure "self-esteem." The questionnaire is scored for the number of items answered (yes or

Table 7.2 *Characteristics of the Four Types of Measurement Scales*

Measurement Scale	Characteristics
Nominal	Groups and labels data only; reports frequencies or percentages.
Ordinal	Ranks data; uses numbers only to indicate ranking.
Interval	Assumes that equal differences between scores really mean equal differences in the variable measured.
Ratio	All of the above, plus true zero point.

Which Statistical Index Is Valid?

Measurements, of course, are not limited to test scores and the like. For example, a widely used measurement is the "index of unemployment" provided by the Bureau of Labor Statistics (BLS). One of its many uses is to study the relationship between unemployment and crime. Its validity for this purpose has been questioned by the author of a recent study who found that, while this index showed no relationship to property crimes, two different indexes that reflected long-term (rather than temporary) unemployment did show substantial relationships. The author concluded, "Clearly, we need to become as interested in the selection of appropriate indicators as we are with the specification of appropriate models and the selection of statistical techniques."*

What do you think? Why did the different indexes give different results?

*M. B. Chamlin (2000). Unemployment, economic theory, and property crime: A note on measurement. *Journal of Quantitative Criminology, 16:* (4): 454.

---

no) in the direction indicating high self-esteem. For a given sample of 60, the researcher finds that the scores range from 30 to 75.

The researcher may now decide to treat scores as interval data, in which case she assumes that equal distances (e.g., 30–34, 35–39, 40–44) in score represent equal differences in self-esteem.* If the researcher is uncomfortable with this assumption, she could use the scores to rank the individuals in her sample from highest (rank 1) to lowest (rank 60). If she were then to use only these rankings in subsequent analysis, she would now be assuming that her instrument provides only ordinal data.

Fortunately, researchers can avoid this choice. They have another option—to treat the data separately according to both assumptions (that is, to treat the scores as ordinal data, and then again as interval data). The important thing to realize is that a researcher must be prepared to defend the assumptions underlying her choice of a measurement scale used in the collection and organization of data.

Preparing Data for Analysis

Once the instruments being used in a study have been administered, the researcher must score the data that have been collected and then organize this data to facilitate analysis.

*Notice that she cannot treat the scores as ratio data, since a score of zero cannot be assumed to represent zero (i.e., "no") self-esteem.

SCORING THE DATA

Collected data must be scored accurately and consistently. If they are not, any conclusions a researcher draws from the data may be erroneous or misleading. Each individual's test (questionnaire, essay, etc.) should be scored using exactly the same procedures and criteria. When a commercially purchased instrument is used, the scoring procedures are made much easier. Usually a scoring manual will be provided by the instrument developer, listing the steps to follow in scoring the instrument, along with a scoring key. It is a good idea to double-check one's scoring to ensure that mistakes have not been made.

The scoring of a self-developed test can produce difficulties, and hence researchers have to take special care to ensure that scoring is accurate and consistent. Essay examinations, in particular, are often very difficult to score in a consistent manner. For this reason, it is usually advisable to have a second person also score the results. Researchers should carefully prepare their scoring plans, in writing, ahead of time and then try out their instrument by administering and scoring it with a group of individuals similar to the population they intend to sample in their study. Problems with administration and scoring can thus be identified early and corrected before it is too late.

TABULATING AND CODING THE DATA

When the data have been scored, the researcher must tally or tabulate them in some way. Usually this is done by transferring the data to some sort of summary data

Table 7.3 *Hypothetical Results of Study Involving a Comparison of Two Counseling Methods*

Score for "Rapport"	Method A	Method B
96–100	0	0
91–95	0	2
86–90	0	3
81–85	2	3
76–80	2	4
71–75	5	3
66–70	6	4
61–65	9	4
56–60	4	5
51–55	5	3
46–50	2	2
41–45	0	1
36–40	0	1
	$N = 35$	35

sheet or card. The important thing is to record one's data accurately and systematically. If categorical data are being recorded, the number of individuals scoring in each category are tallied. If quantitative data are being recorded, the data are usually listed in one or more columns, depending on the number of groups involved in the study. For example, if the data analysis is to consist simply of a comparison of the scores of two groups on a posttest, the data would most likely be placed in two columns, one for each group, in descending order. Table 7.3, for example, presents some hypothetical results of a study involving a comparison of two counseling methods with an instrument measuring "rapport." If pre- and posttest scores are to be compared, additional columns could be added. If subgroup scores will be looked at, these also could be indicated.

When a variety of different kinds of data are collected (i.e., scores on several different instruments) in addition to biographical information (gender, age, ethnicity, etc.), they are usually recorded in a computer or on data cards, one card for each individual from whom data were collected. This facilitates easy comparison and grouping (and regrouping) of data for purposes of analysis. In addition, the data are coded. In other words, some type of code is used to protect the privacy of the individuals in the study. Thus, the names of males and females might be coded as "1" and "2." Coding of data is especially important when data are analyzed by computer, since any data not in numerical form must be coded in some systematic way before they can be entered into the computer. Thus, categorical data, to be analyzed on a computer, are often coded numerically (e.g., pretest scores "1," and posttest scores "2").

The first step in coding data is often to assign an ID number to every individual from whom data has been collected. If there were 100 individuals in a study, for example, the researcher would number them from 001 to 100. If the highest value for any variable being analyzed involves three digits (e.g., 100), then every individual code number must have three digits (e.g., the first individual to be numbered must be 001, not 1).

The next step would be to decide how any categorical data being analyzed are to be coded. Suppose a researcher wished to analyze certain demographic information obtained from 100 subjects who answered a questionnaire. If his study included juniors and seniors in a high school, he might code the juniors as "11" and the seniors as "12." Or, if respondents were asked to indicate which of four choices they preferred (as in certain multiple-choice questions), the researcher might code each of the choices [e.g., (*a*), (*b*), (*c*), (*d*) as "1," "2," "3," or "4," respectively]. The important thing to remember is to ensure that the coding is consistent—that is, once a decision is made about how to code someone, all others must be coded the same way, and this (and any other) coding rule must be communicated to everyone involved in coding the data.

Go back to the **Interactive and Applied Learning Tools** feature at the beginning of the chapter for a listing of interactive and applied activities. Go to the **Online Learning Center** at www.mhhe.com/fraenkel5e or your **Interactive Student CD-ROM** to take practice quizzes and receive immediate feedback, practice with key terms, review chapter content and main ideas, and find annotated Web links.

Main Points

WHAT ARE DATA?

- The term "data" refers to the kinds of information researchers obtain on the subjects of their research.

INSTRUMENTATION

- The term "instrumentation" refers to the entire process of collecting data in a research investigation.

VALIDITY AND RELIABILITY

- An important consideration in the choice of an instrument to be used in a research investigation is validity: the extent to which results from it permit researchers to draw warranted conclusions about the characteristics of the individuals studied.
- A reliable instrument is one that gives consistent results.

OBJECTIVITY AND USABILITY

- Whenever possible, researchers try to eliminate subjectivity from the judgments they make about the achievement, performance, or characteristics of subjects.
- An important consideration for any researcher in choosing or designing an instrument is how easy the instrument will actually be to use.

WAYS TO CLASSIFY INSTRUMENTS

- Research instruments can be classified in many ways. Some of the more common are in terms of who provides the data, the method of data collection, who collects the data, and what kind of response they require from the subjects.
- Research data are data obtained by directly or indirectly assessing the subjects of a study.
- Self-report data are data provided by the subjects of a study themselves.
- Informant data are data provided by other people about the subjects of a study.

TYPES OF INSTRUMENTS

- Many types of researcher-completed instruments exist. Some of the more commonly used are rating scales, interview schedules, tally sheets, flowcharts, performance checklists, anecdotal records, and time-and-motion logs.
- There are also many types of instruments that are completed by the subjects of a study rather than the researcher. Some of the more commonly used of this type are questionnaires; self-checklists; attitude scales; personality inventories; achievement, aptitude, and performance tests; projective devices; and sociometric devices.
- The types of items or questions used in subject-completed instruments can take many forms, but they all can be classified as either selection or supply items. Exam-

ples of selection items include true-false items, multiple-choice items, matching items, and interpretive exercises. Examples of supply items include short-answer items and essay questions.

- An excellent source for locating already available tests is the *ERIC Clearinghouse on Assessment and Evaluation.*
- Unobtrusive measures require no intrusion into the normal course of affairs.

TYPES OF SCORES

- A raw score is the initial score obtained when using an instrument; a derived score is a raw score that has been translated into a more useful score on some type of standardized basis to aid in interpretation.
- Age/grade equivalents are scores that indicate the typical age or grade associated with an individual raw score.
- A percentile rank is the percentage of a specific group scoring at or below a given raw score.
- A standard score is a mathematically derived score having comparable meaning on different instruments.

MEASUREMENT SCALES

- Four types of measurement scales—nominal, ordinal, interval, and ratio—are used in educational research.
- A nominal scale involves the use of numbers to indicate membership in one or more categories.
- An ordinal scale involves the use of numbers to rank or order scores from high to low.
- An interval scale involves the use of numbers to represent equal intervals in different segments on a continuum.
- A ratio scale involves the use of numbers to represent equal distances from a known zero point.

PREPARING DATA FOR ANALYSIS

- Collected data must be scored accurately and consistently.
- Once scored, data must be tabulated and coded.

Key Terms

Achievement test 134
Age-equivalent score 143
Anecdotal record 128
Aptitude test 135
Attitude scale 131
Behavior rating scale 124
Criterion 144
Criterion-referenced
  instrument 144
Data 118
Data-collection
  instrument 123

Derived scores 143
*ERIC Clearinghouse on
  Assessment and
  Evaluation* 120
ERIC/AE Test Locator-
  Search form 120
Evaluative statement 128
Flowchart 126
Generalized statement 129
Grade-equivalent score 143
Graphic rating scale 124

Informant instrument 120
Informants 119
Instrument 118
Instrumentation 118
Interpretive statement 140
Interval scale 145
Interview schedule 125
Matching item 140
Multiple-choice item 140
Nominal scale 145
Norm group 144

Norm-referenced
instrument 144

Objectivity 119

Ordinal scale 145

Percentile 143

Percentile rank 143

Performance checklist 126

Performance
instrument 122

Performance test 136

Personality inventory 132

Procedure 122

Product rating scale 124

Product 122

Projective device 137

Questionnaire 130

Rating scale 123

Ratio scale 147

Raw score 142

Reliability 119

Researcher
instrument 120

Self-checklist 130

Semantic differential 132

Short-answer item 141

Sociometric device 138

Standard score 143

Subject instrument 120

Tally sheet 126

Time-and-motion log 129

True-false item 138

Unobtrusive measure 142

Usability 119

Validity 119

Written-response
instrument 122

For Discussion

1. What type of instrument do you think would be best suited to obtain data about each of the following?
   a. The free-throw shooting ability of a tenth-grade basketball team.
   b. How nurses feel about a new management policy recently instituted in their hospital.
   c. Parental reactions to a proposed campaign to raise money for an addition to the school library.
   d. The "best-liked" boy and girl in the senior class.
   e. The "best" administrator in a particular school district.
   f. How well students in a food management class can prepare a balanced meal.
   g. Characteristics of all students who are biology majors at a midwestern university.
   h. How students at one school compare to students at another school in mathematics ability.
   i. The potential of various high school seniors for college work.
   j. What the members of a kindergarten class like and dislike about school.
2. Which do you think would be the easiest to measure—the "attention-level" of a class, student interest in a poem, or participation in a class discussion? Why? Which would be the hardest to measure?
3. Is it possible to measure a person's "self-concept?" If so, how? What about his or her "body image?"
4. Are there any things (ideas, objects, etc.) that can't be measured? If so, give an example.
5. What type of scale—nominal, ordinal, interval, or ratio—would a researcher be most likely to assume when measuring a person's religious preference? Why? What about his or her mechanical aptitude? Why?
6. Of all the instruments presented in this chapter, which one(s) do you think would be the hardest to use? The easiest? Why? Which one(s) do you think would provide the most dependable information? Why?
7. "Any individual raw score, in and of itself, is meaningless." Would you agree with this statement? Explain.
8. "Derived scores give meaning to individual raw scores." Is this statement true? Explain.
9. It sometimes would not be fair to compare an individual's score on a test to the scores of other individuals taking the same test. Why?

1. American Council on Education (1945). *Helping teachers understand children.* Washington, DC: American Council on Education, pp. 32–33.

2. Ibid., p. 33.

3. A. Likert (1932). A technique for the measurement of attitudes. *Archives de Psychologie, 6:* (140), pp. 173–177.

4. C. Osgood, G. Suci, and P. Tannenbaum (1962). *The measurement of meaning.* Urbana, IL: University of Illinois Press.

5. See, for example, W. J. Popham (1992). *Educational evaluation,* 3rd ed. Englewood Cliffs, NJ: Prentice Hall, pp. 150–173.

6. E. I. Sawin (1969). *Evaluation and the work of the teacher.* Belmont, CA: Wadsworth, p. 176.

7. M. L. Blum (1943). Selection of sewing machine operators. *Journal of Applied Psychology, 27:* (2): 35–40.

8. N. E. Gronlund (1988). *How to construct achievement tests,* 4th ed. Englewood Cliffs, NJ: Prentice Hall, pp. 66–67. Reprinted by permission of Prentice Hall, Inc. Also see Gronlund's (1997) *Assessment of student achievement,* 6th ed. Boston: Allyn & Bacon.

9. Gronlund (1988), pp. 76–77. Reprinted by permission of Prentice Hall, Inc.

10. E. J. Webb, D. T. Campbell, R. D. Schwartz, and L. Sechrest (1966). *Unobtrusive measures: Nonreactive research in the social sciences.* Chicago: Rand McNally.

11. The use of unobtrusive measures is an art in itself. We can only scratch the surface of the topic here. For a more extended discussion, along with many interesting examples, the reader is referred to the book by Webb et al., in note 10.

Notes

Research Exercise Seven: Instrumentation

Decide on the kinds of instruments you will use to measure the dependent variable(s) in your study. Using Problem Sheet 7 (see page 154), name all the instruments you plan to use in your study. If you plan to use one or more already existing instruments, describe each. If you will need to develop an instrument, give two examples of the kind of questions you would ask (or tasks you would have students perform) as a part of each instrument. Indicate how you would describe and organize the data on each of the variables yielding numerical data.

An electronic version of this Problem Sheet that you can fill in and print, save, or e-mail is available on the Online Learning Center at www.mhhe.com/fraenkel5e and on your Interactive Student C-ROM.

A full-sized version of this Problem Sheet that you can fill in or photocopy is in your Student Workbook.

PROBLEM SHEET 7

Instrumentation

1. The question or hypothesis in my study is: _____

2. The types of instruments I plan to use to measure my variables are: _____

   _____

3. Circle one of the following:

   a. I plan to use an existing instrument.

   b. I plan to develop an instrument.

4. If I need to develop an instrument, here are two examples of the kind of questions I would ask (or tasks I would have students perform) as a part of my instrument:

   a. _____

   b. _____

5. These are the existing instruments I plan to use: _____

   _____

6. The independent variable in my study is: _____
   I would describe it as follows (circle the term in each set that applies):

   [quantitative or categorical]   [nominal or ordinal or interval or ratio]

7. The dependent variable in my study is: _____
   I would describe it as follows (circle the term in each set that applies):

   [quantitative or categorical]   [nominal or ordinal or interval or ratio]

8. My study does not have independent/dependent variables. The variable(s) in my study is (are): _____

9. For *each* variable above that yields numerical data, I will treat it as follows (check one in each column): _____

	Independent	*Dependent*	*Other*
Raw score	_____	_____	_____
Age/grade equivalents	_____	_____	_____
Percentile	_____	_____	_____
Standard score	_____	_____	_____

10. I do not have any variables that yield numerical data in my study _____ (✓).

Validity and Reliability

CHAPTER 8

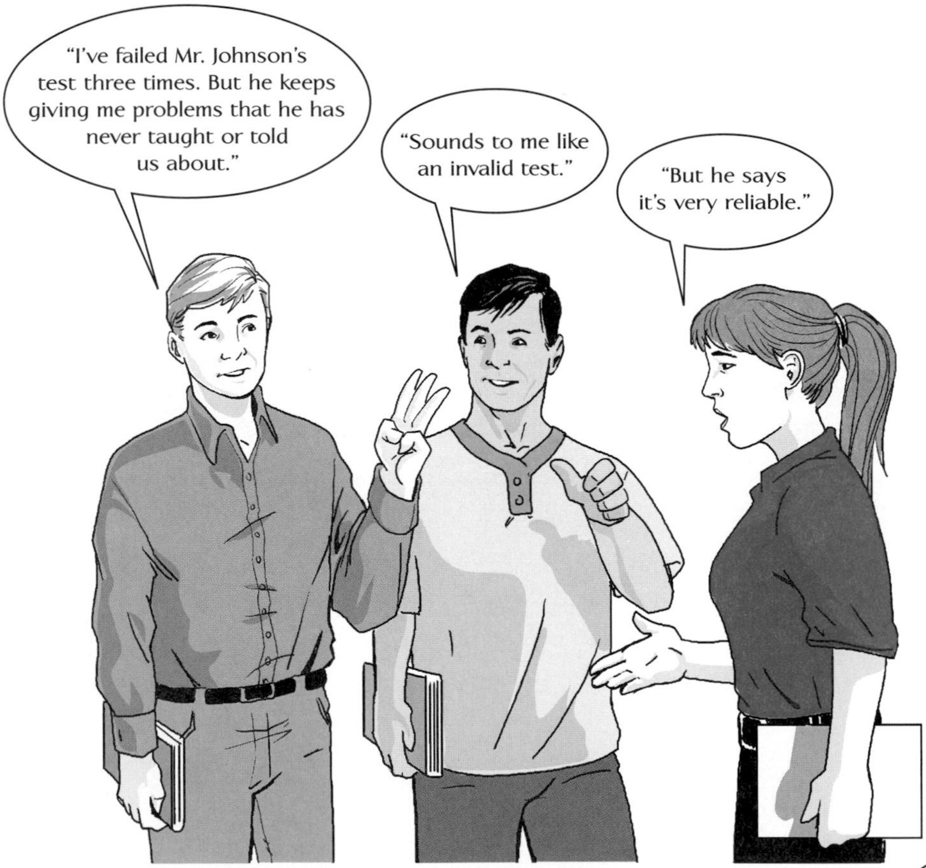

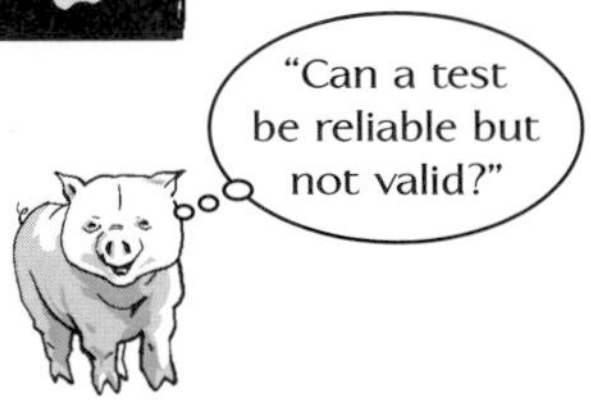

Validity and Reliability

The Importance of Valid Instruments

Reliability

Errors of Measurement
Test-Retest Method
Equivalent-Forms Method
Internal-Consistency Methods
The Standard Error of Measurement (SEMeas)
Scoring Agreement
Validity and Reliability in Qualitative Research

Validity

Content-Related Evidence
Criterion-Related Evidence
Construct-Related Evidence

t isn't fair, Tony!"

"What isn't, Lily?"

"Those tests that Mrs. Leonard gives. Grrr!"

"What about them?"

"Well, take this last test we had on the Civil War. All during her lectures and the class discussions over the last few weeks, we've been talking about the causes and effects of the War."

"So?"

"Well, then on this test, she asked a lot about battles and generals and other stuff that we didn't study."

"Did you ask her 'how come?'"

"Yeah, I did. She said she wanted to test our 'thinking' ability. But she was asking us to think about material she hadn't even gone over or discussed in class. That's why I think she isn't fair."

Lily is correct. Her teacher, in this instance, isn't being fair. Although she isn't using the term, what Lily is talking about is a matter of *validity*. It appears Mrs. Leonard is giving an *invalid* test. What this means, and why it isn't a good thing for a teacher (or any researcher) to do, is largely what this chapter is about.

The Importance of Valid Instruments

The quality of the instruments used in research is very important, for the conclusions researchers draw are based on the information they obtain using these instruments. Accordingly, researchers use a number of procedures to ensure that the inferences they draw, based on the data they collect, are valid and reliable.

"Validity" refers to the appropriateness, meaningfulness, correctness, and usefulness of the inferences a researcher makes. "Reliability" refers to the consistency of scores or answers from one administration of an instrument to another, and from one set of items to another. Both concepts are important to consider when it comes to the selection or design of the instruments a researcher intends to use. In this chapter, therefore, we shall discuss both validity and reliability in some detail.

Validity

Validity is the most important idea to consider when preparing or selecting an instrument for use. More than anything else, researchers want the information they obtain through the use of an instrument to serve their purposes. For example, to find out what teachers in a particular school district think about a recent policy passed by the school board, researchers need both an instrument to record the data and some sort of assurance that the information obtained will enable them to *draw correct conclusions* about teacher opinions. The drawing of correct conclusions based on the data obtained from an assessment is what validity is all about. While it is not essential, the comprehension and use of information is greatly simplified if some kind of score that summarizes the information for each person is obtained. While the ideas that follow are not limited to the use of scores, we discuss them in this context because the ideas are easier to understand, and most instruments provide such scores.

In recent years, **validity** has been defined as referring to the *appropriateness, correctness, meaningfulness,* and *usefulness* of the specific *inferences* researchers make based on the data they collect. **Validation** is the process of collecting and analyzing evidence to support such inferences. There are many ways to collect evidence, and we will discuss some of them shortly. The important point here is to realize that validity refers to the degree to which evidence supports any inferences a researcher makes based on the data he or she collects using a particular instrument. It is the inferences about the specific uses of an instrument that are validated, not the instrument itself.* These inferences should be appropriate, meaningful, correct, and useful.

*This is somewhat of a change from past interpretations. It is based on the set of standards prepared by a joint committee consisting of members of the American Educational Research Association, the American Psychological Association, and The National Council on Measurement in Education. *See* American Psychological Association (1985). *Standards for educational and psychological testing.* Washington, DC: American Psychological Association, pp. 9–18, 19–23.

One interpretation of this conceptualization of validity has been that test publishers no longer have a responsibility to provide evidence of validity. We do not agree; publishers have an obligation to state what an instrument is intended to measure and to provide evidence that it does. Nonetheless, researchers must still give attention to the way in which *they* intend to interpret the information.

An appropriate inference would be one that is relevant—that is, related—to the purposes of the study. If the purpose of a study were to determine what students know about African culture, for example, it would make no sense to make inferences about this from their scores on a test about the physical geography of Africa.

A meaningful inference is one that says something about the *meaning* of the information (such as test scores) obtained through the use of an instrument. What exactly does a high score on a particular test mean? What does such a score allow us to say about the individual who received it? In what way is an individual who receives a high score different from one who receives a low score? And so forth. It is one thing to collect information from people. We do this all the time—names, addresses, birth dates, shoe sizes, car license numbers, and so on. But unless we can make inferences that mean something from the information we obtain, it is of little use. The purpose of research is not merely to collect data, but to use such data to draw warranted conclusions about the people (and others like them) on whom the data were collected.

A useful inference is one that helps researchers make a decision related to what they were trying to find out. Researchers interested in the effects of inquiry-related teaching materials on student achievement, for example, need information that will enable them to infer whether achievement is affected by such materials and, if so, how.

Validity, therefore, depends on the amount and type of evidence there is to support the interpretations researchers wish to make concerning data they have collected. The crucial question is: Do the results of the assessment provide useful information about the topic or variable being measured?

What kinds of evidence might a researcher collect? Essentially, there are three main types.

Content-related evidence of validity refers to the content and format of the instrument. How appropriate is the content? How comprehensive? Does it logically get at the intended variable? How adequately does the sample of items or questions represent the content to be assessed? Is the format appropriate? The content and format must be consistent with the definition of the variable and the sample of subjects to be measured.

Criterion-related evidence of validity refers to the relationship between scores obtained using the instrument and scores obtained using one or more other instruments or measures (often called a criterion). How strong is this relationship? How well do such scores estimate present or predict future performance of a certain type?

Construct-related evidence of validity refers to the nature of the psychological construct or characteristic being measured by the instrument. How well does a measure of the construct explain differences in the behavior of individuals or their performance on certain tasks? We provide further explanation of this rather complex concept later in the chapter.

Figure 8.1 illustrates these three types of evidence.

CONTENT-RELATED EVIDENCE

Suppose a researcher is interested in the effects of a new math program on the mathematics ability of fifth-graders. The researcher expects that students who complete the program will be able to solve a number of different types of word problems correctly. To assess their mathematics ability, the researcher plans to give them a math test containing about 15 such problems. The performance of the students on this test is important only to the degree that it provides evidence of their ability to solve these kinds of problems. Hence, performance on the instrument in this case (the math test) would provide valid evidence of the mathematics ability of these students to the degree that the instrument provides an adequate sample of the types of word problems learned about in the program. If only easy problems are included on the test, or only very difficult or lengthy ones, or only problems involving subtraction, the test would be unrepresentative and hence not provide information from which valid inferences could be made.

One key element in content-related evidence, then, revolves around the adequacy of the sampling. Most instruments (and especially achievement tests) provide only a sample of the kinds of problems that might be solved or questions that might be asked. Content validation, therefore, is partly a matter of determining if the

Figure 8.1 *Illustration of Types of Evidence of Validity*

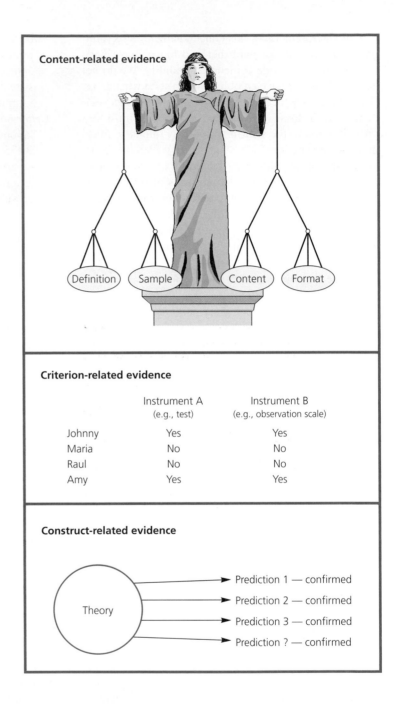

content that the instrument contains is an adequate sample of the domain of content it is supposed to represent.

The other aspect of content validation has to do with the format of the instrument. This includes such things as the clarity of printing, size of type, adequacy of work space (if needed), appropriateness of language, clarity of directions, and so on. Regardless of the adequacy of the questions in an instrument, if they are presented in an inappropriate format (such as giving a test written in English to children whose English is minimal), valid results cannot be obtained. For this reason, it is important that the characteristics of the intended sample be kept in mind.

How does one obtain content-related evidence of validity? A common way to do this is to have someone look at the content and format of the instrument and judge whether or not it is appropriate. The "someone," of course, should not be just anyone, but rather an individual who can be expected to render an intelligent judgment about the adequacy of the instrument in other words, someone who knows enough about what is to be measured to be a competent judge.

The usual procedure is somewhat as follows. The researcher writes out the definition of what he or she wants to measure on a separate sheet of paper and then gives this definition, along with the instrument and a description of the intended sample, to one or more judges. The judges look at the definition, read over the items or questions in the instrument, and place a check mark in front of each question or item that they feel does not measure one or more aspects of the definition (objectives, for example) or other criteria. They also place a check mark in front of each aspect not assessed by any of the items. In addition, the judges evaluate the appropriateness of the instrument format. The researcher then rewrites any item or question so checked and resubmits it to the judges, and/or writes new items for criteria not adequately covered. This continues until the judges approve all the items or questions in the instrument and also indicate that they feel the total number of items is an adequate representation of the total domain of content covered by the variable being measured.

To illustrate how a researcher might go about trying to establish content-related validity, let us consider two examples.

Example 1. Suppose a researcher desires to measure students' ability to *use information that they have previously acquired.* When asked what she means by this phrase, she offers the following definition.

> As evidence that students can use previously acquired information, they should be able to:
>
> 1. Draw a correct conclusion (verbally or in writing) that is based on information they are given.
> 2. Identify one or more logical implications that follow from a given point of view.
> 3. State (orally or in writing) whether two ideas are identical, similar, unrelated, or contradictory.

How might the researcher obtain such evidence? She decides to prepare a written test that will contain various questions for students to answer. Their answers will constitute the evidence she seeks. Here are three examples of the kinds of questions she has in mind, one de-

signed to produce each of the three types of evidence listed above.

1. If A is greater than B, and B is greater than C, then:
   a. A must be greater than C.
   b. C must be smaller than A.
   c. B must be smaller than A.
   d. All of the above are true.
2. Those who believe that increasing consumer expenditures would be the best way to stimulate the economy would advocate:
   a. An increase in interest rates.
   b. An increase in depletion allowances.
   c. Tax reductions in the lower income brackets.
   d. A reduction in government expenditures.
3. Compare the dollar amounts spent by the U.S. government during the past 10 years for (a) debt payments, (b) defense, and (c) social services.

Now, look at each of the questions and the corresponding objective they are supposed to measure. Do you think each question measures the objective it was designed for? If not, why not?*

Example 2. Here is what another researcher designed as an attempt to measure (at least in part) the ability of students to *explain why events occur.*

> Read the directions that follow, and then answer the question.
>
> *Directions:* Here are some facts.
>
> *Fact W:* A camper started a fire to cook food on a windy day in a forest.
> *Fact X:* A fire started in some dry grass near a campfire in a forest.
>
> Here is another fact that happened later the same day in the same forest.
>
> *Fact Y:* A house in the forest burned down.
>
> You are to explain what might have caused the house to burn down (Fact Y). Would Fact W and X be useful as parts of your explanation?
>
> a. Yes, both W and X and the possible cause-and-effect relationship between them would be useful.

---

*We would rate correct answers to questions 1 (choice *d*) and 2 (choice *c*) as valid evidence, although 1 could be considered questionable, since students might view it as somewhat tricky. We would not rate the answers to 3 as valid, since students are not asked to contrast ideas, only facts.)

b. Yes, both W and X would be useful, even though neither was likely a cause of the other.
c. No, because only one of Facts W and X was likely a cause of Y.
d. No, because neither W or X was likely a cause of Y.[1]

Once again, look at the question and the objective it was designed to measure. Does it measure this objective? If not, why not?*

Attempts like these to obtain evidence of some sort (in the above instances, the support of independent judges that the items measure what they are supposed to measure) typify the process of obtaining content-related evidence of validity. As we mentioned previously, however, the qualifications of the judges are always an important consideration, and the judges must keep in mind the characteristics of the intended sample.

CRITERION-RELATED EVIDENCE

To obtain criterion-related evidence of validity, researchers usually compare performance on one instrument (the one being validated) with performance on some other, independent criterion. A **criterion** is a second test or other assessment procedure presumed to measure the same variable. For example, if an instrument has been designed to measure academic ability, student scores on the instrument might be compared with their grade-point averages (the external criterion). If the instrument does indeed measure academic ability, then students who score high on the test would also be expected to have high grade-point averages. Can you see why?

There are two forms of criterion-related validity—predictive and concurrent. To obtain evidence of **predictive validity,** researchers allow a time interval to elapse between administration of the instrument and obtaining the criterion scores. For example, a researcher might administer a science aptitude test to a group of high school students and later compare their scores on the test with their end-of-the-semester grades in science courses.

On the other hand, when instrument data and criterion data are gathered at nearly the same time, and the results are compared, this is an attempt by researchers to obtain evidence of **concurrent validity.** An example

is when a researcher administers a self-esteem inventory to a group of eighth-graders and compares their scores on it with their teachers' ratings of student self-esteem obtained at about the same time.

A key index in both forms of criterion-related validity is the correlation coefficient.* A **correlation coefficient,** symbolized by the letter *r,* indicates the degree of relationship that exists between the scores individuals obtain on two instruments. A positive relationship is indicated when a high score on one of the instruments is accompanied by a high score on the other or when a low score on one is accompanied by a low score on the other. A negative relationship is indicated when a high score on one instrument is accompanied by a low score on the other, and vice versa. All correlation coefficients fall somewhere between +1.00 and –1.00. An *r* of .00 indicates that no relationship exists.

When a correlation coefficient is used to describe the relationship that exists between a set of scores obtained by the same group of individuals on a particular instrument and their scores on some criterion measure, it is called a **validity coefficient.** For example, a validity coefficient of +1.00 obtained by correlating a set of scores

---

*The correlation coefficient, explained in detail in Chapter Ten, is an extremely useful statistic. This is one of its many applications or uses.

"He looks very promising—but let's see how he does on the written test."

---

*We would rate a correct answer to this question as valid evidence of student ability to explain why events occur.

High-Stakes Testing

"High-stakes testing" refers to the use of tests (often only a single achievement test) as the primary, or only basis for decisions having major consequences. For students, such consequences include retention in grade and/or the denial of diplomas and awards. For schools, they include public praise or condemnation, sanctions, and financial rewards or punishments. "In state after state, legislatures, governors, and state boards, supported by business leaders, have imposed tougher requirements in mathematics, English, science, and other fields, together with new tests by which the performance of both students and schools is to be judged."*

For years, tests had been used as one indicator of performance, what was new was exclusive reliance on them. "The backlash, touching virtually every state that has instituted high-stakes testing, arises from a spectrum of complaints. A major complaint is that the focus on testing and obsessive test preparation, sometimes beginning in kindergarten, is killing innovative teaching and curricula and driving out good teachers. Other complaints are that (conversely) the standards on which the tests are based are too vague and that students have not been taught the material on which the tests are based. Or that the tests are unfair to poor and minority students; or to those who lack test-taking skills; or that the tests put too much stress on young children. And some argue that they are too long (in Massachusetts they

can take up to 13 hours!) or too tough or simply not good enough."†

In response, the American Educational Research Association developed a position statement of "conditions essential to sound implementation of high-stakes educational testing programs."‡ It contained 14 specific points, 4 of the most important being that such decisions about students should not be based on test scores alone; tests should be made fairer to all students; tests should match the curriculum; and that the reliability and validity of tests should continually be evaluated.

Two examples of responses to the guidelines were the following:

- "In the face of too much testing with far too severe consequences, the AERA positions, if implemented, would be a step forward relative to current practice."§
- "The statement reflects what is desired for all state tests and assessments. But, just as all students have not yet met the standards, not all state tests and assessments will immediately meet the goals contained in this statement."‖

What do you think? Are the complaints about high-stakes tests warranted?

*P. Schrag (2000). High stakes are for tomatoes. *Atlantic Monthly,* 286:(August): 19.

†Ibid.
‡American Educational Research Association (2000). Position statement of the American Educational Research Association concerning high-stakes testing in pre-12 education. (2000). *Educational Researcher, 29,* (11): 24–35.
§M. Neill (2000). Quoted in Initial responses to AERA's position statement concerning high-stakes testing. *Educational Researcher,* 29:(11): 28.
‖W. Martin (2000). Quoted in Ibid., p. 27.

on a mathematics aptitude test (the predictor) and another set of scores, this time on a mathematics achievement test (the criterion), for the same individuals would indicate that each individual in the group had exactly the same relative standing on both measures. Such a correlation, if obtained, would allow the researcher to predict perfectly math achievement based on aptitude test scores. Although this correlation coefficient would be very unlikely, it illustrates what such coefficients mean. The higher the validity coefficient obtained, the more accurate a researcher's predictions are likely to be.

Gronlund suggests the use of an expectancy table as another way to depict criterion-related evidence.[2] An

expectancy table is nothing more than a two-way chart, with the predictor categories listed down the left-hand side of the chart and the criterion categories listed horizontally along the top of the chart. For each category of scores on the predictor, the researcher then indicates the percentage of individuals who fall within each of the categories on the criterion.

Table 8.1 presents an example. As you can see from the table, 51 percent of the students who were classified outstanding by these judges received a grade of A in orchestra, 35 percent received a B, and 14 percent received a C. Although this table refers only to this particular group, it could be used to predict the scores of other aspiring music students who are evaluated by

Table 8.1 *Example of an Expectancy Table*

Judges' Classification of Music Aptitude	Course Grades in Orchestra (Percentage Receiving Each Grade)			
	A	B	C	D
Outstanding	51	35	14	0
Above average	20	43	37	0
Average	0	6	83	11
Below average	0	0	13	87

these same judges. If a student obtains an evaluation of "outstanding," we might predict (approximately) that he or she would have a 51 percent chance of receiving an A, a 35 percent chance of receiving a B, and a 14 percent chance of receiving a C.

Expectancy tables are particularly useful devices for researchers to use with data collected in schools. They are simple to construct, easily understood, and clearly show the relationship that exists between two measures.

It is important to realize that the nature of the criterion is the most important factor in gathering criterion-related evidence. High positive correlations do not mean much if the criterion measure does not make logical sense. For example, a high correlation between scores on an instrument designed to measure aptitude for science and scores on a physical fitness test would not be relevant criterion-related evidence for either instrument. Think back to the example we presented earlier of the questions designed to measure student ability to explain why events occur. What sort of criteria could be used to establish criterion-referenced validity for those items?

CONSTRUCT-RELATED EVIDENCE

Construct-related evidence is the broadest of the three categories of evidence for validity that we are considering. There is no single piece of evidence that satisfies construct-related validity. Rather, researchers attempt to collect a variety of *different* types of evidence—the more and the more varied the better—that will allow them to make warranted inferences—to assert, for example, that the scores obtained from administering a self-esteem inventory permit accurate inferences about the degree of self-esteem that people who receive those scores possess.

Usually, there are three steps involved in obtaining construct-related evidence of validity: (1) the variable being measured is clearly defined; (2) hypotheses, based on a theory underlying the variable, are formed about how people who possess a "lot" versus a "little" of the variable will behave in a particular situation; and (3) the hypotheses are tested both logically and empirically.

To make the process clearer, let us consider an example. Suppose a researcher interested in developing a pencil-and-paper test to measure "honesty" wants to use a construct-validity approach. First, he defines honesty. Next he formulates a theory about how "honest" people behave as compared to "dishonest" people. For example, he might theorize that honest individuals, if they find an object that does not belong to them, will make a reasonable effort to locate the individual to whom the object belongs. Based on this theory, the researcher might hypothesize that individuals who score high on his "honesty test" will be more likely to attempt to locate the owner of an object they find than individuals who score low on the test. The researcher would then administer the honesty test, separate the names of those who score high and those who score low, and give all of them an opportunity to be honest. He might, for example, leave a wallet with $5 in it lying just outside the test-taking room so that the individuals taking the test can easily see it and pick it up. The wallet displays the name and phone number of the owner in plain view. If the researcher's hypothesis is substantiated, more of the high scorers than the low scorers on the honesty test would attempt to call the owner of the wallet. (This could be checked by having the number answered by a recording machine asking the caller to leave his or her name and number.) This would be one piece of evidence that could be used to support inferences about the honesty of individuals, based on the scores they receive on this test.

We must stress, however, that a researcher must carry out a series of studies to obtain a *variety* of evidence suggesting that the scores from a particular instrument can be used to draw correct inferences about the variable that the instrument purports to measure. It is a broad array of evidence, rather than any one particular type of evidence, that is desired.

Consider a second example. Some evidence that might be considered to support a claim for construct validity in connection with a test designed to measure mathematical reasoning ability might be as follows:

- Independent judges all indicate that all items on the test require mathematical reasoning.
- Independent judges all indicate that the features of the test itself (such as test format, directions, scoring, and reading level) would not in any way prevent students from engaging in mathematical reasoning.
- Independent judges all indicate that the sample of tasks included in the test is relevant and representative of mathematical reasoning tasks.
- A high correlation exists between scores on the test and grades in mathematics.
- High scores have been made on the test by students who have had specific training in mathematical reasoning.
- Students actually engage in mathematical reasoning when they are asked to "think aloud" as they go about trying to solve the problems on the test.
- A high correlation exists between scores on the test and teacher ratings of competence in mathematical reasoning.
- Higher scores are obtained on the test by mathematics majors than by general science majors.

Other types of evidence might be listed for the above task (perhaps you can think of some), but we hope this is enough to make clear that it is not just one type, but many types, of evidence that a researcher seeks to obtain. Determining whether the scores obtained through the use of a particular instrument measure a particular variable involves a study of how the test was developed, the theory underlying the test, how the test functions with a variety of people and in a variety of situations, and how scores on the test relate to scores on other appropriate instruments. Construct validation involves, then, a wide variety of procedures and many different types of evidence, including both content-related and criterion-related evidence. The more evidence researchers have from many different sources, the more confident they become about interpreting the scores obtained from a particular instrument.

Reliability

Reliability refers to the consistency of the scores obtained—how consistent they are for each individual from one administration of an instrument to another and from one set of items to another. Consider, for example, a test designed to measure typing ability. If the test is reliable, we would expect a student who receives a high score the first time he takes the test to receive a high score the next time he takes the test. The scores would probably not be identical, but they should be close.

The scores obtained from an instrument can be quite reliable, but not valid. Suppose a researcher gave a group of eighth-graders two forms of a test designed to measure their knowledge of the Constitution of the United States and found their scores to be consistent: those who scored high on form A also scored high on form B; those who scored low on A scored low on B; and so on. We would say that the scores are reliable. But if the researcher then used these same test scores to predict the success of these students in their physical education classes, she would probably be looked at in amazement. Any inferences about success in physical education based on scores on a Constitution test would have no validity. Now, what about the reverse? Can an instrument that yields unreliable scores permit valid inferences? No! If scores are completely inconsistent for a person, they provide no useful information. We have no way of knowing which score to use to infer an individual's ability, attitude, or other characteristic.

The distinction between reliability and validity is shown in Figure 8.2. Reliability and validity always depend on the context in which an instrument is used. Depending on the context, an instrument may or may not yield reliable (consistent) scores. If the data are unreliable, they cannot lead to valid (legitimate) inferences—as shown in target (*a*). As reliability improves, validity may improve, as shown in target (*b*), or it may not, as shown in target (*c*). An instrument may have good reliability but low validity, as shown in target (*d*). What is desired, of course, is both high reliability and high validity, as target (*e*) shows.

ERRORS OF MEASUREMENT

Whenever people take the same test twice, they will seldom perform exactly the same—that is, their scores or answers will not usually be identical. This may be due to a variety of factors (differences in motivation, energy, anxiety, a different testing situation, and so on), and it is inevitable. Such factors result in **errors of measurement** (see Figure 8.3).

Because errors of measurement are always present to some degree, researchers expect some variation in test scores (in answers or ratings, for example) when an instrument is administered to the same group more than once, when two different forms of an instrument are used, or even from one part of an instrument to another.

Figure 8.2 *Reliability and Validity*

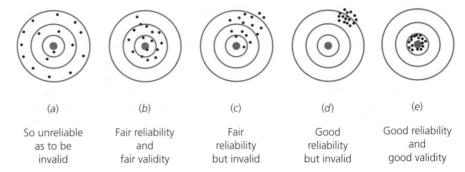

(a)	(b)	(c)	(d)	(e)
So unreliable as to be invalid	Fair reliability and fair validity	Fair reliability but invalid	Good reliability but invalid	Good reliability and good validity

The bulls-eye in each target represents the information that is desired. Each dot represents a separate score obtained with the instrument. A dot in the bulls-eye indicates that the information obtained (the score) is the information the researcher desires.

Reliability estimates provide researchers with an idea of how much variation to expect. Such estimates are usually expressed as another application of the correlation coefficient known as a **reliability coefficient.**

As we mentioned earlier, a validity coefficient expresses the relationship that exists between scores of the same individuals on two *different* instruments. A reliability coefficient also expresses a relationship, but this time it is between scores of the same individuals on the *same* instrument at two different times, or between two parts of the same instrument. The three best-known ways to obtain a reliability coefficient are the test-retest method, the equivalent-forms method; and the internal consistency methods. Unlike other uses of the correla-

tion coefficient, reliability coefficients must range from .00 to 1.00—that is, with no negative values.

TEST-RETEST METHOD

The **test-retest method** involves administering the same test twice to the *same* group after a certain time interval has elapsed. A reliability coefficient is then calculated to indicate the relationship between the two sets of scores obtained.

Reliability coefficients will be affected by the length of time that elapses between the two administrations of the test. The longer the time interval, the lower the reliability coefficient is likely to be, since there is a greater likelihood of changes in the individuals taking the test. In checking for evidence of test-retest reliability, an appropriate time interval should be selected. This interval should be that during which individuals would be assumed to retain their relative position in a meaningful group.

There is no point in studying, or even conceptualizing, a variable that fluctuates wildly in individuals for whom it is measured. When researchers assess someone as academically talented, for example, or skilled in typing or as having a poor self-concept, they assume that this characteristic will continue to differentiate individuals for some period of time. It is impossible to study a variable that has no stability in the individual.

Researchers do not expect all variables to be equally stable. Experience has shown that some abilities (such as writing) are more subject to change than others (such as abstract reasoning). Some personal characteristics (such as self-esteem) are considered to be more stable than others (such as teenage vocational interests).

"I can't believe that my blood pressure is 170 over 110!"

"Maybe it's due to poor reliability of the measurement. Let's wait a few minutes, and check it again."

Figure 8.3 *Reliability of a Measurement*

"Mood" is a variable that, by definition, is considered to be stable for short periods of time—a matter of minutes or hours. But even here, unless the instrumentation used is reliable, meaningful relationships with other (perhaps causal) variables will not be found. For most educational research, stability of scores over a two- to three-month period is usually viewed as sufficient evidence of test-retest reliability. In reporting test-retest reliability coefficients, therefore, the time interval between the two testings should always be reported.

EQUIVALENT-FORMS METHOD

When the **equivalent-forms method** is used, two different but equivalent (also called alternate or parallel) forms of an instrument are administered to the *same* group of individuals during the same time period. Although the questions are different, they should sample the same content and they should be constructed separately from each other. A reliability coefficient is then calculated between the two sets of scores obtained. A high coefficient would indicate strong evidence of reliability—that the two forms are measuring the same thing.

It is possible to combine the test-retest and equivalent-forms methods by giving two different forms of the same test with a time interval between the two administrations. A high reliability coefficient would indicate not only that the two forms are measuring the same sort of performance but also what we might expect with regard to consistency over time.

INTERNAL-CONSISTENCY METHODS

The methods mentioned so far all require two administration or testing sessions. There are several **internal-consistency methods** of estimating reliability, however, that require only a single administration of an instrument.

Split-half Procedure. The **split-half procedure** involves scoring two halves (usually odd items versus even items) of a test separately for each person and then calculating a correlation coefficient for the two sets of scores. The coefficient indicates the degree to which the two halves of the test provide the same results, and hence describes the internal consistency of the test.

The reliability coefficient is calculated using what is known as the Spearman-Brown prophecy formula. A simplified version of this formula is as follows:

$$\frac{\text{Reliability of}}{\text{scores on total test}} = \frac{2 \times \text{reliability for } \frac{1}{2} \text{ test}}{1 + \text{reliability for } \frac{1}{2} \text{ test}}$$

Thus, if we obtained a correlation coefficient of .56 by comparing one half of the test items to the other half, the reliability of scores for the total test would be:

$$\frac{\text{Reliability of}}{\text{scores on total test}} = \frac{2 \times .56}{1 + .56} = \frac{1.12}{1.56} = .72$$

This illustrates an important characteristic of reliability. The reliability of a test (or any instrument) can generally be increased by increasing its length if the items added are similar to the original ones.

Kuder-Richardson Approaches. Perhaps the most frequently employed method for determining internal consistency is the Kuder-Richardson approach, particularly formulas KR20 and KR21. The latter formula requires only three pieces of information—the number of items on the test, the mean, and the standard deviation. Note, however, that formula KR21 can be used only if it can be assumed that the items are of equal difficulty.* A frequently used version of the KR21 formula is the following:

$$\frac{\textbf{KR21 reliability}}{\textbf{coefficient}} = \frac{K}{K - 1} \left[1 - \frac{M(K - M)}{K(SD^2)} \right]$$

where K = number of items on the test, M = mean of the set of test scores, and SD = standard deviation of the set of test scores.[†]

Although this formula may look somewhat intimidating, its use is actually quite simple. For example, if $K = 50$, $M = 40$, and $SD = 4$, the reliability coefficient would be calculated as shown below:

$$\text{Reliability} = \frac{50}{49} \left[1 - \frac{40(50 - 40)}{50(4^2)} \right]$$

$$= 1.02 \left[1 - \frac{40(10)}{50(16)} \right]$$

$$= 1.02 \left[1 - \frac{400}{800} \right]$$

$$= (1.02)(1 - .50)$$

$$= (1.02)(.50)$$

$$= .51$$

---

*Formula KR20 does not require the assumption that all items are of equal difficulty, although it is more difficult to calculate. Computer programs for doing so are commonly available, however, and should be used whenever a researcher cannot assume that all items are of equal difficulty.

[†]See Chapter Ten for an explanation of standard deviation.

Table 8.2 *Methods of Checking Validity and Reliability*

Validity ("Truthfulness")	
Method	**Procedure**
Content-related evidence	Expert judgment
Criterion-related evidence	Relate to another measure of the same variable
Construct-related evidence	Assess evidence on predictions made from theory

Reliability ("Consistency")			
Method	**Content**	**Time Interval**	**Procedure**
Test-retest	Identical	Varies	Give identical instrument twice
Equivalent forms	Different	None	Give two forms of instrument
Equivalent forms/retest	Different	Varies	Give two forms of instrument, with time interval between
Internal consistency	Different	None	Divide instrument into halves and score each or use KR
Observer agreement	Identical	None	Compare scores obtained by two or more observers

Thus, the reliability estimate for scores on this test is .51.

Is a reliability estimate of .51 good or bad, high or low? As is frequently the case, there are some benchmarks we can use to evaluate reliability coefficients. First, we can compare a given coefficient with the extremes that are possible. As you will recall, a coefficient of .00 indicates a complete absence of a relationship, hence no reliability at all, whereas 1.00 is the maximum possible coefficient that can be obtained. Second, we can compare a given reliability coefficient with the sorts of coefficients that are usually obtained for measures of the same type. The reported reliability coefficients for many commercially available achievement tests, for example, are typically .90 or higher when Kuder-Richardson formulas are used. Many classroom tests report reliability coefficients of .70 and higher. Compared to these figures, our obtained coefficient must be judged rather low. For research purposes, a useful rule of thumb is that reliability should be at least .70 and preferably higher.

Alpha Coefficient. Another check on the internal consistency of an instrument is to calculate an **alpha coefficient** (frequently called **Cronbach alpha** after the man who developed it). This coefficient (α) is a general form of the KR20 formula to be used in calculating the reliability of items that are not scored right versus wrong, as in some essay tests where more than one answer is possible.[3]

Table 8.2 summarizes the methods used in checking the validity and reliability of an instrument.

THE STANDARD ERROR OF MEASUREMENT (SEMEAS)

The **standard error of measurement** is an index that shows the extent to which a measurement would vary under changed circumstances (i.e., the amount of **measurement error**). Because there are many ways in which circumstances can vary, there are many possible standard errors for a given score. For example, the standard error will be smaller if it includes only error due to different content (internal consistency or equivalent-forms reliability) than if it also includes error due to the passage of time (test-retest reliability). Under the assumption that errors of measurement are normally distributed (see p. 204 in Chapter Ten), a range of scores can be determined that shows the amount of error to be expected. We show how this is done in Appendix D.

SCORING AGREEMENT

Most tests and many other instruments are administered with specific directions and are scored objectively, that

Figure 8.4 *The Q-E Intelligence Test*

Directions: Read each of the following questions and write your answers on a separate sheet of paper. Suggested time to take the test is ten minutes.

1. There are two people in a room. The first is the son of the second person, but the second person is not the first person's father. How are the two people related?

2. Who is buried in Grant's tomb?

3. Some months have thirty days, some have thirty-one. How many have twenty-eight days?

4. If you had only one match and entered a dark room in which there was an oil lamp, an oil heater, and some firewood, which would you light first?

5. If a physician gave you three pills and told you to take one every half hour, how long would they last?

6. A person builds a house with four sides to it, a rectangular structure, with each side having a southern exposure. A big bear comes wandering by. What color is the bear?

7. A farmer has seventeen sheep. All but nine died. How many did he have left?

8. Divide 30 by $\frac{1}{2}$. Add 10. What is the correct answer?

9. Take two apples from three apples. What do you have?

10. How many animals of each species did Moses take aboard the Ark?

is, with a key that requires no judgment on the part of the scorer. Although differences in the resulting scores with different administrators or scorers are still possible, it is generally considered highly unlikely that they would occur. This is not the case with instruments that are susceptible to differences in administration, scoring, or both, such as essay evaluations. In particular, instruments that use direct observation are highly vulnerable to observer differences. Researchers who use such instruments are obliged to investigate and report the degree of **scoring agreement.** Such agreement is enhanced by training the observers and by increasing the number of observation periods.

Instruments differ in the amount of training required for their use. In general, observation techniques require considerable training for optimum use. Such training usually consists of explaining and discussing the procedures involved, followed by trainees using the instruments as they observe videotapes or live situations. All trainees observe the same behaviors and then discuss any differences in scoring. This process, or some varia-

tion thereon, is repeated until independent observers reach an acceptable level of agreement. What is desired is a correlation of at least .90 among scorers or agreement of at least 80 percent. Usually, even after such training, 8 to 12 observation periods are required to get evidence of adequate reliability over time.

To further illustrate the concept of reliability, let's take an actual test and calculate the internal consistency of the items included within it. Figure 8.4 presents an example of a nontypical intelligence test that we have adapted. Follow the directions and take the test. Then we will calculate the split-half reliability.

Now look at the answer key in the footnote at the bottom of page 171. Give yourself one point for each correct answer. Assume, for the moment, that a score on this test provides an indication of intelligence. If so, each item on the test should be a partial measure of intelligence. We could, therefore, divide the 10-item test into two 5-item tests. One of these five-item tests can consist of all the odd-numbered items, and the other five-item test can consist of all the even-numbered

Person	Score on five-item test 1 (#1, 3, 5, 7, 9)	Score on five-item test 2 (#2, 4, 6, 8, 10)
You	_____	_____
#1	_____	_____
#2	_____	_____
#3	_____	_____
#4	_____	_____
#5	_____	_____

Figure 8.5 *Reliability Worksheet*

items. Now, record your score on the odd-numbered items, and also on the even-numbered items.

We now want to see if the odd-numbered items provide a measure of intelligence similar to that provided by the even-numbered items. If they do, your scores on the odd-numbered items and the even-numbered items should be pretty close. If they are not, then the two five-item tests do not give consistent results. If this is the case, then the total test (the 10 items) probably does not give consistent results either, in which case the score could not be considered a reliable measure.

Ask some other people to take the test. Record their scores on the odd and even sets of items, using the worksheet shown in Figure 8.5.

Take a look at the scores on each of the five-item sets for each of the five individuals, and compare them with your own. What would you conclude about the reliability of the scores? What would you say about any inferences about intelligence a researcher might make based on scores on this test? Could they be valid?*

Note that we have examined only one aspect of reliability (internal consistency) for results of this test. We still do not know how much a person's score might change if we gave the test at two different times (test-retest reliability). We could get a different indication of reliability if we gave one of the five-item tests at one time and the other five-item test at another time, to the same people (equivalent-forms/retest reliability). Try to do this with a few individuals, using a worksheet like the one shown in Figure 8.5.

*You might want to assess the content validity of this test. How would you define intelligence? As you define the term, how would you evaluate this test as a measure of intelligence?

The procedures in Figure 8.5 are the ones typically used by researchers in attempts to establish reliability. Normally, many more people are used, however (at least 100). You should also realize that most tests would have many more than 10 items, since longer tests are usually more reliable than short ones, presumably because they provide a larger sampling of a person's behavior.

In sum, we hope it is clear that a major aspect of research design is the obtaining of reliable and valid information. Because both reliability and validity depend on the way in which instruments are used and on the inferences researchers wish to make from them, researchers can never simply assume that their instrumentation will provide satisfactory information. They can have more confidence if they use instruments on which there is previous evidence of reliability and validity, provided they use the instruments in the same way—that is, under the same conditions as existed previously. Even then, researchers cannot be sure; even when all else remains the same the mere passage of time may have impaired the instrument in some way.

What this means is that there is no substitute for checking reliability and validity as a part of the research procedure. There is seldom any excuse for failing to check internal consistency, since the necessary information is at hand and no additional data collection is required. Reliability over time does, in most cases, require an additional administration of an instrument, but this can often be done. In considering this option, it should be noted that not all members of the sample need be retested, though this is desirable. It is better to retest a randomly selected subsample, or even a convenience subsample, than to have no evidence of retest reliability at all. Another option is to test and retest a different, though very similar, sample.

Obtaining evidence on validity is more difficult but seldom prohibitive. Content-related evidence can usually be obtained since it requires only a few knowledgeable and available judges. It is unreasonable to expect a great deal of construct-related evidence to be obtained, but, in many studies, criterion-related evidence can be obtained. At a minimum, a second instrument should be administered. Locating or developing an additional means of instrumentation is sometimes difficult and occasionally impossible (for example, there is probably no way to validate a self-report questionnaire on sexual behavior), but the results are well worth the time and energy involved. As with retest reli-

Checking Reliability and Validity—An Example

The projective device (Picture Situation Inventory) described on pages 137–138 consists of 20 pictures, each scored on the variables "control need" and "communication" according to a point system. For example, here are some illustrative responses to picture 1 of Figure 7.22. The control need variable, defined as "motivated to control moment-to-moment activities of their students," is scored as follows:

- "I thought you would enjoy something special." (1 point)
- "I'd like to see how well you can do it." (2 points)
- "You and Tom are two different children." (3 points)
- "Yes, I would appreciate it if you would finish it." (4 points)
- "Do it quickly please." (5 points)

In addition to the appeal to content validity, there is some evidence in support of these two measures (control and communication).

Rowan studied relationships between the two scores and several other measures with a group of elementary school teachers.* She found that teachers scoring high on control need were more likely to (1) be seen by classroom observers as imposing themselves on situations and having a higher content emphasis; (2) be judged by interviewers as having more rigid attitudes of right and wrong; and (3) score higher on a test of authoritarian tendencies.

In a study of ability to predict success in a program preparing teachers for inner-city classrooms, evidence was found that the Picture Situation Inventory control score had predictive value.†

Correlations existed between the control score obtained on entrance to the program and a variety of measures subsequently obtained through classroom observation in student teaching and subsequent first-year teaching assignments. The most clear-cut finding was that those scoring higher in control need had classrooms observed as less noisy. The finding adds somewhat to the validity of the measurement, since a teacher with higher control need would be expected to have a quieter room.

The reliability of both measures was found to be adequate (.74 and .81) when assessed by the split-half procedure. When assessed by follow-up over a period of eight years, the consistency over time was considerably lower (.61 and .53), as would be expected.

*N. T. Rowan (1967). The relationship of teacher interaction in classroom situations to teacher personality variables. Unpublished doctoral dissertation. Salt Lake City: University of Utah.

†N. E. Wallen (1971). *Evaluation report to Step-TTT Project.* San Francisco, CA: San Francisco State University.

ability, a subsample can be used or both instruments can be given to a different, but similar, sample.

VALIDITY AND RELIABILITY IN QUALITATIVE RESEARCH

While many qualitative researchers use many of the procedures we have described, some take the position that validity and reliability, as we have discussed them, are either irrelevant or not suited to their research efforts because they are attempting to describe a specific situation or event as viewed by a particular individual. They emphasize instead the honesty, believability, expertise, and integrity of the researcher. We maintain that all researchers should ensure that any inferences they draw that are based on data obtained through the use of an instrument are appropriate, credible, and backed up by evidence of the sort we have described in this chapter.

Answer Key for Q-E Intelligence Test on page 169. 1. Mother and son; 2. Ulysses S. Grant; 3. All of them; 4. The match; 5. One hour; 6. White; 7. Nine; 8. 70; 9. Two; 10. None. (It wasn't Moses, but Noah who took the animals on the ark.)

Is Consequential Validity a Useful Concept?

In recent years, increased attention has been given to a concept called consequential validity, originally proposed by Samuel Messick in 1989.* He intended not to change the core meaning of validity, but to expand it to include two new ideas: "value implications" and "social consequences."

Paying attention to value implications requires the "appraisal of the value implications of the construct label, of the theory underlying test interpretation, and the ideologies in which the theory is imbedded."† This involves expanding the idea of construct-related evidence of validity that we discussed on pages 164–165. "Social consequences" refers to "the appraisal of both potential and actual social consequences of applied testing."

Disagreement with Messick has been primarily with regard to applying his proposal. Using his experience as a developer of a widely used college admissions test battery (ACT) as an example, Reckase systematically analyzed the feasibility of using this concept. He concluded that, although difficult, the critical analysis of value implications is both feasible and useful.‡

However, he argued that assessing the cause-and-effect relationships implied in determining potential and actual social consequences of the use of a test is difficult or impossible, even with a clear intended use such as determining college admissions. Citing the concern of the National Commission on Testing and Public Policy that such tests often undermine vital social policies,§ he argues that obtaining the necessary data seems unlikely and that, by definition, appraising unintended consequences is not possible ahead of time, because one does not know what they are.

What do you think of Messick's proposal?

*S. Messick (1989). Consequential validity. In R. L. Linn (Ed.). *Educational measurement,* 3rd ed. New York: American Council on Education, pp. 13–103.
†Ibid., p. 20.

‡M. D. Reckase (1998). Consequential validity from the test developer's perspective. *Educational Measurement Issues and Practice,* *17:*(2): 13–16.
§National Commission on Testing and Public Policy. *From gatekeeper to gateway: Transforming testing in America* (Technical report). Chestnut Hill, MA: Boston College.

Go back to the **Interactive and Applied Learning Tools** feature at the beginning of the chapter for a listing of interactive and applied activities. Go to the **Online Learning Center** at www.mhhe.com/fraenkel5e or your **Interactive Student CD-ROM** to take practice quizzes and receive immediate feedback, practice with key terms, review chapter content and main ideas, and find annotated Web links.

Main Points   VALIDITY

- It is important for researchers to use valid instruments, for the conclusions they draw are based on the information they obtain using these instruments.
- The term "validity," as used in research, refers to the appropriateness, meaningfulness, correctness, and usefulness of any inferences a researcher draws based on data obtained through the use of an instrument.
- Content-related evidence of validity refers to judgments on the content and logical structure of an instrument as it is to be used in a particular study.
- Criterion-related evidence of validity refers to the degree to which information provided by an instrument agrees with information obtained on other, independent instruments.
- A criterion is a standard for judging; with reference to validity, it is a second instrument against which scores on an instrument can be checked.

- Construct-related evidence of validity refers to the degree to which the totality of evidence obtained is consistent with theoretical expectations.
- A validity coefficient is a numerical index representing the degree of correspondence between scores on an instrument and a criterion measure.
- An expectancy table is a two-way chart used to evaluate criterion-related evidence of validity.

RELIABILITY

- The term "reliability," as used in research, refers to the consistency of scores or answers provided by an instrument.
- Errors of measurement refer to variations in scores obtained by the same individuals on the same instrument.
- The test-retest method of estimating reliability involves administering the same instrument twice to the same group of individuals after a certain time interval has elapsed.
- The equivalent-forms method of estimating reliability involves administering two different, but equivalent, forms of an instrument to the same group of individuals at the same time.
- The internal-consistency method of estimating reliability involves comparing responses to different sets of items that are part of an instrument.
- Scoring agreement requires a demonstration that independent scorers can achieve satisfactory agreement in their scoring.

Key Terms

Alpha coefficient 168

Concurrent validity 162

Construct-related evidence of validity 159

Content-related evidence of validity 159

Correlation coefficient 162

Criterion 162

Criterion-related evidence of validity 159

Cronbach alpha 168

Equivalent-forms method 167

Errors of measurement 165

Expectancy table 163

Internal-consistency methods 167

KR21 reliability coefficient 167

Measurement error 168

Predictive validity 162

Reliability 165

Reliability coefficient 166

Scoring agreement 169

Split-half procedure 167

Standard error of measurement 168

Test-retest method 166

Validation 158

Validity 158

Validity coefficient 162

For Discussion

1. We point out in the chapter that scores from an instrument may be reliable but not valid, yet not the reverse. Why would this be so?
2. What type of evidence—content-related, criterion-related, or construct-related—do you think is the easiest to obtain? the hardest? Why?
3. Would it be possible for a researcher to calculate a correlation coefficient of 3.7 for two sets of scores? Why or why not?
4. In what way(s) might the format of an instrument affect its validity?
5. "There is no single piece of evidence that satisfies construct-related validity." Is this true? If so, explain why this is so.
6. Which do you think is harder to obtain, validity or reliability? Why?
7. Might reliability ever be more important than validity? Explain.
8. How would you assess the Q-E Intelligence Test in Figure 8.4 with respect to validity? Explain.

Notes

1. N. E. Wallen, M. C. Durkin, J. R. Fraenkel, A. J. McNaughton, and E. I. Sawin (1969). *The Taba Curriculum Development Project in Social Studies: Development of a comprehensive curriculum model for social studies for grades one through eight, inclusive of procedures for implementation and dissemination.* Menlo Park, CA: Addison-Wesley, p. 307.

2. N. E. Gronlund (1988). *How to construct achievement tests,* 4th ed. Englewood Cliffs, NJ: Prentice Hall, p. 140.

3. See L. J. Cronbach (1951). Coefficient alpha and the internal structure of tests. *Psychometrika, 16:*297–334.

Research Exercise Eight: Validity and Reliability

Use Problem Sheet 8 to describe how you plan to check on the validity and reliability of scores obtained with your instruments. If you plan to use an existing instrument, summarize what you have been able to learn about the validity and reliability of results obtained with it. If you plan to develop an instrument, explain how you will attempt to ensure validity and reliability. In either case, explain how you will obtain evidence to check validity and reliability.

Problem Sheet 8

Validity and Reliability

1. I plan to use the following *existing* instruments: _____

    _____

    _____

    In summary, I have learned the following about the validity and reliability of scores ob-

    tained with these instruments. _____

    _____

    _____

2. I plan to *develop* the following instruments: _____

    _____

    _____

    I will try to ensure reliability and validity of results obtained with these instruments by:

    _____

3. For each instrument I plan to use:

    a. This is how I will collect evidence to check internal consistency: _____

    _____

    _____

    b. This is how I will collect evidence to check reliability over time (stability): _____

    _____

    _____

    c. This is how I will collect evidence to check validity: _____

    _____

    _____

An electronic version of this Problem Sheet that you can fill in and print, save, or e-mail is available on the Online Learning Center at www.mhhe.com/ fraenkel5e and on your Interactive Student CD-ROM.

A full-sized version of this Problem Sheet that you can fill in or photocopy is in your Student Workbook.

Internal Validity

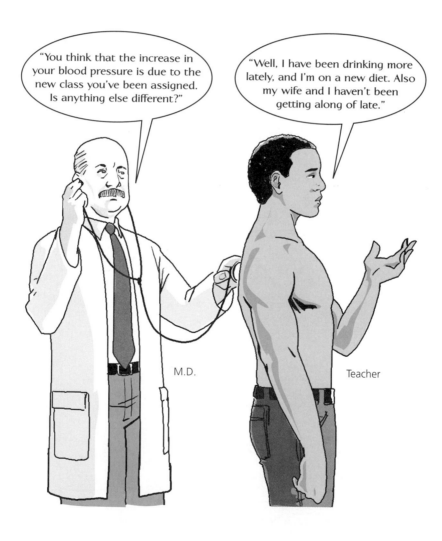

CHAPTER 9

Internal Validity

What Is Internal Validity?

Threats to Internal Validity

Subject Characteristics
Loss of Subjects (Mortality)
Location
Instrumentation
Testing
History
Maturation
Attitude of Subjects
Regression
Implementation
Factors that Reduce the Likelihood of Finding a Relationship

How Can a Researcher Minimize These Threats to Internal Validity?

Objectives

Studying this chapter should enable you to:

- Explain *what is meant by the term "internal validity."*
- Explain *what is meant by a "subject characteristics" threat to internal validity and* give an example *of such a threat.*
- Explain *what is meant by a "mortality" threat to internal validity and* give an example *of such a threat.*
- Explain *what is meant by a "location" threat to internal validity and* give an example *of such a threat.*
- Explain *what is meant by an "instrumentation" threat to internal validity and* give an example *of such a threat.*
- Explain *what is meant by a "testing" threat to internal validity and* give an example *of such a threat.*
- Explain *what is meant by a "history" threat to internal validity and* give an example *of such a threat.*
- Explain *what is meant by a "maturation" threat to internal validity and* give an example *of such a threat.*
- Explain *what is meant by a "subject attitude" threat to internal validity and* give an example *of such a threat.*
- Explain *what is meant by a "regression" threat to internal validity and* give an example *of such a threat.*
- Explain *what is meant by an "implementation" threat to internal validity and* give an example *of such a threat.*
- Identify *various threats to internal validity in published research articles.*
- Suggest *possible remedies for specific examples of the various threats to internal validity.*

Interactive and Applied Learning

After, or while, reading this chapter:

Go to your Interactive Student CD-ROM to:
- Learn More About Internal Validity

Go to your Interactive Student CD-ROM or Student Workbook to do the following activities:
- Activity 9.1: Threats to Internal Validity
- Activity 9.2: What Type of Threat?
- Activity 9.3: Controlling Threats to Internal Validity

Suppose the results of a study show that high school students taught by the inquiry method score higher on a test of critical thinking, on the average, than do students taught by the lecture method. Is this difference in scores due to the difference in methods—to the fact that the two groups have been taught differently? Surely, the researcher who is conducting the study would like to conclude this. Your first inclination may be to think the same. This may not be a legitimate interpretation, however.

What if the students who were taught using the inquiry method were better critical thinkers to begin with? What if some of the students in the inquiry group were also taking a related course during this time at a nearby university? What if the teachers of the inquiry group were simply better teachers? Any of these (or other) factors might explain why the inquiry group scored higher on the critical thinking test. Should this be the case, the researcher may be mistaken in concluding that there is a difference in effectiveness between the two methods, for the obtained difference in results may be due *not* to the difference in methods but to something else.

In any study that either describes or tests relationships, there is always the possibility that the relationship shown in the data is, in fact, due to or explained by, something else. If so, then the relationship observed is not at all what it seems and it may lose whatever meaning it appears to have. Many alternative hypotheses may exist, in other words, to explain the outcomes of a study. These alternative explanations are often referred to as "threats to internal validity," and they are what this chapter is about.

What Is Internal Validity?

Perhaps unfortunately, the term "validity" is used in three different ways by researchers. In addition to internal validity, which we discuss in this chapter, you will see reference to instrument (or measurement) validity, as discussed in Chapter Eight, and external (or generalization) validity, as discussed in Chapter Six.

When a study has **internal validity,** it means that any relationship observed between two or more variables should be unambiguous as to what it means rather than being due to "something else." The "something else" may, as we suggested above, be any one (or more) of a number of factors, such as the age or ability of the subjects, the conditions under which the study is conducted, or the type of materials used. If these factors are not in some way or another controlled or accounted for, the researcher can never be sure that they are not the reason for any observed results. Stated differently, internal validity means that observed differences on the dependent variable are directly related to the independent variable, and not due to some other unintended variable.

Consider this example. Suppose a researcher finds a correlation of .80 between height and mathematics test scores for a group of elementary school students (grades 1–5)—that is, the taller students have higher math scores. Such a result is quite misleading. Why? Because it is clearly a by-product of age. Fifth-graders

are taller and better in math than first-graders simply because they are older and more developed. To explore this relationship further is pointless; to let it affect school practice would be absurd.

Or consider a study in which the researcher hypothesizes that, in classes for educationally handicapped students, teacher expectation of student failure is related to amount of disruptive behavior. Suppose the researcher finds a high correlation between these two variables. Should he or she conclude that this is a meaningful relationship? Perhaps. But the correlation might also be explained by another variable, such as the ability level of the class (classes low in ability might be expected to have more disruptive behavior *and* higher teacher expectation of failure).*

In our experience, a systematic consideration of possible threats to internal validity receives the least attention of all the aspects of planning a study. Often, the possibility of such threats is not discussed at all. Probably this is because their consideration is not seen as an essential step in carrying out a study. Researchers cannot avoid deciding on what variables to study, or how the sample will be obtained, or how the data will be collected and analyzed. They can, however, ignore or simply not think about possible alternative explanations for

*Can you suggest any other variables that would explain a high correlation (should it be found) between a teacher's expectation of failure and the amount of disruptive behavior that occurs in class?

the outcomes of a study until after the study is completed—at which point it is almost always too late to do anything about them. Identifying possible threats during the planning stage of a study, on the other hand, can often lead researchers to design ways of eliminating or at least minimizing these threats.

In recent years many useful categories within which to consider possible threats to internal validity have been identified. Although most of these categories were originally designed for application to experimental studies, some apply to other types of methodologies as well. We discuss the most important of these possible threats in this chapter.

Various ways of controlling for these threats have also been identified. Some of these are discussed in the remainder of this chapter; others are discussed in subsequent chapters.

Threats to Internal Validity

SUBJECT CHARACTERISTICS

The selection of people for a study may result in the individuals (or groups) differing from one another in unintended ways that are related to the variables to be studied. This is sometimes referred to as "selection bias," or a **subject characteristics threat.** In our example of teacher expectations and class disruptive behavior, the ability level of the class fits this category. In studies that compare groups, subjects in the groups to be compared may differ on such variables as age, gender, ability, socioeconomic background, and the like. If not controlled, these variables may "explain away" whatever differences between groups are found. The list of such subject characteristics is virtually unlimited. Some examples of subject characteristics that might affect the results of a study include:

- Age
- Strength
- Maturity
- Gender
- Ethnicity
- Coordination
- Speed
- Intelligence
- Vocabulary
- Attitude
- Reading ability
- Fluency
- Manual dexterity
- Socioeconomic status
- Religious beliefs
- Political beliefs

In a particular study, the researcher must decide, based on previous research or experience, which variables are most likely to create problems, and do his or her best to prevent or minimize their effects. In studies

comparing groups, there are several methods of equating groups, which we discuss in Chapters Thirteen and Sixteen. In correlational studies, there are certain statistical techniques that can be used to control such variables, provided information on each variable is obtained. We discuss these techniques in Chapter Fifteen.

LOSS OF SUBJECTS (MORTALITY)

No matter how carefully the subjects of a study are selected, it is common to "lose" some as the study progresses (see Figure 9.1). This is known as a **mortality threat.** For one reason or another (for example, illness, family relocation, or the requirements of other activities), some individuals may drop out of the study. This is especially true in most intervention studies, since they take place over time.

Subjects may be absent during the collection of data or fail to complete tests, questionnaires, or other instruments. Failure to complete instruments is especially a problem in questionnaire studies. In such studies, it is not uncommon to find that 20 percent or more of the subjects involved do not return their forms. Remember, the actual sample in a study is not the total of those selected but only those from whom data are obtained.

Loss of subjects, of course, not only limits generalizability but also can introduce bias—*if* those subjects who are lost would have responded differently from those from whom data were obtained. Many times this is quite likely, since those who do not respond or who are absent probably act this way for a reason. In the example we presented earlier in which the researcher was studying the possible relationship between amount of disruptive behavior by students in class and teacher expectations of student failure, it is likely that those teachers who failed to describe their expectations to the researcher (and who would therefore be "lost" for the purposes of the study) would differ from those who did provide this information in ways affecting disruptive behavior.

In studies comparing groups, loss of subjects probably will not be a problem if the loss is about the same in all groups. But if there are sizable differences between groups in terms of the numbers who drop out, this is certainly a conceivable alternative explanation for whatever findings appear. In comparing students taught by different methods (lecture versus discussion, for example), one might expect the poorer students in each group to be more likely to drop out. If more of the poorer students drop out of either group, the other method may appear more effective than it actually is.

"I'm afraid my thesis is in big trouble! I lost 25 percent of my experimental group."

"Good grief! What did you do to them?"

Figure 9.1 *A Mortality Threat to Internal Validity*

Mortality is perhaps the most difficult of all the threats to internal validity to control. A common misconception is that the threat is eliminated simply by replacing the lost subjects. No matter how this is done—even if they are replaced by new subjects selected randomly—researchers can never be sure that the replacement subjects respond as those who dropped out would have. It is more likely, in fact, that they would *not*. Can you see why?*

It is sometimes possible for a researcher to argue that the loss of subjects in a study is not a problem. This is done by exploring the reasons for such loss, and then offering an argument as to why these reasons are not relevant to the particular study at hand. Absence from class on the day of testing, for example, probably would not in most cases favor a particular group, since it would be incidental rather than intentional—unless the day and time of the testing was announced beforehand.

Another attempt to eliminate the problem of mortality is to provide evidence that the subjects lost were similar to those remaining on pertinent characteristics such as age, gender, and ethnicity, pretest scores, or other variables that presumably might be related to the

study outcomes. While desirable, such evidence can never demonstrate conclusively that those subjects who were lost would not have responded differently from those who remained. When all is said and done, the best solution to the problem of mortality is to do one's best to prevent or minimize the loss of subjects.

Some examples of a mortality threat include the following:

- A high school teacher decides to teach his two English classes differently. His one o'clock class spends a large amount of time writing analyses of plays, whereas his two o'clock class spends much time acting out and discussing portions of the same plays. Halfway through the semester several students in the two o'clock class are excused to participate in the annual school play—thus being "lost" to the study. If they, as a group, are better students than the rest of their class, their loss will lower the performance of the two o'clock class.

- A researcher wishes to study the effects of a new diet on building endurance in long-distance runners. She receives a grant to study, over a two-year period, a group of such runners who are on the track team at several nearby high schools in a large urban high school district. The study is designed to compare runners who are given the new diet with similar runners in the district who are not given the diet. About 5 percent of the runners who receive the diet and about 20 percent of those who do not receive the diet, however, are seniors, and they graduate at the end of the first year of the study. Because seniors are probably better runners, this loss will cause the remaining "no diet" group to appear "weaker" than the "diet" group.

LOCATION

The particular locations in which data are collected, or in which an intervention is carried out, may create alternative explanations for results. This is called a **location threat.** For example, classrooms in which students are taught by, say, the inquiry method may have more resources (texts and other supplies, equipment, parent support, and so on) available to them than classrooms in which students are taught by the lecture method. The classrooms themselves may be larger, have better lighting, or contain more fully equipped workstations. Such variables may account for higher performance by students. In our disruptive behavior versus teacher expec-

---

*Since those who drop out have done so for a reason, their replacements would be different at least in this respect; thus, they may see things differently or feel differently, and their responses may accordingly be different.

Figure 9.2 *Location Might Make a Difference*

tations example, the availability of support (resources, aides, and parent assistance) might explain the correlation between the major variables of interest. Classes with fewer resources might be expected to have more disruptive behavior and higher teacher expectations of failure.

The location in which tests, interviews, or other instruments are administered may affect responses. Parent assessments of their children may be different when done at home than at school. Student performance on tests may be lower if tests are given in noisy or poorly lighted rooms. Observations of student interaction may be affected by the physical arrangement in certain classrooms. Such differences might provide defensible alternative explanations for the results in a particular study.

The best method of control for a location threat is to hold location constant—that is, keep it the same for all participants. When this is not feasible, the researcher should try to ensure that different locations do not systematically favor or jeopardize the hypothesis. This may require the collection of additional descriptions of the various locations.

Here are some examples of a location threat:

- A researcher designs a study to compare the effects of team versus individual teaching of U.S. history on student attitudes toward history. The classrooms in which students are taught by a single teacher have fewer books and materials than the ones in which students are taught by a team of three teachers.
- A researcher decides to interview counseling and special education majors to compare their attitudes toward their respective master's degree programs. Over a three-week period, he manages to interview

all of the students enrolled in the two programs. Although he is able to interview most of the students in one of the university classrooms, scheduling conflicts prevent this classroom from being available for him to interview the remainder. As a result, he interviews 20 of the counseling students in the coffee shop of the student union (see Figure 9.2).

INSTRUMENTATION

The way in which instruments are used may also constitute a threat to the internal validity of a study. As discussed in Chapter Seven, scores from the instruments used in a study can lack evidence of validity. Lack of this kind of validity, however, does not necessarily present a threat to *internal* validity—but it may.*

Instrument Decay. Instrumentation can create problems if the nature of the instrument (including the scoring procedure) is *changed* in some way or another. This is usually referred to as instrument "decay." This is often the case when the instrument is of a type that permits different interpretations of results (as in essay tests), or is especially long or difficult to score, thereby resulting in fatigue of the scorer. Fatigue often happens when a researcher scores a number of tests one after the other; he or she becomes tired and scores the tests differently (for example, more rigorously at first, more

---

*In general, we expect lack of validity of scores to make it *less* likely that any relationships will be found. There are times, however, when "poor" instrumentation can *increase* the chances of "phony" or "spurious" relationships emerging.

Figure 9.4 *A Data Collector Characteristics Threat*

Figure 9.3 *An Example of Instrument Decay*

generously later) at different times. The principal way to control instrument decay is to schedule data collection and/or scoring so as to minimize changes in any of the instruments or scoring procedures.

Here are some examples of instrument decay:

*   A professor grades 100 essay-type final examinations in a five-hour period without taking a break. Each essay encompasses between 10 and 12 pages. He grades the papers of each class in turn and then compares the results (see Figure 9.3).
*   The administration of a large school district changes its method of reporting absences. Only students who are considered truant (absence is unexcused) are reported as absent; students who have a written excuse (from parents or school officials) are not reported. The district reports a 55 percent decrease in absences since the new reporting system has been instituted.

Data Collector Characteristics. The characteristics of the data gatherers—an inevitable part of most instrumentation—can also affect results. Gender, age, ethnicity, language patterns, or other characteristics of the individuals who collect the data in a study may have an effect on the nature of the data they obtain. If these characteristics are related to the variables being investigated, they may offer an alternative explanation for whatever findings appear. Suppose both male and female data gatherers were used in the prior example of a researcher wishing to study the relationship between disruptive behavior and teacher expectations. It might be that the female data collectors would elicit more confessions of an expectation of student failure on the part of teachers and generate more incidents of disruptive

behavior on the part of students during classroom observations than would the males. If so, any correlation between teacher expectations of failure and the amount of disruptive behavior by students might be explained (at least partly) as an artifact of who collected the data.

The primary ways by which this threat is controlled are by using the same data collector(s) throughout; by analyzing data separately for each collector; or (in comparison-group studies) by ensuring that each collector is used equally with all groups (see Figure 9.4).

Data Collector Bias. There is also the possibility that the data collector(s) and/or scorer(s) may unconsciously distort the data in such a way as to make certain outcomes (such as support for the hypothesis) more likely. Examples include some classes being allowed more time on tests than other classes; interviewers asking "leading" questions of some interviewees; observer knowledge of teacher expectations affecting quantity and type of observed behaviors of a class; and judges of student essays favoring (unconsciously) one instructional method over another.

The two principal techniques for handling this problem are to standardize all procedures, which usually requires some sort of training of the data collectors, and planned ignorance—that is, ensuring that the data collectors lack the information they would need to distort results. They should be either unaware of the hypothesis or unable to identify the particular characteristics of the individuals or groups from whom the data are being collected. Data collectors do not need to be told which method group they are observing or testing or how the individuals they are testing performed on other tests.

Some examples of data collector bias are as follows:

- All teachers in a large school district are interviewed regarding their future goals and their views on faculty organizations. The hypothesis is that those planning a career in administration will be more negative in their views on faculty organizations than those planning to continue teaching. Interviews are conducted by the vice principal in each school. Teachers are likely to be influenced by the fact that the person interviewing them is the vice principal, and this may account for the hypothesis being supported.
- An interviewer unconsciously smiles at certain answers to certain questions during an interview.
- An observer with a preference for inquiry methods observes more "attending behavior" in inquiry- compared to noninquiry-identified classes.
- A researcher is aware, when scoring the end-of-study examinations, which students were exposed to which treatment in an intervention study.

TESTING

In intervention studies, where data are collected over a period of time, it is common to test subjects at the beginning of the intervention(s). By testing, we mean the use of any form of instrumentation, not just "tests." If substantial improvement is found in posttest (compared to pretest) scores, the researcher may conclude that this improvement is due to the intervention. An alternative explanation, however, may be that the improvement is due to the use of the pretest. Why is this? Let's look at the reasons.

Suppose the intervention in a particular study involves the use of a new textbook. The researcher wants to see if students score higher on an achievement test if they are taught the subject using this new text than did students who have used the regular text in the past. The researcher pretests the students before the new textbook is introduced and then posttests them at the end of a six-week period. The students may be "alerted" to what is being studied by the questions in the pretest, however, and accordingly make a greater effort to learn the material. This increased effort on the part of the students (rather than the new textbook) could account for the pre-to-post improvement. It may also be that "practice" on the pretest by itself is responsible for the improvement. This is known as a **testing threat.**

Consider another example. Suppose a counselor in a large high school is interested in finding out whether student attitudes toward mental health are affected by a special unit on the subject. He decides to administer an attitude questionnaire to the students before the unit is introduced and then administer it again after the unit is completed. Any change in attitude scores may be due to the students thinking about and discussing their opinions as a result of the pretest rather than as a result of the intervention.

Notice that it is not always the administration of a pretest per se that creates a possible testing effect, but rather the "interaction" that occurs between taking the test and the intervention. A pretest sometimes can make students more "alert" to or "aware" of what may be about to take place, making them more sensitive to and responsive toward the treatment that subsequently occurs. In some studies, the possible effects of pretesting are considered so serious that such testing is eliminated.

A similar problem is created if the instrumentation process permits subjects to figure out the nature of the study. This is most likely to happen in single-group (correlational) studies of attitudes, opinions, or other variables other than ability. Students might be asked

"How'd you do on the final?"

"I killed it! I remembered the questions on the 'diagnostic' test we took at the beginning of the semester."

Figure 9.5 *A Testing Threat to Internal Validity*

their opinions, for example, about teachers and also about different subjects to test the hypothesis that student attitude toward teachers is related to student attitude toward the subjects taught. They may see a connection between the two sets of questions, especially if they are both included on the same form, and answer accordingly (see Figure 9.5).

Some examples of testing threats are as follows:

- A researcher uses exactly the same set of problems to measure change over time in student ability to solve mathematics word problems. The first administration of the test is given at the beginning of a unit of instruction; the second administration is given at the end of the unit of instruction, three weeks later. If improvement in scores occurs, it may be due to sensitization to the problems produced by the first test and the practice effect rather than to any increase in problem-solving ability.
- A researcher incorporates items designed to measure "self-esteem" and "achievement motivation" in the same questionnaire. The respondents may figure out what the researcher is after and react accordingly.
- A researcher uses pre- and posttests of "anxiety level" to compare students given relaxation training with students in a control group. Lower scores for the "relaxation" group on the posttest may be due to the training, but they also may be due to sensitivity (created by the pretest) to the training.

HISTORY

On occasion, one or more unanticipated, and unplanned for, events may occur during the course of a study that

can affect the responses of subjects. Such an event is referred to in educational research as a **history threat.** In the study we suggested of students being taught by the inquiry versus the lecture method, for example, a boring visitor who "dropped in" on, and spoke to, the lecture class just before an upcoming examination would be an example. Should the visitor's remarks in some way discourage or "turn off" students in the lecture class, they might do less well on the examination than if the visitor had not appeared. Another example involves a personal experience of one of the authors of this text. He remembers clearly the day that President John F. Kennedy died, since he had scheduled an examination for that very day. The author's students at that time, stunned into shock by the announcement of the president's death, were unable to take the examination. Any comparison of examination results taken on this day with the examination results of other classes taken on other days would have been meaningless (see Figure 9.6).

Researchers can never be certain that one group has not had experiences that differ from those of other groups. As a result, they should continually be alert to any such influences that may occur (in schools, for example) during the course of a study. As you will see in Chapter Thirteen, some research "designs" handle this threat better than do others.

Two examples of a history threat follow.

- A researcher designs a study to investigate the effects of simulation games on ethnocentrism. She plans to select two high schools to participate in an experiment. Students in both schools will be given a pretest designed to measure their attitudes toward minority groups. School A will then be given the

Figure 9.6 *A History Threat to Internal Validity*

"I don't see how we're supposed to study with that construction noise outside all the time!"

simulation games during their social studies classes over a three-day period while school B sees travel films. Both schools will then be given the same test to see if their attitude toward minority groups has changed. The researcher conducts the study as planned, but a special documentary on racial prejudice is shown in school A between the pretest and the posttest.

- The achievement scores of five elementary schools whose teachers use a cooperative learning approach are compared with those of five schools whose teachers do not use this approach. During the course of the study, the faculty of one of the schools where cooperative learning is not used is engaged in a disruptive conflict with the school principal.

MATURATION

Often, change during an intervention may be due to factors associated with the passing of time rather than to the intervention itself. This is known as a **maturation threat.** Over the course of a semester, for example, very young students, in particular, will change in many ways simply because of aging and experience. Suppose, for example, that a researcher is interested in studying the effect of special "grasping exercises" on the ability of 2-year-olds to manipulate various objects. She finds that such exercises are associated with marked increases in the manipulative ability of the children over a six-month period. Two-year-olds mature very rapidly, how-

ever, and the improvement in their manipulative ability may be due simply to this fact rather than being a result of the grasping exercises. Maturation is a serious threat only in studies using pre-post data for the intervention group, or in studies that span a number of years. The best way to control for maturation is to include a well-selected comparison group in the study (see Figure 9.7).

Examples of a maturation threat are as follows:

- A researcher reports that students in liberal arts colleges become less accepting of authority between their freshman and senior years and attributes this to the many "liberating" experiences they have undergone in college. This may be the reason, but it also may be because they simply have grown older.
- A researcher tests a group of students enrolled in a special class for "students with artistic potential" every year for six years, beginning when they are age 5. She finds that their drawing ability improves markedly over the years.

ATTITUDE OF SUBJECTS

The way in which subjects view a study and their participation in it can create a threat to internal validity. One example is the well-known "Hawthorne effect," first observed in the Hawthorne plant of the Western Electric Company some years ago.[1] It was accidentally discovered that productivity increased not only when

Figure 9.7 *Could Maturation Be at Work Here?*

improvements were made in physical working conditions (such as an increase in the number of coffee breaks and better lighting) but also when such conditions were unintentionally made worse (for instance, the number of coffee breaks was reduced and the lighting was dimmed). The usual explanation for this is that the special attention and recognition received by the workers were responsible; they felt someone cared about them and was trying to help them. This positive effect resulting from increased attention and recognition of subjects has subsequently been referred to as the **Hawthorne effect.**

It has also been suggested that recipients of an experimental treatment may perform better because of the novelty of the treatment rather than because of the specific nature of the treatment. It might be expected, then, that subjects who know they are part of a study may show improvement as a result of a feeling that they are receiving some sort of special treatment—no matter what this treatment may be (see Figure 9.8).

An opposite effect can occur whenever, in intervention studies, the members of the control group receive no treatment at all. As a result, they may become demoralized or resentful and hence perform more poorly than the treatment group. It may thus appear that the experimental group is performing better as a result of the treatment, when this is not the case.

One remedy for these threats is to provide the control or comparison group(s) with a special treatment and/or novelty comparable to that received by the experimental group. While simple in theory, this is not easy to do in most educational settings. Another possibility, in some cases, is to make it easy for students to believe that the treatment is just a regular part of instruction—that is, not part of an experiment. For example, it is sometimes unnecessary to announce that an experiment is being conducted.

Here are examples of a subject attitude threat:

- A researcher decides to investigate the possible reduction in test anxiety by playing classical music during examinations. She randomly selects 10 freshman algebra classes from all such classes in the five high schools in a large urban school district. In five of these classes, she plays classical music softly in the background during the administration of examinations. In the other five (the control group), she plays no music. The students in the control group, however, learn that music is being played in the other classes and express some resentment when their teachers tell them that the music cannot be played in their class. This resentment may actually cause them to be more anxious during exams or intentionally to inflate their anxiety scores.

- A researcher hypothesizes that critical thinking skill is correlated with attention to detail. He administers a somewhat novel test that provides a separate score for each variable ("critical thinking" and "attention

Figure 9.8 *The Attitude of Subjects Can Make a Difference*

"OK, Juan and Alicia, I know you're going to enjoy this. You're going to be a part of a very important study with a professor from the university. Won't that be exciting?"

Figure 9.9 *Regression Rears Its Head*

to detail") to a sample of eighth-graders. The novelty of the test may confuse some students while others may think it is silly. In either case, the scores of these students are likely to be lower on *both* variables because of the format of the test, not because of any lack of ability. It may appear, therefore, that the hypothesis is supported. Neither score is a valid indicator of ability for such students, so this particular attitudinal reaction creates a threat to internal validity.

REGRESSION

A **regression threat** may be present whenever change is studied in a group that is extremely low or high in its pre-intervention performance. Studies in special education are particularly vulnerable to this threat, since the students in such studies are frequently selected on the basis of previous low performance. The regression phenomenon can be explained statistically, but for our purposes it simply describes the fact that a group selected because of unusually low (or high) performance will, on the average, score closer to the mean on subsequent testing, regardless of what transpires in the meantime. Thus, a class of students of markedly low ability may be expected to score higher on posttests regardless of the effect of any intervention to which they are exposed. Like maturation, the use of an equivalent control or comparison group handles this threat—and this

seems to be understood as reflected in published research.

Some examples of a possible regression threat are as follows:

- An Olympic track coach selects the members of her team from those who have the fastest times during the final trials for various events. She finds that their average time decreases the next time they run, however, which she perhaps erroneously attributes to poorer track conditions (see Figure 9.9).
- Those students who score in the lowest 20 percent on a math test are given special help. Six months later their average score on a test involving similar problems has improved, but not necessarily because of the special help.

IMPLEMENTATION

The treatment or method in any experimental study must be administered by someone—the researcher, the teachers involved in the study, a counselor, or some other person. This fact raises the possibility that the experimental group may be treated in ways that are unintended and not a necessary part of the method, yet which give them an advantage of one sort or another. This is known as an **implementation threat.** It can happen in either of two ways.

Threats to Internal Validity in Everyday Life

Consider the following commonly held beliefs:

- Because "failure" often precedes "suicide," it is therefore the cause of "suicide." (probable history and mortality threat)
- Boys are genetically more talented in mathematics than are girls. (probable subject attitude and history threats)
- Girls are genetically more talented in language than are boys. (probable history and subject attitude threats)
- Minority students are less academically able than students from the dominant culture. (probable subject characteristics, subject attitude, location, instrumentation, and history threats).
- People on welfare are lazy. (probable subject characteristics, location, and history threats)
- Schooling makes students rebellious. (probable maturation and history threats)
- A policy of expelling students who don't "behave" improves a school's test scores. (probable mortality threat)
- Indoctrination changes attitude. (probable testing threat)
- So-called miracle drugs cure intellectual retardation. (probable regression threat)
- Smoking marijuana leads eventually to using cocaine and heroin. (probable mortality threat)

The first way an implementation threat can occur is when different individuals are assigned to implement different methods, and these individuals differ in ways related to the outcome. Consider our previous example in which two groups of students are taught by either an inquiry or a lecture method. The inquiry teachers may simply be better teachers than the lecture teachers.

There are a number of ways to control for this possibility. The researcher can attempt to evaluate the individuals who implement each method on pertinent characteristics (such as teaching ability) and then try to equate the treatment groups on these dimensions (for example, by assigning teachers of equivalent ability to each group). Clearly, this is a difficult and time-consuming task. Another control is to require that each method be taught by all teachers in the study. Where feasible, this is a preferable solution, though it also is vulnerable to the possibility that some teachers may have different abilities to implement the different methods. Still another control is to use *several* different individuals to implement each method, thereby reducing the chances of an advantage to either method.

The second way an implementation threat can occur is when some individuals have a personal bias in favor of one method over the other. Their preference for the method, rather than the method itself, may account for the superior performance of students taught by that method. This is a good reason why a researcher should, if at all possible, *not* be one of the individuals who implements a method in an intervention study. It is sometimes possible to keep individuals who are implementers ignorant of the nature of a study, but it is generally very difficult—in part because teachers or others involved in a study will usually need to be given a rationale for their participation. One solution for this is to allow individuals to choose the method they wish to implement, but this creates the possibility of differences in characteristics discussed above. An alternative is to have all methods used by all implementers, but with their preferences known beforehand. Note that preference for a method as a *result* of using it does not constitute a threat—it is simply one of the by-products of the method itself. This is also true of other by-products. If teacher skill or parent involvement, for example, improves as a *result* of the method, it would not constitute a threat. Finally, the researcher can observe in an attempt to see that the methods are administered as intended.

Examples of an implementation threat are as follows:

- A researcher is interested in studying the effects of a new diet on the physical agility of young children. After obtaining the permission of the parents of the children to be involved, all of whom are first-graders, he randomly assigns the children to an experimental group and a control group. The experimental group is to try the new diet for a period of three months, and the control group is to stay with its regular diet. The researcher overlooks the fact, however, that the teacher of the experimental group is an accomplished instructor of some five years' experience, while the instructor of the control group is a first-year teacher, newly appointed.
- A group of clients who stutter is given a relatively new method of therapy called "generalization training." Both client and therapist interact with people in

Figure 9.10 *Illustration of Threats to Internal Validity*

Note: We are not implying that any of these statements are necessarily true; our guess is that some are and some are not.

*This seems unlikely.

†If these teacher characteristics are *a result* of the type of school, then they do not constitute a threat.

the "real world" as part of the therapy. After six months of receiving therapy, the fluency of these clients is compared with that of a group receiving traditional "in-the-office" therapy. Speech therapists who use new methods are likely to be more generally competent than those working with the comparison group. If so, greater improvement for the "generalization" group may be due not to the new method but rather to the skill of the therapist.

Figure 9.10 illustrates each of the threats we have discussed.

Some Thoughts About Meta-Analysis

As we mentioned in Chapter Five, the main argument in favor of doing a meta-analysis is that the weaknesses in individual studies should balance out or be reduced by combining the results of a series of studies. In short, researchers who do a meta-analysis attempt to remedy the shortcomings of any particular study by statistically combining the results of several (hopefully many) studies that were conducted on the same topic. Thus, the threats to internal validity that we discussed in this chapter should be reduced and generalizability should be enhanced.

How is this done? Essentially by calculating what is called "effect size" (see Chapter Twelve). In its simplest form, researchers conducting meta-analysis do their best to locate all of the studies on a particular topic (i.e., all of the studies having the same independent variable). Once located, effect sizes and an overall average effect size for each dependent variable are calculated.* As an example, Vockell and Asher report an average delta (Δ) of .80 on the effectiveness of cooperative learning.†

*This is not always easy to do. Frequently, published reports lack the necessary information, although it can sometimes be deduced from what is reported.

†E. L. Vockell and J. W. Asher (1995). *Educational research,* 2nd ed. Englewood Cliffs, NJ: Prentice Hall, p. 361.

As we have mentioned, meta-analysis is a way of quantifying replications of a study. It is important to note, however, that the term "replication" is used rather loosely in this context, since the studies that the researcher(s) has collected may have little in common except that they all have the same independent variable. Our concerns are twofold: Merely obtaining several studies, even if they all do have the same independent variable, does not mean that they will necessarily balance out each other's weaknesses—they might all have the *same* weakness. Secondly, in doing a meta-analysis, equal weight is given to both good *and bad* studies—that is, no distinction is made between studies that have been well-designed and conducted and those that have not been so well-designed and/or conducted. Results of a well-designed study in which the researchers used a large random sample, for example, would count the same as results from a poorly controlled study in which researchers used a convenience or purposive sample.

A partial solution to these problems that we support is to combine meta-analysis with judgmental review. This has been done by judging studies as good or bad, and comparing the results; sometimes they agree. If, however, there is a sufficient number of good studies (we would argue for a minimum of seven), we see little to be gained by including poor ones.

Meta-analyses are here to stay, and there is little question that they can provide the research community with valuable information. But we do not think excessive enthusiasm for the technique is warranted. Like many things, it is a tool, not a panacea.

FACTORS THAT REDUCE THE LIKELIHOOD OF FINDING A RELATIONSHIP

In many studies, the various factors we have discussed could also serve to *reduce,* or even prevent, the chances of a relationship being found. For example, if the methods (the treatment) in a study are not adequately implemented—that is, adequately tried—the effect of actual differences between them on outcomes may be obscured. Similarly, if the members of a control or comparison group become "aware" of the experimental treatment, they may increase their efforts because they feel "left out," thereby reducing real differences in achievement between treatment groups that otherwise would be seen. Sometimes, teachers of a control group may unwittingly give some sort of "compensation" to motivate the members of their group, thereby lessening the impact of the experimental treatment. Finally, the use of instruments that produce unreliable scores and/or the use of small samples may result in a reduced likelihood of a relationship or relationships being observed.

How Can a Researcher Minimize These Threats to Internal Validity?

As we have discussed the various threats to internal validity, we have suggested a number of techniques or procedures that researchers can employ to control or minimize the possible effects of these threats. Essen-

Table 9.1 *General Techniques for Controlling Threats to Internal Validity*

	Technique			
Threat	**Standardize Conditions**	**Obtain More Information on Subjects**	**Obtain More Information on Details**	**Choose an Appropriate Design**
Subject characteristics		X		X
Mortality		X		X
Location	X		X	X
Instrumentation	X		X	
Testing				X
History			X	X
Maturation		X		X
Subject attitude	X		X	X
Regression		X		X
Implementation	X		X	X

tially, they boil down to four alternatives. A researcher can try to do any or all of the following.

1. Standardize the conditions under which the study occurs—such as the way(s) in which the treatment is implemented (in intervention studies), the way(s) in which the data are collected, and so on. This helps control for location, instrumentation, subject attitude, and implementer threats.

2. Obtain more information on the subjects of the study—that is, on relevant characteristics of the subjects—and use that information in analyzing and interpreting results. This helps control for a subject characteristics threat and (possibly) a mortality threat.

3. Obtain more information on the details of the study—that is, where and when it takes place, extraneous events that occur, and so on. This helps control for location, instrumentation, history, subject attitude, and implementation threats.

4. Choose an appropriate design. The proper design can do much to control these threats to internal validity.

Because control by design applies primarily to experimental and causal-comparative studies, we shall discuss it in detail in Chapters Thirteen and Sixteen. The four alternatives are summarized in Table 9.1

We want to end this chapter by emphasizing two things. The first is that the likelihood of any of these various threats to internal validity occurring can be greatly reduced by planning; the second is that such planning often requires collecting additional information before a study begins (or while it is taking place). It is often too late to consider how to control these threats once the data in a study have been collected.

Go back to the **Interactive and Applied Learning Tools** feature at the beginning of the chapter for a listing of interactive and applied activities. Go to the **Online Learning Center** at www.mhhe.com/fraenkel5e or your **Interactive Student CD-ROM** to take practice quizzes and receive immediate feedback, practice with key terms, review chapter content and main ideas, and find annotated Web links.

Main Points

THE MEANING OF "INTERNAL VALIDITY"

- When a study lacks internal validity, one or more alternative hypotheses exist to explain the outcomes of the study. These alternative hypotheses are referred to by researchers as "threats to internal validity."
- When a study has internal validity, it means that any relationship observed between two or more variables is unambiguous as to what it means, rather than being due to something else.

THREATS TO INTERNAL VALIDITY

- Some of the more common threats to internal validity are differences in subject characteristics, mortality, location, instrumentation, testing, history, maturation, attitude of subjects, regression, and implementation.
- The selection of people for a study may result in the individuals or groups differing (i.e., the characteristics of the subjects may differ) from one another in unintended ways that are related to the variables to be studied.
- No matter how carefully the subjects of a study (the sample) are selected, it is common to lose some of them as the study progresses. This is known as "mortality." Such a loss of subjects may affect the outcomes of a study.
- The particular locations in which data are collected, or in which an intervention is carried out, may create alternative explanations for any results that are obtained.
- The way in which instruments are used may also constitute a threat to the internal validity of a study. Possible instrumentation threats include changes in the instrument, characteristics of the data collector(s), and/or bias on the part of the data collectors.
- The use of a pretest in intervention studies sometimes may create a "practice effect" that can affect the results of a study. A pretest can also sometimes affect the way subjects respond to an intervention.
- On occasion, one or more unanticipated, and unplanned for, events may occur during the course of a study that can affect the responses of subjects. This is known as a history threat.
- Sometimes change during an intervention study may be due more to factors associated with the passing of time than to the intervention itself. This is known as a maturation threat.
- The attitude of subjects toward a study (and their participation in it) can create a threat to internal validity.
- When subjects are given increased attention and recognition because they are participating in a study, their responses may be affected. This is known as the Hawthorne effect.
- Whenever a group is selected because of unusually high or low performance on a pretest, it will, on the average, score closer to the mean on subsequent testing, regardless of what transpires in the meantime. This is called a regression threat.

- Whenever an experimental group is treated in ways that are unintended and not a necessary part of the method being studied, an implementation threat can occur.

CONTROLLING THREATS TO INTERNAL VALIDITY

- There are a number of techniques or procedures that researchers can use to control or minimize threats to internal validity. Essentially they boil down to four alternatives: (1) standardizing the conditions under which the study occurs; (2) obtaining and using more information on the subjects of the study; (3) obtaining and using more information on the details of the study; and (4) choosing an appropriate design.

Key Terms

Data collector bias 182

Data collector characteristics threat 182

Hawthorne effect 186

History threat 184

Implementation threat 187

Instrument decay 181

Instrumentation threat 181

Internal validity 178

Location threat 180

Maturation threat 185

Mortality threat 179

Regression threat 187

Subject attitude threat 185

Subject characteristics threat 179

Testing threat 183

Threats to internal validity 179

For Discussion

1. Can a researcher prove conclusively that a study has internal validity? Explain.
2. In Chapter Six, we discussed the concept of "external validity." In what ways, if any, are internal and external validity related? Can a study have internal validity, but not external validity? If so, how? What about the reverse?
3. Students often confuse the concept of internal validity with the idea of instrument validity. How would you explain the difference between the two?
4. What threat (or threats) to internal validity might exist in each of the following?
   a. A researcher decides to try out a new mathematics curriculum in a nearby elementary school and to compare student achievement in math with that of students in another elementary school using the regular curriculum. The researcher is not aware, however, that the students in the "new curriculum" school have computers to use in their classrooms.
   b. A researcher wishes to compare two different kinds of textbooks in two high school chemistry classes over a semester. She finds that 20 percent of one group and 10 percent of the other group are absent during the administration of unit tests.
   c. In a study investigating the possible relationship between marital status and perceived social changes during the last five years, men and women interviewers get different reactions from female respondents to the same questions.
   d. Teachers of an experimental English curriculum as well as teachers of the regular curriculum administer both pre- and posttests to their own students.
   e. Eighth-grade students who volunteer to tutor third-graders in reading show greater improvement in their own reading scores than a comparison group that does not participate in tutoring.
   f. A researcher compares the effects of weekly individual and group counseling on the improvement of study habits. Each week the students counseled as a group fill out questionnaires on their progress at the end of their meetings. The students counseled individually, however, fill out the questionnaires at home.
   g. Those students who score in the bottom 10 percent academically in a school in an economically depressed area are selected for a special program of enrichment.

The program includes special games, extra materials, special "snacks," specially colored materials to use, and new books. The students score substantially higher on achievement tests six months after the program is instituted.

h. A group of elderly people are asked to fill out a questionnaire designed to investigate the possible relationship between "activity level" and "sense of life satisfaction."

5. How could you determine whether the threats you identified in each of the situations in question 4 actually exist?
6. Which threats discussed in this chapter do you think are the most important for a researcher to consider? Why? Which do you think would be the most difficult to control? Explain.

Notes

1. F. J. Roethlisberger and W. J. Dickson (1939). *Management and the worker.* Cambridge, MA: Harvard University Press.

Research Exercise Nine: Internal Validity

State the question or hypothesis of your study at the top of Problem Sheet 9. In the spaces indicated, place an *X* after each of the threats to internal validity that apply to your study, explain why they are threats, and describe how you intend to control for those most likely to occur (i.e., prevent them from affecting the outcome of your study).

Problem Sheet 9

Internal Validity

1. My question or hypothesis is: _____

   _____

2. I have placed an *X* in the blank in front of four of the threats listed below that apply to my study. I explain why I think each one is a problem and then explain how I would attempt to control for the threat.

   Threats: _____ Subject characteristics _____ Mortality _____ Location

   _____ Instrumentation _____ Testing _____ History

   _____ Maturation _____ Subject attitude _____ Regression

   _____ Implementation _____ Other

Threat 1: _____ Why? _____

_____

I will control by _____

_____

Threat 2: _____ Why? _____

_____

I will control by _____

_____

Threat 3: _____ Why? _____

_____

I will control by _____

_____

Threat 4: _____ Why? _____

_____

I will control by _____

_____

An electronic version of this Problem Sheet that you can fill in and print, save, or e-mail is available on the **Online Learning Center** at www.mhhe.com/ fraenkel5e and on your **Interactive Student CD-ROM.**

A full-sized version of this Problem Sheet that you can fill in or photocopy is in your **Student Workbook.**

Data Analysis

Part Three introduces the subject of statistics—important tools that
are frequently used by researchers in the analysis of their data.
Chapter Ten presents a discussion of descriptive statistics and provides a number of techniques for summarizing both quantitative and
categorical data. Chapter Eleven deals with inferential statistics—how
to determine whether an outcome can be generalized or not—and
briefly discusses the most commonly used inferential statistics.
Chapter Twelve then places what we have presented in the previous
two chapters in perspective. We provide some techniques for comparing groups and for relating variables within a group. We conclude
the chapter with a summary of recommendations for using both
descriptive and inferential statistics.

Descriptive Statistics

CHAPTER 10

A Normal Distribution?

Descriptive Statistics

Statistics Versus Parameters

Techniques for Summarizing Categorical Data

Two Fundamental Types of Numerical Data

Quantitative Data
Categorical Data

Techniques for Summarizing Quantitative Data

Frequency Polygons
Skewed Polygons
The Normal Curve
Averages
Spreads
Standard Scores and the Normal Curve
Correlation

Objectives

Reading this chapter should enable you to:

· Explain *the difference between a statistic and a parameter.*
· Differentiate *between categorical and quantitative data and give an example of each.*
· Construct *a frequency polygon from data.*
· Explain *what is meant by the terms "normal distribution" and "normal curve."*
· Calculate *the mean, median, and mode for a frequency distribution of data.*
· Calculate *the range and standard deviation for a frequency distribution of data.*
· Explain *what a five-number summary is.*
· Explain *what a boxplot displays.*
· Explain *how any particular score in a normal distribution can be interpreted in standard deviation units.*
· Explain *what a "z score" is and tell why it is advantageous to be able to express scores in z score terms.*
· Explain *how to interpret a normal distribution.*
· Construct *and interpret a scatterplot.*
· Explain *more fully what a correlation coefficient is.*
· Calculate *a Pearson correlation coefficient.*
· Prepare *and interpret a frequency table, a bar graph, and a pie chart.*
· Prepare *and interpret a crossbreak table.*

Interactive and Applied Learning

After, or while reading this chapter:

Go to the Study Guide on the Online Learning Center at www.mhhe.com/fraenkel5e or Interactive Student CD-ROM to:
· Read the Statistics Primer

Go to your Interactive Student CD-ROM to:
· Familiarize yourself with your statistics package
· Learn More About Techniques for Summarizing Quantitative and Categorical Data

Go to your Interactive Student CD-ROM or Student Workbook to do the following activities:
· Activity 10.1: Construct a Frequency Polygon
· Activity 10.2: Comparing Frequency Polygons
· Activity 10.3: Calculating Averages
· Activity 10.4: Calculating the Standard Deviation
· Activity 10.5: Calculating a Correlation Coefficient
· Activity 10.6: Analyzing Crossbreak Tables
· Activity 10.7: Comparing z-Scores

Tim Williams and Jack Martinez have just come from their 9:00 A.M. statistics class.

"I need some coffee," says Tim.

"Yeah, me too," says Jack. "That was a pretty heavy session."

"Let's go over some of the stuff Dr. Fraenkel talked about. He gave some pretty good examples, but it doesn't hurt to see if we can come up with some on our own."

"I agree. You know, I think I finally understand what standard deviation is all about."

"You do? Hey, good going. How about explaining it to me then? I don't quite get it."

"Piece of cake. Think of it this way . . ."

Maybe not exactly a "piece of cake," but we think you'll find the concept fairly easy to understand once you've studied the ideas in this chapter. Read on.

Statistics Versus Parameters

The major advantage of descriptive statistics is that they permit researchers to describe the information contained in many, many scores with just a few indices, such as the mean or median (more about these in a moment). When such indices are calculated for a sample drawn from a population, they are called **statistics;** when they are calculated from the entire population, they are called **parameters.** Because most educational research involves data from samples rather than from populations, we refer mainly to statistics in the remainder of this chapter. We present the most commonly used techniques for summarizing such data. Some form of summary is essential to interpret data collected on any variable—a long list of scores or categorical representations is simply unmanageable.

Two Fundamental Types of Numerical Data

In Chapter Seven, we presented a number of instruments used in educational research. The researcher's intention in using these instruments is to collect information of some sort—measures of abilities, attitudes, beliefs, reactions, and so forth—that will enable him or her to draw some conclusions about the sample of individuals being studied.

As we have seen, such information can be collected in several ways, but it can be reported in only three ways: through words, through numbers, and sometimes through graphs or charts that show patterns or describe relationships. In certain types of research, such as interviews, ethnographic studies, or case studies, researchers often try to describe their findings through a narrative description of some sort. Their intent is not to reduce the information to numerical form but to present it in a descriptive form, and often as richly as possible. We

give some examples of this method of reporting information in Chapters Nineteen, Twenty, and Twenty-One. In this chapter, however, we concentrate on numerical ways of reporting information.

Much of the information reported in educational research consists of numbers of some sort—test scores, percentages, grade point averages, ratings, frequencies, and the like. The reason is an obvious one—numbers are a useful way to simplify information. Numerical information, usually referred to as *data,* can be classified in one of two basic ways: as either categorical or quantitative data.

Just as there are categorical and quantitative variables (see Chapter Three), there are two types of numerical data. Categorical data differ in *kind,* but not in degree or amount. Quantitative data, on the other hand, do differ in *degree* or *amount.*

QUANTITATIVE DATA

Quantitative data are obtained when the variable being studied is measured along a scale that indicates how much of the variable is present. Quantitative data are reported in terms of scores. Higher scores indicate that more of the variable (such as weight, academic ability, self-esteem, or interest in mathematics) is present than do lower scores. Some examples of quantitative data follow.

- The amount of money spent on sports equipment by various schools in a particular district in a semester (the variable is *amount of money spent on sports equipment*).
- SAT scores (the variable is *scholastic aptitude*).
- The temperatures recorded each day during the months of September through December in Omaha, Nebraska, in a given year (the variable is *temperature*).
- The anxiety scores of all first-year students enrolled at San Francisco State University in 2002 (the variable is *anxiety*).

CATEGORICAL DATA

Categorical data simply indicate the total number of objects, individuals, or events a researcher finds in a particular category. Thus, a researcher who reports the number of people for or against a particular government policy, or the number of students completing a program in successive years, is reporting categorical data. Notice that what the researcher is looking for is the frequency of certain characteristics, objects, individuals, or events. Many times it is useful, however, to convert these frequencies into percentages. Some examples of categorical data follow.

- The representation of each ethnic group in a school (the variable is *ethnicity*); for example, Caucasian, 1462 (41 percent); black, 853 (24 percent); Hispanic, 760 (21 percent); Asian, 530 (15 percent).
- The number of male and female students in a chemistry class (the variable is *gender*).
- The number of teachers in a large school district who use (1) the lecture and (2) the discussion method (the variable is *teaching method*).
- The number of each type of tool found in a workroom (the variable is *type of tool*).
- The number of each kind of merchandise found in a large department store (the variable is *type of merchandise*).

You may find it helpful at this point to refer back to Figure 7.25 in Chapter Seven. The ordinal, interval, and ratio scales all pertain to quantitative data; the nominal scale pertains to categorical data.

Techniques for Summarizing Quantitative Data

Note that none of the techniques in this section for summarizing quantitative data is appropriate for categorical data; they are for use only with quantitative data.

FREQUENCY POLYGONS

Listed below are the scores of a group of 50 students on a mid-semester biology test.

64, 27, 61, 56, 52, 51, 3, 15, 6, 34, 6, 17, 27, 17, 24, 64, 31, 29, 31, 29, 31, 29, 29, 31, 31, 29, 61, 59, 56,34, 59, 51, 38, 38, 38, 38, 34, 36, 36, 34, 34, 36, 21, 21, 24, 25, 27, 27, 27, 63

How many students received a score of 34? Did most of the students receive a score above 50? How many received a score below 30? As you can see, when the data are simply listed in no apparent order, as they are here, it is difficult to tell.

Table 10.1 *Example of a Frequency Distribution*[a]

Raw Score	Frequency
64	2
63	1
61	2
59	2
56	2
52	1
51	2
38	4
36	3
34	5
31	5
29	5
27	5
25	1
24	2
21	2
17	2
15	1
6	2
3	1
	$n = 50$

[a]Technically, the table should include all scores, including those for which there are zero frequencies. We have eliminated those to simplify the presentation.

To make any sense out of this data, we must put it into some sort of order. One of the most common ways to do this is to prepare a **frequency distribution.** This is done by listing the scores in rank order from high to low, with tallies to indicate the number of subjects receiving each score (see Table 10.1). Often, the scores in a distribution are grouped into intervals. This results in a **grouped frequency distribution,** as shown in Table 10.2.

Although frequency distributions like the ones in Tables 10.1 and 10.2 can be quite informative, often the information they contain is hard to visualize. To further the understanding and interpretation of quantitative data, it is helpful to present it in a graph. One such graphical display is known as a **frequency polygon.** Figure 10.1 presents a frequency polygon of the data in Table 10.2

The steps involved in the construction of a frequency polygon are as follows:

1. List all scores in order of size, and tally how many students receive each score. Group scores, if necessary, into intervals.*

*Grouping scores into intervals such as five or more is often necessary when there are a large number of scores in the distribution. Generally, 12 to 15 intervals on the *X* axis is recommended.

Table 10.2 *Example of a Grouped Frequency Distribution*

Raw Scores (Intervals of Five)	Frequency
60–64	5
55–59	4
50–54	3
45–49	0
40–44	0
35–39	7
30–34	10
25–29	11
20–24	4
15–19	3
10–14	0
5– 9	2
0– 4	1
	$n = 50$

2. Label the horizontal axis by placing all of the possible scores (or groupings) on that axis, at equal intervals, starting with the lowest score on the left.
3. Label the vertical axis by indicating frequencies, at equal intervals, starting with zero.
4. For each score (or grouping of scores), find the point where it intersects with its frequency of occurrence, and place a dot at that point. Remember that each score (or grouping of scores) with zero frequency must still be plotted.
5. Connect all the dots with a straight line.

As you can see by looking at Figure 10.1, the fact that a large number of the students scored in the middle of this distribution is illustrated quite nicely.[†]

SKEWED POLYGONS

Data can be distributed in almost any shape. If a researcher obtains a set of data in which many individuals received low scores, for example, the shape of the distribution would look something like the frequency polygon shown in Figure 10.2. As you can see, in this particular distribution, only a few individuals received the higher scores. The frequency polygon in Figure 10.2 is said to be **positively skewed** because the tail of the distribution trails off to the right, in the direction of the higher (more *positive*) score values. Suppose the reverse were true. Imagine that a researcher obtained a set of data in which few individuals received relatively low

[†]A common mistake of students is to treat the vertical axis as if the numbers represented specific individuals. They do not. They represent *frequencies.* Each number on the vertical axis is used to plot the number of individuals at each score. In Figure 10.1, the dot above the interval 25–29 shows that 11 persons scored somewhere within the interval 25–29.

Figure 10.1 *Example of a Frequency Polygon*

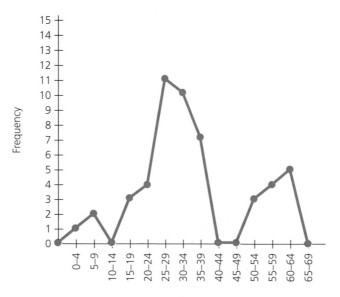

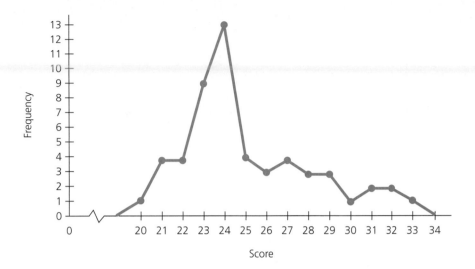

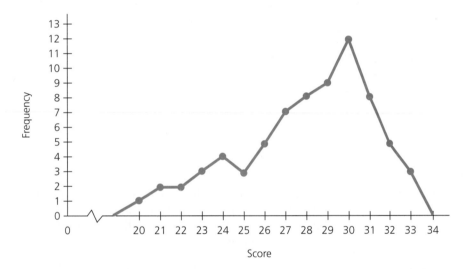

scores. Then the shape of the distribution would look like the frequency polygon in Figure 10.3. This polygon is said to be **negatively skewed,** since the longer tail of the distribution goes off to the left.

Frequency polygons are particularly useful in comparing two (or sometimes more) groups. In Chapter Seven, Table 7.3, we presented some hypothetical results of a study involving a comparison of two counseling methods. Figure 10.4 shows the polygons constructed using the data from Table 7.3.

This figure reveals several important findings. First, it is evident that method B resulted in higher scores, overall, than did method A. Second, it is clear that the scores for method B are more spread out. Third, it is

clear that the reason for method B being higher overall is not that there are fewer scores at the low end of the scale (although this might have happened, it did not). In fact, the groups are almost identical in the number of scores below 61: A=10, B=12. The reason method B is higher overall is that there were fewer cases in the middle range of the scores (between 60 and 75), and more cases above 75. If this is not clear to you, study the shaded areas in the figure. Many times we want to know not only which group is higher overall but also where the differences are. In this example we see that method B results in more variability and that it results in a substantial number of scores higher than those in method A.

Figure 10.4 *Two Frequency Polygons Compared*

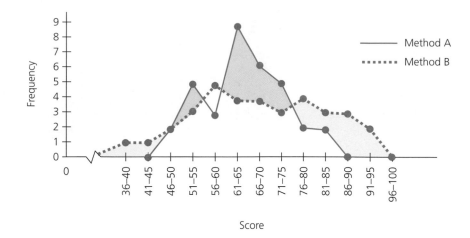

THE NORMAL CURVE

Often researchers draw a smooth curve instead of the series of straight lines in a frequency polygon. The smooth curve suggests that we are not just connecting a series of dots (that is, the actual frequencies of scores in a particular distribution), but rather showing a generalized distribution of scores that is not limited to one specific set of data. These smooth curves are known as **distribution curves.**

Many distributions of data tend to follow a certain specific shape of distribution curve called a **normal distribution.** When a distribution curve is normal, the large majority of the scores are concentrated in the middle of the distribution, and the scores decrease in frequency the farther away from the middle they are, as shown in Figure 10.5

The normal curve is based on a precise mathematical equation. As you can see, it is symmetrical and bell-shaped. The distribution of some human characteristics, such as height and weight, approximate such a curve, while many others, such as spatial ability, manual dex-

terity, and creativity, are often assumed to do so. The normal curve is very useful to researchers, and we shall discuss it in more detail later in the chapter.

AVERAGES

Averages, or **measures of central tendency,** enable a researcher to summarize the data in a frequency distribution with a single number. The three most commonly used averages are the mode, the median, and the mean. Each represents a type of average or typical score attained by a group of individuals on some measure.

The Mode. The **mode** is the most frequent score in a distribution—that is, the score attained by more students than any other score. In the following distribution, what is the mode?

$$25, 20, 19, 17, 16, 16, 16,$$
$$14, 14, 11, 10, 9, 9$$

The mode is 16. What about this distribution?

$$25, 24, 24, 23, 22, 20, 19, 19, 18, 11, 10$$

This distribution (called a bimodal distribution) has two modes, 24 and 19. Because the mode really doesn't tell us very much about a distribution, however, it is not used very often in educational research.

The Median. The **median** is the point below and above which 50 percent of the scores in a distribution fall—in short, the midpoint. In a distribution that contains an uneven number of scores, the median is the middlemost score (provided that the scores are listed in order). Thus, in the distribution 5, 4, 3, 2, 1, the median

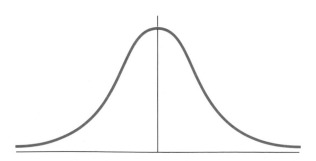

Figure 10.5 *The Normal Curve*

is 3. In a distribution that contains an even number of scores, the median is the point halfway between the two middlemost scores. Thus, in the distribution 70, 74, 82, 86, 88, 90, the median is 84. Hence, the median is not necessarily one of the actual scores in the distribution being summarized.

Note that two very different distributions might have the same median, as shown below:

Distribution 1: 98, 90, 84, 82, 76
Distribution 2: 90, 87, 84, 65, 41

In both distributions, the median is 84.

It may look like the median is fairly easy to determine. This is usually the case with ungrouped data. For grouped data, calculating the median requires somewhat more work. It can, however, be estimated by locating the score that has half of the area under the frequency polygon above it and half below it.

The median is the most appropriate average to calculate when the data result in skewed distributions.

The Mean. The **mean** is another average of all the scores in a distribution.* It is determined by adding up all of the scores and then dividing this sum by the total number of scores. The mean of a distribution containing scores of 52, 68, 74, 86, 95, and 105, therefore, is 80. How did we determine this? We simply added up all the scores, which came to 480, and then divided this sum by 6, the total number of scores. In symbolic form, the formula for computing the mean looks like this:

$$\bar{X} = \frac{\Sigma X}{n}$$

where Σ represents "sum of," X represents any raw score value, n represents the total number of scores, and $\bar{X}$ represents the mean.

Table 10.3 presents a frequency distribution of scores on a test and each of the above measures of central tendency. As you can see, each of these indices tells us something a little different. The most frequent score was 62, but would we want to say that this was the most typical score? Probably not. The median of the scores was 64.5. The mean was 66.7. Perhaps the mean is the best description of the distribution of scores, but it, too, is not totally satisfactory because the distribution is

*Actually, there are several kinds of means (geometric, harmonic, etc.), but their use is specialized and infrequent. We refer here to the arithmetic mean.

Table 10.3 *Example of the Mode, Median, and Mean in a Distribution*

Raw Score	Frequency
98	1
97	1
91	2
85	1
80	5
77	7
72	5
65	3
64	7
62	10
58	3
45	2
33	1
11	1
5	1
	$n = 50$

Mode=62; median=64.5; mean=66.7

skewed. Table 10.3 shows that these indices are only *summaries* of all the scores in a distribution and often do not have the same value. They are not intended to show variation or spread.

Which of the three averages (measures of central tendency), then, is best? It depends. The mean is the only one of the three that uses all the information in a distribution, since every score is used in calculating it, and it is generally preferred over the other two measures. However, it tends to be unduly influenced by extreme scores. (Can you see why?) On occasion, therefore, the median gives a more accurate indication of the typical score in a distribution. Suppose, for example, that the yearly salaries earned by various workers in a small business were as shown in Table 10.4.

The mean of these salaries is $75,000. Would it be correct to say that this is the average yearly salary paid in this company? Obviously it would not. The extremely high salary paid to the owner of the company "inflates" the mean, so to speak. Using it as a summary figure to indicate the average yearly salary would give an erroneous impression. In this instance, the median would be the more appropriate average to calculate, since it would not be as affected by the owner's salary. The median is $27,000, a far more accurate indication of the typical salary for the year.

Table 10.4 *Yearly Salaries of Workers in a Small Business*

Mr. Davis	$ 10,500
Mr. Thompson	20,000
Ms. Angelo	22,500
Mr. Schmidt	24,000
Ms. Wills	26,000
Ms. Brown	28,000
Mr. Greene	36,000
Mr. Adams	43,000
Ms. Franklin	65,000
Mr. Payson (owner)	475,000

SPREADS

While measures of central tendency are useful statistics for summarizing the scores in a distribution, they are not sufficient. Two distributions may have identical means and medians, for example, yet be quite different in other ways. For example, consider these two distributions:

Distribution A: 19, 20, 25, 32, 39
Distribution B: 2, 3, 25, 30, 75

The mean in both of these distributions is 27, and the median in both is 25. Yet you can see that the distribu-

tions differ considerably. In distribution A, the scores are closer together, and tend to cluster around the mean. In distribution B, they are much more spread out. Hence the two distributions differ in what statisticians call **variability.** See Figure 10.7 for further examples.

Thus, measures of central tendency, when presented without any accompanying information of how spread out or dispersed the data are, can be misleading. To say that the average annual income of all the players in the National Basketball Association (NBA) in 1998 was $275,000.00 hides the fact that some players earned far less while someone like Michael Jordan earned more than 5 million. The distribution of players' salaries was skewed to the right and very spread out. Knowing only the mean gives us an inadequate description of the distribution of salaries for players in the NBA (see Figure 10.6).

There is a need, therefore, for measures researchers can use to describe the *spread,* or variability, that exists within a distribution. Let us consider three—the interquartile range, the overall range, and the standard deviation.

Quartiles and the Five-Number Summary. When a distribution is skewed, both the variability and the general shape of the distribution can be described by reporting several *percentiles*. We mentioned percentiles earlier in Chapter Seven. A **percentile** in a set of num-

Figure 10.6 *Averages Can Be Misleading!*

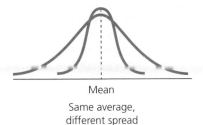 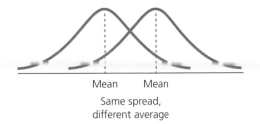

Mean

Same average,
different spread

Mean   Mean

Same spread,
different average

Figure 10.7 *Different Distributions Compared with Respect to Averages and Spreads*

bers is a value such that a certain percentage of the numbers fall below it and the rest of the numbers fall above it.

You may have encountered percentiles if you have ever taken a standardized test such as the SAT and received a report saying "Raw score 630, percentile 84." You received a score of 630, but perhaps more useful is the fact that 84 percent of those who took the examination scored lower than you did.

The median is the 50th percentile. Other percentiles that are important are the 25th percentile, also known as the first quartile (Q_1), and the 75th percentile, the third quartile (Q_3). A useful way to describe a skewed distribution, therefore, is to give what is known as a **five-number summary,** consisting of the lowest score, Q_1, the median, Q_3, and the highest score. The inter-quartile range (IQR) is the difference between the third and first quartiles ($Q_3 - Q_1 = IQR$).

Boxplots. The five-number summary of a distribution can be graphically portrayed by means of a **boxplot.** Boxplots are especially useful in comparing two or more distributions. Figure 10.8 gives boxplots for the distributions of the midterm scores of two classes taking the same biology exam. Each central box has its ends at the quartiles, and the median is marked by the line within the box. The "whiskers" at either end extend to the lowest and highest scores.*

Figure 10.8 permits an immediate comparison between the two classes. Overall, class B did better, but the upper whiskers illustrate that class A had the student with the highest score. Figure 10.8 is but another example of how effectively graphs can convey information.

Though the five-number summary is an extremely useful numerical description of a distribution, it is not the most common. That accolade belongs to a combination of the mean (a measure of center) and the standard deviation (a measure of spread). The *standard deviation*

*Boxplots are sometimes called "box-and-whiskers" diagrams.

and its brother, the *variance,* measure the spread of scores from the mean. They should only be used in conjunction with the mean.

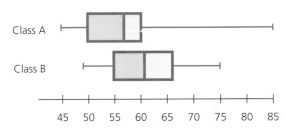

Class A

Class B

45 50 55 60 65 70 75 80 85

Figure 10.8 *Boxplots*

The Range. The overall **range** represents the distance between the highest and lowest scores in a distribution. Thus, if the highest score in a distribution is 89 and the lowest is 11, the range would be 89 – 11, or 78. Because it involves only the two most extreme scores in a distribution, the range is but a crude indication of variability. Its main advantage is that it gives a quick (although rough) estimate of variability.

The Standard Deviation. The **standard deviation** (SD) is the most useful index of variability. It is a single number that represents the spread of a distribution. As with the mean, every score in the distribution is used to calculate it. The steps involved in calculating the standard deviation are straightforward.

1. Calculate the mean of the distribution.

$$\bar{X} = \frac{\Sigma X}{n}$$

2. Subtract the mean from each score. Each result is symbolized $X - \bar{X}$.
3. Square each of these scores $(X - \bar{X})^2$.
4. Add up all the squares of these scores:

$$\Sigma(X - \bar{X})^2.$$

5. Divide the total by the number of scores. The result is called the **variance.**
6. Take the square root of the variance. This is the standard deviation.

The above steps can be summarized as follows:

$$SD = \sqrt{\frac{\Sigma\,(X - \bar{X})^2}{n}}$$

where SD is the symbol for standard deviation, Σ is the symbol for "sum of," X is the symbol for a raw score, $\bar{X}$ is the symbol for the mean, and n represents the number of scores in the distribution.

This procedure sounds more complicated than it is. It really is not difficult to calculate. Table 10.5 illustrates the calculation of the standard deviation of a distribution of 10 scores.

You will notice that the more spread out scores are, the greater the deviation scores will be and hence the

larger the standard deviation. The closer the scores are to the mean, the less spread out they are and hence the smaller the standard deviation. Thus, if we were describing two sets of scores on the same test, and we stated that the standard deviation of the scores in set 1 was 2.7, while the standard deviation in set 2 was 8.3, we would know that there was much less variability in set 1—that is, the scores were closer together.

An important point involving the standard deviation is that if a distribution is normal, then the mean plus or minus three standard deviations will encompass about 99 percent of all the scores in the distribution. For example, if the mean of a distribution is 72 and the standard deviation is 3, then just about 99 percent of the scores in the distribution are somewhere between scores of 63 and 81. Figure 10.9 provides an illustration of standard deviation.

The Standard Deviation of a Normal Distribution. The total area under the normal curve represents all of the scores in a normal distribution. In such a curve, the mean, median, and mode are identical, so the mean falls at the exact center of the curve. It thus is also the most frequent score in the distribution. Because the curve is symmetrical, 50 percent of the scores must fall on each side of the mean.

Here are some important facts about the normal distribution:

- Fifty percent of all the observations (scores, etc.) fall on *each* side of the mean (Figure 10.10).
- In any normal distribution, 68 percent of the observations (scores, etc.) fall within one standard deviation of the mean. Half of these (34 percent) fall within one standard deviation above the mean and the other half within one standard deviation below the mean.
- Another 27 percent of the observations fall between one and two standard deviations away from the mean. Hence 95 percent (68 percent plus 27 percent) fall within two standard deviations of the mean.
- In all, 99.7 percent of the observations fall within three standard deviations of the mean. Figure 10.11 illustrates all three of these facts, often referred to as the **68-95-99.7 rule.**

Hence we see that almost all of the scores in a normal distribution lie between the mean and plus or minus three standard deviations. Only .13 percent of all the scores fall above 3 SD, and .13 percent fall below −3 SD.

Table 10.5 *Calculation of the Standard Deviation of a Distribution*

Raw Score	Mean	$X - \bar{X}$	$(X - \bar{X})^2$
85	54	31	961
80	54	26	676
70	54	16	256
60	54	6	36
55	54	1	1
50	54	−4	16
45	54	−9	81
40	54	−14	196
30	54	−24	576
25	54	−29	841
			$\Sigma = 3640$

$$\text{Variance (SD}^2) = \frac{\Sigma(X - \bar{X})^2}{n}$$

$$= \frac{3640}{10} = 364^a$$

$$\text{Standard deviation (SD)} = \sqrt{\frac{\Sigma(X - \bar{X})^2}{n}}$$

$$= \sqrt{364} = 19.08^b$$

[a]The symbol for the variance of a sample sometimes is shown as s^2; the symbol for the variance of a population is σ^2.
[b]The symbol for the standard deviation of a sample sometimes is shown as s; the symbol for the standard deviation of a population is σ.

Figure 10.9 *Standard Deviations for Boys' and Men's Basketball Teams*

If a set of scores is normally distributed, we can interpret any particular score if we know how far, in standard deviation units, it is from the mean. Suppose, for example, the mean of a normal distribution is 100 and the standard deviation is 15. A score that lies one standard deviation above the mean, therefore, would equal 115. A score that lies one standard deviation below the mean would equal 85. What would a score that lies 1.5 standard deviations above the mean equal?*

We also can determine how a particular individual's score compares with all the other scores in a normal distribution. For example, if a person's score lies exactly one standard deviation above the mean, then we know that slightly more than 84 percent of all the other scores in the distribution lie below his or her score.† If a distribution is normal, and we know the mean and the standard deviation of the distribution, we can determine the percentage of scores that lie above and below any given score (see Figure 10.11). This is one of the most useful characteristics of the normal distribution.

STANDARD SCORES AND THE NORMAL CURVE

Researchers often are interested in seeing how one person's score compares with another's. As we mentioned in Chapter Seven, to determine this, researchers often convert raw scores to derived scores. We described two types of derived scores—age/grade equivalents and percentile ranks—in that chapter, but mentioned another type—standard scores—only briefly. We discuss them now in somewhat more detail, since they are very useful.

Standard scores use a common scale to indicate how an individual compares to other individuals in a

---

*122.5

†Fifty percent of the scores in the distribution must lie below the mean; 34 percent must lie between the mean and +1 SD. Therefore 84 percent (50 percent + 34 percent) of the scores in the distribution must be below +1 SD.

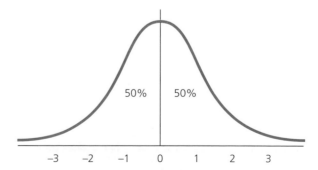

Figure 10.10 *Fifty Percent of All Scores in a Normal Curve Fall on Each Side of the Mean*

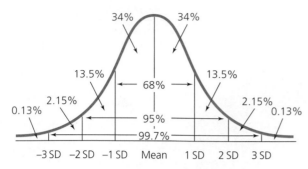

Figure 10.11 *Percentages Under the Normal Curve*

Table 10.6 *Comparisons of Raw Scores and z Scores on Two Tests*

Test	Raw Score	Mean	SD	z Score	Percentile Rank
Biology	60	50	5	+2	98
Chemistry	80	90	10	−1	16

group. These scores are particularly helpful in comparing an individual's relative position on different instruments. The two standard scores that are most frequently used in educational research are *z* scores and *T* scores.

z Scores. The simplest form of standard score is the **z score.** It expresses how far a raw score is from the mean in standard deviation units. A raw score that is exactly on the mean corresponds to a *z* score of zero; a raw score that is exactly one standard deviation above the mean equals a *z* score of +1, while a raw score that is exactly one standard deviation below the mean equals a *z* score of −1. Similarly, a raw score that is exactly two standard deviations above the mean equals a *z* score of +2, and so forth. One *z,* therefore, equals one standard deviation (1 *z* = 1 SD), 2 *z* = 2 SD, −0.5 *z* = −0.5 SD, and so on (see Figure 10.12). Thus, if the mean of a distribution was 50 and the standard deviation was 2, a raw score of 52 would equal a *z* score of +1, a raw score of 46 would equal a *z* score of −2, and so forth.

A big advantage of *z* scores is that they allow raw scores on different tests to be compared. For example, suppose a student received raw scores of 60 on a biol-

ogy test and 80 on a chemistry test. A naive observer might be inclined to infer, at first glance, that the student was doing better in chemistry than in biology. But this might be unwise, for how "well" the student is doing comparatively cannot be determined until we know the mean and standard deviation for each distribution of scores. Let us further suppose that the mean on the biology test was 50, but on the chemistry test it was 90. Also assume that the standard deviation on the biology test was 5, but on the chemistry test it was 10. What does this tell us? The student's raw score in biology (60) is actually two standard deviations *above* the mean (a *z* score of +2), whereas his raw score in chemistry (80) is one standard deviation *below* the mean (a *z* score of −1). Rather than doing better in chemistry, as the raw scores by themselves suggest, the student is actually doing better in biology. Table 10.6 compares both the raw scores, the *z* scores, and the percentile rank of the student on both tests.

Of course, *z* scores are not always exactly one or two standard deviations away from the mean. Actually, researchers apply the following formula to convert a raw score into a *z* score.

$$z \text{ score } = \frac{\text{raw score} - \text{mean}}{\text{standard deviation}}$$

Thus, for a raw score of 80, a mean of 65, and a standard deviation of 12, the *z* score will be:

$$z = \left(\frac{80 - 65}{12}\right) = 1.25$$

Probability and z Scores. Another important characteristic of the normal distribution is that the percentages associated with areas under the curve can be thought of as probabilities. A **probability** is a percent stated in decimal form, and refers to the likelihood of an event occurring. For example, if there is a probability that an event will occur 25 percent of the time, this event can be said to have a probability of .25. Similarly, an event that will probably occur 90 percent of the time

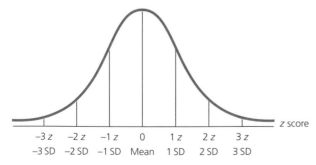

Figure 10.12 *z Scores Associated with the Normal Curve*

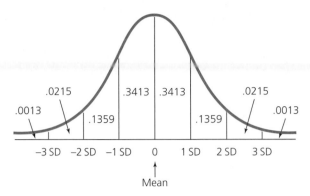

Figure 10.13 *Probabilities Under the Normal Curve*

is said to have a probability of .90. All of the percentages associated with areas under a normal curve, therefore, can be expressed in decimal form and viewed as probability statements. Some of these probabilities are shown in Figure 10.13.

Considering the area under the normal curve in terms of probabilities is very helpful to a researcher. Let us consider an example. We have previously shown that approximately 34 percent of the scores in a normal distribution lie between the mean and 1 SD. Because 50 percent of the scores fall above the mean, roughly 16 percent of the scores must therefore lie above 1 SD (50 − 34 = 16). Now, if we express 16 percent in decimal form and interpret it as a probability, we can say that the probability of randomly selecting an individual from the population who has a score of 1 SD or more

above the mean is .16. Usually this is written as $p = 16$, with the p meaning probability. Similarly, we can determine the probability of randomly selecting an individual who has a score lying at or below −2 SD or lower, or between +1 SD and −1 SD, and so on. Figure 10.13 shows that the probability of selecting an individual who has a score lower than −2 SD is $p = .0228$, or roughly 2 in 100. The probability of randomly selecting an individual who has a score between −1 SD and +1 SD is $p = .6826$, and so forth.

Statistical tables exist (see part of one in Appendix B) that give the proportion of scores associated with any particular z score in the normal distribution (e.g., for $z = 1.10$, the proportion (i.e., the probability) for the area between the mean of $z = 0$ and $z = 1.10$ is .3643, and for the area beyond z, it is .1357). Hence, a researcher can be very precise in describing the position of any particular score relative to other scores in a normal distribution. Figure 10.14 shows a portion of such a table (see Appendix B).

***T* Scores.**   Raw scores that are below the mean of a distribution convert to negative z scores. This is somewhat awkward. One way to eliminate negative z scores is to convert them into T scores. ***T* scores** are simply z scores expressed in a different form. To change a z score to a T score, we simply multiply the z score by 10 and add 50. Thus, a z score of +1 equals a T score of 60 ($1 \times 10 = 10$; $10 + 50 = 60$). A z score of −2 equals a T score of 30 ($−2 \times 10 = −20$; $−20 + 50 = 30$). A z score

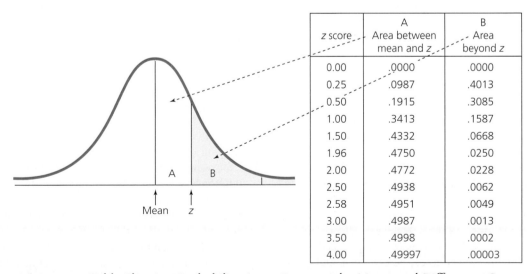

z score	A Area between mean and z	B Area beyond z
0.00	.0000	.0000
0.25	.0987	.4013
0.50	.1915	.3085
1.00	.3413	.1587
1.50	.4332	.0668
1.96	.4750	.0250
2.00	.4772	.0228
2.50	.4938	.0062
2.58	.4951	.0049
3.00	.4987	.0013
3.50	.4998	.0002
4.00	.49997	.00003

Figure 10.14 *Table Showing Probability Areas Between the Mean and Different z Scores*

Figure 10.15 *Examples of Standard Scores*

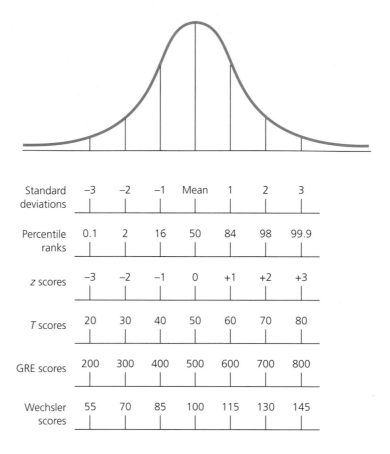

Standard deviations	−3	−2	−1	Mean	1	2	3
Percentile ranks	0.1	2	16	50	84	98	99.9
z scores	−3	−2	−1	0	+1	+2	+3
T scores	20	30	40	50	60	70	80
GRE scores	200	300	400	500	600	700	800
Wechsler scores	55	70	85	100	115	130	145

of zero (which is the equivalent of the mean of the raw scores) equals a *T* score of 50. You should see that a distribution of *T* scores has a mean of 50 and a standard deviation of 10. If you think about it, you should also see that a *T* score of 50 equals the 50th percentile.

When a researcher knows, or can assume, that a distribution of scores is normal, both *T* and *z* scores can be interpreted in terms of percentile ranks because there is then a direct relationship between the two. Figure 10.15 illustrates this relationship. There are other systems similar to *T* scores, which differ only in the choice of values for the mean and standard deviation. Two of the most common, those used with the Graduate Record Examination ($\bar{X} = 500$, SD = 100) and the Wechsler Intelligence Scales ($\bar{X} = 100$, SD = 15), are also illustrated in Figure 10.15.

The Importance of the Normal Curve and z Scores. You may have noticed that the preceding discussion of the use of *z* scores, percentages, and probabilities in relation to the normal curve was always qual-

ified by the words "*if* or *when* the distribution of scores is normal." You should recall that *z* scores can be calculated regardless of the shape of the distribution of original scores. But it is *only* when the distribution is normal that the conversion to percentages or probabilities as described above is legitimate. Fortunately, many distributions *do* approximate the normal curve. This is most likely when a sample is chosen randomly from a broadly defined population. (It would be very unlikely, for example, with achievement scores in a sample that consisted only of gifted students.)

When actual data do not approximate the normal curve, they can be changed to do so. In other words, any distribution of scores can be "normalized." The procedure for doing so is not complicated, but it makes the assumption that the characteristic is "really" normally distributed. Most published tests that permit use of standard scores have normalized the score distributions in order to permit the translation of *z* scores to percentages. This relationship—between *z* scores and percentages of area under the normal curve—is also basic to many inferential statistics.

CORRELATION

In many places throughout this text we have stated that the most meaningful research is that which seeks to find, or verify, relationships among variables. Comparing the performance of different groups is, as you have seen, one way to study relationships. In such studies one variable is categorical—the variable that defines the groups (for example, method A versus method B). The other variable is most often quantitative, and groups are typically compared using frequency polygons, averages, and spreads.

In correlational research, researchers seek to determine whether a relationship exists between two (or more) quantitative variables, such as age and weight or reading and writing ability. Sometimes, such relationships are useful in prediction, but most often the eventual goal is to say something about causation. Although causal relationships cannot be proved through correlational studies, researchers hope eventually to make causal statements as an outgrowth of their work. The totality of studies showing a relationship between incidence of lung cancer and cigarette use is a current example. We will discuss correlational research in further detail in Chapter Fifteen.

Scatterplots. What is needed is a means to determine whether relationships exist in data. A useful technique for representing relationships with quantitative data is the scatterplot. A **scatterplot** is a pictorial representation of the relationship between two quantitative variables.

Scatterplots are easy to construct, provided some common pitfalls are avoided. First, in order to be plotted, there must be a score on each variable for each individual; second, the grouping intervals (if any) within each variable (axis) must be of equal size; third, *each* individual must be represented by one, and only one, point of intersection. We used the data in Table 10.7 to construct the scatterplot in Figure 10.16. The steps involved are the following:

1. Decide which variable will be represented on each axis. It makes no difference which variable is placed on which axis. We have used the horizontal (x) axis for variable 1 and the vertical (y) axis for variable 2.
2. Divide each axis into about 12 to 15 sections. Each point on the axis will represent a particular score or group of scores. Be sure all scores can be included.
3. Group scores if desirable. It was not necessary for us to group scores for variable 1, since all of the scores fall within a 15-point range. For variable 2, however,

representing *each* score on the axis would result in a great many points on the vertical axis. Therefore, we grouped them within *equal sized* intervals of five points each.

4. Plot, for each person, the point where the vertical and horizontal lines for his or her scores on the two variables intersect. For example, Pedro had a score of 12 on variable 1, so we locate 12 on the horizontal axis. He had a score of 41 on variable 2, so we locate that score (in the 40–44 grouping) on the vertical axis. We then draw imaginary lines from each of these points until they intersect, and mark an *X* or a dot at that point.
5. In the same way, plot the scores of all 10 students on both variables. The completed result is a scatterplot.

Interpreting a Scatterplot. How do researchers interpret scatterplots? What are they intended to reveal? Researchers want to know not only *if* a relationship exists between variables, but also *to what degree.* The degree of relationship, if one exists, is what a scatterplot illustrates.

Consider Figure 10.16. What does it tell us about the relationship between variable 1 and variable 2? This question can be answered in several ways.

1. We might say that high scores on variable 1 go with high scores on variable 2 (as in John's case) and that low scores also tend to go together (as in Charles's case).
2. We might say that by knowing a student's score on one variable, we can estimate his or her score on the other variable fairly closely. Suppose, for example, a new student attains a score of 16 on variable 1. What would you predict his or her score would be on variable 2? You probably would *not* predict a score of 75 or one of 25 (we would predict a score somewhere from 45 to 59).
3. The customary interpretation of a scatterplot that looks like this would be that there is a strong or high degree of relationship between the two variables.

Outliers. Outliers are scores or measurements that differ by such large amounts from those of other individuals in a group that they must be given careful consideration as special cases. They indicate an unusual exception to a general pattern. They occur in scatterplots, as well as frequency distribution tables, histograms, and frequency polygons. Figure 10.17 shows the relationship between family cohesiveness and school achieve-

Table 10.7 *Data Used to Construct Scatterplot in Figure 10.16*

Individual	Scores Variable 1	Scores Variable 2	Grouped Scores Variable 2	Frequency of Grouped Scores Variable 2
			75–79	1
Pedro	12	41	70–74	0
John	21	76	65–69	0
Alicia	9	29	60–64	1
Charles	7	21	55–59	0
Bonnie	13	43	50–54	1
Phil	11	37	45–49	0
Sue	7	14	40–44	2
Oscar	18	63	35–39	2
Jean	15	54	30–34	0
Dave	14	39	25–29	1
			20–24	1
			15–19	0
			10–14	1

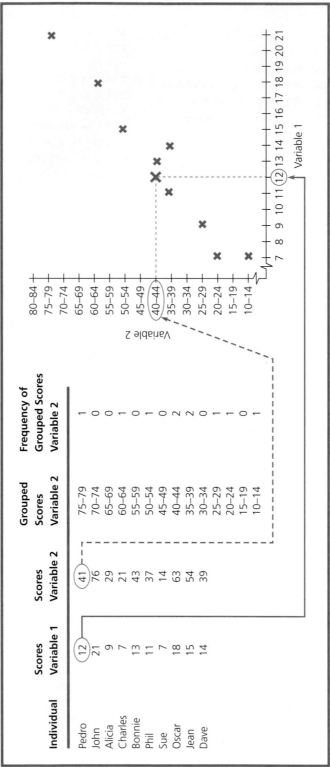

Figure 10.16 *Scatterplot of Data from Table 10.7*

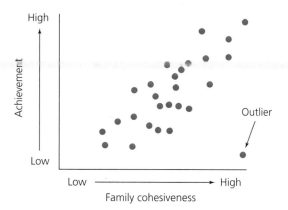

Figure 10.17 *Relationship Between Family Cohesiveness and School Achievement in a Hypothetical Group of Students*

ment. Notice the lonely individual near the lower right corner has a high score in family cohesiveness, but a low score in achievement. Why? The answer should be of interest to the student's teacher.

Correlation Coefficients and Scatterplots. Figure 10.18 presents several other examples of scatterplots. Studying them will help you understand the notion of a relationship and also further your understanding of the correlation coefficient. As we mentioned in Chapter Eight, a **correlation coefficient,** designated by the symbol r, expresses the degree of relationship that exists between two sets of scores.* A positive relationship is indicated when high scores on one variable are accompanied by high scores on the other, low scores on one are accompanied by low scores on the other, and so forth (see Figure 10.19). A negative relationship is indicated when high scores on one variable are accompanied by low scores on the other, and vice versa (Figure 10.20).

You should recall that correlation coefficients are never more than +1.00, indicating a perfect positive relationship, or −1.00, indicating a perfect negative relationship. Perfect positive or negative correlations, however, are rarely, if ever, achieved. If the two variables are highly related, a coefficient somewhat close to +1.00 or −1.00 will be obtained (such as .85 or −.93). The closer the coefficient is to either of these extremes, the greater

*In this context, the correlation coefficient indicates the degree of relationship between two *variables*. You will recall from Chapter Eight that it is also used to assess the reliability and validity of measurements.

the degree of the relationship. If there is no or hardly any relationship, a coefficient of .00 or close to it will be obtained. The coefficient is calculated directly from the same scores used to construct the scatterplot.

The scatterplots in Figure 10.18 illustrate different degrees of correlation. Both positive and negative correlations are shown. Scatterplots (*a*), (*b*), and (*c*) illustrate different degrees of positive correlation, while scatterplots (*e*), (*f*), (*g*), and (*h*) illustrate different degrees of negative correlation. Scatterplot (*d*) indicates no relationship between the two variables involved.

In order to better understand the meaning of different values of the correlation coefficient, we suggest that you try the following two exercises with Figure 10.18.

1. Lay a pencil flat on the paper on scatterplot (*a*) so that the entire length of the pencil is touching the paper. Place it in such a way that it touches or covers as many dots as possible. Take note that there is clearly one "best" placement. You would not, for example, maximize the points covered if you placed the pencil horizontally on the scatterplot. Repeat this procedure for each of the scatterplots, noting what occurs as you move from one scatterplot to another.

2. Draw a horizontal line on scatterplot (*a*) so that about half of the dots are above the line and half are below it. Next draw a vertical line so that about half of the dots are to the left of the line and half are to the right. Repeat the procedure for each scatterplot and note what you observe as you move from one scatterplot to another.

The Pearson Product-Moment Coefficient. There are many different correlation coefficients, each applying to a particular circumstance and each calculated by means of a different computational formula. The one we have been illustrating is the one most frequently used: the **Pearson product-moment coefficient** of correlation. It is symbolized by the lowercase letter r. When the data for both variables are expressed in terms of quantitative scores, the Pearson r is the appropriate correlation coefficient to use. (It is not difficult to calculate, and we'll show you how in Appendix D.) It is designed for use with interval or ratio data.

Eta. Another index of correlation that you should become familiar with is called **eta** (symbolized as η). We shall not illustrate how to calculate eta (since it requires computational methods beyond the scope of this text),

Figure 10.18 *Further Examples of Scatterplots*

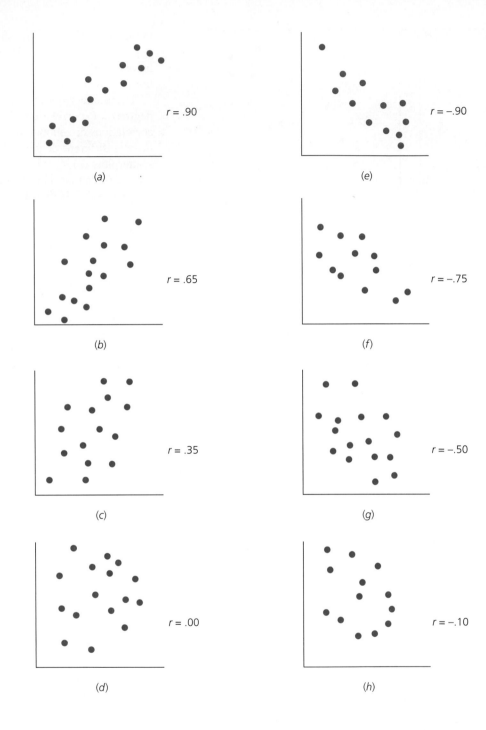

Figure 10.19 *A Perfect Negative Correlation!*

Figure 10.20 *Positive and Negative Correlations*

but you should know that it is used when a scatterplot shows that a straight line is not the best fit for the plotted points. In the examples shown in Figure 10.21, for example, you can see that a curved line provides a much better fit to the data than would a straight line.

Eta is interpreted in much the same way as the Pearson *r*, except that it ranges from .00 to 1.00, rather than from −1.00 to +1.00. Higher values, as with the other correlation coefficients, indicate higher degrees of relationship.

Techniques for Summarizing Categorical Data

THE FREQUENCY TABLE

Suppose a researcher, using a questionnaire, has been collecting data from a random sample of 50 teachers in a large, urban school district. The questionnaire covers many variables related to their activities and interests. One of the variables is "learning activity I use most frequently in my classroom." The researcher arranges her data on this

Figure 10.21 *Examples of Nonlinear (Curvilinear) Relationships*

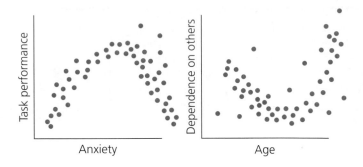

variable (and others) in the form of a frequency table, which shows the frequency with which each type, or category, of learning activity is mentioned. The researcher simply places a tally mark for each individual in the sample alongside the activity mentioned. When she has tallied all 50 individuals, her results look like the following frequency listing.

Response	Tally	Frequency
Lecture	Ⅲ Ⅲ Ⅲ	15
Class discussions	Ⅲ Ⅲ	10
Oral reports	‖‖	4
Library research	‖	2
Seatwork	Ⅲ	5
Demonstrations	Ⅲ ‖‖	8
Audiovisual presentations	Ⅲ ‖	6
		$n = 50$

The tally marks have been added up at the end of each row to show the total number of individuals who listed that activity. Often with categorical data, researchers are interested in proportions, because they wish to make an estimate (if their sample is random) about the proportions in the total population from which the sample was selected. Thus, the total numbers in each category are often changed to percentages. This has been done in Table 10.8, with the categories arranged in descending order of frequency.

BAR GRAPHS AND PIE CHARTS

Two other ways are used to illustrate a difference in proportions. One is to use a **bar graph** portrayal, as shown in Figure 10.22; another is to use a **pie chart,** as shown in Figure 10.23.

THE CROSSBREAK TABLE

When a relationship between two categorical variables is of interest, it is usually reported in the form of a **crossbreak table** (sometimes called a contingency table). The simplest crossbreak is a 2 by 2 table, as shown in Table 10.9. Each individual is tallied in one, and only one, cell that corresponds to the combination of gender and grade level. You will notice that the numbers in each of the cells in Table 10.9 represent totals— the total number of individuals who fit the characteristics of the cell (for example, junior high males). Although percentages and proportions are sometimes calculated for cells, we do not recommend it, as this is often misleading.

It probably seems obvious that Table 10.9 reveals a relationship between teacher gender and grade level. A junior high school teacher is more likely to be female; a high school teacher is more likely to be male. Often, however, it is useful to calculate "expected" frequencies in order to see results more clearly. What do we mean by "expected"? If there is no relationship between variables, we would "expect" the proportion of cases within each cell of the table corresponding to a category of a variable to be identical to the proportion within that category in the entire group. Look, for example, at Table 10.10. Exactly one-half (50 percent) of the total group

Table 10.8 *Frequency and Percentage of Total of Responses to Questionnaire*

Response	Frequency	Percentage of Total (%)
Lecture	15	30
Class discussions	10	20
Demonstrations	8	16
Audiovisual presentations	6	12
Seatwork	5	10
Oral reports	4	8
Library research	2	4
Total	50	100

Correlation in Everyday Life

Many commonplace relationships (true or not) can be expressed as correlations. For example, Boyle's law states that the volume and pressure of a gas vary inversely if kept at a constant temperature. Another way to express this is that the correlation between volume and pressure is –1.00. This relationship, however, is only theoretically true—that is, it exists only for a perfect gas in a perfect vacuum. In real life, the correlation is lower.

Consider the following sayings:

1. "Spare the rod and spoil the child" implies a negative correlation between punishment and spoiled behavior.
2. "Idle hands are the devil's workplace" implies a positive correlation between idleness and mischief.
3. "There's no fool like an old fool" suggests a positive correlation between foolishness and age.
4. "A stitch in time saves nine" suggests a positive correlation between how long one waits to begin a corrective action and the amount of time (and effort) required to fix the problem.
5. "The early bird catches the worm" suggests a positive correlation between early rising and success.
6. "You can't teach an old dog new tricks" implies a negative correlation between age of adults and ability to learn.
7. "An apple a day keeps the doctor away" suggests a negative correlation between the consumption of apples and illness.
8. "Faint heart never won fair maiden" suggests a negative correlation between timidity and female receptivity.

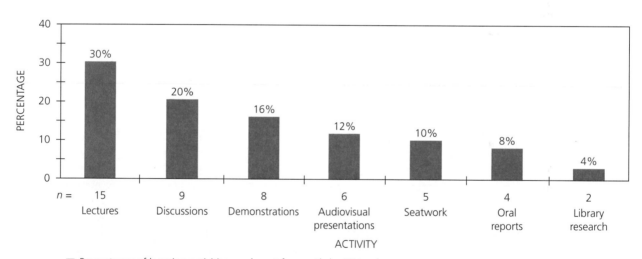

■ Percentages of learning activities used most frequently by 50 teachers

Figure 10.22 *Example of a Bar Graph*

of teachers in this table are female. If gender is unrelated to grade level, we would "expect" that the same proportion (exactly one-half) of the junior high school teachers would be female. Similarly, we would "expect" that one-half of the high school teachers would be female. The "expected" frequencies, in other words, would be 50 female junior high school teachers and 50 female high school teachers, rather than the 60 female junior high school and 40 female high school teachers that were actually obtained. These expected and actual, or "observed," frequencies are shown in

each box (or "cell") in Table 10.10. The expected frequencies are shown in parentheses.*

Comparing expected and actual frequencies makes the degree and direction of the relationship clearer. This is particularly helpful with more complex tables. Look,

*Expected frequencies can also be provided ahead of time, based on theory or prior experience. In this example, the researcher might have wanted to know whether the characteristics of junior high school teachers in a particular school fit the national pattern. National percentages would then be used to determine expected frequencies.

Figure 10.23 *Example of a Pie Chart*

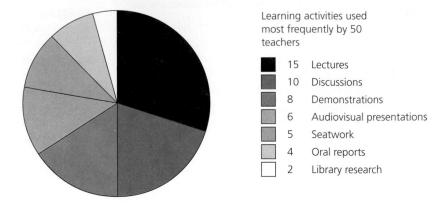

Learning activities used most frequently by 50 teachers

■	15	Lectures
■	10	Discussions
■	8	Demonstrations
■	6	Audiovisual presentations
■	5	Seatwork
■	4	Oral reports
□	2	Library research

Table 10.9 *Grade Level and Gender of Teachers (Hypothetical Data)*

	Male	Female	Total
Junior high school teachers	40	60	100
High school teachers	60	40	100
Total	100	100	200

Table 10.10 *Repeat of Table 10.9 with Expected Frequencies (In Parentheses)*

	Male	Female	Total
Junior high school teachers	40 (50)	60 (50)	100
High school teachers	60 (50)	40 (50)	100
Total	100	100	200

for example, at Table 10.11. This table contains not two, but three, variables.

The researcher who collected and summarized these data hypothesized that appointment to administrative (or other nonteaching) positions rather than teaching positions is related to (1) gender and (2) ethnicity.

While it is possible to examine Table 10.11 in its entirety to evaluate these hypotheses, it is much easier to see the relationships by extracting components of the table. Let us look at the relationship of each variable in the table to the other two variables. By taking two variables at a time, we can compare (1) position and ethnicity; (2) position and gender; and (3) gender and ethnicity. Table 10.12 presents the data for position and ethnicity, Table 10.13 presents the data for position and gender, and Table 10.14 presents the data for gender and ethnicity.

Let us review the calculation of expected frequencies by referring to Table 10.12. This table shows the relationship between ethnicity and position. Since one-sixth of the total group (100/600) are administrators, we would expect 62 whites to be administrators ($\frac{1}{6}$ of 370). Likewise, we would expect 38 of the nonwhites to be administrators ($\frac{1}{6}$ of 230). Since five-sixths of the total group are teachers, we would expect 308 of the whites ($\frac{5}{6}$ of 370), and 192 of the nonwhites ($\frac{5}{6}$ of 230), to be teachers. As you can see, however, the actual frequencies for administrators were 70 (rather than 62) whites, and 30 (rather than 38) nonwhites, and the actual frequencies for teachers were 300 (rather than 308) whites, and 200 (rather than 192) nonwhites. This tells us that

Table 10.11 *Position, Gender, and Ethnicity of School Leaders (Hypothetical Data)*

	Administrators		Teachers		
	White	Nonwhite	White	Nonwhite	Total
Male	50	20	150	80	300
Female	20	10	150	120	300
Total	70	30	300	200	600

Table 10.12 *Position and Ethnicity of School Leaders with Expected Frequencies (Derived from Table 10.11)*

	Administrators	Teachers	Total
White	70 (62)	300 (308)	370
Nonwhite	30 (38)	200 (192)	230
Total	100	500	600

Table 10.13 *Position and Gender of School Leaders with Expected Frequencies (Derived from Table 10.11)*

	Administrators	Teachers	Total
White	70 (50)	230 (250)	300
Female	30 (50)	270 (250)	300
Total	100	500	600

Table 10.14 *Gender and Ethnicity of School Leaders with Expected Frequencies (Derived from Table 10.11)*

	White	Nonwhite	Total
White	200 (185)	100 (115)	300
Female	170 (185)	130 (115)	300
Total	370	230	600

there is a discrepancy between what we would expect (if there is no relationship) and what we actually obtained. Discrepancies between the frequencies expected and those actually obtained can also be seen in Tables 10.13 and 10.14.

An index of the strength of the relationships can be obtained by summing the discrepancies in each table. In

Table 10.12, the sum equals 32, in Table 10.13, it equals 80, and in Table 10.14 it equals 60. The calculation of these sums is shown in Table 10.15. The discrepancy between expected and observed frequencies is greatest in Table 10.13, position and gender; less in Table 10.14, gender and ethnicity; and least in Table 10.12, position and ethnicity. A numerical index showing degree of relationship—the contingency coefficient—will be discussed in Chapter Eleven.

Thus, the data in the crossbreak tables reveal that there is a slight tendency for there to be more white administrators and more nonwhite teachers than would be expected (Table 10.12). There is a stronger tendency toward more white males and nonwhite females than would be expected (Table 10.14). The strongest relationship indicates more male administrators and more female teachers than would be expected (Table 10.13). In sum, the chances of having an administrative position appear to be considerably greater if one is male, and slightly enhanced if one is white.

In contrast to the preceding example, where each variable (ethnicity, gender, role) is clearly categorical, a researcher sometimes has a choice whether to treat data as quantitative or as categorical. Take the case of a researcher who measures self-esteem by a self-report questionnaire scored for number of items answered (yes or no) in the direction indicating high self-esteem. The researcher might decide to use these scores to divide the sample ($n = 60$) into high, middle, and low thirds. He or she might use only this information for each individual and subsequently treat the data as categorical, as is shown, for example, in Table 10.16. Most researchers would advise against treating the data this way, however, since it "wastes" so much information—for example, differences in scores within each category are ignored. A quantitative analysis, by way of contrast, would compare the mean self-esteem scores of males and females.

Table 10.15 *Total of Discrepancies Between Expected and Observed Frequencies in Tables 10.12 Through 10.14*

Table 10.12		Table 10.13		Table 10.14	
(70 vs. 62)	= 8	(70 vs. 50)	= 20	(200 vs. 185)	= 15
(30 vs. 38)	= 8	(30 vs. 50)	= 20	(170 vs. 185)	= 15
(300 vs. 308)	= 8	(230 vs. 250)	= 20	(100 vs. 115)	= 15
(200 vs. 192)	= 8	(270 vs. 250)	= 20	(130 vs. 115)	= 15
Total	32		80		60

Table 10.16 *Crossbreak Table Showing Relationship Between Self-Esteem and Gender (Hypothetical Data)*

Gender	Self Esteem		
	Low	Middle	High
Male	10	15	5
Female	5	10	15

In such situations (i.e., when one variable is quantitative and the other is treated as categorical), correlation is another option. When data on a variable assumed to be quantitative have been divided into two categories, a biserial correlation coefficient can be calculated and interpreted the same as a Pearson *r* coefficient. If the categories are assumed to reflect a true division, calculation of a point biserial coefficient is an option, but must be interpreted with caution.

Go back to the **Interactive and Applied Learning Tools** feature at the beginning of the chapter for a listing of interactive and applied activities. Go to the **Online Learning Center** at www.mhhe.com/fraenkel5e or your **Interactive Student CD-ROM** to take practice quizzes and receive immediate feedback, practice with key terms, review chapter content and main ideas, and find annotated Web links.

Main Points

STATISTICS VERSUS PARAMETERS

- A parameter is a characteristic of a population. It is a numerical or graphic way to summarize data obtained from the population.
- A statistic, on the other hand, is a characteristic of a sample. It is a numerical or graphic way to summarize data obtained from a sample.

TYPES OF NUMERICAL DATA

- There are two fundamental types of numerical data a researcher can collect. Categorical data are data obtained by determining the frequency of occurrences in each of several categories. Quantitative data are data obtained by determining placement on a scale that indicates amount or degree.

TECHNIQUES FOR SUMMARIZING QUANTITATIVE DATA

- A frequency distribution is a two-column listing, from high to low, of all the scores along with their frequencies. In a grouped frequency distribution, the scores have been grouped into equal intervals.
- A frequency polygon is a graphic display of a frequency distribution. It is a graphic way to summarize quantitative data for one variable.
- A graphic distribution of scores in which only a few individuals receive high scores is called a positively skewed polygon; one in which only a few individuals receive low scores is called a negatively skewed polygon.
- The normal distribution is a theoretical distribution that is symmetrical, and in which a large proportion of the scores are concentrated in the middle of the distribution.
- A distribution curve is a smoothed out frequency polygon.
- The distribution curve of a normal distribution is called a normal curve. It is bell-shaped, and its mean, median, and mode are identical.
- There are several measures of central tendency (averages) that are used to summarize quantitative data. The two most common are the mean and the median.
- The mean of a distribution is determined by adding up all of the scores and dividing this sum by the total number of scores.

- The median of a distribution marks the point above and below which half of the scores in the distribution lie.
- The mode is the most frequent score in a distribution.
- The term "variability," as used in research, refers to the extent to which the scores on a quantitative variable in a distribution are spread out.
- The most common measure of variability used in educational research is the standard deviation.
- The range, another measure of variability, represents the difference between the highest and lowest scores in a distribution.
- A five-number summary of a distribution reports the lowest score, the first quartile, the median, the third quartile, and the highest score.
- Five-number summaries of distributions are often portrayed graphically by the use of boxplots.

STANDARD SCORES AND THE NORMAL CURVE

- Standard scores use a common scale to indicate how an individual compares to other individuals in a group. The simplest form of standard score is a *z* score. A *z* score expresses how far a raw score is from the mean in standard deviation units.
- The major advantage of standard scores is that they provide a better basis for comparing performance on different measures than do raw scores.
- The term "probability," as used in research, refers to a prediction of how often a particular event will occur. Probabilities are usually expressed in decimal form.

CORRELATION

- A correlation coefficient is a numerical index expressing the degree of relationship that exists between two quantitative variables. The one most commonly used in educational research is the Pearson *r*.
- A scatterplot is a graphic way to describe a relationship between two quantitative variables.

TECHNIQUES FOR SUMMARIZING CATEGORICAL DATA

- There are a variety of graphic techniques researchers use to summarize categorical data, including frequency tables, bar graphs, and pie charts.
- A crossbreak table is a graphic way to report a relationship between two or more categorical variables.

Key Terms

For Discussion

1. Would you expect the following correlations to be positive or negative? Why?
    a. Bowling scores and golf scores.
    b. Reading scores and arithmetic scores for sixth-graders.
    c. Age and weight for a group of 5-year-olds; for a group of people over 70.
    d. Life expectancy at age 40 and frequency of smoking.
    e. Size and strength for junior high students.
2. Why do you think so many people mistrust statistics? How might such mistrust be alleviated?
3. Could the range of a distribution ever be smaller than the standard deviation of that distribution? Why or why not?
4. Would it be possible for two different distributions to have the same standard deviation but different means? What about the reverse? Explain.
5. "The larger the standard deviation of a distribution, the more heterogeneous the scores in that distribution." Is this statement true? Explain.
6. "The most complete information about a distribution of scores is provided by a frequency polygon." Is this statement true? Explain.
7. Grouping scores in a frequency distribution has its advantages, but also its disadvantages. What might be some examples of each?
8. "Any single raw score, in and of itself, tells us nothing." Would you agree? Explain.
9. The relationship between age and strength is said to be curvilinear. What does this mean? Might there be exceptions to this relationship? What might cause such an exception?

Research Exercise Ten: Descriptive Statistics

Using Problem Sheet 10, state again the question or hypothesis of your study and list your variables. Then indicate how you would summarize the results for each variable in your study. Lastly, indicate how you would describe the relationship between variables 1 and 2.

Problem Sheet 10

Descriptive Statistics

1. The question or hypothesis of my study is: _____

2. My variables are: (1) _____

   (2) _____ (others) _____

3. I consider variable 1 to be: quantitative _____ or categorical _____

4. I consider variable 2 to be: quantitative _____ or categorical _____

5. I would summarize the results for each variable checked below (indicate with a check mark ✓):

	Variable 1:	**Variable 2:**	**Other:**
	_____	_____	_____
a. Frequency polygon			
b. Five-number summary			
c. Box plot			
d. Mean			
e. Median			
f. Percentages			
g. Standard deviation			
h. Frequency table			
i. Bar graph			
j. Pie chart			

6. I would describe the relationship between variables 1 and 2 by (indicate with a check mark ✓):

   a.   Comparison of frequency polygons _____

   b.   Comparison of averages _____

   c.   Crossbreak table(s) _____

   d.   Correlation coefficient _____

   e.   Scatterplot _____

   f.   Reporting of percentages _____

An electronic version of this Problem Sheet that you can fill in and print, save, or e-mail is available on the Online Learning Center at www.mhhe.com/fraenkel5e and on your Interactive Student CD-ROM.

A full-sized version of this Problem Sheet that you can fill in or photocopy is in your Student Workbook.

Inferential Statistics

CHAPTER 11

Inferential Statistics

What Are Inferential Statistics?

The Logic of Inferential Statistics

Sampling Error
Distribution of Sample Means
Standard Error of the Mean
Estimating the Standard Error of the Mean
Confidence Intervals
Confidence Intervals and Probability
Comparing More Than One Sample
The Standard Error of the Difference
Between Sample Means

Inference Techniques

Parametric Techniques for Analyzing Quantitative Data
Nonparametric Techniques for Analyzing Quantitative Data
Parametric Techniques for Analyzing Categorical Data
Nonparametric Techniques for Analyzing Categorical Data
Summary of Techniques
Power of a Statistical Test

Practical Versus Statistical Significance

One- and Two-Tailed Tests
Use of the Null Hypothesis: An Evaluation

Hypothesis Testing

The Null Hypothesis
Hypothesis Testing: A Review

Objectives

Studying this chapter should enable you to:

- Explain *what is meant by the term "inferential statistics."*
- Explain *the concept of sampling error.*
- Describe *briefly how to calculate a confidence interval.*
- State *the difference between a research hypothesis and a null hypothesis.*
- Describe *briefly the logic underlying hypothesis testing.*
- State *what is meant by the terms "significance level" and "statistically significant."*
- Explain *the difference between a one- and a two-tailed test of significance.*
- Explain *the difference between parametric and nonparametric tests of significance.*
- Name *three examples of parametric tests used by educational researchers.*
- Name *three examples of nonparametric tests used by educational researchers.*
- Describe *what is meant by the term "power" with regard to statistical tests.*
- Explain *the importance of random sampling with regard to the use of inferential statistics.*

Interactive and Applied Learning

After, or while, reading this chapter:

🔘 Go to your Interactive Student CD-ROM to:

- Learn More About the Purpose of Inferential Statistics

🔘 📖 Go to your Interactive Student CD-ROM or Student Workbook to do the following activities:

- Activity 11.1: Probability
- Activity 11.2: Learning to Read a *t*-Table
- Activity 11.3: Calculate a *t*-Test
- Activity 11.4: Perform a Chi-Square Test
- Activity 11.5: Conduct a *t*-Test

"**P**aulo, I'm worried."

"Why, Julie?"

"Well, in my job as director of the new elementary math program for the district, I have to find out how well the students in the program are doing. This year, we're testing the fifth-graders."

"Yeah, so? What's to worry about?"

"Well, I gave the end-of-the-semester exam to one of the fifth-grade classes at Hoover Elementary last week. I got the results back just today."

"And?"

"Get this. Their average score was only 65 out of a possible 100 points! Of course this is just one class, but still . . . I'm afraid that it may be true of all the fifth-grade classes."

"Not necessarily, Julie. That would depend on how similar the Hoover kids are to the other fifth-graders in the district. What you need is some way to estimate the average score of all of the district's fifth-graders—but you can't do it from that class."

"I assume you're thinking about some sort of inferential test, eh?"

"Yep, you got it."

How might Julie make such an estimate? To find out, read this chapter.

What Are Inferential Statistics?

Descriptive statistics are but one type of statistic that researchers use to analyze their data. Many times they wish to make inferences about a population based on data they have obtained from a sample. To do this, they use inferential statistics. Let us consider how.

Suppose a researcher administers a commercially available IQ test to a sample of 65 students selected from a particular elementary school district and finds their average score is 85. What does this tell her about the IQ scores of the entire population of students in the district? Does the average IQ score of students in the district also equal 85? Or is this sample of students different, on the average, from other students in the district? If these students are different, how are they different? Are their IQ scores higher—or lower?

What the researcher needs is some way to estimate how closely statistics, such as the mean of the IQ scores, obtained on a sample, agree with the corresponding parameters of the population without actually obtaining data on the entire population. Inferential statistics provide such a way.

Inferential statistics are certain types of procedures that allow researchers to make inferences about a population based on findings from a sample. In Chapter Six we discussed the concept of a random sample and pointed out that obtaining a random sample is desirable because it helps ensure that one's sample is representative of a larger population. When a sample is represen-

tative, all the characteristics of the population are assumed to be present in the sample in the same degree. No sampling procedure, not even random sampling, guarantees a totally representative sample, but the chance of obtaining one is greater with random sampling than with any other method. And the more a sample represents a population, the more researchers are entitled to assume that what they find out about the sample will also be true of that population. Making inferences about populations on the basis of random samples is what inferential statistics is all about.

As with descriptive statistics, the techniques of inferential statistics differ depending on which type of data—categorical or quantitative—a researcher wishes to analyze. This chapter begins with techniques applicable to quantitative data, because they provide the best introduction to the logic behind inference techniques and because most educational research involves such data. Some techniques for the analysis of categorical data are presented at the end of the chapter.

The Logic of Inferential Statistics

Suppose a researcher is interested in the difference between males and females with respect to interest in history. He hypothesizes that female students find history more interesting than do male students. To test the hypothesis, he decides to perform the following study. He obtains one random sample of 30 male history students

Figure 11.1 *Selection of Two Samples from Two Distinct Populations*

from the population of 500 male tenth-grade students taking history in a nearby school district and another random sample of 30 female history students from the female population of 550 tenth-grade history students in the district. All students are given an attitude scale to complete. The researcher now has two sets of data: the attitude scores for the male group and the attitude scores for the female group. The design of the study is shown in Figure 11.1 The researcher wants to know whether or not the male population is different from the female population—that is, is the mean score of the male group on the attitude test any different from the mean score of the female group? But the researcher does not know the means of the two populations. All he has are the means of the two samples. He has to rely on the two samples to provide information about the populations.

Is it reasonable to assume that each sample will give a fairly accurate picture of its population? It certainly is possible, since each sample was randomly selected from its population. On the other hand, the students in each sample are only a small portion of their population, and only rarely is a sample absolutely identical to its parent population on a given characteristic. The data the researcher obtains from the two samples will depend on the individual students selected to be in each sample. If another two samples were randomly selected, their makeup would differ from the original two, their means on the attitude scale would be different, and the researcher would end up with a different set of data. How can the researcher be sure that any particular sample he has selected is, indeed, a representative one? He cannot. Maybe another sample would be better.

SAMPLING ERROR

This is the basic difficulty that confronts us when we work with samples: Samples are not likely to be identical to their parent populations. This difference between a sample and its population is referred to as **sampling error** (see Figure 11.2). Furthermore, no two samples

will be the same in all their characteristics. Two different samples from the same population will not be identical: they will be composed of different individuals, they will have different scores on a test (or other measure), and they will probably have different sample means.

Consider the population of high school students in the United States. It would be possible to select literally thousands of different samples from this population. Suppose we took two samples of 25 students each from this population and measured their heights. What would you estimate our chances would be of finding exactly the same mean height in both samples? Very, very unlikely. In fact, we could probably take sample after sample and very seldom obtain two sets of people having exactly the same mean height.

DISTRIBUTION OF SAMPLE MEANS

All this might suggest that it is impossible to formulate any rules that researchers can use to determine similarities between samples and populations. Not so. Fortunately, large collections of random samples do pattern themselves in such a way that it is possible for researchers to predict accurately some characteristics of the population from which the sample was selected.

Were we able to select an infinite number of random samples (all of the same size) from a population, calculate the mean of each, and then arrange these means into a frequency polygon, we would find that they shape themselves into a familiar pattern. The means of a large number of random samples tend to be normally distributed, unless the size of each of the samples is small (less than 30), *and* the scores in the population are *not* normally distributed. Once sample size reaches 30, however, the **distribution of sample means** is very nearly normal, even if the population is not normally distributed. (We realize that this is not immediately obvious; should you wish more explanation of why this happens to be a fact, consult any introductory statistics text.)

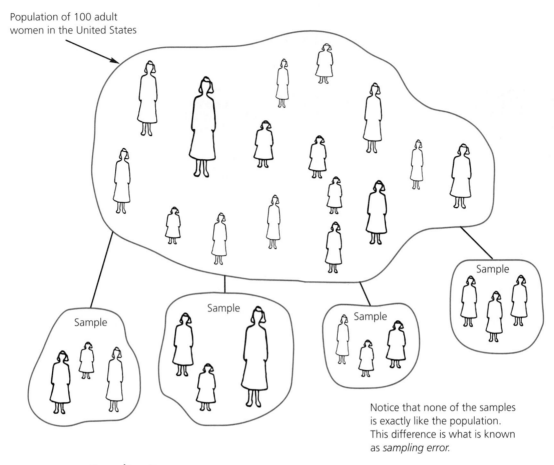

Population of 100 adult women in the United States

Sample

Sample

Sample

Sample

Notice that none of the samples is exactly like the population. This difference is what is known as *sampling error.*

Figure 11.2 *Sampling Error*

Like all normal distributions, a distribution of sample means (called a **sampling distribution**) has its own mean and standard deviation. The mean of a sampling distribution (the "mean of the means") is equal to the mean of the population. In an infinite number of samples, some will have means larger than the population mean and some will have means smaller than the population mean (see Figure 11.3). These data tend to neutralize each other, resulting in an overall average that is equal to the mean of the population. Consider an example. Suppose you have a population of only three scores—1, 2, 3. The mean of this population is 2. Now, take all of the possible types of samples of size two. How many would there be? Nine—(1, 1); (1, 2); (1, 3); (2, 1); (2, 2); (2, 3); (3, 1); (3, 2); (3, 3). The means of these samples are 1, 1.5, 2, 1.5, 2, 2.5, 2, 2.5, and 3, respectively. Add up all these means and divide by nine (that is, 18 ÷ 9), and you see that the mean of these means equals 2, the same as the population mean.

STANDARD ERROR OF THE MEAN

The standard deviation of a sampling distribution of means is called the **standard error of the mean (SEM).** As in all normal distributions, therefore, the 68-95-99.7 rule holds: approximately 68 percent of the sample means fall between ±1 SEM; approximately 95 percent fall between ±2 SEM; and 99.7 percent fall between ±3 SEM (see Figure 11.4).

Thus, if we know or can accurately estimate the mean and the standard deviation of the sampling distribution, we can determine whether it is likely or unlikely that a particular sample mean could be obtained from that population. Suppose the mean of a population is 100, for example, and the standard error of the mean is 10. A sample mean of 110 would fall at +1 SEM; a sample mean of 120 would fall at +2 SEM; a sample mean of 130 would fall at +3 SEM; and so forth.

It would be very unlikely to draw a sample from this population whose mean fell above +3 SEM. Why?

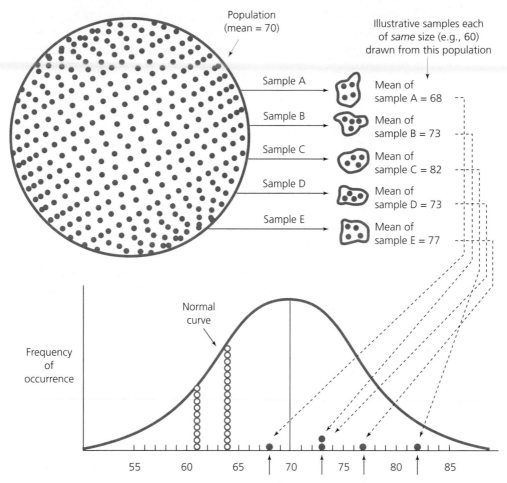

Figure 11.3 *A Sampling Distribution of Means*

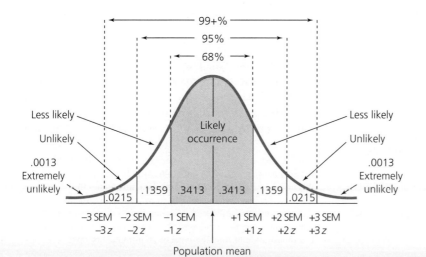

Figure 11.4

Distribution of Sample Means

Because, as in all normal distributions (and remember, the sampling distribution is a normal distribution—of *means*), only 0.0013 of all values (in this case, sample means) fall above +3 SEM. It would not be unusual to select a sample from this population and find that its mean is 105, but selecting a sample with a mean of 130 would be unlikely—very unlikely!

It is possible to use z scores to describe the position of any particular sample mean within a distribution of sample means. We discussed z scores in Chapter Ten. We now want to express means as z scores. Remember that a z score simply states how far a score (or mean) differs from the mean of scores (or means) in standard deviation units. The z score tells a researcher exactly where a particular sample mean is located relative to all other sample means that could have been obtained. For example, a z score of +2 would indicate that a particular sample mean is two standard errors above the population mean. Only about 2 percent of all sample means fall above a z score of +2. Hence, a sample with such a mean would be unusual.

ESTIMATING THE STANDARD ERROR OF THE MEAN

How do we obtain the standard error of the mean? Clearly, we cannot calculate it directly, since we would need, literally, to obtain a huge number of samples and their means.* Statisticians have shown, however, that the standard error can be calculated using a simple formula requiring the standard deviation of the population and the size of the sample. Although we seldom know the standard deviation of the population, fortunately it can be *estimated*† using the standard deviation of the sample. To calculate the SEM, then, simply divide the standard deviation of the sample by the square root of the sample size minus one:

$$\text{SEM} = \frac{\text{SD}}{\sqrt{n-1}}$$

Let's review the basic ideas we have presented so far.

1. The sampling distribution of the mean (or any descriptive statistic) is the distribution of the means (or

other statistic) obtained (theoretically) from an infinitely large number of samples of the same size.
2. The shape of the sampling distribution in many (but not all) cases is the shape of the normal distribution.
3. The SEM (standard error of the mean)—that is, the standard deviation of a sampling distribution of means—can be estimated by dividing the standard deviation of the sample by the square root of the sample size minus one.
4. The frequency with which a particular sample mean will occur can be estimated by using z scores based on sample data to indicate its position in the sampling distribution.

CONFIDENCE INTERVALS

We now can use the SEM to indicate boundaries, or limits, within which the population mean lies. Such boundaries are called **confidence intervals.** How are they determined?

Let us return to the example of the researcher who administered an IQ test to a sample of 65 elementary school students. You will recall that she obtained a sample mean of 85 and wanted to know how much the population mean might differ from this value. We are now in a position to give her some help in this regard.

Let us assume that we have calculated the estimated standard error of the mean for her sample and found it to equal 2.0. Applying this to a sampling distribution of means, we can say that 95 percent of the time the population mean will be between 85 ± 1.96 (2) = 85 ± 3.92 = 81.08 to 88.92. Why ± 1.96? Because the area between ±1.96 z equals 95 percent (.95) of the total area under the normal curve.* This is shown in Figure 11.5.†

Suppose this researcher then wished to establish an interval that would give her more confidence than $p = .95$ in making a statement about the population mean. This can be done by calculating the 99 percent confidence interval. The 99 percent confidence interval is determined in a manner similar to that for determining the 95 percent confidence interval. Given the characteristics of a normal distribution, we know that 0.5 percent of the sample means will lie below –2.58 SEM

---

*If we did have these means, we would calculate the standard error just like any other standard deviation, treating each mean as a score.
†The fact that the standard error is based on an estimated value rather than a known value does introduce an unknown degree of imprecision into this process.

*By looking at the normal curve table in Appendix B, we see that the area between the mean and 1.96 z = .4750. Multiplied by two, this equals .95, or 95 percent, of the total area under the curve.
†Strictly speaking, it is not proper to consider a distribution of population means around the sample mean. In practice, we interpret confidence intervals in this way. The legitimacy of doing so requires a demonstration beyond the level of an introductory text.

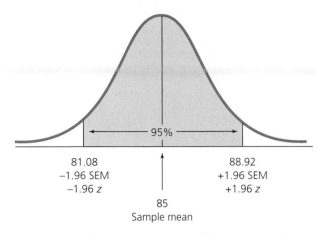

Figure 11.5 *The 95 Percent Confidence Interval*

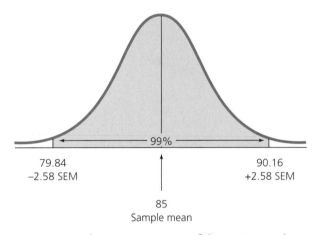

Figure 11.6 *The 99 Percent Confidence Interval*

and another 0.5 percent will lie above +2.58 SEM (see Figure 10.11 in Chapter Ten). Using the previous example, in which the mean of the sample was 85 and the SEM was 2, we calculate the interval as follows: 85 ± 2.58 (SEM) = 85 ± 2.58 (2.0) = 85 ± 5.16 = 79.84 to 90.16. Thus the 99 percent confidence interval lies between 79.84 and 90.16, as shown in Figure 11.6.

Our researcher can now answer her question about approximately how much the population mean differs from the sample mean. While she cannot know exactly what the population mean is, she can indicate the "boundaries" or limits within which it is likely to fall (see Figure 11.7). To repeat, these limits are called confidence intervals. The 95 percent confidence interval spans a segment on the horizontal axis that we are 95 percent certain contains the population mean. The 99

percent confidence interval spans a segment on the horizontal axis within which we are even more certain (99 percent certain) that the population mean falls.* We could be mistaken, of course—the population mean could lie outside these intervals—but it is not very likely.†

CONFIDENCE INTERVALS AND PROBABILITY

Let us return to the concept of probability introduced in Chapter Ten. As we use the term here, **"probability"** is nothing more than predicted relative occurrence, or relative frequency. When we say that something would occur 5 times in 100, we are expressing a probability. We could just as well say the probability is 5 in 100. In our earlier example, we can say, therefore, that the probability of the population mean being *outside* the 81.08–88.92 limits (the 95 percent confidence interval) is only 5 in 100. The probability of it being *outside* the 79.84–90.16 limits (the 99 percent confidence interval) is even less—only 1 in 100. Remember that it is customary to express probabilities in decimal form, e.g., $p = .05$ or $p = .01$. What would $p = .10$ signify?‡

COMPARING MORE THAN ONE SAMPLE

Up to this point we have been explaining how to make inferences about the population mean using data from just one sample. More typically, however, researchers want to compare two or more samples. For example, a researcher might want to determine if there is a difference in attitude between fourth-grade boys and girls in

---

*Notice that it is *not* correct to say that the population mean falls within the 95 percent confidence interval 95 times out of 100. The population mean is a fixed value, and it either does or does not fall within this interval. The correct way to think of a confidence interval is to view it in terms of replicating the study. Suppose we were to replicate the study with another sample and calculate the 95 percent confidence interval for that sample. Suppose we were then to replicate the study once again with a third sample and calculate the 95 percent confidence interval for this third sample. We continue until we have drawn 100 samples and calculated the 95 percent confidence interval for each of these 100 samples. We will find that the population mean lies within 95 percent of these intervals.
†The likelihood of the population mean being outside the 95 percent confidence interval is only 5 percent, and that of being outside the 99 percent confidence interval, only 1 percent. Analogous reasoning and procedures can be used with sample sizes less than 30.
‡A probability of 10 in 100.

Figure 11.7 *We Can Be 99 Percent Confident*

mathematics; whether there is a difference in achievement between students taught by the discussion method as compared to the lecture method; and so forth.

Our previous logic also applies to a difference between means. For example, if a difference between means is found between the test scores of two samples in a study, a researcher wants to know if a difference exists in the populations from which the two samples were selected (Figure 11.8). In essence, we ask the same question we asked about one mean, only this time we ask it about a difference *between* means. Hence we ask, "Is the difference we have found a likely or an unlikely occurrence?" It is possible that the difference can be at-

tributed simply to sampling error—to the fact that certain samples, rather than others, were selected (the "luck of the draw," so to speak). Once again, inferential statistics help us out.

THE STANDARD ERROR OF THE DIFFERENCE BETWEEN SAMPLE MEANS

Fortunately, differences between sample means are also likely to be normally distributed. The distribution of differences between sample means also has its own mean and standard deviation. The mean of the sampling

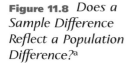

Figure 11.8 *Does a Sample Difference Reflect a Population Difference?*[a]

[a]Question: Does the three-point difference between the means of sample A and sample B reflect a difference between the means of population A and population B?

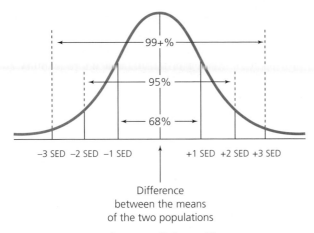

Figure 11.9 *Distribution of the Difference Between Sample Means*

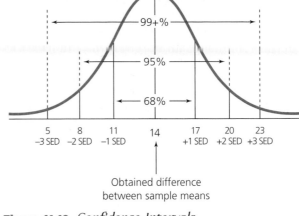

Figure 11.10 *Confidence Intervals*

distribution of differences between sample means is equal to the difference between the means of the two populations. The standard deviation of this distribution is called the **standard error of the difference (SED).** The formula for computing the SED is:

$$SED = \sqrt{(SEM_1)^2 + (SEM_2)^2}$$

where $_1$ and $_2$ refer to the respective samples.

Because the distribution is normal, slightly more than 68 percent of the differences between sample means will fall between ±1 SED (again, remember that the standard error of the difference is a standard deviation); about 95 percent of the differences between sample means will fall between ±2 SED, and 99+ percent of these differences will fall between ±3 SED (Figure 11.9).

Now we can proceed similarly to the way we did with individual sample means. A researcher estimates the standard error of the difference between means, and then uses it, along with the difference between the two sample means and the normal curve, to estimate probable limits (confidence intervals) within which the difference between the means of the two populations is likely to fall.

Let us consider an example. Imagine that the difference between two sample means is 14 raw score points and the calculated SED is 3. Just as we did with one sample population mean, we can now indicate limits within which the difference between the means of the two populations is likely to fall. If we say that the difference between the means of the two populations is between 11 and 17 (±1 SED), we have slightly more than a 68 percent chance of being right. We have somewhat

more than a 95 percent chance of being right if we say the difference between the means of the two populations is between 8 and 20 (±2 SED), and better than a 99 percent chance of being right if we say the difference between the means of the two populations is between 5 and 23 (±3 SED). Figure 11.10 illustrates these confidence intervals.

Suppose the difference between two other sample means is 12. If we calculated the SED to be 2, would it be likely or unlikely for the difference between population means to fall between 10 and 14?*

Hypothesis Testing

How does all this apply to research questions and research hypotheses? You will recall that many hypotheses predict a relationship. In Chapter Ten, we presented techniques for examining data for the existence of relationships. We pointed out in previous chapters that virtually all relationships in data can be examined through one (or more) of three procedures: a comparison of means, a correlation, or a crossbreak table. In each instance, some degree of relationship may be found. If a relationship is found in the data, is there likely to be a similar relationship in the population, or is it simply due to sampling error—to the fact that a particular sample, rather than another, was selected for study? Once again, inferential statistics can help.

*Likely, since 68 percent of the differences between population means fall between these values.

The logic discussed earlier applies to any particular form of a hypothesis and to many procedures used to examine data. Thus, correlation coefficients and differences between them can be evaluated in essentially the same way as means and differences between means; we just need to obtain the standard error of the correlation coefficient(s). The procedure used with crossbreak tables differs in technique, but the logic is the same. We will discuss it later in the chapter.

When testing hypotheses, it is customary to proceed in a slightly different way. Instead of determining the boundaries within which the population mean (or other parameter) can be said to fall, a researcher determines the likelihood of obtaining a sample value (for example, a difference between two sample means) if there is *no* relationship (that is, no difference between the means of the two populations) in the populations from which the samples were drawn. The researcher formulates both a research hypothesis and a null hypothesis. To test the research hypothesis, the researcher must formulate a null hypothesis.

THE NULL HYPOTHESIS

As you will recall, the **research hypothesis** specifies the predicted outcome of a study. Many research hypotheses predict the nature of the relationship the researcher thinks exists in the population, for example: "The population mean of students using method A is greater than the population mean of students using method B."

The **null hypothesis** most commonly used specifies there is *no* relationship in the population, for example: "There is no difference between the population mean of students using method A and the population mean of students using method B." (This is the same thing as saying the difference between the means of the two populations is zero.) Figure 11.11 offers a comparison of research and null hypotheses.

The researcher then proceeds to test the null hypothesis. The same information is needed as before: the knowledge that the sampling distribution is normal, and the calculated standard error of the difference (SED). What is different in a hypothesis test is that instead of using the obtained sample value (e.g., the obtained difference between sample means) as the mean of the sampling distribution (as we did with confidence intervals), we use zero.*

*Actually, any value could be used, but zero is used in virtually all educational research.

We then can determine the probability of obtaining a particular sample value (such as an obtained difference between sample means) by seeing where such a value falls on the sampling distribution. If the probability is small, the null hypothesis is rejected, thereby providing support for the research hypothesis. The results are said to be **statistically significant.**

What counts as "small"? In other words, what constitutes an unlikely outcome? Probably you have guessed. It is customary in educational research to view as unlikely any outcome that has a probability of .05 ($p = .05$) or less. This is referred to as the .05 **level of significance.** When we reject a null hypothesis at the .05 level, we are saying that the probability of obtaining such an outcome is only 5 times (or less) in 100. Some researchers prefer to be even more stringent and choose a .01 level of significance. When a null hypothesis is rejected at the .01 level, it means that the likelihood of obtaining the outcome is only 1 time (or less) in 100.

HYPOTHESIS TESTING: A REVIEW

Let us review what we have said. The logical sequence for a researcher who wishes to engage in hypothesis testing is as follows:

1. State the research hypothesis (e.g., "There is a difference between the population mean of students using method A and the population mean of students using method B").
2. State the null hypothesis (e.g., "There is *no* difference between the population mean of students using method A and the population mean of students using method B," or "The difference between the two population means is zero").
3. Determine the sample statistics pertinent to the hypothesis (e.g., the mean of sample A and the mean of sample B).
4. Determine the probability of obtaining the sample results (i.e., the difference between the mean of sample A and the mean of sample B) if the null hypothesis is true.
5. If the probability is small, reject the null hypothesis, thus affirming the research hypothesis.
6. If the probability is large, do not reject the null hypothesis, which means you cannot affirm the research hypothesis.

Let us use our previous example in which the difference between sample means was 14 points and the SED

(Research hypothesis)

"Jane and Alicia have competed before, and Jane has always won. I predict she'll win today."

(Null hypothesis)

"But she didn't win by much. I predict a tie today."

Figure 11.11 *Research and Null Hypotheses*

was 3 (Figure 11.10). In Figure 11.12 we see that the sample difference of 14 falls far beyond +3 SED; in fact, it exceeds 4 SED. Thus, the probability of obtaining such a sample result is considerably less than .01, and as a result, the null hypothesis is rejected. If the difference in sample means had been 4 instead of 14, would the null hypothesis be rejected?*

Practical Versus Statistical Significance

Just because a result is statistically significant (not due to chance) does not mean that it has any practical or educational value in the real world in which we all work and live. **Statistical significance** only means that one's results are likely to occur by chance less than a certain percentage of the time, say 5 percent. So what? Remember that this only means the observed relationship most likely would not be zero in the population. But it does not mean necessarily that it is *important!* Whenever we have a large enough random sample, almost any result will turn out to be statistically significant. Thus, a very small correlation coefficient, for example, may turn out to be statistically significant but have little

*No. The probability of a difference of 4 is too high—much larger than .05.

(if any) practical significance. In a similar sense, a very small difference in means may yield a statistically significant result but have little educational import.

Consider a few examples. Suppose a random sample of 1000 high school baseball pitchers on the East Coast demonstrate an average fastball speed of 75 mph, while a second random sample of 1000 high school pitchers in the Midwest show an average fastball speed of 71 mph. Now this difference of 4 mph might be statistically significant (due to the large sample size), but we doubt that baseball fans would say that it is of any practical importance. Or suppose that a researcher tries out a new method of teaching mathematics to high school juniors. She finds that those students exposed to method A (the new method) score, on the average, two points higher on the final examination than the students exposed to method B (the older, more traditional method), and that this difference is statistically significant. We doubt that the mathematics department would immediately encourage all of its members to adopt method A on the basis of this two-point difference. Would you?

Ironically, the fact that most educational studies involve smaller samples may actually be an advantage when it comes to practical significance. Because smaller sample size makes it harder to detect a difference even when there is one in the population, a larger difference in means is therefore required to reject the null hypothesis. This is so because a smaller sample results in a larger standard error of the difference in

Figure 11.12
Illustration of When a Researcher Would Reject the Null Hypothesis

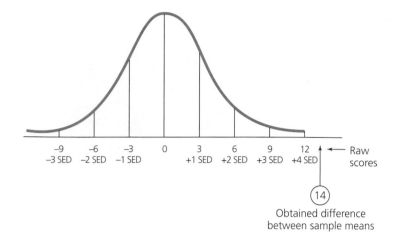

means (SED). Therefore, a larger difference in means is required to reach the significance level (see Figure 11.10). It is also possible that relationships of potential practical significance may be overlooked or dismissed because they are not statistically significant (more on this in the next chapter).

One should always take care in interpreting results—just because one brand of radios is significantly more powerful than another brand statistically does not mean that those looking for a radio should rush to buy one of the first brand.

ONE- AND TWO-TAILED TESTS

In Chapter Three, we made a distinction between directional and nondirectional hypotheses. There is sometimes an advantage to stating hypotheses in directional form that is related to significance testing. We refer again to a hypothetical example of a sampling distribution of differences between means in which the calculated SED equals 3. Previously, we interpreted the statistical significance of an obtained difference between sample means of 14 points. The statistical significance of this difference was quite clear-cut, since it was so large. Suppose, however, that the obtained difference was not 14, but 5.5 points. To determine the probability associated with this outcome, we must know whether the researcher's hypothesis was a directional or a nondirectional one. If the hypothesis was directional, the researcher specified ahead of time (before collecting any data) which group would have the higher mean (for example, the mean score of students using method A would be higher than the mean score of students using method B).

If this had been the case, the researcher's hypothesis would be supported only if the mean of sample A is higher than the mean of sample B. The researcher must decide beforehand that he or she will subtract the mean of sample B from the mean of sample A. A large difference between sample means in the opposite direction would not support the research hypothesis. A difference between sample means of +2 is in the hypothesized direction, therefore, but a difference of −2 (should the mean of sample B be higher than the mean of sample A) is not. Because the researchers' hypothesis can be supported only if he or she obtains a positive difference between the sample means, the researcher is justified in using only the positive tail of the sampling distribution to locate the obtained difference. This is referred to as a **one-tailed test** of statistical significance (Figure 11.13).

At the 5 percent level of significance ($p = .05$), the null hypothesis may be rejected only if the obtained dif-

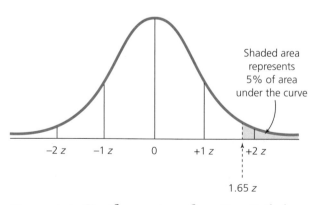

Shaded area represents 5% of area under the curve

1.65 z

Figure 11.13 *Significance Area for a One-Tailed Test*

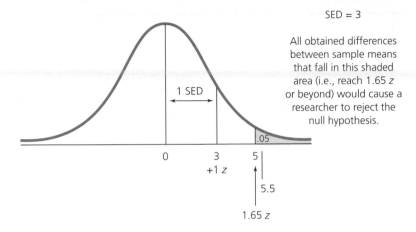

SED = 3

All obtained differences between sample means that fall in this shaded area (i.e., reach 1.65 *z* or beyond) would cause a researcher to reject the null hypothesis.

Figure 11.14 *One-Tailed Test Using a Distribution of Differences Between Sample Means*

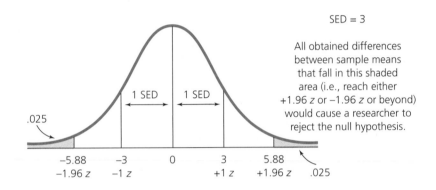

SED = 3

All obtained differences between sample means that fall in this shaded area (i.e., reach either +1.96 *z* or −1.96 *z* or beyond) would cause a researcher to reject the null hypothesis.

Figure 11.15 *Two-Tailed Test Using a Distribution of Differences Between Sample Means*

ference between sample means reaches or exceeds 1.65 SED* in the one tail. As shown in Figure 11.14, this requires a difference between sample means of 5 points or more.† Our previously obtained difference of 5.5 would be significant at this level, therefore, since it not only reaches, but exceeds, 1.65 SED.

What if the hypothesis were nondirectional? If this had been the case, the researcher would not have specified beforehand which group would have the higher mean. In that case, the hypothesis would be supported by a suitable difference in *either* tail. This is called a **two-tailed test** of statistical significance. If the researcher uses the .05 level of significance, this requires that the 5 percent of the total area must include both tails—that is, there is 2.5 percent in each tail. As a re-

sult, a difference in sample means of almost 6 points (either +5.88 or −5.88) is required to reject the null hypothesis (Figure 11.15), since 1.96(3) = 5.88.

USE OF THE NULL HYPOTHESIS: AN EVALUATION

There appears to be much misunderstanding regarding the use of the null hypothesis. First, it often is stated in place of a research hypothesis. While it is easy to replace a research hypothesis (which predicts a relationship) with a null hypothesis (which predicts no relationship), there is no good reason for doing so. As we have seen, the null hypothesis is merely a useful methodological device.

Second, there is nothing sacred about the customary .05 and .01 significance levels—they are merely conventions. It is a little ridiculous, for example, to fail to reject the null hypothesis with a sample value that has a probability of .06. To do so might very well result in what is known as a **Type II error**—this error results when a researcher fails to reject a null hypothesis that is

---

*By looking in the normal curve table in Appendix B, we see that the area beyond 1.65 *z* equals .05, or 5 percent of the area under the curve.
†Since an area of .05 in one tail equals a *z* of 1.65, and the SED is 3, we multiply 1.65(3) to find the score value at this point: 1.65(3) = 4.95, or 5 points.

	Susie has pneumonia.	Susie does not have pneumonia.
Doctor says that symptoms like Susie's occur only 5 percent of the time in healthy people. To be safe, however, he decides to treat Susie for pneumonia.	Doctor is correct. Susie does have pneumonia and the treatment cures her. ☺	Doctor is wrong. Susie's treatment was unnecessary and possibly unpleasant and expensive. **Type I error** (α) ☹
Doctor says that symptoms like Susie's occur 95 percent of the time in healthy people. In his judgment, therefore, her symptoms are a false alarm and do not warrant treatment, and he decides not to treat Susie for pneumonia.	Doctor is wrong. Susie is not treated and may suffer serious consequences. **Type II error** (β) ☹	Doctor is correct. Unnecessary treatment is avoided. ☺

Figure 11.16 *A Hypothetical Example of Type I and Type II Errors*

false. A **Type I error,** on the other hand, results when a researcher rejects a null hypothesis that is true. In our example in which there was a 14-point difference between sample means, for example, we rejected the null hypothesis at the .05 level. In doing so, we realized that a 5 percent chance remained of being wrong—that is, a 5 percent chance that the null hypothesis was true. Figure 11.16 provides an example of Type I and Type II errors.

Finally, there is also nothing sacrosanct about testing an obtained result against zero. In our previous example, for instance, why not test the obtained value of 14 (or 5.5, etc.) against a hypothetical population difference of 1 (or 3, etc.)? Testing only against zero can mislead one into exaggerating the importance of the obtained relationship. We believe the reporting of inferential statistics should rely more on confidence intervals and less on whether a particular level of significance has been attained.

Inference Techniques

It is beyond the scope of this text to treat in detail each of the many techniques that exist for answering inference questions about data. We shall, however, present a brief summary of the more commonly used tests of statistical significance that researchers employ and then illustrate how to do one such test.

In Chapter Ten, we made a distinction between quantitative and categorical data. We pointed out that the type of data a researcher collects often influences the type of statistical analysis required. A statistical technique appropriate for quantitative data, for example, will generally be inappropriate for categorical data.

There are two basic types of inference techniques that researchers use. **Parametric techniques** make various kinds of assumptions about the nature of the population from which the sample(s) involved in the research study are drawn. **Nonparametric techniques,** on the other hand, make few (if any) assumptions about the nature of the population from which the samples are taken. An advantage of parametric techniques is that they are generally more powerful* than nonparametric techniques and hence much more likely to reveal a true difference or relationship if one really exists. Their disadvantage is that often a researcher cannot satisfy the assumptions they require (for example, that the population is normally distributed on the characteristic of interest). The advantage of nonparametric techniques is that they are safer to use when a researcher cannot satisfy the assumptions underlying the use of parametric techniques.

---

*We discuss the power of a statistical test later in this chapter.

Students frequently ask for more specific rules on sample size. Unfortunately, there are no simple answers. However, under certain conditions, some guidelines are available.

The most important condition is random sampling, but there are other specific requirements that are discussed in statistics texts. Assuming these assumptions are met, the following apply:

Sample size required for concluding that a sample *correlation coefficient* is statistically significant (i.e., different from zero in the population) at the .05 level of confidence.

Value of sample r	.05	.10	.15	.20	.25	.30	.40	.50
Sample size required	1539	400	177	100	64	49	25	16

Sample size required for concluding that a *difference in sample means* is statistically significant (i.e., the difference between the means of the two populations is not zero) at the .05 level of confidence. These calculations require that the population standard deviation be known or estimated from the sample standard deviations. Let us assume, for example, that the standard deviation in both populations is 15 and each of the samples is the same size.

Difference between the sample means	2 points	5 points	10 points	15 points
Required size of each sample	434	71	18	8

PARAMETRIC TECHNIQUES FOR ANALYZING QUANTITATIVE DATA*

The *t*-Test for Means. The *t*-test is a parametric statistical test used to see whether a difference between the means of two samples is significant. The test produces a value for *t* (called an obtained *t*), which the researcher then checks in a statistical table (similar to the one shown in Appendix B) to determine the level of significance that has been reached. As we mentioned earlier, if the .05 level of significance is reached, the researcher customarily rejects the null hypothesis and concludes that a real difference does exist.

There are two forms of this *t*-test, a *t*-test for independent means and a *t*-test for correlated means. The *t*-test for independent means is used to compare the mean scores of two *different,* or independent, groups. For example, if two groups of eighth-graders were ex-

posed to two different methods of teaching for a semester and then given the same achievement test at the end of the semester, their achievement scores could be compared using a *t*-test. The *t*-test for correlated means is used to compare the mean scores of the *same* group before and after a treatment of some sort is given, to see if any observed gain is significant, or when the research design involves two matched groups. It is also used when the *same* subjects receive two different treatments in a study.

Analysis of Variance. When researchers desire to find out whether there are significant differences between the means of *more than* two groups, they commonly use a technique called **analysis of variance (ANOVA),** which is actually a more general form of the *t*-test that is appropriate to use with three or more groups. (It can also be used with two groups.) In brief, variation both within and between each of the groups is analyzed statistically, yielding what is known as an *F* value. As in a *t*-test, this *F* value is then checked in a statistical table to see if it is statistically significant. It is interpreted quite similarly to the *t* value, in that the larger the obtained value of *F*, the greater the likelihood that statistical significance exists. When only two groups are

---

*Many texts distinguish between techniques appropriate for nominal, ordinal, and interval scales of measurement (see Chapter Seven). It turns out that in most cases parametric techniques are most appropriate for interval data, while nonparametric techniques are more appropriate for ordinal and nominal data. Researchers rarely know for certain whether their data justify the assumption that interval scales have actually been used.

being compared, the *F* test is sufficient to tell the researcher whether significance has been achieved. When more than two groups are being compared, the *F* test will not, by itself, tell us which of the means are different. A further (but quite simple) procedure, called a post hoc analysis, is required to find this out. ANOVA is also used when more than one independent variable is investigated, as in *factorial designs,* which we discuss in Chapter Thirteen.

Analysis of Covariance. **Analysis of covariance (ANCOVA)** is a variation of ANOVA used when, for example, groups are given a pretest related in some way to the dependent variable and their mean scores on this pretest are found to differ. ANCOVA enables the researcher to adjust the posttest mean scores on the dependent variable for each group to compensate for the initial differences between the groups on the pretest. The pretest is called the *covariate.* How much the posttest mean scores must be adjusted depends on how large the difference between the pretest means is and the degree of relationship between the covariate and the dependent variable. Several covariates can be used in an ANCOVA test, so in addition to (or instead of) adjusting for a pretest, the researcher can adjust for the effect of other variables. (We discuss this further in Chapter Thirteen). Like ANOVA, ANCOVA produces an *F* value, which is then looked up in a statistical table to determine whether it is statistically significant.

Multivariate Analysis of Variance. **Multivariate analysis of variance (MANOVA)** differs from ANOVA in only one respect: it incorporates two or more dependent variables in the same analysis, thus permitting a more powerful test of differences among means. It is justified only when the researcher has reason to believe correlations exist among the dependent variables. Similarly, **multivariate analysis of covariance (MANCOVA)** extends ANCOVA to include two or more dependent variables in the same analysis. The specific value that is calculated is **Wilk's lambda,** a number analogous to *F* in analysis of variance.

The *t*-Test for *r*. This *t*-test is used to see whether a correlation coefficient calculated on sample data is significant—that is, whether it represents a nonzero correlation in the population from which the sample was drawn. It is similar to the *t*-test for means, except that here the statistic being dealt with is a correlation coefficient *r* rather than a difference between means. The test

produces a value for *t* (again called an obtained *t*), which the researcher checks in a statistical probability table to see whether it is statistically significant. As with the other parametric tests, the larger the obtained value for *t,* the greater the likelihood that significance has been achieved.

NONPARAMETRIC TECHNIQUES FOR ANALYZING QUANTITATIVE DATA

The Mann-Whitney *U* Test. The **Mann-Whitney *U* test** is a nonparametric alternative to the *t*-test used when a researcher wishes to analyze ranked data. The researcher intermingles the scores of the two groups and then ranks them as if they were all from just one group. The test produces a value (*U*), whose probability of occurrence is then checked by the researcher in the appropriate statistical table. The logic of the test is as follows: If the parent populations are identical, then the sum of the pooled rankings for *each* group should be about the same. If the summed ranks are markedly different, on the other hand, then this difference is likely to be statistically significant.

The Kruskal-Wallis One-Way Analysis of Variance. The **Kruskal-Wallis one-way analysis of variance** is used when researchers have more than two independent groups to compare. The procedure is quite similar to the Mann-Whitney *U* test. The scores of the individuals in the several groups are pooled and then ranked as though they all came from one group. The sums of the ranks added together for each of the separate groups are then compared. This analysis produces a value (*H*), whose probability of occurrence is checked by the researcher in the appropriate statistical table.

The Sign Test. The **sign test** is used when a researcher wants to analyze two related (as opposed to independent) samples. Related samples are connected in some way. For example, often a researcher will try to equalize groups on IQ, gender, age, or some other variable. The groups are *matched,* so to speak, on these variables. Another example of a related sample is when the same group is both pre- and posttested (that is, tested twice). Each individual, in other words, is tested on two different occasions (as with the *t*-test for correlated means).

This test is very easy to use. The researcher simply lines up the pairs of related subjects and then determines how many times the paired subjects in one group scored higher than those in the other group. If the groups do not differ significantly, the totals for the two groups should be about equal. If there is a marked difference in scoring (such as many more in one group scoring higher), the difference may be statistically significant. Again, the probability of this occurrence can be determined by consulting the appropriate statistical table.

The Friedman Two-Way Analysis of Variance.

If more than two related groups are involved, then the **Friedman two-way analysis of variance** test can be used. For example, if a researcher employs four matched groups, this test would be appropriate.

PARAMETRIC TECHNIQUES FOR ANALYZING CATEGORICAL DATA

t-Test for Proportions. The most commonly used parametric tests for analyzing categorical data are the *t*-tests for a difference in proportions—that is, whether the proportion in one category (e.g., males) is different from the proportion in another category (e.g., females). As is the case with the t-*tests for means,* there are two forms: one for independent proportions and one for correlated proportions. The latter is used primarily when the same group is being compared, as in the proportion of individuals agreeing with a statement before and after receiving an intervention of some sort.

NONPARAMETRIC TECHNIQUES FOR ANALYZING CATEGORICAL DATA

The Chi-Square Test. The **chi-square test** is used to analyze data that are reported in categories. For example, a researcher might want to compare how many male and female teachers favor a new curriculum to be instituted in a particular school district. He asks a sample of 50 teachers if they favor or oppose the new curriculum. If they do not differ significantly in their responses, then we would expect that about the same proportion of males and females would be in favor of (or opposed to) instituting the curriculum.

The chi-square test is based on a comparison between expected frequencies and actual, obtained frequencies. If the obtained frequencies are similar to the expected frequencies, then researchers conclude that the groups do not differ (in our example above, they do not differ in their attitude toward the new curriculum). If there are considerable differences between the expected and obtained frequencies, on the other hand, then researchers conclude that there is a significant difference in attitude between the two groups.

The calculation of chi square is a necessary step in determining the *contingency coefficient*—a descriptive statistic referred to in Chapter Ten.

As with all of these inference techniques, the chi-square test yields a value (χ^2). The chi-square test is not limited to comparing expected and obtained frequencies for only two variables. See Table 10.11 for an example.

After the value for χ^2 has been calculated, we want to determine how likely it is that such a result could occur if there were no relationship in the population—that is, whether the obtained pattern of results does not exist in the population but occurred because of the particular sample that was selected. As with all inferential tests, we determine this by consulting a probability table (Appendix C).

You will notice that the chi-square table in Appendix C has a column headed **"degrees of freedom."** This concept is important in many inferential statistics. In essence, it refers to the number of scores in a frequency distribution that are "free to vary"—that is, that are not fixed. For example, suppose you had a distribution of only three scores, *a, b,* and *c,* that must add up to 10. It is apparent that *a, b,* and *c* can have a number of different values (such as 3, 5, and 2; 1, 6, and 3; 2, 2, and 6) and still add up to 10. But, once any two of these values are fixed—set—then the third is also set—it cannot vary. Thus, should *a* = 3 and *b* = 5, *c must* equal 2. Hence, we say that there are two degrees of freedom in this distribution—any two of the values are "free to vary," so to speak, but once they are set, the third is also fixed. **Degrees of freedom** are calculated in crossbreak tables as follows, using an example of a table with three rows and two columns.

Step 1: Subtract 1 from the number of rows: 3 − 1 = 2

Step 2: Subtract 1 from the number of columns: 2 − 1 = 1

Step 3: Multiply step 1 by step 2: (2)(1) = 2

Thus, in this example, there are two degrees of freedom.

Contingency Coefficient. The final step in the process is to calculate the **contingency coefficient,** symbolized by the letter *C,* to which we referred in Chapter Ten. It is a measure of the degree of association in a contingency table. We show how to calculate both the chi-square test and the contingency coefficient in Appendix D.

Table 11.1 *Contingency Coefficient Values for Different-Sized Crossbreak Tables*

Size of Table (No. of Cells)	Upper limit[a] for C Calculated
2 by 2	.71
3 by 3	.82
4 by 4	.87
5 by 5	.89
6 by 6	.91

[a]The upper limits for unequal-sized tables (such as 2 by 3 or 3 by 4) are unknown but can be estimated from the values given. Thus, the upper limit for a 3 by 4 table would approximate .85.

The contingency coefficient cannot be interpreted in exactly the same way as the correlation coefficient. It must be interpreted by using Table 11.1. This table gives the upper limit for *C,* depending on the number of cells in the crossbreak table.

SUMMARY OF TECHNIQUES

The names of the most commonly used inferential procedures and the data type appropriate to their use are summarized in Table 11.2.

This summary should be useful to you whenever you encounter these terms in your reading. While the details of both mathematical rationale and calculation differ greatly among these techniques, the most important things to remember are as follows.

1. The end product of all inference procedures is the same: a statement of probability relating the sample data to hypothesized population characteristics.
2. All inference techniques assume random sampling. Without random sampling, the resulting probabilities are in error—to an unknown degree.

3. Inference techniques are intended to answer only one question: Given the sample data, what are probable population characteristics? These techniques do *not* help decide whether the data show results that are meaningful or useful—they indicate only the extent to which they may be generalizable.

POWER OF A STATISTICAL TEST

The power of a statistical test is similar to the power of a telescope. Astronomers looking at Mars or Venus with a low-power telescope probably can see that these planets look like spheres, but it is unlikely that they can see much by way of differences. With high-power telescopes, however, they can see such differences as moons and mountains. When the purpose of a statistical test is to assess differences, **power** is the probability that the test will correctly lead to the conclusion that there *is* a difference when, in fact, a difference exists.

Suppose a football coach wants to study a new technique for kicking field goals. He asks a (random) sample of 30 high school players to each kick 30 goals. They take the same "test" after being coached in the new technique. The mean number of goals before coaching is 11.2 and it is 18.8 after coaching—a difference of 7.6. The null hypothesis is that any positive difference (i.e., the number of goals after coaching minus the number of goals before coaching) is a chance difference from the true population difference of zero. A one-tailed *t*-test is the technique used to test for statistical significance.

In this example, the critical value for rejecting the null hypothesis at the .05 level is calculated. Assume the critical value turns out to be 5.8. Any difference in means that is larger than +5.8 would result in rejection of the null hypothesis. Since our difference is 7.6, we

Table 11.2 *Commonly Used Inferential Techniques*

	Parametric	Nonparametric
Quantitative	*t*-test for independent means	Mann-Whitney *U* test
	t-test for correlated means	Kruskal-Wallis one-way analysis of variance
	Analysis of variance (ANOVA)	Sign test
	Analysis of covariance (ANCOVA)	Friedman two-way analysis of variance
	Multivariate analysis of variance (MANOVA)	
	t-test for *r*	
Categorical	*t*-test for difference in proportions	Chi square

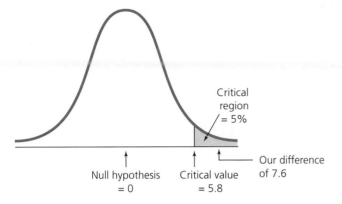

<figure>**Figure 11.17** *Rejecting the Null Hypothesis*</figure>

therefore reject the null hypothesis. Figure 11.17 illustrates this condition.

Now assume that we somehow know that the real difference in the population is actually 8.0. This is shown in Figure 11.18. The dark-shaded part shows the probability that the null hypothesis (which we now "know" to be wrong) will not be rejected by using the critical value of 5.8—that is, it shows how often one would get a value of 5.8 or less, which is not sufficient to cause the null hypothesis to be rejected. This area is beta, and is determined from a *t*-table. The power under this particular "known" value of the population difference is the lightly shaded area 1 − beta. You can see, then, that in this instance, if the real value is 8, a *t*-test using $p = .05$ is unlikely to detect it.

The power (1 − beta) for a series of assumed "true" values can be obtained in the same way. When power is plotted against assumed "real" values, the result is called a power curve, and looks something like Figure 11.19. Comparing such power curves for different tech-

niques (e.g., a *t*-test versus the Mann-Whitney *U* test) indicates their relative efficiency for use in a particular circumstance. Parametric tests (e.g., ANOVA, *t*-tests) are generally, but not always, more powerful than nonparametric tests (e.g., chi-square, Mann-Whitney *U* test).

Clearly, researchers want to use a powerful statistical test—one that can detect a relationship if one exists in the population—if they possibly can. If at all possible, therefore, power should be increased. How might this be done?

There are at least four ways to increase power in addition to the use of parametric tests when appropriate:

1. Decrease sampling error by:
   a. Increasing sample size. An estimate of the necessary sample size can be obtained by doing a statistical power analysis. This requires an estimation of all of the values (except *n* = sample size) used in calculating the statistic you plan to use

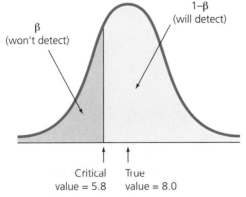

Figure 11.18 *An Illustration of Power Under an Assumed Population Value*

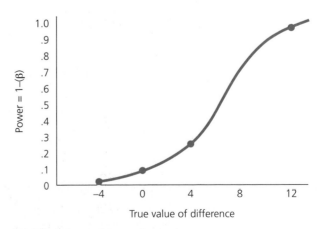

Figure 11.19 *A Power Curve*

Can Statistical Power Analysis Be Misleading?

Can statistical power analysis mislead researchers? An example is provided by a study which found that, in the year following the 1994 federal ban on assault weapons, gun homicides declined 6.7 percent more than would have been expected, based on preexisting trends. This difference was not statistically significant. The authors carried out a statistical power analysis and concluded that a larger sample and longer time period were needed to have a sufficiently powerful statistical test that could detect an effect if any truly existed.*

*C. S. Koper and J. A. Roth (2001). The impact of the 1994 assault weapon ban on gun violence outcomes: An assessment of multiple outcome measures and some lessons for policy evaluation. *Journal of Quantitative Criminology, 17:* (1): pp. 33–74.

Kleck argued that even with a much longer time frame and larger sample (and therefore greater statistical power), the possible impact of the ban is so slight (because assault weapons comprised only two percent of the guns used in crime) that "we could not reliably detect so miniscule an impact."[†] He agreed with the study's authors that the observed decline may well be due to other factors, such as reduced crack use in high-crime neighborhoods (uncontrolled variables). He asked, in light of such known limitations, whether such studies are worth doing. Koper and Roth argued that they are because of the importance of decisions regarding such social policy issues.[‡]

What do you think? Are such studies worth doing?

[†]G. Kleck (2001). Impossible policy evaluations and impossible conclusions: A comment on Koper and Roth. *Journal of Quantitative Criminology, 17:* (1): p. 80.
[‡]C. S. Koper and J. A. Roth (2001). A priori assertions versus empirical inquiry: A reply to Kleck. *Journal of Quantitative Criminology, 17:* (1): pp. 81–88.

and solving for *n* (see, for example, Table D.1 for the formulas used to calculate the *t*-test).*

b. Using reliable measures to decrease measurement error.

2. Controlling for extraneous variables, as these may obscure the relationship being studied.

3. Increasing the strength of the treatment (if there is one), perhaps by using a larger time period.

4. Using a one-tailed test, when such is justifiable.

*Tables are available for estimating sample size based on a combination of desired effect size (Delta, p. 256) and desired level of power. [See Lipsey, M. W. (1990). *Design sensitivity: Statistical power for experimental research*. Newbury Park, CA, Sage.]

Go back to the **Interactive and Applied Learning Tools** feature at the beginning of the chapter for a listing of interactive and applied activities. Go to the **Online Learning Center** at www.mhhe.com/fraenkel5e or your **Interactive Student CD-ROM** to take practice quizzes and receive immediate feedback, practice with key terms, review chapter content and main ideas, and find annotated Web links.

Main Points

WHAT ARE INFERENTIAL STATISTICS?

- Inferential statistics refer to certain procedures that allow researchers to make inferences about a population based on data obtained from a sample.
- The term "probability," as used in research, refers to the predicted relative frequency with which a given event will occur.

SAMPLING ERROR

- The term "sampling error" refers to the variations in sample statistics that occur as a result of repeated sampling from the same population.

THE DISTRIBUTION OF SAMPLE MEANS

- A sampling distribution of means is a frequency distribution resulting from plotting the means of a very large number of samples from the same population.
- The standard error of the mean is the standard deviation of a sampling distribution of means. The standard error of the difference between means is the standard deviation of a sampling distribution of *differences* between sample means.

CONFIDENCE INTERVALS

- A confidence interval is a region extending both above and below a sample statistic (such as a sample mean) within which a population parameter (such as the population mean) may be said to fall with a specified probability of being wrong.

HYPOTHESIS TESTING

- Statistical hypothesis testing is a way of determining the probability that an obtained sample statistic will occur, given a hypothetical population parameter.
- A research hypothesis specifies the nature of the relationship the researcher thinks exists in the population.
- The null hypothesis typically specifies that there is no relationship in the population.

SIGNIFICANCE LEVELS

- The term "significance level" (or "level of significance"), as used in research, refers to the probability of a sample statistic occurring as a result of sampling error.
- The significance levels most commonly used in educational research are the .05 and .01 levels.
- Statistical significance and practical significance are not necessarily the same. Just because a result is statistically significant does not mean that it is practically (i.e., educationally) significant.

TESTS OF STATISTICAL SIGNIFICANCE

- A one-tailed test of significance involves the use of probabilities based on one-half of a sampling distribution because the research hypothesis is a directional hypothesis.
- A two-tailed test, on the other hand, involves the use of probabilities based on both sides of a sampling distribution because the research hypothesis is a nondirectional hypothesis.

PARAMETRIC TESTS FOR QUANTITATIVE DATA

- A parametric statistical test requires various kinds of assumptions about the nature of the population from which the samples involved in the research study were taken.
- Some of the commonly used parametric techniques for analyzing quantitative data include the t-test for means, ANOVA, ANCOVA, MANOVA, and the t-test for r.

PARAMETRIC TESTS FOR CATEGORICAL DATA

- The most common parametric technique for analyzing categorical data is the t-test for differences in proportions.

NONPARAMETRIC TESTS FOR QUANTITATIVE DATA

- A nonparametric statistical technique makes few, if any, assumptions about the nature of the population from which the samples in the study were taken.
- Some of the commonly used nonparametric techniques for analyzing quantitative data are the Mann-Whitney U test, the Kruskal-Wallis one-way analysis of variance, the sign test, and the Friedman two-way analysis of variance.

NONPARAMETRIC TESTS FOR CATEGORICAL DATA

- The chi-square test is the nonparametric technique most commonly used to analyze categorical data.
- The contingency coefficient is a descriptive statistic indicating the degree of relationship that exists between two categorical variables.

POWER OF A STATISTICAL TEST

- The power of a statistical test for a particular set of data is the likelihood of identifying a difference between population parameters when it in fact exists.
- Parametric tests are generally, but not always, more powerful than nonparametric tests.

Key Terms

Analysis of covariance (ANCOVA) 242

Analysis of variance (ANOVA) 241

Chi-square test 243

Confidence interval 232

Degrees of freedom 243

Distribution of sample means 229

Friedman two-way analysis of variance 243

Hypothesis test 235

Inferential statistics 228

Kruskal-Wallis one-way analysis of variance 242

Level of significance 236

Mann-Whitney U test 242

Multivariate analysis of variance (MANOVA) 242

For Discussion

1. If a researcher's hypothesis is that the mean score on a test of critical thinking will be higher for women than for men, should he or she use a one-tailed or two-tailed test of statistical significance? Why?

2. What is wrong with each of the following statements?
   a. Inferential statistics are used to summarize data.
   b. A researcher wants to be very confident that the population mean falls within the 95 percent confidence interval, so she calculates the sample mean ±1 SEM.
   c. All inferential statistics require the assumption of interval scales.
   d. A researcher decides to make his research hypothesis and his null hypothesis identical.
   e. It is sometimes easier to reject the null hypothesis with a two-tailed than with a one-tailed test.
   f. Making inferences about samples is what inferential statistics is all about.

3. What would you say to a researcher who decides to use a .20 level of significance? Why?

4. "Hypotheses can never be proven, only supported." Is this statement true or not? Explain.

5. Is it possible for the results of a study to be of practical importance even though they are not statistically significant? Why or why not?

6. No two samples will be the same in all of their characteristics. Why won't they?

7. The standard error of the mean can never be larger than the standard deviation of the sample. Why?

8. How are z scores related to the standard error of the mean?

9. When might a researcher *not* need to use inferential statistics to analyze his or her data?

Research Exercise Eleven: Inferential Statistics

Using Problem Sheet 11, once again state the question or hypothesis of your study. Summarize the descriptive statistics you would use to describe the relationship you are hypothesizing. Indicate which inference technique(s) is appropriate. Tell whether you would or would not do a significance test and/or calculate a confidence interval, and if not, why. Lastly, describe the type of sample used in your study and explain any limitations that are placed on your use of inferential statistics owing to the nature of the sample.

Problem Sheet 11

Inferential Statistics

1. The question or hypothesis of my study is: _____

   _____

2. The descriptive statistic(s) I would use to describe the relationship I am hypothesizing

   would be: _____

   _____

3. The appropriate inference technique for my study would be: _____

   _____

4. Circle the appropriate word in the sentences below.

   a. I would use a *parametric* or a *nonparametric* technique because: _____

   _____

   b. I *would* or *would not* do a significance test because: _____

   _____

   c. I *would* or *would not* calculate a confidence interval because: _____

   _____

   _____

5. The type of sample used in my study is: _____

6. The type of sample used in my study places the following limitation(s) on my use of

   inferential statistics: _____

   _____

   _____

An electronic version of this Problem Sheet that you can fill in and print, save, or e-mail is available on the **Online Learning Center** at www.mhhe.com/ fraenkel5e and on your Interactive Student CD-ROM.

A full-sized version of this Problem Sheet that you can fill in or photocopy is in your Student Workbook.

Statistics in Perspective

CHAPTER 12

Statistics in Perspective

- **Approaches to Research**

- **A Recap of Recommendations**

- **Comparing Groups: Quantitative Data**
  - Techniques
  - Interpretation

- **Relating Variables Within a Group: Categorical Data**

- **Relating Variables Within a Group: Quantitative Data**
  - Techniques
  - Interpretation

- **Comparing Groups: Categorical Data**
  - Techniques
  - Interpretation

Objectives

Studying this chapter should enable you to:

- Apply *several recommendations when comparing data obtained from two or more groups.*
- Apply *several recommendations when relating variables within a single group.*
- Explain *what is meant by the term "effect size."*
- Describe *briefly how to use frequency polygons, scatterplots, and crossbreak tables to interpret data.*
- Differentiate *between statistically significant and practically significant research results.*

Interactive and Applied Learning

After, or while, reading this chapter:

🔵 Go to your Interactive Student CD-ROM to:
- Learn More About Statistical Versus Practical Significance

🔵 📖 Go to your Interactive Student CD-ROM or Student Workbook to do the following activities:
- Activity 12.1: Statistical Versus Practical Significance
- Activity 12.2: Appropriate Techniques
- Activity 12.3: Interpret the Data
- Activity 12.4: Collect Some Data

Well, the results are in," said Tamara Phillips. "I got the consultant's report about that study we did last semester."

"What study was that?" asked Felicia Lee, as the two carpooled to Eisenhower Middle School, where they both taught eighth-grade social studies.

"Don't you remember? That guy from the university came down and asked some of us who taught social studies to try an inquiry approach?"

"Oh, yeah, I remember. I was in the experimental group—we used a series of "inquiry-oriented" lessons that they designed. They compared the results of our students with those of students who were similar in ability whose teachers did not use those lessons. What did they find out?"

"Well, the report states that those students whose teachers used the inquiry lessons had significantly higher test scores. But I'm not quite sure what that suggests."

"It means that the inquiry method is superior to whatever method the teachers of the other group used, doesn't it?"

"I'm not sure. It depends on whether the significance they're talking about refers to practical or only statistical significance."

"What's the difference?"

This difference—between statistical and practical significance—is an important one when it comes to talking about the results of a study. It is one of the things you will learn about in this chapter.

Now that you are somewhat familiar with both descriptive and inferential statistics, we want to relate them more specifically to practice. What are appropriate uses of these statistics? What are appropriate interpretations of them? What are the common errors or mistakes you should watch out for as either a participant in or consumer of research?

There are appropriate uses for both descriptive and inferential statistics. Sometimes, however, either or both types can be used inappropriately. In this chapter, therefore, we want to discuss the appropriate use of the descriptive and inferential statistics described in the previous two chapters. We will present a number of recommendations that we believe all researchers should consider when they use either type of statistics.

Approaches to Research

Much research in education is done in one of two ways: either two or more groups are compared or variables within one group are related. Furthermore, as you have seen, the data in a study may be either quantitative or categorical. Thus four different combinations of research are possible, as shown in Figure 12.1.

Remember that all groups are made up of individual units. In most cases, the unit is one person and the group is a group of people. Sometimes, however, the unit is itself a group (for example, a class of students). In such cases, the "group" would be a collection of classes. This is illustrated by the following hypothesis: "Teacher friendliness is related to student learning." This hypothesis could be studied with a group of classes and a measure of both teacher "friendliness" and average student learning for each *class.*

Another complication arises in studies in which the same individuals receive two or more different treatments or methods. In comparing treatments, we are not then comparing different groups of people but different groups of scores obtained by the same group at different times. Nevertheless, the statistical analysis fits the comparison group model. We discuss this point further in Chapter Thirteen.

Comparing Groups: Quantitative Data

TECHNIQUES

Whenever two or more groups are compared using quantitative data, the comparisons can be made in a variety of ways: through frequency polygons, calculation of one or more measures of central tendency (averages),

	Data	
	Quantitative	Categorical
Two or more groups are compared		
Variables within one group are related		

Figure 12.1
Combinations of Data and Approaches to Research

and/or calculation of one or more measures of variability (spreads). Frequency polygons provide the most information; averages are useful summaries of each group's performance; and spreads provide information about the degree of variability in each group.

When analyzing data obtained from two groups, therefore, the first thing researchers should do is construct a frequency polygon of each group's scores. This will show all the information available about each group and also help researchers decide which of the shorter and more convenient indices to calculate. For example, examination of the frequency polygon of a group's scores can indicate whether the median or the mean is the most appropriate measure of central tendency to use. When comparing quantitative data from two groups, therefore, we recommend the following:

Recommendation 1: As a first step, prepare a frequency polygon of each group's scores.

Recommendation 2: Use these polygons to decide which measure of central tendency is appropriate to calculate. If any polygon shows extreme scores at one end, use medians for all groups rather than, or in addition to, means.

INTERPRETATION

Once the descriptive statistics have been calculated, they must be interpreted. At this point, the task is to describe, in words, what the polygons and averages tell researchers about the question or hypothesis being investigated. A key question arises: How large does a difference in means between two groups have to be in order to be important? When will this difference *make a difference?* How does one decide? You will recall that this is the issue of practical versus statistical significance that we discussed in Chapter Eleven.

Use Information About Known Groups. Unfortunately, in most educational research, this information is very difficult to obtain. Sometimes, prior experience can be helpful. One of the advantages of IQ scores is that, over the years, many educators have had enough experience with them to make differences between them meaningful. Most experienced counselors, administrators, and teachers realize, for example, that a difference in means of less than 5 points between two groups has little useful meaning, no matter how statistically significant the difference may be. They also know that a difference between means of 10 points is enough to have important implications. At other times, a researcher may have available a frame of reference, or standard, to use in interpreting the magnitude of a difference between means. One such standard consists of

"That's the gist of what I want to say. Now get me some statistics to base it on."

the mean scores of **known groups.** In a study of critical thinking in which one of the present authors participated, for example, the end-of-year mean score for a group of eleventh-graders who received a special curriculum was shown to be higher than is typical of the mean scores of eleventh-graders in general *and* close to the mean score of a group of college students, whereas a comparison group scored lower than both. Because the special-curriculum group also demonstrated a fall-to-spring mean gain that was twice that of the comparison group, the total evidence obtained through comparing their performance with other groups indicated that the gains made by the special-curriculum group were important.

Calculate the Effect Size. Another technique for assessing the magnitude of a difference between the means of two groups is to calculate what is known as **effect size (ES).***

Effect size takes into account the *size* of the difference between means that is obtained, regardless of whether it is statistically significant. One of the most commonly used indexes of effect size is called delta (Δ). It is obtained by dividing the difference between the means of the two groups being compared by the standard deviation of the comparison group. Thus:

$$\Delta = \frac{\text{mean of experimental group} - \text{mean of comparison group}}{\text{standard deviation of comparison group}}$$

When pre-to-post gains in the mean scores of two groups are compared, the formula is modified as follows:

$$\Delta = \frac{\text{mean experimental gain} - \text{mean comparison gain}}{\text{standard deviation of gain of comparison group}}$$

The standard deviation of gain score is obtained by first getting the gain (post – pre) score for each individual and then calculating the standard deviation as usual.[†]

---

*The term "effect size" is used to identify a group of statistical indices, all of which have the common purpose of clarifying the magnitude of relationship. Delta (Δ) is one of the most commonly used of such indices.

[†]There are more effective ways to obtain gain scores, but we will delay a discussion until subsequent chapters.

While delta is a useful tool for assessing the magnitude of a difference between the means of two groups, it does not, in and of itself, answer the question of how large it must be for researchers to consider an obtained difference important. As is the case with significance levels, this is essentially an arbitrary decision. Most researchers consider that any delta of .50 (that is, half a standard deviation of the comparison group's scores) or larger is an important finding. If the scores fit the normal distribution, such a value of delta indicates that the difference in means between the two groups is about one-twelfth the distance between the highest and lowest scores of the comparison group. When assessing the magnitude of a difference between the means of two groups, therefore, we recommend the following:

Recommendation 3: Compare obtained results with data on the means of known groups, if possible.
Recommendation 4: Calculate delta. Interpret a Δ of .50 or larger as important.

Use Inferential Statistics. A third method for judging the importance of a difference between the means of two groups is by the use of **inferential statistics.** It is commonplace to find, even before examining polygons or differences in means, that a researcher has applied an inference technique (a *t*-test, an analysis of variance, and so on) and then used the results as the *only* criterion for evaluating the importance of the results. This practice has come under increasing attack for the following reasons:

1. Unless the groups compared are random samples from specified populations (which is unusual), the results (probabilities, significance levels, and confidence intervals) are to an unknown degree in error and hence misleading.
2. The outcome is greatly affected by sample size. With 100 cases in each of two groups, a mean difference in IQ score of 4.2 points is statistically significant at the .05 level (assuming the standard deviation is 15, as is typical with most IQ tests). Although statistically significant, this difference is so small as to be meaningless in any practical sense.
3. The actual magnitude of difference is minimized or sometimes overlooked.
4. The purpose of inferential statistics is to provide information pertinent to generalizing sample results to populations, not to evaluate sample results.

With regard to the use of inferential statistics, therefore, we recommend the following:

Statistical Inference Tests— Good or Bad?

Our recommendations regarding statistical inference are not free of controversy. At one extreme are the views of Carver* and Schmidt,[†] who argue that the use of statistical inference tests in educational research should be banned. And in 2000 a survey of AERA members (American Educational Research Association) indicated that 19 percent agreed.[‡]

At the other extreme are those who agree with Robinson and Levin that "authors should *first* indicate whether the observed effect is a statistically improbable one, and *only if* it is

should they indicate how *large or important* it is (is it a difference that *makes* a difference)."[§]

Cahan argued to the contrary that the way to avoid misleading conclusions regarding effects is not by using significance tests, but rather using confidence intervals accompanied by increased sample size.[‖]

In 1999 the American Psychological Association Task Force on Statistical Inference recommended that inference tests not be banned, but that researchers should "always provide some effect size estimate when reporting a *p* value," and further that "reporting and interpreting effect sizes in the context of previously reported research is *essential* to good research."[#]

What do you think? Should significance tests be banned in educational research?

*R. P. Carver. (1993). The case against statistical significance testing revisited. *Journal of Experimental Education, 61*:287–292.
[†]F. L. Schmidt. (1996). Statistical significance testing and cumulative knowledge in psychology: Implications for training of researchers. *Psychological Methods, 1*:115–129.
[‡]K. C. Mittag and B. Thompson. (2000). A national survey of AERA members' perceptions of statistical significance tests and other statistical issues. *Educational Researcher, 29*(3):14–19.

[§]D. H. Robinson and J. R. Levin. (1997). Reflections on statistical and substantive significance, with a slice of replication. *Educational Researcher, 26:* (January/February):22.
[‖]S. Cahan (2000). Statistical significance is not a "Kosher Certificate" for observed effects: A critical analysis of the two-step approach to the evaluation of empirical results. *Educational Researcher, 29*(5):34.
[#]L. Wilkinson and the APA Task Force on Statistical Inference (1999). Statistical methods in psychology journals: Guidelines and explanations. *American Psychologist, 54:*599.

Recommendation 5: Consider using inferential statistics only if you can make a convincing argument that a difference between means of the magnitude obtained is important (see Figure 12.2).

Recommendation 6: Do not use tests of statistical significance to evaluate the magnitude of a difference between sample means. Use them only as they were intended: to judge the generalizability of results.

Recommendation 7: Unless random samples were used, interpret probabilities and/or significance levels as crude indices, not as precise values.

Recommendation 8: Report the results of inference techniques as confidence intervals rather than (or in addition to) significance levels.

Relating Variables Within a Group: Quantitative Data

TECHNIQUES

Whenever a relationship between quantitative variables within a single group is examined, the appropriate techniques are the **scatterplot** and the **correlation coeffi-**

cient. The scatterplot illustrates all the data visually, while the correlation coefficient provides a numerical summary of the data. When analyzing data obtained from a single group, therefore, researchers should begin by constructing a scatterplot. Not only will it provide all the information available, but it will help them judge which correlation coefficient to calculate (the choice usually will be between the Pearson *r,* which assumes a straight-line relationship, and eta, which describes a curved or curvilinear relationship).*

Consider Figure 12.3. All of the five scatterplots shown represent a Pearson correlation of about .50. Only in (*a*), however, does this coefficient (.50) completely convey the nature of the relationship. In (*b*) the relationship is understated, since it is a curvilinear one, and eta would give a higher coefficient. In (*c*) the coefficient does not reflect the fan-shaped nature of the relationship. In (*d*) the coefficient does not reveal that there are two distinct subgroups. In (*e*) the coefficient is greatly inflated by a few unusual cases. While these

*Because both of these correlations describe the magnitude of relationship, they are also examples of effect size (see footnote, p. 256).

Figure 12.2 *A Difference That Doesn't Make a Difference!*

illustrations are a bit exaggerated, similar results are often found in real data.

When examining relationships within a single group, therefore, we recommend the following:

> *Recommendation 9:* Begin by constructing a scatterplot.
>
> *Recommendation 10:* Use the scatterplot to determine which correlation coefficient is appropriate to calculate.
>
> *Recommendation 11:* Use *both* the scatterplot and the correlation coefficient to interpret results.

INTERPRETATION

Interpretating scatterplots and correlations presents problems similar to those we discussed in relation to differences in means. How large must a correlation coefficient be to suggest an *important* relationship?

What does an important relationship look like on a scatterplot?

As you can see, doing or evaluating research is not cut and dried; it is not a matter of following a set of rules, but rather requires informed judgment. In judging correlation coefficients, one must first assess their appropriateness, as was done with those in Figure 12.3. If the Pearson correlation coefficient is an adequate summary (and we have shown in Figure 12.3 that this is not always the case), most researchers would agree to the interpretations shown in Table 12.1 when testing a research hypothesis.

As with a comparison of means, the use of inferential statistics to judge the importance of the magnitude of a relationship is both common and often misleading. With a sample of 100, a correlation of only .20 is statistically significant at the .05 level with a two-tailed test. Accordingly, we recommend the follow-

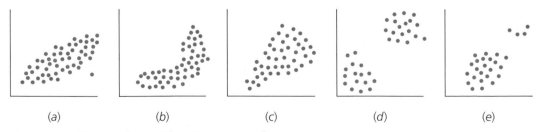

(a)   (b)   (c)   (d)   (e)

Figure 12.3 *Scatterplots with a Pearson r of .50*

Table 12.1 *Interpretation of Correlation Coefficients when Testing Research Hypotheses*

Magnitude of *r*	Interpretation
.00 to .40	Of little practical importance except in unusual circumstances; perhaps of theoretical value.[a]
.41 to .60	Large enough to be of practical as well as theoretical use.
.61 to .80	Very important, but rarely obtained in educational research.
.81 or above	Possibly an error in calculation; if not, a very sizable relationship.

[a]When selecting a very few people from a large group, even correlations this small may have predictive value.

ing when interpreting scatterplots and correlation coefficients:

Recommendation 12: Draw a line that best fits all points in a scatterplot and note the extent of deviations from it. The smaller the deviations all along the line, the more useful the relationship.*

Recommendation 13: Consider using inferential statistics only if you can give a convincing argument for the importance of the size of the relationship found in the sample.

Recommendation 14: Do not use tests of statistical significance to evaluate the magnitude of a relationship. Use them, as they were intended, to judge generalizability.

Recommendation 15: Unless a random sample was used, interpret probabilities and/or significance levels as crude indices, not as precise values.

Recommendation 16: Report the results of inference techniques as confidence intervals rather than as significance levels.

Comparing Groups: Categorical Data

TECHNIQUES

When the data involved are categorical data, groups may be compared by reporting either percentages (or proportions) or frequencies in crossbreak tables. Table 12.2(a) gives a fictitious example.

*Try this with Figure 12.3.

Table 12.2(a) *Gender and Political Preference (Percentages)*

	Percentage of Males	Percentage of Females
Democrat	20	50
Republican	70	45
Other	10	5
Total	100	100

Table 12.2(b) *Gender and Political Preference (Numbers)*

	Males	Females
Democrat	2	30
Republican	7	27
Other	1	3

INTERPRETATION

Once again, we must look at summary statistics-even percentages-carefully. Percentages can be misleading unless the number of cases is also given. At first glance, Table 12.2(a) may look impressive-until one discovers that the data in it represent 60 females and only 10 males. In crossbreak form, Table 12.2(b) represents the actual *numbers,* as opposed to percentages, of individuals.

Table 12.3 illustrates a fictitious relationship between teacher gender and grade level taught. As you can see, the largest number of male teachers is to be found in grade 7, and the largest number of female teachers is to be found in grade 4. Here, too, however, we must ask: How much difference must there be between these frequencies for us to consider them important? One of the limitations of categorical data is that such evaluations are even harder than with quantitative data. One possible approach is to examine prior experience or knowledge. Table 12.3 does suggest a trend toward an

Table 12.3 *Teacher Gender and Grade Level Taught: Case 1*

	Grade 4	Grade 5	Grade 6	Grade 7	Total
Male	10	20	20	30	80
Female	40	30	30	20	120
Total	50	50	50	50	200

Table 12.4 *Teacher Gender and Grade Level Taught: Case 2*

	Grade 4	Grade 5	Grade 6	Grade 7	Total
Male	22	22	25	28	97
Female	28	28	25	22	103
Total	50	50	50	50	200

increasingly larger proportion of male teachers in the higher grades-but, again, is the trend substantial enough to be considered important?

The data in Table 12.4 show the same trend, but the pattern is much less striking. Perhaps prior experience or research shows (somehow) that gender differences become important whenever the within-grade difference is more than 10 percent (or a frequency of 5 in these data). Such knowledge is seldom available, however, which leads us to consider the summary statistic (similar to the correlation coefficient) known as the contingency coefficient (see Chapter Eleven). In order to use it, however, remember that the data *must* be presented in crossbreak tables. Calculating the contingency coefficient is easily done by hand or by computer. You will recall that this statistic is not as straightforward in interpretation as the correlation coefficient, since its interpretation depends on the number of cells in the crossbreak table. Nevertheless, we recommend its use.

Perhaps because of the difficulties mentioned above, most research reports using percentages or crossbreaks rely on inference techniques to evaluate the magnitude of relationships. In the absence of random sampling, their use suffers from the same liabilities as with quantitative data. When analyzing categorical data, therefore, we recommend the following:

Recommendation 17: Whenever possible, place all data into crossbreak tables.

Recommendation 18: To clarify the importance of relationships, patterns, or trends, calculate a contingency coefficient.

Recommendation 19: Do not use tests of statistical significance to evaluate the magnitude of relationships. Use them, as intended, to judge generalizability.

Recommendation 20: Unless a random sample was used, interpret probabilities and/or significance levels as crude indices, not as precise values.

Relating Variables Within a Group: Categorical Data

Although the preceding section involves comparing groups, the reasoning also applies to hypotheses that examine relationships among categorical variables within just one group. A moment's thought shows why. The procedures available to us are the same-percentages or crossbreak tables. Suppose our hypothesis is that, among college students, gender is related to political preference. To test this we must divide the data we obtain from this group by gender and political preference. This gives us the crossbreak in Table 12.2. Because all such hypotheses must be tested by dividing people into groups, the statistical analysis is the same whether seen as one group, subdivided, or as two or more different groups.

A summary of the most commonly used statistical techniques, both descriptive and inferential, as used with quantitative and categorical data, is shown in Table 12.5.

A Recap of Recommendations

You may have noticed that many of our recommendations are essentially the same, regardless of the method of statistical analysis involved. To stress their importance, we want to state them again here, all together, phrased more generally.

We recommend that researchers:

- Use graphic techniques before calculating numerical summary indices. Pay particular attention to outliers.
- Use both graphs and summary indices to interpret results of a study.
- Make use of external criteria (such as prior experience or scores of known groups) to assess the magnitude of a relationship whenever such criteria are available.
- Use professional consensus when evaluating the magnitude of an effect size (including correlation coefficients).
- Consider using inferential statistics only if you can make a convincing case for the importance of the size of the relationship found in the sample.
- Use tests of statistical significance only to evaluate generalizability, not to evaluate the magnitude of relationships.

Table 12.5 *Summary of Commonly Used Statistical Techniques*

	DATA	
	Quantitative	**Categorical**
Two or more groups are compared:		
Descriptive Statistics	• Frequency polygons • Averages • Spreads • Effect size	• Percentages • Bar graphs • Pie charts • Crossbreak (contingency) tables
Inferential Statistics	• *t*-test for means • ANOVA • ANCOVA • MANOVA • MANCOVA • Confidence intervals • Mann-Whitney *U* test • Kruskal-Wallis ANOVA • Sign test • Friedman ANOVA	• Chi square • *t*-test for proportions
Relationships among variables are studied within one group:		
Descriptive Statistics	• Scatterplot • Correlation coefficient (*r*) • eta	• Crossbreak (contingency) tables • Contingency coefficient
Inferential Statistics	• *t*-test for *r* • Confidence intervals	• Chi square • *t*-test for proportions

• When random sampling has not occurred, treat probabilities as approximations or crude indices rather than as precise values.

• Report confidence intervals rather than, or in addition to, significance levels whenever possible.

We also want to make a final recommendation involving the distinction between parametric and nonparametric statistics. Since the calculation of statistics has now become rather easy and quick owing to the availability of many computer programs, we conclude with the following suggestion to researchers:

• Use *both* parametric and nonparametric techniques to analyze data. When the results are consistent, interpretation will thereby be strengthened. When the results are not consistent, discuss possible reasons.

- Suppose a researcher found a correlation of .08 between drinking grapefruit juice and subsequent incidence of arthritis to be statistically significant. Is that possible? [Yes, it is quite possible. If the sample was randomly selected, and the sample size was around 500, a correlation of .08 would be statistically significant at the .05 level. But because of the small relationship (and many uncontrolled variables), we would not stop drinking grapefruit juice based on an r of only .08!]

- Suppose an early intervention program was found to increase IQ scores on average by 12 points, but that this was not statistically significant at the .05 level. How much attention would you give to this report? [We would pay considerable attention. Twelve IQ points is a lot and could be very important if confirmed in replications. Evidently the sample size was rather small (see the information in the box in Chapter Eleven).]

- Suppose the difference in polling preference for a particular candidate was found to be 52 percent for the Democrat as opposed to 48 percent for the Republican, with a margin of error of 2 percent at the .05 level. Would you consider this difference important? [One way of reporting such results is that the probability of the difference being due to chance is less than .01.* In addition, a difference of only four points is of great practical importance since the winner in a two-person election needs only 51 percent of the vote to win. A very similar prediction proved wrong in the 1948 presidential election, when Truman defeated Dewey. (The usual explanations are that the sample was not random and thus not representative, and/or that a lot of people changed their minds before they entered the voting booth.)]

*The SE of each percentage must be 2.00 (the margin of error) divided by 1.96 (the number of standard deviations required at the 5 percent level), or approximately 1.00. The standard error of the difference (SED) equals the square root of $(1^2 + 1^2)$ or 1.4. The difference between 48 percent and 52 percent—4 percent—divided by 1.4 (the SED) equals 2.86, which yields a probability of less than .01.

Go back to the **Interactive and Applied Learning Tools** feature at the beginning of the chapter for a listing of interactive and applied activities. Go to the **Online Learning Center** at www.mhhe.com/fraenkel5e or your **Interactive Student CD-ROM** to take practice quizzes and receive immediate feedback, practice with key terms, review chapter content and main ideas, and find annotated Web links.

Main Points

APPROACHES TO RESEARCH

- A good deal of educational research is done in one of two ways: either two or more groups are compared, or variables within one group are related.
- The data in a study may be either quantitative or categorical.

COMPARING GROUPS USING QUANTITATIVE DATA

- When comparing two or more groups using quantitative data, researchers can compare them through frequency polygons, calculation of averages, and calculation of spreads.
- We recommend, therefore, constructing frequency polygons, using data on the means of known groups, calculating effect sizes, and reporting confidence intervals when comparing quantitative data from two or more groups.

RELATING VARIABLES WITHIN A GROUP USING QUANTITATIVE DATA

- When researchers examine a relationship between quantitative variables within a single group, the appropriate techniques are the scatterplot and the correlation coefficient.
- Because a scatterplot illustrates all the data visually, researchers should begin their analysis of data obtained from a single group by constructing a scatterplot.

- Therefore, we recommend constructing scatterplots and using both scatterplots and correlation coefficients when relating variables involving quantitative data within a single group.

COMPARING GROUPS WHEN THE DATA INVOLVED ARE CATEGORICAL

- When the data are categorical, groups can be compared by reporting either percentages or frequencies in crossbreak tables.
- It is a good idea to report *both* the percentage and the number of cases in a crossbreak table, as percentages alone can be misleading.
- Therefore, we recommend constructing crossbreak tables and calculating contingency coefficients when comparing categorical data involving two or more groups.

RELATING VARIABLES WITHIN A GROUP USING CATEGORICAL DATA

- When you are examining relationships among categorical data within one group, we again recommend constructing crossbreak tables and calculating contingency coefficients.

TWO FINAL RECOMMENDATIONS

- When tests of statistical significance can be applied, it is recommended that they be used to evaluate generalizability only, not to evaluate the magnitude of relationships. Confidence intervals should be reported in addition to significance levels.
- Both parametric and nonparametric techniques should be used to analyze data rather than either one alone.

Categorical data 259	Effect size 256	Quantitative data 254	**Key Terms**
Correlation coefficient 257	Inferential statistics 256	Scatterplot 257	
Descriptive statistics 255	Known groups 256		

1. Give some examples of how the results of a study might be significant statistically, yet unimportant educationally. Could the reverse be true?
2. Are there times when a slight difference in means (e.g., an effect size of less than .50) might be important? Explain your answer.
3. When comparing groups, the use of frequency polygons helps us decide which measure of central tendency is the most appropriate to calculate. How so?
4. Why is it important to consider outliers in scatterplots?
5. "When analyzing data obtained from two groups, the first thing researchers should do is construct a frequency polygon of each group's scores." Why is this important— or is it?
6. Why is it important to use *both* graphs and summary indices (e.g., the means) to interpret the results of a study—or is it?
7. A picture, supposedly, is worth a thousand words. Would this statement also apply to analyzing the results of a study? Can numbers alone ever give a complete picture of a study's results? Why or why not?

For Discussion

Research Exercise Twelve: Statistics in Perspective

Using Problem Sheet 12, once again state the question or hypothesis of your study. Summarize the descriptive and inferential statistics you would use to describe the relationship you are hypothesizing. Then tell how you would evaluate the magnitude of any relationship you might find. Finally, describe the changes in techniques to be used from those you described in Problem Sheets 10 and 11, if any.

An electronic version of this Problem Sheet that you can fill in and print, save, or e-mail is available on the Online Learning Center at www.mhhe.com/ fraenkel5e and on your Interactive Student CD-ROM.

A full-sized version of this Problem Sheet that you can fill in or photocopy is in your Student Workbook.

Problem Sheet 12

Statistics in Perspective

1. The question or hypothesis of my study is: _____
   _____
   _____

2. My expected relationship(s) would be described using the following descriptive statistics: _____
   _____
   _____
   _____

3. The inferential statistics I would use are: _____
   _____
   _____
   _____
   _____

4. I would evaluate the magnitude of the relationship(s) I find by: _____
   _____
   _____
   _____

5. The changes (if any) in my use of descriptive or inferential statistics from those I described in Problem Sheets 10 and 11 are as follows: _____
   _____
   _____
   _____
   _____
   _____

Quantitative Research Methodologies

In Part Four, we begin a more detailed discussion of some of the
methodologies that educational researchers use. We concentrate here
on quantitative research, with a separate chapter devoted to group-
comparison experimental research, single-subject experimental
research, correlational research, causal-comparative research, and
survey research. In each chapter, we not only discuss the method in
some detail, but we also provide examples of published studies in
which the researchers used one of these methods. We conclude
each chapter with an analysis of a particular study's strengths and
weaknesses.

Experimental Research

CHAPTER 13

Experimental Research

The Uniqueness of Experimental Research

Control of Experimental Treatments

Essential Characteristics of Experimental Research

Comparison of Groups
Manipulation of the Independent Variable
Randomization

Evaluating the Likelihood of a Threat to Internal Validity in Experimental Studies

Control of Extraneous Variables

Control of Threats to Internal Validity: A Summary

Group Designs in Experimental Research

Weak Experimental Designs
True Experimental Designs
Quasi-Experimental Designs
Factorial Designs

Objectives

Studying this chapter should enable you to:

- Describe *briefly the purpose of experimental research.*
- Describe *the basic steps involved in conducting an experiment.*
- Describe *two ways in which experimental research differs from other forms of educational research.*
- Explain *the difference between random assignment and random selection and the importance of each.*
- Explain *what is meant by the phrase "manipulation of variables" and describe three ways in which such manipulation can occur.*
- Distinguish *between examples of weak and strong experimental designs and draw diagrams of such designs.*
- Identify *various threats to internal validity associated with different experimental designs.*
- Explain *three ways in which various threats to internal validity in experimental research can be controlled.*
- Explain *how matching can be used to equate groups in experimental studies.*
- Describe *briefly the purpose of factorial and counterbalanced designs and draw diagrams of such designs.*
- Describe *briefly the purpose of a time-series design and draw a diagram of this design.*
- Describe *briefly how to assess probable threats to internal validity in an experimental study.*
- Recognize *an experimental study when you see one in the literature.*

Interactive and Applied Learning

After, or while reading this chapter:

Go to your Interactive Student CD-ROM to:
- Learn More About What Constitutes an Experiment

Go to your Interactive Student CD-ROM or Student Workbook to do the following activities:
- Activity 13.1: Experimental Research Questions
- Activity 13.2: Designing an Experiment
- Activity 13.3: Characteristics of Experimental Research
- Activity 13.4: Random Selection Versus Random Assignment

Does team-teaching improve the achievement of students in high school social studies classes? Abigail Johnson, the principal of a large high school in Minneapolis, Minnesota, having heard encouraging remarks about the idea at a recent educational conference, wants to find out. Accordingly, she asks some of her eleventh-grade world history teachers to participate in an experiment. Three teachers are to combine their classes into one large group. These teachers are to work as a team, sharing the planning, teaching, and evaluation of these students. Three other teachers are assigned to teach a class in the same subject individually, with the usual arrangement of one teacher per class. The students selected to participate are similar in ability, and the teachers will teach at the same time, using the same curriculum. All are to use the same standardized tests and other assessment instruments, including written tests prepared jointly by the six teachers. Periodically during the semester, Mrs. Johnson will compare the scores of the two groups of students on these tests.

This is an example of an experiment—the comparison of a treatment group with a nontreatment comparison group. In this chapter, you will learn about various procedures that researchers use to carry out such experiments, as well as how they try to ensure that it is the experimental treatment rather than some uncontrolled variable that causes the changes in achievement.

Experimental research is one of the most powerful research methodologies that researchers can use. Of the many types of research that might be used, the experiment is the best way to establish cause-and-effect relationships among variables. Yet experiments are not always easy to conduct. In this chapter, we will show you both the power of, and the problems involved in, conducting experiments.

The Uniqueness of Experimental Research

Of all the research methodologies described in this book, **experimental research** is unique in two very important respects: It is the only type of research that directly attempts to influence a particular variable, and, when properly applied, it is the best type for testing hypotheses about cause-and-effect relationships. In an experimental study, researchers look at the effect(s) of at least one independent variable on one or more dependent variables. The **independent variable** in experimental research is also frequently referred to as the *experimental* or **treatment variable.** The **dependent variable,** also known as the **criterion** or **outcome variable,** refers to the results or outcomes of the study.

The major characteristic of experimental research, which distinguishes it from all other types of research, is that researchers *manipulate* the independent variable. They decide the nature of the treatment (that is, what is going to happen to the subjects of the study), to whom

it is to be applied, and to what extent. Independent variables frequently manipulated in educational research include methods of instruction, types of assignment, learning materials, rewards given to students, and types of questions asked by teachers. Dependent variables that are frequently studied include achievement, interest in a subject, attention span, motivation, and attitudes toward school.

After the treatment has been administered for an appropriate length of time, researchers observe or measure the groups receiving different treatments (by means of a posttest of some sort) to see if they differ. Another way of saying this is that researchers want to see whether the treatment made a difference. If the average scores of the groups on the posttest do differ, and researchers cannot find any sensible alternative explanations for this difference, they can conclude that the treatment did have an effect and is likely the cause of the difference.

Experimental research, therefore, enables researchers to go beyond description and prediction, beyond the identification of relationships, to at least a partial determination of what causes them. Correlational studies may demonstrate a strong relationship between socioeconomic level and academic achievement, for instance, but they cannot demonstrate that improving socioeconomic level will necessarily improve achievement. Only experimental research has this capability. Some actual examples of the kinds of experimental studies that have been conducted by educational researchers are as follows:

- Quality of learning with an active versus passive motivational set[1]
- Comparison of computer-assisted cooperative, competitive, and individualistic learning[2]
- An intensive group counseling dropout prevention intervention: . . . isolating at-risk adolescents within high schools[3]
- The effects of student questions and teacher questions on concept acquisition[4]
- Changing teaching practices in mainstream classrooms to improve bonding and behavior of low achievers[5]
- Mnemonic versus nonmnemonic vocabulary-learning strategies for children[6]

Essential Characteristics of Experimental Research

The word **"experiment"** has a long and illustrious history in the annals of research. It has often been hailed as the most powerful method that exists for studying cause and effect. Its origins go back to the very beginnings of history when, for example, primeval humans first experimented with ways to produce fire. One can imagine countless trial-and-error attempts on their part before success was achieved by sparking rocks or by spinning wooden spindles in dry leaves. Much of the success of modern science is due to carefully designed and meticulously implemented experiments.

The basic idea underlying all experimental research is really quite simple: try something and systematically observe what happens. Formal experiments consist of two basic conditions. First, at least two (but often more) conditions or methods are *compared* to assess the effect(s) of particular conditions or "treatments" (the independent variable). Second, the independent variable is directly *manipulated* by the researcher. Change is planned for and deliberately manipulated in order to study its effect(s) on one or more outcomes (the dependent variable). Let us discuss some important characteristics of experimental research in a bit more detail.

COMPARISON OF GROUPS

An experiment usually involves two groups of subjects, an experimental group and a control or a comparison group, although it is possible to conduct an experiment with only one group (by providing all treatments to the same subjects) or with three or more groups. The **experimental group** receives a treatment of some sort (such as a new textbook or a different method of teaching), while the **control group** receives no treatment (or the **comparison group** receives a different treatment). The control or the comparison group is crucially important in all experimental research, for it enables the researcher to determine whether the treatment has had an effect or whether one treatment is more effective than another.

Historically, a pure control group is one that receives no treatment at all. While this is often the case in medical or psychological research, it is rarely true in educational research. The control group almost always receives a different treatment of some sort. Some educational researchers, therefore, refer to comparison groups rather than to control groups.

Consider an example. Suppose a researcher wished to study the effectiveness of a new method of teaching science. He or she would have the students in the experimental group taught by the new method, but the students in the comparison group would continue to be taught by their teacher's usual method. The researcher would not administer the new method to the experimental group and have a control group *do nothing*. Any method of instruction would likely be more effective than no method at all!

MANIPULATION OF THE INDEPENDENT VARIABLE

The second essential characteristic of all experiments is that the researcher actively *manipulates* the independent variables. What does this mean? Simply put, it means that the researcher deliberately and directly determines what forms the independent variable will take and then which group will get which form. For example, if the independent variable in a study is the amount of enthusiasm an instructor displays, a researcher might train two teachers to display different amounts of enthusiasm as they teach their classes.

Although many independent variables in education can be manipulated, many others cannot. Examples of independent variables that can be manipulated include teaching method, type of counseling, learning activities, assignments given, and materials used; examples of independent variables that cannot be manipulated include gender, ethnicity, age, and religious preference.

Researchers can manipulate the kinds of learning activities to which students are exposed in a classroom, but they cannot manipulate, say, religious preference—that is, students cannot be "made into" Protestants, Catholics, Jews, or Muslims, for example, to serve the purposes of a study. To manipulate a variable, researchers must decide who is to get something and when, where, and how they will get it.

The independent variable in an experimental study may be established in several ways—either (1) one form of the variable versus another; (2) presence versus absence of a particular form; or (3) varying degrees of the same form. An example of (1) would be a study comparing the inquiry method with the lecture method of instruction in teaching chemistry. An example of (2) would be a study comparing the use of transparencies versus no transparencies in teaching statistics. An example of (3) would be a study comparing the effects of different specified amounts of teacher enthusiasm on student attitudes toward mathematics. In both (1) and (2), the variable (method) is clearly categorical. In (3), a variable that in actuality is quantitative (*degree* of enthusiasm) is treated as categorical (the effects of only specified *amounts* of enthusiasm will be studied), in order for the researcher to manipulate (that is, to control for) the amount of enthusiasm.

RANDOMIZATION

An important aspect of many experiments is the random assignment of subjects to groups. Although there are certain kinds of experiments in which random assignment is not possible, researchers try to use randomization whenever feasible. It is a crucial ingredient in the best kinds of experiments. Random assignment is similar, but not identical, to the concept of random selection we discussed in Chapter Six. **Random assignment** means that every individual who is participating in the experiment has an equal chance of being assigned to any of the experimental or control conditions being compared. **Random selection,** on the other hand, means that every member of a population has an equal chance of being selected to be a member of the sample. Under random assignment, each member of the sample is given a number (arbitrarily), and a table of random numbers (see Chapter Six) is then used to select the members of the experimental and control groups.

Three things should be noted about the random assignment of subjects to groups. First, it takes place before the experiment begins. Second, it is a *process* of as-

signing or distributing students to groups, not a result of such distribution. This means that you cannot look at two groups that have already been formed and be able to tell, just by looking, whether or not they were formed randomly. Third, the use of random assignment allows the researcher to form groups that, right at the beginning of the study, are *equivalent*—that is, they differ only by chance in any variables of interest. In other words, random assignment is intended to eliminate the threat of additional, or **extraneous,** variables—not only those of which researchers are aware but also those of which they are not aware—that might affect the outcome of the study. This is the beauty and the power of random assignment. It is one of the reasons why experiments are, in general, more effective than other types of research for assessing cause-and-effect relationships.

This last statement is tempered, of course, by the realization that groups formed through random assignment may still differ somewhat. Random assignment ensures only that groups are equivalent (or at least as equivalent as human beings can make them) at the beginning of an experiment.

Furthermore, random assignment is no guarantee of equivalent groups unless both groups are sufficiently large. No one would expect random assignment to result in equivalence if there were only five subjects to be assigned to each group, for example. There are no rules for determining how large groups must be, but most researchers are uncomfortable relying on random assignment if there are fewer than 40 subjects in each group.

Control of Extraneous Variables

Researchers in an experimental study have an opportunity to exercise far more control than in most other forms of research. They determine the treatment (or treatments), select the sample, assign individuals to groups, decide which group will get the treatment, try to control other factors besides the treatment that might influence the outcome of the study, and then (finally) observe or measure the effect of the treatment on the groups when the treatment is completed.

In Chapter Nine, we introduced the idea of internal validity and pointed out that several threats to internal validity exist. It is very important for researchers conducting an experimental study to do their best to *control* for—that is, to eliminate or to minimize the possible effect of—these threats. If researchers are unsure whether another variable might be the cause of a result observed in a study, they cannot be sure what the cause really is. For example, if a researcher attempted to compare the effects of two different methods of instruction on student attitudes toward history but did not make sure that the groups involved were equivalent in ability, then ability might be a possible alternative explanation (rather than the difference in methods) for any differences in attitudes of the groups found on a posttest.

In particular, researchers who conduct experimental studies try their best to ensure that any and all subject characteristics that might affect the outcome of the study are controlled. This is done by ensuring that the two groups are as equivalent as possible on all variables other than the one or ones being studied (that is, the independent variables).

How do researchers minimize or eliminate threats due to subject characteristics? Many ways exist. Here are some of the most common.

Randomization: As we mentioned before, if enough subjects can be randomly assigned to the various groups involved in an experimental study, researchers can assume that the groups are equivalent. This is the best way to ensure that the effects of one or more possible extraneous variables have been controlled.

Hold certain variables constant: The idea here is to eliminate the possible effects of a variable by removing it from the study. For example, if a researcher suspects that gender might influence the outcomes of a study, she could control for it by restricting the subjects of the study to females and by excluding all males. The variable of gender, in other words, has been held constant. However, there is a cost involved (as there almost always is) for this control, as the generalizability of the results of the study are correspondingly reduced.

Build the variable into the design: This solution involves building the variable(s) into the study to assess their effects. It is the exact opposite of the previous idea. Using the preceding example, a researcher would include *both* females and males (as distinct groups) in the design of the study and then analyze the effects of *both* gender and method on outcomes.

Matching: Often pairs of subjects can be matched on certain variables of interest. If a researcher felt that age, for example, might affect the outcome of a study, he might endeavor to match students according to their ages and then assign one member of each pair (randomly if possible) to each of the comparison groups.

Use subjects as their own controls: When subjects are used as their own controls, their performance under both (or all) treatments is compared. Thus, the same students might be taught algebra units first by an inquiry method and later by a lecture method. Another example is the assessment of an individual's behavior during a period of time before and after a treatment is implemented to see whether changes in behavior occur.

Analysis of covariance: As mentioned in Chapter Eleven, analysis of covariance can be used to equate groups statistically on the basis of a pretest or other variables. The posttest scores of the subjects in each group are then adjusted accordingly.

We will shortly show you a number of research designs that illustrate how several of the above controls can be implemented in an experimental study.

Group Designs in Experimental Research

The design of an experiment can take a variety of forms. Some of the designs we present in this section are better than others, however. Why "better"? Because of the various threats to internal validity identified in Chapter Nine: Good designs control many of these threats, while poor designs control only a few. The quality of an experiment depends on how well the various threats to internal validity are controlled.

WEAK EXPERIMENTAL DESIGNS

These designs are referred to as "weak" because they do not have built-in controls for threats to internal validity. In addition to the independent variable, there are a number of other plausible explanations for any outcomes that occur. As a result, any researcher who uses one of these designs has difficulty assessing the effectiveness of the independent variable.

The One-Shot Case Study. In the **one-shot case study design** a single group is exposed to a treatment or event, and a dependent variable is subsequently observed (measured) in order to assess the effect of the treatment. A diagram of this design is as follows:

The One-Shot Case Study Design

X	O
Treatment	Observation
	(Dependent variable)

The symbol *X* represents exposure of the group to the treatment of interest, while *O* refers to observation (measurement) of the dependent variable. The placement of the symbols from left to right indicates the order in time of *X* and *O*. As you can see, the treatment, *X,* comes before observation of the dependent variable, *O.*

Suppose a researcher wishes to see if a new textbook increases student interest in history. He uses the textbook (*X*) for a semester and then measures student interest (*O*) with an attitude scale. A diagram of this example is shown in Figure 13.1.

The most obvious weakness of this design is its absence of any control. The researcher has no way of knowing if the results obtained at *O* (as measured by the attitude scale) are due to treatment *X* (the textbook). The design does not provide for any comparison, so the researcher cannot compare the treatment results (as measured by the attitude scale) with the same group before using the new textbook, or with those of another group using a different textbook. Because the group has not been pretested in any way, the researcher knows nothing about what the group was like before using the text. Thus, he does not know whether the treatment had *any* effect at all. It is quite possible that the students who use the new textbook *will* indicate very favorable attitudes toward history. But the question remains, were these attitudes produced by the new textbook? Unfortunately, the one-shot case study does not help us answer this question. To remedy this design, a comparison could be made with another group of students who had the same course content presented in the regular textbook. (We shall show you just such a design shortly.) Fortunately, the flaws in the one-shot design are so well known that it is seldom used in educational research.

The One-Group Pretest-Posttest Design. In the **one-group pretest-posttest design,** a single group is measured or observed not only after being exposed to a treatment of some sort, but also before. A diagram of this design is as follows:

The One-Group Pretest-Posttest Design

O	X	O
Pretest	Treatment	Posttest

Consider an example of this design. A principal wants to assess the effects of weekly counseling sessions on the attitudes of certain "hard-to-reach" students in her school. She asks the counselors in the program to meet once a week with these students for a period of 10 weeks, during which sessions the students are encouraged to express their feelings and concerns. She uses a 20-item scale to measure student attitudes toward school both immediately before and after the 10-week period. Figure 13.2 presents a diagram of the design of the study.

This design is better than the one-shot case study (the researcher at least knows whether any change occurred), but it is still weak. Nine uncontrolled-for threats to internal validity exist that might also explain the results on the posttest. They are history, maturation, instrument decay, data collector characteristics, data collector bias, testing, statistical regression, attitude of subjects, and implementation. Any or all of these may influence the outcome of the study. The researcher would not know if any differences between the pretest and the posttest are due to the treatment or to one or more of these threats. To remedy this, a comparison group, which does not receive the treatment, could be added. Then if a change in attitude occurs between the pretest and the posttest, the researcher has reason to believe that it was caused by the treatment (symbolized by *X*).

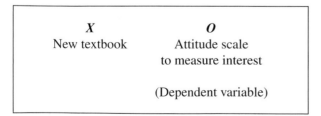

Figure 13.1 *Example of a One-Shot Case Study Design*

O	X	O
Pretest:	Treatment:	Posttest:
Twenty-item attitude scale completed by students	Ten weeks of counseling	Twenty-item attitude scale completed by students
(Dependent variable)		(Dependent variable)

Figure 13.2 *Example of a One-Group Pretest-Posttest Design*

The Static-Group Comparison Design. In the **static-group comparison design,** two already existing, or intact, groups are used. These are sometimes referred to as static groups, hence the name for the design. Comparisons are made between groups receiving different treatments. A diagram of this design is as follows:

The Static-Group Comparison Design

$$X_1 \qquad O$$
$$X_2 \qquad O$$

The dashed line indicates that the two groups being compared are already formed-that is, the subjects are not randomly assigned to the two groups. X_1 and X_2 symbolize the two different treatments. The two O's are placed exactly vertical to each other, indicating that the observation or measurement of the two groups occurs at the same time.

Consider again the example used to illustrate the one-shot case study design. We could apply the static-group comparison design to this example. The researcher would (1) find two intact groups (two classes); (2) assign the new textbook (X_1) to one of the classes but have the other class use the regular textbook (X_2); and then (3) measure the degree of interest of all students in both classes at the same time (for example, at the end of the semester). Figure 13.3 presents a diagram of this example.

X_1	O
New textbook	Attitude scale to measure interest
X_2	O
Regular text	Attitude scale to measure interest

Figure 13.3 *Example of a Static-Group Comparison Design*

Although this design provides better control over history, maturation, testing, and regression threats,* it is more vulnerable not only to mortality and location,† but also, more importantly, to the possibility of differential subject characteristics.

*History and maturation remain possible threats because the researcher cannot be sure that the two groups have been exposed to the same extraneous events or have the same maturational processes.
†Because the groups may differ in the number of subjects lost and/or in the kinds of resources provided.

The Static-Group Pretest-Posttest Design. The **static-group pretest-posttest design** differs from the static-group comparison design only in that a pretest is given to both groups. A diagram for this design is as follows:

The Static-Group Pretest-Posttest Design

$$O \qquad X_1 \qquad O$$
$$O \qquad X_2 \qquad O$$

In analyzing the data, each individual's pretest score is subtracted from his or her posttest score, thus permitting analysis of "gain" or "change." While this provides better control of the subject characteristics threat (since it is the *change* in each student that is analyzed), the amount of gain often depends upon initial performance; that is, the group scoring higher on the pretest is likely to improve more (or in some cases, less), and thus subject characteristics still remains somewhat of a threat. Further, administering a pretest raises the possibility of a testing threat. In the event that the pretest is used to match groups, this design becomes the matching-only pretest-posttest control group design (p. 278), a much more effective design.

TRUE EXPERIMENTAL DESIGNS

The essential ingredient of a true experimental design is that subjects are randomly assigned to treatment groups. As discussed earlier, random assignment is a powerful technique for controlling the subject characteristics threat to internal validity, a major consideration in educational research.

The Randomized Posttest-Only Control Group Design. The **randomized posttest-only control group design** involves two groups, both of which are formed by random assignment. One group receives the experimental treatment while the other does not, and then both groups are posttested on the dependent variable. A diagram of this design is as follows:

The Randomized Posttest-Only Control Group Design

Treatment group	R	X_1	O
Control group	R		O

As before, the symbol X represents exposure to the treatment and O refers to the measurement of the dependent variable. R represents the random assignment of individuals to groups.

In this design, the control of certain threats is excellent. Through the use of random assignment, the threats of subject characteristics, maturation, and statistical regression are well controlled for. Because none of the subjects in the study is measured twice, testing is not a possible threat. This is perhaps the best of all designs to use in an experimental study, provided there are at least 40 subjects in each group.

There are, unfortunately, some threats to internal validity that are not controlled for by this design. The first is mortality. Because the two groups are similar, we might expect an equal dropout rate from each group. However, exposure to the treatment may cause more individuals in the experimental group to drop out (or stay in) than in the control group. This may result in the two groups becoming dissimilar in terms of their characteristics, which in turn may affect the results on the posttest. For this reason researchers should always report how many subjects drop out of each group during an experiment. An attitudinal threat (Hawthorne effect) is possible. In addition, implementation, data collector bias, location, and history threats may exist. These threats can sometimes be controlled by appropriate modifications to this design.

As an example of this design, consider a hypothetical study in which a researcher investigates the effects of a series of sensitivity training workshops on faculty morale in a large high school district. The researcher randomly selects a sample of 100 teachers from all the teachers in the district. The researcher then (1) randomly assigns the teachers in the district to two groups; (2) exposes one group, but not the other, to the training; and then (3) measures the morale of each group using a questionnaire. Figure 13.4 presents a diagram of this hypothetical experiment.

Again we stress that it is important to keep clear the distinction between random selection and random assignment. Both involve the process of randomization, but for a different purpose. Random selection, you will recall, is intended to provide a representative sample. But it may or may not be accompanied by the random assignment of subjects to groups. Random assignment is intended to equate groups, and oftentimes is not accompanied by random selection.

The Randomized Pretest-Posttest Control Group Design. The **randomized pretest-posttest control group design** differs from the randomized posttest-only control group design solely in the use of a pretest. Two groups of subjects are used, with both groups being measured or observed twice. The first measurement serves as the pretest, the second as the posttest.

Random assignment is used to form the groups. The measurements or observations are collected at the same time for both groups. A diagram of this design follows. Notice that an attitudinal threat is controlled by providing a comparison treatment (X_2) for the "control" group.

The Randomized Pretest-Posttest Control Group Design

Treatment group	R	O	X_1	O
Control group	R	O	X_2	O

The use of the pretest raises the possibility of an interaction of testing and treatment threat, since it may "alert" the members of the experimental group, thereby causing them to do better (or more poorly) on the posttest than the members of the control group. A trade-off is that it provides the researcher with a means of checking whether or not the two groups are really similar—that is, whether random assignment actually succeeded in making the groups equivalent. This is particularly desirable if the number in each group is small (less than 30). If the pretest shows that the groups are not equivalent, the researcher can seek to make them so by using one of the matching techniques to be discussed. A pretest is also necessary if the amount of change over time is to be assessed.

Let us use our previous example involving the use of sensitivity workshops to illustrate this design. Figure 13.5 presents a diagram of how this design would be used.

The Randomized Solomon Four-Group Design. The **randomized Solomon four-group design** is an attempt to eliminate the possible effect of a pretest. It involves random assignment of subjects to four groups, with two of the groups being pretested and two not. One of the pretested groups and one of the unpretested groups is exposed to the experimental treatment. All four groups are then posttested. A diagram of this design is as follows:

The Randomized Solomon Four-Group Design

Treatment group	R	O	X_1	O
Control group	R	O	X_2	O
Treatment group	R		X_1	O
Control group	R		X_2	O

The randomized Solomon four-group design combines the pretest-posttest control group and posttest-only control group designs. The first two groups represent the pretest-posttest control group design, while the last two groups represent the posttest-only control

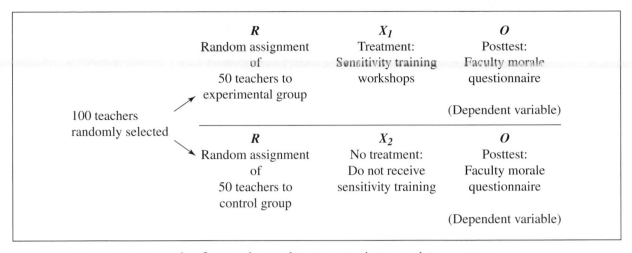

Figure 13.4 *Example of a Randomized Posttest-Only Control Group Design*

group design. Figure 13.6 presents an example of the randomized Solomon four-group design.

The randomized Solomon four-group design provides the best control of the threats to internal validity that we have discussed. A weakness, however, is that it requires a large sample, in that subjects must be assigned to four groups. Furthermore, conducting a study involving four groups at the same time requires a considerable amount of energy and effort on the part of the researcher.

Random Assignment with Matching. In an attempt to increase the likelihood that the groups of subjects in an experiment will be equivalent, pairs of individuals may be matched on certain variables to ensure group equivalence on these variables. The choice of variables on which to match is based on previous research, theory, and/or the experience of the researcher. The members of each matched pair are then assigned to the experimental and control groups at random. This adaptation can be made to both the posttest-only control

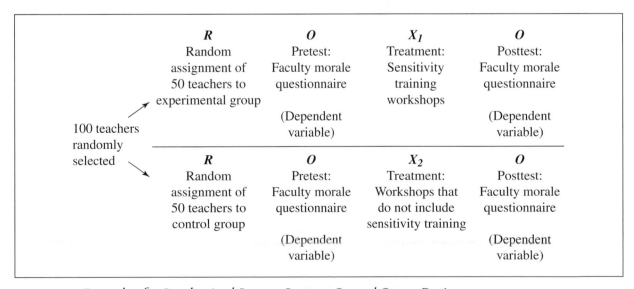

Figure 13.5 *Example of a Randomized Pretest-Posttest Control Group Design*

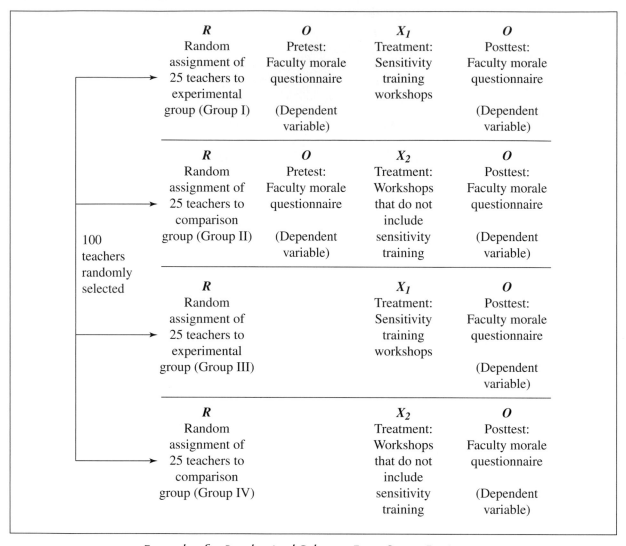

Figure 13.6 *Example of a Randomized Solomon Four-Group Design*

group design, and the pretest-posttest control group design, although the latter is more common. A diagram of these designs is as follows:

The Randomized Posttest-Only Control Group Design, Using Matched Subjects

| Treatment group | M_r | X_1 | O |
| Control group | M_r | | O |

The Randomized Pretest-Posttest Control Group Design, Using Matched Subjects

| Treatment group | O | M_r | X_1 | O |
| Control group | O | M_r | | O |

The symbol M_r refers to the fact that the members of each matched pair are randomly assigned to the experimental and control groups.

Although a pretest of the dependent variable is commonly used to provide scores on which to match, a measurement of any variable that shows a substantial relationship to the dependent variable is appropriate. Matching may be done in either or both of two ways: mechanically or statistically. Both require a score for each subject on *each* variable on which subjects are to be matched.

Mechanical matching is a process of pairing two persons whose scores on a particular variable are similar. Two girls, for example, whose mathematics aptitude

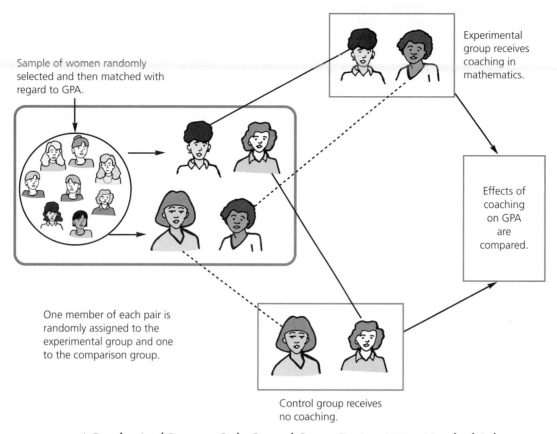

Sample of women randomly selected and then matched with regard to GPA.

Experimental group receives coaching in mathematics.

Effects of coaching on GPA are compared.

One member of each pair is randomly assigned to the experimental group and one to the comparison group.

Control group receives no coaching.

Figure 13.7 *A Randomized Posttest-Only Control Group Design, Using Matched Subjects*

scores and test anxiety scores are similar might be matched on those variables. After the matching is completed for the entire sample, a check should be made (through the use of frequency polygons) to ensure that the two groups are indeed equivalent on each matching variable. Unfortunately, two problems limit the usefulness of mechanical matching. First, it is very difficult to match on more than two or three variables—people just don't pair up on more than a few characteristics, making it necessary to have a very large initial sample to draw from. Second, in order to match, it is almost inevitable that some subjects must be eliminated from the study, because no "matchees" for them can be found. Samples then are no longer random even though they may have been before matching occurred.

As an example of a mechanical matching design with random assignment, suppose a researcher is interested in the effects of academic coaching on the grade point averages (GPA) of low-achieving students in science classes. The researcher randomly selects a sample of 60 students from a population of 125 such students in

a local elementary school and matches them by pairs on GPA, finding that she can match 40 of the 60. She then randomly assigns each subject in the resulting 20 pairs to either the experimental or the control group. Figure 13.7 presents a similar example.

Statistical matching,** on the other hand, does not necessitate a loss of subjects, nor does it limit the number of matching variables. Each subject is given a "predicted" score on the dependent variable, based on the correlation between the dependent variable and the variable (or variables) on which the subjects are being matched. The difference between the predicted and actual scores for each individual is then used to compare experimental and control groups.

When a pretest is used as the matching variable, the difference between the predicted and actual score is called a "regressed gain score." This score is preferable

---

**Statistical "equating" of groups is a more common term that is synonymous with "statistical matching." We believe the meaning for the beginning student is better conveyed by the term "matching."

to the more straightforward gain scores (posttest minus pretest score for each individual) primarily because it is more reliable. We discuss a similar procedure under partial correlation in Chapter Fifteen.

If mechanical matching is used, one member of each matched pair is randomly assigned to the experimental group, the other to the control group. If statistical matching is used, the sample is divided randomly at the outset, and the statistical adjustments are made after all data have been collected. Although some researchers advocate the use of statistical over mechanical matching, statistical matching is not infallible. Its major weakness is that it assumes the relationship between the dependent variable and each predictor variable can be properly described by a straight line rather than being curvilinear. Whichever procedure is used, the researcher must (in this design) rely on random assignment to equate groups on all other variables related to the dependent variable.

QUASI-EXPERIMENTAL DESIGNS

Quasi-experimental designs do not include the use of random assignment. Researchers who employ these designs rely instead on other techniques to control (or at least reduce) threats to internal validity. We shall describe some of these techniques as we discuss several quasi-experimental designs.

The Matching-Only Design. This design differs from random assignment with matching only in that random assignment is not used. The researcher still matches the subjects in the experimental and control groups on certain variables, but he or she has no assurance that they are equivalent on others. Why? Because even though matched, subjects already are in intact groups. This is a serious limitation, but often is unavoidable when random assignment is impossible—that is, when intact groups must be used. When several (say, 10 or more) groups are available for a method study, and the groups can be randomly assigned to different treatments, this design offers an alternative to random assignment of subjects. After the groups have been randomly assigned to the different treatments, the individuals receiving one treatment are matched with individuals receiving the other treatments. The design shown in Figure 13.7 is still preferred, however.

It should be emphasized that matching (whether mechanical or statistical) is never a substitute for random assignment. Furthermore, the correlation between the matching variable(s) and the dependent variable should be fairly substantial. (We suggest at least .40.) Realize also that, unless it is used in conjunction with random assignment, matching only controls for the variable(s) being matched. Diagrams of each of the matching-only control group designs follow.

The Matching-Only Posttest-Only Control Group Design

Treatment group	M	X_1	O
Control group	M_r	X_2	O

The Matching-Only Pretest-Posttest Control Group Design

Treatment group	O	M_r	X_1	O
Control group	O	M_r	X_2	O

The *M* in this design refers to the fact that the subjects in each group have been matched (on certain variables), but not randomly assigned to the groups.

Counterbalanced Designs. **Counterbalanced designs** represent another technique for equating experimental and control groups. In this design, each group is exposed to all treatments, however many there are, but in a different order. Any number of treatments may be involved. An example of a diagram for a counterbalanced design involving three treatments is as follows:

A Three-Treatment Counterbalanced Design

Group I	X_1	O	X_2	O	X_3	O
Group II	X_2	O	X_3	O	X_1	O
Group III	X_3	O	X_1	O	X_2	O

This arrangement involves three groups. Group I receives treatment 1 and is posttested, then receives treatment 2 and is posttested, and last receives treatment 3 and is posttested. Group II receives treatment 2 first, then treatment 3, and then treatment 1, being posttested after each treatment. Group III receives treatment 3 first, then treatment 1, followed by treatment 2, also being posttested after each treatment. The order in which the groups receive the treatments should be determined randomly.

How do researchers determine the effectiveness of the various treatments? Simply by comparing the average scores for all groups on the posttest for each treatment. In other words, the averaged posttest score for all groups for treatment 1 can be compared with the averaged posttest score for all groups for treatment 2, and so on, for however many treatments there are.

This design controls well for the subject characteristics threat to internal validity but is particularly vulnerable to multiple-treatment interference—that is, performance during a particular treatment may be affected by one or more of the previous treatments. Consequently, the results of any study in which the researcher has used a counterbalanced design must be examined carefully. Consider the two sets of hypothetical data shown in Figure 13.8.

The interpretation in study 1 is clear: Method *X* is superior for both groups regardless of sequence and to the same degree. The interpretation in study 2, however, is much more complex. Overall, method *X* appears superior, and by the same amount as in study 1. In both studies, the overall mean for *X* is 12, while for *Y* it is 8. In study 2, however, it appears that the difference between *X* and *Y* depends upon previous exposure to the other method. Group I performed much worse on method *Y* when it was exposed to it following *X,* and group II performed much better on *X* when it was exposed to it after method *Y.* When either *X* or *Y* was given first in the sequence, there was no difference in performance. It is not clear that method *X* is superior in all conditions in study 2, whereas this was quite clear in study 1.

Time-Series Designs. The typical pre- and posttest designs examined up to now involve observations or measurements taken immediately before and after treatment. A **time-series design,** however, involves repeated measurements or observations over a period of time both before and after treatment. It is really an elaboration of the one-group pretest-posttest design presented in Figure 13.2. An extensive amount of data is collected on a single group. If the group scores essentially the same on the pretests and then considerably improves on the posttests, the researcher has more confidence that the treatment is causing the improvement than if just

	Study 1		Study 2	
	Weeks 1-4	*Weeks 5-8*	*Weeks 1-4*	*Weeks 5-8*
Group I	Method $X = 12$	Method $Y = 8$	Method $X = 10$	Method $Y = 6$
Group II	Method $Y = 8$	Method $X = 12$	Method $Y = 10$	Method $X = 14$
Overall Means: Method $X = 12$; Method $Y = 8$			Method $X = 12$; Method $Y = 8$	

Figure 13.8 *Results (Means) from a Study Using A Counterbalanced Design*

one pretest and one posttest is given. An example might be when a teacher gives a weekly test to his or her class for several weeks before giving them a new textbook to use, and then monitors how they score on a number of weekly tests after they have used the text. A diagram of the basic time-series design is as follows:

A Basic Time-Series Design

$$O_1 \quad O_2 \quad O_3 \quad O_4 \quad O_5 \quad X \quad O_6 \quad O_7 \quad O_8 \quad O_9 \quad O_{10}$$

The threats to internal validity that endanger use of this design include history (something could happen between the last pretest and the first posttest), instrumentation (if, for some reason, the test being used is changed at any time during the study), and testing (due to a practice effect). The possibility of a pretest-treatment interaction is also increased with the use of several pretests.

The effectiveness of the treatment in a time-series design is basically determined by analyzing the pattern of test scores that results from the several tests. Figure 13.9 illustrates several possible outcome patterns that might result from the introduction of an experimental variable (*X*).

The vertical line indicates the point at which the experimental treatment is introduced. In this figure, the change between time periods 5 and 6 gives the same kind of data that would be obtained using a one-group pretest-posttest design. The collection of additional data before and after the introduction of the treatment, however, shows how misleading a one-group pretest-posttest design can be. In (A), the improvement is

shown to be no more than that which occurs from one data collection period to another—regardless of method. You will notice that performance does improve from time to time, but no trend or overall increase is apparent. In (B), the gain from periods 5 to 6 appears to be part of a trend already apparent before the treatment was begun (quite possibly an example of maturation). In (D) the higher score in period 6 is only temporary, as performance soon approaches what it was before the treatment was introduced (suggesting an extraneous event of transient impact). Only in (C) do we have evidence of a consistent effect of the treatment.

The time-series design is a strong design, although it is vulnerable to history (an extraneous event could occur after period 5) and instrumentation (owing to the several test administrations at different points in time). The extensive amount of data collection required, in fact, is a likely reason why this design is infrequently used in educational research. In many studies, especially in schools, it simply is not feasible to give the same instrument eight to ten times. Even when it is possible, serious questions are raised concerning the validity of instrument interpretation with so many administrations. An exception to this is the use of unobtrusive devices that can be used over many occasions, since interpretations based on them should remain valid.

FACTORIAL DESIGNS

Factorial designs extend the number of relationships that may be examined in an experimental study. They

Figure 13.9 *Possible Outcome Patterns in a Time-Series Design*

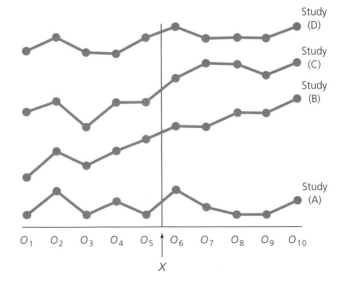

are essentially modifications of either the posttest-only control group or pretest-posttest control group designs (with or without random assignment), which permit the investigation of additional independent variables. Another value of a factorial design is that it allows a researcher to study the **interaction** of an independent variable with one or more other variables, sometimes called moderator variables. **Moderator variables** may be either treatment variables or subject characteristic variables. A diagram of a factorial design is as follows:

Factorial Design

Treatment	R	O	X_1	Y_1	O
Control	R	O	X_2	Y_1	O
Treatment	R	O	X_1	Y_2	O
Control	R	O	X_2	Y_2	O

This design is a modification of the pretest-posttest control group design. It involves one treatment variable having two levels (X_1 and X_2), and one moderator variable, also having two levels (Y_1 and Y_2). In this example, two groups would receive the treatment (X_1) and two would not (X_2). Both groups receiving the treatment would differ on Y, however, as would the two groups not receiving the treatment. Because each variable, or factor, has two levels, the above design is called a 2 by 2 factorial design. This design can also be illustrated as follows:

Alternate Illustration of a 2 by 2 Posttest-Only Factorial Design

	X_1	X_2
Y_1		
Y_2		

Consider the example we have used before of a researcher comparing the effectiveness of inquiry and lecture methods of instruction on achievement in history. The independent variable in this case (method of instruction) has two levels—inquiry (X_1) and lecture (X_2). Now imagine the researcher wants to see whether achievement is also influenced by class size. In that case, Y_1 might represent small classes and Y_2 might represent large classes.

As we suggest above, it is possible using a factorial design to assess not only the separate effect of each independent variable but also their joint effect. In other

Class size	Method	
	Inquiry (X_1)	Lecture (X_2)
Small (Y_1)		
Large (Y_2)		

Figure 13.10 *Using a Factorial Design to Study Effects of Method and Class Size on Achievement*

words, the researcher is able to see how one of the variables might moderate the other (hence the reason for calling these variables "moderator" variables).

Let us continue with the example of the researcher who wished to investigate the effects of method of instruction and class size on achievement in history. Figure 13.10 illustrates how various combinations of these variables could be studied in a factorial design.

Factorial designs, therefore, are an efficient way to study several relationships with one set of data. Let us emphasize again, however, that their greatest virtue lies in the fact that they enable a researcher to study interactions between variables.

Figure 13.11, for example, illustrates two possible outcomes for the 2 by 2 factorial design shown in Figure 13.10. The scores for each group on the posttest (a 50-item quiz on American history) are shown in the boxes (usually called *cells*) corresponding to each combination of method and class size.

In study (*a*) in Figure 13.11, the inquiry method was shown to be superior in both small and large classes, and small classes were superior to large classes for both methods. Hence no interaction effect is present. In study (*b*), students did better in small than in large classes with both methods; however, students in small classes did better when they were taught by the inquiry method, but students in large classes did better when they were taught by the lecture method. Thus, even though students did better in small than in large classes in general, how well they did depended on what method they were taught by. As a result, the researcher cannot say that either method was always better; it depends on the size of the class in which students were taught. There is an interaction, in other words, between class size and method, and this in turn affects achievement.

Suppose a factorial design was *not* used in study (*b*). If the researcher simply compared the effect of the two methods, without taking class size into account, he or

(a) No interaction between class size and method

Method

Class size	Inquiry (X_1)	Lecture (X_2)	Mean
Small (Y_1)	46	38	42
Large (Y_2)	40	32	36
Mean =	43	35	

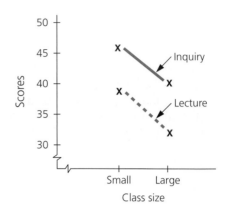

(b) Interaction between class size and method

Method

Class size	Inquiry (X_1)	Lecture (X_2)	Mean
Small (Y_1)	48	42	45
Large (Y_2)	32	38	36
Mean =	40	40	

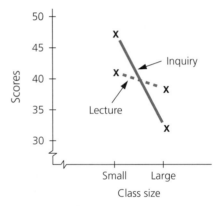

Figure 13.11 *Illustration of Interaction and No Interaction in a 2 by 2 Factorial Design*

she would conclude that there was no difference in their effect on achievement (notice that the means of both groups = 40). The use of a factorial design enables us to see that the effectiveness of the method, in this case, depends on the size of the class in which it is used. It appears that an interaction exists between method and class size. Figure 13.12 illustrates an example of an interaction effect.

A factorial design involving four levels of the independent variable and using a modification of the posttest-only control group design was employed by Tuckman.[7] In this design, the independent variable is type of instruction, and the moderator is amount of motivation. It is a 4 by 2 factorial design (see Figure 13.13). Many additional variations are also possible, such as 3 by 3, 4 by 3, and 3 by 2 by 3 designs. Factorial designs can be used to investigate more than two variables, although rarely are more than three variables studied in one design.

Control of Threats to Internal Validity: A Summary

Table 13.1 presents our evaluation of the effectiveness of each of the preceding designs in controlling the threats to internal validity that we discussed in Chapter Nine. You should remember that these assessments reflect our judgment; not all researchers would necessarily agree. We have assigned two pluses (++) to indicate a *strong* control (the threat is *unlikely* to occur); one plus (+) to indicate *some* control (the threat *might* occur); a minus (–) to indicate a *weak* control (the threat *is* likely to occur); and a question mark (?) to those threats whose likelihood, owing to the nature of the study, we cannot determine.

You will notice that these designs are most effective in controlling the threats of subject characteristics, mortality, history, maturation, and regression. Note that mortality is controlled in several designs because any

Figure 13.12 *An Interaction Effect*

A little drink can be fun . . .

as can a drive around town . . .

but watch out for the interaction.

subject lost is lost to both the experimental and control methods, thus introducing no advantage to either. A location threat is a minor problem in the time-series design because the location where the treatment is administered is usually constant throughout the study; the same is true for data collector characteristics, although such characteristics may be a problem in other designs if different collectors are used for different methods. This is usually easy to control, however. Unfortunately,

time-series designs do suffer from a strong likelihood of instrument decay and data collector bias, since data (by means of observations) must be collected over many trials, and the data collector can hardly be kept in the dark as to the intent of the study.

Unconscious bias on the part of data collectors is not controlled by any of these designs, nor is an implementation or attitudinal effect. Either implementers or data collectors can, unintentionally, distort the results of a

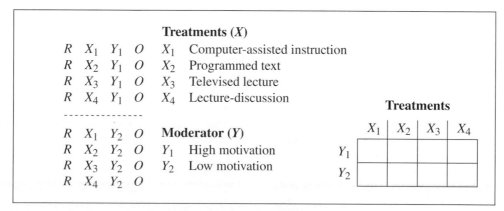

Figure 13.13 *Example of a 4 by 2 Factorial Design*

Table 13.1 *Effectiveness of Experimental Designs in Controlling Threats to Internal Validity*

Design	Subject Characteristics	Mortality	Location	Instrument Decay	Data Collector Characteristics	Data Collector Bias	Testing	History	Maturation	Attitudinal	Regression	Implementation
One-shot case study	–	–	–	(NA)	–	–	(NA)	–	–	–	–	–
One group pre-posttest	–	?	–	–	–	–	–	–	–	–	–	–
Static-group comparison	–	–	–	+	–	–	+	?	+	–	–	–
Randomized posttest-only control group	++	+	–	+	–	–	++	+	++	–	++	–
Randomized pre-post-test control group	++	+	–	+	–	–	+	+	++	–	++	–
Solomon four-group	++	++	–	+	–	–	++	+	++	–	++	–
Randomized posttest-only control group with matched subjects	++	+	–	+	–	–	++	+	++	–	++	–
Matching-only pre- posttest control group	+	+	–	+	–	–	+	+	+	–	+	–
Counterbalanced	++	++	–	+	–	–	+	++	++	++	++	–
Time-series	++	–	+	–	–	–	–	–	+	–	++	–
Factorial with randomization	++	++	–	++	–	–	+	+	++	–	++	–
Factorial without randomization	?	?	–	++	–	–	+	+	+	–	?	–

Key: (++) = strong control, threat unlikely to occur; (+) = some control, threat may possibly occur; (–) = weak control, threat likely to occur; (?) = can't determine; (NA) = threat does not apply.

study. The data collector should be kept ignorant as to who received which treatment, if this is feasible. It should be verified that the treatment is administered and the data collected as the researcher intended.

As you can see in Table 13.1, a testing threat may be present in many of the designs, although its magnitude depends on the nature and frequency of the instrumentation involved. It can occur only when subjects respond to an instrument on more than one occasion.

The attitudinal (or demoralization) effect is best controlled by the counterbalanced design since each subject receives both (or all) special treatments. In the remaining designs, it can be controlled by providing another

"special" experience during the alternative treatment. Special mention should be made of the double-blind (see p. 266) experiment. Such studies are common in medicine, but hard to arrange in education. The key element is that neither the subjects nor the researcher know the identity of those receiving each treatment. This is most easily accomplished by means of a *placebo* (sometimes a sugar pill) which is indistinguishable from the actual medicine.

Regression is not likely to be a problem except in the single-group pretest-posttest design, since it should occur equally in experimental and control conditions if it occurs at all. It could, however, possibly occur in a nonequivalent (no random assignment) pretest-posttest control group design, if there are large initial differences between the two groups.

Evaluating the Likelihood of a Threat to Internal Validity in Experimental Studies

An important consideration in planning an experimental study or in evaluating the results of a reported study is the likelihood of possible threats to internal validity. As we have shown, there are a number of possible threats to internal validity that may exist. The question that a researcher must ask is: How likely is it that any *particular* threat exists in *this* study?

To aid in assessing this likelihood, we suggest the following procedures.

Step 1: Ask: What specific factors either are known to affect the dependent variable or may logically be expected to affect this variable? (Note that researchers need *not* be concerned with factors unrelated to what they are studying.)

Step 2: Ask: What is the likelihood of the comparison groups differing on each of these factors? (A difference between groups cannot be explained away by a factor that is the same for all groups.)

Step 3: Evaluate the threats on the basis of how likely they are to have an effect and plan to control for them. If a given threat cannot be controlled, this should be acknowledged.

The importance of step 2 is illustrated in Figure 13.14. In each diagram, the thermometers depict the performance of subjects receiving method A compared to those receiving method B. In diagram (*a*), subjects receiving method A performed higher on the posttest

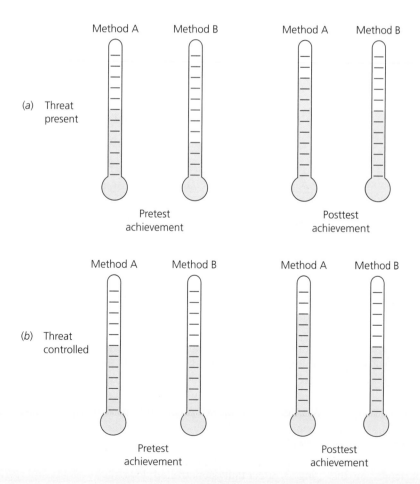

Figure 13.14 *Guidelines for Handling Internal Validity in Comparison Group Studies*

but *also* performed higher on the pretest; thus, the difference in pretest achievement accounts for the difference on the posttest. In diagram (*b*), subjects receiving method A performed higher on the posttest but did *not* perform higher on the pretest; thus, the posttest results *cannot* be explained by, or attributed to, different achievement levels prior to receiving the methods.

Let us consider an example to illustrate how these different steps might be employed. Suppose a researcher wishes to investigate the effects of two different teaching methods (for example, lecture versus inquiry instruction) on critical thinking ability of students (as measured by scores on a critical thinking test). The researcher plans to compare two groups of eleventh-graders, one group being taught by an instructor who uses the lecture method, the other group being taught by an instructor who uses the inquiry method. Assume that intact classes will be used rather than random assignment to groups. Several of the threats to internal validity discussed in Chapter Nine are considered and evaluated using the steps just presented. We would argue that this is the kind of thinking researchers should engage in when planning a research project.

Subject Characteristics. Although there are many possible subject characteristics that might affect critical thinking ability, we identify only two here-initial critical thinking ability (a) and gender (b).

1. **Variable (a).** *Step 1:* Posttreatment critical thinking ability of students in the two groups is almost certainly related to initial critical thinking ability. *Step 2:* Groups may well differ unless randomly assigned or matched. *Step 3:* Likelihood of having an effect unless controlled: high.
2. **Variable (b).** *Step 1:* Posttreatment critical ability may be related to gender. *Step 2:* If groups differ significantly in proportions of each gender, threat exists. Although possible, this is unlikely. *Step 3:* Likelihood of having an effect unless controlled: low.

Mortality. *Step 1:* Likely to affect posttreatment scores on any measure of critical thinking since those subjects who drop out or are otherwise lost would likely have lower scores. *Step 2:* Groups probably would not differ in numbers lost, but this should be verified. *Step 3:* Likelihood of having an effect unless controlled: moderate.

Location. *Step 1:* If location of implementation of treatment and/or of data collection differs for the two groups, this could affect posttreatment scores on the critical thinking test. Posttreatment scores would be expected to be affected by such resources as class size, availability of reading materials, films, and so forth. *Step 2:* May differ for groups unless controlled for by standardizing locations for implementation and data collection. The classrooms using each method may differ systematically unless steps are taken to ensure resources are comparable. *Step 3:* Likelihood of having an effect unless controlled: moderate to high.

Instrumentation.

1. **Instrument decay.** *Step 1:* May affect any outcome. *Step 2:* Could differ for groups. This should not be a major problem, providing all instruments used are carefully examined and any alterations found are corrected. *Step 3:* Likelihood of having an effect unless controlled: low.
2. **Data collector characteristics.** *Step 1:* Might affect scores on critical thinking test. *Step 2:* Might differ for groups unless controlled by using the same data collector(s) for all groups. *Step 3:* Likelihood of having an effect unless controlled: moderate.
3. **Data collector bias.** *Step 1:* Could certainly affect scores on critical thinking test. *Step 2:* Might differ for groups unless controlled by training implementers in administration of the instrument and/or keeping them ignorant as to which treatment group is being tested. *Step 3:* Likelihood of having an effect unless controlled: high.

Testing. *Step 1:* Pretesting, if used, might well affect posttest scores on critical thinking test. *Step 2:* Presumably the pretest would affect both groups equally, however, and would not be likely to interact with method, since instructors using each method are teaching critical thinking skills. *Step 3:* Likelihood of having an effect unless controlled: low.

History. *Step 1:* Extraneous events that might affect critical thinking skills are difficult to conjecture, but they might include such things as a special TV series on thinking, attendance at a district workshop on critical thinking by some students, or participation in certain extracurricular activities (e.g., debates) that occur during the course of the study. *Step 2:* In most cases, these events would likely affect both groups equally and hence are not likely to constitute a threat. Such events should be noted and their impact on each group assessed to the degree possible. *Step 3:* Likelihood of having an effect unless controlled: low.

Maturation. *Step 1:* Could affect outcome scores since critical thinking is presumably related to individual growth. *Step 2:* Presuming that the instructors teach each method over the same time period, maturation should not be a threat. *Step 3:* Likelihood of having an effect unless controlled: low.

Attitudinal Effect. *Step 1:* Could affect posttest scores. *Step 2:* If the members of either group perceive that they are receiving any sort of "special attention," this could be a threat. The extent to which either treatment is "novel" should be evaluated. *Step 3:* Likelihood of having an effect unless controlled: low to moderate.

Regression. *Step 1:* Unlikely to affect posttest scores unless subjects are selected on the basis of extreme scores. *Step 2:* Unlikely, though possible, to affect groups differently. *Step 3:* Likelihood of having an effect unless controlled: low.

Implementation. *Step 1:* Instructor characteristics are likely to affect posttreatment scores. *Step 2:* Because different instructors teach the methods, they may well differ. This could be controlled by having several instructors for each method, by having each instructor teach both methods, or by monitoring instruction. *Step 3:* Likelihood of having an effect unless controlled: high.

The trick, then, to identifying threats to internal validity is, first, to think of different variables (conditions, subject characteristics, and so on) that might affect the outcome variable of the study and, second, to decide, based on evidence and/or experience, whether these things would affect the comparison groups differently. If so, this may provide an alternative explanation for the results. If this seems likely, a threat to internal validity of the study may indeed be present and needs to be minimized or eliminated. It should then be discussed in the final report on the research project.

Control of Experimental Treatments

The designs discussed in this chapter are all intended to improve the internal validity of an experimental study. As you have seen, each has its advantages and disadvantages and each provides a way of handling some threats but not others.

Another issue, however, cuts across all designs. While it has been touched upon in earlier sections, particularly in connection with location and implementation threats, it deserves more attention than it customarily receives. The issue is that of researcher control over the experimental treatment(s). Of course, an essential requirement of a well-conducted experiment is that researchers have control over the treatment—that is, they control the what, who, when, and how of it. A clear example of researcher control is the testing of a new drug; clearly, the drug is the treatment and the researcher can control who administers it, under what conditions, when it is given, to whom, and how much. Unfortunately, researchers seldom have this degree of control in educational research.

In the ideal situation, a researcher can specify precisely the ingredients of the treatment; in actual practice, many treatments or methods are too complex to describe precisely. Consider the example we have previously given of a study comparing the effectiveness of inquiry and lecture methods of instruction. What, exactly, is the individual who implements each method to do? Researchers may differ greatly in their answers to this question. Ambiguity in specifying exactly what the person who is to conduct the treatment is to do leads to major problems in implementation. How are researchers to train teachers to implement the methods involved in a study if they can't specify the essential characteristics of those methods? Even supposing that adequate specification can be achieved and training methods developed, how can researchers be sure the methods are implemented *correctly?* These problems must be faced by any researcher using any of the designs we have discussed.

A consideration of this issue frequently leads to consideration (and assessment) of possible trade-offs. The greatest control is likely to occur when the researcher is the one implementing the treatment; this, however, also provides the greatest opportunity for an implementation threat to occur. The more the researcher diffuses implementation by adding other implementers in the interest of reducing threats, however, the more he or she risks distortion or dilution of the treatment. The extreme case is presented by the use of existing treatment groups— that is, groups located by the researcher that already are receiving certain treatments. Most authors refer to these as causal-comparative or *ex post facto* studies, (see Chapter Sixteen) and do not consider them to fall under the category of experimental research. In such studies, the researcher must locate groups receiving the specified treatment(s) and then use a matching-only design or, if sufficient lead time exists before implementation of the treatment, a time-series design. We are not

Significant Findings in Experimental Research

In our opinion, some of the most important research in social psychology, with obvious implications for education, has been that on the effects of cooperative social interaction on negative attitudes, or the tendency of people to dislike others. A series of experimental studies begun in the 1940s led to the generalization that liking for group members, including those of different backgrounds and ethnicity, is increased by cooperative activities that lead to a successful outcome.* A recent application of this finding is the "jigsaw technique," which requires each member of a group to teach other members a section of material to be learned.† Experimental studies generally support the effectiveness of this procedure.

*W. G. Stephan (1985). Intergroup relations. In G. Lindzey and E. Aronson (Eds.), *Handbook of social psychology*. New York: Random House.
†E. Aronson, C. Stephan, J. Sikes, N. Blaney, and M. Snapp (1978). *The jigsaw classroom*. Beverly Hills: Sage.

persuaded that such studies, if treatments are carefully identified, are necessarily inferior with respect to cause-effect conclusions compared with studies in which treatments are assigned to teachers (or others) by the researcher. Both are equally open to most of the threats we have discussed. The existing groups are more susceptible to subject characteristics, location, and regression threats than true experiments, but not necessarily more so than quasi-experiments. One would expect fewer problems with an attitudinal effect, since existing practice is not altered. Greater history and maturation threats exist because the researcher would have less control. Implementation is difficult to assess. Teachers who are already implementing a new method may be enthusiastic if they initially chose the method, but they also may be better teachers. On the other hand, teachers assigned to a method that is new to them may be either enthusiastic or resentful. We conclude that both types of study are legitimate.

An Example of Experimental Research

In the remainder of this chapter, we present a published example of experimental research. Along with a reprint of the actual study itself, we critique the study, identify its strengths, and discuss areas we think could be improved. We also do this at the end of Chapters Fourteen to Seventeen and Nineteen to Twenty-Three, in each case analyzing the type of study discussed in the chapter. In selecting the studies for review, we used the following criteria:

- The study had to exemplify typical, but not outstanding, methodology and permit constructive criticism.

- The study had to have enough interest value to hold the attention of students, even though specific professional interests may not be directly addressed.
- The study had to be concisely reported.

In total, these studies represent the diversity of special interests in the field of education.

In critiquing each of these studies, we used a series of categories and questions that should, by now, be familiar to you. They are:

Purpose/justification: Is it logical? Is it convincing? Is it sufficient? Do the authors show how the results of the study would have important implications for theory, practice, or both? Are assumptions made explicit?

Definitions: Are major terms clearly defined? If not, are they clear in context?

Prior research: Has previous work on the topic been covered adequately? Is it clearly connected to the present study?

Hypotheses: Are they stated? Implied? Appropriate for the study?

Sampling: What type of sample is used? Is it a random sample? If not, is it adequately described? Do the authors recommend or imply generalizing to a population? If so, is the target population clearly indicated? Are possible limits to generalizing discussed?

Instrumentation: Is it adequately described? Is evidence of adequate reliability presented? Is evidence of validity provided? How persuasive is the evidence or the argument for validity of inferences made from the instruments?

Internal validity: What threats are evident? Were they controlled? If not, were they discussed?

Data analysis: Are data summarized and reported appropriately? Are descriptive and inferential statistics (if any) used appropriately? Are the statistics interpreted correctly? Are limitations discussed?

Results: Are they clearly presented? Is the written summary consistent with the data reported?

Interpretations/discussion: Do the authors place the study in a broader context? Do they recognize limitations of the study, especially with regard to population and ecological generalizing of results?

Journal of Educational Research. (1996). Vol. 89, pp. 187–191.
Address correspondence to Judith R. Lampe. Lubbock Independent School District, 1628 19th Street, Lubbock, TX 79401.

Effects of Cooperative Learning Among Hispanic Students in Elementary Social Studies

Judith R. Lampe
Lubbock Independent School District, Texas

Gene R. Rooze
Mary Tallent-Runnels
Texas Tech University

Abstract

Justification

Explain further

Although research has indicated that cooperative learning enhances student achievement, promotes self-esteem, and improves interpersonal relations, few studies have focused on cooperative learning in elementary social studies. There is a close affinity between the goals of citizenship education and social skills promoted by cooperative learning. This investigation determined differences between achievement and self-esteem of Hispanic fourth graders who received instruction using cooperative learning or traditional instruction. Results indicated higher achievement with cooperative learning. Although self-esteem was apparently higher for boys than for girls, regardless of treatment, this result was inconclusive. Making connections between social studies goals and cooperative learning offers a valuable tool for improving social studies education.

During the past 15 years, research has indicated that cooperative-learning groups enhance student achievement (Johnson & Johnson, 1989; Slavin, 1990, 1991; Webb, 1989). Peer interaction is central to the success of cooperative learning as it relates to cognitive understanding. Cognitive developmental theories such as Vygotsky's (1978) emphasize that intellectual growth is a dynamic social-interactive process. Active verbalization, especially when it involves explanation, often leads to cognitive restructuring and an increase in understanding. Comprehension is facilitated as learners, some of whom might normally "tune out" or refuse to speak out in a traditional setting, become actively involved in the learning process through group interaction. According to

Weak —

Stahl and VanSickle (1992), every cooperative-learning strategy, when used appropriately, can enable students to move beyond the text, memorization of basic facts, and learning lower level skills.

In addition to its academic benefits, cooperative learning has been found to promote self-esteem, interpersonal relations, and improved attitudes toward school and peers. In a competitively structured classroom, except for the few "winners" or students who succeed, self-esteem can suffer. Likewise, self-esteem and approval of classmates can be lower in individualistic learning situations than in cooperative ones (Johnson, Johnson, & Maruyama, 1984). When competition is promoted, students may learn to value winning at all costs, and cooperation may be discouraged (Conrad, 1988). Although advocates of cooperative learning are not opposed to all competition, they do oppose inappropriate competition (Johnson & Johnson, 1991). One cooperative learning model, Teams-Games-Tournament, builds a competitive phase into part of the instructional strategy (Stahl & VanSickle, 1992). Inappropriate competition, however, tends to widen the existing differences among students' academic knowledge and abilities, which, in turn, can widen negative perceptions of others on the basis of gender, race, or ethnicity (Stahl, 1992).

Use of circled terms is weak here.

Cooperative-learning groups have also been found to equalize the status and respect of all group members, regardless of gender (Glassman, 1989; Johnson, Johnson, & Stanne, 1986). Research by Klein (1985) revealed that competitively structured classrooms have the effect of favoring boys or reinforcing sex role stereotypes that may limit opportunities for girls. Studies in traditional classrooms have consistently shown that boys have more interactions with teachers than girls do (Brophy & Good, 1974; Cooper & Good, 1983) and that in our culture boys are often socialized to be assertive and demanding, whereas girls are to be responsible and compliant. In a comprehensive study (Martinez & Dukes, 1991) on self-esteem and ethnicity among students in Grades 7 through 12 (*N* = 13,489), minorities and women generally reported lower levels of self-esteem than White males did. Within each race or ethnic category, satisfaction-with-self averages for girls were lower than those for boys. A particularly interesting finding regarding satisfaction-with-self was that male Hispanics reported the highest satisfaction of any ethnic group, including White males.

> What is the importance of this?

PURPOSE

There have been numerous empirical studies that confirm cooperative learning to be an effective way to structure learning activities (Johnson, Johnson, Holubec, & Roy, 1984; Montague & Tanner, 1987; Slavin, 1991). However, there is surprisingly little research that emphasizes social studies and even less that focuses on social studies at the elementary level. Furthermore, no studies of which we are aware have investigated the effects of cooperative learning and the interaction of gender on social studies and self-esteem at the fourth-grade level in a Hispanic, low-socioeconomic population. Thus, our purpose in the present study was to determine differences between the social studies achievement and self-esteem of Hispanic, economically disadvantaged, fourth-grade male and female students who participated in cooperative-learning groups and those who received instruction using a traditional approach. Therefore, we addressed the following questions in this study:

> Problem statement

1. Is there a difference in the social studies achievement self-esteem of fourth-grade students according to the treatments of cooperative learning or traditional instruction and according to gender across treatment groups?
2. Is there a difference in the social studies achievement of fourth-grade students according to the treatments of cooperative learning or traditional instruction and according to gender across treatment groups?

> Repeated in #2. This should be deleted.
>
> Implied hypotheses

METHOD

Participants

This 12-week study was conducted in eight 4th-grade social studies classrooms (*N* = 105) in two elementary schools in the Southwest with low-socioeconomic, Hispanic populations. Percentages of the student populations receiving free or reduced lunches were 78% free and 10% reduced at School A and 88% free and 5% reduced at School B. Twenty-five boys and 26 girls received instruction based on cooperative learning; 24 boys and 30 girls received traditional, teacher-directed instruction. School district administrators assigned this research study to eight intact classrooms at two elementary schools; two classes of each treatment group were represented at each school. Teachers were randomly assigned by the researchers to the cooperative-learning treatment groups. They had received training in cooperative-learning group strategies through Johnson and Johnson "Brown Book" workshops, consultation with the researchers, sample lessons, and supplemental materials. Teachers using the traditional approach also had experience in cooperative-learning methodology but agreed to teach the content in a whole-class, textbook-centered teacher-directed format. All of the female teachers (one Hispanic and

> Convenience sample
> Hispanics only, or all students?
> Assigned on what basis?
> Good, but only four in each method
> Limits generalizeability
> Attitude and implementation threats to internal validity

Unclear

To balance
experience

(the remaining Anglo) were deemed as performing effectively by their superiors. The most experienced teacher (approximately 20 years) and most inexperienced teacher (2 years) were assigned to the cooperative-learning treatment group. All of the remaining teachers were between 25 and 35 years of age and averaged 10 years of teaching experience.

Instruments

Good, but only
controls these
variables

Who did testing?
Example would help

Good idea

Why 5th grade?

Acceptable

Because random assignment of treatment groups to students was not possible, we used pretest scores from researcher-constructed social studies unit tests and the Coopersmith Self-Esteem Inventory, School Form (Coopersmith, 1984), as covariates to determine equivalence of groups. Prior to the beginning of each of the two units, the social studies pretest was administered. Then at the end of each unit, the sample social studies test was given as a posttest to measure achievement in social studies. In an effort to increase content validity, we developed these criterion-referenced objective tests by using the publisher's fourth-grade test data bank as a source. In constructing the 30-item multiple-choice tests, we included a variety of items that incorporated fact-recall, interpreting graphics (charts and maps), identifying cause and effect, drawing conclusions, sequencing, and inferencing. These social studies unit tests were piloted prior to the experiment with fifth-grade students in the same school system and yielded a .78 Pearson product-moment test-retest reliability coefficient and a .79 Kuder-Richardson Formula 20 reliability coefficient for interitem consistency. The interval for the test-retest analysis was 23 days.

Operational definition

Good, but should have
been checked

Both scales probably
similar

To measure self-esteem, the Coopersmith Self-Esteem Inventory, School Form, was administered both as a pretest and posttest, before and after the 12-week treatment period. The school form consists of 50 items, resulting in a total self score and subscale scores of General Self, Social Self-Peers, Home-Parents, and School-Academic. Reliability coefficients (K-R 20s) for measuring internal consistency were reported by Kimball (1972) to be between (87) and (92) when administered to 7,600 public schoolchildren in Grades 4 through 8. This sample included students of all socioeconomic ranges and Black and Hispanic students. The concurrent validity coefficient was reported to be .83 when the Coopersmith Self-Esteem Inventory was compared with the Hare Self-Esteem Scale (Mitchell, 1985).

Treatment Procedures

During the 12-week period, both treatment groups studied the same content material on Texas history drawn from two 4th-grade Scott, Foresman and Company (1988) social studies units titled "Settling Our State" and "A Changing Texas." During the treatment period, students in the cooperative-learning classrooms were instructed by teachers who followed the guidelines of Johnson, Johnson, and Holubec (1990), also known as "Brown Book Training" for structuring heterogeneous cooperative-learning groups. Teachers incorporated the basic elements of cooperative learning into the group experience: positive interdependence, face-to-face interaction, individual accountability, social skill development, and group processing. In addition, teachers specified both the academic and social skill objectives, explained the tasks and goal structures,

Presumably shown by
observation

assigned roles within the groups, and described the procedures for the learning activity. Group interaction was evidenced by much student-student talking; they often sat in groups on the floor as they worked on their mutual group goal. Students took turns reading the social studies content to each other and then discussed it by asking questions, summarizing, and clarifying each other's understandings.

Many different types of cooperative-learning group interactions were experienced. Jigsaw II groups and Group Investigation project groups were formed for some lessons as students worked together on their specified tasks. Examples of group activities included (a) writing letters from a historical character's perspective, (b) developing and using flash cards on Texas history, (c) discussing controversial issues (Civil War and slavery), and (d) becoming "experts" on a certain aspect of Texas history in a specialized group and then teaching the content to another base group (Jigsaw II strategy). Teachers in the cooperative learning classrooms acted as facilitators of learning as they formed groups, made placement decisions, specified tasks, assigned roles, monitored, intervened only when necessary, evaluated, and performed group processing.

Good description

While the cooperative-learning groups studied social studies content using group interaction, the traditional groups learned the same content about Texas history from the same two 4th-grade textbook units, but did so during instruction in a whole-class, teacher-directed, textbook-centered approach. Instead of discussing the material, helping each other, or developing projects in groups, students read the assigned reading material silently, completed worksheets independently at their seats, did individual reports on Texas history, watched filmstrips, or engaged in discussions with the teacher in response to teacher questions. Traditional classrooms were characterized by a quiet, orderly atmosphere with the students seated at their desks, and teachers in these classrooms dispensed facts, served as resources, or provided information. Observations of both treatment conditions were documented by researcher field notes.

Good description

More detail needed

DATA ANALYSIS AND RESULTS

Data were analyzed using analysis of covariance (ANCOVA) to explore differences among groups. First, a two-way ANCOVA was performed with social studies achievement as the dependent variable and the social studies pretest as the covariate. Another two-way ANCOVA was then conducted with the Coopersmith Self-Esteem posttest as the dependent variable and the Coopersmith Self-Esteem pretest as the covariate. The independent variables for both analyses were treatment and gender. The two treatment conditions were cooperative learning and traditional, teacher-directed instruction.

Better to combine pretest achievement and self-esteem as covariates in both analyses

The interaction of the covariate with treatment that was used to test for homogeneity of regression for the self-esteem test was not statistically significant, $F(1, 102) = 0$, $p = .95$. The homogeneity of regression tests for the interaction between the covariate and gender was also not statistically significant, $F(1, 102) = .79$, $p = .38$. This indicated that the assumption of parallelism of slopes was met and lends support for the use of ANCOVA in this study. For the social studies achievement test, the interaction of the covariate with gender used to test for homogeneity of regression was not statistically significant, $F(1, 95) = 0$, $p = 1$. For the interaction of the covariate with treatment, the test for homogeneity of regression was statistically significant $F(1, 95) = 28.96$, $p = .0001$. This departure from linearity sometimes results in biased estimates of treatment (Kirk, 1982). Therefore, our next step was to plot the regression lines for the covariate by treatment interaction. When these lines were plotted, they were both positive, and the slopes were only slightly different. Therefore, we concluded that the use of this covariate was appropriate.

Good

Means and standard deviations of raw scores for the social studies achievement pretests and posttests, as well as the adjusted means for the social studies achievement posttest, are shown in Table 1. Results of the ANCOVA revealed a statistically significant main effect for treatment, $F(1, 93) = 25.72$, $p < .001$, as shown in Table 2, favoring cooperative learning over traditional instruction; however, no statistically significant effects were found for gender or for an interaction between treatment and gender on social studies achievement. The correlation r between the pretest and the posttest was .67, $p = .001$.

But $p = .065$; see Table 2

The raw score means, standard deviations, and the adjusted means for self-esteem reflect similar scores for both treatment groups (Table 3). Results of the ANCOVA for self-esteem revealed no main effect for treatment and no statistically significant interaction between treatment

Statistical significance is irrelevant here

Table 1 *Observed Means, Adjusted Means, and Standard Deviations for Achievement, by Treatment and Gender*

	Cooperative Learning			Traditional		
Group	n	M	SD	n	M	SD
Pretest						
Boys	22	24.77	6.43	(23)	21.04	5.13
Girls	23	23.44	4.07	29	21.17	5.02
Total	45	24.09	5.33	53	21.11	5.02
Posttest						
Boys	22	48.73	3.32	24	33.33	9.81
		(46.32)			(35.07)	
Girls	23	44.87	9.63	29	37.00	10.34
		(43.95)			(38.59)	
Total						
obs. mean	45	46.98	3.83	53	35.34	10.17
adj. mean		(45.07)			(37.02)	

Note: Adjusted means are presented in parentheses.

24?

Sample reduced by 6 in cooperative method and by 1 in traditional method

Table 2 *Analysis of Covariance of Social Studies Achievement*

Source of variation	SS	df	MS	F	p
Within cells	5,557.73	93	59.76		
Regression	3,142.57	1	3,142.57	52.29	.001
Treatment	1,537.13	1	1,537.13	25.72	.001
Gender	8.01	1	8.01	.13	.715
Treatment by gender	209.14	1	209.14	3.50	0.065

Marginally significant

Table 3 *Observed Means, Adjusted Means, and Standard Deviations for Self-Esteem, by Treatment and Gender*

	Cooperative Learning			Traditional		
Group	n	M	SD	n	M	SD
Pretest						
Boys	25	54.88	11.86	24	59.67	13.00
Girls	26	61.58	16.13	30	61.23	13.31
Total	51	58.29	14.46	54	60.54	13.07
Posttest						
Boys	25	62.40	13.47	24	66.67	14.73
		(65.27)			(66.46)	
Girls	26	61.31	19.37	30	59.67	14.63
		(59.87)			(58.45)	
Total						
obs. mean	51	61.84	16.58	54	62.78	14.95
adj. mean		(62.53)			(62.09)	

Note that boys increase, girls decrease

Note: Adjusted means are presented in parentheses.

and gender; however, a statistically significant main effect for gender was revealed, $F(1, 100) =$ 6.68, $p < .011$, favoring boys over girls, regardless of treatment group. The correlation between the pretest and the posttest was .60, $p = .001$. An effect size was calculated for the main effect for the gender result because it appeared difficult to explain, (eta squared = .066) (Thompson, 1994).

Eta = $\sqrt{.066}$ = .26

CONCLUSIONS AND DISCUSSION

Achievement

The results of this study indicated that there was a difference in the social studies achievement of 4th-grade students according to the treatment of cooperative-learning or traditional instruction. The cooperative-learning group instructional approach was a more effective way than traditional instruction to structure learning in 4th-grade social studies. However, no difference in social studies achievement was found according to gender across treatment groups. Both boys and girls profited from participation in cooperative-learning groups. This points out the need for educators to provide opportunities for all students to engage in cooperative-learning groups in elementary social studies. It is not suggested that all social studies content be studied using cooperative-learning groups; however, social studies educators are encouraged to recognize the effectiveness and benefits of this alternative approach and structure more cooperative-learning-group lessons in their classrooms.

Suggestive treatment by gender interaction

A possible explanation for the effectiveness of cooperative learning in this study involves the students' active involvement in the learning process through frequent verbalization in both an extensive and intensive way. Extensive interaction was apparent through the variety of exchanges—summarizing, explaining, clarifying, encouraging, probing, extending, and questioning. Intensive interaction was exhibited by the on-task behavior, the high level of motivation, and the "eye-to-eye," "knee-to-knee" communication posturing as the students interacted in cooperative-learning groups.

Observational data

With little research having been conducted in social studies on cooperative learning in Hispanic, low-socioeconomic populations, a major contribution of this study is that the cooperative-learning instructional approach (can) be more effective than the traditional approach for producing achievements gains in such a population. In an effort to meet the needs of an increasingly diverse, multicultural student population, cooperative learning provides social studies educators with an effective instructional approach for enhancing the success of our youth.

This is weak

Self-Esteem

No difference was found in the self-esteem of 4th-grade students according to the treatment of cooperative learning or traditional instruction. Although prior research indicated that cooperative-learning groups can equalize the status and respect of all group members regardless of gender, this study demonstrated no such equivalence. Although differences in self-esteem

Note that girls decrease

Table 4 *Analysis of Covariance of Self-Esteem*

Source of variation	SS	df	MS	F	p
Within cells	17,125.40	100	171.25		
Regression	7,808.14	1	7,808.14	45.59	.001
Treatment	.34	1	.34	.00	(.001) ◄ Clearly incorrect
Gender	1,143.84	1	1,143.84	6.68	.001
Treatment by gender	43.99	1	43.99	.26	.613

were not attributable to the type of instructional approach used, the results did indicate that gains in self-esteem were related to one's gender across treatment groups; boys outscored girls on the posttest regardless of whether we used cooperative learning or traditional, teacher-directed instruction.

Right

However, because of the small effect size for this analysis, these results should be interpreted with caution. There appears to be an effect; however, considering the small size, we find the results to be inconclusive. Although the current findings of the discrepancy in gains between boys' and girls' self-esteem may be related to the ethnicity factor previously reported in the Martinez and Dukes study (1991), the small effect size and short length of the study (12 weeks) cannot be regarded as conclusive evidence. It is suggested that differences in self-esteem for boys and girls according to ethnicity be explored further in research studies of greater length across the curriculum, including the social studies.

Overgeneralizing

In summary, cooperative learning provides a valuable instructional approach for social studies education. In addition, teachers working with Hispanic populations should consider cooperative learning in planning productive activities for their students. Making connections between social studies goals and cooperative-learning strategies is likely to enhance the possibility of developing knowledgeable, responsible, and participating citizens for our pluralistic society.

References

Brophy, J., & Good, T. (1974). *Teacher-student relationships: Causes and consequences.* New York: Holt, Rinehart & Winston.

Conrad, B. (1988). Cooperative learning and prejudice reduction. *Social Education, 52*(4), 283–286.

Cooper, H., & Good, T. (1983). *Pygmalion grows up: Studies in the expectation communication process.* New York: Longman.

Coopersmith, S. (1984). *Coopersmith self-esteem inventories* (3rd printing). Palo Alto, CA: Consulting Psychologists Press.

Glassman, P. (1980). *A study of cooperative learning in mathematics, writing, and reading in the intermediate grades: A focus upon achievement, attitudes, and self-esteem by gender, race, and ability group.* Dissertation, Hofstra University, New York.

Johnson, D., & Johnson, R. (1989). *Cooperation and competition: Theory and research.* Edina, MN: Interaction Book Company.

Johnson, D., & Johnson, R. (1991). *Learning together and alone: Cooperative, competitive, and individualistic learning* (3rd ed.). Englewood Cliffs, NJ: Prentice-Hall.

Johnson D., Johnson, R., & Holubec, E. (1990). *Cooperation in the classroom.* Edina, MN: Interaction Book Company.

Johnson, D., Johnson, R., Holubec, E., & Roy, P. (1984). *Circles of learning.* Alexandria, VA: Association for Supervision and Curriculum Development.

Johnson, D., Johnson, R., & Maruyama, G. (1984). Interdependence and interpersonal attraction among heterogeneous and homogeneous individuals: A theoretical formulation and a meta-analysis of the research. *Review of Educational Research, 53,* 5–54.

Johnson, R., Johnson, D., & Stanne, M. (1986). Comparison of computer assisted cooperative, competitive, and individualistic learning. *American Educational Research Journal, 23,* 382–392.

Kimball, O. (1972). Development of norms for the Coopersmith Self-Esteem Inventory: Grades four through eight (Doctoral dissertation, Northern Illinois University, 1972). *Dissertation Abstracts International, 34,* 1131–1132.

Kirk, R. (1982). *Experimental design* (2nd ed.). Belmont, CA: Brooks/Cole.

Klein, S. (Ed.). (1985). *Handbook for achievement of sex equity through education.* Baltimore, MD: The Johns Hopkins University Press.

Martinez, R., & Dukes, R. (1991). Ethnic and gender differences in self-esteem. *Youth and Society, 22(3),* 318–338.

Mitchell, J. (Ed.). (1985). *The ninth mental measurements yearbook.* Lincoln, NE: The University of Nebraska.

Montague, M., & Tanner, M. (1987). Reading strategy groups for content area instruction. *Journal of Reading, 30,* 716–725.

Scott, Foresman and Company. (1988). *Texas: The study of our state.* Fourth-grade textbook. Scott, Foresman.

Slavin, R. (1990). *Cooperative learning: Theory, research, and practice.* Englewood Cliffs, NJ: Prentice-Hall.

Slavin, R. (1991). Synthesis of research on cooperative learning. *Educational Leadership, 48,* 71–82.

Stahl, R. (1992). From "academic strangers" to successful members of a cooperative learning group: An inside-the-learner perspective. In *Cooperative learning in the social studies classroom: An invitation to social study.* Washington, DC: National Council for the Social Studies.

Stahl, R., & VanSickle, R. (1992). Cooperative learning as effective social study within the social studies classroom: Introduction and an invitation. In *Cooperative learning in the social studies classroom: An invitation to social study.* Bulletin No. 87. Washington, DC: National Council for the Social Studies.

Thompson, B. (1994). *The concept of statistical significance testing.* ERIC/AE Digest, Report No. (EDO-TM-94-1). Washington, DC: ERIC Clearinghouse on Assessment and Evaluation. (ERIC Document Reproduction Service No. ED 366 654)

Vygotsky, L. (1978). *Thought and Language.* Cambridge, MA: MIT Press.

Webb, N. (1989). Peer interaction and learning in small groups. *International Journal of Educational Research, 13,* 21–39.

Analysis of the Study

PURPOSE/JUSTIFICATION

The purpose of this study is partly clear at the outset: To study the effects of cooperative learning with Hispanic students in elementary social studies. Under "Purpose," we learn that the students are economically disadvantaged fourth-graders. It is clear in the introduction that the effects studied are social studies achievement (later clarified as unit tests) and self-esteem. The introduction (actually a summary of prior research) reviews several empirical and theoretical justifications for studying cooperative learning and for the position that it improves achievement and self-esteem. We think the case could be made more forcefully and that it is especially weakened by the frequent use of the words "can" and "may," since the question is not whether these effects *can* occur, but whether they *do*. The major justification for this study is that there appears to have been few studies focused on elementary social studies and none focused on the effects relative to gender with fourth-grade, low-income Hispanic students. While this kind of justification is common—that is, using a group that hasn't been studied yet—it is nevertheless weak. Why is it important to study this method and these outcomes with this group?

Probably little justification is needed for studying achievement since this is presumably what schools are primarily about. Self-esteem is more controversial, being viewed by some as a fuzzy-minded frill. Citations in the introduction provide a beginning justification for looking at gender and ethnicity in relation to self-esteem that could be connected to the prior arguments that were made for cooperative learning. It may have seemed obvious to the authors why it is important to find out whether cooperative learning improves achievement and self-esteem, and particularly for girls, but their report would be greatly strengthened by spelling it out. The assertion in the abstract that "there is a close affinity between the goals of citizenship education and social skills promoted by cooperative learning" is not obvious and requires explanation. There appear to be no ethical issues involving confidentiality, risk, or deception.

DEFINITIONS

Specific definitions, as such, are not provided; we believe they should be. Cooperative learning is "defined" by descriptions of what occurred during the study ("Brown Book Training," Jigsaw II, Group Investigation) that are not likely to be familiar to the general readership of the *Journal of Educational Research.* Further description provides a pretty good idea of what occurred and is consistent with most definitions of cooperative learning. Description of the traditional classrooms serves to clarify further the differences between the two methods.

Social studies achievement is operationally defined (by implication) as the score on criterion-referenced unit tests based on two specified units on Texas history published by Scott, Foresman ("Settling Our State" and "A Changing Texas"). The reader is provided with little help in assessing what is considered achievement in this context. Self-esteem is also defined operationally as a score on the Coopersmith Self-Esteem Inventory. Once again, a reader unfamiliar with this scale is given little help in defining self-esteem. Inclusion of the definition that accompanies the manual for this scale would be helpful.

PRIOR RESEARCH

As mentioned under "Purpose," the review of general literature on cooperative learning appears to be adequate, and a justification for studying cooperative learning as a means of enhancing the self-esteem of Hispanic girls can be inferred. We object to the description of higher self-esteem reported by Hispanic males as "interesting" without discussion of its meaning or importance.

HYPOTHESES

Although not stated—and we think they should be—two directional hypotheses seem clearly implied in the two questions that are stated. They are:

- When compared to traditional instruction, cooperative learning will result in greater gains in achievement and self-esteem.
- The gains under cooperative learning, as compared to traditional instruction, will be greater for girls than for boys.

SAMPLE

As is common (unfortunately), a convenience sample was used. Description of students is limited to gender breakdown and income level (free and reduced-cost lunches). It is unclear whether income applies to all students, or to Hispanic students only. As eight classrooms would be expected to include approximately 240 to 280 students, the proportion of Hispanic students was probably about 45 percent. It is unclear how the selection of the eight classrooms at two schools by district administrators would affect generalizability. It is unclear to us as to what population of students the results could be generalized. Finally, the sample size is the group on whom data is collected and analyzed—in this case, $N = 98$ for achievement, not 105 as implied. The original sample size of 105 is correct for self-esteem since no loss occurred.

INSTRUMENTATION

The achievement test was a 30-item, multiple-choice test selected from the publisher's bank of test items. Priority was given to items requiring higher-level thinking skills, although factual recall items were also included. Some examples would be helpful for checking content validity. The authors are to be commended for piloting the test (although we are confused as to the piloting with fifth-graders since the items and units are intended for fourth-graders!). The resulting reliability coefficients (.78 and .79) are acceptable, although not as high as commonly obtained with achievement tests. This is probably due to the test having fewer items than usual. No evidence of validity is presented; the authors appear to assume content validity.

The Coopersmith test is widely used and generally highly regarded. There is considerable evidence to suggest that both internal consistency and short-term stability are adequate for the present study. Nevertheless, internal consistency should have been checked for these particular students, especially since it is so easy to do. The validity of all self-esteem scales is frequently debated and a matter for concern. The correlation with another self-esteem scale is suspect since the two scales are probably very similar. Inclusion of another instrument (such as an essay or teacher ratings) would greatly enhance the claim to validity.

PROCEDURES/INTERNAL VALIDITY

The design of the study fits the quasi-experimental format with "matching" done statistically through analysis of covariance. Procedures are straightforward; each class was taught the same content over 12 weeks, half of the classrooms using each method. Students took both achievement and self-esteem tests before and after the units were taught. Validation of treatments by observation is commendable, although more detail would be helpful.

With regard to possible threats to internal validity, the use of pretests to control statistically for the subject characteristics threat is appropriate. It does not, however, ensure that the methods groups are equated on variables not included, such as family income. The treatment groups are approximately balanced on gender, with a slightly higher proportion of girls in the traditional method (55 percent versus 51 percent).

Although there was a slightly higher loss of subjects in the achievement data for the cooperative learning group (six compared to one), this probably does not create a serious bias. A location threat seems unlikely since assignment of method to teacher/classes was done randomly within each of the two schools. An instrumentation threat is unlikely since instrument decay should affect all comparisons equally; all scoring is mechanical and presumably the same data collectors were used in all classrooms. A testing threat should not exist since pretesting should affect both comparison groups equally. Maturation should be the same in both groups. History is a possible threat, but it seems unlikely that experiences would have been different for the two method groups. No regression threat exists.

We think that two important threats to internal validity do exist, however. The first is attitude of subjects, since the "traditional" teachers had experience in cooperative learning, but agreed to teach the units in a traditional format. More information as to students' prior experience with cooperative learning would help in evaluating the likelihood of this threat. The second threat is implementation, since only one of the eight teachers was Hispanic and it is likely that this would affect outcomes; it would help to know which method she used. Differences in teacher skill, motivation, and method preference could also affect results.

DATA ANALYSIS

Attention to possible violation of statistical assumptions is a positive feature. Analysis of covariance is perhaps appropriate as a means of assessing whether differences in means are attributable to the independent variables, but is not a justifiable basis for assessing generalizability, since random samples were not used.* We would suggest combining the pretests for achievement and self-esteem as covariate in both analyses.

*For a discussion of the rationale for this, see the Carver reference in the suggested readings for Chapter Eleven, listed on the CD-ROM that accompanies this text.

RESULTS

The difference between method groups in achievement is impressive. Calculation of effect size (Delta) gives $45.07 - 37.02/10.17 = .79$, which is considerably larger than the usual criterion of .50. The difference between methods in self-esteem is clearly minimal (the probability of .001 given in Table Four as "Treatment" is obviously an error). The overall difference between boys and girls in achievement is minimal. However, we think the interaction is of more importance than is suggested by the probability of .065 (see Table Two). For boys, the Delta of $1.15 = \dfrac{(46.32 - 37.07)}{9.81}$ indicates the cooperative method to be substantially more effective, whereas the Delta for girls of $.52 = \dfrac{(43.95 - 38.59)}{10.34}$ suggests less relative effectiveness for girls.

For self-esteem, the overall difference between boys and girls, although yielding a $p < .001$ results in a Delta of .46, suggesting a marginally important difference. This value is consistent with the reported Eta squared of .066. Eta equals the square root of .066, which equals .26, a very modest correlation. Mean scores increased from pre- to posttesting for boys under both methods, whereas the means of the girls decreased slightly under both methods.

DISCUSSION

We agree that the findings are consistent with the hypothesis that cooperative learning is more effective than "traditional" instruction with regard to achievement. We think that more should have been made of the suggestive gender/method interaction. With respect to self-esteem, we agree that the suggestive gender difference should be interpreted with caution.

It is appropriate for the authors to suggest explanations for the outcomes and to indicate that observation verified that the major characteristics of the cooperative-learning method were present. More detail would have strengthened this argument. While we did not identify many major threats to internal validity, we think that the two we did identify (attitude and implementation, and possibly history), should have been discussed.

As with most educational research, the use of a convenience sample severely limits generalization, particularly since the sample is not well described and since all teachers had previous experience in cooperative learning, including the teachers who used the traditional method. This limitation is not acknowledged by the authors in their recommendations.

Go back to the **Interactive and Applied Learning Tools** feature at the beginning of the chapter for a listing of interactive and applied activities. Go to the **Online Learning Center** at www.mhhe.com/fraenkel5e or your **Interactive Student CD-ROM** to take practice quizzes and receive immediate feedback, practice with key terms, review chapter content and main ideas, and find annotated Web links.

Main Points

THE UNIQUENESS OF EXPERIMENTAL RESEARCH

- Experimental research is unique in that it is the only type of research that directly attempts to influence a particular variable, and it is the only type that, when used properly, can really test hypotheses about cause-and-effect relationships. Experimental designs are some of the strongest available for educational researchers to use in determining cause and effect.

ESSENTIAL CHARACTERISTICS OF EXPERIMENTAL RESEARCH

- Experiments differ from other types of research in two basic ways-comparison of treatments *and* the direct manipulation of one or more independent variables by the researcher.

RANDOMIZATION

- Random assignment is an important ingredient in the best kinds of experiments. It means that every individual who is participating in the experiment has an equal chance of being assigned to any of the experimental or control conditions that are being compared.

CONTROL OF EXTRANEOUS VARIABLES

- The researcher in an experimental study has an opportunity to exercise far more control than in most other forms of research.
- Some of the most common ways to control for the possibility of differential subject characteristics (in the various groups being compared) are randomization, holding certain variables constant, building the variable into the design, matching, using subjects as their own controls, and the statistical technique of ANCOVA.

WEAK EXPERIMENTAL DESIGNS

- Three weak designs that are occasionally used in experimental research are the one-shot case study design, the one-group pretest-posttest design, and the static-group design. They are considered weak because they do not have built-in controls for threats to internal validity.
- In a one-shot case study, a single group is exposed to a treatment or event, and its effects assessed.
- In the one-group pretest-posttest design, a single group is measured or observed both before and after exposure to a treatment.
- In the static-group comparison design, two intact groups receive different treatments.

TRUE EXPERIMENTAL DESIGNS

- The essential ingredient of a true experiment is random assignment of subjects to treatment groups.

- The randomized posttest-only control group design involves two groups formed by random assignment and receiving different treatments.
- The randomized pretest-posttest control group design differs from the randomized posttest-only control group only in the use of a pretest.
- The randomized Solomon four-group design involves random assignment of subjects to four groups, with two being pretested and two not.

MATCHING

- To increase the likelihood that groups of subjects will be equivalent, pairs of subjects may be matched on certain variables. The members of the matched groups are then assigned to the experimental and control groups.
- Matching may be either mechanical or statistical.
- Mechanical matching is a process of pairing two persons whose scores on a particular variable are similar.
- Two difficulties with mechanical matching are that it is very difficult to match on more than two or three variables, and that in order to match, some subjects must be eliminated from the study, since no matches can be found..
- Statistical matching does not necessitate a loss of subjects.

QUASI-EXPERIMENTAL DESIGNS

- The matching-only design differs from random assignment with matching only in that random assignment is not used.
- In a counterbalanced design, all groups are exposed to all treatments, but in a different order.
- A time-series design involves repeated measurements or observations over time, both before and after treatment.

FACTORIAL DESIGNS

- Factorial designs extend the number of relationships that may be examined in an experimental study.

Key Terms

For Discussion

1. An occasional criticism of experimental research is that it is very difficult to conduct in schools. Would you agree? Why or why not?

2. Are there any cause-and-effect statements you can make that you believe would be true in most schools? Would you say, for example, that a sympathetic teacher "causes" elementary school students to like school more?

3. Are there any advantages to having more than one independent variable in an experimental design? If so, what are they? What about more than one dependent variable?

4. What designs could be used in each of the following studies? (*Note:* More than one design is possible in each instance.)

    a. A comparison of two different ways of teaching spelling to first-graders.

    b. The effectiveness of weekly tutoring sessions on the reading ability of third-graders.

    c. A comparison of a third-period high school English class taught by the discussion method with a third-period (same high school) English class taught by the lecture method.

    d. The effectiveness of reinforcement in decreasing stuttering in students with this speech defect.

    e. The effects of a year-long weight-training program on a group of high school athletes.

    f. The possible effects of age, gender, and method on student liking for history.

5. What flaw can you find in each of the following studies?

    a. A teacher tries out a new mathematics textbook with her class for a semester. At the end of the semester, she reports that the class's interest in mathematics is markedly higher than she has ever seen it in the past with other classes using another text.

    b. A teacher divides his class into two subgroups, with each subgroup being taught spelling by a different method. Each group listens to the teacher instruct the other group while they wait their turn.

    c. A researcher calls for eighth-grade students to volunteer to tutor third-grade students who are having difficulty in reading. She compares their effectiveness as tutors with a control group of students who are assigned to be tutors (they do not volunteer). The volunteers have a much greater level of improvement in reading among the students they tutor than the students do who were assigned to tutor.

    d. A teacher decides to try out a new textbook in one of her social studies classes. She uses it for four weeks and then compares this class's scores on a unit test with the scores of her previous classes. All classes are studying the same material. During the unit test, however, a fire drill occurs, and the class loses about 10 minutes of the time allotted for the test.

    e. Two groups of third-graders are compared with regard to running ability, subsequent to different training schedules. One group is tested during physical education class in the school gymnasium, while the other is tested after school on the football field.

f. A researcher compares a third-period English class with a fifth-period chemistry class in terms of student interest in the subject taught. The English class is taught by the discussion method, while the chemistry class is taught by the lecture method.

1. C. A. Benware and E. L. Deci (1984). Quality of learning with an active versus passive motivational set. *American Educational Research Journal, 21*(4):755–766.

2. R. T. Johnson, D. W. Johnson, and M. B. Stanne (1986). Comparison of computer-assisted cooperative, competitive, and individualistic learning. *American Educational Research Journal, 23*(3):382–392.

3. J. S. Catterall (1987). An intensive group counseling dropout prevention intervention: Some cautions on isolating at-risk adolescents within high schools. *American Educational Research Journal, 24*(4):521–540.

4. A. G. Gilmore and C. W. McKinney (1986). The effects of student questions and teacher questions on concept acquisition. *Theory and Research in Social Education, 14*(3):225–244.

5. J. D. Hawkins, H. J. Doueck, and D. M. Lishner (1988). Changing teaching practices in mainstream classrooms to improve bonding and behavior of low achievers. *American Educational Research Journal, 25*(1):31–50.

6. J. R. Levin, C. B. McCormick, G. E. Miller, J. K. Berry, and M. Pressley (1982). Mnemonic versus nonmnemonic vocabulary-learning strategies for children. *American Educational Research Journal, 19*(1):121–136.

7. B. W. Tuckman (1994). *Conducting educational research,* 4th ed. New York: Harcourt Brace Jovanovich, p. 152.

Notes

Research Exercise Thirteen: Research Methodology

Using Problem Sheet 13, once again state the question or hypothesis of your study and identify which methodology you plan to use. Then describe, in as much detail as you can, the procedures of your study, including analysis of results—that is, *what* you intend to do, *when, where,* and *how.* Lastly, indicate any unresolved problems you see at this point in your planning.

An electronic version of this Problem Sheet that you can fill in and print, save, or e-mail is available on the Online Learning Center at www.mhhe.com/ fraenkel5e and on your Interactive Student CD-ROM.

A full-sized version of this Problem Sheet that you can fill in or photocopy is in your Student Workbook.

Problem Sheet 13

Research Methodology

You should complete Problem Sheet 13 once you have decided which of the methodologies described in Chapters 13–17 and 20–23 you plan to use. You might wish to consider, however, whether your research question could be investigated by other methodologies.

1. The question or hypothesis of my study is: _____

   _____

   _____

2. The methodology I intend to use is: _____

   _____

   _____

3. A brief summary of *what* I intend to do, *when, where,* and *how* is as follows: _____

   _____

   _____

   _____

   _____

   _____

   _____

   _____

   _____

4. The major problems I foresee at this point include the following: _____

   _____

   _____

   _____

   _____

Single-Subject Research

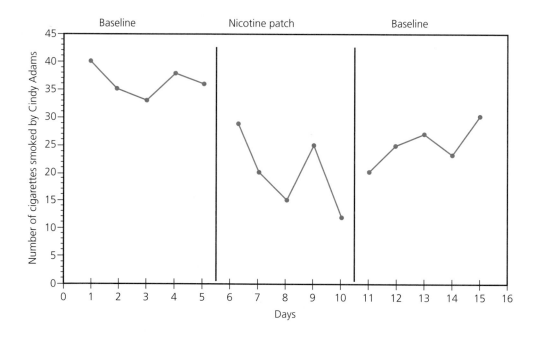

CHAPTER 14

Single-Subject Research

Essential Characteristics of Single-Subject Research

Single-Subject Designs

The Graphing of Single-Subject Designs
The A-B Design
The A-B-A Design
The A-B-A-B Design
The B-A-B Design
The A-B-C-B Design
Multiple-Baseline Designs

Threats to Internal Validity in Single-Subject Research

Control of Threats to Internal Validity in Single-Subject Research
External Validity in Single-Subject Research:
The Importance of Replication
Other Single-Subject Designs

Objectives

Studying this chapter should enable you to:

- Describe *briefly the purpose of single-subject research.*
- Describe *the essential characteristics of such research.*
- Describe *two ways in which single-subject research differs from other forms of experimental research.*
- Explain *what a baseline is and why it is used.*
- Explain *what an A-B design is.*
- Explain *what a reversal (A-B-A) design is.*
- Explain *what an A-B-A-B design is.*
- Explain *what a B-A-B design is.*
- Explain *what an A-B-C-B design is.*
- Explain *what a multiple-baseline design is.*
- Identify *various threats to internal validity associated with single-subject studies.*
- Explain *three ways in which threats to internal validity in single-subject studies can be controlled.*
- Discuss *the external validity of single-subject research.*
- Critique *research articles that involve single-subject designs.*

Interactive and Applied Learning

After, or while, reading this chapter:

🔘 Go to your Interactive Student CD-ROM to:
- Learn More About Essential Characteristics of Single-Subject Research

🔘 📖 Go to your Interactive Student CD-ROM or Student Workbook to do the following activities:
- Activity 14.1: Single-Subject Research Questions
- Activity 14.2: Characteristics of Single-Subject Research
- Activity 14.3: Analyze Some Single-Subject Data

asmin Wong, a third-grade teacher in a small elementary school in San Diego, California, finds her teaching continually interrupted by Alex, a student who can't seem to keep quiet. Distressed, she asks herself what she might do to control this student and wonders whether some kind of "time-out" activity might work. With this in mind, she asks some of the other teachers in the school whether brief periods of removing Alex from the class might decrease the frequency of his disruptive behavior.

This question is exactly the sort that can be answered best by means of a single-subject A-B-A-B design. What an A-B-A-B design involves, and how it works, is but one of the things (as well as some other ideas about single-subject research) that you will learn about in this chapter.

Essential Characteristics of Single-Subject Research

All of the designs described in the previous chapter on experimental research involve the study of groups. At times, however, group designs are not appropriate for a researcher to use, particularly when the usual instruments are not pertinent and observation must be the method of data collection. Sometimes there are just not enough subjects available to make the use of a group design practical. In other cases, intensive data collection on a very few individuals makes more sense. Researchers who wish to study children who suffer from multiple handicaps (who are both deaf and blind, for example) may have only a small number of children available to them, say six or less. It would make little sense to form two groups of three each in such an instance. Further, each child would probably need to be observed in great detail.

Single-subject designs are adaptations of the basic time-series design shown in Figure 13.9 in the previous chapter. The difference is that data are collected and analyzed for only one subject at a time. They are most commonly used to study the changes in behavior an individual exhibits after exposure to an intervention or treatment of some sort. Developed primarily in special education, where much of the usual instrumentation is inappropriate, single-subject designs have been used by researchers to demonstrate that children with Down syndrome, for example, are capable of far more complex learning than was previously believed.

Single-Subject Designs

THE GRAPHING OF SINGLE-SUBJECT DESIGNS

Single-subject researchers primarily use line graphs to present their data and to illustrate the effects of a par-ticular intervention or treatment. Figure 14.1 presents an illustration of such a graph. The dependent (outcome) variable is displayed on the vertical axis (the ordinate or y-axis). For example, if we were teaching a self-help skill to a severely limited child, the number of correct responses would be shown on the vertical axis.

The horizontal axis (the abscissa or x-axis) is used to indicate a sequence of time, such as sessions, days, weeks, trials, or months. A rough rule of thumb is to have the horizontal axis anywhere from one and one-half to two times as long as the vertical axis.

A description of the *conditions* involved in the study is listed just above the graph. The first condition is usually the **baseline,** followed by the intervention (the independent variable). *Condition lines,* indicating when the condition has changed, separate the conditions. The round dots are *data points.* They represent the data collected at various times during the study. They are placed on the graph by finding the intersection of the time when the data point was collected (e.g., session 6) and the results at that time (six correct responses). These data points are then connected to illustrate trends in the data. Lastly, there is a figure caption near the bottom of the graph, which is a summary of the figure, usually listing both the independent and the dependent variables.

THE A-B DESIGN

The basic approach of researchers using an A-B design is to collect data on the same subject, operating as his or her own control, under two conditions or phases. The first condition is the pretreatment condition, typically called (as mentioned before) the *baseline period,* and identified as **A.** During the baseline period, the subject is assessed for several sessions until it appears that his or her typical behavior has been reliably determined. The baseline is extremely important in single-subject research since it is the best estimate of what would have occurred if the intervention were not applied. Enough

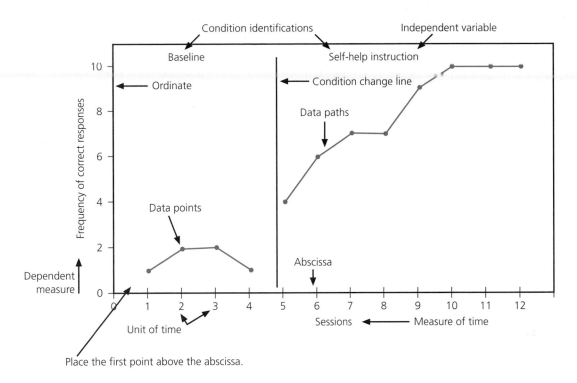

Percentage of correct responses across baseline and self-help conditions

Figure 14.1 *Single-Subject Graph*

data points must be obtained to determine a clear picture of the existing condition; certainly one should collect a minimum of three data points before implementing the intervention. The baseline, in effect, provides a comparison to the intervention condition.

Once the baseline condition has been established, a treatment or intervention condition, identified as **B,** is introduced and maintained for a period of time. Typically, though not necessarily, a highly specific behavior is taught during the intervention condition, with the instructor serving as the data collector—usually by recording the number of correct responses (e.g., answers to questions) or behaviors (e.g., looking at the teacher) given by the subject during a fixed number of trials.

As an example of an A-B design, consider a researcher interested in the effects of verbal praise on a particularly nonresponsive junior high school student during instruction in mathematics. The researcher could observe the student's behavior for, say, five days while instruction in math is occurring, then praise him verbally for five sessions and observe his behavior immediately after the praise. Figure 14.2 illustrates this A-B design.

As you can see, five measures were taken before the intervention and five more during the intervention. Looking at the data in Figure 14.2, the intervention appears to have been effective. The amount of responsiveness after the intervention (the praise) increased markedly. However, there is a major problem with the A-B design. Similar to the one-shot case study that it resembles, the researcher does not know whether any behavior change occurred *because* of the treatment. It is possible that some other variable (other than praise) actually caused the change, or even that the change would have occurred naturally, without any treatment at all. Thus the A-B design fails to control for various threats to internal validity; it does not determine the effect of the independent variable (praise) on the dependent variable (responsiveness), while ruling out the possible effect(s) of extraneous variables. As a result, researchers usually try to improve on the A-B design by using an A-B-A design.*

*Another option is to replicate this design with additional individuals with treatment beginning at different times, thereby reducing the likelihood that the passage of time or other conditions are responsible for changes.

Figure 14.2 *An A–B Design*

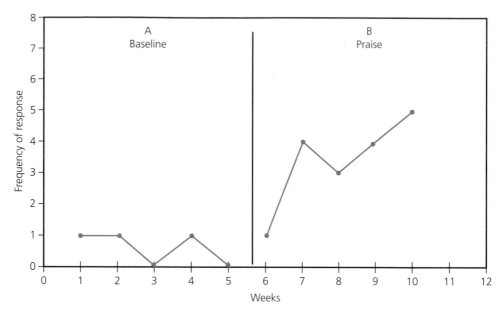

Frequency of response across baseline and praise conditions

THE A-B-A DESIGN

When using an **A-B-A design** (sometimes called *reversal* designs), researchers simply add another baseline period. This improves the design considerably. If the behavior is different during the treatment period than during either baseline period, we have stronger evidence for the effectiveness of the intervention. In our previous example, the researcher could, after having praised the student for say, six days, eliminate the praise and observe the student's behavior for another five days when no praise is forthcoming. Threats to internal validity are now reduced, because it is unlikely that something occurred at the precise time the intervention was presented to cause an increase in the behavior, and at the precise time the intervention was removed to cause a decrease in the behavior. Figure 14.3 illustrates the A-B-A design.

Although the decrease in threats to internal validity is a definite advantage of the A-B-A design, there is a significant ethical disadvantage to this design. It involves the ethics of leaving the subjects in the "A" condition. It is unlikely that many researchers would feel comfortable about ending this type of study without some degree of final improvement being shown. As a result, an extension of this design—the A-B-A-B design, is frequently used.

THE A-B-A-B DESIGN

In the **A-B-A-B design,** two baseline periods are combined with two treatment periods. This further strengthens any conclusion about the effectiveness of the treatment, because it permits the effectiveness of the treatment to be demonstrated *twice*. In fact, the second treatment can be extended indefinitely if a researcher so desires. If the behavior of the subject is essentially the same during both treatment phases, and better (or worse) than both baseline periods, the likelihood of another variable being the cause of the change is decreased markedly. Another advantage here is evident— the ethical problem of leaving the subject(s) without an intervention is avoided.

To implement an A-B-A-B design in the previous example, the researcher would reinstate the experiment treatment, B (praise), for five days after the second baseline period and observe the subject's behavior. As with the A-B-A design, the researcher hopes to demonstrate that the dependent variable (responsiveness) changes whenever the independent variable (praise) is applied. If the subject's behavior changes from the first baseline to the first treatment period, from the first treatment to the second baseline, and so on, the researcher has evidence that praise is indeed the cause of the change. Figure 14.4 illustrates the results of a hypothetical study involving an A-B-A-B design.

Notice that a clear baseline is established, followed by an increase in response during treatment, followed by a decrease in response when treatment is stopped, followed by an increase in response once the treatment is instituted again. This pattern provides fairly strong

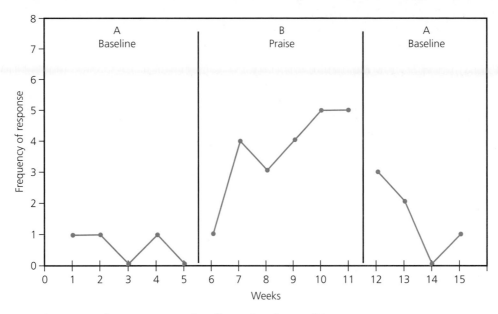

Frequency of response across baseline and praise conditions

Figure 14.3 *An A–B–A Design*

evidence that it is the treatment, rather than history, maturation, or something else that is responsible for the improvement.

Although evidence such as that shown in Figure 14.4 would be considered a strong argument for causation, you should be aware that the A-B-A and A-B-A-B designs suffer from limitations: the possibility of data-collector bias (the individual who is giving the treat-ment also usually collects the data) and the possibility of an instrumentation effect (the need for an extensive number of data-collection periods) can lead to changes in the conditions of data collection.

THE B-A-B DESIGN

Occasionally there are times when an individual's be-havior is so severe or disturbing (e.g., excessive fighting

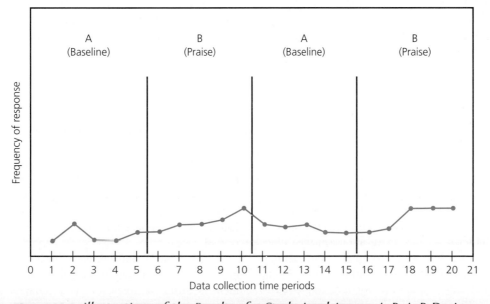

Figure 14.4 *Illustrations of the Results of a Study Involving an A–B–A–B Design*

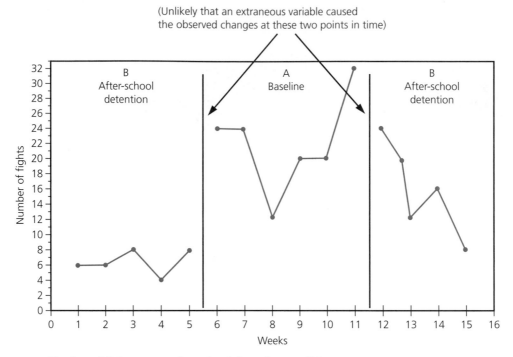

Number of fights across after-school detention conditions

Figure 14.5 *A B–A–B Design*

both in and outside of class) that a researcher cannot wait for a baseline to be established. In such cases, a B-A-B design may be used. This design involves a treatment followed by a baseline followed by a return to the treatment. Other times when this design is applicable might be when there is a lack of behavior—for example, if the subjects have never exhibited the desired (e.g., paying attention) behaviors in the past—or when an intervention is already ongoing (e.g., an after-school detention program) and a researcher wishes to establish its effect. Figure 14.5 illustrates the B-A-B design.

THE A-B-C-B DESIGN

The A-B-C-B design is a further modification of the A-B-A design. The "C" in this design refers to a variation of the intervention in the "B" condition. In the first two conditions, the baseline and intervention data are collected. During the "C" condition, the intervention is *changed* to control for any extra attention the subject may have received during the "B" phase. For example, in our earlier example, one might argue that it was not the praise that was responsible for any improved re-

sponsiveness (should that occur) on the part of the subject, but rather the extra attention that the subject received.

The "C" condition, therefore, might be praise given no matter how the subject responds (i.e., whether he offers responses or not). Thus, as shown in Figure 14.6, a conclusion could be reached that *selective* praise is critical for improved responsiveness, as compared to the mere increase in overall praise.

MULTIPLE-BASELINE DESIGNS

An alternative to the A-B-A-B design is the multiple-baseline design. **Multiple-baseline designs** are typically used when it is not possible or ethical to withdraw a treatment and return to the baseline condition. When a multiple-baseline design is used, researchers do more than collect data on one behavior for one subject in one setting; they collect on several behaviors for one subject, obtaining a baseline for each during the *same* period of time.

When using a multiple-baseline design across behaviors, the researcher systematically applies the treatment at different times for each behavior until all of

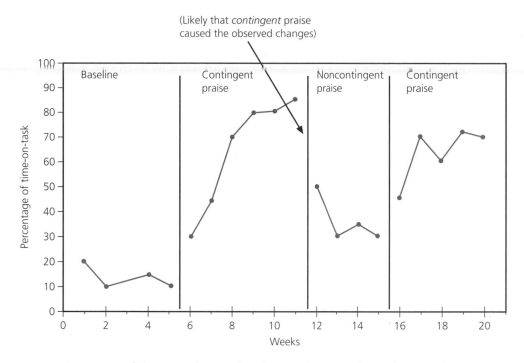

Percentage of time-on-task across baseline, contingent praise, and noncontingent praise conditions

Figure 14.6 *An A–B–C–B Design*

them are undergoing the treatment. If behavior changes in each case only after the treatment has been applied, the treatment is judged to be the cause of the change. It is important that the behaviors being treated, however, remain independent of each other. If behavior 2, for example, is affected by the introduction of the treatment to behavior 1, then the effectiveness of the treatment cannot be determined. A diagram of a multiple-baseline design involving three behaviors is shown in Figure 14.7

In this design, treatment is applied first to change behavior 1, then behavior 2, and then behavior 3 until all three behaviors are undergoing the treatment. For example, a researcher might investigate the effects of "time-out" (removing a student from class activities for a period of time) on decreasing various undesirable behaviors of a particular student. Suppose the behaviors

are (a) talking out of turn; (b) tearing up worksheets; and (c) making derogatory remarks toward another student. The researcher would begin by applying the treatment ("time-out") first to behavior 1, then to behavior 2, and then to behavior 3. At that point, the treatment will have been applied to all three behaviors. The more behaviors that are eliminated or reduced, the more effective the treatment can be judged to be. How many times the researcher must apply the treatment is a matter of judgment and depends on the subjects involved, the setting, and the behaviors the researcher wishes to decrease or eliminate (or encourage). Multiple-baseline designs also are sometimes used to collect data on *several* subjects with regard to a *single* behavior, or to measure a subject's behavior in two or more *different* settings.

Behavior 1	*O O O O X O X O X O X O X O X O X O X O X O X O*
Behavior 2	*O O O O O O O X O X O X O X O X O X O X O*
Behavior 3	*O O O O O O O O O O X O X O X O X O X O*

Figure 14.7 *A Multiple-Baseline Design*

Figure 14.8
Illustration of Multiple-Baseline Design

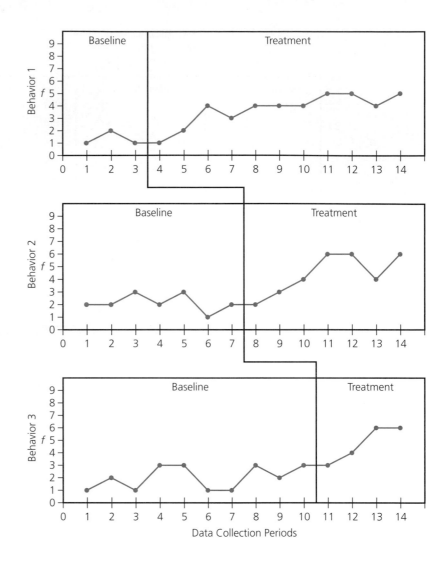

An illustration of the effects of a treatment in a hypothetical study using a multiple-baseline design is shown in Figure 14.8. Notice that each of the behaviors involved changed only when the treatment was introduced. Figure 14.9 illustrates the design applied to different settings.

In practice, the results of studies like those described here rarely fit the ideal model in that the data points often show more fluctuation, making trends less clear-cut. This feature makes data-collector bias even more of a problem, particularly when the behavior in question is more complex than just a simple response such as picking up an object. Data-collector bias in multiple-baseline studies remains a serious concern.

Threats to Internal Validity in Single-Subject Research

As we mentioned earlier, there are unfortunately several threats to the internal validity of single-subject studies. Some of the most important involve the length of the baseline and intervention conditions, the number of variables changed when moving from one condition to another, the degree and speed of any change that occurs, whether or not the behavior returns to baseline levels, the independence of behaviors, and the number of baselines. Let us discuss each of these in more detail.

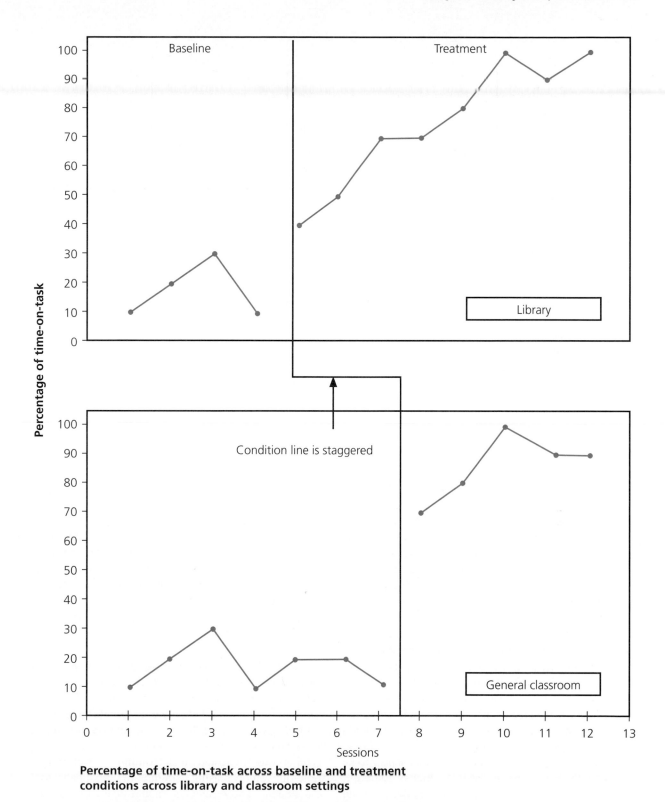

Percentage of time-on-task across baseline and treatment
conditions across library and classroom settings

Figure 14.9 *A Multiple-Baseline Design Applied to Different Settings*

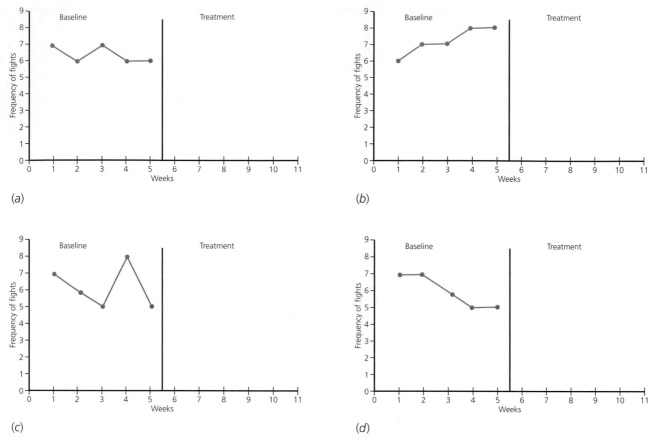

Figure 14.10 *Variations in Baseline Stability*

Condition Length. Condition length refers to how long the baseline and intervention conditions are in effect. It is essentially the number of data points gathered during a condition. A researcher must have enough data points (a minimum of three) to establish a clear pattern or trend. Take a look at Figure 14.10(*a*). The data shown in the baseline condition appear to be stable, and hence it would be appropriate for the researcher to introduce the intervention. In Figure 14.10(*b*), the data points appear to be moving in a direction opposite to that which is desired, and hence here too it would be appropriate for the researcher to introduce the intervention. In Figure 14.10(*c*), the data show a lot of variability; no trend has been established, and hence the researcher should stay in the baseline condition for a longer period of time. Note that the data in Figure 14.10(*d*) appear to be moving in the *same* direction as that which is desired. If the baseline condition were to be ended at this time and the intervention introduced, the effects of the intervention might be difficult to determine.

In the real world, of course, it is often difficult to obtain enough data points to see a clear trend. Often there are practical problems such as a need to begin the study due to a shortage of time or an ethical concern such as a subject displaying very dangerous behavior. Nevertheless, the stability of data points must always be taken into account by those who conduct (and those who read) single-subject studies.

Number of Variables Changed When Moving from One Condition to Another. This is one of the most important considerations in single-subject research. It is important that only one variable be changed at a time when moving from one condition to another. For instance, consider our previous example where a researcher was interested in determining the effects of "time-out" on decreasing certain undesirable behaviors of a student. The researcher should take care that the only treatment he or she introduces during the intervention condition is the time-out experience. This is chang-

Important Findings in Single-Subject Research

For a long time, it was thought that there were many things, including independent living skills, that severely intellectually limited or emotionally disturbed children and adults could not be expected to learn. A series of studies in the 1960s, however, proved that they could learn a great deal through procedures known originally as operant conditioning;

and more recently as behavior management or applied behavioral analysis.* Recent studies have refined these methods.†

*G. J. Bensberg, C. N. Colwell, and R. H. Cassel. (1965). Teaching the profoundly retarded self-help activities by behavior shaping techniques. *American Journal of Mental Deficiency, 69:*674–679; O. I. Lovaas, L. Freitag, K. Nelson, and C. Whalen. (1967). The establishment of imitation and its use for the development of complex behavior in schizophrenic children. *Behavior Research and Therapy, 5:*171–181.

†M. Wolery, D. B. Bailey, and G. Sugai. (1998). *Effective teaching principles and practices of applied behavior analysis with exceptional students.* Needham, MA: Allyn and Bacon.

ing only one variable. If the researcher were to introduce not only the time-out experience, *but also* another experience (e.g., counseling the student during the time-out) as well, he or she would be changing *two* variables. In effect, the treatment is confounded. The intervention now consists of two variables mixed together. Unfortunately, the only thing now that the researcher can conclude is whether the combined treatment was or was not effective. He or she would not know if it was the counseling or the time-out that was the cause. Thus, when analyzing a single-subject design, it is always important to determine whether only one variable at a time has been changed. If this is not the case, any conclusions that are drawn may be erroneous.

Degree and Speed of Change. Researchers must also take into account the magnitude with which the data change at the time the intervention condition is implemented (i.e., when the independent variable is introduced or removed). Look, for example, at Figure 14.11(*a*). The baseline condition reveals that the data have stability. When the intervention is introduced, however, the subject's behavior does not change for a period of three sessions. This does not indicate a very strong experimental effect. If the independent variable (whatever it may be) were effective, one would assume that the subject's behavior would change more quickly. It is possible, of course, that the independent variable was effective, but not of sufficient strength to bring about an immediate change (or the behavior may have been resistant to change). Nevertheless, researchers must consider all such possibilities if there is a slow or delayed change once the intervention is introduced. Figure 14.11(*b*) indicates there was a fairly immediate change, but it was of small magnitude. Only in Figure 14.11(*c*) do we see a dramatic and rapid change once

the intervention is introduced. A researcher would be more likely to conclude that the independent variable was effective in this case than he or she would in either of the other two.

Return to Baseline Level. Look at Figure 14.12(*a*). Notice that in returning to the baseline condition, there was not a rapid change in behavior. This suggests that something else may have occurred when the intervention condition was introduced. We would expect that the behavior of the subject would return to baseline levels fairly quickly if the intervention was the causal factor in changing the subject's behavior. The fact that the subject's behavior did not return to the original baseline level suggests that one or more extraneous variables may have produced the effects observed during the intervention condition. On the other hand, look at Figure 14.12(*b*). Here we see that the change from intervention to baseline levels was abrupt and rapid. This suggests that the independent variable was likely the cause of the changes in the dependent variable. Note, however, that, because the treatment was intended to have a lasting impact, a slower return to baseline may be desirable, though it does complicate interpretation.

Independence of Behaviors. This concern is most applicable to multiple-baseline studies. Imagine, for a moment, that a researcher is investigating various methods of teaching history. The researcher defines two separate behaviors that she is going to measure. These include (1) ability to locate the central idea, and (2) ability to summarize the important points in various historical documents. The researcher obtains baseline data for each of these skills, and then implements an intervention (providing worksheets that give clues about how to locate important ideas in historical documents). The

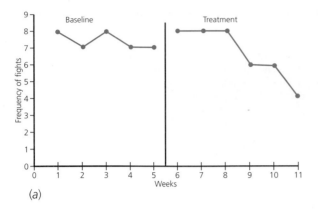

(a)

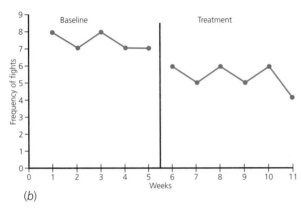

(b)

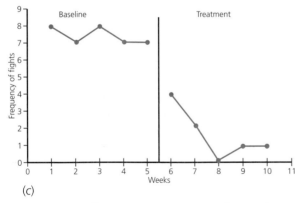

(c)

Figure 14.11 *Differences in Degree and Speed of Change*

subject's ability to locate the central idea in a document improves quickly and considerably. However, the subject's ability to summarize important points also improves. It is quite evident that these two skills are not independent. They appear to be related in some way, conceivably dependent on the same underlying cognitive ability, and hence they improved together.

Number of Baselines. In order to have a multiple-baseline design, a researcher must have at least two baselines. Although the baselines begin at the same time, the interventions are introduced at different times. As we mentioned earlier, the chances that an extraneous variable caused the results when using a multiple-baseline design across two behaviors are lessened since it is less likely that the same extraneous event caused the observed changes for both behaviors at different times. The chances that an extraneous event caused the changes in a multiple-baseline design across three behaviors, therefore, is even less.

Thus, the greater the number of baselines, the greater the probability that the intervention is the cause of any changes in behavior, since the chances that an extraneous variable caused the changes is correspondingly decreased the more behaviors we have.

There is a problem with a large number of baselines, however. The more baselines there are, the longer the later behaviors must remain in baseline—that is, are kept from receiving the intervention. For example, if we follow the recommendation mentioned earlier of establishing stable data points before we introduce the intervention condition, this would mean that the first behavior is in baseline for a minimum of three sessions, the second for six sessions, and the third for nine. Should we use four baselines, the fourth behavior would be in baseline condition for 12 sessions! This is a very long time for a behavior to be kept from receiving the intervention. As a general rule, however, it is important to remember that the fewer the number of baselines, the less likely it is we can conclude that it is the intervention rather than some other variable that causes any changes in behavior that occur.

CONTROL OF THREATS TO INTERNAL VALIDITY IN SINGLE-SUBJECT RESEARCH

Single-subject designs are most effective in controlling for subject characteristics, mortality, testing, and history threats; they are less effective with location, data-collector characteristics, maturation, and regression threats; and they are definitely weak when it comes to instrument decay, data-collector bias, attitudinal, and implementation threats.

A location threat is most often only a minor threat in multiple-baseline studies, because the location where the treatment is administered is usually constant

Examples of Studies Conducted Using Single-Subject Designs

- Determining the collateral effects of peer tutor-training on a student with severe disabilities (an A-B design).[*]
- Effects of training in rapid decoding on the reading comprehension of adult learners (an A-B-A design).[†]

- Self-recording: Effects on reducing off-task behavior with a high school student with an attention-deficit hyperactivity disorder (an A-B-A-B design).[‡]
- Assessing the acquisition of first-aid treatments by elementary-aged children (a multiple-baseline across subjects design).[§]
- The effects of a self-management procedure on the classroom and academic behavior of students with mild handicaps (A multiple-baseline across settings design).[‖]

[*]R. C. Martella, N. E. Marchand-Martella, K. R. Young, and C. A. McFarland. (1995). *Behavior Modification, 19*:170–191.
[†]A. Tan, D. W. Moore, R. S. Dixon, and T. Nichelson (1994). *Journal of Behavioral Education, 4*:177–189.

[‡]K. G. Stewart and T. F. McLaughlin. (1992). *Child and Family Behavior Therapy 14*(3), pp. 53–59.
[§]N. E. Marchand-Martella, R. C. Martella, M. Agran, and K. R. Young. (1991). *Child and Family Behavior Therapy 13* (4), pp. 29–43.
[‖]D. J. Smith, J. R. Nelson, K. R. Young, and R. P. West. (1992). *School Psychology Review, 21*:59–72.

throughout the study. The same is true for data-collector characteristics, although such characteristics can be a problem if the data collector is changed over the course of the study.

Single-subject designs unfortunately do suffer from a strong likelihood of instrument decay and data-collector bias, since data must be collected (usually by means of observations) over many trials, and the data collector can hardly be kept in the dark as to the intent of the study.

Neither implementation nor attitudinal effect threats are well controlled-for in single-subject research. Either implementers or data collectors can, unintentionally, distort the results of a study. Data-collector bias is a particular problem when the same person is both implementer (e.g., acting as the teacher) and data collector. A second observer, recording independently, reduces this threat but increases the amount of staff needed to complete the study. A testing threat is usually not a threat, since presumably the subject cannot affect observational data.

EXTERNAL VALIDITY AND SINGLE-SUBJECT RESEARCH: THE IMPORTANCE OF REPLICATION

Single-subject studies are weak when it comes to **external validity**—i.e., generalizability. One would hardly advocate use of a treatment shown to be effective with only one subject! As a result, studies involving single-subject designs that show a particular treatment to be effective in changing behaviors must rely on replications—across individuals rather than groups—if such results are to be found worthy of generalization.

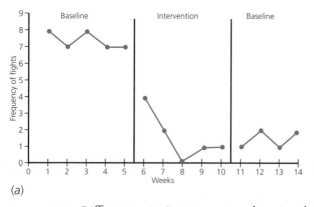

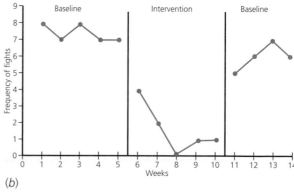

Figure 14.12 *Differences in Return to Baseline Conditions*

OTHER SINGLE-SUBJECT DESIGNS

There are a variety of other, less used designs that fall within the single-subject category. One is the **multi-treatment design,** which introduces a different treatment into an A-B-A-B design (i.e., A-B-A-C-A). The **alternating treatments design** alternates two or more different treatments after an initial baseline period (e.g., A-B-C-B-C). A variation of this is illustrated in the study analysis in this chapter, which eliminates the baseline, becoming a B-C-B, B-C-B-C, or B-C-B-C-B design. The **multi-probe design** differs from a multiple-baseline design only in that fewer data points are used, in an attempt to reduce the data-collection burden and avoid threats to internal validity. Finally, features of all these designs can be combined.*

*For a more detailed discussion of various types of single-subject designs, see D. H. Barlow and M. Hersen (1984). *Single-case experimental designs: Strategies for studying behavior change,* 2nd ed. New York: Pergamon Press.

An Example of Single-Subject Research

In the remainder of this chapter, we present a published example of single-subject research followed by a critique of its strengths and weaknesses. As we did in our critique of the group comparison experimental research study in Chapter Thirteen, we use the concepts introduced in earlier parts of the book in our analysis.

From: *Journal of Applied Behavior Analysis, 23*(4):515–524, 1990.

Effects of Choice Making on the Serious Problem Behaviors of Students with Severe Handicaps

Kathleen Dyer
The May Institute

Glen Dunlap
Florida Mental Health Institute
University of South Florida

Vincent Winterling
University of Kentucky

Abstract

This study assessed the impact of choice making on the serious problem behaviors of three students with severe autism and/or mental retardation. In the context of within-subject reversal designs, the results showed consistently reduced levels of problem behaviors (e.g., aggression) when the students were given opportunities to make choices among instructional tasks and reinforcers. Additional data showed no systematic differences in the rate of correct responding between the two conditions. The results are discussed in relation to the continuing search for effective, nonintrusive solutions to the occurrence of serious problem behavior.

Descriptors: severely handicapped, choice behavior, problem behavior, autistic children

A growing emphasis of research and practice has been on the development of effective, non-intrusive techniques for managing the serious problem behaviors of persons with developmental disabilities (Horner et al., in press). Numerous authors have argued in favor of restricting the use of invasive procedures and promoting the development of positive, educative approaches to behavior management (e.g., Evans and Meyer, 1985; Lovaas and Favell, 1987). It has been recognized by many that continued progress in this area will rely on applied research designed to delineate and document interventions that are both effective and respectful of a person's dignity (Bannerman, Sheldon, Sherman, and Harchick, 1990; Dunlap, 1985; Horner et al., in press).

One rapidly expanding research emphasis has been on the effects of learners' preferences and choice-making opportunities (Guess, Benson, and Siegel-Causey, 1985; Houghton, Bronicki and Guess, 1987; Kishi, Teeluck-singh, Zollers, Park-Lee, and Meyer, 1988; Parsons and Reid, 1990;

The importance of these behaviors with this population could be emphasized

This investigation was supported by Cooperative Agreement G0087CO234 from the National Institute on Disability and Rehabilitation Research. However, the opinions expressed herein do not necessarily reflect the opinions or policies of the supporting agency, and no official endorsement should be inferred.

The authors are grateful to Jeff Amero and Michele Taylor for serving as teachers, and to Cynthia Dollman, Mark Ellison, Beth Brookfield, Jennifer Karr, Jenny Turner, Paul Reedy, Kit Hoffman, Jeffrey K. Withstandly, and Lynn Foster Johnson for assistance in data collection and manuscript and figure preparation. Appreciation is extended to Steven C. Luce and Edward K. Morris for their helpful comments.

Correspondence and requests for reprints should be sent to Kathleen Dyer, The May Institute, Box 703, 100 Sea View Street, Chatham, Massachusetts 02633, or to Glen Dunlap, Department of Child & Family Studies, Florida Mental Health Institute, University of South Florida, Tampa, Florida 33612-3899.

Shevin and Klein, 1984). The success of procedures using choice and preference for individuals with severe handicaps has been documented in studies showing reductions in social avoidance behavior (Koegel, Dyer, & Bell, 1987), increases in spontaneous communication (Dyer, 1987; Peck, 1985), and improvements in task performance (Mithaug & Mar, 1980; Parsons, Reid, Reynolds, and Bumgarner, 1990). There has also been some suggestion that choice making may result in reductions in serious problem behaviors, for example, Dyer (1987) showed that when children with autism were given choices of preferred rewards, decreases were shown in stereo-typed self-stimulatory behaviors that had been reduced previously only with contingent restraint. This study also indicated that there were improvements in other problem behaviors, but these in-dications came from global ratings of on-task behavior rather than from direct observations of specific responses. Therefore, the purpose of the present experiment was to expand the litera-ture on choice making by focusing explicitly on the serious problem behaviors (including aggres-sion and self-injury) of school-age students with severe handicaps. In this case, a choice-making package was implemented in which students were permitted to make selections of rewards as well as the tasks and materials with which they could be engaged.

Purpose is clear

METHOD

Subjects

Definitions would help here

No mention is made of the intended population

Three children (Lori, Mary, and George) participated in this experiment. All of the children ex-hibited high levels of serious disruptive behavior such as aggression, self-injury, and tantrums. The behaviors resulted in placement in a residential treatment center for Lori and Mary. George had also been institutionalized because of his problem behaviors, but at the time of this study he was living at home and receiving assessment and training services from a university-based program. Lori was 5 years old, and Mary and George were 11. Lori was diagnosed as having a developmen-tal delay with autistic features, Mary as having pervasive developmental delay with autistic features, and George as having severe mental retardation. On the Vineland Social Maturity Scale, Lori and Mary were estimated to have social age scores of 1.8 years and 1.0 years, respectively. George re-ceived an adaptive behavior composite of 1.5 years on the Vineland Adaptive Behavior Scales. Lori was nonverbal and used gestures and a small number of signs to communicate. Mary had a vo-cabulary of approximately 10 words that served requesting functions. George was primarily echolalic, but he occasionally used phrases of two to four words to express needs and desires.

Good descriptions

Before the experimental sessions were conducted, each child received pretraining on how to express choices. Lori and Mary were taught to point to a preferred object when presented with two objects and the statement, "Show me which one you want." For George, the pretraining involved teaching him to discriminate such questions as "What do you want to work on?" and to limit his selections to the materials that were available and designated as options. Prior to the experiment, the children were also exposed to sessions in which definitions of the dependent variables were developed and the teachers were trained to use the procedures.

Not clear to us

Setting

All sessions were conducted with one-to-one teacher-student ratios in rooms located on the campuses of the residential center or the university. The rooms contained at least one table, sev-eral chairs, instructional tasks, and videotape equipment. Sessions ranged in length from 10 to 20 min, with no more than four sessions per day and 5 days between sessions.

Selection of Tasks and Reinforcers

During all sessions in each experimental condition, three to four educational tasks were used for each student. The students had demonstrated the ability to perform each of the tasks during

Table 1 *Tasks and Reinforcers for Each Student in Each of the Experimental Conditions*

Student	Tasks	Reinforcers
Lori	Nine-piece puzzle	Soda
	Inserting sticks into a slot	Crackers
	Shape box	M&M candies
Mary	Seven-piece puzzle	Teddy bear
	Inserting pennies into a bank	Cookie
	Inserting buttons into a slot	Juice
George	Large form puzzle	Crackers
	Stacking disks onto a spindle	Soda
	Sorting spoons by color	Juice
	Labeling picture cards[a]	Candy
		Potato sticks

[a]Used only in the final choice condition.

previous educational activities. The tasks involved prevocational and preacademic skills and were selected because they could be handled easily in table work sessions and because they were judged by the students' teachers to be of approximately equivalent preference.

Also used in each session were three to five preferred stimuli that were reported by the children's teachers to be functional reinforcers in other contexts. These preferred stimuli were used as reinforcers for correct performance on instructional tasks. The schedules of reinforcement, determined by the teachers, were *variable-ratio schedules* (e.g., *VR3, VR5*) that were maintained throughout all phases of the experiment. Table 1 lists the tasks and reinforcers available for each child.

Reinforcement is provided as an intermittent pattern

Dependent Variables

The primary dependent variable in this experiment was the percentage of intervals that included instances of serious problem behavior. Problem behaviors were defined individually for each child and included aggression (biting, hitting, kicking, pinching, and scratching) and object misuse (throwing, tearing, banging, and ⟨destroying⟩ objects) for all 3 children, tantrums (screaming, ⟨whining,⟩ and crying) and bolting (moving more than 2 ft from the table) for Lori and George, and self-injury (slapping the face or body, punching self, head banging, elbow and wrist banging, and ⟨forcefully⟩ pressing objects to the face) for Lori. For a self-hit or self-slap to be scored, it had to be *forceful* and be initiated from a distance of more than 6 in. Measures of problem behavior were obtained with a 30-s continuous-interval system of data recording.

Ambiguous terms

To obtain measures of *task performance,* correct responses were counted and then translated into measures of rate for each task. To be scored as a correct response, performance on the educational materials had to conform to the task definitions. Responses that were prompted with physical assistance were not counted as correct. Response definitions for each child's tasks are as follows:

A second dependent variable

Lori. A correct response on the puzzle was scored when Lori placed one puzzle piece into its accompanying space on the template. The stick task involved inserting sticks into a small hole on top of a can. A correct response for this task was scored when one stick was put completely into the slot. A correct response on the shape box was scored when Lori placed a block into its accompanying hole in a container.

Mary. A correct response on the puzzle was scored when Mary placed one puzzle piece into its accompanying space on the template. The button task involved inserting buttons into a small hole on top of a can, with a correct response being scored when one button was put completely through the slot. A correct response on the penny task was scored when Mary put a penny into a slot in a bank.

George. A correct response on the puzzle task was scored when a puzzle piece was inserted into its appropriate place. A correct response on the stacking spindles was counted when a donut-shaped disk was placed successfully on a spindle. Plastic spoons were sorted by color and a correct response was recorded when a spoon was placed in its appropriate receptacle. Responses to the picture cards were scored as correct when George accurately labeled a picture upon request.

Reliability of Dependent Variables

Reliability measures were obtained for each of the dependent variables during the experiment or from videotape obtained throughout each experimental condition. Interobserver agreement on the occurrence of problem behaviors was assessed for 21% of the experimental sessions, and reliability of the task performance data was assessed for 61% of the sessions. An agreement in the recording of problem behavior was counted when two independent observers scored a 30-s interval in an identical manner.

Observer agreement only

Interobserver agreement for problem behavior was calculated by dividing the number of agreements by the sum of agreements plus disagreements and multiplying the obtained quotient by 100. Percentage agreement for problem behavior was 92% (range, 75% to 100%); occurrence reliability was 92% (range, 75% to 100%); nonoccurrence reliability was 91% (range, 75% to 100%). Reliability for rate of correct responding was calculated by dividing the smallest frequency count (obtained by one observer) by the largest frequency count (obtained by the other observer) and multiplying the quotient by 100. Percentage agreement for rate of correct responding was 96% (range, 80% to 100%).

Design and Experimental Conditions

Modified A-B-A-B design

Defines choice vs. no-choice

To demonstrate replicability of treatment effects, reversal designs (Barlow and Hersen, 1984) were used, with the order of conditions alternated across children. For each child, two conditions were presented, a choice condition and a no-choice condition. In the choice condition, the child was provided with opportunities to choose from the available selection of tasks and reinforcers. George indicated his selections verbally, and Mary and Lori indicated their selections by pointing. If a task was completed during a session, the child was asked to choose new materials. The children were also permitted to continue work on the same materials if they chose. Also, if the child voluntarily requested a change in materials, such a change was permitted. Reinforcers were also selected, but the opportunity to select a reinforcer was provided in accordance with the prevailing reinforcement schedule.

Why "in some" and not others?

In the no-choice condition, the same tasks and reinforcers were provided, but always according to an independent schedule and always at the teacher's initiation. To keep the teaching sessions as natural as possible, the specific scheduling of tasks ⟨in some⟩ of the no-choice conditions was left to the discretion of the teacher. In other no-choice conditions, teachers were given explicit instructions to maintain an equal balance of tasks within the sessions. Any expression of choice that occurred during this condition was followed by a brief explanation that the schedule must be followed (e.g., "We need to do this other work now.").

In all experimental conditions, problem behaviors were addressed according to guidelines set forth in each child's regular program. In general, problem behaviors were ignored whenever possible and aggressive responses were blocked in a protective manner. For all three children, physical prompts were used occasionally to continue instruction. For example, if the child engaged in excessive motor activity that prevented attending to task-related instructions, he or she was prompted with verbal and occasional physical guidance to sit quietly. In accordance with her on-going habilitation plan, some of Mary's problem behaviors were managed with additional con-tingencies. Specifically, Mary's aggression was followed by a brief regime of contingent exercise, and her instances of object misuse were followed by 5 s of corrective positive practice. All pro-cedures were used in the same manner across all conditions in the experiment.

Teachers and Observers

All teachers had extensive experience in the use of behavioral techniques with severely hand-icapped children, including a minimum of 1 year supervised practicum in clinic settings. The ob-servers had extensive backgrounds in the recording of operationally defined behavior of children with disabilities. Before any experimental data were recorded, each observer was trained to record each of the dependent variables until interobserver agreement reached at least 80% for three consecutive practice sessions. To control for the potential effects of experimenter bias, the teachers were naive with respect to the experimental hypothesis for 59% of the experimental sessions.

What about observer bias?

Acceptable

Why not 100%?

Results

The data points in Figure A show the percentage of intervals with problem behavior during each session for each experimental condition in the reversal analyses. Each child exhibited lower levels of problem behavior during the choice condition. When choices were first presented to Mary, her problem behavior decreased to a low of 5% during the last session in the condition. A reversal to the no-choice condition resulted in an immediate increase in problem behavior, with an average of 78% across the condition. During the subsequent choice condition, Mary's prob-lem behavior decreased to a low of 0%. The remaining two graphs reveal essentially the same effects for the other 2 children. That is, the choice condition always produced lower levels of problem behavior than did the no-choice condition.

For George and Mary, a subset of their problem behavior (i.e., aggression) was considered to be a most urgent and severe problem (Lori did not display aggression during the experiment). To assess the potential effects of choices on George and Mary's aggressive behaviors, the videotapes were reviewed, and the data on aggressive behavior were separated from the pool of problem behaviors for these two children. The shaded portions of Figure A show the results of this analy-sis. Both Mary and George showed higher levels of aggression in the no-choice condition than in the choice condition. Mary's aggressive behavior decreased to 0 during the last two sessions of both choice conditions, and George did not display any aggressive behavior during any of the sessions in the choice condition.

Data for rate of correct unprompted responding across all experimental conditions are shown in Table 2. These data show no consistent differences in rate of responding across the conditions.

Very low rate of correct response

Data were also collected on the relative proportions of tasks and reinforcers that were pre-sented by the teachers in the no-choice condition and those that were presented (i.e., selected by the children) in the choice condition. These data are shown in Table 3. All of the children se-lected all of the tasks in the choice condition that were presented in the no-choice condition. Al-though there was some evidence of preference (e.g., Mary appeared to favor the pennies and buttons over the puzzle), in general there were few consistent differences across tasks and conditions.

The data for reinforcer presentation and selection are also presented in Table 3. All of the chil-dren selected all of the reinforcers in the choice condition that were presented in the no-choice condition. During the choice condition, however, a somewhat higher proportion of crackers and candy were selected by George and Lori, respectively.

Figure A

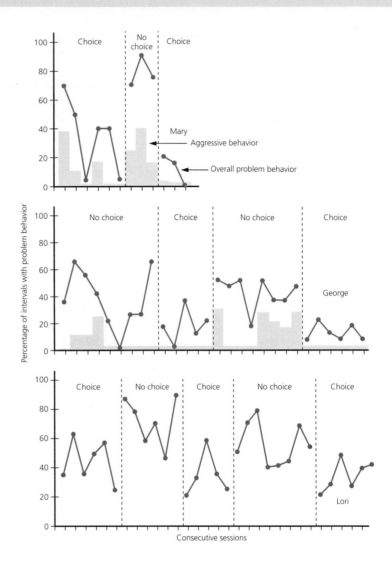

In summary, the principal findings from this investigation are that (a) the choice conditions always produced lower levels of problem behavior than did the no-choice conditions, (b) during the choice conditions, levels of serious aggressive behaviors were lower for Mary and nonexistent for George, and (c) there were no systematic differences in the rate of unprompted correct responding across both conditions. In addition, it is important to note that all of the children selected all of the tasks and reinforcers during the choice condition that were presented by the teachers during the no-choice condition.

DISCUSSION

The results of this experiment add to the literature by providing direct evidence that choice making can produce reductions in specific, objectively measured problem behaviors. Although the magnitude of the differences was not always great, a clear distinction was demonstrated by the reversal design. Additionally, whereas other studies used preference assessments that were conducted before each session (Dyer, 1987; Koegel et al., 1987), this study proved that simply providing choices of preferred reinforcers and maintenance tasks during the session reduced

Table 2 *Rate of Unprompted Correct Responding Across Each Experimental Condition*

Child	Condition	Task			
Mary		**Pennies**	**Button**	**Puzzle**	
	Choice	3.61	7.58	1.00	
	No choice	5.30	6.00	0.20	
	Choice	7.00	6.00		
George		**Sorting spoons**	**Stacking spindles**	**Rubber puzzles**	**Picture cards**
	No choice	6.36	10.49	7.89	
	Choice	8.60	9.00	8.00	
	No choice	6.70	10.47		
	Choice	6.75	70.65		3.81
Lori		**Sticks**	**Blocks**	**Puzzle**	
	Choice	5.49	4.13	1.67	
	No choice	7.06	6.89	7.90	
	Choice	8.07	6.40	8.60	
	No choice	7.00	7.02	6.84	
	Choice	9.19	6.75	9.55	

Are these means?

Table 3 *Proportion of Therapist Presentation and Child Selection of Tasks and Reinforcers*

Child	Condition	Tasks				Reinforcers				
Mary		**Pennies**	**Button**	**Puzzle**		**Cookie**	**Juice**	**Stuffed animals**		
	Choice	.29	.59	.12		.50	.20	.30		
	No choice	.25	.25	.50		.67	.33			
	Choice	.40	.40	.20		.42	.13	.45		
George		**Sorting spoons**	**Stacking spindles**	**Rubber puzzles**	**Picture cards**	**Crackers**	**Candy**	**Soda**	**Juice**	**Potato Sticks**
	No choice	.41	.46	.14		.26	.35	.0	.39	.0
	Choice	.60	.27	.13		.83	.0	.07	.10	.0
	No choice	.50	.45	.04		.36	.29	.0	.35	.0
	Choice	.17	.33		.50	.60	.05	.11	.03	.21
Lori		**Sticks**	**Blocks**	**Puzzles**		**Candy**	**Crackers**	**Sosda**		
	Choice	.41	.24	.35		.65	.16	.19		
	No choice	.38	.27	.35		.33	.33	.34		
	Choice	.32	.27	.41		.78	.12	.10		
	No choice	.31	.34	.35		.35	.28	.37		
	Choice	.36	.21	.43		.69	.21	.10		

problem behavior. Thus, it may not be necessary to conduct daily preference assessments to achieve positive results. Indeed, such assessments can be time consuming and, thus, impractical for many practitioners in applied settings. The present procedure of making choices available on a continuing basis was demonstrated to be effective and may be more efficient than previously reported strategies.

It is important to note that although the provision of choice-making opportunities systematically influenced problem behavior, there were no effects on the rate of responding on the instructional tasks. Similar results were found by Cox (1988), who suggested that systematic differences in performance across choice and no-choice conditions might not occur in tasks that have been previously acquired by the study participants. Thus, it is important to evaluate the effects of this procedure on new skills.

Because the independent variable in this study was a package that permitted choices of both reinforcers and tasks, the effects of each element on problem behavior cannot be separated. However, the data on the children's selection of tasks and reinforcers offer some suggestions. Specifically, because Mary selected the puzzle at a relatively low rate during the choice condition, it is possible that this task was less preferred and that the problem behavior served an escape function during the no-choice condition (Carr and Durand, 1985). In contrast, George and Lori selected a particular reinforcer at a relatively high rate during the choice condition. This suggests that for these children, the reinforcers provided by engaging in the task competed with the reinforcers provided by engaging in problem behavior (Dyer, 1987; Lovaas and Newsom, 1976).

It might be argued that similar results could be achieved by having the teachers deliver optimal proportions of preferred tasks and reinforcers rather than by providing choices. However, a number of studies (e.g., Dyer, 1987; Green et al., 1988; Parsons et al., 1990) have shown that teachers' selections are not as effective in identifying reinforcers as is a procedure of systematic assessment of preferred stimuli. Also, in the present study, Mary's teacher was naive with respect to the experimental hypothesis during all but the last session, and Lori's teacher was naive throughout the entire experiment. Further, during Lori's sessions in the no-choice conditions, the proportions of tasks and reinforcers were nearly equivalent. These controls reduce the potential for the beneficial effects of choice to be influenced by teacher selection of preferred tasks and reinforcers. Additional studies should address this issue by implementing a yoking procedure in which equivalent proportions of tasks and reinforcers are presented in the no-choice and choice conditions.

Another possible explanation for the results is that the opportunity to choose tasks as well as reinforcers may have been a reinforcer in itself. This hypothesis is supported by a study conducted by Brigham and Sherman (1973) in which children of normal development responded at higher rates during a condition in which they were allowed to choose their reinforcers, as opposed to a condition in which the experimenter selected the reinforcers. Because the reinforcers were the same in both conditions, the authors suggested that the opportunity to choose may have been as important as the reinforcers provided. Along these lines, Monty, Geller, Savage, and Perlmuter (1979) found that college students exhibited improved performance in a learning task when they were offered an attractive choice compared to a condition in which they were offered an unattractive choice. These authors suggested that the positive effects of choice-making opportunities may be attributed to the extent to which a subject perceives control in the situation.

To control for possible sequence effects in this investigation, the order of choice and no-choice conditions was counterbalanced across children. However, it is noteworthy that George's aggression increased in the second no-choice condition. This effect was also reported anecdotally by teachers from classrooms in which choice-making opportunities were introduced and then taken away (Dyer, Williams, Santarcangelo, and Luce, 1987). Given these observations, it is important to investigate the potentially deleterious effects of withholding opportunities for control (i.e., choice) after a period in which choice-making opportunities are provided.

Margin notes:

Right!

Unclear rationale

Good

Rationale is unclear to us

Good control of sequence

Good point; alternative explanation of result

The children who participated in this study appeared to have preference for specific tangible reinforcers (George and Lori) or tasks (Mary). It is important to determine whether similar results would be found by students who were motivated primarily by social reinforcement. In addition, there is a need for controlled studies examining the effect of choice making on problem behavior in natural settings. In this regard, pilot data collected by the authors suggest that choice-making strategies can be integrated into a variety of everyday activities (Dunlap, Dunlap, Clarke, and Robbins, 1990; Garling, Carroll, Luce, and Dyer, 1987) and that these options can effectively reduce levels of problem behavior.

Good qualification of results

In summary, this study suggests that choice-making options provide a simple strategy that *can be used* to reduce serious problems exhibited by students with severe handicaps. The fact that these results contribute to a growing body of literature that stresses the importance of increasing personal autonomy for persons with severe handicaps indicates that this is an important area of future investigation.

Rather weak conclusion

References

Bannerman, D. J., Sheldon, J. B., Sherman, J. A., and Harchik, A. E. (1990). Balancing the right to habilitation with the right to personal liberties: The rights of people with developmental disabilities to eat too many doughnuts and take a nap. *Journal of Applied Behavior Analysis, 23:*79–89.

Barlow, D. H., and Hersen, M. (1984). *Single-case experimental designs.* New York: Pergamon Press.

Brigham, T. A., and Sherman, J. A. (1973). Effects of choice and immediacy of reinforcement on single response and switching behavior of children. *Journal of the Experimental Analysis of Behavior, 19:*425–435.

Carr, E. G., and Durand, V. M. (1985). Reducing behavior problems through functional communication training. *Journal of Applied Behavior Analysis, 18:*111–126.

Cox, S. (1988, December). The effects of choice-making on the production rate of three tasks performed by four students with severe handicaps. In E. Siegel-Causey (Chair), *Choice-making as a means of empowerment session: The role of choice-making in the lives of persons with severe handicaps. Implications for teachers, researchers, and personnel preparation programs.* Paper presented at the meeting of the Association for Persons with Severe Handicaps, Washington, DC.

Dunlap, G. (1985). Review of *An educative approach to behavior problems. Journal of the Association for Persons with Severe Handicaps, 10:*237–238.

Dunlap, G., Dunlap, L. K., Clarke, M., and Robbins, F. R. (1990). *Functional assessment and curricular revision in solving the serious behavior challenges of a student with multiple disabilities.* Manuscript submitted for publication.

Dyer, K. (1987). The competition of autistic stereotypes behavior with usual and specially assessed reinforcers. *Research in Developmental Disabilities, 8:*607–626.

Dyer, K. Williams, L., Santarcangelo, S., and Luce, S. C. (1987, November). *Training teachers to use "motivational" techniques: Effects on spontaneous communication and severe disruptive behavior for students with severe handicaps.* Poster presented at the meeting of the Association for the Advancement of Behavior Therapy, Boston.

Evans, I. M., and Meyer, L. H. (1985). *An educative approach to behavior problems.* Baltimore: Paul H. Brookes.

Garling, S. C., Carroll, H., Luce, S. C., and Dyer, K. (1987, October). *Reduction of disruptive mealtime behaviors: A comparison of choice-making options versus more restrictive time-out contingencies.* Poster presented at the annual Berkshire Conference on Behavior Analysis and Behavior Therapy, Amherst, MA.

Green, C. W., Reid, D. H., White, L. K., Halford, R. C., Brittain, D. P., and Gardner, S. M. (1988). Identifying reinforcers for persons with profound handicaps: Staff opinion versus systematic assessment of preferences. *Journal of Applied Behavior Analysis. 21:*31–43.

Guess, D., Benson, H. S., and Siegel-Causey, E. (1985). Concepts and issues related to choice-making and autonomy among persons with severe disabilities. *Journal of the Association for Persons with Severe Handicaps, 10:*79–86.

Horner, R. H., Dunlap, G., Koegel, R. L., Carr, E. G., Sailor, W., Anderson, J., Albin, R. W., and O'Neill, R. E. (in press). Toward a technology of "nonaversive" behavioral support. *Journal of the Association for Persons with Severe Handicaps.*

Houghton, J., Bronicki, G. J., and Guess, D. (1987). Opportunities to express preferences and make choices among students with severe disabilities in classroom settings. *Journal of the Association for Persons with Severe Handicaps, 12:*18–27.

Kishi, G., Teelucksingh, B., Zollers, N., Park-Lee, S., and Meyer, L. H. (1988). Daily decision-making in community residences: A social comparison of adults with and without mental retardation. *American Journal on Mental Retardation, 92:*430–435.

Koegel, R. L., Dyer, D., and Bell, L. K. (1987). The influence of child-preferred activities on autistic children's social behavior. *Journal of Applied Behavior Analysis, 20:*243–252.

Lovaas, O. I., and Favell, J. E. (1987). Protection for clients undergoing aversive/restrictive interventions. *Education and Treatment of Children, 10:*311–325.

Lovaas, O. I., and Newsom, C. D. (1976). Behavior modification with psychotic children. In H. Leitenberg (Ed.), *Handbook of behavior modification and behavior therapy* (pp. 303–360). Englewood Cliffs, NJ: Prentice Hall.

Mitchaug, D. E., and Mar, D. K. (1980). The relation between choosing and working prevocational tasks in two severely retarded young adults. *Journal of Applied Behavior Analysis, 13:*177–182.

Monty, R. A., Geller, E. S., Savage, R. E., and Perlmuter, L. C. (1979). The freedom to choose is not always so choice. *Journal of Experimental Psychology, 37:*170–178.

Parsons, M. B., and Reid, D. H. (1990). Asessing food preferences among persons with profound mental retardation: Providing opportunities to make choices. *Journal of Applied Behavior Analysis, 23:*183–195.

Parsons, M. B., Reid, D. H., Reynolds, J., and Bumgarner, M. (1990). Effects of chosen versus assigned jobs on the work performance of persons with severe handicaps. *Journal of Applied Behavior Analysis, 23:*253–258.

Peck, C. A. (1985). Increasing opportunities for social control by children with autism and severe handicaps: Effects on student behavior and perceived classroom climate. *Journal of the Association for Persons with Severe Handicaps, 10:*183–193.

Shevin, M., and Klein, N. K. (1984). The importance of choice-making skills for students with severe disabilities. *Journal of the Association for Persons with Severe Handicaps, 9:*159–166.

Analysis of the Study

PURPOSE/JUSTIFICATION

The purpose is suggested in the abstract and made clear at the end of the introduction, though a clearer statement might have been made, such as: "The purpose is to investigate the efficacy of student choice of task and reinforcers in reducing problem behaviors of severely handicapped children." The study is justified as an extension of previous research and by arguments favoring this (and other) nonintrusive methods. Ways in which this study differs from prior research are made clear. There appear to be no problems regarding risk, confidentiality, or deception.

PRIOR RESEARCH

Several references support the authors' rationale. While little detail is provided, the outcomes of prior studies are given.

DEFINITIONS

No definitions are provided as such and would be helpful. In further descriptions, the essential terms do become clear (i.e., the particular problem behaviors of each child are described under "Dependent Variables"; "choice-making" is defined under "Design and Experimental Conditions," and "students with severe handicaps" is defined under "Subjects"). While these descriptions clarify the use of these terms in this study, the authors clearly intend them to apply more generally and therefore should have defined them accordingly (e.g., "choice" is defined as "providing the student the opportunity to decide what task to work on from a selection provided by the teacher and to choose among several reinforcers previously identified by the teacher"; "problem behavior" is defined as "any behavior that is a major impediment to teaching"). Note that use of the term "such as" in clarifying "serious disruptive behavior" (under "Subjects") is not satisfactory, because it does not indicate what other behaviors (e.g., "object misuse" under "Dependent Variables") are included by the authors, in addition to aggression, self-injury, and tantrums.

HYPOTHESES

None are stated. However, a directional hypothesis is clearly implied (that all three children will demonstrate less problem behavior when given a choice of tasks and reinforcers than when these are determined by the teacher). It is unclear what the researchers expected with respect to the other dependent variable (task performance).

SAMPLE

Because this type of design requires collecting extensive data on very few subjects, generalization is extremely tenuous, as the authors acknowledge indirectly in their suggestion of further studies with different students.* Because the study was, in effect, replicated across three different subjects differing in age, gender, and diagnostic descriptions as well as in the nature of their disruptive behavior, the authors could have made a somewhat stronger argument for generalization of their findings to other severely handicapped students exhibiting disruptive behavior. Limitations to ecological generalization *are* addressed in the authors' recommendation that studies be done in natural, as opposed to contrived, settings and on the acquisition of *new* skills.

INSTRUMENTATION

The basic instrumentation is observational tallying of specific, identified behaviors in 30-second intervals during each session of 10 to 20 minutes. For disruptive behavior, the score used in analysis was the percentage of intervals in which the behavior occurred during each session. For task performance, the score used was the rate of correct responses (presumably obtained by dividing correct responses by total responses) during each session.

The authors' discussion of reliability addresses only observer agreement for which the data are satisfactory. A sizable proportion of sessions were observed by two observers, and the overall agreement across sessions is above 90 percent, although as low as 75 percent for problem behavior in individual sessions.

As is common in this design, consistency across time and content is not specifically addressed. Considerable inconsistency across sessions is expected and shown in Figure A. In this study, time is mixed in with differences in both task and reinforcer, though these could have been systematically compared to determine consistency across tasks and reinforcers. The important question is

*As is customary in studies using this design, the authors do not indicate the basis for selecting these particular children. This is unfortunate since it raises the possibility that those selected were those most likely to provide data supporting the hypothesis.

whether, despite the fluctuations from session to session, there is sufficient consistency within *conditions* to permit differences *between* conditions to emerge. Visual inspection of Figure A strongly indicates that this is the case. Again, as is customary in such studies, long-term reliability and content reliability are of minimal concern, since the focus of the research is on behaviors demonstrated within a highly specified context.

With regard to instrument validity, the absence of discussion reflects reliance on logical or face validity. It is customarily argued that the extent to which behaviors are precisely described *and* the high degree of observer agreement is sufficient evidence that the variable being tallied is, indeed, the intended variable. While this argument is much more persuasive in studies of this type than in studies assessing more ambiguous variables, such as reading ability or assertiveness, one can question whether observation of "whining," "forceful" pressing of objects to the face, and "destroying" objects is entirely objective. That one observer's "whine" may be another's "complaint" is suggested by the occasional disagreement among observers. In total, however, we would agree that what was observed was, indeed, disruptive behavior.

PROCEDURES/INTERNAL VALIDITY

Procedures are described in considerable detail. It is implied that the experimental teachers were the students' regular teachers, but this should be made clear. This design is an A-B-A-B design, but it does not contain a baseline since the authors' purpose is to compare the effectiveness of two methods rather than to see if either is effective. Thus A and B represent different treatments. This design provides good control over several threats to internal validity (subject characteristics, mortality, testing, history, maturation, regression, location, and data-collector characteristics). Instrument decay and implementer effects are minimal problems in this study. While observers might become less accurate, the alternation of conditions makes it unlikely that one condition was affected more than the other. Each teacher implemented both methods; it is unclear why teachers were unaware of the experimental hypothesis in only 59 percent of experimental sessions. In any case, teachers were obviously aware of the difference in treatments, so implementation is a major threat. However, the finding of similar results for three different teachers is evidence that effectiveness of the "choice" method is not due to teacher characteristics. Data-collector bias remains a possible threat but is reduced by using two observers in many sessions. It was probably impossible to keep observers ignorant of the condition being observed. The authors recognize a possible attitudinal threat in that disruptive behavior during "no-choice" may be due to resentment after having "choice" removed. Unfortunately, only one of the three subjects received the no-choice treatment first. This subject did not show greater overall disruptive behavior in the second no-choice condition, but did show an increase in aggressive behavior, an indication that this explanation of results may be important.

DATA ANALYSIS

Results for "disruptive behavior" are shown in the customary charts. In addition, tables present data on the proportions of usage of various tasks and reinforcers (Table 3) and on rate of correct response (Table 2). The latter are presumably means, although this is unclear.

RESULTS

The study findings are clearly presented and justified in the data. Differences between choice and no-choice conditions consistently favor the choice condition in reducing disruptive behavior for all three children. The data show no consistent differences in task performance across conditions and few consistencies across task and reinforcer preferences. One peculiar result that is not discussed is the generally low rate of successful task performance on tasks identified as within the subjects' response capabilities.

DISCUSSION

The authors recognize limitations on ecological generalizability, as mentioned previously. They also suggest replication with different students and recognize an attitudinal threat to internal validity. They recognize correctly that their study cannot determine the relative importance of the two types of choice (task versus reinforcer). We find the discussion of this point confusing. While the points raised may be good ones, too little data and/or supporting argument is provided. Similarly we do not see why naiveté on the part of teachers is relevant: if teachers had assigned preferred tasks or reinforcers, the data should have been less supportive of the hypothesis and there seems to be no reason for teachers to assign less preferred ones.* In addition, it is unclear why two different methods of scheduling the "no-choice" condition were used.

The major conclusion of the authors is that the treatment studied (choice-making) *can* produce reductions in specific problem behaviors and they indicate how it is more efficient than previous (daily preference) methods. We find this wording perplexing. When this method of research with severely handicapped students began, it was important to demonstrate that such teaching methods *could* influence behavior since many professionals were skeptical—and this provided a rationale for studying only one or two subjects. Today, however, it is expected that such treatments *will* affect behavior; the question remains as to which are more effective. Thus, we would have concluded that the choice method was *more* effective than the more common teacher determination of task and reinforcer. This seems a significant finding provided subsequent studies control the attitudinal and implementation threats to internal validity and obtain similar results.

*The authors also discuss the possibility that the effectiveness of the choice method may be due to the provision of choice itself rather than the nature of what is chosen. Note that this is not a threat to internal validity because this interpretation is consistent with the hypothesis—it simply attempts to explain further the reason for the method's effectiveness.

Go back to the **Interactive and Applied Learning Tools** feature at the beginning of the chapter for a listing of interactive and applied activities. Go to the **Online Learning Center** at www.mhhe.com/fraenkel5e or your **Interactive Student CD-ROM** to take practice quizzes and receive immediate feedback, practice with key terms, review chapter content and main ideas, and find annotated Web links.

Main Points

ESSENTIAL CHARACTERISTICS OF SINGLE-SUBJECT RESEARCH

- Single-subject research involves the extensive collection of data on one subject at a time.
- An advantage of single-subject designs is that they can be applied in settings where group designs are difficult to put into play.

SINGLE-SUBJECT DESIGNS

- Single-subject designs are most commonly used to study the changes in behavior an individual exhibits after exposure to a treatment or intervention of some sort.
- Single-subject researchers primarily use line graphs to present their data and to illustrate the effects of a particular intervention or treatment.
- The basic approach of researchers using an A-B design is to expose the same subject, operating as his or her own control, to two conditions or phases.
- When using an A-B-A design (sometimes called a reversal design), researchers simply add another baseline period to the A-B design.
- In the A-B-A-B design, two baseline periods are combined with two treatment periods.
- The B-A-B design is used when an individual's behavior is so severe or disturbing that a researcher cannot wait for a baseline to be established.
- In the A-B-C-B design, the "C" condition refers to a variation of the intervention in the "B" condition. The intervention is changed during the "C" phase typically to control for any extra attention the subject may have received during the "B" phase.

MULTIPLE-BASELINE DESIGNS

- Multiple-baseline designs are used when it is not possible or ethical to withdraw a treatment and return to baseline.

- When a multiple-baseline design is used, researchers do more than collect data on one behavior for one subject in one setting; they collect on several behaviors for one subject, obtaining a baseline for each during the same period of time.
- Multiple-baseline designs also are sometimes used to collect data on several subjects with regard to a single behavior, or to measure a subject's behavior in two or more different settings.

THREATS TO INTERNAL VALIDITY IN SINGLE SUBJECT RESEARCH

- Several threats to internal validity exist with regard to single-subject designs. These include the length of the baseline and intervention conditions, the number of variables changed when moving from one condition to another, the degree and speed of any change that occurs, whether or not the behavior returns to baseline levels, the independence of behaviors, and the number of baselines.

CONTROLLING THREATS IN SINGLE-SUBJECT STUDIES

- Single-subject designs are most effective in controlling for subject characteristics, mortality, testing, and history threats.
- They are less effective with location, data-collector characteristics, maturation, and regression threats.
- They are especially weak when it comes to instrument decay, data-collector bias, attitude, and implementation threats.

EXTERNAL VALIDITY AND SINGLE-SUBJECT RESEARCH

- Single-subject studies are weak when it comes to generalizability.
- It is particularly important to replicate single-subject studies to determine whether they are worthy of generalization.

OTHER SINGLE-SUBJECT DESIGNS

- Variations on the basic designs discussed in this chapter include the A-B-A-C-A design; the A-B-C-B-C design; and the multi-probe design.

Key Terms

A-B design 308
A-B-A design 310
A-B-A-B design 310
A-B-C-B design 312
Alternating treatments design 320

B-A-B design 311
Baseline 308
External validity of single-subject studies 319
Multiple-baseline design 312

Multi-treatment design 320
Multi-probe design 320
Single-subject design 308

For Discussion

1. Could single-subject designs be implemented in secondary schools? If so, what difficulties do you think one might encounter?
2. Professor Jones has a very difficult student in his introductory statistics class who keeps interrupting the other students in the class when they attempt to answer the professor's questions. How might the professor use one of the designs described in this chapter to reduce the student's interruptions?

3. Can you suggest any instances where a B-A-B design might be required in a typical elementary school? What might they be?

4. Would random sampling be possible in single-subject research? Why or why not?

5. Which do you think is easier to conduct, single-subject or group comparison research? Why?

6. What sorts of questions lend themselves better to single-subject as opposed to other kinds of research?

7. What sorts of behaviors might require only a few data points to establish a baseline? Give some examples.

8. When might it be unethical to stop the intervention to return to baseline in an A-B-A design? Give an example.

9. In terms of difficulty, how would you rate single-subject research on a scale of 1 to 10. What do you think is the most difficult aspect of this kind of research? Why?

Correlational Research

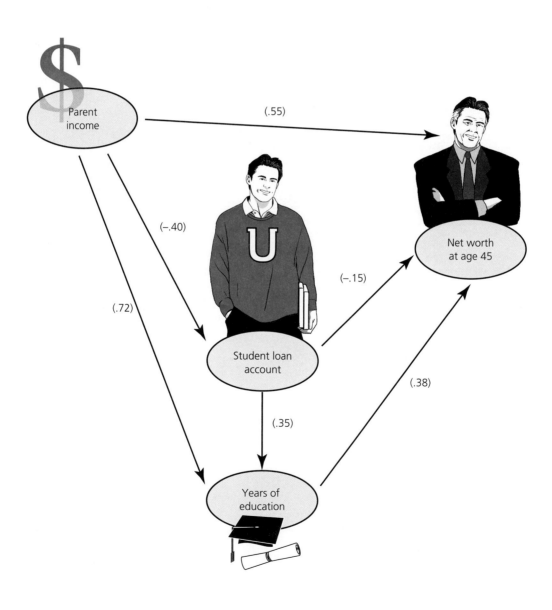

CHAPTER 15

Correlational Research

The Nature of Correlational Research

Purposes of Correlational Research

Explanatory Studies
Prediction Studies
More Complex Correlational Techniques

Basic Steps in Correlational Research

Problem Selection
Sample
Instruments
Design and Procedures
Data Collection
Data Analysis and Interpretation

Evaluating Threats to Internal Validity in Correlational Research

Threats to Internal Validity in Correlational Research

Subject Characteristics
Location
Instrumentation
Testing Mortality

What Do Correlation Coefficients Tell Us?

Objectives

Studying this chapter should enable you to:

- Describe *briefly what is meant by associational research.*
- State *the two major purposes of correlational studies.*
- Distinguish *between predictor and criterion variables.*
- Explain *the role of correlational studies in exploring causation.*
- Explain *how a scatterplot can be used to predict an outcome.*
- Describe *what is meant by a prediction equation.*
- Explain *briefly the main ideas underlying multiple correlation, factor analysis, and path analysis.*
- Identify *and* describe *briefly the steps involved in conducting a correlational study.*
- Interpret *correlation coefficients of different magnitude.*
- Explain *the rationale underlying partial correlation.*
- Describe *some of the threats to internal validity that exist in correlation studies and* explain *how to identify them.*
- Discuss *how to control for these threats.*
- Recognize *a correlation study when you come across one in the educational research literature.*

Interactive and Applied Learning

After, or while, reading this chapter:

🔘 Go to your Interactive Student CD-ROM to:
- Learn More About What Correlation Coefficients Tell Us

🔘 📖 Go to your Interactive Student CD-ROM or Student Workbook to do the following activities:
- Activity 15.1: Correlational Research Questions
- Activity 15.2: What Kind of Correlation?
- Activity 15.3: Think Up an Example
- Activity 15.4: Match the Correlation Coefficient to Its Scatterplot
- Activity 15.5: Calculate a Correlation Coefficient

J ustine Gibbs, a high school biology teacher, was bothered last year by the fact that many of her 10th-grade students had considerable difficulty learning many of the concepts in biology while some learned them rather easily. Before the semester begins this year, therefore, she would like to be able to predict which sorts of individuals are likely to have trouble learning these concepts. If she could make some fairly accurate predictions in this regard, she might be able to suggest some corrective measures (e.g., special tutorial sessions) so that more students would not have difficulty in her biology classes.

The appropriate methodology called for here is *correlational* research. What Gibbs might do is to collect different kinds of data on her students that might be related to the difficulties they do—or do not—have when it comes to biology. Any variables that might be related to success—or failure—in biology (e.g., their anxiety toward the subject, their previous knowledge, how well they understand abstractions, their performance in other science courses, etc.) would be useful. This might give her some ideas about how those students who learn biological concepts easily differ from those who find them difficult. This, in turn, might help her to predict who might have trouble learning in biology next semester. This chapter, therefore, describes for Ms. Gibbs (and you) what correlational research is all about.

The Nature of Correlational Research

Correlational research, like causal-comparative research (which we discuss in Chapter Sixteen), is an example of what is sometimes called *associational research*. In associational research, the relationships among two or more variables are studied without any attempt to influence them. In their simplest form, correlational studies investigate the possibility of relationships between only two variables, although investigations of more than two variables are common. In contrast to experimental research, however, there is no manipulation of variables in correlational research.

Correlational research is also sometimes referred to as a form of descriptive research because it describes an existing relationship between variables. The way it describes this relationship, however, is quite different from the descriptions found in other types of studies. A correlational study describes the degree to which two or more quantitative variables are related, and it does so by using a correlation coefficient.*

When a correlation is found to exist between two variables, it means that scores within a certain range on one variable are associated with scores within a certain range on the other variable. You will recall that a positive correlation means high scores on one variable tend to be associated with high scores on the other variable, while low scores on one are associated with low scores on the other. A negative correlation, on the other hand, means high scores on one variable are associated with low scores on the other variable, and low scores on one are associated with high scores on the other (Table 15.1). As we also have indicated before, relationships like those shown in Table 15.1 can be illustrated graphically through the use of scatterplots. Figure 15.1, for example, illustrates the relationship shown in Table 15.1(A.)

Purposes of Correlational Research

Correlational research is carried out for one of two basic purposes—either to help explain important human behaviors or to predict likely outcomes.

*Although associations among two or more categorical variables can also be studied, such studies are not usually referred to as correlational. They are similar with respect to overall design and threats to internal validity, however, and we discuss them further in Chapter Sixteen.

Table 15.1 *Three Sets of Data Showing Different Directions and Degrees of Correlation*

(A) r = +1.00		(B) r = −1.00		(C) r = 0	
X	Y	X	Y	X	Y
5	5	5	1	2	1
4	4	4	2	5	4
3	3	3	3	3	4
2	2	2	4	1	5
1	1	1	5	4	2

Important Findings in Correlational Research

Ⓞne of the most famous, and controversial, examples of correlational research is that relating frequency of tobacco smoking to incidence of lung cancer. When these studies began to appear, many argued for smoking as a major cause of lung cancer. Opponents did not argue for the reverse—that is, that cancer caused smoking—for the obvious reason that smoking occurred first. They did, however, argue that both smoking and lung cancer were caused by other factors such as genetic predisposition, lifestyle (sedentary occupations might result in more smoking and less exercise), and environment (smoking and lung cancer might be more prevalent in smoggy cities).

Despite a persuasive theory—smoking clearly could irritate lung tissue—the argument for causation was not sufficiently persuasive for the surgeon general to issue warnings until experimental studies showed that exposure to tobacco smoke did result in lung cancer in animals.

EXPLANATORY STUDIES

A major purpose of correlational research is to clarify our understanding of important phenomena by identifying relationships among variables. Particularly in developmental psychology where experimental studies are especially difficult to design, much has been learned by analyzing relationships among several variables. For example, correlations found between variables such as complexity of parent speech and rate of language acquisition have taught researchers much about how language is acquired. Similarly, the discovery that, among variables related to reading skill, auditory memory shows a substantial correlation with reading ability has expanded our understanding of the complex phenomenon of reading. The current belief that smoking causes lung cancer, although based in part on experimental studies of animals, rests heavily on correlational evidence of the relationship between amount of smoking and the incidence of lung cancer (see the More About Research insert above).

Researchers who conduct explanatory studies often investigate a number of variables they believe are related to a more complex variable, such as motivation or learning. Variables found not to be related or only slightly related (i.e., when correlations below .20 are obtained) are then dropped from further consideration, while those found to be more highly related (i.e., when correlations beyond +.40 or −.40 are obtained) often serve as the focus of additional research, using an experimental design, to see whether the relationships are indeed causal.

Let us say a bit more here about causation. Although the discovery of a correlational relationship does not establish a causal connection, most researchers who engage in correlational research are probably trying to gain some idea about cause and effect. A researcher who carried out the fictitious study whose results are illustrated in Figure 15.2, for example, would probably be inclined to hypothesize that a teacher's expectation of failure is a partial (or at least a contributing) cause of the amount of disruptive behavior his or her students display in class.

It must be stressed, however, that correlational studies *do not,* in and of themselves, establish cause and effect. In the previous example, one could just as well argue that the amount of disruptive behavior in a class would cause a teacher's expectation of failure, or that *both* teacher expectation and disruptive behavior were caused by some third factor—such as the ability level of the class.

The possibility of causation is strengthened, however, if a time lapse occurs between measurement of the

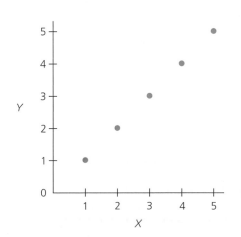

Figure 15.1 *Scatterplot Illustrating a Correlation of +1.00*

Table 15.2 *Teacher Expectation of Failure and Amount of Disruptive Behavior for a Sample of 12 Classes*

Class	Teacher Expectation of Failure (Ratings)	Amount of Disruptive Behavior (Ratings)
1	10	11
2	4	3
3	2	2
4	4	6
5	12	10
6	9	6
7	8	9
8	8	6
9	6	8
10	5	5
11	5	9
12	7	4

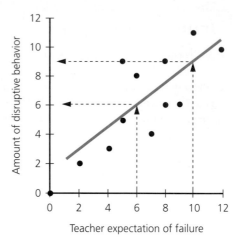

Figure 15.2 *Prediction Using a Scatterplot*

variables being studied. If the teacher's expectations of failure were measured before assigning students to classes, for example, it would seem unreasonable to assume that class behavior (or, likewise, the ability level of the class) would cause their failure expectations. The reverse, in fact, would make more sense. Certain other causal explanations, however, remain persuasive, such as the socioeconomic level of the students involved. Teachers might have higher expectations of failure for economically poor students. Such students also might exhibit a greater amount of disruptive behavior in class regardless of their teacher's expectations. The search for cause and effect in correlational studies, therefore, is fraught with difficulty. Nonetheless, it can be a fruitful step in the search for causes. We return to this matter later in the discussion of threats to internal validity in correlational research.

PREDICTION STUDIES

A second purpose of correlational research is that of **prediction:** If a relationship of sufficient magnitude exists between two variables, it becomes possible to predict a score on either variable if a score on the other variable is known. Researchers have found, for example, that high school grades are highly related to college grades. Hence, high school grades can be used to predict college grades. We would predict that a person who has a high GPA in

high school would be likely to have a high GPA in college. The variable that is used to make the prediction is called the **predictor variable;** the variable about which the prediction is made is called the **criterion variable.** Hence, in the above example, "high school grades" would be the predictor variable, and "college grades" would be the criterion variable. As we mentioned in Chapter Eight, prediction studies are also used to determine the predictive validity of measuring instruments.

Using Scatterplots to Predict a Score. Prediction can be illustrated through the use of scatterplots. Suppose, for example, that we obtain the data shown in Table 15.2 from a sample of 12 classes. Using these data, we find a correlation of .71 between the variables "teacher expectation of failure" and "amount of disruptive behavior."

Plotting the data in Table 15.2 produces the scatterplot shown in Figure 15.2. Once a scatterplot such as this has been constructed, a straight line, known as a **regression line**, can be calculated mathematically. The calculation of this line is beyond the scope of this text, but a general understanding of its use can be obtained by looking at Figure 15.2. The regression line comes the closest to all of the scores depicted on the scatterplot of any straight line that could be drawn. A researcher can then use the line as a basis for prediction. Thus, as you can see, a teacher with an "expectation of failure" score of 10 would be predicted to have a class with an "amount of disruptive behavior" score of 9, and a teacher with an expectation score of 6 would be predicted to have a class with a "disruptive behavior" score of 6. Similarly, a second regression line can be drawn to predict a "teacher expectation of failure" score if we know his or her class's "amount of disruptive behavior" score.

Being able to predict a score for an individual (or group) on one variable from knowing the individual's (or group's) score on another variable is extremely useful. A school administrator, for example, could use Figure 15.2 (if it were based on real data) to (1) identify and select teachers who are likely to have less disruptive classes; (2) provide training to those teachers who are predicted to have a large amount of disruptive behavior in their classes; or (3) plan for additional assistance for such teachers. Both the teachers and students involved should benefit accordingly.

A Simple Prediction Equation. Although scatterplots are fairly easy devices to use in making predictions, they are inefficient when pairs of scores from a large number of individuals have been collected. Fortunately, the regression line we just described can be expressed in the form of a **prediction equation,** which has the following form:

$$Y_1' = a + bX_1$$

where Y_1' = the predicted score on Y (the criterion variable) for individual i, X_1 = individual i's score on X (the predictor variable), and a and b are values calculated mathematically from the original scores. For any given set of data, a and b are constants.

We mentioned earlier that high school GPA has been found to be highly related to college GPA. In this example, therefore, the symbol Y' stands for the predicted first-semester college GPA (the criterion variable), and X_1 stands for the individual's high school GPA (the predictor variable). Let us assume that $a = .18$ and $b = .73$. By substituting in the equation, we can predict a student's first-semester college GPA. Thus, if an individual's high school GPA is 3.5, we would predict that his or her first semester college GPA would be 2.735 (that is, $.18 + .73 \times 3.5 = 2.735$). We later can compare the student's actual first semester college GPA to the predicted GPA. If there is a close similarity between the two, we gain confidence in using the prediction equation to make future predictions.

This predicted score will not be exact, however, and hence researchers also calculate an index of prediction error, known as the *standard error of estimate.* This index gives an estimate of the degree to which the predicted score is likely to be incorrect. The smaller the standard error of estimate, the more accurate the pre-

diction. This index of error, as you would expect, is much larger for small values of r than for large r's.*

Furthermore, if we have more information on the individuals about whom we wish to predict, we should be able to decrease our errors of prediction. This is what a technique known as multiple regression (or multiple correlation) is designed to do.

MORE COMPLEX CORRELATIONAL TECHNIQUES

Multiple Regression. Multiple regression is a technique that enables researchers to determine a correlation between a criterion variable and the best combination of *two or more* predictor variables. Let us return to our previous example involving the high positive correlation that has been found to exist between high school GPA and first-semester college GPA. Suppose it is also found that a high positive correlation ($r = .68$) exists between first-semester college GPA and the verbal scores on the Scholastic Aptitude Test (SAT) of the college entrance examination, and a moderately high positive correlation ($r = .51$) exists between the mathematics scores on the SAT and first-semester college GPA. It is possible, using a multiple regression prediction formula, to use *all three* of these variables to predict what a student's GPA will be during his or her first semester in college. The formula is similar to the simple prediction equation, except that it now includes more than one predictor variable and more than two constants. It takes the following form:

$$Y' = a + b_1X_1 + b_2X_2 + b_3X_3$$

where Y' once again stands for the predicted first-semester college GPA, a, b_1, b_2, and b_3 are constants, X_1 = the high school GPA, X_2 = the verbal SAT score, and X_3 = the mathematics SAT score. Let us imagine that $a = .18$, $b_1 = .73$, $b_2 = .0005$, and $b_3 = .0002$. We know that the student's high school GPA is 3.5. Suppose his or her SAT verbal and mathematics scores are 580 and 600, respectively. Substituting in the formula, we would predict that the student's first semester GPA would be 3.15.

$$Y' = .18 + .73(3.5) + .0005(580)$$
$$+ .0002(600)$$
$$= .18 + 2.56 + .29 + .12$$
$$= 3.15$$

*If the reason for this is unclear to you, refer again to the scatterplots in Figures 15.2 and 10.18.

Again, we could later compare the actual first-semester college GPA obtained by this student with the predicted score to determine how accurate our prediction was.

The Coefficient of Multiple Correlation. The **coefficient of multiple correlation,** symbolized by *R,* indicates the strength of the correlation between the combination of the predictor variables and the criterion variable. It can be thought of as a simple Pearson correlation between the actual scores on the criterion variable and the predicted scores on that variable. In the previous example, we used a combination of high school GPA, SAT verbal score, and SAT mathematics score to predict that a particular student's first-semester college GPA would be 3.15. We then could obtain that same student's *actual* first-semester college GPA (it might be 2.95, for example). If we did this for 100 students, we could then calculate the correlation (*R*) between predicted and actual GPA. If *R* turned out to be +1.00, for example, it would mean that the predicted scores correlate perfectly with the actual scores on the criterion variable. An *R* of +1.00, of course, would be most unusual to obtain. In actual practice, *R*s of .70 or .80 are considered quite high. The higher *R* is, of course, the more reliable a prediction will be. Figure 15.3 illustrates the relationships among a criterion and

two predictors. The amount of college GPA accounted for by high school GPA (about 36 percent) is increased by about 13 percent by adding test score as a second predictor.

The Coefficient of Determination. The square of the correlation between a predictor and a criterion variable is known as the **coefficient of determination,** symbolized by r^2. If the correlation between high school GPA and college GPA, for example, equals .60, then the coefficient of determination would equal .36. What does this mean? In short, the coefficient of determination indicates the percentage of the variability among the criterion scores that can be attributed to differences in the scores on the predictor variable. Thus, if the correlation between high school GPA and college GPA for a group of students is .60, 36 percent $(.60)^2$ of the differences in the college GPAs of those students can be attributed to differences in their high school GPAs.

The interpretation of R^2 (for multiple regression) is similar to that of r^2 (for simple regression). Suppose in our example that used three predictor variables, the multiple correlation coefficient is equal to .70. The coefficient of determination, then, is equal to $(.70)^2$, or .49. Thus, it would be appropriate to say that 49 percent of the variability in the criterion variable is predictable on the basis of the three predictor variables. Another way of saying this is that high school GPA, verbal SAT scores, and mathematics SAT scores (the three predictor variables), taken together, account for about 49 percent of the variability in college GPA (the criterion variable).

The value of a prediction equation depends on whether it can be used with a *new* group of individuals. Researchers can never be sure the prediction equation they develop will work successfully when it is used to predict criterion scores for a new group of persons. In fact, it is quite likely that it will be less accurate when so used, since the new group is not identical to the one used to develop the prediction equation. The success of a particular prediction equation with a new group, therefore, usually depends on the group's similarity to the group used to develop the prediction equation originally.

Discriminant Function Analysis. In most prediction studies, the criterion variable is quantitative—that is, it involves scores that can fall anywhere along a continuum from low to high. Our previous example of college

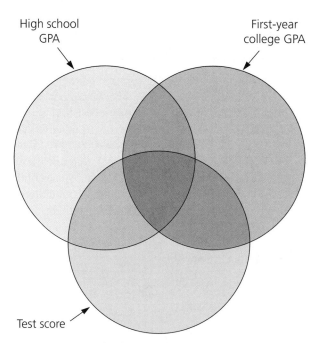

High school GPA

First-year college GPA

Test score

Figure 15.3 *Multiple Correlation*

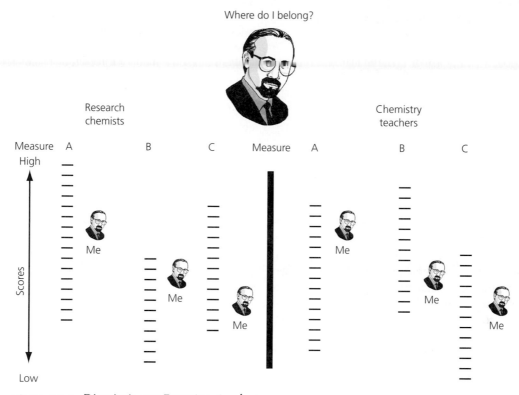

Figure 15.4 *Discriminant Function Analysis*

GPA is a quantitative variable, for scores on the variable can fall anywhere at or between 0.00 and 4.00. Sometimes, however, the criterion variable may be a categorical variable—that is, it involves membership in a group (or category) rather than scores along a continuum. For example, a researcher might be interested in predicting whether an individual is more like engineering majors or business majors. In this instance, the criterion variable is dichotomous—an individual is either in one group or the other. Of course, a categorical variable can have more than just two categories (for example, engineering majors, business majors, education majors, science majors, and so on). The technique of multiple regression cannot be used when the criterion variable is categorical; instead, a technique known as **discriminant function analysis** is used. The purpose of the analysis and the form of the prediction equation, however, is similar to multiple regression. Figure 15.4 illustrates the logic; note that the scores of the individual represented by the six faces remain the same for each measure! The person's score is compared first to the scores of research chemists, and then to the scores of chemistry teachers.

Factor Analysis. When a number of variables are investigated in a single study, analysis and interpretation of data can become rather cumbersome. It is often desirable, therefore, to reduce the number of variables by grouping those that are moderately or highly correlated with one another into *factors.*

Factor analysis is a technique that allows a researcher to determine if many variables can be described by a few factors. The mathematical calculations involved are beyond the scope of this book, but the technique essentially involves a search for "clusters" of variables, all of which are correlated with each other. Each cluster represents a factor. Studies of group IQ tests, for example, have suggested that the many specific scores used could be explained as a result of a relatively small number of factors. While controversial, these results did provide one means of comprehending the mental abilities required to perform well on such tests. They also led to new tests designed to test these identified abilities more effectively.

Path Analysis. **Path analysis** is used to test the likelihood of a causal connection among three or more

Table 15.3 *Correlation Matrix for Variables in Student Alienation Study*

	School Enjoyment	Number of Friends	Alienation
Relevance of courses	.65	.24	−.48
School enjoyment		.58	−.53
Number of friends			−.27

variables. Some of the other techniques we have described can be used to explore theories about causality, but path analysis is far more powerful than the rest. Although a detailed explanation of this technique is too technical for inclusion here, the essential idea behind path analysis is to formulate a theory about the possible causes of a particular phenomenon (such as student alienation)—that is, to identify causal variables that could explain why the phenomenon occurs—and then to determine whether correlations among all the variables are consistent with the theory.

Suppose a researcher theorizes as follows: (1) certain students are more alienated in school than others because they do not find school enjoyable and because they have few friends; (2) they do not find school enjoyable partly because they have few friends and partly because they do not perceive their courses as being in any way related to their needs; and (3) perceived relevance of courses is related slightly to number of friends. The researcher would then measure each of these variables ("degree of alienation," "personal relevance of courses," "enjoyment in school," and "number of friends") for a number of students. Correlations between pairs of each of the variables would then be calculated. Let us imagine that the researcher obtains the correlations shown in the correlation matrix in Table 15.3.

What does this table reveal about possible causes of student alienation? Two of the variables (relevance of courses at −.48 and school enjoyment at −.53) shown in the table are sizable predictors of such alienation. Nevertheless, to remind you again, just because these variables predict student alienation you should not assume that they cause it. Furthermore, something of a problem exists in the fact that the two predictor variables correlate with *each other*. As you can see, school enjoyment and perceived relevance of courses not only predict student alienation, but they also correlate highly with each other ($r = .65$). Now, does perceived relevance of courses affect student alienation independently of school enjoyment? Does school enjoyment affect stu-

dent alienation independently of perception of course relevance? Path analysis can help the researcher determine the answers to these questions.

Path analysis, then, involves four basic steps. First, a theory that links several variables is formulated to explain a particular phenomenon of interest. In our example, the researcher theorized the following causal connections: (1) When students perceive their courses as being unrelated to their needs, they will not enjoy school; (2) if they have few friends in school, this will contribute to their lack of enjoyment, and (3) the more a student dislikes school, and the fewer friends he or she has, the more alienated he or she will be. Second, the variables specified by the theory are then measured in some way.* Third, correlation coefficients are computed to indicate the strength of the relationship between each of the pairs of variables postulated in the theory. And, fourth, relationships among the correlation coefficients are analyzed in relation to the theory.

Path analysis variables are typically shown in the type of diagram in Figure 15.5.† Each variable in the theory is shown in the figure. Each arrow indicates a hypothesized causal relationship in the direction of the arrow. Thus, liking for school is hypothesized to influence alienation; number of friends influences school enjoyment, and so on. Notice that in this example all of the arrows point in one direction only. This means that the first variable is hypothesized to influence the second variable, but not vice versa. Numbers similar (but not identical) to correlation coefficients are calculated for each pair of variables. If the results were as shown in Figure 15.5, the causal theory of the researcher would be supported. Do you see why?‡

Structural Modeling. Structural modeling is a sophisticated method for exploring and possibly confirming causation among several variables. Its complexity is beyond the scope of this text. Suffice it to say that it combines multiple regression, path analysis, and factor

---

*Note that this step is very important. The measures must be valid representations of the variables. The results of the path analysis will be invalid if this is not the case.

†The process of path analysis and the diagrams drawn are, in practice, often more complex than the one shown here.

‡Because alienation is "caused" primarily by lack of enjoyment (−.55) and number of friends (−.60). The perceived lack of relevance of courses does contribute to degree of alienation, but primarily because relevance "causes" enjoyment. Enjoyment is partly caused by number of friends. Perceived relevance of courses is only slightly caused by number of friends.

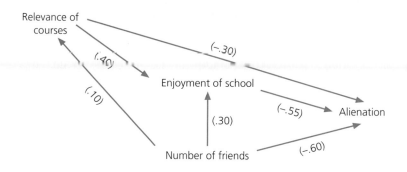

Figure 15.5 *Path Analysis Diagram*

analysis. The computations are greatly simplified by use of computer programs; the computer program most widely used is probably LISREL.[1]

Basic Steps in Correlational Research

PROBLEM SELECTION

The variables to be included in a correlational study should be chosen based on a sound rationale growing out of experience or theory. The researcher should have some reason for thinking certain variables may be related. As always, clarity in defining variables will avoid many problems later on. In general, three major types of problems are the focus of correlational studies:

1. Is variable *X* related to variable *Y?*
2. How well does variable *P* predict variable *C?*
3. What are the relationships among a large number of variables and what predictions can be made that are based on them?

Almost all correlational studies will revolve around one of these types of questions. Some examples of published correlational studies are as follows.

- The accuracy of principals' judgments of teacher performance.[2]
- Teacher clarity and its relationship to student achievement and satisfaction.[3]
- Factors associated with the drug use of fifth- through eighth-grade students.[4]
- Moral development and empathy in counseling.[5]
- The relationship among health beliefs, health values, and health promotion activity.[6]
- The relationship of student ability and small-group interaction to student achievement.[7]
- Predicting students' outcomes from their perceptions of classroom psychosocial environment.[8]

SAMPLE

The sample for a correlational study, as in any type of study, should be selected carefully and, if possible, randomly. The first step in selecting a sample, of course, is to identify an appropriate population, one that is meaningful and from which data on *each* of the variables of interest can be collected. The minimum acceptable sample size for a correlational study is considered by most researchers to be no less than 30. Data obtained from a sample smaller than 30 may give an inaccurate estimate of the degree of relationship that exists. Samples larger than 30 are much more likely to provide meaningful results.

INSTRUMENTS

The instruments used to measure the two (or more) variables involved in a correlational study may take any one of a number of forms (see Chapter Seven), but they must yield quantitative data. Although data sometimes can be collected from records of one sort or another (grade transcripts, for example), most correlational studies involve the administration of some type of instrument (tests, questionnaires, and so on) and sometimes observation. As with any study, whatever instruments are used must yield reliable scores. In an explanatory study, the instruments must also show evidence of validity. If they do not truly measure the intended variables, then any correlation that is obtained will not be an indication of the intended relationship. In a prediction study, it is not essential that we know what variable is actually being measured—if it works as a predictor, it is useful. However, prediction studies are most likely to be successful, and certainly more satisfying, if we know what we are measuring!

DESIGN AND PROCEDURES

The basic design used in a correlational study is quite straightforward. Using the symbols introduced in our discussion of experimental designs in Chapter Thirteen, this design can be diagrammed as shown below:

Design for a Correlational Study

Observations

Subjects	O_1	O_2
A	—	—
B	—	—
C	—	—
D	—	—
E	—	—
F	—	—
G	—	—
etc.		

As you can see, two (or more) scores are obtained from *each* individual in the sample, one score for each variable of interest. The pairs of scores are then correlated, and the resulting correlation coefficient indicates the degree of relationship between the variables.

Notice, again, that we cannot say that the variable being measured by the first instrument (O_1) is the cause of any differences in scores we may find in the variable being measured by the second instrument (O_2). As we have mentioned before, three possibilities exist:

1. The variable being measured by O_1 may cause the variable being measured by O_2.
2. The variable being measured by O_2 may cause the variable being measured by O_1.
3. Some third, perhaps unidentified and unmeasured, variable may cause *both* of the other variables.

Different numbers of variables can be investigated in correlational studies, and sometimes quite complex statistical procedures are used. The basic research design for all correlational studies, however, is similar to the one just shown. An example of data obtained with a correlational design is shown in Table 15.4.

DATA COLLECTION

In an explanatory study, all the data on both variables will usually be collected within a fairly short time. Often, the instruments used are administered in a single session, or in two sessions one immediately after the other. Thus, if a researcher were interested in measuring the relationship between verbal aptitude and memory, a test of verbal aptitude and another of memory would be administered closely together in time to the same group of subjects. In a prediction study, the measurement of

Table 15.4 *Example of Data Obtained in a Correlational Design*

Student	(O_1) Self-Esteem	(O_2) Mathematics Achievement
José	25	95
Felix	23	88
Rosita	25	96
Phil	18	81
Jenny	12	65
Natty	23	73
Lina	22	92
Jill	15	71
Jack	24	93
James	17	78

the criterion variables often takes place sometime after the measurement of the predictor variables. If a researcher were interested in studying the predictive value of a mathematics aptitude test, the aptitude test might be administered just prior to the beginning of a course in mathematics. Success in the course (the criterion variable, as indicated by course grades) would then be measured at the end of the course.

DATA ANALYSIS AND INTERPRETATION

As we have mentioned previously, when variables are correlated, a **correlation coefficient** is produced. This coefficient will be a decimal, somewhere between 0.00 and +1.00 or −1.00. The closer the coefficient is to +1.00 or −1.00, the stronger the relationship. If the sign is positive, the relationship is positive, indicating that high scores on the one variable tend to go with high scores on the other variable. If the sign is negative, the relationship is negative, indicating that high scores on the one variable tend to go with low scores on the other variable. Coefficients that are at or near .00 indicate that no relationship exists between the variables involved.

What Do Correlation Coefficients Tell Us?

It is important to be able to interpret correlation coefficients sensibly since they appear so frequently in articles about education and educational research. Unfortunately, they are seldom accompanied by scatterplots, which usually help interpretation and understanding.

The meaning of a given correlation coefficient depends on how it is applied. Correlation coefficients below .35 show only a slight relationship between variables. Such relationships have almost no value in any predictive sense. (It may, of course, be important to know that certain variables are not related. Thus we would expect to find a very low correlation, for instance, between years of teaching experience and number of students enrolled.) Correlations between .40 and .60 are often found in educational research and may have theoretical or practical value, depending on the context. A correlation of at least .50 must be obtained before any crude predictions can be made about individuals. Even then such predictions will be subject to sizable errors. Only when a correlation of .65 or higher is obtained can individual predictions that are reasonably accurate for most purposes be made. Correlations over .85 indicate a close relationship between the variables correlated and are useful in predicting individual performance, but correlations this high are rarely obtained in educational research, except when checking on reliability.

As we illustrated in Chapter Eight, correlation coefficients are also used to check the reliability and validity of scores obtained from tests and other instruments used in research; when so used, they are called reliability and validity coefficients. When used to check reliability of scores, the coefficient should be at least .70, preferably higher; many tests achieve reliability coefficients of .90. The correlation between two different scorers, working independently, should be at least .90. When used to check validity of scores, the coefficient should be at least .50, and preferably higher.

Threats to Internal Validity in Correlational Research

Recall from Chapter Nine that a major concern to researchers is that extraneous variables may "explain" any results that are obtained.* A similar concern applies

---

*It can be argued that such threats are irrelevant to the predictive use of correlational research. The argument is that one can predict even if the relationship is an artifact of other variables. Thus, predictions of college achievement can be made from high school grades even if both are highly related to socioeconomic status. While we agree with the practical utility of such predictions, we believe that research should seek to illuminate relationships that have at least the potential for explanation.

to correlational studies. A researcher who conducts a correlational study should always be alert to alternative explanations for relationships found in the data. What might account for any correlations that are reported as existing between two or more variables?

Consider again the hypothesis that teacher expectation of failure is positively correlated with student disruptive behavior. A researcher conducting this study would almost certainly have a cause-and-effect sequence in mind, most likely that teacher expectation is a partial cause of disruptive behavior. Why? Because disruptive behavior is undesirable (because it clearly interferes with both academic learning and a desirable classroom climate). Thus, it would be helpful to know what might be done to reduce it. While teacher expectation of failure *might* be considered the dependent variable, it seems less likely since such expectations would be of little interest if they have no effect on students.

If, indeed, the researcher's intentions are as we have described, he might have carried out an experiment. However, it is difficult to see how "teacher expectation" could be experimentally manipulated. It might, however, be possible to study whether attempts to *change* teacher expectations result in subsequent *changes* in amount of disruptive behavior, but such a study requires developing and implementing training methods. Before embarking on such development and implementation, therefore, one might well ask whether there is any relationship between the primary variables. This is why a correlational study is an appropriate first step.

A positive correlation resulting from such a study would most likely be viewed as at least some evidence to suggest that modifying teacher expectations would result in less disruptive behavior, thereby justifying further experimental efforts. (It may also be that some principals or teacher-trainers would wish to institute mechanisms for changing teacher expectations before waiting for experimental confirmation, just as the medical profession began warning about the effects of smoking in the absence of conclusive experimental evidence.) Before investing time and resources in developing training methods and carrying out an experiment, the researcher needs to be as confident as possible that he is not misinterpreting his correlation. If the relationship he has found really reflects the opposite cause-and-effect sequence (student behavior causing teacher expectations), or if *both* are a result of other causes, such as student ability or socioeconomic status, changes in teacher expectation are *not* likely to be accompanied by a reduction in disruptive behavior. The former problem (direction of cause and effect) can be largely eliminated by assessing teacher expectations *prior to* direct involvement with the student group. The latter problem—of other causes—is the one we turn to now.

Some of the threats we discussed in Chapter Nine do not apply to correlational studies. Implementation, history, maturation, attitude of subjects, and regression threats are not applicable since no intervention occurs. There are some threats, however, that do apply.

SUBJECT CHARACTERISTICS

Whenever two or more characteristics of individuals (or groups) are correlated, there exists the possibility that yet *other* characteristics can explain any relationships that are found. In such cases, the other characteristics can be controlled through a statistical technique known as **partial correlation.** Let us illustrate the logic involved by using the example of the relationship between teachers' expectations of failure and the amount of disruptive behavior by students in their classes. This relationship is shown in Figure 15.6(*a*).

The researcher desires to control, or "get rid of," the variable of "ability level" for the classes involved, since it is logical to assume that it might be a cause of variation in the other two variables. In order to control for this variable, the researcher needs to measure the ability level of each class. She can then construct scatterplots as shown in Figure 15.6(*b*) and (*c*). Scatterplot (*b*) shows the correlation between amount of disruptive behavior and class ability level; scatterplot (*c*) shows the correlation between teacher expectation of failure and class ability level.

The researcher can now use scatterplot (*b*) to predict the "disruptive behavior" score for class 1, based on the ability score for class 1. In doing so, the researcher would be assuming that the regression line shown in scatterplot (*b*) correctly represents the relationship between these variables (class ability level and amount of disruptive behavior) in the data. Next, the researcher subtracts the *predicted* disruptive behavior score from the *actual* disruptive behavior score. The result is called the adjusted disruptive behavior score—that is, the score has been "adjusted" by taking out the influence of ability level. For class 1, the predicted disruptive behavior score is 7 (based on a class ability score of 5). In actuality this class scored 11 (higher than expected), so the adjusted score for amount of disruptive behavior is (11 − 7), or 4.

The same procedure is then followed to adjust teacher expectation scores for class ability level, as shown in scatterplot (*c*) (10 − 7 = 3). After repeating this process for the entire sample of classes, the researcher is now in a position to determine the correlation between the *adjusted* disruptive behavior scores and the *adjusted* teacher expectation scores. The result is the correlation between the two major variables with the effect of class ability eliminated, and thus controlled. Methods of calculation, involving the use of relatively simple formulas are available to greatly simplify this procedure.[9] Figure 15.7 shows another way to think about partial correlation. The top circles illustrate (by amount of overlap) the correlation between A and B. The bottom circles show the same overlap but reduced by "taking out" the overlap of C with A and B. What remains (the diagonally lined section) illustrates the partial correlation of A and B with the effects of C removed.

LOCATION

A location threat is possible whenever all instruments are administered to each subject at a specified location, but the location is different for different subjects. It is not uncommon for researchers to encounter differences in testing conditions, particularly when individual tests are required. In one school, a comfortable, well-lit, and ventilated room may be available. In another, a custodian's closet may have to do. Such conditions can increase (or decrease) subject scores. If both measures are not administered to all subjects under the same conditions, the conditions rather than the variables being studied may account for the relationship. If only part of a group, for example, responds to instruments in an uncomfortable, poorly lit room, they might score lower on an achievement test and respond more negatively to a rating scale measuring student "liking for school," thus producing a misleading correlation coefficient.

Similarly, conditions in different schools may account for observed relationships. A high negative correlation between amount of disruptive behavior in class and achievement may be simply a reflection of differing resources. Students in schools with few science materials can be expected to do poorly in science and also to be disruptive because of boredom or hostility. The only solutions to location problems such as these are either to measure the extraneous variables (such as resource level) and use partial correlation or to determine correlations separately for each location, provided the number of students at each location is sufficiently large (a minimum *n* of 30).

Figure 15.6
Scatterplots for Combinations of Variables

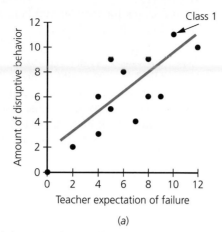

(a)

Amount of disruptive behavior in class as related to teacher expectation of failure

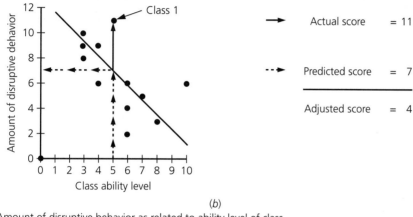

(b)

Amount of disruptive behavior as related to ability level of class

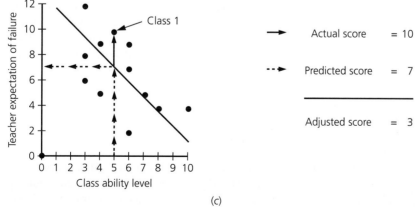

(c)

Teacher expectation of failure as related to ability level of class

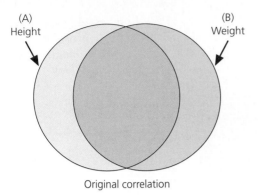

Original correlation

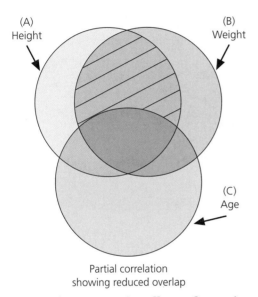

Partial correlation
showing reduced overlap

Figure 15.7 *Eliminating the Effects of Age Through Partial Correlation*

INSTRUMENTATION

Instrument Decay. In any study using a particular instrument many times, thought must be given to the possibility of instrument decay. This is most likely in observational studies since most other correlational studies do not use instruments many times (with the same subjects at least). When both variables are measured by an observational device at the same time, care must be taken to ensure that observers don't become tired, bored, or inattentive (this may require using additional observers). In a study in which observers are asked to record (during the same time period) both the number of "thought questions" asked by the teacher and the attentiveness of students, for example, a tired (or bored) observer might miss instances of each, resulting

in low scores for the class on both variables, and thus distortion in the correlation.

Data-collector Characteristics. Characteristics of data collectors can create a threat if different persons administer both instruments. Gender, age, or ethnicity, for example, may affect specific responses, particularly with opinion or attitudinal instruments, as well as the seriousness with which respondents answer certain questions. One might expect an Air Force colonel in uniform, for example, to engender different scores on instruments measuring attitudes toward the military and (separately) toward the aerospace industry than a civilian data collector. If each data collector gives both instruments to several groups, the correlation between these scores will be higher as a result of the impact of the data collector. Fortunately, this threat is easily avoided by having each instrument administered by a different individual.

Data-collector Bias. Another instrumentation threat can result from unconscious bias on the part of the data gatherers whenever both instruments are given or scored by the same person. It is not uncommon, particularly with individually administered performance tests, for the same person to administer both tests to the same student, and even during the same time period. It is likely that the observed or scored performance on the first test will affect the way in which the second test is administered and/or scored. It is almost impossible to avoid expectations based on the first test, and these may well affect the examiner's behavior on the second testing. A high score on the first test, for example, may lead to examiner expectation of a high score on the second, resulting in students being given additional time or encouragement on the second test. While precise instructions for administering instruments are helpful, a better solution is to have different administrators for each test.

TESTING

The experience of responding to the first instrument that is administered in a correlational study may influence subject responses to the second instrument. Students asked to respond first to a "liking for teacher" scale, and then shortly thereafter to a "liking for social studies" scale are likely to see a connection. You can imagine them saying, perhaps, something like, "Oh, I see, if I don't like the teacher, I'm not supposed to like the subject." To the extent that this happens, the results obtained can be misleading. The solution is to administer instruments, if possible, at different times and in different contexts.

MORTALITY

Mortality, strictly speaking, is not a problem of internal validity in correlational studies since anyone "lost" must be excluded from the study—correlations cannot be obtained unless a researcher has a score for each person on *both* of the variables being measured.

There are times, however, when loss of subjects may make a relationship more (or less) likely in the remaining data, thus creating a threat to *external* validity. Why external validity? Because the sample actually studied is often not the sample initially selected, because of mortality. Let us refer again to the study hypothesizing that teacher expectation of failure would be positively correlated with amount of disruptive student behavior. It might be that those teachers who refused to participate in the study were those who had a very low expectation of failure—who, in fact, expected their students to achieve at unrealistically high levels. It also seems likely that the classes of those same teachers would exhibit a lot of disruptive behavior as a result of such unrealistic pressure from these teachers. Their loss would serve to *increase* the correlation obtained. Because there is no way to know whether this possibility is correct, the only thing the researcher can do is to try to avoid losing subjects.

Evaluating Threats to Internal Validity in Correlational Studies

The evaluation of specific threats to internal validity in correlational studies follows a procedure similar to that for experimental studies.

Step 1: Ask: What are the specific factors that are known to affect one of the variables being correlated or which logically could affect it? It does not matter which variable is selected.

Step 2: Ask: What is the likelihood of each of these factors also affecting the *other* variable being correlated with the first? We need not be concerned with any factor unrelated to either variable. A fac-

tor must be related to *both* variables in order to be a threat.*

Step 3: Evaluate the various threats in terms of their likelihood and plan to control them. If a given threat cannot be controlled, this should be acknowledged and discussed.

As we did in Chapter Thirteen, let us consider an example to show how these steps might be applied. Suppose a researcher wishes to study the relationship between social skills (as observed) and job success (as rated by supervisors) of a group of severely disabled young adults in a career education program. Listed below again are several threats to internal validity discussed in Chapter Nine and our evaluation of each.

Subject Characteristics. We consider here only four of many possible characteristics.

1. **Severity of handicap.** *Step 1:* Rated job success can be expected to be related to severity of handicap. *Step 2:* Severity of handicap can also be expected to be related to social skills. Therefore, severity should be assessed and controlled (using partial correlation). *Step 3:* Likelihood of having an effect unless controlled: high.

2. **Socioeconomic level of parents.** *Step 1:* Likely to be related to social skills. *Step 2:* Parental socioeconomic status not likely to be related to job success for this group. While it is desirable to obtain socioeconomic data (to find out more about the sample), it is not of high priority. *Step 3:* Likelihood of having an effect unless controlled: low.

3. **Physical strength and coordination.** *Step 1:* May be related to job success. *Step 2:* Strength and coordination not likely to be related to social skills. While desirable to obtain such information, it is not of high priority. *Step 3:* Likelihood of having an effect unless controlled: low.

4. **Physical appearance.** *Step 1:* Likely to be related to social skills. *Step 2:* Also likely to be related to rated job success. Therefore, this variable should be assessed and controlled (again by using partial correlation). *Step 3:* Likelihood of having an effect unless controlled: high.

---

*This rule must be modified with respect to data-collector and testing threats, where knowledge about the first instrument (or scores on it) may influence performance or assessment on the second instrument.

Mortality. *Step 1:* Subjects "lost" are likely to have poorer job performance. *Step 2:* Lost subjects are also more likely to have poorer social skills. Thus, loss of subjects can be expected to reduce magnitude of correlation. *Step 3:* Likelihood of having an effect unless controlled: moderate to high.

Location. *Step 1:* Because the subjects of the study would (inevitably) be working at different job sites and under different conditions, location may well be related to rated job success. *Step 2:* If social skill is observed on site, it may be related to the specific site conditions. While it is possible that this threat could be controlled by independently assessing the job site environments, a better solution would be to assess social skills at a common site such as that used for group training. *Step 3:* Likelihood of having an effect unless controlled: high.

Instrumentation.

1. **Instrument decay.** *Step 1:* Instrument decay, if it has occurred, is likely to be related to how accurately social skills are measured. Observations should be scheduled, therefore, to preclude this possibility. *Step 2:* Instrument decay would be unlikely to affect job ratings. Therefore, its occurrence would not be expected to account for any relationship found between the major variables. *Step 3:* Likelihood of having an effect unless controlled: low.
2. **Data-collector characteristics.** *Step 1:* Might well be related to job ratings since interaction of data collectors and supervisors is a necessary part of this study. *Step 2:* Characteristics of data collectors presumably would not be related to their observation of social skills; nevertheless, to be on the safe side, this possibility should be controlled by having the same data collectors observe all subjects. *Step 3:* Likelihood of having an effect unless controlled: moderate.

3. **Data-collector bias.** *Step 1:* Ratings of job success should not be subject to data-collector bias, since different supervisors will rate each subject. *Step 2:* Observations of social skills may be related to preconceptions of observers about the subjects, *especially* if they have prior knowledge of job success ratings. Therefore, observers should have no knowledge of job ratings. *Step 3:* Likelihood of having an effect unless controlled: high.
4. **Testing.** *Step 1:* In this example, performance on the first instrument administered cannot, of course, be affected by performance on the second. *Step 2:* In this study, scores on the second instrument cannot be affected by performance on the first, since the subjects are unaware of their performance on the first instrument. *Step 3:* Likelihood of having an effect unless controlled: zero.

Rationale for the Process of Evaluating Threats in Correlational Studies. We will try to demonstrate the logic behind the principle that a factor must be related to both correlated variables in order to explain a correlation between them. Consider the three scatterplots shown in Figure 15.8, which represent the scores of a group of individuals on three variables: *A, B,* and *C.* Scatterplot 1 shows a substantial correlation between *A* and *B;* scatterplot 2 shows a substantial correlation between *A* and *C;* scatterplot 3 shows a zero correlation between *B* and *C.*

Suppose the researcher is interested in determining whether the correlation between variables *A* and *B* can

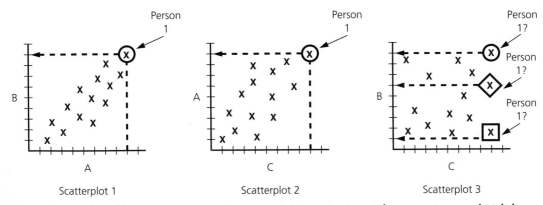

Figure 15.8 *Scatterplots Illustrating How a Factor (C) May Not Be a Threat to Internal Validity*

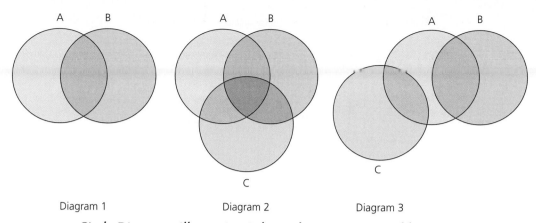

Diagram 1   Diagram 2   Diagram 3

Figure 15.9 *Circle Diagrams Illustrating Relationships Among Variables*

be "explained" by variable *C. A* and *B,* in other words, represent the variables being studied, while *C* represents a third variable being evaluated as a potential threat to internal validity. If the researcher tries to explain the correlation between *A* and *B* as due to *C,* he or she cannot. Here's why.

Suppose we say that person 1, shown in scatterplot 1, is high on *A* and *B because* he or she is high on *C.* Sure enough, being high on *C would* predict being high on *A.* You can see this in scatterplot 2. However, being high on *C* does *not* predict being high on *B,* because although some individuals who scored high on *C* did score high on *B,* others who scored high on *C* scored in the middle or low on *B.* You can see this in scatterplot 3.

Another way of portraying this logic is with circle diagrams, as shown in Figure 15.9.

Diagram 1 in Figure 15.9 illustrates a correlation between *A* and *B.* This is shown by the overlap in circles; the greater the overlap, the greater the correlation. Diagram 2 shows a third circle, *C,* which represents the additional variable that is being considered as a possible threat to internal validity. Because it is correlated with *both A* and *B,* it may be considered a possible

explanation for at least part of the correlation between them. This is shown by the fact that circle *C* overlaps *both A* and *B.* By way of contrast, diagram 3 shows that whereas *C* is correlated with *A,* it is *not* correlated with *B* (there is no overlap). Because *C* overlaps only with *A* (i.e., it does not overlap with *both* variables), it *cannot* be considered a possible alternative explanation for the correlation between *A* and *B.* Diagram 3, in other words, shows what the three scatterplots in Figure 15.8 do, namely, that *A* is correlated with *B,* and that *A* is correlated with *C,* but that *B* is *not* correlated with *C.*

An Example of Correlational Research

In the remainder of this chapter, we present a published example of correlational research, followed by a critique of its strengths and weaknesses. As we did in our critique of the experimental and single-subject studies analyzed in Chapters Thirteen and Fourteen, we use several of the concepts introduced in earlier parts of the book in our analysis.

Research Report

Journal of Research and Development in Education, 30(2) Winter, 1997, pp. 113–117.

The Relationship Between Time to Completion and Achievement on Multiple-Choice Items

William E. Herman
State University of New York College at Potsdam

This study explored the relationship between the time needed to complete multiple-choice examinations in the college classroom and student exam performance. The results indicated that these variables are relatively unrelated and students tended to employ a fairly consistent test-taking tempo on relatively untimed exams. The implications of this research suggest that students, teachers, and test examiners need to better understand the metacognitive and behavioral elements of test-taking tempo and probably need not worry about the order of finish on such classroom examinations.

Unclear

The rate with which students finish a (relatively) untimed classroom examination and the performance level of students who complete such examinations has fascinated researchers for many decades. The beliefs of students related to this aspect of test taking has important implications for the study of test anxiety, test administration, and test taking. One student shared the following beliefs in response to an open-ended survey question related to thoughts and feelings when the first person in class turns in his or her test.

"I think that I am too slow and I must hurry up."
"I must be dumb or stupid for not catching up."
"I feel that I should have studied more."

Some students appear to be convinced that those who finish the examination early must obtain high scores while those who take longer to finish an examination must receive lower scores. Johnston (1977) suggested that many professors believe that students who finish objective examinations very quickly or are among the last to finish are either the best or poorest students in class. Terranova (1972) pointed out that a belief about the order of examination completion "may be the basis for the apparent discomfort exhibited by the other students when it is obvious that the first few have completed a test" (p. 81).

The relationship between speed and accuracy on tests or examinations has been explored with different types of students (e.g., Kindergarten–12, undergraduate, graduate), different types of achievement (e.g., ability, multiple-choice examinations, essay examinations, true/false examinations), and various different subject areas. Various research paradigms have been used to study these variables resulting in different theoretical explanations of the findings.

Good review of research

The consistent finding of no relationship between the test scores and order of finishing predominates the literature (Beaulieu & Frost, 1994; Bridges, 1985; Burack, 1967; Ebel, 1972; Foos, 1989; Freeman, 1923; Johnston, 1977; Lester, 1991; Michael & Michael, 1969; Nevo & Spector, 1979; Paul & Rosenkoetter, 1980; Terranova, 1972). Occasionally, an unexplainable statistically significant relationship can be found in the midst of the prevailing results. An exploration of the possibility of a curvilinear relationship between these variables has also proved to be a rarity (Michael & Michael, 1969; Nevo & Spector, 1979).

Fewer researchers have explored the consistency of time needed to complete examinations over two or more testing circumstances. Positive relationships for the time used for finishing two

Note: This research was supported by a grant from the NYS/UUP Affirmative Action Committee.

examinations have been reported which suggests considerable stability of this test-time-to-completion variable (Bridges, 1985; Freeman, 1923; Nevo & Spector, 1979). Stability of academic achievement from one testing to another point in time (e.g., mid-semester/final examination) has also been found (Nevo & Spector, 1979).

Nevo and Spector (1979) explained the lack of relationship between time to completion and examination performance on the basis of the personality trait of "personal tempo in test taking," which was operationally defined as the time needed to complete the examination. The authors further suggested that native tendencies or learned factors such as general intelligence, mastery of content, test wiseness, reflection, and caution may operate differentially among students in order to produce the lack of linear and curvilinear relationships found in the study.

Operational definition??

The notion of a variable like personal tempo in test taking is indirectly supported by studies which observed and measured a wide variety of performance tasks. Mishima (1951) and Rimoldi (1951) both observed the fairly consistent variable of task tempo while studying individual differences in performance on a variety of untimed tasks, such as motor activities, reaction times to stimuli, expressive drawing, reasoning, and recognition tasks.

Good detail

Since the word *speed* was never mentioned in the instructions to subjects performing these tasks, the authors were willing to assume that the subjects worked at a pace that the authors described as the subjects' own natural congenial way. The retesting of subjects on repeated attempts at these tasks generated correlation coefficients which ranged from + .60 to + .95. Such results provide tentative support for the concept of a personal test taking tempo variable; it also suggests the need for further research on this topic.

Justification

The research literature is replete with evidence that shows a lack of relationship between examination performance and time to completion. An obvious explanation for such findings is less clear. The purpose of the current study was to further investigate the taking of college-level examinations and the time needed to complete such examinations. The study differs from most of the previous studies in the following ways: (a) personal tempo in test taking was also explored as a tool to better understand the relationship between these variables and (b) a descriptive analysis was employed to better interpret the results.

Purpose
Why do this?

Justification

METHOD

Participants

A total of 130 undergraduate students at a small midwestern suburban Catholic college participated in the study. The median age at the institution was 29 years. Females constituted 82% of the student body. The religious preference of students was 58% Roman Catholic, 34% other Christian, and 8% non-Christian. Approximately 65% of the students were part-time students. Nearly 95% of students commuted to campus; most students worked part-time or full-time.

Convenience sample

Helpful demographics

The sample was determined to be representative of the college population. Participants were drawn from one introductory psychology course, two developmental psychology courses, and one educational psychology course. Class size varied from 21 to 40 students.

How determined?
Which college population?

Instruments

The time to completion variable was operationalized as the time needed (to the nearest minute) in order to complete a virtually untimed classroom examination. Since this study was conducted within the normal activities of the course, examination time was recorded in an inconspicuous manner so as to reduce the likelihood that test taking tempo was influenced by the presence of the researcher.

Unclear

Good procedure

Examination performance was defined as the number of correct responses to 100 multiple-choice questions. Midsemester and final examination performance measures were available on

See page l67

Validity is not
discussed.

Right

See p. 342.

No random sampling

Good clarification

Good clarification

subjects. The Kuder-Richardson reliability estimates for the classroom examination scores ranged from +.79 to +.94, which is somewhat better than most teacher-made tests (Diederich, 1973).

RESULTS

The Pearson product-moment correlation coefficients are presented in Table 1 for the consistency measures of time to completion and examination achievement on the midsemester and final examinations. Table 1 depicts fairly stable relationships for both time to completion and examination performance. The coefficients of determination for the correlations which ranged from +.59 to +.87 indicated that about 35% to 76% of the variation in time to completion and final examination performance could be explained by a linear relationship with measurements obtained at the time the midsemester examination was given.

The relationship between time to completion and examination achievement was explored separately for midsemester and final examinations (Table 2). The resultant correlation coefficients were low and not statistically significant (p > .05). Although the range of coefficients extended from +.27 to −.30, the coefficients of determination for these values suggest that 0.04% to 9% of variance in examination performance could be explained by differences in time to completion variables.

Table 2 also demonstrates consistency of the directionality of the relationships (+ or −) from the midsemester to final examination. An analysis of the scatterplots generated from the data gave no indication of a curvilinear relationship between these variables. Gender differences were found to be negligible.

The lack of either linear or nonlinear relationships between time to completion and examination performance gave rise to a descriptive analysis of the data. Table 3 offers a descriptive analysis of one typical class in terms of first and last finishers. The lack of linear relationship as demonstrated by low correlation coefficients between time to completion and examination performance can be seen on a single-case basis in terms of great variance in examination scores

Table 1 *Correlations for Stability of Time and Achievement*

Class	n	r Time to Completion (Midsemester/Final)	n	r Exam Performance (Midsemester/Final)
PSY 101	38	.59**	39	.87**
PSY 240	22	.75**	22	.83**
EDU 312	35	.83**	35	.83**
PSY 240	31	.65**	34	.68**

$**p < .01$

Table 2 *Correlations Between Time to Completion and Achievement*

Class	n	r Midsemester Exam Results–Time	n	r Final Exam Results–Time
PSY 101	40	−.26	38	−.11
PSY 240	21	−.30	22	−.21
EDU 312	36	.14	35	.27
PSY 240	32	.03	32	−.02

Table 3 *Descriptive Example of First and Last Finishers on Exams*

Midsemester Exam:

Order of Finish	Name	Time	Exam Score	Order of Finish	Name	Time	Exam Score
1.	M. Jones	46 min.	83	*30.	K. Webb	81 min.	84
*2.	S. Anders	47 min.	94	31.	T. Sands	83 min.	47
3.	A. Dove	48 min.	72	32.	G. Thomas	83 min.	92
*4.	F. Carson	48 min.	44	33.	C. Frost	85 min.	80
*5.	H. Fisk	49 min.	73	*34.	D. Beck	87 min.	80
*6.	S. Smith	50 min.	71	*35.	S. Locke	89 min.	79
7.	J. Voss	54 min.	76	*36.	S. Pound	90 min.	43
*8.	B. Call	55 min.	73	37.	L. Nord	95 min.	74
@9.	W. Hall	56 min.	63	*38.	R. Rand	100 min.	41
10.	D. Mills	56 min.	72	39.	D. Kolp	102 min.	52

Descriptive Statistics for the entire Midsemester Exam
Mean Time = 69.54   Mean Score = 70.08
SD Time = 15.25   *SD* Score = 15.32
N = 39   *N* = 39

Final Exam:

Order of Finish	Name	Time	Exam Score	Order of Finish	Name	Time	Exam Score
*1.	H. Fisk	41 min.	79	29.	K. Rust	76 min.	89
*2.	S. Smith	41 min.	72	*30.	S. Locke	76 min.	78
*3.	S. Anders	50 min.	87	31.	L. Carr	76 min.	83
*4.	F. Carson	51 min.	43	*32.	D. Beck	77 min.	86
5.	T. Doers	58 min.	76	@33.	W. Hall	79 min.	68
6.	S. Feldman	61 min.	72	*34.	K. Webb	82 min.	85
7.	J. Berry	62 min.	38	35.	J. Kirth	83 min.	77
*8.	B. Call	62 min.	86	36.	F. Marcs	84 min.	50
9.	K. Wonders	62 min.	71	*37.	R. Rand	88 min.	47
10.	P. Johns	62 min.	79	*38.	S. Pound	95 min.	45

Descriptive Statistics for the entire Final Exam
Mean Time = 68.68   Mean Score = 74.84
SD Time = 11.41   *SD* Score = 14.98
N = 38   *N* = 38

Code: * indicates a consistent time to completion from midsemester exam to final exam.
   @ indicates a rare instance where a student dramatically changes his/her tempo of test-taking (first to last).

Special Note: Pseudonyms were used for the names of all students.

within each of the first and last finisher groups. Exactly half of each group of first and last fin-ishers demonstrated fairly consistent results for both the time to completion and achievement measures (note asterisks*).

The relationship between time to completion and examination performance variables from the midsemester examination to the final examination can also be seen from the actual cases de-picted in Table 3. The uncharacteristic reversal of one case (see @ W. Hall) in terms of time to completion (W. Hall went from first finisher to last finisher) failed to account for any appreciable gain in exam performance.

An analysis of examination performance for the three groups (first, last, and middle finishers) further highlights the correlational analyses. Mean examination performances for the midsemester examination were 72.1, 67.2, and 68.32, respectively. The similar mean examination outcomes for the final examination were 70.3, 70.8, and 68.9, respectively. Standard deviations for the same groups in order of finish on the midsemester examination were 12.86, 19.21, and 15.27 and the final examination were 16.68, 17.24, and 11.66. The differences in means and variances were not found to be statistically significant.

Better to use Delta
See p. 256.

DISCUSSION

Same or different
tasks?
Evidence of reliability

The consistency measures represented by the correlation coefficients for time to completion (+.59 to +.83) and achievement (+.68 to +.87) in this study agree with previous findings (Bridges, 1985; Mishima, 1951; Nevo & Spector, 1979; Rimoldi, 1951). Such results suggest that students tend to approach examinations in a fairly consistent tempo in the same course as measured by time to completion and earn fairly similar scores on examinations from one testing to another in the course.

The descriptive results in the current study support the correlational findings related to the consistency of time to completion from one examination to the next examination. Such findings are also supported by previous research, which found that only one subject in two classes of the first/last five finishers ($N = 26$) and first/last 10 finishers ($N = 97$) completed the examination by finishing early on one examination and late on another (Johnston, 1977).

Good interpretation

Time to completion from one examination to the next examination in a course would not always be consistent based upon several possible scenarios: students might change their test-taking strategies based upon their preparedness or lack of preparedness for an examination, students might find some examinations easier or more difficult than others in terms of reading or item difficulty, and students could become more distracted on some examinations. The strength of the consistency measures on achievement from one point-in-time to the next suggests that classroom achievement and examination performance are complex variables where a radical change in only test-taking tempo alone is not likely to result in improved achievement.

The lack of the relationship between time to completion and achievement (−.30 to +27) also closely matches the findings of other studies (Beaulieu & Frost, 1994; Bridges, 1985; Burack, 1967; Ebel, 1972; Foos; 1989; Freeman, 1923; Lester, 1991; Nevo & Spector, 1979; Terranova, 1972). Although this outcome has puzzled researchers for decades, the improved understanding of the personal tempo variable would seem to explain a good deal of the lack of a linear or nonlinear relationship between time to completion and examination achievement.

Right

The descriptive and correlational findings in this study argue against the analysis that "those students who are among the first to finish an objective exam are likely to get especially high or especially low scores" (Johnston, 1977, p. 149). The current findings also are at odds with the "speculation that perhaps there is a tendency for better students to finish early on tests" (Paul & Rosenkoetter, 1980, p. 109).

Interest in this field of study would seem to have been revitalized in the past decade-and-a-half with the publication of several studies in this area. Unfortunately, none of the five post-1980s studies even referenced the groundbreaking tempo work in this area published by Nevo and Spector (1979).

Good suggestion

The results of the current study argue for additional research in the areas of personal test tempo during examinations and personality trait variables that lead to tempo dispositions which are likely to extend across tasks. The mediating variables related to examination completion time would seem to include: information processing speed, reading ability, test anxiety, and personal strategies used during the test-taking situation.

SUMMARY

The accumulated evidence related to test takers who finish first, last, or somewhere in the middle compared to other test takers on a relatively untimed classroom examination seems to indicate indistinguishable levels of examination performance. This finding lends support for the conscious destruction of the myth that the rate of finishing such an examination is related to how well students will perform on these examinations. Teachers and students should become more aware of personal tempo as a consistent variable that is unrelated to examination performance in the classroom and strive to change ineffective test-taking behaviors while maintaining successful strategies. Teachers and test-takers must be informed that on relatively untimed examinations "students who see others turn in their examination papers early need not panic," because this order of finish "will probably not be related to how well they do" (Michael & Michael, 1969, p. 513).

We agree

Good suggestion

References

Beaulieu, R. P., & Frost, B. (1994). Another look at the time-score relationship. *Perceptual and Motor Skills, 78*(1):40–42.

Bridges, K. R. (1985). Test-completion speed: Its relationship to performance on three course-based objective examinations. *Educational and Psychological Measurement, 45:*29–35.

Burack, B. (1967). Relationship between course examination scores and time taken to finish the examination, revisited. *Psychological Reports, 20:*164.

Diederich, P. B. (1973). *Short-cut statistics for teacher-made tests.* Princeton, NJ: Educational Testing Service.

Ebel, R. L. (1972). *Essentials of educational measurement* (2nd ed.). Englewood Cliffs, NJ: Prentice-Hall.

Foos, P. W. (1989). Completion time and performance on multiple-choice and essay tests. *Bulletin of the Psychonomic Society, 27*(2):179–180.

Freeman, F. N. (1923). Note on the relation between speed and accuracy or quality of work. *Journal of Educational Research, 7:*87–89.

Johnston, J. J. (1977). Exam-taking speed and grades. *Teaching of Psychology, 4*(3):148–149.

Lester, D. (1991). Speed and performance on college course examinations. *Perceptual and Motor Skills, 73:*1090.

Michael, J. J., & Michael, W. B. (1969). The relationship of performance on objective achievement examinations to the order in which students complete them. *Educational and Psychological Measurement, 29:*511–513.

Mishima, J. (1951). Fundamental research on the constancy of mental tempo. Japanese *Journal of Psychology, 22:*12–28.

Nevo, B., & Spector, A. (1979). Personal tempo in taking tests of the multiple-choice type. *Journal of Educational Research, 73:*75–78.

Paul, C. A., & Rosenkoetter, J. S. (1980). The relationship between the time taken to complete an examination and the test score received. *Teaching of Psychology, 7*(2):108–109.

Rimoldi, N. J. A. (1951). Personal tempo. *Journal of Abnormal and Social Psychology, 46:*282–303.

Terranova, C. (1972). Relationship between test scores and test time. *Journal of Experimental Education, 40*(3):81–83.

Analysis of the Study

PURPOSE/JUSTIFICATION

The purpose is stated toward the end of the introduction: "to further investigate the taking of college-level examinations and the time needed to complete such examinations." While such "further study" purposes are commonly stated, we think a more focused purpose is desirable (e.g., "to investigate the relationship between test performance and personal test-taking style or tempo").

The study is justified in two ways. The first is practical, that is, to clarify student and teacher beliefs that are thought to be incorrect and potentially harmful. The second is the clarification of previous research that found no correlation between performance and time to complete an examination, which the author believes the concept of "tempo" may largely explain. An unstated assumption appears to be that student performance on course examinations is important to all concerned and that such examinations should not have lessened validity because of extraneous variables such as test-taking style of those taking the examination.

DEFINITIONS

The key variables are "achievement on multiple-choice examinations," "time to completion," and "personal tempo."

- Achievement on multiple-choice examinations is defined as "number of correct responses to 100 multiple-choice questions." In actuality, the definition should include the following addition: ". . . on midterm and final examinations in four psychology courses." This is an operational definition.
- Time to completion is defined operationally (say the authors) as "the time needed to complete a virtually untimed classroom examination." Technically, this is not an operational definition until the examinations are identified. We are unclear as to what is meant by the term "virtually untimed."
- Personal tempo is defined in a prior study (Nevo & Spector, 1979) as "time needed to complete the examination," but this is not the definition pertaining to this study. The implied definition is something like "speed of completion of untimed tasks that is consistent across tasks and over time."

PRIOR RESEARCH

The author appears to have reviewed all of the research since 1960 on this specific topic as well as at least some of the theoretical speculation. This review is well summarized and discussed.

HYPOTHESES

No hypotheses are explicitly stated, but two seem clearly implied:

- Low correlations will be found between examination scores and time to examination completion.
- Consistency will be found across examinations in "time to completion."

SAMPLE

The sample is a convenience sample of 130 students in four psychology classes at a suburban Catholic college. Demographics provided are helpful in judging generalizability. The statement that "the sample was determined to be representative of the college population" is almost certainly incorrect if it refers to the general college population. While it may be true with respect to this particular college, it cannot be based on the manner of sample selection and must rest on argumentation or descriptive data, neither of which is provided.

INSTRUMENTATION

The only actual instruments used were the midterm and final examinations. More description of them would be helpful—presumably they covered typical topics in the three psychology courses with a mix of recall and application items. Internal consistency reliability is adequate to good (.79 to .94). Stability from midterm to final (probably about two months) is good considering that the content covered would differ from midterm to final. Validity is not addressed, possibly because it is not considered crucial—that is, the relationship to time to completion can be studied regardless of what the examination actually measures. Generalization of results, however, is hampered by this lack of clarity. Because the "tempo" variable is based on the two "time to completion" scores, the effort to enhance validity by inconspicuous timing is commendable. Validity of this measurement rests primarily on its obvious content validity.

PROCEDURES/INTERNAL VALIDITY

Procedures are straightforward and adequately described (except for the "virtually untimed" feature, which probably means that time was called for a few late finishers). With respect to internal validity, the question is whether other variables could account for the low correlations between examination score and "time to completion." Interestingly, a subject characteristics threat, "personal tempo," is offered as the explanation for this result—that is, a student's preference for working fast or slow is unrelated to examination score. Data-collector characteristics could conceivably account for a substantial correlation (nasty demeanor lowers both examination score and time to completion), but not for such low correlations. Data-collector bias could exist if knowledge of "time to completion" affected examination scores, but these were presumably machine scored. Instrument decay and testing threats do not exist. The loss of four students in the midterm analysis is not enough to raise the possibility of a mortality threat.

With respect to the substantial correlations of "time to completion," midterm versus final, the question remains as to what other variables besides the postulated "personal tempo" might explain them.* It is possible to conjecture situational variables such as inferior lighting or "cheating opportunity" or "student dislike of instructor," which would be the same from midterm to final, but these seem far-fetched. Of more concern is the generality of this "trait" beyond the particular class. While the variation from .59 to .83 (see Table 1) may be sampling error, it may also reflect differences from class to class.

*Personal tempo might, of course, be itself explained by such variables as task anxiety, competitiveness or other personal characteristics, but these do not discount the interpretation—they refine it further.

DATA ANALYSIS

The reported correlations are appropriate; the author is to be commended for determining, from scatterplots, that no curvilinear relations (see text, pp. 217–218) were present. Results of significance tests are reported without the necessary qualifications resulting from the lack of random sampling. Differences among means are better interpreted by the use of Delta (see text, p. 256) than by highly questionable tests of statistical significance. Deltas computed from the data provided support for the conclusion of minor differences.

RESULTS AND DISCUSSION

Results are clearly and accurately presented. The inclusion of individual patterns adds clarity. Results are discussed in the light of other research. Appropriate speculation as to reasons for departure from "personal tempo" are given, although the results suggest that such departures are relatively rare. The implications for classroom teaching and for further research are clear and useful. The author should have discussed the limits on generalizability that are created by the use of a convenience sample, however, although these limits are partially offset (with respect to hypothesis #1 only) by similar findings from other studies—which is a kind of replication. Further, the author seems sometimes to overgeneralize the evidence for generality across tasks of the "personal tempo" characteristic. More discussion of the Mishima and the Rimoldi studies listed in the references would have helped, since it is unclear whether they examined consistency across tasks—that is, were those who were early finishers on one task also early finishers on others.

Go back to the **Interactive and Applied Learning Tools** feature at the beginning of the chapter for a listing of interactive and applied activities. Go to the **Online Learning Center** at www.mhhe.com/fraenkel5e or your **Interactive Student CD-ROM** to take practice quizzes and receive immediate feedback, practice with key terms, review chapter content and main ideas, and find annotated Web links.

Main Points

THE NATURE OF CORRELATIONAL RESEARCH

- The major characteristic of correlational research is seeking out associations among variables.

PURPOSES OF CORRELATIONAL RESEARCH

- Correlational studies are carried out either to help explain important human behaviors or to predict likely outcomes.
- If a relationship of sufficient magnitude exists between two variables, it becomes possible to predict a score on either variable if a score on the other variable is known.
- The variable that is used to make the prediction is called the predictor variable.
- The variable about which the prediction is made is called the criterion variable.
- Both scatterplots and regression lines are used in correlational studies to predict a score on a criterion variable.
- A predicted score is never exact. As a result, researchers calculate an index of prediction error, which is known as the "standard error of estimate."

COMPLEX CORRELATIONAL TECHNIQUES

- Multiple regression is a technique that enables a researcher to determine a correlation between a criterion variable and the best combination of two or more predictor variables.
- The coefficient of multiple correlation (R) indicates the strength of the correlation between the combination of the predictor variables and the criterion variable.
- The value of a prediction equation depends on whether it predicts successfully with a new group of individuals.
- When the criterion variable is categorical rather than quantitative, discriminant function analysis (rather than multiple regression) must be used.
- Factor analysis is a technique that allows a researcher to determine whether many variables can be described by a few factors.
- Path analysis is a technique used to test a theory about the causal connections among three or more variables.

BASIC STEPS IN CORRELATIONAL RESEARCH

- These include, as in most research, selecting a problem, choosing a sample, selecting or developing instruments, determining procedures, collecting and analyzing data, and interpreting results.

CORRELATION COEFFICIENTS AND THEIR MEANING

- The meaning of a given correlation coefficient depends on how it is applied.
- Correlation coefficients below .35 show only a slight relationship between variables.

- Correlations between .40 and .60 may have theoretical and/or practical value depending on the context.
- Only when a correlation of .65 or higher is obtained can reasonably accurate predictions be made.
- Correlations over .85 indicate a very strong relationship between the variables correlated.

EVALUATING THREATS TO INTERNAL VALIDITY IN CORRELATIONAL RESEARCH

- Threats to the internal validity of correlational studies include subject characteristics, location, instrument decay, data collection, and testing.
- Results of correlational studies must always be interpreted with caution, because they may suggest, but they cannot establish, causation.

Key Terms

Coefficient of determination 342

Coefficient of multiple correlation 342

Correlation coefficient 346

Correlational research 338

Criterion variable 340

Discriminant function analysis 342

Explanatory studies 339

Factor analysis 343

Multiple regression 341

Partial correlation 348

Path analysis 343

Prediction 340

Prediction equation 341

Prediction studies 340

Predictor variable 340

Regression line 340

For Discussion

1. Which type of relationship would a researcher be more pleased to have the results of a study reveal—positive or negative—or would it matter? Explain.
2. What is the difference between an effect and a relationship? Which is more important, or can this be determined?
3. Are there any types of instruments that could *not* be used in a correlational study? If so, why?
4. Would it be possible for a correlation to be statistically significant, yet educationally insignificant? If so, give an example.
5. Why do you suppose people often interpret correlational results as proving causation?
6. What is the difference, if any, between the *sign* of a correlation and the *strength* of a correlation?
7. "Correlational studies, in and of themselves, do not establish cause and effect." Is this true? Why or why not?
8. "The possibility of causation (in a correlational study) is strengthened if a time lapse occurs between measurement of the variables being studied." Why?
9. To interpret correlation coefficients sensibly, it is a good idea to show the scatterplots on which they are based. Why is this? Explain.

Notes

1. K. G. Joreskog and D. Sorbom (1988). LISREL VII. Analysis of linear structural relationships by maximum likelihood and least squares methods: Statistical package for the social sciences. New York: McGraw-Hill.

2. D. M. Medley and H. Coker (1987). The accuracy of principals' judgments of teacher performance. *Journal of Educational Research, 80*(4):242–247.

3. C. V. Hines, D. R. Cruickshank, and J. J. Kennedy (1985). Teacher clarity and its relationship to student achievement and satisfaction. *American Educational Research Journal, 22*(1):87–100.

4. L. D. Ried, O. B. Martinson, and L. C. Weaver (1987). Factors associated with the drug use of fifth-through eighth-grade students. *Journal of Drug Education, 17*(2):149–161.

5. J. T. Bowman and T. G. Reeves (1987). Moral development and empathy in counseling. *Counselor Education and Supervision, 6:*293–297.

6. N. Brown, A. Muhlenkamp, L. Fox, and M. Osborn (1983). The relationship among health beliefs, health values, and health promotion activity. *Western Journal of Nursing Research, 5*(2):155–163.

7. S. R. Swing and P. L. Peterson (1982). The relationship of student ability and small-group interaction to student achievement. *American Educational Research Journal, 19*(2):259–274.

8. B. J. Fraser and D. L. Fisher (1982). Predicting students' outcomes from their perceptions of classroom psychosocial environment. *American Educational Research Journal, 19*(4):498–518.

9. D. E. Hinkle, W. Wiersma, and S. G. Jurs (1981). *Applied statistics for the behavioral sciences.* Chicago: Rand McNally.

Causal–Comparative Research

CHAPTER 16

Is there a difference between natural grass and Astro-turf?

Causal-Comparative Research

What Is Causal-Comparative Research?

Similarities and Differences
Between Causal-Comparitive
and Correlational Research
Similarities and Differences
Between Causal-Comparitive
and Experimental Research

Associations Between Categorical Variables

Steps Involved in Causal-Comparative Research

Problem Formulation
Sample
Instrumentation
Design

Data Analysis

Threats to Internal Validity in Causal-Comparative Research

Subject Characteristics
Other Threats

Evaluating Threats to Internal Validity in Causal-Comparative Studies

Objectives

Studying this chapter should enable you to:

- Explain *what is meant by the term "causal-comparative research."*
- Describe *briefly how causal-comparative research is both similar to, yet different from, both correlational and experimental research.*
- Identify *and describe briefly the steps involved in conducting a causal-comparative study.*
- Draw *a diagram of a design for a causal-comparative study.*
- Describe *how data are collected in causal-comparative research.*
- Describe *some of the threats to internal validity that exist in causal-comparative studies and* discuss *how to control for these threats.*
- Recognize *a causal-comparative study when you come across one in the educational research literature.*

Interactive and Applied Learning

After, or while, reading this chapter:

Go to your Interactive Student CD-ROM to:
- Learn More About Important Causal-Comparative Research

Go to your Interactive Student CD-ROM or Student Workbook to do the following activities:
- Activity 16.1: Causal-Comparative Research Questions
- Activity 16.2: Analyze Some Causal-Comparative Data

oseph Perea has just completed his first year of teaching chemistry in a small high school in rural Idaho. His method of teaching involved primarily lecturing to his students. At the end of the year faculty party, he is discussing the year with Mary Roberts, one of the other teachers in the school.

"Ah, Mary, I'm a bit discouraged. Things did not turn out the way I had hoped."

"How come?"

"A lot of my students didn't seem to like my teaching very much. And they didn't do well on the final exam that I gave."

"You know, Joe, Bruce (Bruce Washington, who taught chemistry last year) used some 'inquiry science' materials. I remember him saying that his students really liked them. Maybe you should try them next term."

"I wonder whether his approach would work for me?"

An appropriate method for this kind of question is a *causal-comparative* study. What that involves is what this chapter is about.

What Is Causal-Comparative Research?

In causal-comparative research, investigators attempt to determine the cause *or* consequences of differences that *already exist* between or among groups of individuals. As a result, it is sometimes viewed, along with correlational research, as a form of associational research, since both describe conditions that already exist. A researcher might observe, for example, that two groups of individuals differ on some variable (such as teaching style) and then attempt to determine the *reason* for, or the *results* of, this difference. The difference between the groups, however, has *already occurred.* Because both the effect(s) and the alleged cause(s) have already occurred, and hence are studied in retrospect, causal-comparative research is also referred to sometimes as ex post facto (from the Latin for "after the fact") research. This is in contrast to an experimental study, in which a researcher *creates* a difference between or among groups and then compares their performance (on one or more dependent variables) to determine the effects of the created difference.

The group difference variable in a causal-comparative study is either a variable that cannot be manipulated (such as ethnicity) or one that might have been manipulated but for one reason or another has not been (such as teaching style). Sometimes, ethical constraints prevent a variable from being manipulated, thus preventing the effects of variations in the variable from being examined by means of an experimental study. A researcher might be interested, for example, in the effects of a new diet on very young children. Ethical considerations, however, might prevent the researcher from

deliberately varying the diet to which the children are exposed. Causal-comparative research, however, would allow the researcher to study the effects of the diet if he or she could find a group of children who have *already been exposed* to the diet. The researcher could then compare them with a similar group of children who had not been exposed to the diet. Much of the research in medicine and sociology is causal-comparative in nature.

Another example is the comparison of scientists and engineers in terms of their originality. As in correlational research, explanations or predictions can be made from either variable to the other: originality could be predicted from group membership, or group membership could be predicted from originality. However, most such studies attempt to explore causation rather than to foster prediction. Are "original" individuals more likely to become scientists? Do scientists become more original as they become immersed in their work? And so forth. Notice that if it were possible, a correlational study might be preferable, but that it is not appropriate when one of the variables (in this case, the nature of the groups) is a categorical variable.

Following are some examples of different types of causal-comparative research.

Type 1: Exploration of *effects* (dependent variable) caused by membership in a given group
Question: What differences in abilities are caused by gender?
Research hypothesis: Females have a greater amount of linguistic ability than males.

Type 2: Exploration of *causes* (independent variable) of group membership
Question: What causes individuals to join a gang?

Research hypothesis: Individuals who are members of gangs have more aggressive personalities than individuals who are not members of gangs.

Type 3: Exploration of the *consequences* (dependent variable) of an intervention

Question: How do students taught by the inquiry method react to propaganda?

Research hypothesis: Students who were taught by the inquiry method are more critical of propaganda than are those who were taught by the lecture method.

Causal-comparative studies have been used frequently to study the differences between males and females. They have demonstrated the superiority of girls in language and of boys in math at certain age levels. The attributing of these differences to gender—as cause—must be tentative. One could hardly view "gender" as being caused by ability, but there are many other probable links in the causal chain, including societal expectations of males and females.

The basic causal-comparative approach, therefore, is to begin with a noted difference between two groups and to look for possible causes for, or consequences of, this difference. A researcher might be interested, for example, in the reason(s) why some individuals become addicted to alcohol while others develop a dependence on pills. How can this be explained? Descriptions of the two groups (alcoholics and pill poppers) might be compared to see if their characteristics differ in ways that might account for the difference in choice of drug.

Sometimes causal-comparative studies are conducted solely as an alternative to experiments. Suppose, for example, that the curriculum director in a large, urban high school district is considering implementing a new English curriculum. The director might try the curriculum out experimentally, selecting a few classes at random throughout the district, and compare student performance in these classes with comparison groups who continue to experience the regular curriculum. This might take a considerable amount of time, however, and be quite costly in terms of materials, teacher preparation workshops, and so on. As an alternative, the director might consider a causal-comparative study and compare the achievement of students in school districts that are currently using this curriculum with the achievement of students in similar districts that do not use the new curriculum. If the results show that students in districts (similar to his) with the new curriculum are

achieving higher scores in English, the director would have a basis for going ahead and implementing the new curriculum in his district. Like correlational studies, causal-comparative investigations often identify relationships that later are studied experimentally.

Despite their advantages, however, causal-comparative studies do have serious limitations. The most serious lie in the lack of control over threats to internal validity. Because the manipulation of the independent variable has already occurred, many of the controls we discussed in Chapter Thirteen cannot be applied. Thus, considerable caution must be expressed in interpreting the outcomes of a causal-comparative study. As with correlational studies, relationships can be identified, but causation cannot be fully established. As we have pointed out before, the alleged cause may really be an effect, the effect may be a cause, or there may be a third variable that produced both the alleged cause and effect.

SIMILARITIES AND DIFFERENCES BETWEEN CAUSAL-COMPARATIVE AND CORRELATIONAL RESEARCH

Causal-comparative research is sometimes confused with correlational research. Although similarities do exist, there are notable differences.

Similarities. Both causal-comparative and correlational studies are examples of associational research—that is, researchers who conduct them seek to explore relationships among variables. Both attempt to explain phenomena of interest. Both seek to identify variables that are worthy of later exploration through experimental research, and both often provide guidance for subsequent experimental studies. Neither permits the manipulation of variables by the researcher, however. Both attempt to explore causation, but, in both cases, causation must be argued; the methodology alone does not permit causal statements.

Differences. Causal-comparative studies typically compare two or more groups of subjects, while correlational studies require a score on each variable for each subject. Correlational studies investigate two (or more) quantitative variables, whereas causal-comparative studies typically involve at least one categorical variable (group membership). Correlational studies often analyze data using scatterplots and/or correlation

How Should Research Methodologies Be Classified?

Opinions differ as to how the different types of research methodology should be classified. No single system for classifying research methods has been widely accepted. To be sure, clear distinctions have been drawn between experimental and nonexperimental methods and between group-comparison and single-subject forms of experimental research. However, different authors use different categories to describe nonexperimental research, with the most common being the ones we use in this text (correlational, causal-comparative, and survey). These categories, however, are mostly a matter of convenience and custom rather than reflecting essential differences. Correlational and causal-comparative methods differ largely in the nature of the variables investigated (quantitative versus categorical) and the methods of data analysis. Survey research differs from the other two primarily in its purpose. We must admit that such a system is not very satisfying.

Recently, Johnson has proposed a new means of classification.* He suggests using a combination of *purpose* (descriptive, predictive, or explanatory) and *time frame* (retrospective, cross-sectional or longitudinal) to identify different methods. Such combinations produce a total of nine different types. While we would agree that his typology is logically more consistent, we do not find it useful nor appropriate for an introductory text. Why? Because the steps involved in correlational, causal-comparative, and survey research are quite different, and we believe strongly that students need to learn these steps. We see no reason to increase the complexity involved in doing so. We also note that a fairly recent survey of teachers of educational research showed that 80 percent favored retaining the correlational versus causal-comparative distinction, apparently finding it useful despite its deficiencies.[†]

*B. Johnson (2001). Towards a new classification of nonexperimental quantitative research. *Educational Researcher, 30*(2): 3–13.
[†]Allyn and Bacon (1996). *Research methods survey.* Boston: Allyn & Bacon.

---

coefficients, while causal-comparative studies often compare averages or use crossbreak tables.

SIMILARITIES AND DIFFERENCES BETWEEN CAUSAL-COMPARATIVE AND EXPERIMENTAL RESEARCH

Similarities. Both causal-comparative and experimental studies typically require at least one categorical variable (group membership). Both compare group performances (average scores) to determine relationships. Both typically compare separate groups of subjects.*

Differences. In experimental research, the independent variable is manipulated; in causal-comparative research, no manipulation takes place. Causal-comparative studies are likely to provide much weaker evidence for causation than do experimental studies. In experimental research, the researcher can sometimes assign subjects to treatment groups; in causal-comparative research, the groups are already formed—the researcher must locate them. In experimental studies, the researcher has much greater flexibility in formulating the structure of the design.

Steps Involved in Causal-Comparative Research

PROBLEM FORMULATION

The first step in formulating a problem in causal-comparative research is usually to identify and define the particular phenomena of interest and then to consider possible causes for, or consequences of, these phenomena. Suppose, for example, that a researcher is interested in student creativity. What causes creativity? Why are a few students highly creative while most are not? Why do some students who initially appear to be creative seem to lose this characteristic? Why do others who at one time are not creative later become so? And so forth.

The researcher speculates, for example, that high-level creativity might be caused by a combination of social failure, on the one hand, and personal recognition

*Except in counterbalanced, time-series, or single-subject experimental designs (see Chapters Thirteen and Fourteen).

for artistic or scientific achievement, on the other. The researcher also identifies a number of alternative hypotheses that might account for a difference between highly creative and noncreative students. Both the quantity and quality of a student's interests, for example, might account for differences in creativity. Highly creative students might tend to have many diverse interests. Parental encouragement to explore ideas might also account partly for creativity, as might some types of intellectual skills.

Once possible causes of the phenomena have been identified, they are (usually) incorporated into a more precise statement of the research problem the researcher wishes to investigate. In this instance, the researcher might state the objective of his research as "to examine possible differences between students of high and low creativity." Note that differences in a number of variables can be investigated in a causal-comparative study in order to determine which variable (or combination of variables) seems most likely to cause the phenomena (creativity, in this case) being studied. This testing of several alternative hypotheses is a basic characteristic of good causal-comparative research, and whenever possible should be the basis for identifying the variables on which the comparison groups are to be contrasted. This provides a rational basis for selection of the variables to be investigated, rather than relying on what is often called the "shotgun" approach, in which a large number of measures are administered simply because they seem interesting or are available. They also serve to remind the researcher that the findings of a causal-comparative study are open to a variety of causal explanations.

SAMPLE

Once the researcher has formulated the problem statement (and hypotheses, if any) the next step is to select the sample of individuals to be studied. The important thing here is to define carefully the characteristic to be studied and then to select groups that differ in this characteristic. In the above example, this means defining as clearly as possible the term "creativity." If possible, operational definitions should be employed. A highly creative student might be defined, for example, as one who "has developed an award-winning scientific or artistic product."

The researcher also needs to think about whether the group obtained using the operational definition is likely to be reasonably homogeneous in terms of factors causing creativity. For example, are students who are creative in science similar to students who are creative in art with respect to causation? This is a very important question to ask. If creativity has different "causes" in different fields, the search for causation is only confused by combining students from such fields. Do ethnic, age, or gender differences produce differences in creativity? The success of a causal-comparative study depends in large degree on how carefully the comparison groups are defined.

It is very important to select groups that are homogeneous with regard to at least some important variables. For example, if the researcher assumes that the same causes are operating for all creative students, regardless of gender, ethnicity, or age, he or she may find no differences between comparison groups simply because too many other variables are involved. If all creative students are treated as a homogeneous group, no differences may be found between highly creative and noncreative students, whereas if only creative and noncreative female art students were compared, differences might be found.

Once the defined groups have been selected, they can be matched on one or more variables. This process of matching controls certain variables, thereby eliminating any group differences on these variables. This is desirable in type 1 and type 3 studies (see pp. 368–369) since the researcher wants the groups as similar as possible in order to explain differences on the dependent variable(s) as being due to group membership. Matching is not as appropriate in type 2 studies, because the researcher presumably knows little about the extraneous variables that might be related to group differences and as a result cannot match on them.

INSTRUMENTATION

There are no limits on the types of instruments that may be used in causal-comparative studies. Achievement tests, questionnaires, interview schedules, attitudinal measures, observational devices—any of the devices discussed in Chapter Seven can be used.

DESIGN

The basic causal-comparative design involves selecting two or more groups that differ on a particular variable of interest and comparing them on another variable or variables. No manipulation is involved. The groups differ in one of two ways: One group either possesses a characteristic (often called a criterion) that the other does not, or the groups differ on known characteristics. These two variations of the same basic design (sometimes called a criterion-group design) are as follows:

The Basic Causal-Comparative Designs

	Group	Independent variable	Dependent variable
(a)	I	C (Group possesses characteristic)	O (Measurement)
	II	$-C$ (Group does not possess characteristic)	O (Measurement)
(b)	I	C_1 (Group possesses characteristic 1)	O (Measurement)
	II	C_2 (Group possesses characteristic 2)	O (Measurement)

The letter C is used in this design to represent the presence of the characteristic. The dashed line is used to show that intact groups are being compared. Examples of these causal-comparative designs are presented in Figure 16.1.

Threats to Internal Validity in Causal-Comparative Research

Two weaknesses in causal-comparative research are lack of randomization and inability to manipulate an independent variable. As we have mentioned, random assignment of subjects to groups is not possible in causal-comparative research since the groups are already formed. Manipulation of the independent variable is not possible because the groups have already been exposed to the independent variable.

SUBJECT CHARACTERISTICS

The major threat to the internal validity of a causal-comparative study is the possibility of a subject characteristics threat. Because the researcher has had no say in either the selection or formation of the comparison groups, there is always the likelihood that the groups are not equivalent on one or more important variables other than the identified group membership variable (Figure 16.2). A group of girls, for example, might be older than a comparison group of boys.

There are a number of procedures that a researcher can use to reduce the chance of a subject characteristics threat in a causal-comparative study. Many of these are also used in experimental research (see Chapter Thirteen).

Matching of Subjects. One way to control for an extraneous variable is to match subjects from the comparison groups on that variable. In other words, pairs of subjects, one from each group, are found that are similar on that variable. Students might be matched on GPA, for example, in a study of attitudes. Individuals with similar GPAs would be matched. If a match cannot be found for a particular subject, he or she is then eliminated from the study. As you have probably realized, the problem with matching is often that just this happens—matches cannot be found for many subjects, and hence the size of the sample involved is accordingly reduced. Matching becomes even more difficult when the researcher tries to match on two or more variables.

(a)	Group	Independent variable	Dependent variable
	I	C Dropouts	O Level of self-esteem
	II	$(-C)$ Nondropouts	O Level of self-esteem

(b)	Group	Independent variable	Dependent variable
	I	C_1 Counselors	O Amount of job satisfaction
	II	C_2 Teachers	O Amount of job satisfaction

Figure 16.1 *Examples of the Basic Causal-Comparative Design*

Figure 16.2 *A Subject Characteristics Threat*

Finding or Creating Homogeneous Subgroups. Another way to control for an extraneous variable is either to find, or restrict one's comparison to, groups that are relatively homogeneous on that variable. In the attitude study, the researcher could either seek to find two groups that have similar GPAs (say, all 3.5 GPA or above) or form subgroups that represent various levels of the extraneous variable (divide the groups into high, middle, and low GPA subgroups, for example), and then compare the comparable subgroups (low GPA subgroup with the other low GPA subgroup, and so on).

Statistical Matching. The third way to control for an important extraneous variable is to match the groups on that variable, using the technique of statistical matching. As described in Chapter Thirteen, statistical matching adjusts scores on a posttest for initial differences on some other variable that is assumed to be related to performance on the dependent variable.

OTHER THREATS

The likelihood of the remaining threats to internal validity depends on the type of study being considered. In nonintervention studies, the main additional concerns are loss of subjects, location, instrumentation, and sometimes history and maturation. If the persons who are lost to data collection are different from those who remain (as is often probable), *and* if more are lost from one group than the other(s), internal validity is threatened. If unequal numbers are lost, an effort should be made to determine the probable reasons.

A *location* threat is possible if the data are collected under different conditions for different groups. Similarly, if different data collectors are used with different groups, an *instrumentation* threat is introduced. Fortunately, it is usually relatively easy to ensure that variations in location and data collectors do not exist.

The possibility of a *data-collector bias* can usually be controlled, as in experimental studies, by ensuring that whoever collects the data lacks any information that might bias results. *Instrument decay* may occur in observational studies, and with repeated administration of the same test to the same group(s). It can be controlled as in experimental studies.

In intervention-type studies, in addition to the threats just discussed, all of the remaining threats that we discussed in Chapter Thirteen may be present. Unfortunately, most are harder to control in causal-comparative studies than in experimental research. The fact that the researcher does not directly manipulate the treatment variable makes it more likely that a *history* threat may exist. It may also mean that the length of the treatment time may have varied, thus creating a possible *maturation* threat. An *attitude* threat is less likely because nothing "special" is introduced. *Regression* may be a threat if one of the groups was initially selected on the basis of extreme scores. Finally, a *pretest/treatment interaction* effect, as in experimental studies, may exist if a pretest was used in the study. As we mentioned in Chapter 13 (see pp. 287–288), we think both experimental and causal-comparative intervention studies are useful.

Evaluating Threats to Internal Validity in Causal-Comparative Studies

The evaluation of specific threats to internal validity in causal-comparative studies involves a set of steps similar to those presented in Chapter Thirteen for experimental studies.

> *Step 1:* Ask: What specific factors either are known to affect the variable on which groups are being compared, or may logically be expected to affect this variable? Note that this is the dependent variable for type 1 and type 3 studies (pp. 368–369), but the independent variable for type 2 studies. As we mentioned with regard to experimental studies, the researcher need not be concerned with factors unrelated to what is being studied.
>
> *Step 2:* Ask: What is the likelihood of the comparison groups differing on each of these factors? (Remember that a difference between groups *cannot* be explained away by a factor that is the same for all groups.)
>
> *Step 3:* Evaluate the threats on the basis of how likely they are to have an effect and plan to control for them. If a given threat cannot be controlled, this should be acknowledged.

Again, let us consider an example to illustrate how these steps might be employed. Suppose a researcher wishes to explore possible causes of students "dropping out" in inner-city high schools. He or she hypothesizes three possible causes: (1) family instability, (2) low student self-esteem, and (3) lack of a support system related to school and its requirements. The researcher compiles a list of recent dropouts and randomly selects a comparison group of students still in school. He or she then interviews students in both groups to obtain data on each of the three possible causal variables.

As we did in Chapters Thirteen and Fifteen, we list below a number of the threats to internal validity discussed in Chapter Nine, followed by our evaluation of each as they might apply to this study.

Subject Characteristics. Although there are many possible subject characteristics that might be considered, we deal with only four here—socioeconomic level of the family, gender, ethnicity, and marketable job skills.

1. **Socioeconomic level of the family.** *Step 1:* Socioeconomic level may be related to all three of the hypothesized causal variables. *Step 2:* Socioeconomic level can be expected to be related to dropping out versus staying in school. It should therefore be controlled by some form of matching. *Step 3:* Likelihood of having an effect unless controlled: high.

2. **Gender.** *Step 1:* Gender may also be related to each of the three hypothesized causal variables. *Step 2:* It may well be related to dropping out. Accordingly, the researcher should either restrict this study only to males or females or ensure that the comparison group has the same gender proportions as the dropout group.* *Step 3:* Likelihood of having an effect unless controlled: high.

3. **Ethnicity.** *Step 1:* Ethnicity may also be related to all three of the hypothesized causal variables. *Step 2:* It may be related to dropping out. Therefore, the two groups should be matched with respect to ethnicity. *Step 3:* Likelihood of having an effect unless controlled: moderate to high.

4. **Marketable job skills.** *Step 1:* Job skills may be related to each of the three hypothesized causal variables. *Step 2:* They are likely to be related to dropping out, since students often drop out if they are able to make money working. It would be desirable, therefore, to assess job skills and then control by some form of matching. *Step 3:* Likelihood of having an effect unless controlled: moderate to high.

Mortality. *Step 1:* It is probable that refusing to be interviewed is related to each of the three hypothesized causal variables. *Step 2:* It is also probable that more students in the dropout group will refuse to be interviewed (since they may be working, it may be harder to arrange time for an interview) than will students in the comparison group. The only solution would be to make every effort to get cooperation for the interviews from all subjects in both groups. *Step 3:* Likelihood of having an effect unless controlled: high.

---

*This is an example of stratifying a sample—in this case, the comparison group.

Location. *Step 1:* While it seems unlikely that the causal variables would differ for different schools, this might be the case. *Step 2:* It is quite likely that location (that is, the specific high schools involved in the study) is related to dropping out. (Dropout rates typically differ in different schools.) The best solution is to analyze the data separately for each school. *Step 3:* Likelihood of having an effect unless controlled: moderate.

Instrumentation.

1. **Instrument decay.** *Step 1:* Instrument decay in this study means interviewer fatigue. This certainly could affect the information obtained from students in both groups. *Step 2:* The fatigue factor could be different for the two groups, depending on how interviews are scheduled; the solution is to try to schedule interviews to prevent fatigue from occurring. *Step 3:* Likelihood of having an effect unless controlled: moderate.
2. **Data-collector characteristics.** *Step 1:* Can be expected to influence the information obtained on the three hypothesized causal variables; for this reason, training of interviewers to standardize the interview process is very important. *Step 2:* Despite such training, different interviewers might elicit different information. Therefore, interviewers should be balanced across the two groups, that is, each interviewer should be scheduled to do the same number of interviews with each group. *Step 3:* Likelihood of having an effect unless controlled: moderate.
3. **Data-collector bias.** *Step 1:* Bias might well be related to information obtained on the three hypothesized causal variables. *Step 2:* Might differ for the two groups, for example, interviewer might behave differently when interviewing dropouts. The solution is to keep interviewers ignorant as to which group subjects belong to. To do this, care has to be taken both with questions to be asked and in training interviewers. *Step 3:* Likelihood of having an effect unless controlled: high.

Other Threats. Implementation, history, maturation, attitudinal, and regression threats do not affect this kind (type 2) of causal-comparative study.

The trick to identifying threats to internal validity in causal-comparative studies (as in experimental studies) is, first, to think of various things (conditions, other variables, and so on) that might affect the outcome variable of the study. Then, second, to decide, based on evidence or experience, whether these things would be likely to affect the comparison groups differently. If so, this may provide an alternative explanation for the results. If this seems likely, a threat to internal validity of the study may indeed be present and needs to be controlled. Many of these threats can be greatly reduced if causal-comparative studies are replicated. Figure 16.3 summarizes the process of evaluating the presence of threats to internal validity.

Data Analysis

The first step in analyzing data in a causal-comparative study is to construct frequency polygons and then calculate the mean and standard deviation of each group if the variable is quantitative. These descriptive statistics are then assessed for magnitude (see Chapter Twelve). A statistical inference test may or may not be appropriate, depending on whether random samples were used from identified populations (such as creative versus noncreative high school seniors). The most commonly used test in causal-comparative studies is a *t*-test for differences between means. When more than two groups are used, then either an analysis of variance or an analysis of covariance is the appropriate test. Analysis of covariance is particularly helpful in causal-comparative research because a researcher cannot always match the comparison groups on all relevant variables other than the ones of primary interest. As mentioned in Chapter Eleven, analysis of covariance provides a way to match groups "after the fact" on such variables as age, socioeconomic status, aptitude, and so on. Before analysis of covariance can be used, however, the data involved need to satisfy certain assumptions.[1]

The results of a causal-comparative study must be interpreted with caution. As with correlational studies, causal-comparative studies are good at identifying relationships between variables, but they do not prove cause and effect.

There are two ways to strengthen the interpretability of causal-comparative studies. First, as we mentioned earlier, alternative hypotheses should be formulated and investigated whenever possible. Second, if the dependent variables involved are categorical, the relationships among all of the variables in the study should be examined using the technique of discriminant function analysis, which we briefly described in Chapter Fifteen.

The most powerful way to check on the possible causes identified in a causal-comparative study, of course, is to perform an experiment. The presumed cause (or causes) identified can sometimes be manipulated. Should

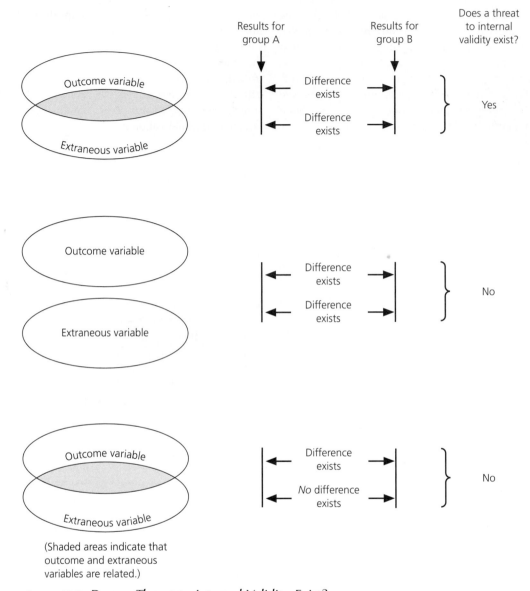

(Shaded areas indicate that outcome and extraneous variables are related.)

Figure 16.3 *Does a Threat to Internal Validity Exist?*

differences between experimental and control groups now be found, the researcher then has a much better reason for inferring causation.

Associations Between Categorical Variables

Up to this point our discussion of associational methods has considered only the situations in which (1) one variable is categorical and the other(s) is quantitative (causal-comparative); and (2) both variables are quantitative (correlational). It is also possible to investigate associations between categorical variables. Both crossbreak tables (see Chapter Ten) and contingency coefficients are used. An example of a relationship between categorical variables is shown in Table 16.1.

As was true with correlation, such data can be used for purposes of prediction and, with caution, in the search for cause and effect. Knowing that a person is a teacher, and male, for example, we can predict, with some degree of confidence (on the basis of the data in Table 16.1), that he teaches either junior or senior high

Significant Findings in Causal-Comparative Research

A widely cited causal-comparative study was conducted by two researchers in the 1940s.* They compared two groups of 500 boys, one group identified as juvenile delinquents based on their having been institutionalized (7 months on average), and a second group not so identified. Both groups were from the same "high-risk" area of Boston. Pairs of boys, one from each group, were matched on ethnicity, IQ, and age.

The major differences they found between the groups were that the boys in the delinquent group had more solid muscular bodies, were more energetic and extroverted, were more unconventional and defiant, were less methodical and abstract, and came from less cohesive, less affectionate families. Combining these characteristics resulted in a table for predicting probable delinquency that has received considerable validation in other settings over the years.† Nonetheless, argument continues as to the nature of cause and effect and as to the desirability of using such predictive information. It could be used either for benevolent intervention (as envisioned by the researchers who did the original study) or to stigmatize and coerce.

*S. Gluek and E. Gluek (1950). *Unraveling juvenile delinquency.* Cambridge, MA: Harvard University Press.

†S. Gluek and E. Gluek (1974). *Of delinquency and crime.* Springfield, IL: C. Thomas.

---

school, since 76 percent of males who are teachers do so. We can also estimate how much in error our prediction is likely to be. Based on the data in Table 16.1, the probability of our prediction being in error is 40/170, or .24. In this example, the possibility that gender is a major *cause* of teaching level seems quite remote—there are other variables, such as historical patterns of teacher preparation and hiring, that make more sense when one tries to explain the relationship.

There are no techniques analogous to partial correlation (see Chapter Fifteen) or the other techniques that have evolved from correlational research that can be used with categorical variables. Further, prediction from crossbreak tables is much less precise than from scatterplots. Fortunately, there are relatively few questions of interest in education that involve two categorical variables. It is common, however, to find a researcher treating variables that are conceptually quantitative (and measured accordingly) as if they were categorical. For example, a researcher arbitrarily may divide a set of quantitative scores into high, middle, and low groups. Nothing is gained by this procedure and it suffers from two serious defects: the loss of the precision that is acquired through the use of correlational techniques, and the essential arbitrariness of the division into groups. How does one decide which score separates "high" scores from "middle" scores, for example? In general, therefore, such arbitrary division should be avoided.*

An Example of Causal-Comparative Research

In the remainder of this chapter, we present a published example of causal-comparative research, followed by a critique of its strengths and weaknesses. As we did in our critiques of the different types of research studies we analyzed in other chapters, we use concepts introduced in earlier parts of the book in our analysis.

Table 16.1 *Grade Level and Gender of Teachers (Hypothetical Data)*

Grade Level	Males	Females	Total
Elementary	40	70	110
Junior High	50	40	90
Senior High	80	60	140
Total	170	170	340

*There are times when a quantitative variable is justifiably treated as a categorical variable. For example, creativity is generally considered to be a quantitative variable. One might, however, establish criteria for dividing this continuum into only two categories—"highly creative" and "typically creative"—as a way of studying relationships with other variables more efficiently, as was done in our earlier example.

Professional School Counseling, 4:2 (December 2000): 86–94.

Personal, Social, and Family Characteristics of Angry Students

Dale Fryxell, Ph.D.
Chaminade University, Honolulu, HI.

Douglas C. Smith, Ph.D.
University of Hawaii, Honolulu.

Amid growing public concern about youth violence in school settings, school and mental health counselors are increasingly being asked to play a leadership role in establishing policies with regard to violence prevention and school safety. Although school violence is a complex issue with multiple causal pathways, one potentially important variable is the high degree of anger and hostility existing among some students today. Anger-related problems are among the most common reasons for referral to school counselors (Smith & Furlong, 1994). Interest in anger and hostility as precursors of aggressive behavior can be seen in the growing number of anger management programs currently operating within school settings (Larson, 1994; Smith, Larson, DeBaryshe, & Salzman, 2000).

Justification and prior research

Children identified as manifesting high levels of anger and hostility at school appear to be at risk for a number of behavioral, social, academic, and physical concerns (Smith & Furlong, 1994). Longitudinal research suggests that angry, aggressive children are likely to grow up to be angry, aggressive adults (Elliot, Huizinga, & Ageton, 1985; Kazdin, 1987; Olweus, 1979). Thus, it is important to identify children manifesting anger-related problems early and to provide appropriate interventions. With regard to specific outcomes for children and adolescents, the few studies available suggest that high levels of anger and hostility are associated with poorer academic performance (Smith, Adelman, Nelson, Taylor, & Phares, 1987; Smith, Furlong, Bates, & Laughlin, 1998) and with a wide range of social and behavioral difficulties both in and out of school (Lochman, White, & Wayland, 1991; Smith et al., 1998). Deffenbacher and colleagues (Deffenbacher, Lynch, Oetting, & Kemper, 1996; Liebsohn, Oetting, & Deffenbacher, 1994) have provided some promising directions for future research with initial findings linking high levels of anger in youth to increased risk for substance abuse, delinquency, interpersonal difficulties, vocational and school-related problems, and other maladaptive behaviors.

In examining causal influences on anger, hostility, and aggression in children, Greenberg, Speltz, and DeKlyen (1993) proposed a four-factor model that includes family stressors, parent discipline styles, attachment relationships, and within-child characteristics such as individual temperaments. Tolan, Guerra, and Kendall (1995) suggested that researchers consider multiple developmental-ecological pathways to children's antisocial behavior. These might include both individual and interpersonal characteristics as well as contextual variables, including specific cultural and community contexts. In most cases, it appears that such factors mutually influence children's behavior. For example, Patterson and colleagues (Patterson, 1982; Patterson, DeBaryshe, & Ramsey, 1989; Reid & Patterson, 1991) suggested that individual temperament and dispositions with regard to anger and aggression are shaped and modified through interactions both within and outside the family. Specifically, early coercive family interactions serve as models of aggressive behaviors, and children are themselves reinforced for such behaviors by avoidance of negative stimuli. Degrees of nurturance and family support are also critical determinants of children's social and emotional development (Reid & Patterson, 1991).

Personal factors include personality traits, disposition, reactivity, and temperament. In terms of anger and hostility, these factors might include a propensity to react intensely to perceived transgressions. It might also include such social-cognitive processes as causal attributions, which assess intentionality on the part of others. Previous research indicates that aggressive children frequently attribute intentionality to negative actions by peers, thereby justifying aggressive retaliation (Dodge, 1991).

Prior research

School factors include not only the immediate physical environment, size of school, and general school climate, but also such variables as attitudes of teachers and administrators, discipline policies, and student academic performance. Smith et al. (1987) concluded that at least some of the anger and hostility expressed by students in school settings may be the result of academic failures and/or lack of academic competence.

Peer relationships are also important determinants of anger and hostility at school. It is becoming increasingly clear that students who lack social competence and have few friends at school are more prone to aggressive behavior. In a longitudinal study of emotional competence and peer relations (Eisenberg et al., 1995), it was determined that the frequency of children's negative emotions such as anger and the inability to effectively regulate negative feelings were inversely related to peer acceptance.

Too strong

Most of the above-cited work has focused on understanding the complex interplay between individual and contextual factors involved in children's displays of aggressive behavior. Clearly more work is needed to provide a more detailed picture both of the factors promoting high levels of anger and hostility in youth and the impact of anger and hostility upon social, behavioral, and academic functioning.

Type 2 study
Type 1 study
(see page 368)

The purpose of the present research was to address this need by collecting descriptive data on personal, family, peer, and school factors associated with students manifesting anger-related problems at school. In conceptualizing this study, we decided to use a modified case-study approach focusing on detailed analyses of a relatively small number of angry, hostile, and aggressive preadolescents. Given the perceived importance of including multiple sources of information, we interviewed not only students but also their parents and teachers. We supplemented semi-structured interviews with school record reviews and standardized measures of behavior, attitudes at school, self-esteem, and academic performance.

Purpose

METHOD

Participants

Participants for this study were 24 high-anger, elementary-age students identified on the basis of teacher ratings and standardized assessment and an equal number of low-anger students who served as a comparison sample. Both groups were drawn from 12 elementary schools in the Honolulu, Hawaii, area. In general, all schools serve an economically and ethnically diverse population in a high-density area of the city.

Convenience sample

The 24 students comprising the high-anger group included 20 males and 4 females equally distributed between fifth and sixth grades. The mean age for this group was 10.5 years. The ethnic distribution of this group mirrored the composition of the community from which it was drawn and included six Caucasians, four Pacific Islanders, one Native American, one Hispanic, and the remainder Asian-American children of Japanese, Chinese, Korean, and/or Filipino descent.

Unclear

The 24 students in the low-anger sample included 8 males and 16 females equally distributed between fifth and sixth grades. The mean age for this group was 10.6 years. Ethnic distribution of this group included three Caucasians, five Pacific Islanders, one African-American, two Hispanics, and the remainder Asian-American including Japanese, Chinese, Korean, and Filipino youth.

Gender imbalance

Instruments

Group used?

The Behavioral Assessment System for Children (BASC)—Aggression subscale (Reynolds & Kamphaus, 1992) was used to measure teachers' perceptions of students' physical and verbal aggression at school. Items are scored according to a 4-point Likert-like format with 1 being "not at all" and 4 being "all the time." The 14-item aggression subscale has an internal consistency of .95 and test-retest reliability of .91 (Reynolds & Kamphaus, 1992).

Too strong

The Self-Perception Profile for Children (SPP; Harter, 1985) is a 36-item measure of perceived self-worth, which consists of six subscales including scholastic competence, social acceptance, athletic competence, physical appearance, behavioral conduct, and global self-worth. Items are scored according to a 4-point Likert-like scale with 1 being "not at all like me" and 4 being "very much like me." Internal consistency for the SPP has been established as ranging from .71 to .82 (Harter, 1985).

Procedure

Teachers in each of the 12 participating fifth- and sixth-grade classrooms were asked to nominate as many students as they wished from their classes who fit the criteria of "high" and "low" anger at school. High-anger students were defined as those students who displayed frequent emotional outbursts related to feelings of anger; demonstrated a consistent cynical, hostile, or angry attitude; or were involved in frequent incidents of fighting or acting out in an angry, aggressive manner. Low-anger students were defined as those students who rarely or never displayed these characteristics.

Definitions

As an additional screening measure, all students in the 12 classrooms were administered the Multidimensional School Anger Inventory (MSAI; Smith et al., 1998), which yields subscale scores in the areas of anger arousal, cynical hostility, and negative anger expression. Both internal consistency of subscales and construct validity of the scale have been well-established (Smith et al., 1998). Internal consistency of the MSAI subscales ranged from .58 to .88. Criterion-related validity has been established as ranging from .39 to .54 between MSAI subscales and other measures of anger and aggression.

Too strong

What are they?

The 24 students designated as high anger in this study were those students nominated by their teachers as manifesting anger-related problems at school who also scored in the top one third of their class on one or more subscales of the MSAI. The 24 students designated as low-anger were those students nominated by their teachers as manifesting relatively few anger-related problems at school and who scored in the bottom one third of their class on one or more subscales of the MSAI.

Operational definition

The total sample of 48 students comprising both high- and low-anger groups was individually interviewed by one of six trained graduate students. All interviews took place at each child's school and included semi-structured interview questions designed to elicit information with regard to school experiences, friendships, perceptions of self, home environment, and specific anger experiences. In addition, the students completed the Behavioral Assessment System for Children and the Self-Perception Profile for Children. Teachers for each student were also individually interviewed and asked to complete both semi-structured interviews and a portion of the BASC. Teacher interview questions elicited information about teachers' backgrounds, perceptions of students' functioning at school, and specific impressions with regard to students' anger. Finally, parents of the high- and low-anger students were individually interviewed and asked to provide information in response to semi-structured questions about family demographics, students' developmental histories, social and leisure activities, anger experiences, and future expectations.

Helpful detail

In order to facilitate analysis of qualitative data, we coded student, teacher, and parent responses to open-ended questions on a 3-point Likert scale where higher scores represented more problematic, dysfunctional environments, feelings, behaviors, and attitudes, and lower scores indicated more positive and prosocial functioning.

Results

Data from parent, teacher, and student interviews were organized according to four major domains—personal, family, peer, and school factors. Personal variables included participants' gender and ethnicity, perceived self-worth as measured by the SPP, and both negative self-descriptions and anger-related self-descriptions in response to semi-structured interview questions. Family variables included parents' marital status and teachers' perceptions of parent support. Peer variables included number of friends reported by participants, extent of teasing, and general peer relations as reported by teachers and students. School variables included students' grade point average (GPA), most recent Stanford Achievement Test (SAT) scores, attitudes and motivation toward school, and academic performance as reported by teachers.

Good detail

Within each domain, results are reported first according to the relationship between global anger scores on the MSAI and other relevant outcome variables. This is followed by descriptions of contrasts between high- and low-anger groups on selected variables of interest. These descriptions were compiled from student, teacher, and parent responses to semi-structured interviews and are reported as qualitative findings.

Personal Domain

For the entire sample of students comprising both high- and low-anger groups, moderate but statistically significant negative correlations were found between MSAI global scores and the physical appearance, behavioral conduct, and global self-worth scales of the SPP ($r = -.35$, $-.45$, and $-.45$, respectively; $p < .05$). Global anger was essentially unrelated to perceived athletic competence on the SPP ($r = .07$). A moderate positive correlation was found between anger-related self-descriptions and MSAI global scores ($r = .45$, $p < .05$), indicating that students reporting high levels of anger at school also tended to characterize themselves as angry in various other aspects of their lives.

These probabilities are inappropriate.

With regard to specific differences between the high- and low-anger groups in this study, a number of personal domain variables distinguished the two. Most dramatic were the disproportions among genders in the two groups, with males comprising roughly 83% of students in the high-anger group but only 33% of students in the low-anger group. Interestingly, there were no differences in the ethnic composition of each group. Roughly equal numbers of Caucasians, Pacific Islanders, and Asian-Americans were identified as manifesting either high levels or low levels of anger at school.

Right!

Unclear

Several themes emerged from qualitative analysis of student, teacher, and parent interviews with regard to personal characteristics of students. One pertained to the nature of self-descriptions reported by high- and low-anger students. Negative self-descriptions or self-derogatory comments were much more common among students in the high-anger group. One student, for example, stated that "sometimes I don't want to be myself." Another described himself as "not very popular because I don't have many friends." Yet another stated that "I don't like anything about myself." Other negative terms used in the self-descriptions of high-anger students included *weird, bad,* and *lazy.* In contrast, self-descriptions of low-anger students were overwhelmingly positive with only occasional references to undesirable personal qualities.

Frequencies needed here

Also included in some of the participants' self-descriptions was information relating to their experience of anger. When asked what things they would like to change about themselves, all of the high-anger students acknowledged problems in controlling or regulating anger. One participant described himself as a person who "gets angry easily." Another stated that "I lose my temper fast." A third participant described himself as "mad when I don't get my own way."

Good specificity

Another participant stated that he would like to "change my temper" but indicated "you can't change that." In contrast, only one of the low-anger participants mentioned anger control as something she would like to change about herself. In this case, she stated that she would like to change her frequency of "getting really angry at my sisters."

Family Domain

Biserial *r*?
r = ?

A significant inverse relationship was found betwesen teacher ratings of parental support and students' level of anger ($r = .53$, $p < .05$). Interestingly, there was no relationship between parents' marital status and the degree of school anger reported by their children. Students from divorced, separated, single parent, and intact families were equally represented between high- and low-anger groups.

How many?

Teachers' responses to semi-structured interviews provided some of the more interesting qualitative information regarding the home life of their students. In many cases, families of high-anger students were described by teachers as facing significant challenges, including economic, occupational, and interpersonal woes. One teacher described her student's home life as an environment where "mom and dad often quarrel" and where "the student hides from the father to escape his anger." Another teacher described her student's home life as "up and down" because the father is often away due to military duty, and the mother faces long working hours. Two of the participants in the high-anger group had particularly distressing family backgrounds. One had never known her real mother and spent several years living with grandparents before being taken back by her remarried father. Another was described by his teacher as concerned that his real father could show up at any time to kidnap both him and his younger sister and take them away from their mother. Indeed, only a small minority of the high-anger group were described by teachers as having even moderately positive, supportive family lives.

How many?

How many?

Definition?

On the other hand, teachers described the majority of the families of low-anger participants as extremely supportive and positive. Typical descriptors included "extremely supportive, a lot of parental involvement" and "excellent family, parents are very involved in school, very giving people, encouraging." Even the families of low-anger students from divorced or separated parents were described in mostly positive terms. For example, one teacher mentioned that her student "lives with a mom who is very supportive and on top of things; is very involved with her daughter."

Peer Domain

Low *r*'s

Significant inverse correlations were found between MSAI global scores and the number of friends students reported having at school ($r = -.32$, $p < .05$) and teacher ratings of social relationships ($r = -.64$, $p < .01$). Significant positive relationships were found between the extent of teasing experienced by students and their level of anger ($r = .43$, $p < .05$ and between self-reported anger and the perceived anger level of friends ($r = .34$, $p < .05$). This latter finding is interesting in that it implies that angry students at school tend to associate with like-minded peers.

r = ?

On the other hand, global anger scores were essentially unrelated to students' perceptions of their own social competence (as evidenced by SPP scores), to number of friends outside of school, and to overall satisfaction with friends. Thus, it appears that although teachers report social difficulties experienced by high-anger students, the students themselves may not acknowledge such problems other than the fact of simply having fewer friends at school.

Qualitative analysis of student and teacher interviews suggested several themes related to high- and low-anger students' interpersonal functioning. First, teachers described all of the low-anger students as having positive relationships and interactions with their classmates. One low-anger student was described, for example, as "well liked by her peers; looked up to as a role model; has many friends; is really accepting of others." Another was described as "well liked;

very friendly; has a high tolerance for other people; has lots of friends." Teacher descriptions of high-anger students, on the other hand, were laced with comments about difficulties building and maintaining friendships. One teacher described her student as "not getting along very well; very poor relationships; the low man on the totem pole; less power; very defensive and can't let things go." Another participant was described as "an outcast; other students don't accept her; she says things in a sly, devious manner." Yet another participant was described as "a loner . . . no close friends, no attachments."

The social portrait painted by teachers of high-anger students was not always so bleak, however. A number of students in this group were described by their teachers as having positive relationships with their classmates. A few were described as "getting along well with others" and one was described as "the cool guy in class; bad but popular." *N = ?*

Some interesting qualitative data regarding students' interpersonal functioning were also obtained from interviews with parents. Once again, all the parents of low-anger students described their children's relationships with others in positive terms. Typcial responses included "gets along with others, has a lot of friends," or "she is friendly and outgoing, so she gets along well with other children." The majority of parents of the high-anger group also saw their children as having positive relationships with others. Only a few concerns were noted. One parent said that his daughter "did not get along with other children very good and only had one or two close friends." Another parent described her son as "having okay relationships" but stated that "he still isn't close to any of his friends."

Another important theme pertaining to peer relationships related to teasing at school. Participants in the high-anger group were more likely to admit to being teased by others both within and outside the classroom. The reasons for being teased could be classified into four general themes including: a) appearance, e.g., "fatty," "scareface," "small;" b) ability, e.g., "stupid," "junk art;" c) names, e.g., "tiffy-taffy;" d) behavior, e.g., "because I like a boy," "because of the way I act." Appearance was the most often cited reason for being teased by both high- and low-anger students, although this appeared more frequently in the responses of high-anger students. Teasing with regard to ability occurred almost exclusively among the experiences of high-anger students. *Frequencies in each?*

School Domain

Moderate, significant inverse relationships were found between MSAI global scores and school success as measured by GPA ($r = -.57$, $p < .05$), school work habits ($r = -.56$, $p < .05$), and school-related personal and social attitudes ($r = -.71$, $p < .05$). In addition, participants who scored higher on their SAT were less likely to experience high levels of anger and hostility at school ($r = -.47$, $p < .05$). A significant inverse relationship was also found between teacher and student ratings of academic ability and anger ($r = -.33$ and $-.36$, respectively; $p < .05$). In addition, students in the low-anger group were much more likely to be categorized as intrinsically motivated than were students in the high-anger group (42% vs. 0%, respectively). *These correlations are worth noting.*

Percentages here are helpful.

Most of the qualitative information pertaining to students' school performances was obtained from semi-structured interviews with teachers. Only one high-anger student was described as an above average student academically, and this included a qualifier. She stated that the student "is very smart, but is sometimes lazy." Laziness or lack of motivation was a common theme among teacher descriptions of the high-anger group. One teacher said of her student, "If he didn't have to, he wouldn't do anything except sit and draw . . . he tries to just get by." Another teacher described her student as "a girl that if I let her, will just do enough to get by."

In addition to motivational problems, some high-anger students were described as having social or emotional problems that interfered with their academics. One teacher described her student in the following manner: "He has made good progress (academically), but social and emotional problems pull him down." Another student was described as "an average student that lacks confidence." A third was described as "one who gives up easily and is easily frustrated."

Teachers identified several participants from the high-anger group as below average academically. These students were described as "very low in most areas," "nonexistent academics," or "has a difficult time in all subject areas."

A sharp contrast was found in teacher descriptions of the academic performance of low-anger students. The vast majority of these students were classified as average or above average academically. Of these, most were described as being highly motivated at school. Only one of the low-anger students was described in terms indicating that motivation was a concern.

Teachers also provided information on the kinds of strategies used to motivate students in the two groups. As a group, high-anger students were more likely to be motivated by the prospect of obtaining material rewards (i.e., extrinsic factors). Low-anger students, although still responsive to external rewards, were considerably more likely to be motivated by factors intrinsic to the task (i.e., sense of accomplishment, for the sake of learning) than were students from the high-anger group. One high-anger student was described by his teacher as "unmotivated; nothing seems to work at school."

DISCUSSION

Change of purpose

The intent of this study was to examine possible risk factors related to the development and expression of anger in preadolescents. The results support a conceptualization of anger development in children based on multiple pathways across four domains including individual, school, family, and peer factors. In general, it appears that cumulative positive and negative experiences at home, in school, and with peers have a major impact on the frequency and intensity of anger experienced at school. This conclusion was evidenced throughout the data where preadolescents who had negative experiences and relationships across domains were also more likely to experience high levels of anger. There also appears to be an additive effect across domains, in which negative experiences within one domain have an impact on the relationships and experiences within other domains.

Unclear

The data don't show that it is the same students across domains.

One possible interpretation of the data is that individual traits and dispositions are first shaped within the family and home environment and later modified through interactions and experiences in school and with peers. Through these interactions and experiences, the child develops a sense of self-worth, abilities to regulate emotions, perceptions about themselves as social beings, and feedback on appropriate behavioral conduct. The first environment normally experienced by a child is the home, where initial socialization and development takes place. In this domain, parental support as well as family stability was found to be related to level of anger at school. Preadolescents who had little parental support were at risk for experiencing chronic anger. Further findings indicate that having positive relationships and interactions at home is likely to influence subsequent relations outside the home both in school and with peers.

Causation

Causation

In addition to family factors, school was also an important contributor to students' overall levels of anger. Participants in the high-anger group had lower academic GPAs, nonacademic GPAs, and achievement scores as measured by the SAT than did participants in the low-anger group. Zagar, Arbit, Hughes, Busell, and Busch (1989) discovered similar patterns in achievement test scores among a sample of juvenile delinquents. The high-anger participants were also more likely to have low levels of motivation, poor work habits, and negative attitudes towards school. Overall, the results from this study support the view that low-achieving preadolescents are more at risk for anger-related problems than their higher achieving peers.

Social skills also appear to play an important role in chronic anger at school. Preadolescents who have poor social skills and who have difficulty making and keeping friends manifest more anger problems. Further, it was interesting to note that angry students tend to associate themselves more often with angry peers. In this study, conflicting information was obtained from the participant and teacher interviews regarding friendship. The majority of students in both the high- and low-anger groups felt that they had friends and about equal numbers from both groups thought that they had either enough friends or wished they had more friends. The teachers, however, had a somewhat different view of their students' social relationships. The teachers described all of the low-anger students as having positive relationships with peers while only half of the high-anger participants were described as having positive relationships with peers. The parents of both groups generally saw their children as having positive relationships with other children. The related topic of teasing was identified as a common problem for preadolescents with chronic anger as they saw themselves as more frequent victims of teasing than did the low-anger children. Further, high-anger children were more likely to be teased based on some lack of ability than were low-anger children.

Clarifies

Frequency should be given.

IMPLICATIONS FOR SCHOOL COUNSELORS

Results of this study suggest there are strong patterns within each of the four life domains associated with chronically angry preadolescent youth. This pattern of risk factors may help in the assessment and identification of students experiencing chronic anger and its associated impact on future health and development (Williams & Williams, 1995). This information is especially important given the body of research linking anger to such diverse negative consequences as coronary heart disease (Seigel, 1992), cancer, depression, family violence (Smith & Furlong, 1994; Smith & Christensen, 1992), and the use of drugs and alcohol (Lochman, 1992; Scherwitz & Rugilies, 1992). Efforts, therefore, to assess, identify, treat, and prevent chronic anger and the negative consequences associated with it must begin as early as possible.

Prior research

The rationale for conducting this study with fifth and sixth grade students was that they are about to enter a turbulent stage in their lives. Adolescence is a time when emotions such as anger can become heightened. Thus, it is important to identify students most at risk for chronic anger and teach them the skills they need to deal with their anger before its consequences become more severe.

Justification

Several important risk factors associated with chronically angry students are discussed to help in identifying students needing anger management skill training or intervention. These student groups include:

- Preadolescent youth who are not getting sufficient emotional or material support at home. This group may include children from divorced or separated parents or those who live in single-parent households.
- Preadolescent youth who for various reasons (e.g., ability, motivation) do poorly in school.
- Students who are identified by their teachers as having difficulty making and keeping friends, who are constant victims of teasing, or who have poor social skills. Teachers should play an active role in observing and identifying those students who are commonly left out or who are subjected to ridicule from their peers.
- Preadolescent youth with low self-worth or low self-esteem. Both teachers and parents may play a crucial role in assisting students to acquire new skills for boosting self esteem.
- Students who self-select themselves as having a problem with anger. Preadolescent youth in this study appeared capable of understanding their difficulties with anger. This may be an especially important strategy, because many preadolescents, especially females, may express anger in more indirect ways not readily observable by others.

School counselors and other mental health professionals functioning within school settings may want to consider some of the findings from this study in developing anger management programs for youth. These include the following:

1. Include family members in anger management programs. It appears that the home life and family structure of students are strongly associated with anger. Thus, programs should be designed to include parents and other family members as integral parts of the intervention.
2. Provide anger management or emotional control programs as part of prenatal or early childhood parenting programs so that parents will have the skills and strategies necessary to act as emotional coaches for their children.
3. Include anger prevention and/or emotional regulation components as part of counseling for individuals or groups who are at risk for chronic anger. For example, a student taking part in a school counseling group for students who are going through divorce will most likely benefit from a comprehensive anger management program. In addition, a student identified as at risk for dropping out of school in the future because of academic failure may benefit from a program which teaches anger management skills.
4. All children could potentially benefit from anger management or emotional regulation programs that teach positive social skills and methods for building and maintaining friendships with peers. With these skills, children could help each other deal with anger problems and, in turn, become part of an angry child's social support system. Schools could also benefit from school-wide anger management programs aimed at developing the skills of teachers for identifying, understanding, and working with students who may have trouble controlling their anger. By learning proactive strategies, they could possibly prevent many angry and aggressive outbreaks and also learn to help students control and deal with their anger.

LIMITATIONS OF THE STUDY AND FUTURE DIRECTIONS

This study was not able to capture possible genetic, biological, neurological, and many early developmental characteristics, which may play an important role in the development of chronic anger. Future studies may want to consider intergenerational family patterns related to chronic levels of anger to determine the contributions of both genetic and environmental factors. There was some support for the notion that chronic anger and hostility tends to be present in both children and adults within the same family. For example, the interviewer comments about a father of one of the high-anger students indicated that the father was "pretty hostile" during the interview. He refused to answer several of the questions and made comments during the interview such as "this is taking too much time," or "I'll give you a few more minutes."

Little evidence provided

Further, it was found that preadolescent males were more likely to be identified as chronically angry than were females. Additional research is needed to determine why this appears to be true. The question of whether males are more genetically predisposed to anger or whether they are just socialized to be more angry is an interesting one. Achenbach (1982) found some developmental stability in the aggressive behavior displayed by males, but did not find this same stability in females. Achenbach attributed some of the aggressive behavior displayed by males to their more muscular body type. This muscular structure makes males more effective users of aggression and thus, they find it more rewarding. Future studies may want to control for gender by selecting and comparing high-anger males and females with low-anger students of the same sex.

We agree.

An additional limitation of this study was that students, teachers, and parents may have been reluctant to disclose information that was embarrassing or negative in nature. In two of the interviews with high-anger students, information was given which had to be reported to school personnel as possible instances of child abuse. The parents of one of these students asked that her child discontinue participation in the study. Abuse, which was identified by Lewis (Lewis, Lovely, Yeager, & Femina, 1989) as one of the most important contributors to the development of violent behavior, was not likely to be admitted to during the interviews with either parents or children. In fact, during the sample selection process, some of the parents may have refused to give consent for their child to participate due to a fear that their child may expose negative information about the family.

Threats to internal validity

A concluding thought: Consistent with the theme of early intervention, a logical next step in trying to understand the risk factors associated with chronic anger and how it may develop in children would be to conduct similar studies with younger cohorts of children. Such studies could use a similar research design and could be conducted not only in the earlier grades of elementary school but also in preschool and Headstart programs. A further interesting next step would be to follow some of the students who participated in this study into the future to track the course and consequences of anger into adolescence and adulthood.

References

Achenbach, T. (1982). *Developmental psychopathology*. New York: John Wiley.

Deffenbacher, J. L., Lynch, R. S., Oetting, E. R., & Kemper, C. C. (1996). Anger reduction in early adolescents. *Journal of Counseling Psychology, 43:*149–157.

Dodge, K. A. (1991). The structure and function of reactive and proactive aggression. In D. J. Pepler & K. H. Rubins (Eds.), *Development and treatment of childhood aggression* (pp. 201–218). Hillsdale, NJ: Lawrence Earlbaum.

Eisenberg, N., Fabes, R. A., Murphy, B., Maszk, P., Smith, M., & Karbon, M. (1995). The role of emotionality and regulation in children's social functioning: A longitudinal study. *Child Development, 66:*1360–1384.

Elliot, D. S., Huizinga, D., & Ageton, S. S. (1985). *Explaining delinquency and drug use*. Beverly Hills, CA: Sage.

Greenberg, M. T., Speltz, M. L., & DeKlyen, M. (1993). The role of attachment in the early development of disruptive behavior problems. *Development and Psychopathology, 3:*413–430.

Harter, S. (1985). *Self-perception profile for children*. Denver, CO: University of Denver.

Kazdin, A. E. (1987). Treatment of antisocial behavior in children: Current status and future directions. *Psychological Bulletin, 102:*187–203.

Larson, J. D. (1994). Violence prevention in the schools: A review of selected programs and procedures. *School Psychology Review, 23:*151–164.

Lewis, D. D., Lovely, R., Yeager, C., & Femina, D. D. (1989). Toward a theory of the genesis of violence: A follow-up study of delinquents. *Journal of the American Academy of Child and Adolescent Psychiatry, 28:*431–436.

Liebsohn, M. T., Oetting, E. R., & Deffenbacher, J. L. (1994). Effects of trait anger on alcohol consumption and consequences. *Journal of Child and Adolescent Substance Abuse, 3:*17–32.

Lochman, J. E. (1992). Cognitive-behavioral intervention with aggressive boys: Three-year follow-up and preventative effects. *Journal of Consulting and Clinical Psychology, 60:*426–432.

Lochman, J. E., White, K. J., & Wayland, K. K. (1991). Cognitive-behavioral assessment and treatment with aggressive children. In P. C. Kendall (Ed.), *Child and adolescent therapy: Cognitive-behavioral procedures* (pp. 25–65). New York: Guilford.

Olweus, D. (1979). Stability of aggressive reaction patterns in males: A review. *Psychological Bulletin, 86:*852–875.

Patterson, G. R. (1982). *Coercive family process*. Eugene, OR: Castalia.

Patterson, G. R., DeBaryshe, B. D., & Ramsey, E. (1989). A developmental perspective on antisocial behavior. *American Psychologist, 2:*329–335.

Reid, J. B., & Patterson, G. R. (1991). Early prevention and intervention with conduct problems: A social interactional model for the integration of research and practice. In G. Stoner, M. R. Schinn, & H. M. Walker (Eds.), *Interventions for achievement and behavior problems* (pp. 725–739). Washington, DC: National Association of School Psychologists.

Reynolds, C. R., & Kamphaus, R. W. (1992). *Behavior Assessment System for Children.* Circle Pines, MN: American Guidance Service.

Scherwitz, L., & Rugilies, R. (1992). Life-style and hostility. In H. S. Friedman (Ed.), *Hostility, coping, and health* (pp. 77–98). Washington, DC: American Psychological Association.

Siegel, J. M. (1992). Anger and cardiovascular health. In H. S. Friedman (Ed.), *Hostility, coping, and health* (pp. 49–64). Washington, DC: American Psychological Association.

Smith, D.C., Adelman, H. S., Nelson, P., Taylor, L., & Phares, V. (1987). Perceived control at school and problem behavior and attitudes. *Journal of School Psychology, 25:*167–176.

Smith, D. C. & Furlong, M. J. (1994). Correlates of anger, hostility, and aggression in children and adolescents. In M. J. Furlong & D. C. Smith (Eds.), *Anger, hostility, and aggression: Assessment, prevention, and intervention strategies for youth* (pp. 15–38). New York: John Wiley.

Smith, D. C., Furlong, M. E., Bates, M., & Laughlin, J. (1998). Development of the Multidimensional School Anger Inventory for Males. *Psychology in the Schools, 35:*1–15.

Smith, D. C., Larson, J. D., DeBaryshe, B., & Salzman, M. (2000). Anger management for youth: What works and for whom? In D. S. Sandhu & C. B. Aspy (Eds.), *Violence in American schools: A practical guide for counselors* (pp. 217–230). Alexandria, VA: American Counseling Association.

Smith, T. W., & Christensen, A. J. (1992). Hostility, health, and social contexts. In H. S. Friedman (Ed.), *Hostility, coping, and health* (pp. 33–48). Washington, DC: American Psychological Association.

Tolan, P. H., Guerra, N. G., & Kendall, P. C. (1995). A developmental-ecological perspective on antisocial behavior in children and adolescents: Toward a unified risk and intervention framework. *Journal of Consulting and Clinical Psychology, 63:*579–584.

Williams, R. B., & Williams, V. (1995). *Anger kills.* New York: Times Books.

Zagar, R., Arbit, J., Hughes, J. R., Busell, R. E., & Busch, K. (1989). Developmental and disruptive behavior disorders among delinquents. *Journal of the American Academy of Child and Adolescent Psychiatry, 28:*437:440.

Analysis of the Study

PURPOSE/JUSTIFICATION

The purpose is stated near the end of the introduction as addressing the need "to provide a more detailed picture both of the factors promoting high levels of anger and hostility in youth and the impact of anger and hostility upon social, behavioral, and academic functioning." Extensive justification is provided on grounds of practical necessity and prior research. What is not clear to us is how the present study was intended to add to the body of prior knowledge, particularly in distinguishing causes of anger from consequences. There appear to be no problems of confidentiality, risk, or deception.

DEFINITIONS

Although definition of all the variables in this study might seem excessive, we think some should have been provided, especially for those emphasized in outcomes. For example, "family support," "social skills," "positive relationships with peers," and "low level of motivation." Such terms may seem clear, but their ambiguity is illustrated by the "typical descriptions" for "supportive families" that are given as "extremely supportive, a lot of parental involvement" (in what?) and "excellent family, parents are very involved in school, very giving people, encouraging." These suggest that the term includes more than encouragement and availability to their children. The primary term, "anger" is operationally defined as "teacher nomination of students who did or did not display frequent emotional outbursts related to feelings of anger, demonstrated a consistent cynical, hostile, or angry attitude or were involved in frequent incidents of fighting or acting out in an angry, aggressive manner." This definition suggests that "angry" is implicitly defined in terms of behavior, not feelings.

PRIOR RESEARCH

The authors cite numerous pertinent references in the introduction (and in the implications) pertaining to both causes and effects of anger in students. These are appropriately organized and summarized.

HYPOTHESES

None are stated but many are implied (i.e., that student anger is related to lack of parental support, parent mar-ital status, number of friends, extent of teasing, general peer relations, GPA, SAT scores, attitude and motivation toward school, and teacher perception of academic performance). Many of these appear to be directional. Other themes emerged from the qualitative analysis of interview data.

SAMPLE

The sample is a convenience sample of fifth- and sixth-graders drawn from 12 elementary schools in Honolulu. Consequently, generalization beyond these schools is not justified methodologically nor is argumentation provided for such generalization. Some description is provided of the schools as serving an economically and ethnically diverse population. The ethnic distribution of students is predominantly Asian-American (over 50 percent). The implications of this are not discussed. The identification of students for high- and low-anger groups is well described.

INSTRUMENTATION

Formal instruments given to students and teachers are well described. We think, however, that use of the term "established" in relation to the validity of the SPP and MSAI and the internal consistency of the MSAI is unfortunate in light of coefficients as low as .71 and .39 and without description of the groups involved. More description of the semi-structured interview questions is needed, partly to assess how much interviewer bias might have affected responses. Scoring agreement on the Likert scales should be reported since they are, apparently, those used in quantitative analyses.

PROCEDURES/INTERNAL VALIDITY

Procedures are adequately described. Internal validity is always a problem in causal-comparative studies. This study is a combination of types 1 and 2 (pp. 368–369). The high- and low-anger groups may differ in many ways other than level of anger. Two such variables are gender and ethnicity. The authors, in their limitations section, suggest controlling gender in future studies; it seems to us there was good reason to have controlled it (by matching or same-sex selection) in this study. Ethnicity was not controlled, but the groups are similar, although not identical. Many of the variables in this study are subject characteristics, but none were controlled. A mortality threat is likely, because some parents, presumably in the high-anger group, refused permission. A data-collector threat is possible because it is unclear whether interviewers were balanced across groups. Data-collector bias is possible, especially with the open-ended questions; presumably this was addressed in training. An instrumentation threat seems likely, as is discussed in the limitations section. Though less likely, instrument decay and location threats are possible. Implementation, attitude, and regression threats do not apply.

DATA ANALYSIS

The use of correlation coefficients (presumably the biserial r—see p. 222) is appropriate but, we think, less satisfactory than using means, standard deviations, and, where feasible, frequency polygons (see pp. 201–203). Significant tests are of little value because of the lack of random sampling; the magnitude of r indicates importance.

RESULTS

Results are appropriately presented. Too much is made of low values of r, even though statistically significant. Because the study clearly focuses on practical, as distinct from theoretical, uses, we would pay little attention to correlations below .50. We would have emphasized the following correlations with degree of anger: $-.53$ with parental support; $-.64$ with (positive) social relationships; $-.57$ with GPA; $-.56$ with (positive) work habits; $-.71$ with (positive) attitude; and, because it is consistent with GPA, $-.47$ with SAT scores. Qualitative differences between anger groups that seem important are that the high anger group indicated: much greater desire to control anger (all versus one), more negative self-descriptions (frequencies would be helpful here and in subsequent comparisons), more family problems, more often teased at school, and less motivated by factors intrinsic to school tasks.

DISCUSSION

This section is generally consistent with the results and attempts to provide an integration. It highlights some suggestive findings, for example, that parents' and teachers' perceptions of student social relations differed markedly in the high-anger group and that for them, teasing may be more related to lack of academic ability.

The statement that effects are cumulative across domains, while it may well be true, is not justified from the data provided in the report. The reason is that data are presented separately for each domain with no data on individuals across domains. The authors commendably address several limitations, but omit others. We are concerned with the implications regarding causality. In offering one possible interpretation of the data, inappropriate statements are made (i.e., the data *do not* "indicate that having positive relationships at home is likely to *influence* subsequent relations outside the home both in school and with peers." Nor do results show that "school was also an important *contributor* to students' overall levels of anger." While these are plausible interpretations, the findings can just as legitimately be used to support the reverse (e.g., that student anger is an important contributor to poor school achievement and attitude and to poor parental support or that both variables are caused by other variables.

Causal-comparative study findings cannot determine the nature of causality and are therefore poorly suited to distinguishing causes of anger from effects. In addition to the problem of causality, the threats to internal validity in this study are severe. As one example, because the anger groups differ dramatically in gender composition, it is important to assess whether gender is related to other outcome variables and could, therefore, account for the relationships (see pp. 372–373). Recognizing that the sample is atypical of U.S. schools in general, and of our experience, we nevertheless think it likely that gender differences could account for a large portion of the relationships found.

The problems with causality are avoided by the redefinition of purpose (in the discussion section) as identification of risk factors related to the development and expression of anger in preadolescents. As such, risk factors would include low family support, poor academic performance, teacher assessment as having poor social relationships, low intrinsic motivation for school, and so forth. The danger here is one of overgeneralization. In a society prone to oversimplification, it is easy to forget that, with correlations even as high as .71, many (perhaps most) students identified by one or a combination of these factors will be misidentified as angry or anger-prone. Students so identified should get help in coping with such problems *if* their existence is verified. We agree that students who identify themselves as needing help with anger should get it.

Go back to the **Interactive and Applied Learning Tools** feature at the beginning of the chapter for a listing of interactive and applied activities. Go to the **Online Learning Center** at www.mhhe.com/fraenkel5e or your **Interactive Student CD-ROM** to take practice quizzes and receive immediate feedback, practice with key terms, review chapter content and main ideas, and find annotated Web links.

Main Points

THE NATURE OF CAUSAL-COMPARATIVE RESEARCH

- Causal-comparative research, like correlational research, seeks to identify associations among variables.
- Causal-comparative research attempts to determine the cause or consequences of differences that already exist between or among groups of individuals.
- The basic causal-comparative approach is to begin with a noted difference between two groups and then to look for possible causes for, or consequences of, this difference.
- There are three types of causal-comparative research (exploration of effects, exploration of causes, exploration of consequences), which differ in their purposes and structure.
- When an experiment would take a considerable length of time and be quite costly to conduct, a causal-comparative study is sometimes used as an alternative.
- As in correlational studies, relationships can be identified in a causal-comparative study, but causation cannot be fully established.

CAUSAL-COMPARATIVE VERSUS CORRELATIONAL RESEARCH

- The basic similarity between causal-comparative and correlational studies is that both seek to explore relationships among variables. When relationships are identified through causal-comparative research (or in correlational research), they often are studied at a later time by means of experimental research.

CAUSAL-COMPARATIVE VERSUS EXPERIMENTAL RESEARCH

- In experimental research, the group membership variable is manipulated; in causal-comparative research, the group differences already exist.

STEPS IN CAUSAL-COMPARATIVE RESEARCH

- The first step in formulating a problem in causal-comparative research is usually to identify and define the particular phenomena of interest, and then to consider possible causes for, or consequences of, these phenomena.
- The important thing in selecting a sample for a causal-comparative study is to define carefully the characteristic to be studied and then to select groups that differ in this characteristic.
- There are no limits to the kinds of instruments that can be used in a causal-comparative study.
- The basic causal-comparative design involves selecting two groups that differ on a particular variable of interest and then comparing them on another variable or variables.

THREATS TO INTERNAL VALIDITY IN CAUSAL-COMPARATIVE RESEARCH

- Two weaknesses in causal-comparative research are lack of randomization and inability to manipulate an independent variable.
- A major threat to the internal validity of a causal-comparative study is the possibility of a subject selection bias. The chief procedures that a researcher can use to reduce this threat include matching subjects on a related variable or creating homogeneous subgroups, and the technique of statistical matching.
- Other threats to internal validity in causal-comparative studies include location, instrumentation, and loss of subjects. In addition, type 3 studies are subject to implementation, history, maturation, attitude of subjects, regression, and testing threats.

DATA ANALYSIS IN CAUSAL-COMPARATIVE STUDIES

- The first step in a data analysis of a causal-comparative study is to construct frequency polygons.
- Means and standard deviations are usually calculated if the variables involved are quantitative.
- The most commonly used inference test in causal-comparative studies is a *t*-test for differences between means.
- Analysis of covariance is particularly useful in causal-comparative studies.
- The results of causal-comparative studies should always be interpreted with caution, because they do not prove cause and effect.

ASSOCIATIONS BETWEEN CATEGORICAL VARIABLES

- Both crossbreak tables and contingency coefficients can be used to investigate possible associations between categorical variables, although predictions from crossbreak tables are not precise. Fortunately, there are relatively few questions of interest in education that involve two categorical variables.

Key Terms

Causal-comparative research 368

Correlational research 369

For Discussion

1. Suppose a researcher was interested in finding out what factors cause delinquent behavior in teenagers. What might be a suitable comparison group for the researcher to use in investigating this question?
2. Could observation be used in a causal-comparative study? If so, how?
3. Can you suggest any other threats to internal validity besides those we mention in this chapter that might endanger a causal-comparative study?
4. When, if ever, might a researcher prefer to conduct a causal-comparative study rather than an experimental study? Suggest an example.
5. What sorts of questions might lend themselves better to causal-comparative research than to experimental research? Why?
6. Which do you think would be easier to conduct, causal-comparative or experimental research? Why?
7. Is random assignment possible in causal-comparative research? What about random selection? Explain.

8. Suppose a researcher was interested in the effects of team teaching on student attitudes toward history. Could such a topic be studied by means of causal-comparative research? If so, how?

9. What sorts of variables might it be wise for a researcher to think about controlling for in a causal-comparative study? What sorts of variables, if any, might be irrelevant?

10. Might a researcher ever study the exact same variables in an experimental study that he or she studied in a causal-comparative study? If so, why?

11. We state in the text that, in general, quantitative variables should not be collapsed into categorical variables because (a) the decision to do so is almost always an arbitrary one, and (b) too much information is lost by doing so. Can you suggest any quantitative variables that, for these reasons, should not be collapsed into categorical variables? Can you suggest some quantitative variables that could justifiably be treated as categorical variables?

12. Suppose a researcher reports a higher incidence of childhood sexual abuse in adult women who have eating disorders than in a comparison group of women without eating disorders. Which variable is more likely to be the cause of the other? What other variables could be alternative or contributing causes?

13. Are there any research questions that cannot be studied by the causal-comparative method?

14. A professor at a private women's college wishes to assess the degree of alienation present in undergraduates as compared to graduate students at her institution, using an instrument that she has developed.
    a. Which method, causal-comparative or experimental, would you recommend she use in her inquiry? Why?
    b. Would the fact that the researcher plans to use an instrument that she herself developed make any difference in your recommendation?

1. The interested reader is referred to J. D. Elashoff (1969). Analysis of covariance: A delicate instrument. *American Educational Research Journal, 6:*383–399.

Notes

Survey Research

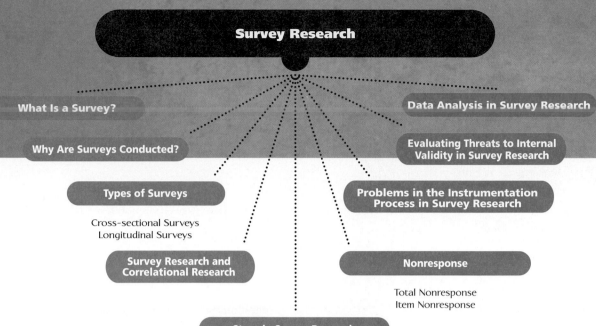

CHAPTER 17

Survey Research

What Is a Survey?

Why Are Surveys Conducted?

Types of Surveys
Cross-sectional Surveys
Longitudinal Surveys

Survey Research and
Correlational Research

Steps in Survey Research
Defining the Problem
Identifying the Target Population
Choosing the Mode of Data Collection
Selecting the Sample
Preparing the Instrument
Preparing the Cover Letter
Training Interviewers
Using an Interview to Measure Ability

Data Analysis in Survey Research

Evaluating Threats to Internal
Validity in Survey Research

Problems in the Instrumentation
Process in Survey Research

Nonresponse
Total Nonresponse
Item Nonresponse

Objectives

Studying this chapter should enable you to:

- Explain *what a survey is.*
- Name *three types of surveys conducted in educational research.*
- Explain *the purpose of surveys.*
- Explain *the difference between a cross-sectional and a longitudinal survey.*
- Describe *how survey research differs from other types of research.*
- Describe *briefly how mail surveys, telephone surveys, and face-to-face interviews differ and state two advantages and disadvantages of each type.*
- Describe *the most common pitfalls in developing survey questions.*
- Explain *the difference between a closed-ended and an open-ended question.*
- Explain *why nonresponse is a problem in survey research and name two ways to improve the rate of response in surveys.*
- Name *two threats to instrument validity that can affect survey results.* Explain *how such threats can be controlled.*
- Describe *possible threats to internal validity in survey research.*
- Recognize *an example of survey research when you come across it in the educational literature.*

Interactive and Applied Learning

After, or while, reading this chapter:

Go to your Interactive Student
CD-ROM to:
- Learn More About Taking a Census

Go to your Interactive
Student CD-ROM or Student
Workbook to do the following
activities:
- Activity 17.1 Survey Research Questions
- Activity 17.2 Types of Surveys
- Activity 17.3 Open- vs. Close-Ended Questions
- Activity 17.4 Conduct a Survey

om Martinez, the principal of Grover Creek High School, is meeting with his vice principal, Jesse Sullivan.

"I wish I knew how more of the faculty felt about this after-school detention program we've implemented this year," says Tom. "Jose Alcazar stopped me in the hall yesterday to say he thinks it's not working."

"Why?"

"He says many of the faculty think it doesn't do any good, so they don't even bother to send any students there."

"Really?" answers Jesse. "I've heard just the opposite. Just today, at lunch, Becky and Felicia were saying they think it's great!"

"Hmm, that's interesting. It seems we need more data."

A survey is an appropriate way for Tom and Jesse to get such data. How to conduct a survey is what this chapter is about.

What Is a Survey?

Researchers are often interested in the opinions of a large group of people about a particular topic or issue. They ask a number of questions, all related to the issue, to find answers. For example, imagine that the chairperson of the counseling department at a large university is interested in determining how students who are seeking a master's degree feel about the program. She decides to conduct a survey to find out. She selects a sample of 50 students from among those currently enrolled in the master's degree program and constructs questions designed to elicit their attitudes toward the program. She administers the questions to each of the 50 students in the sample in face-to-face interviews over a two-week period. The responses given by each student in the sample are coded into standardized categories for purposes of analysis, and these standardized records are then analyzed to provide descriptions of the students in the sample. The chairperson draws some conclusions about the opinions of the sample, which she then generalizes to the population from which the sample was selected, in this case, all of the graduate students seeking a master's degree in counseling from this university.

The previous example illustrates the three major characteristics that most surveys possess.

1. Information is collected from a group of people in order to *describe* some aspects or characteristics (such as abilities, opinions, attitudes, beliefs, and/or knowledge) of the population of which that group is a part.
2. The main way in which the information is collected is through *asking questions;* the answers to these

questions by the members of the group constitute the data of the study.
3. Information is collected from a *sample* rather than from every member of the population.

Why Are Surveys Conducted?

The major purpose of surveys is to describe the characteristics of a population. In essence, what researchers want to find out is how the members of a population distribute themselves on one or more variables (for example, age, ethnicity, religious preference, attitudes toward school). As in other types of research, of course, the population as a whole is rarely studied. Instead, a carefully selected sample of respondents is surveyed and a description of the population is inferred from what is found out about the sample.

Researchers might be interested in describing how certain characteristics (age, gender, ethnicity, political involvement, and so on) of teachers in inner-city high schools are distributed within the group. The researcher would select a sample of teachers from inner-city high schools to survey. Generally, in a descriptive survey such as this, researchers are not so much concerned with why the observed distribution exists as with what the distribution *is*.

Types of Surveys

There are two major types of surveys that can be conducted—a cross-sectional survey and a longitudinal survey.

CROSS-SECTIONAL SURVEYS

A **cross-sectional survey** collects information from a sample that has been drawn from a predetermined population. Furthermore, the information is collected at just one point in time, although the time it takes to collect all of the data desired may take anywhere from a day to a few weeks or more. Thus, a professor of mathematics might collect data from a sample of all the high school mathematics teachers in a particular state about their interests in earning a master's degree in mathematics from his university, or another researcher might take a survey of the kinds of personal problems experienced by students at 10, 13, and 16 years of age. All these groups could be surveyed at approximately the same point in time.

When an entire population is surveyed, it is called a **census.** The prime example is the census conducted by the U.S. Bureau of the Census every 10 years, which attempts to collect data about everyone in the United States.

LONGITUDINAL SURVEYS

In a **longitudinal survey,** on the other hand, information is collected at different points in time in order to study changes over time. Three longitudinal designs are commonly employed in survey research: trend studies, cohort studies, and panel studies.

In a **trend study,** different samples from a population whose members may change are surveyed at different points in time. For example, a researcher might be interested in the attitudes of high school principals toward the use of flexible scheduling. He would select a sample each year from a current listing of high school principals throughout the state. Although the population would change somewhat and the same individuals would not be sampled each year, if random selection was used to obtain the samples, the responses obtained each year could be considered representative of the population of high school principals. The researcher would then examine and compare responses from year to year to see whether any trends are apparent.

Whereas a trend study samples a population whose members may change over time, a **cohort study** samples a particular population whose members do not change over the course of the survey. Thus, a researcher might want to study growth in teaching effectiveness of all the first-year teachers who had graduated the past year from San Francisco State University. The names of all of these teachers would be listed, and then a different sample would be selected from this listing at different times.

In a **panel study,** on the other hand, the researcher surveys the *same* sample of individuals at different times during the course of the survey. Because the researcher is studying the same individuals, she can note changes in their characteristics or behavior and explore the reasons for these changes. Thus, the researcher in our previous example might select a sample of last year's graduates from San Francisco State University who are first-year teachers and survey the same individuals several times during the teaching year. Loss of individuals is a frequent problem in panel studies, however, particularly if the study extends over a fairly long period of time.

Following are the titles of some published reports of surveys that have been conducted by educational researchers.

- The status of state history instruction.[1]
- Dimensions of effective school leadership: The teacher's perspective.[2]
- Teacher perceptions of discipline problems in a central Virginia middle school.[3]
- Two thousand teachers view their profession.[4]
- Grading problems: A matter of communication.[5]
- Peers or parents: Who has the most influence on cannabis use?[6]
- A career ladder's effect on teacher career and work attitudes.[7]
- Ethical practices of licensed professional counselors: A survey of state licensing boards.[8]

Survey Research and Correlational Research

It is not uncommon to find researchers examining the relationship of responses to one question in a survey to another, or of a score based on one set of survey questions to a score based on another set. In such instances, the techniques of correlational research described in Chapter Fifteen are appropriate.

Suppose a researcher is interested in studying the relationship between attitude toward school of high school students and their outside-of-school interests. A questionnaire containing items dealing with these two variables could be prepared and administered to a sample of high school students, and then relationships could be determined by calculating correlation coefficients or by preparing contingency tables. The researcher may find that students who have a positive attitude toward school also have a lot of outside interests, while those who have a negative attitude toward school have few outside interests.

Steps in Survey Research

DEFINING THE PROBLEM

The problem to be investigated by means of a survey should be sufficiently interesting and important enough to motivate the individuals surveyed to respond. Trivial questions usually get what they deserve—they're tossed into the nearest wastebasket. We would not be surprised to learn that you have done this yourself to a survey questionnaire you considered unimportant or found boring.

Researchers need to define clearly their objectives in conducting a survey. Each question to be asked should relate to one or more of the survey's objectives. One strategy for defining survey questions is to use a hierarchical approach, beginning with the broadest, most general questions, and ending with the most specific. Richard Jaeger gives a detailed example of such a survey on the question of why many public school teachers "burn out" and leave the profession within a few years. He suggests three general factors—economics, working conditions, and perceived social status—around which to structure possible questions for the survey. Here are the questions he developed with regard to economic factors.

I. Do economic factors cause teachers to leave the profession early?
   A. Do teachers leave the profession early because of inadequate yearly income?
      1. Do teachers leave the profession early because their monthly income during the school year is too small?
      2. Do teachers leave the profession early because they are not paid during the summer months?
      3. Do teachers leave the profession early because their salary forces them to hold a second job during the school year?
      4. Do teachers leave the profession early because their lack of income forces them to hold a different job during the summer months?
   B. Do teachers leave the profession early because of the structure of their pay scale?
      1. Do teachers leave the profession early because the upper limit on their pay scale is too low?
      2. Do teachers leave the profession early because their rate of progress on the pay scale is too slow?
   C. Do teachers leave the profession early because of inadequate fringe benefits?
      1. Do teachers leave the profession early because their health insurance benefits are inadequate?
      2. Do teachers leave the profession early because their life insurance benefits are inadequate?
      3. Do teachers leave the profession early because their retirement benefits are inadequate?[9]

A hierarchical set of research questions like this can help researchers identify large categories of issues, suggest more specific issues within each category, and conceive of possible questions. By determining whether a proposed question fits the purposes of the intended survey, researchers can eliminate those that do not. This is important since the length of a survey's questionnaire or interview schedule is a crucial factor in determining the survey's success.

IDENTIFYING THE TARGET POPULATION

Almost anything can be described by means of a survey. That which is studied in a survey is called the **unit of analysis.** Although typically people, units of analysis can also be objects, clubs, companies, classrooms, schools, government agencies, and others. For example, in a survey of faculty opinion about a new discipline policy recently instituted in a particular school district, each faculty member sampled and surveyed would be the unit of analysis. In a survey of urban school districts, the school district would be the unit of analysis.

Survey data are collected from a number of individual units of analysis to describe those units; these descriptions are then summarized to describe the population that the units of analysis represent. In the example given above, data collected from a sample of faculty members (the unit of analysis) would be summarized to describe the population that this sample represents (all of the faculty members in that particular school district).

As in other types of research, the group of persons (objects, institutions, and so on) that is the focus of the

Table 17.1 *Advantages and Disadvantages of Survey Data-Collection Methods*

	Direct Administration	Telephone	Mail	Interview
Comparative cost	Lowest	Same	Same	High
Facilities needed?	Yes	No	No	Yes
Require training of questioner?	Yes	Yes	No	Yes
Data-collection time	Shortest	Short	Longer	Longest
Response rate	Very high	Good	Poorest	Very high
Group administration possible?	Yes	No	No	Yes
Allow for random sampling?	Possibly	Yes	Yes	Yes
Require literate sample?	Yes	No	Yes	No
Permit follow-up questions?	No	Yes	No	Yes
Encourage response to sensitive topics?	Somewhat	Somewhat	Best	Weak
Standardization of responses	Easy	Somewhat	Easy	Hardest

study is called the target population. To make trustworthy statements about the target population, it must be very well defined. In fact, it must be so well defined that it is possible to state with certainty whether or not a particular unit of analysis is a member of this population. Suppose, for example, that the target population is defined as "all of the faculty members in a particular school district." Is this definition sufficiently clear so that one can state with certainty who is or is not a member of this population? At first glance, you may be tempted to say yes. But what about administrators who also teach? What about substitute teachers, or those who teach only part-time? What about student teachers? What about counselors? Unless the target population is defined in sufficient detail so that it is unequivocally clear as to who is, or is not, a member of it, any statements made about this population, based on a survey of a sample of it, may be misleading or incorrect.

CHOOSING THE MODE OF DATA COLLECTION

There are four basic ways to collect data in a survey: by administering the survey instrument "live" to a group; by mail; by telephone; or through face-to-face interviews. Table 17.1 presents a summary of the advantages and the disadvantages of each of the four survey methods, which are discussed below.

Direct Administration to a Group. This method is used whenever a researcher has access to all (or most) of the members of a particular group in one place. The instrument is administered to all members of the group at the same time and usually in the same place. Exam-

ples would include students being given a questionnaire to complete in their classrooms or workers at their job settings. The chief advantage of this approach is the high rate of response—often close to 100 percent (usually in a single setting). Other advantages include a generally low cost factor, plus the fact that the researcher has an opportunity to explain the study and answer any questions that the respondents may have before they complete the questionnaire. The chief disadvantage is that there are not many types of surveys that can use samples of individuals that are collected together as a group.

Mail Surveys. When the data in a survey are collected by mail, the questionnaire is sent to each individual in the sample by mail, with a request that it be completed and then returned by a given date. The advantages of this approach are that it is relatively inexpensive and it can be accomplished by the researcher alone (or with only a few assistants). It also allows the researcher to have access to samples that might be hard to reach in person or by telephone (such as the elderly), and it permits the respondents to take sufficient time to give thoughtful answers to the questions asked.

The disadvantages of mail surveys are that there is less opportunity to encourage the cooperation of the respondents (through building rapport, for example) or to provide assistance (through answering their questions, clarifying instructions, and so on). As a result, mail surveys have a tendency to produce low response rates. Mail surveys also do not lend themselves well to obtaining information from certain types of samples (such as individuals who are illiterate).

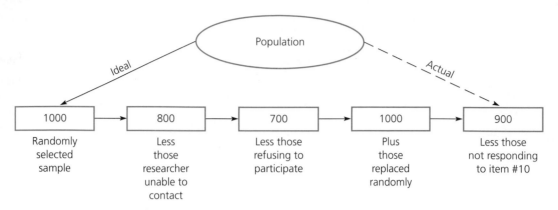

Figure 17.1 *Example of an Ideal Versus an Actual Telephone Sample for a Specific Question*

Telephone Surveys. In a telephone survey, of course, the researcher (or his or her assistants) asks questions of the respondents over the telephone. The advantages of telephone surveys are they are cheaper than personal interviews, can be conducted fairly quickly, and lend themselves easily to standardized questioning procedures. They also allow the researcher to assist the respondent (by clarifying questions, asking follow-up questions, encouraging hesitant respondents, and so on), permit a greater amount of follow-up (through several callbacks), and provide better coverage in certain areas where personal interviewers often are reluctant to go.*

The disadvantages of telephone surveys are that access to some samples (obviously, those without telephones and those whose phone numbers are unlisted) is not possible. Telephone interviews also prevent visual observation of respondents and are somewhat less effective in obtaining information about sensitive issues or personal questions. Generally, telephone surveys are reported to result in a 5 percent lower response rate than that obtained by personal interviews.[10] Figure 17.1 illustrates the difficulty sometimes encountered when obtaining a research sample by telephone.

*Computers are being used more and more in telephone surveys. Typically, an interviewer sits in front of a computer screen. A central computer randomly selects a telephone number and dials it. The interviewer, wearing a headset, hears the respondent answer the phone. On the computer screen appears a typed introduction, such as "Hello, my name is _____," for the interviewer to read, followed by the first question for him or her to ask. The interviewer then types the respondent's answer into the computer. The answer is immediately stored inside the central computer. The next question to be asked then appears on the screen, and the interviewer continues the questioning.

Personal Interviews. In a personal interview, the researcher (or trained assistant) conducts a face-to-face interview with the respondent. As a result, this method has many advantages. It is probably the most effective way there is to enlist the cooperation of the respondents in a survey. Rapport can be established, questions can be clarified, unclear or incomplete answers can be followed up, and so on. Face-to-face interviewing also places less of a burden on the reading and writing skills of the respondents and, when necessary, permits spending more time with respondents.

The biggest disadvantage of face-to-face interviews is that they are more costly than either mail or telephone surveys. They also require a trained staff of interviewers, with all that implies in terms of training costs and time. The total data collection time required is also likely to be quite a bit longer than in either of the other two methods. It is possible, too, that the lack of anonymity (the respondent is obviously known to the interviewer, at least temporarily) may result in less valid responses to personally sensitive questions. Last, some types of samples (individuals in high crime areas, workers in large corporations, students, and so on) are often difficult to contact in sufficient numbers.

SELECTING THE SAMPLE

The subjects to be surveyed should be selected (randomly, if possible) from the population of interest. Researchers must ensure, however, that the subjects they intend to question possess the information the researcher wants to obtain and that they will be willing to answer these questions. Individuals who possess the necessary information but who are uninterested in the topic of the survey (or who do not see it as important)

Important Findings in Survey Research

Probably the most famous example of survey research is that done by the sociologist Alfred Kinsey and his associates on the sexual behavior of American men (1948)* and women (1953).† While these studies are best known for their shocking (at the time) findings concerning the frequency of various sexual behaviors, they are equally noteworthy for their methodological competence. Using very large (although not random) samples totaling some 12,000 men and 8,000 women, Kinsey and his associates were meticulous in comparing results from different samples (replication), and in ex-

amining reliability through retesting and validity through internal cross-checking and comparison with spouses or other partners. One of the more unusual aspects of the basic data-gathering process—individual interviews—was the interview schedule that contained 521 items, (although the minimum per respondent was 300). The same information was elicited in several different questions, all asked in rapid-fire succession so as to minimize conscious distortion.

A recent study came to somewhat different conclusions regarding sexual behavior. The researchers used an interview procedure very similar to that used in the Kinsey studies, but claimed a superior sampling procedure. They selected a random sample of 4369 adults from a list of nationwide home addresses, with the household respondent also chosen at random. While the final participation rate of 79 percent (sample=3500) is high, 79 percent of a random sample is no longer a random sample.‡

*A. C. Kinsey, W. B. Pomeroy, and C. E. Martin (1948). *Sexual behavior in the human male.* Philadelphia: Saunders.
†A. C. Kinsey, W. B. Pomeroy, C. E. Martin, and P. H. Gebhard (1953). *Sexual behavior in the human female.* Philadelphia: Saunders.

‡E. Laumann, R. Michael, S. Michaels, and J. Gagnon (1994). *The social organization of sexuality.* Chicago: University of Chicago Press.

are unlikely to respond. Accordingly, it is often a good idea for researchers to conduct a preliminary inquiry among potential respondents to assess their receptivity. Frequently, in school-based surveys, a higher response rate can be obtained if a questionnaire is sent to persons in authority to administer to the potential respondents rather than sending it to the respondents themselves. For example, a researcher might ask classroom teachers to administer a questionnaire to their students rather than asking the students directly.

Some examples of samples that have been surveyed by educational researchers are as follows:

- A sample of all students attending an urban university concerning their views on the adequacy of the general education program at the university.
- A sample of all faculty members in an inner-city high school district as to the changes needed to help "at-risk" students learn more effectively.
- A sample of all such students in the same district concerning their views on the same topic.
- A sample of all women school superintendents in a particular state concerning their views as to the problems they encounter in their administrations.
- A sample of all the counselors in a particular high school district concerning their perceptions as to the adequacy of the school counseling program.

PREPARING THE INSTRUMENT

The most common types of instruments used in survey research are the **questionnaire** and the **interview schedule** (see Chapter Seven).* They are virtually identical, except that the questionnaire is usually self-administered by the respondent, while the interview schedule is administered verbally by the researcher (or trained assistant). In the case of a mailed or self-administered questionnaire, the appearance of the instrument is very important to the overall success of the study. It should be attractive and not too long† and the questions should be as easy to answer as possible. The questions in a survey, and the way they are asked, are of crucial importance. Floyd Fowler points out that there are four practical standards that all survey questions should meet:

1. Is this a question that can be asked exactly the way it is written?
2. Is this a question that will mean the same thing to everyone?

*Tests of various types can also be used in survey research, as when a researcher uses them to describe the reading proficiency of students in a school district. We restrict our discussion here, however, to the description of preferences, opinions, and beliefs.
†This is very important. Long questionnaires discourage people from completing and returning them.

3. Is this a question that people can answer?
4. Is this a question that people will be willing to answer, given the data-collection procedures?[11]

The answers to each of the previous questions for every question in a survey should be "yes." Any survey question that violates one or more of these standards should be rewritten.

In the case of a personal interview or a telephone survey, the manner of the questioner becomes of paramount importance. He or she must ask the questions in such a way that the subjects of the study want to respond.

In either case, the audience to whom the questions are to be directed should be clearly identified. Specialized or unusual words should be avoided if possible, or if they must be used, defined clearly in the instructions written on the instrument. The most important thing for researchers to keep in mind, however, is that whatever type of instrument is used, the *same* questions must be asked of all respondents in the sample. Furthermore, the conditions under which the questionnaire is administered or the interview is conducted should be as similar as possible for all respondents.

Types of Questions. The nature of the questions and the way they are asked are extremely important in survey research. Poorly worded questions can doom a survey to failure. Hence, they must be clearly written in a manner that is easily understandable by the respondents.[12]

Most surveys rely on multiple-choice or other forms of what are called **closed-ended questions.** Multiple-choice questions allow a respondent to select his or her answer from a number of options. They may be used to measure opinions, attitudes, or knowledge.

Closed-ended questions are easy to use, score, and code for analysis on a computer. Because all subjects respond to the same options, standardized data are provided. They are somewhat more difficult to write than open-ended questions, however. They also pose the possibility that an individual's true response is not present among the options given. For this reason, the researcher usually should provide an "other" choice for each item, where the subject can write in a response that the researcher may not have anticipated. Some examples of closed-ended questions are the following:

1. Which subject do you like *least?*
   a. Social studies
   b. English
   c. Science
   d. Mathematics
   e. Other (specify)

2. Rate each of the following parts of your master's degree program by circling the number under the phrase that describes how you feel.

	Very dissatisfied	Dissatisfied	Satisfied	Very satisfied
a. Coursework	1	2	3	4
b. Professors	1	2	3	4
c. Advising	1	2	3	4
d. Requirements	1	2	3	4
e. Cost	1	2	3	4
f. Other (specify)	1	2	3	4

Open-ended questions allow for more individualized responses, but they are sometimes difficult to interpret. They are also often hard to score, since so many different kinds of responses are received. Furthermore, respondents sometimes do not like them. Some examples of open-ended questions are as follows:

1. What characteristics of a person would lead you to rate him or her as a good administrator?
2. What do you consider to be the most important problem facing classroom teachers in high schools today?
3. What were the three things about this class you found most useful during the past semester?

Generally, therefore, closed-ended or short-answer questions are preferable, although sometimes researchers find it useful to combine both formats in a single question, as shown in the following example of a question using both open- and closed-ended formats.

1. Please rate and comment on each of the following aspects of this course:

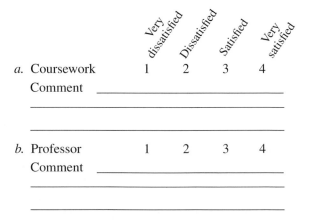

Table 17.2 presents a brief comparison of the advantages and disadvantages of closed-ended and open-ended questions.

Table 17.2 *Advantages and Disadvantages of Closed-Ended Versus Open-Ended Questions*

Closed-Ended	Open-Ended
Advantages	
• Enhances consistency of reponse across respondents. • Easier and faster to tabulate. • More popular with respondents.	• Allows more freedom of response. • Easier to construct. • Permits follow-up by interviewer.
Disadvantages	
• May limit breadth of responses. • Takes more time to construct. • Requires more questions to cover the research topic.	• Responses tend to be inconsistent in length and content across respondents. • Both questions and responses subject to misinterpretation. • Harder to tabulate and synthesize.

Some Suggestions for Improving Closed-Ended Questions. There are a number of relatively simple tips that researchers have found to be of value in writing good survey questions. A few of the most frequently mentioned ones follow.[13]

1. Be sure the question is *unambiguous.*
   Poor: Do you spend a lot of time studying?
   Better: How much time do you spend each day studying?
   a. More than 2 hours.
   b. One to 2 hours.
   c. Thirty minutes to 1 hour.
   d. Less than 30 minutes.
   e. Other (specify). _____
2. Keep the focus as simple as possible.
   Poor: Who do you think are more satisfied with teaching in elementary and secondary schools, men or women?
   a. Men are more satisfied.
   b. Women are more satisfied.
   c. Men and women are about equally satisfied.
   d. Don't know.
   Better: Who do you think are more satisfied with teaching in elementary schools, men or women?
   a. Men are more satisfied.
   b. Women are more satisfied.
   c. Men and women are about equally satisfied.
   d. Don't know.

3. Keep the questions short.
   Poor: What part of the district's English curriculum, in your opinion, is of the most importance in terms of the overall development of the students in the program?
   Better: What part of the district's English curriculum is the most important?
4. Use common language.
   Poor: What do you think is the principal reason schools are experiencing increased student absenteeism today?
   a. Problems at home.
   b. Lack of interest in school.
   c. Illness.
   d. Don't know.
   Better: What do you think is the main reason students are absent more this year than previously?
   a. Problems at home.
   b. Lack of interest in school.
   c. Illness.
   d. Don't know.
5. Avoid the use of terms that might bias responses.
   Poor: Do you support the superintendent's "no smoking" policy on campus grounds while school is in session?
   a. I support the policy.
   b. I am opposed to the policy.
   c. I don't care one way or the other about the policy.
   d. I am undecided about the policy.
   Better: Do you support a policy of "no smoking" on campus grounds while school is in session?
   a. I support the policy.
   b. I am opposed to the policy.
   c. I don't care one way or the other about the policy.
   d. I am undecided about the policy.
6. Avoid leading questions.
   Poor: What rules do you consider necessary in your classes?
   Better: Circle each of the following that describes a rule you set in your classes.
   a. All homework must be turned in on the date due.
   b. Students are not to interrupt other students during class discussions.
   c. Late homework is not accepted.
   d. Students are counted tardy if they are more than 5 minutes late to class.
   e. Other (specify) _____

7. Avoid double negatives.

Poor: Would you not be opposed to supervising students outside of your classroom?

    a. Yes.

    b. No.

    c. Undecided.

Better: Would you be willing to supervise students outside of your classroom?

    a. Yes.

    b. No.

    c. Undecided.

Pretesting the Questionnaire. Once the questions to be included in the questionnaire or the interview schedule have been written, the researcher is well-advised to try them out with a small sample similar to the potential respondents. A "pretest" of the questionnaire or interview schedule can reveal ambiguities, poorly worded questions, questions that are not understood, and unclear choices, and can also indicate whether the instructions to the respondents are clear.

Overall Format. The format of a questionnaire—how the questions look to the respondents—is very important in encouraging them to respond. Perhaps the most important rule to follow is to ensure that the questions are spread out—that is, uncluttered. No more than one question should be presented on a single line. When respondents have to spend a lot of time reading a question, they quickly become discouraged from continuing.

There are a variety of ways to present the response categories from which respondents are asked to choose. Earl Babbie suggests that boxes, as shown in the question below, are the best.[14]

Have you ever taught an advanced placement class?

[   ] Yes

[   ] No

Sometimes, certain questions will apply to only a portion of the subjects in the sample. When this is the case, follow-up questions can be included in the questionnaire. For example, a researcher might ask respondents if they are familiar with a particular activity, and then ask those who say "yes" to give their opinion of the activity. The follow-up question is called a **contingency question**—it is contingent upon how a respondent answers the first question. If properly used, contingency questions are a valuable tool to use in surveys, in that they can make it easier for a respondent to answer a

"Next question: I believe that life is a constant striving for balance, requiring frequent tradeoffs between morality and necessity, within a cyclic pattern of joy and sadness, forging a trail of bittersweet memories until one slips, inevitably, into the jaws of death. Agree or disagree?"

given question and also improve the quality of the data a researcher receives. Although there are a variety of contingency formats that might be used, the easiest to prepare is simply to set off the contingency question by indenting it, enclosing it in a box, and connecting it to the base question by means of an arrow to the appropriate response, as follows:

Have you ever taught an advanced placement class?

[   ] Yes

[   ] No

> If yes: Have you ever attended a workshop in which you received special training to teach such classes?
>
> [   ] Yes
>
> [   ] No

A clear and well-organized presentation of contingency questions is particularly important in interview schedules. An individual who receives a questionnaire in the mail can reread a question if it is unclear the first time through. If an interviewer becomes confused,

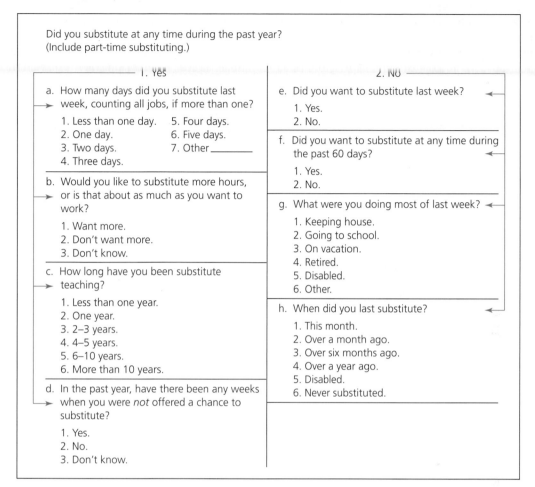

Figure 17.2 *Example of Several Contingency Questions in an Interview Schedule*

Adapted from E. S. Babbie (1973). *Survey research methods.* Belmont, CA: Wadsworth, p. 149.

however, or reads a question poorly or in an unclear manner, the whole interview may become jeopardized. Figure 17.2 illustrates a portion of an interview schedule designed to determine certain characteristics of substitute teachers that includes several contingency questions.

PREPARING THE COVER LETTER

Mailed surveys require something that telephone surveys and face-to-face personal interviews do not—a cover letter explaining the purpose of the questionnaire. Ideally, the cover letter also motivates the members of the sample to respond.

The cover letter should be brief and addressed specifically to the individual being asked to respond. It should explain the purpose of the survey, emphasize the importance of the topic of the research, and (it is hoped) engage the respondent's cooperation. If possible, it should indicate a willingness on the part of the researcher to share the results of the study once it is completed. Confidentiality and anonymity of the respondents should be assured.* It also helps if the researcher obtains the sponsorship of an institution of some importance that is known to the respondent. The specific deadline date by which the completed questionnaire is to be returned should be indicated, and the letter should be individually signed by the researcher.

*If done under a university (or other agency) sponsorship, the letter should indicate that the study has been approved by the "Research with Human Subjects" review committee.

Every effort should be made to avoid the appearance of a form letter. Finally, the return should be made as easy as possible; hence, enclosing a stamped, self-addressed envelope is always a good idea. Figure 17.3 presents an example of a cover letter.

TRAINING INTERVIEWERS

Both telephone and face-to-face interviewers need to be trained beforehand. Many suggestions have been made in this regard, and we have space to mention only a few of them here.[15] Telephone interviewers need to be shown how to engage their interviewees so that they do not hang up on them before the interview has even begun. They need to know how to explain quickly the purpose of their call, and why it is important to obtain information from the respondent. They need to learn how to ask questions in a way so as to encourage those they call to respond honestly.

Face-to-face interviewers need all of the above and more. They need to learn how to establish rapport with their interviewees and to put them at ease. If a respondent seems to be resistant to a particular line of questioning, the interviewer needs to know how to move on to a new set of questions and return to the previous questions later. The interviewer needs to know when and how to "follow up" on an unusual answer or one that is ambiguous or unclear. Interviewers also need training in gestures, manner, facial expression, and dress. A frown at the wrong time can discourage a respondent from even attempting to answer a question! In sum, the general topics to be covered in training interviewers should always include at least the following:

1. Procedures for contacting respondents and introducing the study. All interviewers should have a common understanding of the purposes of the study.
2. The conventions that are used in the design of the questionnaire with respect to wording and instructions for skipping questions (if necessary) so that interviewers can ask the questions in a consistent and standardized way.
3. Procedures for probing inadequate answers in a nondirective way. *Probing* refers to following up incomplete answers in ways that do not favor one particular answer over another. Certain kinds of standard probes, such as asking "Anything else?" "Tell me more," or "How do you mean that?" usually will handle most situations.

4. Procedures for recording answers to open-ended and closed-ended questions. This is especially important with regard to answers to open-ended questions, which interviewers are expected to record verbatim.
5. Rules and guidelines for handling the interpersonal aspects of the interview in a nonbiasing way. Of particular importance here is for interviewers to focus on the task at hand and to avoid expressing their views or opinions (verbally or with body language) on any of the questions being asked.[16]

USING AN INTERVIEW TO MEASURE ABILITY

Although the interview has been used primarily to obtain information on variables other than cognitive ability, an important exception can be found in the field of developmental and cognitive psychology. Interviews have been used extensively in this field to study both the content and processes of cognition. The best-known example of such use is to be found in the work of Jean Piaget and his colleagues. They used a semistructured sequence of contingency questions to determine a child's cognitive level of development.

Other psychologists have used interviewing procedures to study thought processes and sequences employed in problem solving. While not used extensively to date in educational research, an illustrative study is that of Peter Freyberg and Roger Osborne, who studied student understanding of basic science concepts. They found frequent and important misconceptions of which teachers were often unaware. Teachers often assumed that students used such terms as "gravity," "condensation," "conservation of energy," and "wasteland community" in the same way as they did themselves. Many 10-year-olds and even some older children, for example, believed that condensation on the outside of a water glass was caused by water getting through the glass. One 15-year-old displayed ingenious (although incorrect) thinking as shown in the following excerpt:

(Jenny, aged 15): Through the glass—the particles of water have gone through the glass, like diffusion through air—well, it hasn't got there any other way. (Researcher): A lot of younger people I have talked to have been worried about this water . . . it troubles them. (Jenny): Yes, because they haven't studied things like we have studied. (Researcher): What have you studied which helps?

COLLEGE OF EDUCATION

San Francisco State University

October 1, 200–

Mr. Robert R. Johnson
Social Studies Department
Oceana High School
Pacifica, California 96321

Dear Mr. Johnson,

The Department of Secondary Education of San Francisco State University prepares over 100 student teachers every year to teach in the public and private schools of California. It is our goal to help our graduates become as well prepared as possible to teach in today's schools. The enclosed questionnaire is designed to obtain your views on ideas you can offer to improve the quality of our training program. Your suggestions will be considered in planning for revisions in the program in the coming academic year. We will also provide you with a copy of the results of our study.

We will greatly appreciate it if you will complete the questionnaire and return it in the enclosed stamped, self-addressed envelope by October 18th. We realize your schedule is a busy one and that your time is valuable, but we are sure that you want to improve the quality of teacher training as much as we do. Your responses will be kept completely confidential; we ask for no identifying information on the questionnaire form. The study has been approved by the University's Research with Human Subjects review committee.

We want to thank you in advance for your cooperation.

William P. Jones
Chair of the Department

Figure 17.3 *Cover Letter for Use in a Survey*

(Jenny): Things that pass through air, and concentrations and how things diffuse.[17]

Freyberg and Osborne make the argument that teachers and curriculum developers must have such information on student conceptions if they are to teach effectively. They have also shown how such research can improve the content of achievement tests by including items specifically directed at common misconceptions.

Nonresponse

In almost all surveys, some members of the sample will not respond. This is referred to as **nonresponse.** It may be due to a number of reasons (lack of interest in the topic being surveyed, forgetfulness, unwillingness to be surveyed, and so on), but it is a major problem that seems to be increasing in recent years as more and more people seem (for whatever reason) to be unwilling to participate in surveys.

Why is nonresponse a problem? The chief reason is that those who do not respond will very likely differ from the respondents with regard to answers to the survey questions. Should this be the case, any conclusions drawn on the basis of the respondents' replies will be misleading and not a true indication of the views of the population from which the sample was drawn.

TOTAL NONRESPONSE

Graham Kalton points out that total nonresponse can occur in interview surveys for any of the following reasons: intended respondents can refuse to be interviewed, not be at home when the interviewer calls, be unable to take part in the interview for various reasons (such as illness, deafness, inability to speak the language), or sometimes cannot even be located.[18] Of these, refusals and not-at-homes are the most common.

In mail surveys, a few questionnaires may not be deliverable, and occasionally a few respondents will return their questionnaires unanswered as an indication of their refusal to participate. Generally, however, all that is known about most mail survey nonresponse is that the questionnaire has not been returned. The reason for the lack of return may be any of the ones we have already mentioned.

A variety of techniques are employed by survey researchers to reduce nonresponse. In interview surveys, the interviewers are carefully trained to be courteous, to ask questions pleasantly and sensitively, to dress conservatively, or to return to conduct an interview at a more appropriate time if the situation warrants. Assurances of anonymity and confidentiality are made (this is done in mailed surveys as well). Questions are usually organized to start with fairly simple and nonthreatening questions. Not-at-homes are treated by callbacks (a second, third, or even a fourth visit) on different days and at different times during the day. Sometimes appointments are set up at a convenient time for the respondent. Mailed questionnaires can be followed up with a reminder letter and often a second or sometimes even a third mailing. A frequently overlooked technique is the offering of a tangible reward as an inducement to respond. There is nothing inappropriate about paying (in some manner) respondents for providing information.

Nonresponse is a serious problem in many surveys. Some observers have stated that response rates for uncomplicated face-to-face surveys by nongovernment survey organizations are about 70 to 75 percent. Refusals make up the majority of nonrespondents in face-to-face interviews, with not-at-homes constituting most of the remainder. Telephone surveys generally have somewhat lower response rates than face-to-face surveys (respondents simply hang up). Response rates in mail surveys are quite varied, ranging from as low as 10 percent to as high as 90 percent.[19] Furthermore, nonresponse is not evenly spread out among various subgroups within the United States. Nonresponse rates in face-to-face interview surveys, for example, are much higher in inner cities than in other locations.

A procedure commonly used to handle nonresponse, especially in telephone surveys, is *random replacement,*

which is continuing to add randomly selected cases until the desired sample size is reached. This method does not work for the same reason mentioned earlier: Those who are not contacted or who refuse to respond probably would have answered differently than those who do respond. Remember: A random sample requires that the sample actually comprises those who are originally selected.

In addition to doing as much as possible to reduce nonresponse, researchers should obtain, during the survey or in other ways, as much demographic information as they can on respondents. This not only permits a more complete description of the sample, but also may support an argument for representativeness—*if* it turns out that the sample is very similar to the population with regard to those demographics that are pertinent to the study (Figure 17.4). These may include gender, age, ethnicity, family size, and so forth. Needless to say, all such data must be reported, not just those that support the claim of representativeness. Such an argument is always inconclusive since it is impossible to obtain data on all pertinent variables (or even to be sure as to what they all are), but it is an important feature of any survey that has a substantial nonresponse (we would say over 10 percent). A major difficulty with this suggestion is that the needed demographics may not be available for the population. In any case, the nonresponse rate should always be reported.

ITEM NONRESPONSE

Partial gaps in the information provided by respondents can also occur for a variety of reasons: The respondent may not know the answer to a particular question; he or she may find certain questions embarrassing or perhaps irrelevant; the respondent may be pressed for time, and the interviewer may decide to skip over part of the questions; the interviewer may fail to record an answer. Sometimes during the data analysis phase of a survey, the answers to certain questions are thrown out because they are inconsistent with other answers. Some answers may be unclear or illegible.

Item nonresponse is rarely as high as total nonresponse. Generally it varies according to the nature of the question asked and the mode of data collection. Very simple demographic questions usually have almost no nonresponse. Kalton estimates that items dealing with income and expenditures may experience item nonresponse rates of 10 percent or more, while extremely sensitive or difficult questions may produce nonresponse rates that are much higher.[20]

Figure 17.4
*Demographic
Data and
Representativeness*

Listed below is a summary of some of the more common suggestions for increasing the response rate in surveys.

1. *Administration of the questionnaire or interview schedule:*
   - Make conditions under which the interview is conducted, or the questionnaire administered, as simple and convenient as possible for each individual in the sample.
   - Be sure that the group to be surveyed knows something about the information you want to sobtain.
   - Train face-to-face or telephone interviewers in how to ask questions.
   - Train face-to-face interviewers in how to dress.
2. *Format of the questionnaire or interview schedule:*
   - Be sure that sufficient space is provided for respondents (or the interviewer) to fill in the necessary biographical data that is needed (age, gender, grade level taught, and so on).
   - Specify in precise terms the objectives the questionnaire or interview schedule is intended to achieve—exactly what kind of information is wanted from the respondents?

- Be sure each item in the questionnaire or interview schedule is related to one of the objectives of the study—that is, it will help obtain information about the objective.
- Use closed-ended (e.g., multiple-choice) rather than or in addition to open-ended (e.g., free response) questions.
- Ensure that no psychologically threatening questions are included.
- Eliminate any leading questions.
- Check for ambiguity of items with a panel of judges. Revise as needed.
- Pretest the questionnaire or interview schedule with a small group similar to the sample to be surveyed.

Problems in the Instrumentation Process in Survey Research

Several threats to the validity of the instrumentation process in surveys can cause individuals to respond differently than they might otherwise. Suppose, for example, that a group of individuals is brought together to

Is Low Response Rate Necessarily a Bad Thing?

As pointed out by some researchers, "A basic tenet of survey research is that high response rates are better than low response rates. Indeed, a low rate is one of the few outcomes or features that—taken by itself—is considered to be a major threat to the usefulness of a survey."* Two recent studies of telephone response rates, however, suggest that this is not necessarily true. In one instance, the authors used an omnibus questionnaire that included demographic, behavioral, attitudinal, and knowledge items. In the other, the researcher used data from the *Index of Consumer Sentiment* (a measure of consumer opinions about the economy). In both studies, a comparison of response rates of 60 to 70 percent to rates substantially lower (i.e., 20 to 40 percent) showed minimal differences in substantive answers.

The implication is that the substantial expense of attaining higher rates may not be worth it. It is pointed out that "observing (the) little effect of nonresponse when comparing response rates of 60 to 70 percent with rates much lower does not mean that the surveys with 60 to 70 percent response rates do not themselves suffer from significant nonresponse bias,"[†] that is, a 90 percent rate may have given different results from the 60 percent rate. Further, these results should not be generalized to other types of questions or respondents other than those in these particular surveys.

*R. Curtin, S. Presser, and E. Singer (2000). The effects of response rate changes on the Index of Consumer Sentiment. *Public Opinion Quarterly, 64:*413.

[†]S. Keeter, C. Miller, A. Kohut, R. Groves, and S. Prosser (2000). Consequences of reducing nonresponse in a large national telephone survey. *Public Opinion Quarterly, 64:*125–148.

---

be interviewed all in one place, and an extraneous event (say, a fire drill) occurs during the interview process. The event might upset or otherwise affect various individuals, causing them to respond to the interview questions differently than they would had the event not occurred.

Whenever researchers do not take care in preparing their questionnaires—if questions are leading or insensitive, for example—it may cause individuals to respond differently. If the conditions under which individuals are questioned in interview studies are somewhat unusual (during the dinner hour; in poorly lit rooms; and so on), they may react in certain ways unrelated to the nature of the questions themselves.

Finally, the characteristics of a data collector (such as garish dress, insensitivity, rudeness, and use of offensive language) can affect how individuals respond, causing them to react in part to the data collector rather than to the questions. There is also the possibility of an unconscious bias on the part of the data collector, as when he or she asks leading questions of some individuals but not others.

Evaluating Threats to Internal Validity in Survey Research

There are four main threats to internal validity in survey research: mortality, location, instrumentation, and instrument decay. A mortality threat arises in longitudinal studies unless all of the data on "lost" subjects are deleted, in which case the problem becomes one of appropriate generalization. A location threat can occur if the collection of data is carried out in places that may affect responses (e.g., a survey of attitudes toward the police conducted in a police station). Instrument decay can occur in interview surveys if the interviewers get tired or are rushed. This, as well as defects in the instruments themselves, not only may reduce the validity of the information obtained but also may introduce a systematic bias.

Data Analysis in Survey Research

After the answers to the survey questions have been recorded, there remains the final task of summarizing the responses in order to draw some conclusions from the results. The total size of the sample should be reported, along with the overall percentage of returns. The percentage of the total sample responding for each item should then be reported. Finally, the percentage of respondents who chose each alternative for each question should be given. For example, a reported result might be as follows: "For item 26, regarding the approval of a no-smoking policy while school is in session, 80 percent indicated they were in favor of such a policy, 15 percent indicated they were not in favor, and 5 percent said they were neutral."

An Example of Survey Research

In the remainder of this chapter, we present a published example of survey research, followed by a critique of its strengths and weaknesses. As we did in our critiques of the different types of research studies we analyzed in other chapters, we use several of the concepts introduced in earlier parts of the book in our analysis.

From: *Journal of Research in Personality* (1997), 31(1): 21–31.

Jobs, Careers, and Callings:
People's Relations to Their Work

Amy Wrzesniewski
University of Michigan

Clark McCauley
Bryn Mawr College

Paul Rozin
University of Pennsylvania

Barry Schwartz
Swarthmore College

We present evidence suggesting that most people see their work as either a Job (focus on financial rewards and necessity rather than pleasure or fulfillment: not a major positive part of life), a Career (focus on advancement), or a Calling (focus on enjoyment of fulfilling, socially useful work). Employees at two work sites (n = 196) with a wide range of occupations from clerical to professional were unambiguous in seeing their work primarily in terms of a Job, Career, or Calling. Differences in respondents' relations to their work could not be reduced in demographic or occupational differences; an homogenous subset of 24 college administrative assistants were, like the total sample of respondents, distributed evenly across Job, Career, and Calling. © 1997 Academic Press

Work constitutes more than one-third of waking life for most human adults, and there is a substantial psychological literature devoted to the study of work. Satisfaction with work varies widely across individuals (Staw & Ross, 1985) and seems to constitute a substantial part of the subjective quality of life (Loscocco & Roschelle, 1991). In a measure of general life satisfaction, work satisfaction was found to account for 20% of the variance of the entire measure (Campbell, Converse, & Rodgers, 1976). Quality of life, in turn, can have a major effect on life stress and on health (Adler & Matthews, 1994). There is strong evidence for the belief that dispositional factors are related to job attitudes (Staw, Bell & Clausen, 1986; Staw & Ross, 1985). This suggests that the way individuals view work may be a function of stable traits, not just reflections of the work itself. It is possible that these traits interact with the objective characteristics of the work (Hackman & Oldham, 1980; Hulin & Blood, 1968; Schneider, 1983). For these reasons, we believe it is important to understand the subjective experience of work: how individuals differ in their experience of the work they do.

The inspiration for our approach came from *Habits of the Heart,* in which Bellah *et al.* (1985) argue that there are three distinct relations people can have to their work: as Jobs, Careers, and Callings (see also Schwartz, 1986, 1994). The distinctions, drawn starkly, are these: People who

This research was supported by funding from the John D. and Catherine T. MacArthur Foundation Network on Health-Related Behaviors. Correspondence concerning this article should be addressed to Amy Wrzesniewski, Department of Psychology, University of Michigan, 525 E. University, Ann Arbor, MI 48109-1109. E-mail: amywvtz@umich.edu.

have (Jobs) are only interested in the material benefits from work and do not seek or receive any other type of reward from it. The work is not an end in itself, but instead is a means that allows individuals to acquire the resources needed to enjoy their time away from the Job. The major interests and ambitions of Job holders are not expressed through their work. In contrast, people who have (Careers) have a deeper personal investment in their work and mark their achievements not only through monetary gain, but through advancement within the occupational structure. This advancement often brings higher social standing, increased power within the scope of one's occupation, and higher self-esteem for the worker (Bellah *et al.*, 1985, p. 66). Finally, people with (Callings) find that their work is inseparable from their life. A person with a Calling works not for financial gain or Career advancement, but instead for the fulfillment that doing the work brings to the individual. The word "calling" was originally used in a religious context, as people were understood to be "called" by God to do morally and socially significant work (see Weber, 1956, 1963). While the modern sense of "calling" may have lost its religious connection (but see Davidson & Caddell, 1994, for evidence that the religious connection still matters), work that people feel called to do is usually seen as socially valuable—an end in itself—involving activities that may, but need not be, pleasurable.

The Job—Career—Calling distinction is not necessarily dependent upon occupation. Within any occupation, one could conceivably find individuals with all three kinds of relations to their work. Although one might expect to find a higher number of Callings among those in certain occupations, for example, teachers and Peace Corps employees, it is plausible that salespersons, medical technicians, factory workers, and secretaries could view their work as a Calling. Such people could love their work and think that it contributes to making the world a better place.

Although this tripartite set of relations to work has not been explored by psychologists, it is related to some aspects of work that have received considerable attention. One is work satisfaction, which has been found to be sensitive to many different conditions of work, including actual work tasks, work organization, pay, supervision, benefits, promotional structure, and coworkers (Locke & Latham, 1990). While we expect that work satisfaction would be highest for Callings and lowest for Jobs, we do not believe that the Job, Career, Calling distinction is defined entirely by its potential relation to job satisfaction. For example, a successful career in business or bureaucracy might be just as satisfying as a calling.

Another analysis of work that is related to the present one contrasts intrinsic and extrinsic motivation to work. An ambitious recent study on this issue includes the formulation of a scale, the Work Preference Inventory, to assess intrinsic versus extrinsic work motivations. Amabile, Hill, Hennessey, & Tighe (1994) analyzed the extrinsic orientation into two subfactors: compensation and outward orientation. Correspondingly, intrinsic motivation is analyzed into challenge and enjoyment. We presume that intrinsic motivation is most associated with Callings, and extrinsic motivation is most associated with Jobs, with Careers somewhat closer to extrinsic than intrinsic motivation. However, we do not see the distinction between Careers and either Jobs or Callings as neatly falling on the intrinsic–extrinsic dimension. For example, a Calling might be neither challenging nor enjoyable and a Career might be both.

We believe the Job–Career–Calling distinction has not previously been explicit in the psychology of work. Amabile *et al.'s* (1994) Work Preference Inventory, Hall's (1968) "sense of calling" sub-scale, and some work on work involvement and identification (Lodahl & Kejner, 1965) all relate to issues raised by the tripartite work classification, but none of these research directions proposes or accounts for the three distinct relations to work that are the focus of the present study.

The questionnaire developed and reported on in this paper was designed to provide initial evidence of the usefulness of the Job–Career–Calling distinctions. We asked how easy it is for people to classify themselves along these lines, what features of each dimension may be most

Definition #1

Theory

Definition #2

Definition #3

Hypothesis?

Related literature

Justification

Is this the purpose?

Table 1 *Paragraphs Describing Job, Career, and Calling*

Job

　　Mr. A. works primarily to earn enough money to support his life outside of his job. If he was financially secure, he would no longer continue with his current line of work, but would really rather do something else instead. Mr. A's job is basically a necessity of life, a lot like breathing or sleeping. He often wishes the time would pass more quickly at work. He greatly anticipates weekends and vacations. If Mr. A lived his life over again, he probably would not go into the same line of work. He would not encourage his friends and children to enter his line of work. Mr. A is very eager to retire.

Career

　　Mr. B basically enjoys his work, but does not expect to be in his current job five years from now. Instead, he plans to move on to a better, higher level job. He has several goals for his future pertaining to the positions he would eventually like to hold. Sometimes his work seems a waste of time, but he knows that he must do sufficiently well in his current position in order to move on. Mr. B can't wait to get a promotion. For him a promotion means recognition of his good work, and is a sign of his success in competition with his coworkers.

Calling

　　Mr. C's work is one of the most important parts of his life. He is very pleased that he is in this line of work. Because what he does for a living is a vital part of who he is, it is one of the first things he tells people about himself. He tends to take his work home with him and on vacations, too. The majority of his friends are from his place of employment, and he belongs to several organizations and clubs relating to his work. Mr. C feels good about his work because he loves it, and because he thinks it makes the world a better place. He would encourage his friends and children to enter his line of work. Mr. C would be pretty upset if he were forced to stop working, and he is not particularly looking forward to retirement.

Appears to have
context validity

significant, what objective and psychological features of occupations or persons are related to each dimension, and what the correlates of viewing one's work as a Job, Career, or Calling might be, in terms of measures of work and life satisfaction and physical health.

METHOD

The Questionnaire

　　The questionnaire was titled the "University of Pennsylvania Work–Life Questionnaire" and the terms "job," "career," and "calling" did not appear in it (except for a job satisfaction question—see below). On the first page of the questionnaire appeared three separate paragraphs describing Job, Career, and Calling according to the definitions offered by Bellah et al. (1985) and Schwartz (1986, 1994) (Mr. A, Mr. B, Mr. C; Table 1). The instructions were first to read all three paragraphs and then to indicate how much the respondent was like Mr. A, Mr. B, and Mr. C, on a scale ranging from "very much," "somewhat," "a little," or "not at all like me" (scored 3–0).[1]

Clear rationale
　　On the second spage of the questionnaire appeared 18 true–false items asking about specific aspects of relations to work that are relevant to the Job, Career, Calling distinction (Table 2). Almost all of the true–false items appeared in the prose of at least one of the paragraphs. Of the true–false items, 5 were intended to probe *behaviors* related to work, while the other 13 examined *feelings* about work.

　　Next appeared three items taken from Campbell *et al.* (1976) that asked for self-rating of satisfaction with life (SATLIFE), health (SATHEALTH), and job (SATJOB) on a seven-point scale (1 = completely dissatisfied to 7 = completely satisfied). Next was a self-rating of health (Health; 1 = poor, 2 = fair, 3 = good, 4 = excellent) and a self-rating of occupational status (SOCSTAND; 1 = bottom social standing to 9 = top social standing). In order to gauge work sat-

[1]Future versions of this scale should be in terms of "A" rather than "Mr. A." and so forth.

Table 2 *Eighteen True–False Items, with Percent Answering "True" and Relations to Job, Career, and Calling Paragraphs* (n = 196)

Item	% True	Correlations with paragraph scores		
		Job	Career	Calling
I find my work rewarding. (REWARD)	84	−46*	−13	33*
I am eager to retire. (RETIRE)	36	49*	−01	−41*
My work makes the world a better place. (BETTERWORLD)	62	−35*	−04	28*
I am very conscious of what day of the work week it is and I greatly anticipate weekends. I say, "Thank God it's Friday!" (TGIF)	62	40*	08	−41*
I tend to take my work with me on vacations. (VACATION)	15	−20*	05	42*
I expect to be in a higher level job in five years. (HIGHERLEVEL)	49	−11	58*	−06
I would choose my current work life again if I had the opportunity. (CHOOSEAGAIN)	50	−47*	−19	48*
I feel in control of my work life. (INCONTROL)	68	−27*	−16	20*
I enjoy talking about my work to others (TALKWORK)	68	−48*	05	40*
I view my job primarily as a stepping stone to other jobs. (STEPPINGSTONE)	26	06	55*	−13
My primary reason for working is financial—to support my family and lifestyle. (FINANCIAL)	64	54*	0	−58
I expect to be doing the same work in five years. (SAMEWORK)	54	−05	−47*	22
If I was financially secure, I would continue with my current line of work even if I was no longer paid. (STILLWORK)	25	−32*	−11	47*
When I am not at work, I do not think much about my work. (THINKWORK)	51	24*	−19	−33*
I view my job as just a necessity of life, much like breathing or sleeping. (NECESSITY)	50	48*	01	−29*
I never take work home with me. (TAKEHOME)	31	21*	−05	32*
My work is one of the most important things in my life. (WORKIMPORTANT)	48	−41*	−04	59*
I would not encourage young people to pursue my kind of work. (NOTENCOURAGE)	25	39*	02	−31*

Note: Decimal points omitted from tabeled correlations. Item abbreviations appear in parentheses.

*$p < .05$, two-tailed. Job and Calling items coded "1" for responses indicating Calling and "0" otherwise; remaining items coded "1" for response indicating Career.

isfaction in another manner, respondents were asked to rank hobbies, work, and friends based upon the amount of satisfaction they received from each (WORKRANK).

Finally, several demographic items appeared at the end of the questionnaire, including occupation, age, sex, years of education (SCHOOL), income, years in current position (JOBYEARS), hours worked per week, days missed per year excluding vacation (DAYSMISS), marital status, and number of children. Income was divided into five categories (from under $25,000 to over $75,000) and age was recorded in years. Respondents were assigned to occupational levels based upon the occupational prestige score given in their occupations by the Nakao & Treas (in press) 1989 General Social Survey (OCCSTATUS). The occupational prestige scale ranges from 0–100, and respondents were divided into levels by increments of 10; therefore, a respondent with an occupation that scores 26 was assigned to the third occupational level.

Respondents

Very limiting

The respondents were 76 (out of 130) employees of a major state university student health service, and 162 (out of 283) non-faculty employees of a small liberal arts college (total 238 out of 413 employees) who volunteered to complete the questionnaire. Only respondents reporting working at least 35 or more hours per week were retained, leaving a total of 196 respondents for analysis.

Self-selected sample

The two work sites were surveyed at different times. Some minor additions and deletions of questions were made after the first site (student health service) was surveyed, but all questions reported in this study were identical in the two samples. The questionnaires were completed anonymously.

RESULTS

Characteristics of the Respondents

Of the 196 respondents, 79% were female, with a mean age of 42 years (range 21–69). This sample included individuals in a range of occupations, including physicians, nurses, administrators, pharmacists, health educators, librarians, supervisors, computer programmers and analysts, medical technicians, administrative assistants, and clerical employees. The income distribution of the respondents was: <$25,000/year, 39%; 25,000–34,999, 28%; 35,000–49,999, 18%;

Helpful demographics

50,000–74,999, 13%; >75,000, 3%. The distribution of occupational status (OCCSTATUS), as defined above, was level 3 (3%), level 4 (19%), level 5 (12%), level 6 (34%), level 7 (29%), level 8 (2%), and level 9 (2%).

Categorization of Respondents

A respondent was placed into the category corresponding to the paragraph to which the respondent gave the highest rating. A small number of respondents misunderstood the instructions and rated only one paragraph, presumably the one that was most like them. Others rated two or more paragraphs as being equally like them. These two groups of respondents (total

Questionable procedure

$n = 61$) were not included in the analyses in which respondents are categorized by the highest rated paragraph, but were included in analyses of correlations of particular paragraph scores with the various outcome variables and in analyses focusing on responses to the true–false items.

As shown in Table 3 (top), respondents are clear in expressing how they view their work. Mean relevance ratings for the highest rated paragraph are 2.5, 2.4, and 2.4 for Job, Career, and Calling respondents; the mean ratings for the other paragraphs range from .23 to .70. The standard deviations indicate that there is practically no overlap in relevance ratings: essentially all those viewing work as a Job, for instance, rated the Job paragraph as "very much" or "somewhat like me" and rated Career and Calling as "not at all" or "a little like me."

A subsample; $n = 196 - 61$

In this sample of 135 employees, nearly equal numbers of respondents viewed work as a Job, Career, or Calling (44, 43, and 48, respectively). Furthermore, Job and Calling paragraph ratings were strongly and inversely related [$r (n = 135) = -.52, p < .01$], whereas Career ratings were not correlated (r's $= -.14$ and $-.01$) with either Calling or Job (correlations not tabled). Consistent with the descriptions of the three dimensions, Calling respondents ranked work as relatively

Table 3 *Means of Characteristics of 135 Respondents Viewing Work as Job, Career, or Calling*

	Job (n = 44)	Career (n = 43)	Calling (n = 48)
Paragraph ratings			
JOB	2.5 (0.7)	0.7 (0.6)	0.2 (0.4)
CAREER	0.5 (0.7)	2.4 (0.6)	0.5 (0.7)
CALLING	0.2 (0.4)	0.6 (0.7)	2.4 (0.6)
Demographics			
AGE	43.0[a] (8.0)	37.1[b] (10.0)	44.9[a] (10.7)
INCOME	1.9[a] (1.1)	1.8[a] (0.9)	2.5[b] (1.3)
SCHOOL	14.8[a] (2.4)	15.1[a] (2.3)	16.6[b] (2.4)
SOCSTAND	4.5[a] (2.0)	5.2[a] (1.7)	6.0[b] (1.4)
OCCSTATUS	5.5[a] (1.2)	5.2[a] (1.3)	6.5[b] (1.2)
JOBYEARS	6.7[b] (4.5)	4.8[a] (3.7)	8.1[b] (7.4)
Well-being			
SATLIFE	4.5[a] (1.1)	4.7[a] (1.1)	5.5[b] (1.0)
SATHEALTH	5.3 (1.4)	5.4 (1.4)	5.6 (1.2)
SATJOB	4.2[a] (1.5)	4.6[a] (1.4)	5.7[b] (1.2)
WORKRANK	2.6[a] (.54)	2.4[a] (.66)	1.6[b] (.74)
HEALTH	3.2 (.07)	3.3 (0.7)	3.3 (0.6)
DAYSMISS	3.2[a] (2.1)	4.3[a] (2.9)	2.0[b] (2.1)

Note: Table includes only respondents who rated all three paragraphs, and rated no more than one dimension as most like them. Some means are based on 1–4 fewer respondents than column *n* because of missing data. Standard deviations appear in parentheses. Means in the same row that do not share the same superscript (*a* or *b*) differ at $p < .05$ two-tailed.

more important in comparison to hobbies and friends (mean rank 1.6) than did Career or Calling respondents (mean ranks 2.6 and 2.4; see Table 3).

Relation of Dimensions to the 18 True–False Items

All but three of the true–false items appeared in at least one paragraph, and we examined responses to these items chiefly in order to confirm our expectation about the correlation of items with paragraph scores. That is, the true–false items provided the opportunity to test our expectation that each hypothesized feature of Job, Career, and Calling would individually correlate higher with the rating of the paragraph in which the feature appeared than with ratings of the other two paragraphs.

As shown in Table 2, the correlations of true–false items with their corresponding paragraph ratings were generally significant and substantial (.25 to .55). The significant correlations include the three statements that were not included in any of the paragraphs, "I enjoy talking about my work with others" (positively with Calling and negatively with Job), "My primary reason for working is financial—to support my family and lifestyle" (positively with Job and negatively with Calling), and "I am very conscious of what day of the work week it is and I greatly anticipate weekends. I say, 'Thank God It's Friday!' '" (positively with Job and negatively with Calling). The only surprise was the extent to which Job and Calling items correlated equally well (in opposite directions) with both Job and Calling paragraph ratings. Career items correlated only with ratings of the Career paragraph. In short, responses to the true–false items give the same picture as the intercorrelations of paragraph ratings already described: Job and Calling are inversely related, whereas Career is independent of both Job and Calling.

Concurrent Validity: see text, p. 162

Not substantial

Not clear to us

See text, p. 343

Sum = 51%

These are not factor loadings.

A principal components factor analysis of the matrix of intercorrelations of the 18 true–false items revealed four factors with eigenvalues greater than 1.00: 4.91, 2.09, 1.64, and 1.25. The rotated factors accounted respectively for 27.30, 11.60, 9.09, and 6.92% of the total variance. Of these factors, the first was identified by item loadings as representing the Job/Calling dimension. Because the responses of those who view work as a Job or Calling are often judged to be opposite responses to the same items, it is possible that the same factor can be representing both dimensions. The items with the highest loadings were CHOOSEAGAIN, WORKIMPORTANT, TALK-WORK, STILLWORK, FINANCE, AND NECESSITY (all loadings > .54; see Table 2 for full items). The second factor was identified by item loadings as probably representing the Career dimension. The items with the highest loadings were HIGHERLEVEL, SAMEWORK, and STEPPINGSTONE (all loadings > .55) and the only other item with a loading above .40 was THINKWORK.

Relation of Dimensions to Demographic Characteristics

Table 3 shows difference also in JOBYEARS.

Delta would be preferable here.

Table 3 presents the mean scores on demographic variables for those respondents who view work as a Job, Career, or Calling. With the exception of age, with Career respondents younger than Job respondents by an average of 6 years, there were no significant differences between Career and Job respondents. Compared with Job and Career respondents, however, Calling respondents were significantly better paid (INCOME) and better educated (SCHOOL), and had occupations higher in both self-perceived status (SOCSTAND) and objective prestige level (OCC-STATUS).

Relation of Dimensions to Well-Being

We suggested that Callings would generally be associated with greater life, health, and job satisfaction and with better health. Results were consistently in this direction, with Job respondents scoring lowest and Calling respondents highest on all four of these measures (Table 3). Calling respondents reported notably and significantly higher life and job satisfaction than Job and Career respondents. Calling respondents also ranked work satisfaction significantly higher (relative to hobbies and friends) than did Job and Career respondents (WORKRANK, Table 3). In contrast, differences between Job and Career respondents on satisfaction and two health measures were all small and non-significant.

Although this study was not directed at assessing work performance, we did include one relevant measure: self report of days of work missed. Calling respondents missed significantly fewer days than either Job or Career respondents; Career and Job respondents did not differ significantly in days missed (Table 3).

Results from 24 Administrative Assistants

Alternative explanation

A control for internal validity

Since respondents who viewed their work as a Calling did work of significantly higher occupational status than respondents in the other two groups, the data reported here could be taken to make the fairly obvious point that people in relatively high-status occupations think more positively about their work and have more interesting and challenging work than people in relatively low-status occupations. We were able to assess this possibility by analyzing the results from a subset of our respondents. The largest single occupational group represented in our sample consisted of 24 administrative assistants at the college work site. This group was analyzed separately in order to determine both whether the Job, Career, Calling distinction might be made within a single occupation, and if so, whether the dimensions might relate to well-being variables.

Surprisingly, the administrative assistants produced a broad and rather equal distribution of work orientations: 9 respondents saw themselves as having Jobs, 7 had Careers, and 8 had Callings. Table 4 presents a comparison of means for those respondents who view work as a Job,

Table 4 *Means of Characteristics of 24 Administrative Assistants Viewing Work as Job, Career, or Calling*

	Job (n = 0)[a]	Career (n = 7)[b]	Calling (n = 9)[c]
Paragraph ratings			
JOB	2.6 (0.7)	0.2 (0.5)	0.3 (0.5)
CAREER	0.9 (0.8)	2.0 (0.8)	0.5 (0.8)
CALLING	0.0 (0.0)	0.6 (0.6)	2.1 (0.8)
Demographics			
AGE	44.9 (7.8)	47.3 (8.9)	47.1 (12.7)
INCOME	1.3 (1.0)	1.4 (0.5)	1.3 (0.5)
SCHOOL	14.7 (2.0)	14.1 (2.2)	15.0 (1.8)
SOCSTAND	4.6 (1.5)	6.7 (1.4)	5.1 (1.7)
OCCSTATUS*			
JOBYEARS	4.2 (3.3)	6.8 (3.8)	9.2 (8.5)
Well-being			
SATLIFE	4.1 (1.4)	4.9 (1.5)	5.3 (1.6)
SATHEALTH	5.6 (1.7)	6.1 (0.9)	5.6 (1.4)
SATJOB	3.8 (1.8)	5.1 (0.7)	5.3 (1.8)
WORKRANK	2.7 (0.5)	2.0 (0.6)	1.9 (1.0)
HEALTH	3.1 (0.8)	3.6 (0.5)	3.6 (0.5)
DAYSMISS	2.6 (1.6)	1.0 (1.0)	2.1 (2.4)

Note: p levels not marked on this table because of small *n*.

[a]*n* = 8 for CAREER, CALLING, and SATJOB.

[b]*n* = 5 for JOB and CALLING.

[c]*n* = 6 for JOB and CAREER; *n* = 7 for SOCSTAND.

*All administrative assistants shared the same occupational status rating.

Career, or Calling parallel to the comparison for all respondents in Table 3. Although Table 4 results will not support statistical analysis—given the small total of administrative assistants—nevertheless the results are descriptively quite striking. The Job–Career–Calling distinction emerged just about as clearly for administrative assistants as for the total sample. Respondents with Jobs, Careers, and Callings were very similar in age, income, and education, but may have differed in self-perceived social standing of their occupation (Career highest) and years in present position (Career between Job and Calling). Particularly notable is the fact that, descriptively, the difference between Job and Calling respondents was about the same for the homogenous subgroup as for the total group. For SATLIFE, SATJOB, and WORKRANK, the mean difference between Job and Calling respondents was about the same magnitude for administrative assistants (Table 4) as for all occupations together (Table 3).

As already noted, the results for our small sample of administrative assistants cannot have more than heuristic value. Nevertheless, we believe they are important in showing that the Job–Career–Calling distinction can be made clearly even within a group of persons relatively homogenous in occupation and background, and that these orientations may have some interesting correlates even within the homogenous group.

DISCUSSION

We believe that we have demonstrated that it is easy for most people to assign themselves to one of the three Job, Career, or Calling dimensions, based on degree of agreement with three paragraphs representing the three work-relations. The differentiation of the three orientations

Margin notes: Number is not the major issue. / Good justification. / The sample does not justify this statement.

was clearer and easier than we had anticipated. In accord with our predictions, we presented evidence indicating highest life and work satisfaction for respondents who see their work as a Calling—even when income, education, and occupation are at least roughly controlled (the administrative assistants).

Our results offer some support for our suggestion that being in a Calling is related to better health. This suggestion came out of the growing literature relating lifestyle and other social factors to health (see, e.g., Adler, Boyce, & Chesney, 1993, on SES and health). Although respondents in a Calling were not higher than others on self-reported health, they did, in our total sample report missing fewer days of work. Whether missing fewer days is better interpreted as better health or better motivation for work cannot be established in this initial study.

In addition to the evidence favoring the meaningfulness of the Job, Career, Calling distinction and its linkage to satisfaction and other outcome variables, we note three somewhat surprising results of this study.

1. Although there are no doubt relations between occupation and distribution of people across the Job–Career–Calling dimension, it is clear that all three dimensions can be well represented in at least some occupations. We demonstrated this for the case of administrative assistants.

2. While Job and Calling seem to fall on a single dimension, having to do with work as fulfillment versus work as a boring necessity, self-perception as having a Career seems to be orthogonal to this dimension. A Career, as represented in this study, focuses on promotion and associated change in the kind of work performed. Furthermore, the concern with advancement that seems to mark a Career does not appear to confer much advantage over a Job in the various well-being variables we assessed.

3. Satisfaction with life and with work may be more dependent on how an employee sees his or her work than on income or occupational prestige. Our evidence for this claim is that the absolute size of Job vs. Calling differences is about the same in the homogenous sample of administrative assistants as in the total sample of respondents.

Respondents in lower level occupations are likely to see themselves as having either a Job or a Career. The prevalence of Career in lower status occupations may be at least partially a function of age; Career respondents tend to be the youngest respondents. This interpretation implies that younger employees may be willing to work harder than their older counterparts, in order to advance within their organizations. If true, this would have important implications for managers trying to generate higher levels of productivity. It is possible, however, that the link between youth and Career means not a willingness of younger employees to work harder, but rather an expectation held by younger employees that they will eventually move on to better positions. This interpretation would predict more hope but not harder working habits for more youthful employees. Indeed it may be that many younger people who think they have Careers later become resigned to having only a Job.

We believe that our results offer initial support for the value of viewing work according to the Job–Career–Calling distinction. But many important questions remain. Because the Amabile *et al.* (1994) paper came out after we had completed our study, we were unable to introduce some of the advances made in that study into our own. Amabile *et al.* (1994) identified "challenge" as an important factor in the intrinsic–extrinsic distinction. Our paragraphs did not represent this concept well, and it might be a critical feature that differentiates both Careers and Callings from Jobs. Our Career dimension has the "thinnest" definition, focusing almost entirely on the single dimension of advancement. Challenge might enrich this dimension, and make Career less unidimensional.

Future work should relate the Amabile intrinsic–extrinsic distinction to Jobs, Careers, and Callings. Future work might also address the relation between Job, Career, and Calling and meas-

Marginal annotations:

Slight difference

Right

Right

Seems reasonable

But not by much and not in sample of 24

Limitation recognized

ures of work performance, as well as the distribution and predictors of Job, Career, and Calling with the steps of a well-marked ladder of Career advancement, such as is found in some large corporations or in the armed forces. Most critically, since we can find people who locate themselves along each dimension in at least some occupations, we can begin to ask how the same work can be a Calling for one person and a Job for another. This issue may require moving beyond the questionnaire methods of the present study; interviews of considerable depth may be necessary in order to develop hypotheses about how an individual comes to understand her work in terms of Job, Career, or Calling.

Good suggestions

References

Adler, N., Boyce, W. T., & Chesney, M. A. (1993). Socioeconomic inequalities in health: No easy solution. *Journal of the American Medical Association, 269:*3140–3145.

Adler, N., & Matthews, K. (1994). Health psychology: Why do some people get sick and some stay well? *Annual Review of Psychology, 45:*229–259.

Amabile, T. M., Hill, K. G., Hennessey, B. A., & Tighe, E. M. (1994) The work preference inventory: Assessing intrinsic and extrinsic motivational orientations. *Journal of Personality & Social Psychology, 66:*950–967.

Bellah, R. N., Madsen, R., Sullivan, W. M., Swidler, A., & Tipton, S. M. (1985). *Habits of the heart.* New York: Harper & Row.

Campbell, A., Converse, P. E., & Rodgers, W. L. (1976). *The quality of American life.* New York: Russell Sage Foundation.

Davidson, J. C., & Caddell, D. P. (1994). Religion and the meaning of work. *Journal for the Scientific Study of Religion, 33:*135–147.

Hackman, J. R., & Oldham, G. R. (1980). *Work redesign,* Reading, MA: Addison–Wesley.

Hall, R. H. (1968). Professionalism and bureaucratization. *American Sociological Review, 33:*92–104.

Hullin C. L., & Blood, M. R. (1968). Job enlargement, individual differences, and worker responses. *Psychological Bulletin, 69:*41–55.

Locke, E. A., & Latham, G. P. (1990). Work motivation and satisfaction: Light at the end of the tunnel. *Psychological Science, 4:*240–246.

Lodahl, T. M., & Kejner, M. (1965). The definition and measurement of job involvement. *Journal of Applied Psychology, 49:*24–33.

Loscocco, K. A., & Roschelle, A. R. (1991). Influences on the quality of work and nonwork life: Two decades in review. *Journal of Vocational Behavior, 39:*182–225.

Nakao, K., & Treas, J. (1994). Updating occupational prestige and socioeconomic scores: How the new measures measure up. *Sociological Methodology, 24:*1–72.

Schneider, B. (1983). Interactional psychology and organizational behavior. *Research in Organizational Behavior, 5:*1–31.

Schwartz, B. (1986) *The battle for human nature: Science, morality, and modern life.* New York: Norton.

Schwartz, B. (1994). *The costs of living: How market freedom erodes the best things in life.* New York: Norton.

Staw, B. M., Bell, N. E., & Clausen, J. A. (1986). The dispositional approach to job attitudes. *Administrative Science Quarterly, 31:*56–77.

Staw, B. M., & Ross, J. (1985). Stability in the midst of change: A dispositional approach to job attitudes. *Journal of Applied Psychology, 70:*469–480.

Weber, M. (1958). *The Protestant ethic and the spirit of capitalism.* New York: Scribner.

Weber, M. (1963). *The sociology of religion.* Boston: Beacon.

Analysis of the Study

PURPOSE/JUSTIFICATION

A clear statement of purpose would be helpful. A very general statement appears at the end of the first paragraph, that is, "to understand the subjective experience of work: how individuals differ in their experience of the work they do." The last paragraph of the introduction suggests the purpose of the study is to "provide initial evidence of the usefulness of the Job-Career-Calling distinctions." We think that the purpose of this survey was, in addition, to assess the paragraph instrument and to study relationships between these different orientations and other variables, including demographics and work and life satisfaction.

We think that a good justification is provided for both the importance of the study and for the theoretical orientation. The authors state that no research has been focused on the topic of their investigation.

DEFINITIONS

The primary categorical variable (Job-Career-Calling) is clearly defined both constitutively and operationally. While definition of some other variables (e.g., "satisfaction with life, health and job") would be helpful, we do not consider this a major omission.

PRIOR RESEARCH

Research review is minimal, and used primarily to justify the study. The vast literature on work satisfaction should, we think, have received more attention. A study that developed a scale used in the present study is mentioned, but only briefly.

HYPOTHESES

The report would be much improved by a clear statement of hypotheses. We think there are at least two: (1) that respondents will be readily divided into the three "types" of work orientation, and (2) that work orientation will be related to job satisfaction.

SAMPLE

The sample is a convenience sample consisting of employees of two colleges. Generalizability is further hampered by the fact that only 58 percent actually participated and did so as volunteers—introducing a very probable bias. This limitation is somewhat reduced by the purpose of the study—to show that the orientation types are identifiable, at least with some college employees—but clearly limits conclusions. The sample is described in terms of gender, age, occupation, income, and occupational status, which is helpful in deciding where results might be generalized.

INSTRUMENTATION

The main focus of the study was to determine whether the instrument the researchers developed does identify work orientation types. It appears to have content validity. Although the results indicate that it is effective (i.e., valid for this purpose), reliability data should be provided. It is important to know whether other parallel paragraphs would have classified individuals the same and, even more importantly—given the authors' assumption of persistence of orientation—how stable results are over time. Concurrent validity is addressed through a comparison of "paragraph" scores with true-false item responses. While results are generally as expected, we disagree that correlations as low as .25 are "substantial." Correlations with individual items must be expected to be lower than those with scores based on multiple items, but even here correlations this low have little meaning. More impressive evidence would consist of correlations with less-similar instruments, such as ratings by colleagues. The predicted finding of relationships to work satisfaction is supportive of construct validity.

INTERNAL VALIDITY

Because this survey examines relationships, internal validity must be addressed. While applicable to all of the relationships reported, we limit ourselves to those between orientation type and job and life satisfaction where the finding is higher satisfaction among "Calling" type than Job or Career. We think a testing threat is likely because the content of the paragraphs is so similar to "job satisfaction." The authors point out that job satisfaction is not identical with orientation type, but we think the instrument suggests otherwise. This seems much less the case with "life satisfaction." The authors point out that Job and Career orientation types were very similar on "subject characteristics," with the possible exception of age. However, the Calling orientation is better paid, better educated, and held higher-status jobs. In order to control these threats, the subgroup of administrative assistants was analyzed, suggesting that none of these variables account for the relationship between "Calling" and satisfaction. The authors properly point out the tentativeness of this conclusion. A location threat is also possible since at least two locations were used in the collection of data, but it seems unlikely.

DATA ANALYSIS

Use of the highest-rated paragraph to designate "type" is appropriate, but elimination of 61 individuals who misunderstood directions or who "tied" further limits the sample. Inclusion of these 61 people in correlations with other variables complicates interpretation (since there is no longer a single sample) and seems unnecessary since the sample size is adequate without them ($n = 196 - 61 = 135$). Reporting of means and standard deviations on other variables within each type is appropriate. Reporting of probabilities is inferior to reporting Delta as a descriptive indicator and completely indefensible as an index of generalizability—because of the nature of the sample.

RESULTS

In general, results are adequately presented, with the exception of the reference to Table 2 in the discussion of factor analysis, which implies that the values in the table are factor loadings; they are not. We have previously criticized the reporting of probabilities. The authors give the size of the subsample as the reason for not reporting probabilities in Table 4, but sample size is not the issue; it is the complete failure to ensure randomness. We are unclear as to the meaning of results on "work rank" (Table 3). Does the lower mean for the "Calling" orientation indicate that work for this group ranks lower or higher in comparison with hobbies and friends?

DISCUSSION

We agree with the major conclusion that the paragraph scale effectively identified work orientation. The overlap among orientation categories is minimal; 95 percent of job scores should fall between 1.1 and 3.9 [$2.5 \pm 2(.7)$], whereas means for the other orientations are 0.7 and 0.2. This must be qualified by recalling that some unreported number (less than 61) had tied "type" scores. The statement that it is easy for "most people" to assign themselves to "type" should be limited to this particular sample. The authors sometimes report their findings as suggestive (e.g., relationships to health), but at other times imply too much generalizability (e.g., work satisfaction and career orientation). Finally, we think that the authors make too much of small differences in the case of "missed days of work" and age differences among "types."

Go back to the **Interactive and Applied Learning Tools** feature at the beginning of the chapter for a listing of interactive and applied activities. Go to the **Online Learning Center** at www.mhhe.com/fraenkel5e or your **Interactive Student CD-ROM** to take practice quizzes and receive immediate feedback, practice with key terms, review chapter content and main ideas, and find annotated Web links.

Main Points

MAJOR CHARACTERISTICS OF SURVEY RESEARCH

- Most surveys possess three basic characteristics: (1) the collection of information (2) from a sample (3) by asking questions, in order to describe some aspects of the population of which the sample is a part.

THE PURPOSE OF SURVEY RESEARCH

- The major purpose of all surveys is to describe the characteristics of a population.
- Rarely is the population as a whole studied, however. Instead, a sample is surveyed and a description of the population is inferred from what the sample reveals.

TYPES OF SURVEYS

- There are two major types of surveys that can be conducted: cross-sectional surveys and longitudinal surveys.
- Three longitudinal designs commonly employed in survey research are trend studies, cohort studies, and panel studies.
- In a trend study, different samples from a population whose members change are surveyed at different points in time.
- In a cohort study, different samples from a population whose members do *not* change are surveyed at different points in time.
- In a panel study, the same sample of individuals is surveyed at different times over the course of the survey.
- Surveys are not suitable for all research topics, especially those that require observation of subjects or the manipulation of variables.

STEPS IN SURVEY RESEARCH

- The focus of study in a survey is called the unit of analysis.
- As in other types of research, the group of persons that is the focus of the study is called the target population.
- There are four basic ways to collect data in a survey: by direct administration of the survey instrument to a group, by mail, by telephone, or by personal interview. Each has both advantages and disadvantages.
- The sample to be surveyed should be selected randomly if possible.
- The most common types of instruments used in survey research are the questionnaire and the interview schedule.

QUESTIONS ASKED IN SURVEY RESEARCH

- The nature of the questions, and the way they are asked, are extremely important in survey research.
- Most surveys use some form of closed-ended question.
- The survey instrument should be pretested with a small sample similar to the potential respondents.
- A contingency question is a question whose answer is contingent upon how a respondent answers a prior question to which the contingency question is related. Well-organized and sequenced contingency questions are particularly important in interview schedules.

THE COVER LETTER

- A cover letter is a letter sent to potential respondents in a mail survey explaining the purpose of the survey questionnaire.

INTERVIEWING

- Both telephone and face-to-face interviewers need to be trained before they administer the survey instrument.
- Both total and item nonresponse are major problems in survey research that seem to be increasing in recent years. This is a problem because those who do not respond are very likely to differ from the respondents in terms of how they would answer the survey questions.

THREATS TO INTERNAL VALIDITY IN SURVEY RESEARCH

- Threats to the internal validity of survey research include location, instrumentation instrument decay, and mortality.

DATA ANALYSIS IN SURVEY RESEARCH

- The percentage of the total sample responding for each item on a survey questionnaire should be reported, as well as the percentage of the total sample who chose each alternative for each question.

Census 397

Closed-ended question 402

Cohort study 397

Contingency question 404

Cover letter 405

Cross-sectional survey 397

Direct administration of survey instrument to a group 399

Interview schedule 401

Item nonresponse 408

Longitudinal survey 397

Mail survey 399

Nonresponse 407

Open-ended question 402

Panel study 397

Personal interview 400

Questionnaire 401

Survey 396

Telephone survey 400

Trend study 397

Unit of analysis 398

Key Terms

For Discussion

1. For what kinds of topics might a personal interview be superior to a mail or telephone survey? Give an example.
2. When might a telephone survey be preferable to a mail survey? To a personal interview?
3. Give an example of a question a researcher might use to assess each of the following characteristics of the members of a teachers group:
   a. Their income.
   b. Their teaching style.
   c. Their biggest worry.
   d. Their knowledge of teaching methods.
   e. Their opinions about homogeneous grouping of students.
4. Suppose a researcher is interested in finding out how elementary school administrators feel about elementary school counseling. Give an example of a contingency question that could be used in a personal interview.
5. Which mode of data collection—mail, telephone, or personal interview—would be best for each of the following surveys?
   a. The reasons why some students drop out of college before they graduate.
   b. The feelings of high school teachers about special classes for the gifted.
   c. The attitudes of people about raising taxes to pay for the construction of new schools.
   d. The duties of secondary school superintendents in a midwestern state.
   e. The reasons why individuals of differing ethnicity did or did not decide to enter the teaching profession.
   f. The opinions of teachers about the idea of minimum competency testing before permanent tenure would be granted.
   g. The opinions of parents of students in a private school about the elimination of certain subjects from the curriculum.

6. Listed below are some definitions of target populations from which a sample is to be selected and surveyed. See if you can improve (make more precise) the definitions of each:
   a. "All of the counselors in the school."
   b. "All of the parents of the students in our school."
   c. "All of the administrators in the school district."
   d. "All chemistry students."
   e. "All of the teachers of the gifted."
7. Look at each of the three open-ended questions in the example on p. 402. See if you can restate them in a closed-ended form.
8. Try to restate one of the closed-ended questions on page 403 in a contingency format.
9. What suggestions can you offer, beyond those given in this chapter, for improving the rate of response in surveys?

Notes

1. J. L. Blaga and L. E. Nielsen (1983). The status of state history instruction. *Journal of Social Studies Research, 7*(1): 45–57.

2. J. J. Blase (1987). Dimensions of effective school leadership: The teacher's perspective. *American Educational Research Journal, 24*(4): 589–610.

3. J. Tlou and C. Bennett (1983). Teacher perceptions of discipline problems in a central Virginia middle school. *Journal of Social Studies Research, 7*(2): 37–59.

4. C. I. Chase (1985). Two thousand teachers view their profession. *Journal of Educational Research, 79*(1): 12–18.

5. J. Raths, M. Wojtaszek-Healy, and C. Kubo Della-Plana (1987). Grading problems: A matter of communication. *Journal of Educational Research, 80*(3): 133–137.

6. M. A. Sheppard, M. S. Goodstadt, and M. M. Willett (1987). Peers or parents: Who has the most influence on cannabis use? *Journal of Drug Education, 17*(2): 123–128.

7. A. Weaver Hart (1987). A career ladder's effect on teacher career and work attitudes. *American Educational Research Journal, 24*(4): 479–504.

8. B. Herlihy, M. Healy, E. Piel Cook, and P. Hudson (1987). Ethical practices of licensed professional counselors: A survey of state licensing boards. *Counselor Education and Supervision,* September: 69–76.

9. R. M. Jaeger (1988). Survey research methods in education. In Richard M. Jaeger (ed.), *Complementary methods for research in education.* Washington, DC: American Educational Research Association, pp. 308–310.

10. R. M. Grovers and R. L. Kahn (1979). *Surveys by telephone: A national comparison with personal interviews.* New York: Academic Press.

11. F. J. Fowler, Jr. (1984). *Survey research methods.* Beverly Hills, CA: Sage Publications, p. 101.

12. The development of survey questions is an art in itself. We can only begin to deal with the topic here. For a more detailed discussion, see J. M. Converse and S. Presser (1986). *Survey questions: Handcrafting the standardized questionnaire.* Beverly Hills, CA: Sage.

13. For further suggestions, see N. E. Gronlund (1988). *How to construct achievement tests.* Englewood Cliffs, NJ: Prentice Hall.

14. E. S. Babbie (1973). *Survey research methods.* Belmont, CA: Wadsworth, p. 145.

15. For a more detailed discussion, see Fowler, op. cit., Chapter 7.

16. Ibid., pp. 109–110.

17. P. Freyberg and R. Osborne (1981). Who structures the curriculum: Teacher or learner? *Research Information for Teachers,* Number Two. SET, Hamilton, New Zealand.

18. G. Kalton (1983). *Introduction to survey sampling.* Beverly Hills, CA: Sage, p. 64.

19. Ibid., p. 66.

20. Ibid., p. 67.

Introduction to Qualitative Research

Part Five begins our discussion of qualitative research. We devote a

separate chapter to the nature of qualitative research, and follow it

with two chapters on the main techniques that qualitative

researchers use to collect and analyze their data. These include

observation, interviewing, and content analysis. We provide some

examples of published studies in which researchers use these tech-

niques, along with our analysis of the strengths and weaknesses of

their investigations.

The Nature of Qualitative Research

CHAPTER 18

The Nature of Qualitative Research

```
What Is Qualitative Research?          Qualitative and Quantitative
                                        Research Reconsidered

General Characteristics of             Ethics and Qualitative Research
Qualitative Research

Philosophical Assumptions              Internal Validity in
Underlying Qualitative as              Qualitative Research
Opposed to Quantitative Research

Postmodernism                          Generalization in
                                        Qualitative Research

Steps in Qualitative Research     Approaches to Qualitative
                                  Research
                              Biography
                              Phenomenology
                              Grounded Theory
                              Case Studies
                     Ethnographic and Historical Research
                     Sampling in Qualitative Research
```

Objectives

Studying this chapter should enable you to:

- Explain *what is meant by the term "qualitative research."*
- Describe *five general characteristics that most qualitative studies have in common.*
- Describe *briefly the philosophic assumptions underlying qualitative and quantitative research.*
- Describe *briefly some of the steps involved in qualitative research.*
- Describe *at least three ways that qualitative research differs from quantitative research.*
- Describe *briefly at least four different approaches to qualitative research.*
- Describe *the type of samples that are used in qualitative research, and give some examples of these types.*
- Explain *how generalizing differs in qualitative and quantitative research.*
- Describe *briefly how matters of ethics affect qualitative research.*
- Suggest *some ways that qualitative and quantitative approaches to research might be used together.*

Interactive and Applied Learning

After, or while reading this chapter:

Go to your Interactive Student CD-ROM to:
- Learn More About Mixed Designs and Their Limitations

Go to your Interactive Student CD-ROM or Student Workbook to do the following activities:
- Activity 18.1: Qualitative Research Questions
- Activity 18.2: Qualitative vs. Quantitative Research
- Activity 18.3: Approaches to Qualitative Research

H ey, Brendan."

"Oh, hi, Melissa. Where've you been?"

"I just came from my research class. We're just starting to learn about qualitative research."

"What's that?"

"Well, sometimes a researcher wants to obtain an in-depth look at a particular individual, say, or a specific situation. Maybe even a particular set of instructional materials."

"Yeah?"

"When they do, they ask some interesting questions. Instead of asking something like 'What do people think about this?' or 'What would happen if I do this?' qualitative researchers ask, 'How do these people act?' or 'How are things done?' or 'How do people give meaning to their lives?'"

"How come?"

"Because what they want to get at is some idea of the *quality* of the experiences that people have."

"Sounds different. Tell me more."

We shall indeed "tell Brendan (and you) more" about qualitative research. The nature of qualitative research, and how it differs from quantitative resarch, is what this chapter is all about.

What Is Qualitative Research?

Most of the questions being asked by researchers who use the methodologies discussed in previous chapters involve the extent to which various learnings, attitudes, or ideas exist, or how well or how accurately they are being developed. Thus, possible avenues of research included comparisons between alternative methods of teaching (as in experimental research); examining research among variables (as in correlational relationships); comparing groups of individuals in terms of existing differences on certain variables (as in causal-comparative research); or interviewing different groups of educational professionals, such as teachers, administrators, and counselors (as in survey research). These methods are frequently referred to as "quantitative research."

As we mentioned in Chapter One, however, researchers might wish to obtain a more holistic impression of teaching and learning than answers to the above questions can provide. A researcher might wish to know more than just "to what extent" or "how well" something is done. He or she might wish to obtain a more complete picture, for example, of what goes on in a particular classroom or school.

Consider the teaching of history in secondary schools. Just how do history teachers teach their subject? What kinds of things do they do as they go about their daily routine? What sorts of things do students do? In what kinds of activities do they engage? What are the explicit and implicit "rules of the game" in history classes that seem to help or hinder the process of learning?

To gain some insight into these concerns, a researcher might try to document or portray the everyday experiences of students (and teachers) in history classrooms. The focus would be on only one classroom (or a small number of them at most). The researcher would observe the classroom on as regular a basis as possible and attempt to describe, as fully and as richly as possible, what he or she sees.

The above example points to the fact that many researchers are more interested in the *quality* of a particular activity than in how often it occurs or how it would otherwise be evaluated. Research studies that investigate the quality of relationships, activities, situations, or materials are frequently referred to as **qualitative research.** This type of research differs from the methodologies discussed in earlier chapters in that there is a greater emphasis on holistic description—that is, on describing in detail all of what goes on in a particular activity or situation rather than on comparing the effects of a particular treatment (as in experimental research), say, or on describing the attitudes or behaviors of people (as in survey research).

We believe that educational research increasingly is, and should be, a mixture of quantitative and qualitative approaches (We'll discuss this in more detail later in the chapter.) However, to assist you in understanding the many types of research that exist, we think it useful to

Table 18.1 *Quantitative Versus Qualitative Research*

Quantitative Methodologies	Qualitative Methodologies
Preference for precise hypotheses stated at the outset.	Preference for hypotheses that emerge as study develops.
Preference for precise definitions stated at the outset.	Preference for definitions in context or as study progresses.
Data reduced to numerical scores.	Preference for narrative description.
Much attention to assessing and improving reliability of scores obtained from instruments.	Preference for assuming that reliability of inferences is adequate.
Assessment of validity through a variety of procedures with reliance on statistical indices.	Assessment of validity through cross-checking sources of information (triangulation).
Preference for random techniques for obtaining meaningful samples.	Preference for expert informant (purposive) samples.
Preference for precisely describing procedures.	Preference for narrative/literary descriptions of procedures.
Preference for design or statistical control of extraneous variables.	Preference for logical analysis in controlling or accounting for extraneous variables.
Preference for specific design control for procedural bias.	Primary reliance on researcher to deal with procedural bias.
Preference for statistical summary of results.	Preference for narrative summary of results.
Preference for breaking down complex phenomena into specific parts for analysis.	Preference for holistic description of complex phenomena.
Willingness to manipulate aspects, situations, or conditions in studying complex phenomena.	Unwillingness to tamper with naturally occurring phenomena.

point out the essential differences between quantitative and qualitative research. Table 18.1 compares the distinctive features of each approach.

General Characteristics of Qualitative Research

Many different types of qualitative methodologies exist, but there are certain general features that characterize most qualitative research studies. Not all qualitative studies will necessarily display all of these characteristics with equal strength. Nevertheless, taken together, they give a good overall picture of what is involved in this type of research. Robert Bogdan and Sari Knopp Biklen describe five such features.[1]

1. The **natural setting** is the direct source of data, and the researcher is the key instrument in qualitative research. Qualitative researchers go directly to the particular setting in which they are interested to observe and collect their data. They spend a considerable amount of time actually being in a school, sitting in on faculty meetings, attending parent-teacher association meetings, observing teachers in their classrooms and in other locales, and in general directly observing and interviewing individuals as they go about their daily routines.

   Sometimes they come equipped only with a pad and a pencil to take notes, but often they use sophisticated audio- and videotaping equipment. Even when such equipment is used, however, the data are collected right at the scene and supplemented by the researcher's observations and insights about what occurred. As Bogdan and Biklen point out, qualitative researchers go to the particular setting of interest because they are concerned with *context*—they feel that activities can best be understood in the actual settings in which they occur. They also feel that human behavior is vastly influenced by the setting in which such behavior takes place, and, hence, whenever possible they visit such settings.

2. *Qualitative data are collected in the form of words or pictures rather than numbers.* The kinds of data collected in qualitative research include interview transcripts, field notes, photographs, audio recordings, videotapes, diaries, personal comments, memos, official records, textbook passages, and anything else that can convey the actual words or actions of people. In their search for understanding, qualitative researchers do not usually attempt to reduce their data to numerical symbols,[2] but rather

seek to portray what they have observed and recorded in all of its richness. Hence, they do their best not to ignore anything that might lend insight to a situation. Gestures, jokes, conversational gambits, artwork or other decorations in a room—all are noted by qualitative researchers. To a qualitative researcher, no data are trivial or unworthy of notice.

3. *Qualitative researchers are concerned with process as well as product.* Qualitative researchers are especially interested in *how* things occur. Hence, they are likely to observe how people interact with each other; how certain kinds of questions are answered; the meanings that people give to certain words and actions; how people's attitudes are translated into actions; how students seem to be affected by a teacher's manner, or gestures, or comments; and the like.

4. *Qualitative researchers tend to analyze their data inductively.* Qualitative researchers do not, usually, formulate a hypothesis beforehand and then seek to test it out. Rather, they tend to "play it as it goes." They spend a considerable amount of time collecting their data (again, primarily through observing and interviewing) before they decide what are the important questions to consider. As Bogdan and Biklen suggest, qualitative researchers are not putting together a puzzle whose picture they already know. They are *constructing* a picture that takes shape as they collect and examine the parts.[3]

5. *How people make sense out of their lives is a major concern to qualitative researchers.* A special interest of qualitative researchers lies in the perspectives of the subjects of a study. Qualitative researchers want to know what the participants in a study are thinking and why they think what they do. Assumptions, motives, reasons, goals, and values—all are of interest and likely to be the focus of the researcher's questions. It also is not uncommon for a researcher to show a completed videotape or the contents of his or her notes to a participant to check on the accuracy of the researcher's interpretations. In other words, the researcher does his or her best to capture the thinking of the participants from the *participants'* perspective (as opposed to the researcher merely reporting what he or she thinks) as accurately as possible.

Table 18.2 presents a summary of the main characteristics of qualitative research.

Philosophical Assumptions Underlying Qualitative as Opposed to Quantitative Research

Differences between quantitative and qualitative researchers are often discussed in terms of differing **paradigms** or *worldviews*—that is, differences in the basic set of beliefs or assumptions that guide the way they approach their investigations. These assumptions are related to the views they hold concerning the nature of reality, the relationship of the researcher to that which he or she is studying, the role of values in a study, and the process of research itself.

The quantitative approach is associated with the philosophy of **positivism,** which emerged in the nineteenth century. Perhaps the person most responsible for the development and spread of this philosophy was Auguste Comte (1798–1857). In 1824 he wrote, "I believe that I shall succeed in having it recognized . . . that there are laws as well-defined for the development of the human species as for the fall of a stone."[4] Comte argued that the "positive" stage of human knowledge is reached when people begin to rely on empirical data, reason, and the development of scientific laws to explain phenomena. The scientific method, positivists believe, is the surest way to produce effective knowledge.

Although positivism has changed somewhat over the years, a basic premise is that there exists a reality "out there," independent of us, waiting to be discovered, that is driven by stable natural laws. The task of science is to discover the nature of this reality and how it works. A related emphasis is on breaking complex phenomena down into manageable pieces for study and eventual reassembly into the whole. The researcher's role is that of a "disinterested scientist," standing apart from that which is being studied, with his or her biases and values excluded through experimental design and control.

Challenges to the philosophy of positivism have come from many directions and continue to be debated. In general, qualitative researchers are sympathetic to the issues raised by critical researchers that we described in Chapter One, and they present their methods as an alternative to the quantitative approach. Many of them advocate a more "artistic," as opposed to a "scientific," approach to research. Further, their goals are often different; this is illustrated by the preference of

Table 18.2 *Major Characteristics of Qualitative Research*

1. **Naturalistic inquiry**	Studying real-world situations as they unfold naturally; nonmanipulative, unobtrusive, and noncontrolling; openness to whatever emerges—lack of predetermined constraints on outcomes.
2. **Inductive analysis**	Immersion in the details and specifics of the data to discover important categories, dimensions, and interrelationships; begin by exploring genuinely open questions rather than testing theoretically derived (deductive) hypotheses.
3. **Holistic perspective**	The *whole* phenomenon under study is understood as a complex system that is more than the sum of its parts; focus is on complex interdependencies not meaningfully reduced to a few discrete variables and linear, cause-effect relationships.
4. **Qualitative data**	Detailed, thick description; inquiry in depth; direct quotations capturing people's personal perspectives and experiences.
5. **Personal contact and insight**	The researcher has direct contact with and gets close to the people, situation, and phenomenon under study; researcher's personal experiences and insights are an important part of the inquiry and critical to understanding the phenomenon.
6. **Dynamic systems**	Attention to process; assumes change is constant and ongoing whether the focus is on an individual or an entire culture.
7. **Unique case orientation**	Assumes each case is special and unique; the first level of inquiry is being true to, respecting, and capturing the details of the individual cases being studied; cross-case analysis follows from and depends on the quality of individual case studies.
8. **Context sensitivity**	Places findings in a social, historical, and temporal context; dubious of the possibility or meaningfulness of generalizations across time and space.
9. **Empathic neutrality**	Complete objectivity is impossible; pure subjectivity undermines credibility; the researcher's passion is understanding the world in all its complexity—not proving something, not advocating, not advancing personal agendas, but understanding; the researcher includes personal experience and empathic insight as part of the relevant data, while taking a neutral nonjudgmental stance toward whatever content may emerge.
10. **Design flexibility**	Open to adapting inquiry as understanding deepens and/or situations change; avoids getting locked into rigid designs that eliminate responsiveness; pursues new paths of discovery as they emerge.

Source: Reprinted from Michael Quinn Patton (1990). *Qualitative evaluation and research methods,* 2nd ed. Newbury Park, CA: Sage, pp. 40–41.

some for fostering multiple interpretations of events, depending on how they are perceived by the individuals involved. This is the opposite of what almost all physical scientists (and most social scientists) advocate.

Table 18.3 reveals the basic differences between the two approaches with regard to these philosophic assumptions.

Postmodernism

Recently, a number of scholars have begun to question whether research (and educational research in particular) can really contribute to an understanding of human behavior. These scholars, usually referred to as **postmodernists,** criticize the relevance of mainstream research as we have described it in many of the chapters in this text. They present an even more intensive critique of such research, in fact, than do the critical researchers we described in Chapter One.

Postmodernists offer a number of criticisms of traditional research, but perhaps the most common are the following two: first, they deny the existence of underlying structures (e.g., meaning, laws) in the domain of social behavior. Michel Foucault, in fact, argues that all knowledge and truth are products of history, power, and social interests and, hence, cannot be "discovered," as positivists, for example, believe.[5] Second, they argue that all naturally occurring (i.e., nonmathematical) languages are inevitably made up of ambiguous terms that change over time and that all statements that use these languages, therefore, cannot be verified.[6] Postmodernism has had an impact on all intellectual disciplines, including an increasing discussion of its implications for educational research.

Table 18.3 *Differing Philosophical Assumptions of Quantitative and Qualitative Researchers*

Assumptions of Quantitative Researchers	Assumptions of Qualitative Researchers
There exists a reality "out there," independent of us, waiting to be known. The task of science is to discover the nature of reality and how it works.	The individuals involved in the research situation construct reality; thus, realities exist in the form of multiple mental constructions.
Research investigations can potentially result in accurate statements about the way the world really is.	Research investigations produce alternative visions of what the world is like.
It is possible for the researcher to remove him- or herself—to stand apart—from that which is being researched.	It is impossible for the researcher to stand apart from the individuals he or she is studying.
Facts stand independent of the knower and can be known in an undistorted way.	Values are an integral part of the research process.
Facts and values are distinct from one another.	Facts and values are inextricably intertwined.
The proper design of research investigations will lead to accurate conclusions about the nature of the world.	The initial ambiguity that occurs in a study is desirable.
The purpose of educational research is to explain and be able to predict relationships. The ultimate goal is the development of laws that make prediction possible.	The purpose of educational research is *verstehen*, that is, *understanding* of what things mean to others. Highly generalizable "laws," as such, can never be found.

What do you think? Can "truth" be verified? Or is it "a product of history, power, and social interests" as postmodernists claim?

Steps in Qualitative Research

The steps involved in conducting a qualitative research study are not as distinct as they are in quantitative research; they often overlap and are sometimes even conducted concurrently. All qualitative studies have a distinct starting and ending point, however. They begin when the researcher identifies the phenomenon he or she wishes to study, and they end when the researcher draws whatever final conclusions he or she wishes to make.

Although the steps involved in qualitative research are not as distinct as they are in quantitative studies (they aren't even necessarily sequential), several steps can be identified. Let us describe them briefly.

1. *Identification of the phenomenon to be studied.* Before any study can begin, the researcher must identify the particular phenomenon he or she is interested in investigating. Suppose, for example, a researcher wishes to conduct a study to investigate the interaction between minority and nonminority students in an inner-city high school. The phenomenon of interest here is "student interaction," specifically in an inner-city school. Admittedly, this is a rather general topic, but it does provide a starting point from which the researcher can proceed. Stated as a research

question, the researcher might ask: "To what extent and in what ways do minority and nonminority students in an inner-city high school interact?"

Such a question suggests what are known as **foreshadowed problems.** All qualitative studies begin with such problems—they are akin to the overall statement of the problem that we discussed in Chapter Two. They give the researcher something to look for. They should not be considered restrictive or limiting, however, since their purpose is to provide direction, to serve as a guide. For example, as the investigation of the question mentioned above proceeds, it may become evident that extracurricular as well as in-school activities need to be looked at, so the kinds of participation by students in such activities would be observed and analyzed. Foreshadowed problems are often reformulated several times during the course of a qualitative study.

2. *Identification of the participants in the study.* The participants in the study constitute the sample of individuals who will be observed (interviewed, etc.)—in other words, the subjects of the study. In almost all qualitative research, the sample is a **purposive sample** (see Chapter Six). Random sampling ordinarily is not feasible, since the researcher wants to ensure that he or she obtains a sample that is uniquely suited to the intent of the study. In the current example, inner-city high school students are the subjects of interest, but not just any group of such students will do. They must be found in a particular inner-city high school or schools.

Controversies in Research

Clarity and Postmodernism

Are the concepts and language that postmodernists use unnecessarily difficult to understand? Such criticisms are frequently made not only by education students, but by others as well. Alison Jones, for example, argues that this difficulty results from the fact that most students lack historical exposure to the context of the issues.* Mark Constas believes that proponents of postmodernism in educational research need to provide better clarification† and (as paraphrased by Wanda Pillow) that some theorists "exhibit symptoms such as speaking gibberish, while others wander aimlessly (and mean-inglessly), and still others are in a state of paralysis."‡ Patti Lather counters that the search for clarity is part of the "humanist romance of knowledge as cure" and that the role of postmodernists is to question "taken-for-granted structures of intelligibility."§ (4, p. 540). These would include such concepts as "truth," "progress," "rationality," "gender," and "race."

Pillow argues that Constas misses the point. "Why, around questions of postmodernism's influence on educational research, are we still pursuing questions of truth and intelligibility? Perhaps what we need more of are examples of what postmodern research looks like, does, and is committed to. That is, less about attempts to contain what it is, and more working examples of what it may be."∥

*A. Jones (1997). Teaching post-structuralist feminist theory in education: Student resistances. *Gender and Education, 9* (3):266–269.
†M. A. Constas (1998). Deciphering postmodern educational research. *Educational Researcher, 27* (9):36–42.

‡W. S. Pillow (2000). Deciphering attempts to decipher postmodern educational research. *Educational Researcher, 29* (June–July):21–24.
§P. Lather (1996). Troubling clarity: The politics of accessible language. *Harvard Educational Review* 66(3) pp. 525–554.
∥Pillow (2000), p. 23.

3. *Generation of hypotheses.* Contrary to most quantitative studies, hypotheses are not posed at the beginning of the study by the researcher. Instead, they emerge from the data as the study progresses. Some are almost immediately discarded; others are modified or replaced. New ones are formulated. A typical qualitative study may begin with few, if any, hypotheses being posed by the researcher at the start, but with several being formulated, reconsidered, dropped, and modified as the study proceeds. In the current example, a researcher might hypothesize originally that interaction in an inner-city high school between minority and nonminority students, outside of daily class sessions, will be minimal. As he or she observes the daily goings-on in the school, the hypothesis may be modified a number of times as the researcher becomes more aware of times and places where the students actually do interact fairly regularly and frequently.

4. *Data collection.* There is no "treatment" in a qualitative study, nor is there any "manipulation" of subjects. The participants in a qualitative study are not divided into groups, with one group being exposed to a treatment of some sort and the effects of this treatment then measured in some way. Data are not collected at the "end" of the study. Rather, the collection of data in a qualitative research study is on-going. The researcher is continually observing people, events, and occurrences, often supplementing his or her observations with in-depth interviews of selected participants and the examination of various documents and records relevant to the phenomenon of interest.

5. *Data analysis.* Analyzing the data in a qualitative study essentially involves analyzing and synthesizing the information the researcher obtains from various sources (e.g., observations, interviews, documents) into a coherent description of what he or she has observed or otherwise discovered. Hypotheses are not usually tested by means of inferential statistical procedures, as is the case with experimental or associational research, although some statistics, such as percentages, may be calculated if it appears they can illuminate specific details about the phenomenon under investigation. Data analysis in qualitative research, however, relies heavily on description; even when certain statistics are calculated, they tend to be used in a descriptive rather than an inferential sense. We shall discuss the collection and analysis of data in qualitative research in some detail in Chapter Nineteen.

6. *Interpretations and conclusions.* In qualitative research, interpretations are made continuously throughout the course of a study. Whereas quantitative researchers usually leave the drawing of

Figure 18.1 *How Qualitative and Quantitative Researchers See the World*

conclusions to the very end of their research, qualitative researchers tend to formulate their interpretations as they go along. As a result, one finds the researcher's conclusions in a qualitative study more or less integrated with other steps in the research process. A qualitative researcher who is observing the ongoing activities of an inner-city classroom, for example, is likely to write up not only what he or she sees each day but also his or her interpretations of those observations.

Approaches to Qualitative Research

One finds a number of approaches to qualitative research. John Creswell, for example, has identified five, including biography, phenomenology, grounded theory, case studies, and ethnography.[7] Although these five by no means exhaust the variety of approaches that exist, we include them here because "they represent different discipline traditions, have detailed procedures, and . . . are popular in the human and social sciences."[8] We would add historical research. Although it is possible to find two or more variations or combinations of these approaches within a single study, we separate and describe them here as "pure" approaches to research design in order to simplify understanding. Let us present a brief description of each.

BIOGRAPHY

A **biographical study** is "the study of a single individual and his or her experiences as told to the researcher or found in documents and archival material.[9] An important aspect of some biographical studies is that the subject recalls one or more special events (an "epiphany") in his or her life. The author of the biography describes, in some detail, the setting or context within which the epiphany occurred. Lastly, the author is actively present during the study and openly acknowledges that his or her report is an interpretation of the subject's experiences.

Different forms of biographical study exist, including *biographies* (life stories written by a person other than the one being studied); *autobiographies* (life stories written by persons about themselves); *life histories* (a combination of biography and autobiography); and *oral histories* (in which the researcher gathers personal recollections, usually from a variety of individuals).

Biographies are not easy to do, for a number of reasons:

1. The researcher must collect an extensive amount of information about his or her subject.
2. The researcher must have a clear understanding of the historical period within which the subject lived in order to position the subject accurately within that period.
3. The researcher needs a "sharp eye" to uncover the various aspects of the subject's life.

Portraiture: Art, Science, or Both?

Portraiture is a recent variation on biography. It first appeared in 1983 in a book by Sara Lawrence-Lightfoot entitled *The Good High School: Portraits of Character and Culture.**

It won the outstanding book award from the American Educational Research Association in 1984. Its distinctive feature is that the researcher plays an avowedly interactive role with the person being portrayed. In a subsequent book, Lawrence-Lightfoot and her co-author, Hoffman-Davis, argued that portraiture meets the criteria to be considered a science.[†] They described the process as follows: "They (the portraitist and the person being described) both express their views and together define meaning-making," that is, getting the essence of the subject. Although the portraitist's "soul echoes through the piece," she or he works very hard not to simply produce a self-portrait."[‡]

*Sarah Lawrence-Lightfoot (1983). *The good high school: Portraits of character and culture.* New York: Basic Books.
[†]Sara Lawrence-Lightfoot and J. Hoffman-Davis (1997). *The art and science of portraiture.* San Francisco: Jossey-Bass.
[‡]Ibid. pp. 103, 105.

The controversy in this instance is not about the value of the method in producing powerful and useful results; that was demonstrated in *The Good High School,* but rather, whether the method can be considered "scientific," as its proponents argue. Portraitists cannot, of course, claim generalization beyond the subject(s) portrayed; they can adopt the position only that generalization is left to the reader.

Like all biographers, portraitists can claim only that other researchers would arrive at essentially the same descriptions and conclusions as they have. The nature of the interaction between the portraitist and the individual being portrayed makes triangulation virtually impossible—there is no other source for the portraitist to check his or her descriptions with. Fenwick English has argued that the "objective of portraiture to capture the "essence" of the subject is implicitly a quest for a stable truth which, in turn, requires the portraitist to become omniscient." He argues, further, that "the claim that the reader of portraiture can construct his or her own interpretations from 'thick description' ignores the complete dependence of the reader on a finished product from which there can be no independent access to information and alternative explanations" of that which has been described by the portraitist.[§]

What do you think? Is portraiture science?

[§]Fenwick W. English (2000). A critical appraisal of Sara Lawrence-Lightfoot's portraiture as a method of educational research. *Educational Researcher, 29:*21.

---

4. The researcher needs to be able to bring him- or herself into the account and acknowledge his or her views on the subject.[10]

In sum, then, the authors of biographical studies focus on a single individual, often describe special or important events in the individual's life, place the individual within a historical context, and try to place themselves in the study by acknowledging that the study is their interpretation of the subject's life.

PHENOMENOLOGY

A researcher undertaking a **phenomenological study** investigates various reactions to, or perceptions of, a particular phenomenon (e.g., the experience of teachers in an inner-city high school). The researcher hopes to gain some insight into the world of his or her participants and to describe their perceptions and reactions (e.g., what it is like to teach in an inner-city high school). Data are usually collected through in-depth interviewing. The researcher then attempts to identify and describe aspects of each individual's perceptions and reactions to their experience in some detail.

Phenomenologists generally assume that there is some commonality to the perceptions that human beings have in how they interpret similar experiences, and they seek to identify, understand, and describe these commonalities. This commonality of perception is referred to as the *essence*—the essential characteristic(s)—of the experience. It is the essential structure of a phenomenon that researchers want to identify and describe. They do so by studying multiple perceptions of the phenomenon as experienced by different people, and by then trying to determine what is common to these perceptions and reactions. This searching for the essence of an experience is the cornerstone—the defining characteristic—of phenomenological research.

Here are some examples of the kinds of topics that might serve as the focus for a phenomenological study. The experiences of:

• African American students in a predominantly white high school.

- Teachers who have used the inquiry approach in teaching ninth-grade social studies.
- Civil rights workers in the South during the 1960s.
- Nurses who work in the operating room of a large medical center.

Like biographies, phenomenological studies are not easy to do. The researcher must get the participants in a phenomenological study to relive in their minds the experiences they have had, not an easy task. Often, a number of tape-recorded interview sessions are necessary. Once completed, the researcher must search through each subject's statements for those that are especially relevant—those that appear to be particularly meaningful to the subject in describing his or her experience in relation to the phenomenon of interest. He or she then clusters these statements into *themes,* those aspects of the subjects' experiences that they had in common. The researcher then attempts to describe the fundamental features of the experience that have been described by most (hopefully all) of the participants in the study.

In sum, then, researchers who conduct phenomenological studies search for the "essential structure" of a single phenomenon by interviewing, in depth, a number of individuals who have experienced the phenomenon. The researcher extracts what he or she considers to be relevant statements from each subject's description of the phenomenon, and then clusters these statements into themes. He or she then integrates these themes into a narrative description of the phenomenon.

GROUNDED THEORY

In a **grounded theory study,** the researchers intend to generate a theory that is "grounded in data systematically gathered and analyzed."[11] Grounded theories are not generated before a study begins, but are formed inductively from the data that are collected during the study itself. In other words, researchers start with the data they have collected and then develop generalizations after they look at the data. A. Strauss and J. Corbin put it this way: "One does not begin with a theory, then prove it. Rather, one begins with an area of study and what is relevant to that area is allowed to emerge."[12]

Researchers doing a grounded theory study use what is called the *constant comparative method.* There is a continual interplay between the researcher, his or her data, and the theory that is being developed. Potential categories for grouping items of data are created, tried out, and discarded until a "fit" between theory and data

is achieved. David Lancy describes the process as follows:

> In a study of parental influence on children's reading of storybooks, Kelly Draper and I videotaped 32 parent-child pairs as they read to each other. We had few if any preconceptions about what we would find, only that we hoped that distinct patterns would emerge and that these would be associated with the children's evident ease/difficulty in learning to read. I spent literally dozens of hours viewing these videotapes, developing, using, and casting aside various categories until I found two clusters of characteristics which I called "reductionist" and "expansionist" that accounted for a large portion of the variation among parents' reading/listening styles. I was, of course, guided in my search for appropriate categories by my [experience] with the setting and by the transcripts of our interview with each parent.[13]

The data in a grounded theory study are collected primarily through one-on-one interviews, focus group interviews, and participant observation by the researcher(s). But it is an ongoing process. Data are collected and analyzed, a theory is suggested, more data are collected, the theory is revised, then more data are collected, the theory is further developed, clarified, revised, and the process continues.

Let us consider a hypothetical example of a grounded theory study. Suppose that a researcher is interested in how principals try to maintain and enhance morale among the teachers in their schools. He or she might conduct a series of in-depth interviews with a number of principals in a few large urban high schools. Suppose the researcher finds that these principals utilize a variety of strategies to keep morale high, including frequent one-on-one "praise sessions" to reward good teaching, acknowledging the efforts of teachers through written and oral commendations at faculty meetings, writing supportive letters and placing them in the teacher's personnel files, providing extra resources, replacing unnecessary meetings by providing routine information in writing, advising faculty of policy changes in advance and asking for their input and approval before implementing such, and so forth.

In addition, the researcher not only observes how the principals interact with their faculties and listen to what they have to say, but also interviews some of their teachers, and continually examines and thinks about the data he or she has collected through the interviews and observations. Gradually, the researcher develops a theory about what effective principals do to maintain and enhance morale among their teachers. The theory is then modified over time as the researcher observes and interviews more and more principals and teachers. The point to stress here, however, is that the researcher does not go in with a theory ahead of time; rather he or she develops a theory out of the data that are collected—that is, one that is *grounded* in the data. This approach is obviously highly dependent on the insight of the individual researcher.

CASE STUDIES

The study of "cases" has been around for some time. Students in medicine, law, business, and the social sciences often study cases as a part of their training. What **case study** researchers have in common is that they call the object of their research cases, and they focus their research on the study of such cases. The studies of Piaget and Vigotsky for example, have contributed much to our understanding of cognitive and moral development.[14]

What is a case? A **case** involves the study of just one individual, classroom, school, or program. Typical cases are a student who has trouble learning to read, a social studies classroom, a private school, and a national curriculum project. For some researchers, a case is not just an individual or situation that can easily be identified (e.g., a particular individual, classroom, organization, or project), but may be an event (e.g., a campus celebration), an activity (e.g., learning to use a computer), or an ongoing process (e.g., student teaching).

Consider the following examples. Sometimes much can be learned from studying just one individual, one classroom, one school, or one school district. For example, there are some students who learn a second language rather easily. In hopes of gaining insight into why this is the case, one such student could be observed on a regular basis to see if there are any noticeable patterns or regularities in the student's behavior. The student, as well as his or her teachers, counselors, parents, and friends, might also be interviewed in depth. A similar series of observations (and interviews) might be conducted with a student who finds learning another language very difficult. As much information as possible (study style, attitudes toward the language, approach to the subject, behavior in class, and so on) would be collected. The hope here is that through the study of a somewhat unique individual, insights can be gained that will suggest ways to help other language students in the future.

Similarly, a detailed study might be made of a single school. There might be a particular elementary school in a given school district, for example, that is noteworthy for its success with at-risk students. A researcher might visit the school on a regular basis, observing what goes on in classrooms, during recess periods, in the hallways and lunchroom, during faculty meetings, and so on. Faculty members, administrators, support staff, and counselors could be interviewed. Again, as much information as possible (such as teaching strategies, administrative style, school activities, parental involvement, attitudes of faculty and staff toward students, classroom and other activities) would be collected. Here too, the hope would be that through the study of a single rather unique case (only in this instance not an individual but a school) valuable insights would be gained.

Robert Stake has identified three types of case studies.[15] In an **intrinsic case study,** the researcher is primarily interested in understanding a specific individual or situation. He or she describes, in detail, the particulars of the case in order to shed some light on what is going on. Thus, a researcher might study a particular student in order to find out why that student is having trouble learning to read. Another researcher might want to understand how a school's student council operates. A third might wish to determine how effectively (or whether) an after-school detention program is working. All three of these examples involve the study of a single case. The researcher's goal in each instance is to understand the case in all its parts, including its inner workings. Intrinsic case studies are often used in exploratory research when researchers seek to learn about some little-known phenomenon by studying it in depth.

In an **instrumental case study,** on the other hand, a researcher is interested in understanding something more than just a particular case. In an instrumental case study, the researcher is interested in studying the particular case only as a means to some larger goal. A researcher might study how Mrs. Brown teaches phonics, for example, in order to learn something about phonics as a method or about the teaching of reading in general. The researcher's goal in such studies is more global and less focused on the particular individual, event, program, or school being studied. Researchers who conduct such studies are more interested in drawing conclusions that apply beyond a particular case than they are in conclusions that apply to just one specific case.

Third, there is the **multiple- or collective case study** in which a researcher studies multiple cases at the same time as part of one overall study. For example, a researcher might choose several cases to study because he or she is interested in the effects of mainstreaming children with disabilities into regular classrooms. Instead of studying the results of such mainstreaming in just a single classroom, the researcher studies its impact in a number of different classrooms.

Which is to be preferred, multiple- or single-case designs? Multiple-case designs have both advantages and disadvantages when compared to single-case designs. The results of multiple-case studies are often considered more compelling, and they are more likely to lend themselves to valid generalization. On the other hand, certain types of cases (the rare case, the critical case for testing a theory, or the case that permits a researcher to observe a phenomenon previously inaccessible to scientific study) require single-case research. Furthermore, multiple-case studies often require extensive resources and time. Any decision to undertake multiple-case studies, therefore, cannot be taken lightly. Robert Yin argues that researchers who do undertake multiple-case studies, therefore, should employ what he calls "replication logic." Here is his rationale:

> Thus, if one has access to only three cases of a rare, clinical syndrome in . . . medical science, the appropriate research design is one in which the same results are predicted for each of the three cases, thereby producing evidence that the three cases did indeed involve the same syndrome. If similar results are obtained from all three cases, replication (of results) is said to have taken place.[16]

ETHNOGRAPHIC AND HISTORICAL RESEARCH

With regard to the remaining two approaches to qualitative research, we shall not describe them here because each is discussed in detail in later chapters. We selected these two to discuss in greater depth because they represent distinctly different approaches. Ethnographic research focuses on the study of culture. Historical research concentrates exclusively on the past. We will discuss them in Chapters Twenty-One and Twenty-Two.

SAMPLING IN QUALITATIVE RESEARCH

Researchers who engage in some form of qualitative research are likely to select a *purposive sample* (see Chapter Six)—that is, they select a sample they feel will yield the best understanding of whatever it is they wish to study. At least eight types of purposive sampling have been identified.[17] These include:

- a *typical* sample, one that is considered or judged to be typical or representative of that which is being studied (e.g., a class of elementary school pupils selected because they are judged to be typical third-graders).
- a *critical* sample, one that is considered to be particularly enlightening because it is so unusual or exceptional (e.g., selecting individuals who have attained high achievement despite some serious physical limitations).
- a *homogeneous* sample, in which all of the members possess a certain trait or characteristic (e.g., a group of high school students all judged to possess exceptional artistic talent).
- a *theoretical* sample, one that helps the researcher to understand a concept or theory (e.g., selecting a group of tribal elders to assess the relevance of Piagetian theory to the education of Native Americans).
- a *snowball* sample, one selected as need arises during the conduct of a study (e.g., during the interviewing of a group of principals, they recommend others who also should be interviewed because they are particularly knowledgeable about the subject of the research).
- an *opportunistic* sample, one chosen during a study to take advantage of new conditions or circumstances that have arisen (e.g., interviewing eyewitnesses to a fracas at a high school football game).
- a *confirming* sample, one that is obtained to validate or disconfirm preliminary findings (e.g., follow-up interviews with students in order to verify reasons some students drop out).
- a sample of *maximal variation,* one selected in order to represent a diversity of perspectives or characteristics (e.g., a group of students who possess a wide variety of attitudes toward recent school policies).

Generalization in Qualitative Research

A **generalization** is usually thought of as a statement or claim of some sort that applies to more than one individual, group, object, or situation. Thus, when a researcher makes a statement, based on a review of the literature, that there is a negative correlation between age and amount of interest in school (older children are less interested in school than younger children), he or she is making a generalization.

The value of a generalization is that it allows us to have expectations (and sometimes to make predictions) about the future. Although a generalization might not be true in every case (e.g., some older children may be more interested in school than some younger children), it describes, more often than not, what we would expect to find. Almost all researchers hope that useful generalizations can be derived from their research. A limitation of qualitative research is that there is seldom methodological justification for generalizing the findings of a particular study. While this limitation also applies to many quantitative studies, it is almost inevitable given the nature of qualitative research. Because of this, **replication** of qualitative studies is even more important than it is in quantitative research.

Elliot Eisner points out that not only ideas, but also skills and images, can be generalized.[18] We generalize a skill when we apply it in a different situation than the one in which we learned the skill. Images also generalize. As Eisner points out, it is this fact—that images generalize—that leads a qualitative researcher to look for certain characteristics in a classroom, certain ways of teaching, that he or she can apply elsewhere. Once a researcher has an image of "excellence" in teaching, for example, he or she can apply this image to a variety of situations. "For qualitative research, this means that the creation of an image—a vivid portrait of excellent teaching, for example—can become a prototype that can be used in the education of teachers or for the appraisal of teaching."[19] In Elliott Eisner's words:

Direct contact with the qualitative world is one of our most important sources of generalization. But . . . we do not need to learn everything first-hand. We listen to storytellers and learn about how things were, and we use what we have been told to make decisions about what will be. We see photos and learn what to expect on our forthcoming trip to Spain. We see the play *On the Waterfront* and learn something about corruption in the shipping industry and, more important, about the conflicts and tensions between two brothers. We see the film *One Flew over the Cuckoo's Nest* and understand a bit more about how people survive in an institution that is hell-bent on their domestication. . . .

Attention to the particular, to the case, is descriptive not only of the case, but of other cases like it. When Sarah Lawrence-Lightfoot writes about the Brookline High School or the George Washington Carver High School or the John F. Kennedy High School, she tells us more than just what those particular schools are like; we

learn something about what makes a good high school.[20] Do all high schools have to be good in the same way? No. Can some high schools share some of their characteristics? Yes. Can we learn from Lawrence Lightfoot what to look for? Certainly.[21]

There is little question, we think, that generalization is possible in qualitative research. But it is a different type of generalization than that which is found in much quantitative research. In many experimental and quasi-experimental studies, the researcher generalizes from the sample under investigation to the population of interest (see Chapter Six). Note that it is the researcher who does the generalizing.[22] He or she is likely to suggest to practitioners that the findings are of value and can (sometimes they say "should") be applied in their situations.

In qualitative studies, on the other hand, the researcher may also generalize, but it is much more likely that any generalizing to be done will be by interested practitioners—by individuals who are in situations similar to the one(s) investigated by the researcher. It is the practitioner, rather than the researcher, who judges the applicability of the researcher's findings and conclusions, who determines whether the researcher's findings fit his or her situation. Eisner makes this clear:

The researcher might say something like this: "This is what I did and this is what I think it means. Does it have any bearing on your situation? If it does and if your situation is troublesome or problematic, how did it get that way and what can be done to improve it?"[23]

It is worth noting that not all qualitative researchers look at generalizing in the same way. Some are concerned less "with the question of whether their findings are generalizable, but rather with the question of to *which* other settings and subjects they are generalizable.[24] Bogdan and Biklen give an example:

In the study of an intensive care unit at a teaching hospital, we studied the ways professional staff and parents communicate about the condition of the children. As we concentrated on the interchanges, we noticed that the professional staff not only diagnosed the infants but sized up the parents as well. These parental evaluations formed the basis for judgments the professionals made about what to say to parents and how to say it. [When we reflected] about parent-teacher conferences in public schools and other situations where professionals have information about children to which parents might want access, we began to see parallels. . . . One tack we are presently exploring is the extent to which the findings of the intensive care unit are generalizable not to other settings of the same substantive type, but to other settings, such as schools, in which professionals talk to parents.[25]

Qualitative investigators, then, are less definitive, less certain about the conclusions they draw from their research. They tend to view them as ideas to be shared, discussed, and investigated further. Modification in different circumstances and under different conditions will almost always be necessary.

Internal Validity in Qualitative Research

To the extent that a qualitative study does not attempt to explore relationships, internal validity is, strictly speaking, irrelevant. However, because qualitative research is so dependent on the researcher in both collecting and interpreting information, an important consideration, even in purely descriptive studies, is researcher bias. Further, qualitative studies frequently do contain interpretations involving relationships. Examples of this occur in the studies evaluated in Chapters Nineteen to Twenty-Three. When this is the case, attention should be given to assessing and, where possible, controlling each of the threats discussed in Chapter Nine. Though more difficult in qualitative research, it is sometimes possible, as discussed in the Chapter Twenty study critique, to control particular threats. The exception is historical research wherein control is, we think, virtually impossible.

Ethics and Qualitative Research

Ethical concerns affect qualitative research just as much as they do any of the other kinds of research that we have considered in this book. Nevertheless, a few points bear repeating because of their importance.

First, unless otherwise agreed to, the identities of all who participate in a qualitative study should always be protected; care should be taken to ensure that none of the information collected would embarrass or harm them. If confidentiality cannot be maintained, participants must be so informed and given the opportunity to withdraw from the study.

Second, participants should always be treated with respect. It is especially important in qualitative studies to seek the cooperation of all subjects in the research endeavor. Usually, subjects should be told of the researcher's interests and should give their permission to proceed. Researchers should never lie to subjects nor record any conversations using a hidden tape recorder or other mechanical apparatus.

Third, researchers should do their best to ensure that no physical or psychological harm will come to anyone who participates in the study. This seems rather obvious, perhaps, but researchers sometimes are placed in a difficult position because they find, inadvertently, that subjects *are* being harmed. Consider the following example. In certain studies in state institutions for the mentally handicapped, researchers have witnessed the physical abuse of residents. What is their ethical responsibility in such cases? Here is what two researchers who observed such abuse firsthand had to say:

> In the case of physical abuse, the solution may seem obvious at first: Researcher or not, you should intervene to stop the beatings. In some states, it is illegal not to report abuse. That was our immediate disposition. But, through our research, we came to understand that abuse was a pervasive activity in most such institutions nationally, not only part of this particular setting. Was blowing the whistle on one act a responsible way to address this problem or was it a way of getting the matter off our chests? Intervention may get you kicked out. Might not continuing the research, publishing the results, writing reports exposing national abuse, and providing research for witnesses in court (or being an expert witness) do more to change the conditions than the single act of intervention? Was such thinking a copout, an excuse not to get involved?[26]

What do you think?

As the above excerpt reveals, ethical concerns are difficult ones indeed. Two other points deserve mention. Many researchers are concerned that subjects do not get very much in return from participating in a research investigation. After all, the studies that researchers do often lead to the advancement of their careers. They help professors to get promoted. Study results are frequently reported in books that bring their authors royalty checks. Researchers get to talk about what they have learned; their work, when well done, helps them to gain the respect of their colleagues. But what do subjects get? Participants often (perhaps usually) do not have a chance to reciprocate and/or tell what their lives are like. As a result, subjects sometimes get misrepresented or even demeaned. Accordingly, some researchers have tried to design studies in which researcher and participants are more like partners in an investigation where the subjects definitely have a say.

Furthermore, there is another ethical concern, somewhat related to the above, that must be addressed. This occurs when there is the possibility that certain research findings, in the hands of the powerful, may lead to actions that could actually hurt subjects (or people in similar circumstances), and/or lead to public policies or public attitudes that are actually harmful to certain groups. What a researcher might see as "a sympathetic portrayal of people living in a housing project might be read by others as proving prejudices about poor people being irresponsible and prone to violence."[27] The ethical point to stress here, then, is this: While researchers can never be sure how their findings will be received, they must always be sure to think carefully about the implications of their work, who the results of this work may affect, and how.

We offer, then, a number of specific questions that we think all researchers, no matter what kind of research they prefer, should think about before, during, and after the completion of any study they undertake:

- Is the study being contemplated *worth* doing?
- Do the researchers have the necessary *expertise* to carry out a study of good quality?
- Have the participants in the study been given *full information* about what the study will involve?
- Have the participants willingly given their *consent to participate?*
- Who will *gain* from this research?
- Is there a *balance* between gains and costs for both researchers and participants?
- Who, if anyone, might be *harmed* (physically or psychologically) in this study, and to what degree? What is to be done should harmful, illegal, or wrongful behavior be witnessed?
- Will the participants in the study be *deceived* in any way?
- Will *confidentiality* be assured?
- Who *owns the data* that will be collected and analyzed in this study?
- How will the results of the study be *used?* Is there any possibility for misuse? If so, how?

Qualitative and Quantitative Research Reconsidered

Can qualitative and quantitative approaches be used together? Of course. And often they should be. In survey research, for example, it is common not only to prepare a closed-ended (e.g., multiple-choice) questionnaire for people to answer in writing, but also to conduct open-ended personal interviews with a random sample of the respondents. Descriptive statistics are sometimes used to provide quantitative details in an otherwise qualitative study. Many historical studies include a combination of qualitative and quantitative methodologies, and their final reports present both kinds of data.

Nevertheless, it must be admitted that carrying out a sophisticated quantitative study *and* an in-depth qualitative investigation at the same time is difficult to pull off successfully. Indeed, it is *very* difficult. Oftentimes what is produced is a study that is neither a good qualitative nor a good quantitative piece of work.

Which is the better approach—qualitative or quantitative? Although we hear this question a lot, we think it's pretty much a waste of energy. Oftentimes you will hear overly zealous advocates of one or the other approach disparaging the other. They say theirs is the best (indeed, sometimes the only) method to use if one wants to do really useful research on important questions, while the other is badly flawed and can only lead to spurious or trivial results. But here is what two eminent qualitative researchers have to say:

> . . . there is no best method. It all depends on what you are studying and what you want to find out. If you want to find out what the majority of the American people think about a particular issue, survey research which relies heavily on quantitative design in picking your sample, designing and pretesting your instrument, and analyzing the data is best. If you want to know about the process of change in a school and how the various school members experience change, qualitative methods will do a better job. Without a doubt there are certain questions and topics that the qualitative approach will not help you with, and the same is true of quantitative research.[28]

We agree. The important thing is to know what questions can best be answered by which method or combination of methods.

It is worth noting that increased attention is being given to mixed-method studies. For example, Creswell describes three types of **mixed-method designs.**[29]

1. In a **triangulation design,** the researcher simultaneously collects both quantitative and qualitative data, compares results, and then uses those findings to see whether they validate each other.
2. In an **explanatory design,** the researcher first collects and analyzes quantitative data, and then obtains qualitative data to follow up and refine the quantitative findings.

3. In an **exploratory design,** the researcher first collects qualitative data and then uses the findings to give direction to quantitative data collection. This data is then used to validate or extend the qualitative findings.

Consider an example. Fraenkel used a modified triangulation design to study four high school social studies teachers identified by their peers as outstanding. He attempted to paint a portrait of what happens on a daily basis in their classrooms and to identify effective teacher techniques and behaviors. To this end, he used several qualitative techniques including extensive in-class observation using a daily log and interviews with teachers and students. He also used a number of quantitative instruments, including performance checklists, rating scales, and discussion flowcharts. His general approach was qualitative in that no specific hypotheses were initially formulated, but rather emerged as the study progressed. He developed detailed descriptions of each teacher's behaviors, teaching style, and techniques and compared the teachers for similarities and differences. Triangulation was achieved by comparing not only teacher interviews, student interviews, and observations, but also by comparing these with the quantitative measures of classroom interaction and achievement. An illustrative finding was that all four teachers emphasized small-group work, as shown by observation, teacher interviews, and student ratings. Overall, the findings of the study supported frequently recommended teaching strategies, but also suggested some that have not received much attention in the literature. These include extensive personal involvement in the lives of students, consciously promoting social interaction in and out of class, and consciously attending to nonverbal cues. Although primarily designed as a qualitative study, this does fit the definition of a triangulation, mixed-method design.[30]

Go back to the **Interactive and Applied Learning Tools** feature at the beginning of the chapter for a listing of interactive and applied activities. Go to the **Online Learning Center** at www.mhhe.com/fraenkel5e or your **Interactive Student CD-ROM** to take practice quizzes and receive immediate feedback, practice with key terms, review chapter content and main ideas, and find annotated Web links.

Main Points

THE NATURE OF QUALITATIVE RESEARCH

- The term "qualitative research" refers to research investigations of the *quality* of relationships, activities, situations, or materials.
- The natural setting is a direct source of data and the researcher is a key part of the instrumentation process in qualitative research.
- Qualitative data are collected mainly in the form of words or pictures and seldom involve numbers. Content analysis is a primary method of data analysis.
- Qualitative researchers are especially interested in how things occur and particularly in the perspectives of the subjects of a study.
- Qualitative researchers do not, usually, formulate a hypothesis beforehand and then seek to test it. Rather, they allow hypotheses to emerge as a study develops.
- Qualitative and Quantitative Research differ in the philosophic assumptions that underlie the two approaches.

STEPS INVOLVED IN QUALITATIVE RESEARCH

- The steps involved in conducting a qualitative study are not as distinct as they are in quantitative studies. They often overlap and sometimes are even conducted concurrently.
- All qualitative studies begin with a *foreshadowed problem,* the particular phenomenon the researcher is interested in investigating.

- Researchers who engage in a qualitative study of some type usually select a purposive sample. Several types of purposive samples exist.
- There is no "treatment" in a qualitative study, nor is there any manipulation of variables.
- The collection of data in a qualitative study is ongoing.
- Conclusions are drawn continuously throughout the course of a qualitative study.

APPROACHES TO QUALITATIVE RESEARCH

- A biographical study tells the story of the special events in the life of a single individual.
- A researcher studies an individual's reactions to a particular phenomenon in a phenomenological study. He or she attempts to identify the commonalities among different individual perceptions.
- In a grounded theory study, a researcher forms a theory inductively from the data collected as a part of the study.
- A case study is a detailed study of one or (at most) a few individuals or other social units, such as a classroom, a school, or a neighborhood.

GENERALIZATION IN QUALITATIVE RESEARCH

- Generalizing is possible in qualitative research, but it is of a different type than that found in quantitative studies. Most likely it will be done by interested practitioners.

ETHICS AND QUALITATIVE RESEARCH

- The identities of all participants in a qualitative study should be protected, and they should be treated with respect.

RECONSIDERING QUALITATIVE AND QUANTITATIVE RESEARCH

- Aspects of both qualitative and quantitative research often are used together in a study. Increased attention is being given to such mixed-method studies.
- Whether qualitative or quantitative research is the most appropriate boils down to what the researcher involved wants to find out.

Key Terms

For Discussion

1. What do you see as the greatest strength of qualitative research? The biggest weakness?
2. Are there any topics or questions that could *not* be studied using a qualitative approach? If so, give an example. Is there any type of information that qualitative research cannot provide? If so, what might it be?
3. Qualitative researchers are sometimes accused of being too subjective. What do you think a qualitative researcher might say in response to such an accusation?
4. Qualitative researchers say that "complete" objectivity is impossible. Would you agree? Explain your reasoning.
5. "The essence of all good research is understanding, rather than an attempt to prove something." What does this statement mean?
6. "All researchers are biased to at least some degree. The important thing is to be aware of one's biases!" Is just being "aware" enough? What else might one do?
7. Qualitative researchers often say that "the whole is greater than the sum of its parts." What does this statement mean? What implications does it have for educational research?
8. Would it be possible to use random sampling in qualitative research? Would it be desirable? Explain.
9. In what way is generalization in qualitative research different from generalization in quantitative research—or is it?
10. What do you think is the ethical responsibility of researchers should they witness an instance of physical abuse in a study they are conducting?

Notes

1. R. C. Bogdan and S. K. Biklen (1998). *Qualitative research for education: An introduction to theory and methods,* 3rd ed. Boston: Allyn & Bacon.

2. Recently, however, some qualitative researchers have begun to use statistical procedures to clarify their data. See, for example, M. B. Miles and A. M. Huberman (1994). *Qualitative data analysis,* 2nd ed. Beverly Hills, CA: Sage.

3. Bogdan and Biklen, op. cit., p. 6.

4. H. R. Bernard (2000). *Social research methods: Qualitative and quantitative approaches.* Thousand Oaks, CA: Sage.

5. M. Foucault (1972). *The archaeology of knowledge.* New York: Harper and Row.

6. J. Derrida (1972). Discussion: Structure, sign, and plot in the discourse of the human sciences. In R. Macksey and E. Donato (eds.), *The structuralist controversy.* Baltimore: Johns Hopkins University Press, pp. 242–272.

7. John W. Creswell (1998). *Qualitative inquiry and research design: Choosing among five traditions.* Thousand Oaks, CA: Sage.

8. Ibid., p. 9.

9. Ibid., p. 57.

10. Ibid., p. 30.

11. Ibid., p. 51.

12. A. Strauss, and J. Corbin (1994). Grounded theory methodology: An overview. In A. Denzin and Y. Lincoln (eds.), *Handbook of qualitative research.* Thousand Oaks, CA: Sage, p. 273.

13. David F. Lancy (2001). *Studying children in schools: Qualitative research traditions.* Prospect Heights: Waveland Press, p. 9.

14. J. Piaget (1936/1963). *The origins of intelligence in the child.* New York: Norton; J. Piaget (1932/1965). *The moral judgment of the child.* New York: Free Press; L. S. Vigotsky (1914/1962). *Thought and language.* Cambridge, MA: MIT Press.

15. Robert Stake (1997). *The art of case study research.* Thousand Oaks, CA: Sage.

16. Robert K. Yin (1994). *Case study research: Design and methods.* Thousand Oaks, CA: Sage.

17. Adapted from John W. Creswell (2002). *Educational research: Planning, conducting, and evaluating qualitative and quantitative research.* Columbus, OH: Merrill Prentice Hall, pp. 194–197.

18. E. W. Eisner (1991). *The enlightened eye: Qualitative inquiry and the enhancement of educational practice.* New York: Macmillan.

19. Ibid., p. 199.

20. S. L. Lightfoot (1983). *The good high school.* New York: Basic Books.

21. Eisner, op. cit., pp. 202–203.

22. Remember that a researcher is entitled to generalize only if his or her sample has been randomly selected from the population. Many times, such is not the case.

23. Eisner, op. cit., p. 204.

24. Bogdan and Biklen, op. cit., p. 33.

25. Ibid.

26. Ibid., p. 46.

27. Ibid., p. 47.

28. Ibid., p. 39.

29. Creswell, op. cit., pp. 564–578.

30. Jack R. Fraenkel (1994). A portrait of four social studies teachers and their classes: With special attention paid to identification of teaching techniques and behaviors that contribute to student learning. In D. S. Tierney (ed.) *1994 yearbook of California education research.* San Francisco: Caddo Gap Press.

Observation
and Interviewing

CHAPTER 19

Observation and Interviewing

Observation

Participant Observation
Nonparticipant Observation
Naturalistic Observation
Simulations
Observer Effect
Observer Bias
Coding Observational Data
The Use of Technology

Validity and Reliability in Qualitative Research

Interviewing

Types of Interviews
Key-Actor Interviews
Types of Interview Questions
Interviewing Behavior
Focus Group Interviews
Recording Interview Data
Ethics in Interviewing: The Necessity of Informed Consent
Data Collection and Analysis
in Qualitative Research

Objectives

Studying this chapter should enable you to:

- Explain *what is meant by the term "observational research."*
- Describe *at least four different roles an observer can take in a qualitative study.*
- Explain *what is meant by the term "participant observation."*
- Explain *what is meant by the term "nonparticipant observation" and describe two different forms of nonparticipant observation studies that educational researchers conduct.*
- Explain *what is meant by the term "naturalistic observation."*
- Describe *what a simulation is and how it might be used by a researcher.*
- Give one example of *a coding scheme that might be used in observational research.*
- Describe *what is meant by the term "observer effect."*
- Explain *what is meant by the term "observer bias."*
- Describe *the type of sampling that occurs in observational studies.*
- Describe *briefly four types of interviews qualitative researchers use.*
- Explain *what a "key actor" is.*
- Give an example of *at least six types of interview questions.*
- List *at least three expectations that exist for all interviews.*
- Describe *at least five techniques good interviewers use.*
- Explain *what a focus group interview is.*
- Describe *briefly why an informed consent form is needed in interview research.*
- Give *at least four procedures qualitative researchers use to check on or enhance validity and reliability in qualitative studies.*

Interactive and Applied Learning

After, or while, reading this chapter:

🎧 Go to your Interactive Student CD-ROM to:
- Learn More About Interviews and Observations

🎧 📖 Go to your Interactive Student CD-ROM or Student Workbook to do the following activities:
- Activity 19.1: Observer Roles
- Activity 19.2: Types of Interviews
- Activity 19.3: Types of Interview Questions
- Activity 19.4: Do Some Observational Research

What was it like to be a student teacher?"

"Well, uh, (laughs), it's sort of, uh, hard to describe. I guess I liked it, now that it's all over (laughs). But there were times, uh, . . . I had a lot of trouble at first with discipline. You know controlling the kids. Couldn't seem to manage them. Especially when they wouldn't sit down and started wandering around the room. Teaching isn't easy, you know, even for the old pros. And there I was, just a beginner. Not even sure I wanted to be a teacher. I was older, too, than most of the other student teachers. Didn't have a lot in common with them, me having been in the military and all. But then, things changed."

"What happened?"

"Well, I sort of got the hang of it. I learned some things. Began to learn my craft, you might say (smiles). I learned to control them better. I, uh, didn't take any guff, you know (laughs). Oh, I wasn't mean or anything like that, just firm. Yeah! You know, uh, uh, they respect it if you're firm. You got to be. They don't like wishy-washy teachers. Took me a while to learn that. But then I got better at explaining things too, and that made it easier to control the kids. And I set up some rules. They had to be in their seats when the bell rang, and they got points if they were. I had an election for a class president who I had sit at the front of the room and whose job was to keep order. That worked great. And then I had a weekly 'class meeting' where we talked about things they liked and things they thought could be improved. And I also . . ."

The above conversation is part of an in-depth interview between a qualitative researcher and a 55-year-old retired Air Force Major who has returned to school to get a middle school teaching credential. In-depth interviewing is one of the staples of qualitative research. It is one of the things we shall discuss in some detail in this chapter.

Qualitative researchers use three main techniques to collect and analyze their data: observing people as they go about their daily activities and recording what they do; conducting in-depth interviews with people about their ideas, their opinions, and their experiences; and analyzing documents or other forms of communication (content analysis). Interviews can provide us with information about people's attitudes, their values, and what they think they do. If you want to know what they actually do, however, there is no substitute for watching them or examining documents and other forms of communication that they create. In this chapter, we discuss observation and interviewing in some detail. We will discuss the analysis of documents in Chapter Twenty.

Observation

Certain kinds of research questions can best be answered by *observing* how people act or how things look. For example, researchers could interview teachers about how their students behave during class discussions of sensitive issues, but a more accurate indication of their activities would probably be obtained by actually observing such discussions while they take place.

The degree of observer participation can vary considerably. There are four different roles that a researcher can take, ranging on a continuum from complete participant to complete observer.

PARTICIPANT OBSERVATION

In **participant observation** studies, researchers actually participate in the situation or setting they are observing.

When a researcher takes on the role of a *complete participant* in a group, his identity is not known to any of the individuals being observed. The researcher interacts with members of the group as naturally as possible and, for all intents and purposes (so far as they are concerned), is one of them. Thus, a researcher might arrange to serve for a year as an actual teacher in an inner-city classroom and carry out all of the duties and responsibilities that are a part of that role, but not reveal that he is also a researcher. Such covert observation is suspect on ethical grounds.

When a researcher chooses the role of *participant-as-observer,* he participates fully in the activities in the group being studied, but also makes it clear that he is doing research. As an example, the researcher described above might tell the faculty that he is a researcher and intends to describe as thoroughly and accurately as he can what goes on in the school over the course of a year's time.

Participant observation can be *overt,* in that the researcher is easily identified and the subjects know that they are being observed, or *covert,* in which case the researcher disguises his or her identity and acts just like any of the other participants. For example, a researcher might ask a ninth-grade geography teacher to allow him or her to observe one of that teacher's classes over the course of a semester. Both teacher and students would know the researcher's identity. This would be an example of overt observation. Overt participant observation is a key ingredient in ethnographic research, which we will discuss in more detail in Chapter Twenty-One.

On the other hand, another researcher might take the trouble to become certified as an elementary school teacher and then spend a period of time actually teaching in an elementary school while he or she at the same time observes what is going on. No one would know the researcher's identity (with the possible exception of the district administration from whom permission would have been obtained beforehand). This would be an example of covert observation. Covert participant observation, although likely to produce more valid observations of what really happens, is often criticized on ethical grounds. Observing people without their knowledge (and/or recording their comments without their permission) seems to some a highly questionable practice.

Is it ethical to observe people without their knowledge? What about so-called passive deception, such as that involved in observing people as they go about their business in public places, like restaurants and airports? Or what about observing children's schoolyard activities from a distance using a telephoto lens? What do you think?

NONPARTICIPANT OBSERVATION

In a **nonparticipant observation** study, researchers do not participate in the activity being observed but rather "sit on the sidelines" and watch; they are not directly involved in the situation they are observing.

When a researcher chooses the role of *observer-as-participant,* she identifies herself straight off as a researcher, but makes no pretense of actually being a member of the group she is observing. An example here might be a university professor who is interested in what goes on in an inner-city school. The researcher

might conduct a series of interviews with teachers in the school, visit classes, attend faculty meetings and collective bargaining negotiations, talk with principals and the superintendent, and talk with students, but she would not attempt to participate in the activities of the group other than superficially. She remains essentially (and does not hide the fact that she is) an interested observer who is doing research.

Finally, the role of *complete observer* is just that—a role at the opposite extreme from the role of complete participant. The researcher observes the activities of a group without in any way becoming a participant in those activities. The subjects of the researcher's observations may, or may not, realize they are being observed. An example would be a researcher who observes the activities that go on daily in a school lunchroom.*

Each of the observer roles we have described has both advantages and disadvantages. The complete participant is probably most likely to get the truest picture of a group's activities, and the others less so, but the ethical question involving covert observation remains. The complete observer is probably least likely to affect the actions of the group being studied, the others more so. The participant-as-observer, since he or she is an actual member of the group being studied, will have some (and often an important) effect on what the group does. The participant-as-observer and the observer-as-participant are both likely, in varying degrees, to focus the attention of the group on the activities of the researcher and away from their normal routine, thereby making their activities no longer typical. Figure 19.1 indicates how approaches to observation can vary.

NATURALISTIC OBSERVATION

Naturalistic observation involves observing individuals in their natural settings. The researcher makes no effort whatsoever to manipulate variables or to control the activities of individuals, but simply observes and records what happens as things naturally occur. The activities of students at an athletic event, the interactions between students and teachers on the playground, or the activities of very young children in a nursery, for example, are probably best understood through naturalistic observation.

*Note that many of the techniques described in Chapter Seven are also examples of nonparticipant observation frequently used in both qualitative and quantitative studies.

Figure 19.1 *Variations in Approaches to Observation*

Role of the Observer		
Full-participant observation	Partial participation	Onlooker; observer is an outsider
How the Observer Is Portrayed to Others		
Participants know that observations are being made and they know who is making them.	Some but not all of the participants know the observer.	Participants do not know that observations are being made or that there is someone observing them.
How the Purpose of the Observation Is Portrayed to Others			
The purpose of the observation is fully explained to all involved.	The purpose of the observation is explained to some of the participants.	No explanation is given to any of the participants.	False explanations are given; participants are deceived about the purpose of the observation.
Duration of the Observations		
A single observation of limited duration (e.g., 30 minutes).	Multiple observations; long-term duration (e.g., months, even years).	
Focus of the Observations		
Narrow focus: Only a single element or characteristic is observed.	Broad focus: Holistic view of the activity or characteristic being observed and all of its elements is sought.	

Much of the work of the famous child psychologist Jean Piaget involved naturalistic observation. Many of his conclusions on the cognitive development of children grew out of watching his own children as they developed, and they have stimulated other researchers to do further research in this area. Insights obtained as a result of naturalistic observation, in fact, often serve as the basis for more formal experiments.

SIMULATIONS

To investigate certain variables, researchers sometimes will *create* a situation and ask subjects to act out, or *simulate,* certain roles. In **simulations,** the researcher, in effect, actually tells the subjects what to do (but not how to do it). This permits a researcher to observe what happens in certain kinds of situations, including those that occur fairly infrequently in schools or other educational settings. For example, individuals might be asked to portray a counselor interacting with a distraught parent, a teacher disciplining a student, or two administrators discussing their views on enhancing teacher morale.

There are two main types of role-playing simulations used by researchers in education—individual role playing and team role playing. In individual role playing, a person is asked to role-play how he or she thinks a particular individual might act in a given situation. The researcher then observes and records what happens. Here is an example:

> You are an elementary school counselor. You have an appointment with a student who is frequently abusive toward his teachers. The student has just arrived for his 9:00 A.M. appointment with you and is sitting before you in your office. What do you say to this student?

In team role playing, a group of individuals is asked to act out a particular situation, with the researcher again observing and recording what goes on. Particular attention is paid to how the members of the group interact. Here is an example:

> You and five of your faculty colleagues have been appointed as a temporary special committee to discuss and come up with solutions to the problem of student cutting of classes, which has been increasing this semester. Many of the faculty support a "get tough" policy and have openly advocated suspending students who are frequent cutters. The group's assignment is to come up with other alternatives that the faculty will accept. What do you propose?

The main disadvantage to simulations, as you might have recognized, is their artificiality. Situations are being acted out, and there is no guarantee that what the researcher sees is what would normally occur in a real-life situation. The results of a simulation often serve as hypotheses in other kinds of research investigations.

OBSERVER EFFECT

The presence of an observer can have a considerable effect on the behavior of those being observed, and hence on the outcomes of a study. Also the data reported (that which the observer records) inevitably to some extent reflect the biases and viewpoints of the observer. Let us consider each of these facts a bit further.

There is always the problem of reactivity in observational research. Getting around the reactivity problem involves staying around long enough to get people used to the observer's presence. As Bernard suggests, eventually "people just get plain tired of trying to manage your impression and they act naturally. In [spot sampling] research, the trick is to catch a glimpse of people in their natural activities before they see you coming on the scene—before they have a chance to modify their behavior."[1]

Unless a researcher is concealed, it is quite likely that he or she will have some effect on the behavior of those individuals who are being observed. Two things can happen, particularly if an observer is unexpected. First, he or she is likely to arouse curiosity and result in a lack of attention to the task at hand, thus producing other-than-normal behavior. An inexperienced researcher who records such behavior might easily be misled. It is for this reason that researchers who observe in classrooms, for example, usually alert the teacher beforehand and ask to be introduced. They then may spend four to five days in the classroom before starting to record observations (to enable the students to become accustomed to their presence and go about their usual activities).

The second thing that can happen is that the behavior of those who are being observed might be influenced by the researcher's purpose. For example, suppose a researcher was interested in observing whether social studies teachers ask "high-level questions" during class discussions of controversial issues. If the teachers are aware of what the researcher is looking for, they may tend to ask more questions than normal, thus giving a distorted impression of what really goes on during a typical class discussion. The data obtained by the researcher's observation would not be representative of how the teachers normally behave. It is for this reason that many researchers argue that the participants in a study should not be informed of the study's purposes until after the data have been collected. Instead, the researchers should meet with the participants before the study begins and tell them that they cannot be informed of the purpose of the study since it might affect the study's outcomes. As soon as the data have been collected, however, the researcher should promise to reveal the findings to those who are interested.

OBSERVER BIAS

Observer bias refers to the possibility that certain characteristics or ideas of observers may bias what they "see." Over the years, qualitative researchers have continually had to deal with the charge that it is very easy for their prejudices to bias their data. But this is something with which all researchers must deal. It is probably true that no matter how hard observers try to be impartial, their observations will possess some degree of bias. No one can be totally objective, as we all are influenced to some degree by our past experiences, which in turn affect how we see the world and the people within it. Nevertheless, all researchers should do their best to become aware of, and try to control, their biases.

What qualitative researchers try to do is to study the subjective factors objectively. They do this in a number of ways. They spend a considerable amount of time at the site, getting to know their subjects and the environment (both physical and cultural) in which they live. They collect copious amounts of data and check their perceptions against what the data reveal. Realizing that most situations and settings are very complex, they do their best to collect data from a variety of perspectives, using a variety of formats. Not only do they prepare extremely detailed field notes, but they attempt to reflect on their own subjectivity as a part of these field notes. Often they work in teams so that they can check each other's observations against another's (Figure 19.2). Although they realize (as should all researchers) that one's biases can never be completely eliminated from one's observations, the important thing is to reflect on how one's own attitudes may influence what one perceives.

A related concern here is **observer expectations.** If researchers know they are to observe subjects who have certain characteristics (such as a certain IQ range, ethnicity, or religion), they may "expect" a certain type of behavior, which may not be how the subjects normally behave. It is in this regard that audiotapings and

Figure 19.2 *The Importance of a Second Observer as a Check on One's Conclusions*

videotapings are so valuable, as they allow researchers to check their observations against the impressions of others.

CODING OBSERVATIONAL DATA

Over the years, quantitative researchers have developed a number of coding schemes to use when they observe. A **coding scheme** is a set of categories (e.g., "gives directions"; "asks questions"; "praises") that an observer uses to record the frequency of a person's or group's behavior. Coding schemes have been used to measure interactions between parents and adolescent children in a laboratory setting;[2] interactions of college students who drank alcohol in a group setting;[3] doctor-patient interactions in the office of family physicians;[4] and student-teacher interactions in a classroom.[5] One such coding scheme, primarily used in quantitative research, was developed by Amidon and Flanders more than 30 years ago, but is still in use.[6] It is shown in Figure 19.3.

These schemes require the observer to judge and categorize behavior at it occurs. This is in contrast to more qualitative approaches that attempt to describe all or most of what occurs in a given situation. At a later time, these data are coded into categories that emerge as the analysis proceeds. This is particularly true in ethnographic research. We shall give an example of this type of coding in Chapter Twenty.

THE USE OF TECHNOLOGY

Even with a fixed coding scheme like the one shown in Figure 19.3, however, the observer must still choose from among alternatives when coding the behavior of people. When is someone being "critical," for example, or "encouraging"? Recording the behavior of people on film or video, instead, permits the researcher to repeatedly view the behavior of an individual or a group and then decide how to code it at a later, usually more relaxed and convenient, time.

Furthermore, a major difficulty in observing people is the fact that much that goes on may be missed by the observer. This is especially true when several behaviors of interest are occurring rapidly in an educational setting. In addition, sometimes a researcher wants to have someone else (such as an expert on the topic of interest) offer his or her insights about what is happening. A researcher who observes a number of children's play sessions in a nursery school setting, for example, might want to obtain the ideas of a qualified child psychologist or an experienced teacher of preschool children about what is happening.

To overcome these obstacles, researchers may use audiotapes or videotapes to record their observations. These have several advantages. The tapes may be replayed several times for continued study and analysis. Experts or interested others can also hear and/or see

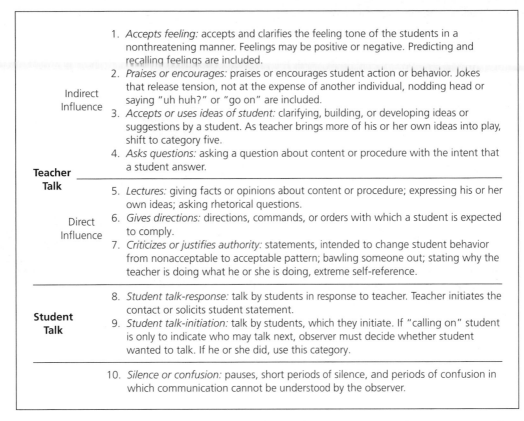

		1. *Accepts feeling:* accepts and clarifies the feeling tone of the students in a nonthreatening manner. Feelings may be positive or negative. Predicting and recalling feelings are included.
Teacher Talk	Indirect Influence	2. *Praises or encourages:* praises or encourages student action or behavior. Jokes that release tension, not at the expense of another individual, nodding head or saying "uh huh?" or "go on" are included.
		3. *Accepts or uses ideas of student:* clarifying, building, or developing ideas or suggestions by a student. As teacher brings more of his or her own ideas into play, shift to category five.
		4. *Asks questions:* asking a question about content or procedure with the intent that a student answer.
	Direct Influence	5. *Lectures:* giving facts or opinions about content or procedure; expressing his or her own ideas; asking rhetorical questions.
		6. *Gives directions:* directions, commands, or orders with which a student is expected to comply.
		7. *Criticizes or justifies authority:* statements, intended to change student behavior from nonacceptable to acceptable pattern; bawling someone out; stating why the teacher is doing what he or she is doing, extreme self-reference.
Student Talk		8. *Student talk-response:* talk by students in response to teacher. Teacher initiates the contact or solicits student statement.
		9. *Student talk-initiation:* talk by students, which they initiate. If "calling on" student is only to indicate who may talk next, observer must decide whether student wanted to talk. If he or she did, use this category.
		10. *Silence or confusion:* pauses, short periods of silence, and periods of confusion in which communication cannot be understood by the observer.

Figure 19.3 *The Amidon/Flanders Scheme for Coding Categories of Interaction in the Classroom*

Source: E. J. Amidon and J. B. Hough (1967). *Interaction analysis: Theory, research, and application.* Reading, MA: Addison-Wesley.

what the researcher observed and offer their insights accordingly. And a permanent record of certain kinds of behaviors is obtained for comparison with later or different samples.

There are a few disadvantages to such tapings, however, which also should be noted. Videotapings are not always the easiest to obtain and usually require trained technicians to do the taping unless the researcher has had some training and experience in this area. Often several microphones must be set up, which can distort the behavior of those being observed. Prolonged taping can be expensive. Audiotapings are somewhat easier to do, but they of course record only verbal behavior. Furthermore, sometimes it is difficult to distinguish among different speakers when one hears only their recorded voices. Noise is difficult to control and often seriously interferes with the understanding of content. Nevertheless, if these difficulties can be overcome, the use of audio- and videotaping offers considerable promise to researchers as a way to collect, store, and analyze data.

Interviewing

A second method used by qualitative researchers to collect data is to *interview* selected individuals. Interviewing (i.e., the careful asking of relevant questions) is an important way for a researcher to check the accuracy of—to verify or refute—the impressions he or she has gained through observation. Fetterman, in fact, describes interviewing as the most important data-collection technique a qualitative researcher possesses.[7]

The purpose of interviewing people is to find out what is on their mind—what they think or how they feel about something. As Patton has remarked:

We interview people to find out from them those things we cannot directly observe. The issue is not whether observational data is more desirable, valid, or meaningful than self-report data. The fact of the matter is that we cannot observe everything. We cannot observe feelings, thoughts, and intentions. We cannot observe behaviors that took place at some previous point in time. We cannot observe situations that preclude the presence of an observer. We cannot observe how people have organized the world and the meanings they attach to what goes on in the world. We have to ask people questions about those things.[8]

TYPES OF INTERVIEWS

Interviews are of four types: structured, semistructured, informal, and retrospective. Although these different types often blend and merge into one another, we shall describe them separately in order to clarify how they differ.

Structured and **semistructured interviews** are verbal questionnaires. Rather formal, they consist of a series of questions designed to elicit specific answers on the part of respondents. Often they are used to obtain information that can later be compared and contrasted. For example, a researcher interested in how the characteristics of teachers in inner-city and suburban schools differ might conduct a structured interview (i.e., asking a set of structured questions) with a group of inner-city high school teachers to obtain background information about them—their education, their qualifications, their previous experience, their out-of-school activities, and so on—in order to compare this data with the same data (i.e., answers to the same questions) obtained from a group of teachers who teach in the suburbs. In qualitative research, structured and semistructured interviews are often best conducted toward the end of a study, as they tend to shape responses to the researcher's perceptions of how things are. They are most useful for obtaining information to test a specific hypothesis that the researcher has in mind.

Informal interviews are much less formal than structured or semistructured interviews. They tend to resemble casual conversations, pursuing the interests of both the researcher and the respondent in turn. They are the most common type of interview in qualitative research. They do not involve any specific type or sequence of questions or any particular form of questioning. The primary intent of an informal interview is to find out what people think and how the views of one individual compare with those of another.

Although at first glance they seem like they would be easy to conduct, informal interviews are probably the most difficult of all interviews to do well. Issues of ethics appear almost immediately. Researchers often need to make some sensitive decisions as an informal interview progresses. When, for example, is a question too personal to pursue? To what extent should the re-

"How do I feel? I feel that your question is trivial, courts sensationalism, and is designed to appeal to appallingly base instincts. Additionally, it demeans my intelligence. Next question."

searcher "dig deeper" into how an individual feels about something? When is it more appropriate to refrain from probing further about an individual's response? How, in fact, does a researcher establish a climate of ease and familiarity while at the same time trying to learn in some detail about a respondent's life?

Although informal interviews offer the most natural type of situation for the collection of data, there is always some degree of artificiality present in any type of interview. A skillful interviewer, however, soon learns to begin with nonthreatening questions to put a respondent at ease before he or she poses more personal and (potentially) threatening questions. Always, an atmosphere of trust, cooperation, and mutual respect must be established by the researcher if he or she is to obtain accurate information. Planning and asking good questions, while developing and maintaining an atmosphere of mutual trust and respect, is an art that anyone who wishes to do competent qualitative research must master.

Retrospective interviews can be structured, semistructured, or informal. A researcher who conducts a retrospective interview tries to get a respondent to recall and then reconstruct from memory something that has happened in the past. A retrospective interview is the least likely of the four interview types to provide accurate, reliable data for the researcher.

Table 19.1 summarizes some of the major interviewing strategies that are employed in educational research.

Table 19.1 *Interviewing Strategies Used in Educational Research*

Type of Interview	Characteristics	Strengths	Weaknesses
Informal conversational interview	Questions emerge from the immediate context and are asked in the natural course of things; there is no predetermination of question topics or wording.	Increases the salience and relevance of questions; interviews are built on and emerge from observations; the interview can be matched to individuals and circumstances.	Different information collected from different people with different questions. Less systematic and comprehensive if certain questions do not arise "naturally." Data organization and analysis can be quite difficult.
Interview guide approach	Topics and issues to be covered are specified in advance, in outline form; interviewer decides sequence and wording of questions in the course of the interview.	The outline increases the comprehensiveness of the data and makes data collection somewhat systematic for each respondent. Logical gaps in data can be anticipated and closed. Interviews remain fairly conversational and situational.	Important and salient topics may be inadvertently omitted. Interviewer flexibility in sequencing and wording questions can result in substantially different responses from different perspectives, thus reducing the comparability of responses.
Standardized open-ended interview	The exact wording and sequence of questions are determined in advance. All interviewees are asked the same basic questions in the same order. Questions are worded in a completely open-ended format.	Respondents answer the same questions, thus increasing comparability of responses; data are complete for each person on the topics addressed in the interview. Reduces interviewer effects and bias when several interviewers are used. Permits evaluation users to see and review the instrumentation used in the evaluation. Facilitates organization and analysis of the data.	Little flexibility in relating the interview to particular individuals and circumstances; standardized wording of questions may constrain and limit naturalness and relevance of questions and answers.
Closed, fixed-response interview	Questions and response categories are determined in advance. Responses are fixed; respondent chooses from among these fixed responses.	Data analysis is simple; responses can be directly compared and easily aggregated; many questions can be asked in a short time.	Respondents must fit their experiences and feelings into the researcher's categories; may be perceived as impersonal, irrelevant, and mechanistic. Can distort what respondents really mean or have experienced by so completely limiting their response choices.

Source: Reprinted from Michael Quinn Patton (1990). *Qualitative evaluation and research methods,* 2nd ed. Newbury Park, CA: Sage, pp. 288–289.

The first three strategies are more likely (although not exclusively) to be utilized in qualitative studies, the fourth more likely (but again, not exclusively) in quantitative studies. The reader is reminded, however, that it is not uncommon to find several of these strategies being employed in the same study.

KEY-ACTOR INTERVIEWS

Some people in any group are more informed about the culture and history of their group, as well as more articulate, than others. Such individuals, traditionally called *key informants*, are especially useful sources of information. Fetterman prefers the term **"key actors"** to describe such individuals to avoid the stigma attached to the term "informant," as well as the historical roots that underlie the term.[9] Key actors are especially knowledgeable individuals and thus often excellent sources of information. They can often provide detailed information about a group's past and about contemporary happenings and relationships as well as the everyday nuances—the ordinary details—that others might miss. They offer insights that are often invaluable to a researcher. Fetterman gives an example of a key actor who proved helpful to him in a study of school dropouts.

> James was a long-term janitor in the Detroit dropout program [a program that Fetterman was studying]. He grew up in the local community with many of the students and was extraordinarily perceptive about the differences between the serious and less serious students in the program, as well as between the serious and less serious teachers. I asked him whether he thought the students were obeying the new restrictions against smoking, wearing hats in the building, and wearing sneakers. He said, "You can tell from the butts on the floor that they is still smokin', no matter what dey tell yah. I know, cause I gotta sweep 'em up. . . . It's mostly the new ones, don't yah know, like Kirk, and Dyan, Tina. You can catch 'em almost any ol' time. I seen 'em during class in the hallways, here (in the cafeteria), and afta hours." He provided empirical evidence to support his observations—a pile of cigarette butts he had swept up while we were talking.[10]

Here is another example from Fetterman's research.

> In a study of a gifted and talented education program, my most insightful and helpful key actor was a school district supervisor. He told about the politics of the school district and how to avoid the turf disputes during my study. He drove me around the community to teach me how to identify each of the major neighborhoods and pointed out corresponding socioeconomic differences that proved to have an important impact on the study. He also described the cyclical nature of the charges of elitism raised against the program by certain community members and a former school board member. He confided that his son (who was eligible to enter the program) had decided not to enter. This information opened new doors to my perception of peer pressure in that community.[11]

As you can see, a key actor can be an extremely valuable source of information. Accordingly, re-searchers need to take the time to seek out and establish a bond of trust with these individuals. The information they provide can serve as a cross-check on data the researcher obtains from other interviews, from observations, and from content analysis. But the musings of a key actor must also be viewed with some caution. Care must be taken to ensure that a key actor is not merely providing information he or she thinks the researcher wants to hear. This is why a researcher needs to seek out multiple sources of information in any study.

TYPES OF INTERVIEW QUESTIONS

Patton has identified six basic types of questions that can be asked of people. Any or all of these questions might be asked during an interview. The six types are (1) background or demographic questions, (2) knowledge questions, (3) experience or behavior questions, (4) opinion or values questions, (5) feelings questions, and (6) sensory questions.[12]

Background or **demographic questions** are routine sorts of questions about the background characteristics of the respondents. They include questions about education, previous occupations, age, income, and the like.

Knowledge questions are questions researchers ask to find out what factual information (as contrasted with their opinions, beliefs, and attitudes) respondents possess. Knowledge questions about a school, for example, might include queries about the kinds of courses available for students to take, graduation requirements, the sorts of extracurricular activities provided, school rules, enrollment policies, and the like. From a qualitative perspective, what the researcher wants to find out is what the respondents consider to be factual information (as opposed to beliefs or attitudes).

Experience or **behavior questions** are questions a researcher asks to find out what a respondent is currently doing or has done in the past. Their intent is to elicit descriptions of experience, behaviors, or activities that could have been observed but (for reasons such as the researcher not being present) were not. Examples might include, "If I had been in your class during the past semester, what kinds of things would I have been doing?" or "If I were to follow you through a typical day here at your school, what experiences would I be likely to see you having?"

Opinion or **values questions** are questions researchers ask to find out what people *think* about some topic or issue. Answers to such questions call attention to the respondent's goals, beliefs, attitudes, or values.

Examples might include such questions as, "What do you think about the principal's new policy concerning absenteeism?" or "What would you like to see changed in the way things are done in your U.S. history class?"

Feelings questions are questions a researcher asks to find out how respondents *feel* about things. They are directed toward the emotional responses of people to their experiences. Examples might include such questions as, "How do you feel about the way students behave in this school?" or "To what extent are you anxious about going to gym class?"

Feelings and opinion questions are often confused. It is very important for anyone who wishes to be a skillful interviewer to be able to distinguish between the two types of questions and to know when to ask each. To find out how someone feels about an issue is not the same thing as finding out their opinion about the issue. Thus, the question, "What do you think (what is your opinion) about your teacher's homework policy?" asks for the respondent's *opinion*—what he or she thinks—about the policy. The question, "How do you feel (what do you like or dislike) about your teacher's homework policy?" asks how the respondent *feels* about (his or her attitude toward) the policy. The two, although they appear somewhat similar, ask for decidedly different kinds of information.

Sensory questions are questions a researcher asks to find out what a respondent has seen, heard, tasted, smelled, or touched. Examples might include questions such as, "When you enter your classroom, what do you see?" or "How would you describe what your class sounds like?" Although this type of question could be considered as a form of experience or behavior question, it is often overlooked by researchers during an interview. Further, such questions are sufficiently distinct to warrant a category of their own.

INTERVIEWING BEHAVIOR

A set of expectations exists for all interviews. Here are some of the most important.

- *Respect the culture of the group being studied.* It would be insensitive, for example, for a researcher to wear expensive clothing while conducting an interview with an impoverished, inner-city high school youth. Of course, a researcher may commit an occasional faux pas inadvertently, but most interviewees will forgive such. A constant disregard for a group's traditions and values, however, is bound to impede the researcher's efforts to obtain reliable and valid information.

- *Respect the individual being interviewed.* Those who agree to be interviewed give up time they might spend elsewhere to answer the researcher's questions. An interview, therefore, should not be viewed as an opportunity to criticize or evaluate the interviewee's actions or ideas; rather, it is an opportunity to learn from the interviewee. A classroom teacher, a student, a counselor, a school custodian—all have work to do, and hence every researcher is well reminded not to waste their time. Interviews should start and end at the scheduled times and be conducted courteously. Further, the researcher should pick up on cues given by the interviewee. As Fetterman points out, "repeated glances at a watch are usually a clear signal that the time is up. Glazed eyes, a puzzled look, or an impatient scowl is an interviewee's way of letting the questioner know that something is wrong. The individual is lost, bored, or insulted. Common errors involve spending too much time talking and not enough time listening, failing to make questions clear, and making an inadvertently insensitive comment."[13] (Figure 19.4 illustrates an example where the interviewee is *not* respected)

- *Be natural.* "Acting like an adolescent does not win the confidence of adolescents, it only makes them suspicious."[14] Deception in any form has no place in an interview.

- *Develop an appropriate rapport with the participant.* Here you have to be careful, for dangers lurk. Seidman points out the problem: "Rapport implies getting along with each other, a harmony with, a conformity to, an affinity for one another. The problem is that, carried to an extreme, the desire to build rapport with the participant can transform the interviewing relationship into a full 'We' relationship in which the question of whose experience is being related and whose meaning is being made is critically confounded.[15] He goes on to describe an incident that occurred in a study he conducted in a community college:

In our community college study, one participant invited my wife and me to his house for dinner after (an) interview . . . I had never had such an invitation from a participant . . . and I did not quite know what to do. I did not want to appear ungracious, so we accepted. My wife and I went to dinner at his home. We had a wonderful California backyard cookout and it was a pleasure to spend

Figure 19.4 *An Interview of Dubious Validity*

time with the participant and his family. But a few days later, when I met him at his faculty office for the third interview, he was so warm and familiar toward me, that I could not retain the distance that I needed to explore his responses. I felt tentative as an interviewer because I did not want to risk violating the spirit of hospitality that he had created by inviting us to his home.[16]

- *Ask the same question in different ways during the interview.* This enables the researcher to check his or her understanding of what the interviewee has been saying, and may even shed new light on the topic being discussed.

- *Ask the interviewee to repeat an answer or statement when there is some doubt about the completeness of a remark.* This can stimulate discussion when an interviewee tends to respond with terse, short answers to the researcher's questions.

- *Vary who controls the flow of communication.* In a formal, structured interview, it is often necessary for the researcher to control the asking of questions and the pace of the discussion. In informal interviews, particularly during the exploratory or initial phase of an interview, it is often wise to let the interviewee ramble a bit in order to establish a sense of trust and cooperation.

- *Avoid leading questions.* Leading questions presume an answer, as in questions like "You wanted to do that, of course?" or "Your friends talked you into that,

didn't they?" or "How much did that upset you?" Each of these questions leads the participant to respond in a certain way. More appropriate versions of these questions would be "What did you want to do?" and "Why did you do that?" and "How did you feel about that?"

Instead of leading questions, interviewers often ask **open-ended questions.** Open-ended questions indicate an area to be explored without suggesting to the participant how it should be explored. They do not presume an answer. Here are some examples: "What was the meeting like for you?" or "Tell me what your student teaching experience was like?" There are many possibilities for open-ended questions and many ways of asking them. Perhaps none is better than simply asking "What was that like for you" when an interviewer wants to get at a participant's subjective experience.

- Do not ask **dichotomous questions,** that is, questions that permit a "yes-no" answer, when you are trying to get a complete picture. Here are some examples: "Were you satisfied with your assignment?" "Have you changed as a result of teaching at Adams School?" "Was that a good experience for you?" "Did you know what to do when you were asked to do that?" And so forth.

The problem with dichotomous questions is that they do not encourage the respondent to talk. Often-

Figure 19.5 *Don't Ask More Than One Question at a Time*

times, when an interviewer is having trouble getting a participant to talk, it is because he or she is asking a string of dichotomous questions.

Patton presents what is perhaps the classic example of a series of dichotomous questions in the following conversation between a teenager and his parent. The teen has just returned home from a date:

Do you know that you're late?
Yeah.
Did you have a good time?
Yeah.
Did you go to a movie?
Yeah.
Was it a good movie?
Yeah, it was okay.
So, it was worth seeing?
Yeah, it was worth seeing.
I've heard a lot about it. Do you think I would like it?
I don't know. Maybe.
Anything else you'd like to tell me about your evening?
No, I guess that's it.
(Teenager goes upstairs to bed. One parent turns to the other and says: "It sure is hard to get him to talk to us.")[17]

As you can see, the problem with asking dichotomous questions is that they can easily turn an inter-

view into something more like a test or interrogation than an interview.

- *Ask only one question at a time.* Asking more than one question is a common error made by novice interviewers, and you sometimes see this on poorly designed questionnaires as well. Rather than asking only a single question and allowing the participant to respond, the interviewer asks several questions one after the other without allowing the interviewee to answer (see Figure 19.5). Here is an example:

What was that like for you? Did you participate? You said you found it difficult. Was it difficult for you or for the other people who were participating as well? And how do you think they felt about it?

- *Don't interrrupt.* This is perhaps the most important technique there is in good interviewing. Don't interrupt participants when they are talking. And this is especially true when a participant says something that the interviewer finds particularly interesting. Often it is tempting to interrupt the speaker to pursue this interesting item. To do so, however, may interrupt the participant's train of thought. It is better to simply jot down a brief note and then follow up on it later, when there is a pause in the conversation.

How Not to Interview

A hypothetical situation involving a researcher interviewing a teacher who has just finished using her district's new mathematics curriculum.)

RESEARCHER: This is a very important topic, but don't be nervous. *(Fails to establish rapport)*

TEACHER: Okay.

RESEARCHER: I assume you had prior experience working with this type of mathematics materials?

TEACHER: Well, yes, a little.

RESEARCHER: That's too bad. I was hoping you would be more experienced *(Indicates desired response)*

TEACHER: Well, actually, now that I think about it, I did use similar materials a year or so ago. *(Gives desired response)*

RESEARCHER: Oh, where was that? *(Irrelevant comment)*

TEACHER: In Utah.

RESEARCHER: Really? I'm from Utah—how did you like it there? *(Loses focus)*

TEACHER: I loved it. Skiing was great!

RESEARCHER: I'm a tennis player myself.

TEACHER: What's this got to do with math?

FOCUS GROUP INTERVIEWS

A **focus group** interview is an interview with a small group (usually four to eight) people who are asked to think about a series of questions asked by the interviewer. The participants are seated together in a group and get to hear one another's responses to the questions. Often they offer additional comments beyond what they originally had to say once they hear the other responses. They may agree or disagree; consensus is neither necessary nor desired. The object is to get at what people really think about an issue or issues in a social context where the participants can hear the views of others and consider their own views accordingly.

We should stress, however, that a focus group interview is not a discussion. Neither is it a problem-solving session, nor is it a decision-making group. It is an *interview.*[18]

RECORDING INTERVIEW DATA

No matter what kind of interview one conducts, and no matter how carefully one prepares the questions to be asked during the interview, all will be to no avail if the interviewer does not capture what the person being interviewed actually says. While the interview is going on, therefore, it is essential to record as faithfully as possible what the participant has to say. Some method for recording an interviewee's words exactly is required.

A tape-recorder, therefore, is often considered to be an indispensable part of any qualitative researcher's equipment. "Tape recorders do not 'tune out' conversations, change what has been said because of interpreta-tion (either conscious or unconscious), or record words more slowly than they are spoken."[19]

Using a tape recorder, however, does not eliminate the need for taking notes. As Patton points out:

> Notes can serve at least two purposes: (1) Notes taken during the interview can help the interviewer formulate new questions as the interview moves along, particularly where it may be appropriate to check out something that was said earlier; and (2) taking notes about what is said will facilitate later analysis, including locating important quotations from the tape itself . . . the failure to take notes will often indicate to the respondent that nothing of importance is being said.[20]

ETHICS IN INTERVIEWING: THE NECESSITY FOR INFORMED CONSENT

In-depth interviews ask participants to reveal much about their lives. During such interviews, a measure of intimacy can be developed between interviewers and participants that can lead participants to describe events in their lives that, if misused, could leave them very vulnerable. Participants deserve to be protected from such vulnerability. Furthermore, interviewers also need to be protected against any misunderstanding on the part of participants as to the nature and purpose of the interview itself.

Thus, we believe that it is ethically desirable in this instance for interviewers to obtain the informed consent of individuals they are about to interview. The consent of a participant should be obtained, therefore, on an informed consent form. We suggest that any such form include points similar to the ones provided in the form on p. 59 in Chapter Four.

DATA COLLECTION AND ANALYSIS IN QUALITATIVE RESEARCH

As pointed out in Chapter Eighteen and described previously, there are important differences between quantitative and qualitative approaches to data collection and analysis. Although qualitative research can, and sometimes does, make use of structured instruments such as those described in Chapter Seven, the preference is for less structured, open-ended data collection with structuring taking place later through content analysis or emergent themes (Chapter Twenty) as the means of data analysis. While other descriptive statistics are often relevant, the most commonly used is reporting of frequencies. As the use of mixed models continues to increase, we expect to see more use of quantitative analysis in conjunction with more customary qualitative analyses.

Validity and Reliability in Qualitative Research

In Chapter Eight, we introduced the concepts of validity and reliability as they apply to the use of instruments in educational research. These two concepts are also very important in qualitative research, only here they apply to the observations researchers make and to the responses they receive to the interview questions asked. A fundamental concern in qualitative research, in fact, revolves around the degree of confidence researchers can place in what they have seen or heard. In other words, how can researchers be sure that they are not being misled?

You will recall that **validity** refers to the appropriateness, meaningfulness, and usefulness of the inferences researchers make based on the data they collect, while **reliability** refers to the consistency of these inferences over time, location, and circumstances.

In a qualitative study, much depends on the perspective of the researcher. All researchers have certain biases. Accordingly, different researchers see some things more clearly than others. Qualitative researchers use a number of techniques, therefore, to check their perceptions in order to ensure that they are not being misinformed—that they are, in effect, seeing (and hearing) what they think they are. These procedures for checking on or enhancing validity and reliability include the following:

- Using a variety of instruments to collect data. When a conclusion is supported by data collected from a number of different instruments, its validity is

thereby enhanced. This kind of checking is often referred to as **triangulation** (See Figure 21.1 in Chapter Twenty-One).

- Checking one informant's descriptions of something (a way of doing things or a reason for doing something) against another informant's descriptions of the same thing. Discrepancies in descriptions *may* mean the data are invalid.*
- Learning to understand and, where appropriate, speak the vocabulary of the group being studied. If researchers do not understand what informants mean when they use certain terms (especially slang) or if they take such terms to mean something that they do not, the recording of invalid data will surely result.
- Writing down the questions asked (in addition to the answers received). This helps researchers make sense at a later date out of answers recorded earlier, and helps them reduce distortions owing to selective forgetting.
- Recording personal thoughts while conducting observations and interviews. Responses that seem unusual or incorrect can be noted and checked later against other remarks or observations.
- Asking one or more participants in the study to review the accuracy of the research report. This is frequently referred to as *member*-checking.
- Obtaining an individual outside of the study to review and evaluate the report. This is called an *external audit.*
- Documenting the sources of remarks whenever possible and appropriate. This helps researchers make sense out of comments that otherwise might seem misplaced.
- Documenting the basis for inferences.
- Describing the context in which questions are asked and situations are observed.
- Using audiotapes and videotapes when possible and appropriate.
- Drawing conclusions based on one's understanding of the situation being observed and then acting on these conclusions. If these conclusions are invalid, the researcher will soon find out after acting on them.
- Interviewing individuals more than once. Inconsistencies over time in what the same individual reports may suggest that he or she is an unreliable informant.

*Not necessarily, of course. It may simply mean a difference in viewpoint or perception.

Table 19.2 *Qualitative Research Questions, Strategies, and Data-Collection Techniques*

Purpose of the Study	Possible Research Questions	Research Strategies	Examples of Data-Collection Techniques
Exploratory: • To investigate a little-understood event, situation, or circumstance • To identify or discover important variables • To generate hypotheses for further research	• What is happening in this school? • What are the important themes or patterns in the ways teachers behave in this school? • How are these themes or patterns linked together?	• Case study • Observation • Field study	• Participant observation • Nonparticipant observation • In-depth interviewing • Selected interviewing
Descriptive: • To document an event, situation, or circumstance of interest	What are the important behaviors, events, attitudes, processes, and/or structures occurring in this school?	• Case study • Field study • Ethnography • Observation	• Participant observation • Nonparticipant observation • In-depth interviewing • Written questionnaire • Content analysis
Explanatory: • To explain the forces causing an event, situation, or circumstance • To identify plausible causal networks shaping an event, situation, or circumstance	• What events, beliefs, attitudes, and/or policies are shaping the nature of this school? • How do these forces interact to shape this school?	• Case study • Field study • Ethnography	• Participant observation • Nonparticipant observation • In-depth interviewing • Written questionnaire • Content analysis
Predictive: • To predict the outcomes of an event, situation, or circumstance • To forecast behaviors or actions that might result from an event, situation, or circumstance	• What is likely to occur in the future as a result of the policies now in place at this school? • Who will be affected, and in what ways?	• Observation • Interview	• In-depth interviewing • Written questionnaire • Content analysis

• Observing the setting or situation of interest over a period of time. The length of an observation is extremely important in qualitative research. Consistency over time with regard to what researchers are seeing or hearing is a strong indication of reliability. Furthermore, there is much about a group that does not even begin to emerge until some time has passed and the members of the group become familiar with, and willing to trust, the researcher.

Table 19.2 summarizes a number of purposes, research questions, strategies, and data-collection techniques used in qualitative research.

An Example of Qualitative Research

In the remainder of this chapter, we present a published example of an interview-type qualitative study, followed by a critique of its strengths and weaknesses. As we did in our critiques of the different types of research studies we analyzed in other chapters, we use concepts introduced in earlier parts of the book in our analysis.

From: *Journal of Teacher Education, 45*:5 (1994): 346–353.

Why Students of Color Are Not Entering Teaching: Reflections from Minority Teachers

June A. Gordon
University of Washington

The choice of teaching as a career and the persistence through the process culminating in a teaching position result from a complex and highly varied array of influences upon the individual. For this study, I designed interviews with teachers of color to obtain expert perceptions of how those influences work within communities of color. The interviews of minority teachers is one component in a larger effort to understand how to both increase the number of teachers of color and improve the preparation of all teachers for work in schools with a diverse student population. These efforts require full awareness of the differences between individuals within racial categories as well as the power of socialization into professionalism and hence the middle-class (Apple, 1988; Goodlad, 1990; Durkheim, 1961).

Purpose

REVIEW OF LITERATURE

A shortage of minority teachers is embedded in a context of school desegregation, higher education elitism, racism, poverty, and urban decay. A much larger potential supply of teachers exists among ethnic and urban communities than is evident from the current minority student enrollment in teacher education programs in universities with traditionally white student bodies (Haberman, 1989). The continuing success of historically African American colleges in attracting prospective teachers is part of this evidence (Allen, Epps & Haniff, 1991; Clark, 1987; LeMelle & LeMelle, 1969). While racism and poverty have slowed academic achievement in urban communities, the lack of active recruitment and community partnerships on the part of teacher education programs has contributed to the low enrollment of students of color in those programs. Adding to this situation is the inertia of the teaching profession and its training programs resulting from selection criteria and forms of recruitment which perpetuate stereotypes of teaching based on the typical teacher at middle-class suburban schools (Apple, 1978; Etzioni, 1969). Efforts to enhance the teaching profession through increased testing and longer training have so far only worsened the prospects for students of color (Witty, 1986; Gifford, 1986; Pofahl, 1987). Many see the problem not solvable in the present social conditions.

Needs a reference

Nevertheless, no matter what one's orientation to public schooling, consensus exists on the need for more minority teachers. The reasons include increasingly low academic performance of minority youth (Dentzer & Wheelock, 1990; Moore & Pachon, 1985), inability and/or unwillingness of middle-class teachers to teach low-income minority children (Book, Byers & Freeman, 1983), desire for minorities to educate their own people (Hilliard, 1988), need for all children to experience a multiethnic teaching force (Banks & Banks, 1989), high cost of prisons and welfare (Doston & Bolden, 1990), and desire for a more honest representation in the curriculum of the diversity of ideas and skills that have contributed to the development of the nation (Gay, 1990). In addition, there are economic and world market competitive concerns suggesting the need to develop more adequately the human potential of all citizens (Sowell, 1983).

Good documentation

The question remains: Why then do so few students of color enter the field of teaching if the needs are so great? The research and commentary in the field offer both the view that people of color do not choose teaching as a career because incentives such as salary, prestige, and social

Research or opinion?
Is this a
comprehensive
review?

Justification

mobility are low relative to alternative careers now available (Robinson, 1981; Dupre, 1986) and the view that people of color still face significant impediments in gaining access to and success in teacher education (Goodlad, 1990; Ogbu, 1974). Acceptance of either or both of the two views provokes wonderment why any person of color would enter the field of teaching. Research is necessary to understand the reasons for the decline in minority teachers entering the teaching profession (Mercer, 1982; Merino & Quintanar, 1988).

STATEMENT OF PURPOSE

Assumption

Purpose

I based this research on the premise that minority teachers are a crucial source of both knowledge and numbers requisite to provide an adequate education not only for the rising numbers of minority youth in our cities, but for all children. By understanding more thoroughly the reasons for the lack of minority participation in teacher education programs, teacher education might implement more effective programs to better prepare all teachers to work in multicultural settings and provide access and support for all individuals with the appropriate commitment and competence for careers in public school teaching.

METHODOLOGY

Sample
How many at each
location?

In this article I describe one part of a much larger research project in which I explored the impediments that people of color have faced and continue to face in their search for an adequate education. Over a two-year period I conducted face-to-face, semi-structured interviews with 140 teachers of color in Cincinnati, Ohio; Seattle, Washington; and Long Beach, California. Six interview questions brought a wealth of information which, if I consolidated them into one article, would lose integrity and depth. For this reason I focus on one of the research questions at this time: *Why do you think students of color are not going into teaching?*

The interview questions I selected to probe for answers to the research questions included:

- *Why do you think students of color are not going into teaching?*
- *Why did you choose teaching as a career?*
- *Do you recommend teaching to others? Why, why not?*
- *Are teachers respected in your community? Has the image of teachers changed over time in your community?*
- *How can we attract and recruit more students of color into the field of teaching?*
- *What changes would you make in the teacher training experience to better prepare all teachers to work with students from diverse economic, ethnic, and linguistic backgrounds?*

Operational definition
See text p. 31.

Ambiguous

How known?

Convenience sample

In this study the terms *minority teacher* and *teacher of color* include individuals who school districts have identified as being from one of four ethnic categories used for official reporting: Latino/Hispanic, African American/Black, Asian American, and Native American. The teachers of color I selected as the most appropriate group to interview met the following criteria: they selected teaching as a career and completed a teacher education program; are working in the field, often in urban schools; are usually working with students of color who could choose teaching as a career; and represent strong views held within communities of color as to perceptions of teaching and teacher education.

I selected Cincinnati, Seattle, and Long Beach largely on the basis of accessibility; I knew someone in each city who could assist me in gaining access to the district. The school district administration in each city made the choices of schools in each district for interviewing. I asked that the administration select schools which had a balance between all four ethnic groups mentioned above; geographic variation within the city; economic variation among the schools; and schools from all grade levels: high school, middle, and elementary.

I selected semi-structured, face-to-face interviewing as the most appropriate research strategy because of the intense and critical nature of the topic under scrutiny and the informants involved. This form of qualitative research offers the advantages of focusing on the specific experience and perceptions of individuals engaged in the area of interest. Conceptual models prompt qualitative research rather than vice versa; real-life examples provide illustrative evidence rather than the basis for testing hypothetical deductions needed in the formation of theory (Sirotnik, 1989). Partlett and Hamilton (1972) contend that this discovery of apparent contradictions makes face-to-face interviewing valuable. Rather than ironing out unusual responses, qualitative researchers welcome unfamiliar utterances and encourage sensitivity to context.

Justification

RESULTS

Seventeen themes emerged from the responses to the question: *Why do you think students of color are going into the field of teaching?* I have classified them into three areas for further consideration: educational experiences, cultural and community concerns, and social and economic obstacles.

Wasn't "not" omitted here?

While non-minority teachers may share some of the impediments interviewees expressed in these interviews, certain issues, particularly pertaining to educational and cultural/community concerns, are more common to the minority experience than to that of White European Americans. After listing the themes, respondents elaborated on their interpretation of the question.

Not clear to us

EDUCATIONAL EXPERIENCE: INTERVIEW RESPONSES

Not Graduating from High School

Approximately one-fourth of the informants specifically indicated low graduation rates as the primary cause of the shortage of teachers of color. This perception was particularly strong for Latino and Native American teachers who saw the school failure of children from their ethnic groups as the main reason for their absence from college campuses and, therefore, from the

Quantification is helpful.

Table 1 *Respondent Themes*

Educational Experience
    not graduating from high school
    lack of preparation
    negative experience in school
    poor student discipline/lack of respect
    teachers not prepared for diversity
    lack of support in college

Cultural and Community Concerns
    lack of academic encouragement
    racelessness
    absence of role models
    low status
    too much education for the return
    teaching not attractive to some ethnic groups

Social and Economic Obstacles
    low pay
    negative image
    poor school conditions
    more opportunities elsewhere
    racism

Good examples

teaching profession. As one Latino teacher stated, *Hispanics don't even think of career; they don't make it through high school.* Native American informants corroborated this pessimistic outcome for their own people. *Indians have one of the highest drop-out rates; they can't get into college. They have the lowest graduation rate; only two percent go on to college.*

Lack of Adequate Preparation

How many?

(Several) teachers believed that the reason that few minority students select teaching as a career is that *They can't keep up; so they do something less difficult than teaching.* Two other comments supported this perception: *There are gaps in the education of students of color . . . The preparation to get into college is overwhelming, especially for minorities.*

Negative Experience in School

Quantification is helpful.

Almost (one-third) of the responses noted negative experiences in school as a reason students of color opt not to stay in education for their life work. Some of the more poignant responses were in this area: *The 40 percent drop-out rate for minorities is due to what happens in the classroom . . . How can you expect somebody to survive a system that doesn't expect them to be successful? Education, as it's set up for minority students, is teaching them to be failures . . . If kids are getting turned off of K-12 education, why would they want to teach anyone else? It [boarding school] was like a prison to them; it's slow to change that mentality.*

Poor Student Discipline/Lack of Respect

Nearly one-half of the informants noted lack of respect that teachers receive from students in the classroom as one of the reasons many students of color are not selecting teaching as a profession. *They see teachers have a hard time. They don't want to be subject to it. They know what they put their teachers through . . . I can only speak for Vietnamese people. Teaching is not worth the trouble. There's too much freedom in America; students use freedom to intimidate the teacher.*

Teachers Not Prepared for Diversity

Almost one-fourth of the informants saw the lack of teacher preparation to work with diversity as a source of turning students of color away from teaching. While some respondents felt that teachers of color were better at handling students of color, the vast majority admitted to being at a loss as to how to work with inner-city youth. *I wasn't trained for the inner city. I never experienced some of the things that these kids live; I came to Detroit; it frightened me, coming from a small Southern town. . . . I've never lived in a ghetto, in the South we were just poor; Cincinnati was my first urban experience. . . . I was in a small town before [in Florida]. I have very little in common with, or understanding of, poor urban kids. . . . I wasn't raised that way . . . Teaching in L.A. is different from my experience being raised in Seattle. I hadn't been around that many Black people. I had to take classes at UCLA to learn about people different from my own.*

Lack of Support in College

One fifth of the informants questioned the rhetoric of concern for students of color. One African American woman spoke candidly, *I live in the [Black] community and I know what it thinks of the [university]. It is viewed as not a positive environment for minorities. The community does not see it as a friendly place. No one [from the university] comes into the schools to promote teaching; no one encourages minorities to apply. There is no program that supports minorities throughout their undergraduate experience. I went to [the university] and I know.*

For some, college is too expensive for most students of color and they are not aware of the alternative funding that is available for them. The following views exemplify these feelings, *Most kids that go to college are middle class; The poor can't go to college.*

CULTURAL AND COMMUNITY CONCERNS:
INTERVIEW RESPONSES

Lack of Academic Encouragement

While some students of color might not enter teaching because of lack of academic encouragement that they receive from parents not aware of or involved in formal schooling, significant discouragement comes from counselors and middle-class parents who know the benefits of an education. Much of this bias against the field is based on parental and student experiences, but it is also an issue of elitism and racism as reflected in these comments: *Parents don't encourage kids to go into teaching. Even if they're not middle-class, parents will encourage their children to be doctors and lawyers. . . . Counselors don't recommend teaching to Indians. Rather [they recommend] drafting and business. . . . My parents didn't want me to go into teaching, even though they were educators; my parents stressed lucrative jobs.* One Latino teacher commented, [Latino] *Parents have a different view of education. It's not the same as Asian or Anglo. Education is important, but it isn't the most important thing. Parents are dealing with survival, not long-range goals.* Another Latino added, *It is a luxury to think about what you want to do in the future, about going to college. This image comes from their own community; the environment is one of survival.*

How many mentioned these things?

Racelessness

Fear that demonstrating an interest in school will be equated with acting White and adopting the dominant culture's values impede many minority urban youth from putting forth their best effort. This condition had been called *racelessness* since it implies that individuals give up their own racial identity in the process of becoming educated. Approximately one-eighth of the informants mentioned this attitude as a major impediment to students of color rejecting teaching as a career choice. One African American teacher commented, *I confront students daily who say, 'You can't make me learn.' It's not cool to be educated. There is a thin wall between success and failure. Blacks can easily turn off from you.* Another informant lamented, *I have one student who told me that he didn't want to be seen carrying books home, so he keeps one there and one in class.* Elaborating on a possible source of this condition, a Latino explained, *Parents have this attitude and it is passed on to their kids. So they feel they have to go against the system because it goes against them. Why should we do like the White kids do?* A Native American respondent commented, *Education is the equivalent to going to learn how to be a White man.*

Absence of Role Models

One-fifth of the informants contended that one way to get students hooked into education, as well as improve discipline, is to increase the participation of positive minority role models in schools. *The Black community is more respectful of Black teachers than White. Black parents fear racism might enter into discipline. They think that Black teachers will be more fair. The more educated you are the more confident; Black kids play games, tell middle-class White teachers what they want to hear, and White middle-class teachers fall for it; but Black teachers will call them on it.*

But the complications of race, class and even age overcome this simple proposition: *Black teachers are looked upon negatively by Black parents. Black teachers are viewed as not as qualified as White. Blacks have been conditioned to think that Blacks are inferior; White kids won't* listen to me because I'm Black. They assume I'm stupid and lack respect. And Black kids won't listen to me because I'm Black; it has to do with denigration and self-hate. They'll listen to White teacher more because higher status. Lower-class Black parents trust an older Black teacher more than a younger Black teacher but middle-class parents want a younger teacher. The Black community has lots of types of people. The middle-class is emulating White society, not accepting our own segment of the population. One teacher summarized the resulting conclusion, expressed in a variety of ways by informants, by the words, Just because you're a minority it doesn't mean that you know how to work with kids. Sometimes it can be worse if you're a minority and a bad teacher. Kids will say, 'I don't want to grow up like her/him.' The difficulty is that there are so few minorities [in teaching].

Are these all different respondents?

Low Status

Almost half (47 of 114) of the informants identified the low status of teachers as the main reason students of color are not entering the field of teaching: As a minority, you don't get the respect that you deserve and as a teacher you don't get it either; so why be a teacher?

Too Much Education for the Return

One-eighth of the informants claimed that the extra year many colleges of education require for certification discourages students from selecting teaching. Five years in college and more is too much for the benefits of teaching. We are very practical people; Minority people go to college to get a job, not to listen to some special lectures or learn for learning's sake. Why should a Black person go to school an extra year to end up with a job that pays less than those that only take four years?

SOCIAL AND ECONOMIC OBSTACLES: INTERVIEW RESPONSES

Low Pay

While one-half of all informants stated low pay as the main reason that students of color are not entering teaching, their responses were mixed. My wife gets $10,000 more than I do working at Cincinnati Bell; she gets $63,000. My brother got $42,000 straight out of college; he's an aerospace engineer; What we get is not enough money when compared to doctors and lawyers. Another lamented, There was a teacher here who had three kids. Her husband left her and she had to quit and go on welfare to support them because she couldn't do it on a teacher's salary; The money is too low to afford a house, investments. We don't even make enough to retire on.

Others countered by stating, I don't think that money is the real issue. It's a myth. The union is working against us. By advocating for more income for teachers, they give a bad image of the profession. It's an irony. They have to say that we are poorly paid in order to get more money, but then, everyone thinks that it's [teaching] a low-paying job . . . Money is in the street. That's not what it's about. If you don't value the same things as the dominant culture, they go hustle on street; they'll get money their own way . . . You can't put monetary value on self-worth. Education must be viewed not by material gains received but by the improvement of their well-being, regardless of socioeconomic status. Money can't be the issue with any profession."

Negative Image

Almost one half of the respondents believed that a professional image is particularly important to people of color. The negative image of teaching in urban areas is that you are looked down on; no one wants to battle against the image . . . Minorities are looking for something *where they will be valued . . . Minorities want status even though a lot of us want to help people.* The image of teachers as middle-class females makes it difficult, some say, to identify with the role of teacher. Teaching has a *wimpish image* and does not represent *machismo. As long as the majority of teachers are women, it will be negatively perceived as a 'nice' profession. Females are seen as less than capable . . . A common view in the Black community is that if you're interested in music, art, or elementary education, you must be gay.* An art teacher claimed, *Teachers are seen as little old maids and goody two shoes. Teachers are seen as tall children. Teachers are viewed as baby-sitters; their roles are ill-defined; society doesn't value* [*them*].

Poor School Conditions

A little more than one-eighth of the informants noted the physical conditions of schools, especially in the inner city, as a cause for the low rate of minority participation in the field of education. *Minority kids coming from segregated schools look at their rundown schools, the poor supplies. It's not a condition, an environment, that makes you want to go back. On the other hand, kids coming from nice, well-supplied schools might be more interested in teaching . . . Minorities will enter the teaching force when teachers are treated at least as well as secretaries. Here we have to paint our own rooms with our own money. We have no privacy, no telephone in case of emergency. We clean our own rooms, have no secretarial help, and have to buy our own supplies.*

More Opportunities Elsewhere

One-third of the informants thought that students of color could get top jobs easily. *A Black male can get paid a lot more in other fields, it's wide open. They could be lawyers or bank presidents, why would they want to be teachers?* For some Latino teachers the perspective was more constrained, *There are so few minorities in higher education that those who are in college tend to go into more lucrative fields . . . Few Hispanics have degrees, those that do are goal-directed to other careers.*

Racism

About one-eighth of the interviews specified racism as a deterrent for students. *The racial aspect is always there. Why should minorities go back into schools as teachers when there has been so much prejudice for so long. . . . My granddaughter was doing great until she told them that she was an Indian, then they treated her differently and her grades dropped, then she had problems.* However, according to the informants, racism does not stop once there is a degree in hand, as a young African American male described: *I wanted to come home to Cincinnati to teach, but never got a response from the district, so I had to do another job, loading trucks, because I couldn't get hired as a teacher.* A teacher from Honduras explained, *You always have to struggle through the system, then you still have to keep proving yourself even if you make it into teaching. People don't believe you are qualified because of your accent.* A Chinese woman agreed: *Asians can't get jobs here teaching because of their accent. Americans need to be more realistic. If there is something that I can teach you in math or science, which does not need a great deal of language proficiency, why can't I teach? Americans need to learn from other cultures.* A gay Native American had to call up the school district and beg to work. He said *Hey, I teach math and science; I'm a Native American, why won't you hire me?*

DISCUSSION

Many teachers cited negative experiences in school as the most common educational reason students of color were not selecting teaching as a career. The experiences entailed lack of adequate academic preparation and poor counseling for students of color as well as lack of adequate preparation on the part of teachers to work with students from diverse backgrounds, resulting in students dropping out or being pushed out of the system. Social and economic obstacles included low pay and the negative image that teachers have in our society. The most revealing finding, however, came under cultural and community concerns: students are being discouraged from entering the teaching profession on all sides. Students not academically successful are told that they cannot survive the rigors of college. Lower-income students are either told that they cannot afford college or they are tracked into programs that match their parents' vocations. Middle-class children of color are told that they should strive for a career other than teaching given that their chances of teaching in low status urban schools are great. Academically successful students of color are told that their opportunities are limitless, that colleges are waiting to recruit them. Parents who have struggled and perhaps not survived formal schooling steer their children away from education seeing it as the source of their present predicament. Parents who see education as an avenue out of poverty and low-status pressure their children to move into high-status professions away from community and service occupations.

CONCLUSION

In this research I suggest that educators view the lack of interest in teaching on the part of students of color from a narrow, privileged perspective. The popular literature and jargon of the media have led to the belief that the cause of the shortage of minority teachers is low pay (Robinson, 1981; Dupre, 1986). As I have demonstrated, low pay is but one of many causes for students of color not selecting teaching. As several of the informants stated even if the pay were increased, the situation would not change. There are far more serious and more complex issues to address.

Since teacher education has failed and continues to fail to provide the majority of all teachers with the skills to succeed in inner city schools, there is a search for a short cut, a quick answer, a placebo that will get the profession through the next few years: recruit minority teachers to work in the inner cities, to work with their own people. This assumes a great deal. The voices of teachers of color who have traveled the path and continue their sojourn in urban classrooms make clear that a great deal more must be discussed and understood if public school teaching will ever attract students of color. Teachers of color are products of the same educational system as white teachers (Hale-Benson, 1982; Rist, 1970). Those who have made it into teaching have not only survived the system but have succeeded in it (Mercer, 1992). Most are middle class and have come from families removed from the realities of inner cities (Grant, 1989; Montero-Sieburth, 1989; Kluckhohn, 1962). As the interviews demonstrate, token representation of minority teachers will in and of itself not attract more students of color to the profession. The improvement of the education of all children is necessary so that they can choose their vocation in life. To do this all teachers must be better equipped to work with all children. The informants' responses provide an insight into the impediments that people of color face in their reach for a career in teaching and suggestions to improve the likelihood that students of color might select teaching as a career choice.

Not reported earlier

Respondent opinion

We agree.

Change to "suggest" (?)

Good point

References

Allen, W. R., Epps, E. G., & Hanniff, N. Z. (1991). *College in Black and White: African American students in predominantly White and in historically Black public universities.* New York: SUNY Press.

Apple, M. W. (1986). *Teachers and texts: A political economy of class and gender relations in education.* New York: Methuen.

Apple, M. W. (1988). Redefining equality. *Teachers College Record, 90,* 167–184.

Banks, J. A., & Banks, C. A. (1989). *Multicultural education: Issues and perspectives.* Boston: Allyn and Bacon.

Book, C., Byers, J., & Freeman, D. (1983). Student expectations and teacher education traditions with which we can and cannot live. *Journal of Teacher Education, 34,* 9–13.

Clark, V. L. (1987). Teacher education at historically Black institutions in the aftermath of the Holmes/Carnegie reports. *Planning and Change, 18,* 74–89.

Dentzer, E., & Wheelock, A. (1990). *Locked in/locked out: Tracking in Boston public schools.* Boston: Massachusetts Advocacy Center.

Doston, G. A., & Bolden, S. H. (1991). *The impact of nationwide school reform on the recruitment and retention of Black males in teacher education: A philosophical perspective.* Paper presented at the Fifth Annual Conference on Recruitment and Retention of Minorities in Education, Lexington, Kentucky.

Dupre, B. B. (1986). Problems regarding the survival of future Black teachers in education. *Journal of Negro Education, 55,* 56–66.

Durkheim, E. (1961). *Moral education: A study in the theory and application of sociology of education.* Glencoe, IL: The Free Press.

Etzioni, A. (1969). *The semi-professions and their organizations: Teachers, nurses, and social workers.* New York: The Free Press.

Gay, G. (1990). Achieving educational equality through curriculum desegregation. *Phi Delta Kappan,* September, 56–62.

Gifford, B. R. (1986). Excellence and equity in teacher competency testing: A policy perspective. *Journal of Negro Education, 55,* 251–271.

Grant, C. A. (1989). Urban teachers: Their new colleagues and curriculum. *Phi Delta Kappan, 70* (19), 251–271.

Haberman, M. (1989). More minority teachers. *Phi Delta Kappan, 70* (10), 771–776.

Hale-Benson, J. E. (1982). *Black children: Their roots, culture, and learning styles.* Baltimore: Johns Hopkins University.

Hilliard, A. G. (1988). Reintegration for education: Black community involvement with black schools. *Urban League Review, 11* (1,2), 251–271.

Kluckhohn, C. (1962). *Culture and behavior.* New York: The Free Press of Glencoe.

LeMelle, T. J. & LeMelle, W. J. (1969). *The Black college: A strategy for relevancy.* Praeger Special Studies in U.S. Economic and Social Development. New York: Frederick A. Praeger.

Mercer, W. A. (1982). Future Black teacher: A vanishing breed. *Negro Educational Review, 33,* 251–271.

Merino, B. J., & Quintanar, R. (1988). *The recruitment of minority students into teaching careers: A status report of effective approaches.* University of Colorado, Boulder, CO: Far West Regional Holmes Group.

Montero-Sieburth, M. (1989). Restructuring teachers' knowledge for urban settings. *Journal of Negro Education, 58.*

Moore, J. W., & Pachon, H. (1985). *Hispanics in the United States.* New Jersey: Prentice-Hall.

Oakes, J. (1985). *Keeping track: How schools structure inequality.* New Haven: Yale University Press.

Ogbu, J. U. (1974). *The next generation: An ethnography of education in an urban neighborhood.* New York: Academic Press.

Pofahl, M. (1987). *The educational testing service and a theory of cultural reproduction.* Unpublished manuscript.

Rist, R. (1970). Student social class and teacher expectations: The self-fulfilling prophecy in ghetto education. *Harvard Educational Review, 40,* 416–451.

Robinson, P. (1981). *Perspectives on the sociology of education.* London: Routledge & Kegan Paul.

Sirotnik, K. A. (1989). *Studying the education of educators: Methodology.* Technical Report No. 3. University of Washington, Seattle, Washington: Center for Educational Renewal.

Sowell, T. (1983). *The economics and politics of race.* New York: William Morrow.

Witty, E. P. (1986). Testing teacher performance. *Journal of Negro Education, 55* (3), 358–367.

Analysis of the Study

PURPOSE/JUSTIFICATION

This report states two purposes. First, in paragraph one, is "to understand how to both increase the number of teachers of color and improve the preparation of all teachers for work in schools with a diverse student population"—a "knowledge" purpose. This leads to a "practice" purpose—"teacher education might implement more effective programs" as stated under the statement of purpose. Several arguments are presented, most with references, as to why this purpose is important. The assumption that "minority teachers are a crucial source of both knowledge and numbers requisite to provide an adequate education" is identified under "Statement of Purpose," but we are unclear as to the relevance of "numbers requisite to." In our opinion, the study is well justified.

DEFINITIONS

"Minority teacher," used interchangeably with "teacher of color," is clearly defined as Latino/Hispanic, African-American/black, Asian American, or Native American as identified by the school district—the latter an operational definition. This definition is muddied by the additional criteria for selection discussed under "Methodology," since some of the criteria are ambiguous.

PRIOR RESEARCH

A fairly extensive review is provided in support of the need for the study; we must presume it is an adequate sampling of the various topics. It is unclear whether the four references that directly address the research question are research studies or commentary and whether they exhaust the topic.

HYPOTHESES

No hypotheses are stated (apparently deliberately—see the last paragraph of the methodology section), as is appropriate in a study designed to be purely descriptive.

SAMPLE

The sample is a convenience sample, but it is subject to certain criteria requested for schools—that is, a balance of the four ethnic groups involved in the study, geo-graphic variation within the city, economic variation, and including all grade levels. In addition to the above, descriptive information includes the cities used: Cincinnati, Seattle, and Long Beach. It appears that the sample included only teachers who were currently teaching and "often in urban schools; are usually working with students of color who could choose teaching as a career; and represent strong views . . . " It is unclear to us how the last two criteria were assessed unless based on information obtained during the interview. The latter criterion—"represent strong views"—suggests more of a purposive sampling. It would be helpful to have the numbers in each ethnic group.

INSTRUMENTATION AND DATA ANALYSIS

As is common in qualitative studies, interviews were the primary source of information. We think the method is well justified. No data on reliability or validity are provided, nor would it be easy to do so with such an open-ended focus question. Reporting extent of agreement with a second "reader" on theme categorization for at least a subsample of responses would be helpful.

Some effort to check reliability by follow-up questions would strengthen confidence in the data if it were appropriate. Reinterviewing a subsample at a later date might be feasible. Probably the best evidence of validity would consist of comparison of responses (in total and as categorized) with answers to other questions that were used in the overall study, since almost all have a bearing on the question used for this report. The statement that subjects elaborated on interpretations "after listing the themes" is unclear, since the themes were developed subsequently by the author. Providing percentages of respondents who mentioned each theme is a helpful use of quantitative data.

INTERNAL VALIDITY

The author's purpose is not to study relationships; hence internal validity is, strictly speaking, irrelevant. Studies such as this one provide no clear controls over researcher bias, which may affect both data collection and analysis. Because the findings imply that specific factors such as "cultural and community concerns" discourage minority students more than "majority culture students" from entering teaching, other factors, such as low pay, are alternative explanations for any particular factor.

RESULTS AND DISCUSSION

As is customary in such studies, we must, for the most part, accept at face value the author's summary of responses as well as their categorization—a content analysis. It is very helpful to have examples for each of the 17 themes; we must assume that they are representative. While we are prepared to accept the overall theme descriptions, it is unclear how many respondents did or would agree with some of the examples. It seems that classification of this content would be relatively straightforward, but evidence that others would classify in the same way would add credibility.

While the discussion and conclusion sections are consistent with the results presented, they contain assertions that go beyond these results, for example, "Since teacher education has failed and continues to fail to provide the majority of all teachers with the skills to succeed in inner city schools, there is a search for a short cut . . ." While this may very well be true, the author should make clear that it does not follow from the results of *this* study. We also think the author should qualify conclusions by indicating that they are often the assessments of respondents—not necessarily fact.

Lastly, we think the purpose of the study—to clarify reasons why minority students are not entering teaching—was achieved.

Go back to the **Interactive and Applied Learning Tools** feature at the beginning of the chapter for a listing of interactive and applied activities. **Go to the Online Learning Center** at www.mhhe.com/fraenkel5e or your **Interactive Student CD-ROM** to take practice quizzes and receive immediate feedback, practice with key terms, review chapter content and main ideas, and find annotated Web links.

Main Points

OBSERVER ROLES

- There are four roles that an observer can play in a qualitative research study, ranging from complete participant, to participant-as-observer, to observer-as-participant, to complete observer. The degree of involvement of the observer in the observed situation diminishes accordingly for each of these roles.

PARTICIPANT VERSUS NONPARTICIPANT OBSERVATION

- In participant observation studies, the researcher actually participates as an active member of the group in the situation or setting he or she is observing.
- In nonparticipant observation studies, the researcher does not participate in an activity or situation, but observes "from the sidelines."
- The most common forms of nonparticipant observation studies include naturalistic observation and simulations.
- A simulation is an artificially created situation in which subjects are asked to act out certain roles.

OBSERVATION TECHNIQUES

- A coding scheme is a set of categories an observer uses to record a person's or group's behaviors.
- Even with a fixed coding scheme in mind, an observer must still choose what to observe.
- A major problem in all observational research is that much that goes on may be missed.

OBSERVER EFFECT

- The term "observer effect" refers to either the effect the presence of an observer can have on the behavior of the subjects or observer bias in the data reported. The use of audio- and videotapings is especially helpful in guarding against this effect.
- For this reason, many researchers argue that the participants in a study should not be informed of the study's purpose until after the data have been collected.

OBSERVER BIAS

- Observer bias refers to the possibility that certain characteristics or ideas of observers may affect what they observe.

SAMPLING IN OBSERVATIONAL STUDIES

- Researchers who engage in observation usually must choose a purposive sample.

INTERVIEWING

- A major technique commonly used by qualitative researchers is that of in-depth interviewing.
- One purpose of interviewing the participants in a qualitative study is to find out how they think or feel about something. Another purpose is to provide a check on the researcher's observations.
- Interviews may be structured, semistructured, informal, or retrospective.
- The six types of questions asked by interviewers are background or demographic questions, knowledge questions, experience or behavior questions, opinion or values questions, feelings questions, and sensory questions.
- Respect for the individual being interviewed is a paramount expectation in any proper interview.
- Key actors are people in any group who are more informed about the culture and history of the group, and who also are more articulate, than others.
- A focus group interview is an interview with a small fairly homogeneous group of people who respond to a series of questions asked by the interviewer.
- The most effective characteristic of a good interviewer is a strong interest in people and in listening to what they have to say.

RELIABILITY AND VALIDITY IN QUALITATIVE RESEARCH

- An important check on the validity and reliability of the researcher's interpretations in qualitative research is to compare one informant's description of something with another informant's description of the same thing.
- Another, although more difficult, check on reliability/validity is to compare information on the same topic with different information—triangulation.
- Efforts to ensure reliability and validity include use of proper vocabulary, recording questions used as well as personal reactions, describing content, and documenting sources.

Key Terms

Background (or demographic) question 458

Coding scheme 454

Dichotomous question 460

Experience (or behavior) question 458

External audit 463

Feelings question 459

Focus group 462

Informal interview 456

Key actor 458

Knowledge question 458

Member checking 463

Naturalistic observation 451

Nonparticipant observation 451

Observation 450

Observer bias 453

Observer effect 453

Observer expectations 453

Open-ended question 460

Participant observation 450

Reliability in qualitative research 463

Retrospective interview 456

Semi-structured interview 456

Sensory question 459

Simulation 452

Structured interview 456

Triangulation 463

Validity in qualitative research 463

Values (or opinion) question 458

For Discussion

1. "Observing people without their knowledge and/or recording their comments without their permission is unethical." Would you agree with this statement? Explain your reasoning.
2. Which do you think is more likely to produce valid information—participant or nonparticipant observation? Why?
3. Are there any kinds of behaviors that should *not* be observed? Explain your thinking. If so, give an example.
4. What would you say is the biggest advantage of participant observation? The biggest disadvantage?
5. "A major difficulty in observing people is that much that goes on may be missed by the observer." Is this always true? Are there any ways to decrease what is missed during observational research? If so, give an example of what might be done.
6. Is "observer effect" inevitable? Why or why not?
7. "What qualitative researchers try to do is to study the subjective objectively?" What does this mean?
8. Is there any kind of data that cannot be obtained through observation? Through interviews? If so, why?
9. Of the six types of questions we described on pages 458–459 in this chapter, which do you think interviewees would find the hardest to answer? The easiest? Why?
10. What would you say is the most important quality or characteristic an interviewer should possess? Why?
11. Which do you think would be hardest to master and do well, observing or interviewing? Why?
12. Interviewers are frequently advised to "be natural." What do you think that means? Is it possible? Desirable? Always a good idea or not? Explain your thinking.

Notes

1. H. R. Bernard (2000). *Social research methods. Qualitative and quantitative approaches.* Thousand Oaks, CA: Sage, p. 388.

2. D. R. Papini, N. Datan, and K. A. McCluskey-Fawcett (1988). An observational study of affective and assertive family interactions during adolescence. *Journal of Youth and Adolescence, 17:*477–492.

3. R. Lindman, P. Jarvinen, and J. Vidjeskog (1987). Verbal interactions of aggressively and nonaggressively predisposed males in a drinking situation. *Aggressive Behavior, 13:*187–196.

4. M. A. Stewart (1984). What is a successful doctor-patient interview? A study of interactions and outcomes. *Social Science and Medicine, 19:*167–175.

5. B. Devet (1990). A method for observing and evaluating writing lab tutorials. *Writing Center Journal, 10:*75–83.

6. E. J. Amidon and J. B. Hough (1967). *Interaction analysis: Theory, research, and application.* Reading, MA: Addison-Wesley.

7. M. Fetterman (1989). *Ethnography: Step by Step.* Thousand Oaks, CA: Sage.

8. M. Q. Patton (1990). *Qualitative evaluation and research methods,* 2nd ed. Thousand Oaks, CA: Sage.

9. Fetterman, op. cit., p. 58. Fetterman points out that the term "informant" has its roots in anthropological work conducted in colonial settings, specifically in African nations formerly within the British Empire. He refers the reader to E. E. Pritchard (1940). *The Nuer: A description of the modes of livelihood and political institutions of a nilotic people.* New York: Oxford University Press. The term also conjures up an image of clandestine activities that he finds objectionable (as do we) and not compatible with ethical research.

10. Ibid., pp. 59–60.

11. Ibid.

12. Patton, op. cit., pp. 290–293.

13. Fetterman, op. cit., p. 55.

14. Ibid., p. 56.

15. I. E. Seidman (1991). *Interviewing as qualitative research: A guide for researchers in education and the social sciences.* New York: Teacher's College Press, p. 73.

16. Ibid., pp. 73–74.

17. Patton, op. cit., pp. 297–298.

18. Patton, op. cit., p. 335.

19. Ibid., p. 348.

20. Ibid., pp. 348–349.

Content Analysis

CHAPTER 20

Content Analysis

- **What Is Content Analysis?**
- **Some Applications**
- **Categorization in Content Analysis**
- **Steps Involved in Content Analysis**
  - Determine Objectives
  - Define Terms
  - Specify the Unit of Analysis
  - Locate Relevant Data
  - Develop a Rationale
  - Develop a Sampling Plan
  - Formulate Coding Categories
  - Reliability and Validity
  - Analyze Data
- **An Illustration of Content Analysis**
- **Using the Computer in Content Analysis**
- **Advantages of Content Analysis**
- **Disadvantages of Content Analysis**

Objectives

Studying this chapter should enable you to:

- Explain *what a content analysis is.*
- Explain *the purpose of content analysis.*
- Name *three or four ways content analysis can be used in educational research.*
- Explain *why a researcher might want to do a content analysis.*
- Summarize *an example of content analysis.*
- Describe *the steps involved in doing a content analysis.*
- Describe *the kinds of sampling that can be done in content analysis.*
- Describe *the two ways to code descriptive information into categories.*
- Describe *two advantages and two disadvantages of content analysis research.*
- Recognize *an example of content analysis research when you come across it in the educational literature.*

Interactive and Applied Learning

After, or while, reading this chapter:

Go to your Interactive Student CD-ROM to:
- Learn More About Content Analysis

Go to your Interactive Student CD-ROM or Student Workbook to do the following activities:
- Activity 20.1: Content Analysis Research Questions
- Activity 20.2: Do a Content Analysis
- Activity 20.3: Advantages vs. Disadvantages of Content Analysis

arrah Hallowitz, a middle school English teacher, is becoming more and more concerned about the ways that women are presented in the literature anthologies she has been assigned to use in her courses. She worries that her students are getting a limited view of the roles that women can play in today's world. After school one day, she asks Roberta, another English teacher, what she thinks. "Well," says Roberta, "Funny you should ask me that. Because I have been kind of worried about the same thing. Why don't we check this out?"

How could they "check this out?" What is called for here is content analysis. Darrah and Roberta need to take a careful look at the ways women are portrayed in the various anthologies they are using. They might find that such studies have been done or they might do one themselves. That is what this chapter is about.

As we mentioned in Chapter Nineteen, the third method that qualitative researchers use to collect and analyze data is what is customarily referred to as *content analysis*, of which the analysis of documents is a major part.

What Is Content Analysis?

Much of human activity is not directly observable or measurable, nor is it always possible to get information from people who might know of such activity from first-hand experience. **Content analysis** is a technique that enables researchers to study human behavior in an indirect way, through an analysis of their communications.* It is just what its name implies: the analysis of the usually, but not necessarily, written contents of a communication. Textbooks, essays, newspapers, novels, magazine articles, cookbooks, songs, political speeches, advertisements, pictures—in fact, the contents of virtually any type of communication can be analyzed. A person's or group's conscious and unconscious beliefs, attitudes, values, and ideas often are revealed in their communications.

In today's world, there is a tremendously large number of communications of one sort or another (newspaper editorials, graffiti, musical compositions, magazine articles, advertisements, films, etc.). Analysis of such communications can tell us a great deal about how human beings live. To analyze these messages, a researcher needs to organize a large amount of material. How can this be done? By developing appropriate categories, ratings, or scores that the researcher can use for subsequent comparison in order to illuminate what he or she is investigating. This is what content analysis is all about.

By using this technique, a researcher can study (indirectly) anything from trends in child-rearing practices (by comparing them over time), or differences in such practices among various groups of people, to types of heroes people prefer, to the extent of violence on television. Through an analysis of literature, popular magazines, songs, comic strips, cartoons, and movies, the different ways in which sex, crime, religion, education, ethnicity, affection and love, or violence and hatred have been presented at different times can be revealed. The rise and fall of fads can be noted. From such data, researchers can make comparisons about the attitudes and beliefs of various groups of people separated by time, geographic locale, culture, or country.

Content analysis as a methodology is often used in conjunction with other methods, in particular historical and ethnographic research. It can be used in any context in which the researcher desires a means of systematizing and (often) quantifying data. It is extremely valuable in analyzing observation and interview data.

Let us consider an example. In a series of studies during the 1960s and 1970s, George Gerbner and his colleagues did a content analysis of the amount of violence appearing on television.[1] They selected for their study all of the dramatic television programs that were broadcast during a single week in the fall of each year (in order to make comparisons from year to year) and looked for incidents that involved violence.

They videotaped each program and then developed a number of measures that trained coders used to analyze each of the programs. *Prevalence,* for example, referred to the percentage of programs that included one or more

*Many things produced by human beings (e.g., pottery, weapons, songs) were not originally intended as communications, but subsequently have been viewed as such. For example, the pottery of the Mayans tells us much about their culture.

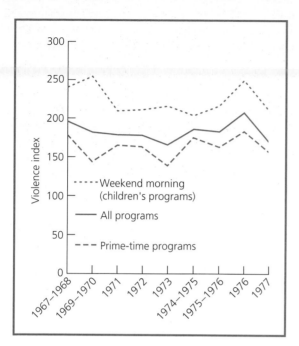

Figure 20.1 *TV Violence and Public Viewing Patterns*

incidents of violence; *rate* referred to the number of violent incidents occurring in each program; and *role* referred to the individuals who were involved in the violent incidents. (The individuals who committed the violent act or acts were categorized as "violents," while the individuals against whom the violence was committed were categorized as "victims.")[2]

Gerbner and his associates used these data to report two scores: a *program score,* based on prevalence and rate; and a *character score,* based on role. They then calculated a *violence index* for each program, which was determined by the sum of these two scores. Figure 20.1 shows one of the graphs they presented to describe the violence index for different types of programs between 1967 and 1977. It suggests that violence was higher in children's programs than in other types of programs and that there was little change during the 10-year period.

Some Applications

Content analysis is a method that has wide applicability in educational research. For example, it can be used to:

- Describe trends in schooling over time (e.g., the back-to-basics movement) by examining professional and/or general publications.
- Understand organizational patterns (e.g., by examining charts, outlines, etc., prepared by school administrators).
- Show how different schools handle the same phenomena differently (e.g., curricular patterns, school governance).
- Infer attitudes, values, and cultural patterns in different countries (e.g., through an examination of what sorts of courses and activities are—or are not—sponsored and endorsed).
- Compare the myths that people hold about schools with what actually occurs within them (e.g., by comparing the results of polls taken of the general public with literature written by teachers and others working in the schools).
- Gain a sense of how teachers feel about their work (e.g., by examining what they have written about their jobs).
- Gain some idea of how schools are perceived (e.g., by viewing films and television programs depicting same).

Content analysis can also be used to supplement other, more direct methods of research. Attitudes toward women who are working in so-called men's occupations, for example, can be investigated in a variety of ways: questionnaires; in-depth interviews; participant observations; and/or content analysis of magazine articles, television programs, newspapers, films, and autobiographies that touch on the subject.

Lastly, content analysis can be used to give researchers insights into problems or hypotheses that they can then test by more direct methods. A researcher might analyze the content of a student newspaper, for example, to obtain information for devising questionnaires or formulating questions for subsequent in-depth interviews with members of the student body at a particular high school.

Categorization in Content Analysis

All procedures that are called content analysis have certain characteristics in common. These procedures also vary in some respects, depending on the purpose of

Important Findings in Content Analysis Research

One of the classic examples of content analysis was done almost 50 years ago by Whiting and Child.* Their method was to have at least two judges assign ratings on 17 characteristics of child-rearing and on the presence or absence of 20 different explanations of illness for 75 "primitive societies" in addition to the United States. Examples of character-

istics are: dependence socialization anxiety, age at weaning, and age at toilet training. Ratings were based on ethnographic material on each society (see Chapter Twenty-One), available at the Yale Institute of Human Relations, which varied from one printed page to several hundred pages.

Psychoanalytical theory provided the basis for a series of correlational hypotheses. Among the researchers' conclusions were that explanations of illness are related to both early deprivation and severity of training (e.g., societies that weaned earliest were more likely to explain illness as due to eating, drinking, or verbally instigated spells). Another finding was that the U.S. (middle-class) sample was, by comparison, quite severe in its child-rearing practices, beginning both weaning and toilet training earlier than other societies and accompanying both with exceptionally harsh penalties.

*M. W. Whiting and I. L. Child (1953). *Child training and personality.* New Haven, CT: Yale University Press.

the analysis and the type of communication being analyzed.

All must at some point convert (i.e., *code*) descriptive information into *categories*. There are two ways that this might be done:

1. The researcher determines the categories before any analysis begins. These categories are based on previous knowledge, theory, and/or experience. For example, we used predetermined categories to describe and evaluate a series of journal articles pertaining to social studies education (see pp. 490–492).
2. The researcher becomes very familiar with the descriptive information collected and allows the categories to emerge as the analysis continues. An example of this is shown on page 488.

Steps Involved in Content Analysis

DETERMINE OBJECTIVES

Decide on the specific objectives you want to achieve. There are several reasons why a researcher might want to do a content analysis.

- *To obtain descriptive information about a topic:* Content analysis is a very useful way to obtain information that describes an issue or topic. For example, a content analysis of child-rearing practices in different countries could provide descriptive infor-

mation that might lead to a consideration of different approaches within a particular society. Similarly, a content analysis of the ways various historical events are described in the history textbooks of different countries might shed some light on why people have different views of history (e.g., Adolf Hitler's role in World War II).

- *To formulate* **themes** *(i.e., major ideas) which help to organize and make sense out of large amounts of descriptive information.* Themes are typically groupings of codes which emerge either during or after the process of developing codes. An example is shown on p. 488.
- *To check other research findings:* Content analysis is helpful in validating the findings of a study or studies using other research methodologies. Statements of textbook publishers concerning what they believe is included in their company's high school biology textbooks (obtained through interviews), for example, could be checked by doing a content analysis of such textbooks. Interviews with college professors as to what they say they teach could be verified by doing a content analysis of their lesson plans.
- *To obtain information useful in dealing with educational problems:* Content analysis can help teachers plan activities to help students learn. A content analysis of student compositions, for example, might help teachers pinpoint grammatical or stylistic errors. A content analysis of math assignments might reveal deficiencies in the ways students attempt to solve word problems. While such analyses are simi-

lar to grading practices, they differ in that they provide more specific information, such as the relative frequency of different kinds of mistakes.

* *To test hypotheses:* Content analysis can also be used to investigate possible relationships or to test ideas. For example, a researcher might hypothesize that in social studies textbooks, minority individuals are not portrayed as playing much of a role in the history of our country, but that this situation has changed in recent years. A content analysis of a sample of texts published over the last 20 years would reveal if this is the case.

DEFINE TERMS

As in all research, investigators and/or readers are sure to incur considerable frustration unless important terms such as "violence," "minority individuals," and "back-to-basics" are clearly defined, either beforehand or as the study progresses.

SPECIFY THE UNIT OF ANALYSIS

What, exactly, is to be analyzed? Words? Sentences? Phrases? Paintings? The units to be used for conducting and reporting the analysis should be specified before the researcher begins the analysis.

LOCATE RELEVANT DATA

Once the researcher is clear about the objectives and units of analysis, he or she must locate the data (e.g., textbooks, magazines, songs, course outlines, lesson plans) that will be analyzed and that are relevant to the objectives. The relationship between content to be analyzed and objectives of the study should be clear. One way to help ensure this is to have a specific research question (and possibly a hypothesis) in mind beforehand, and then to select a body of material in which the question or hypothesis can be investigated.

DEVELOP A RATIONALE

The researcher needs a conceptual link to explain how the data are related to the objectives. The choice of content should be clear, even to a disinterested observer. Often, the link between question and content is quite obvious. A logical way to study bias in advertisements, for example, is to study the contents of newspaper and magazine advertisements. At other times, the link is not so obvious, however, and needs to be explained. Thus, a researcher who is interested in changes in attitudes toward a particular group (e.g., police officers) over time might decide to look at how they were portrayed in short stories appearing in magazines published at different times. The researcher must assume that changes in how police officers were portrayed in these stories indicate a change in attitudes toward them.

Many content analyses use available material. But it is also common for a researcher to generate his or her own data. Thus, open-ended questionnaires might be administered to a group of students in order to determine how they feel about a new curriculum that had recently been introduced, and then the researcher would analyze their responses. Or a series of open-ended interviews might be held with a group of students to assess their perceptions of the strengths and weaknesses of the school's counseling program, and these interviews would be coded and analyzed.

DEVELOP A SAMPLING PLAN

Once these steps have been accomplished, the researcher develops a sampling plan. Novels, for example, may be sampled at one or any number of levels, such as words, phrases, sentences, paragraphs, chapters, books, or authors. Television programs can be sampled by type, channel, sponsor, producer, or time of day shown. Any form of communication may be sampled at any conceptual level that is appropriate.

One of the *purposive sampling designs* described in Chapter Eighteen is most commonly used. For example, a researcher might decide to obtain transcribed interviews from several students because all of them are exceptionally talented musicians. Or a researcher might select from among the minutes of school board meetings only those that described meetings in which specific curriculum changes were recommended.

The sampling techniques discussed in Chapter Six can also be used in content analysis. For example, a researcher might decide to select a **random sample** of chemistry textbooks, curriculum guides, laws pertaining to education that were passed in the state of California, lesson plans prepared by history teachers in an inner-city high school, or an elementary principal's daily bulletins. Another possibility would be to number all the songs recorded by the Benny Goodman big band and then select a random sample of 50 to analyze.

Stratified sampling also can be used in content analysis. A researcher interested in school board policies in a particular state, for example, might begin by grouping school districts by geographic area and size, and then use random or systematic sampling to select particular districts. Stratification ensures that the sample is representative of the state in terms of district size and location. A statement of policies would then be obtained from each district in the sample for analysis.

Cluster sampling can also be used. In the example just described, if the unit of analysis were the minutes of board meetings rather than formal policy statements, the minutes of all meetings during an academic year could be analyzed. Each randomly selected district would thus provide a cluster of meeting minutes. If minutes of only one or two meetings were randomly selected from each district, however, this would be an example of two-stage random sampling (see page 101).

There are, of course, less desirable ways to select a sample of content to be analyzed. One could easily select a convenience sample of content that would make the analysis virtually meaningless. An example would be assessing the attitudes of American citizens toward free trade by studying articles published only in the *National Review* or *The Progressive*. An improvement over convenience sampling would be, as mentioned earlier, purposive sampling. Rather than relying on simply their own or their colleagues' judgments as to what might be appropriate material for analysis, researchers should, when possible, rely on evidence that the materials they select are, in fact, representative. Thus, deciding to analyze letters to the editor in *Time* magazine in order to study public attitudes regarding political issues might be justified by previous research showing that the letters in *Time* agreed with polling data, election results, and so on.

FORMULATE CODING CATEGORIES*

After the researcher has defined as precisely as possible what aspects of the content are to be investigated, he or she needs to formulate categories that are relevant to the investigation (Figure 20.2). The categories should be so explicit that another researcher could use them to examine the same material and obtain substantially the same results—that is, find the same frequencies in each category.

Example. Suppose a researcher is interested in the accuracy of the images or concepts presented in high school English texts. She wonders whether the written or visual content in these books is biased in any way, and if it is, how. She decides to do a content analysis to obtain some answers to these questions.

She must first plan how to select and order the content that is available for analysis—in this case, the textbooks. Pertinent categories must be developed that will allow her to identify that which she thinks is important.

Let us imagine that the researcher decides to look, in particular, at how women are presented in these texts. She would first select the sample of textbooks to be analyzed—that is, which texts she will read (in this case, perhaps, all of the textbooks used at a certain grade level in a particular school district). Categories could then be formulated. How are women described? What traits do they possess? What are their physical, emotional, and social characteristics? These questions suggest categories for analysis that can, in turn, be broken down into even smaller coding units such as those shown in Table 20.1.

Another researcher might be interested in investigating whether different attitudes toward intimate human relationships are implied in the mass media of the United States, England, France, and Sweden. Films would be an excellent and accessible source for this

*An exception to this step occurs when the researcher counts instances of a particular characteristic (e.g., of violence, as in the Gerbner study), or uses a rating system, as was done in the Whiting & Child study.

Table 20.1 *Coding Categories for Women in Social Studies Textbooks*

Physical Characteristics	Emotional Characteristics	Social Characteristics
Color of hair	Warm	Race
Color of eyes	Aloof	Religion
Height	Stable, secure	Occupation
Weight	Anxious, insecure	Income
Age	Hostile	Housing
Hairstyle	Enthusiastic	Age
etc.	etc.	etc.

Figure 20.2 *What Categories Should I Use?*

analysis, although the categories and coding units within each category would be much more difficult to formulate. For instance, three general categories could be formed using Karen Horney's typology of relationships: "going toward," "going away from," and "going against."[3] This would be an example of categories formulated ahead of time. The researcher would then look for instances of these concepts expressed in the films. Other units of behavior such as hitting someone, expressing a sarcastic remark, kissing or hugging, and refusing a request are illustrations of other categories that might emerge from familiarity with the data.

Another way to analyze the content of mass media is to use "space" or "time" categories. For example, in the past few years, how many inches of newsprint have been devoted to student demonstrations on campuses? How many minutes have television news programs devoted to urban riots? How much time has been used for programs that deal with violent topics compared to non-violent topics?

The process of developing categories that emerge from the data is often complex. An example of coding an interview is shown in Figure 20.3. It is a transcript of an interview with a teacher regarding curriculum change. In this example, both the category codes and the initial themes are identified in the text and annotated in the margins, along with reminders to the researcher.

Manifest Versus Latent Content. In doing a content analysis, a researcher can code either or both the manifest and the latent content of a communication. How do they differ? The **manifest content** of a communication refers to the obvious, surface content—the words, pictures, images, and so on that are directly accessible to the naked eye or ear. No inferences as to underlying meaning are necessary. To determine, for example, whether a course of study encourages the development of critical thinking skills, a researcher might simply count the number of times the word "thinking" appears in the course objectives listed in the course outline.

The **latent content** of a document, on the other hand, refers to the meaning underlying what is said or shown. To get at the underlying meaning of a course outline, for example, a researcher might read through

Codes	Transcript	Themes
	INTERVIEWER: Lucy, what do you perceive as strengths of Greenfield as a community and how that relates to schools?	
Close-knit community	**LUCY:** Well, I think Greenfield is a fairly (close-knit) (community.) I think people are interested in what goes on. . . . We like to keep track of what our kids are doing, and feel a connection to them because of that. The downside of that	
Health of community, or community values	perhaps is that kids can feel that we are looking TOO close. . . . you said the (health of the community) itself is reflected in schools. . . . I think . . . this is a pretty conservative community overall, and look to make sure that what is being talked about in the schools really carries out the (community's) (values.). . . . (And I think there might be a tendency to hold back a little bit too much because of that idealization of "you know, we learned the basics, the reading, the writing, and the	Sense of community
Change is threatening	arithmetic"). So you know, any (change is threatening). . . . Sometimes that can get in the way of trying to do different things.	
	INTERVIEWER: In terms of looking at leadership strengths in the community, where does Greenfield set in a continuum with planning process, . . . forward thinking, visionary people. . . .	Potential theme: Leaders
Visionary skills of talented people	**LUCY:** I think there are people that have wonderful (visionary) (skills.) I would say that the community as a whole . . . would not reflect that . . . I think we have some incredibly talented people who become frustrated when they try to implement what they see as their . . .[4]	

Figure 20.3 *An Example of Coding an Interview*

the entire outline or a sample of pages, particularly those describing the classroom activities and homework assignments to which students will be exposed. The researcher would then make an overall assessment as to the degree to which the course is likely to develop critical thinking. Although the researcher's assessment would surely be influenced by the appearance of the word "thinking" in the document, it would not depend totally on the frequency with which the word (or its synonyms) appeared.

There seems little question that both methods have their advantages and disadvantages. Coding the manifest content of a document has the advantage of ease of coding and *reliability*—another researcher is likely to arrive at the same number of words or phrases counted. It also lets the reader of the report know exactly how the term "thinking" was measured. On the other hand, it would be somewhat suspect in terms of *validity*. Just counting the number of times the word "thinking" appears in the outline for a course

would not indicate all the ways in which this skill is to be developed, nor would it necessarily indicate "critical" thinking.

Coding the latent content of a document has the advantage of getting at the underlying meaning of what is written or shown, but it comes at some cost in reliability. It is likely that two different researchers may come to different assessments of the degree to which a particular course outline is likely to develop critical thinking. An activity or assignment judged by one researcher as especially likely to encourage critical thinking might be seen by a second researcher as ineffective. A commonly used criterion is 80 percent agreement. But even if a single researcher does all the coding, there is no guarantee that he or she will remain constant in the judgments made or standards used. Furthermore, the reader would likely be uncertain as to exactly how the overall judgment was made.

The best solution therefore is to use both methods whenever possible. A given passage or excerpt should

Table 20.2 *Sample Tally Sheet (Newspaper Editorials)*

Newspaper ID Number	Location	Circulation	Number of Editorials Coded	Subjective Evaluation[a]	Number of Pro-Abortion Editorials	Number of Anti-Abortion Editorials
101	A	3,000,000	29	3	0	1
102	B	675,000	21	3	1	1
103	C	425,000	33	4	2	0
104	D	1,000,000	40	1	0	8
105	E	550,000	34	5	7	0

[a]Categories within the subjective evaluation: 1 = very conservative; 2 = somewhat conservative; 3 = middle-of-the-road; 4 = moderately liberal; 5 = very liberal.

receive close to the same description if a researcher's coding of the manifest and latent contents is reasonably reliable and valid. However, if a researcher's (or two or more researchers') assessments, using the two methods, are not fairly close (it is unlikely that there would ever be perfect agreement), the results should probably be discarded, and perhaps the overall intent of the analysis reconsidered.

RELIABILITY AND VALIDITY

Although it is seldom done, we believe that some of the procedures for checking **reliability** and **validity** (see Chapter Eight) could at least in some instances be applied to content analysis. In addition to assessing the agreement between two or more categorizers, it would be useful to know how the categorizations by the same researcher agree over a meaningful time period (test-retest method). Furthermore, a kind of equivalent-forms reliability could be done by selecting a second sample of materials or dividing the original sample in half. One would expect, for example, that the data obtained from one sample of editorials would agree with those obtained from a second sample. Another possibility would be to divide each unit of analysis in the sample in half for comparison. Thus, if the unit of analysis is a novel, the number of derogatory statements about foreigners in odd-numbered chapters should agree fairly well with the number in even-numbered chapters.

With respect to validity, we think it should often be possible not only to check manifest against latent content but also to compare either or both with results from different instruments. For example, the relative frequency of derogatory and positive statements about for-

eigners found in editorials would be expected to correspond with that found in letters to the editor, if both reflected popular opinion.

ANALYZE DATA

Counting is an important characteristic of some content analysis. Each time a unit in a pertinent category is found, it is "counted." Thus, the end product of the coding process must be numbers. It is obvious that counting the frequency of certain words, phrases, symbols, pictures, or other manifest content requires the use of numbers. But even coding the latent content of a document requires the researcher to represent those coding decisions with numbers in each category.

It is also important to record the *base,* or reference point, for the counting. It would not be very informative, for example, merely to state that a newspaper editorial contained 15 anti-Semitic statements without knowing the overall length of the editorial. Knowing the number of speeches a senator makes in which she argues for balancing the budget doesn't tell us very much about how fiscally conservative she is if we don't know how many speeches she has made on economic topics since the counting began.

Let us suppose that we want to do a content analysis of the editorial policies of newspapers in various parts of the United States. Table 20.2 illustrates a portion of a tally sheet that might be used to code such editorials. The first column lists the newspapers by number (each newspaper could be assigned a number to facilitate analysis). The second and third columns list location and circulation, respectively. The fourth column lists the number of editorials coded for each paper. The fifth column shows the subjective assessment by the researcher of each newspaper's editorial policy (these might later be compared with the objective measures obtained). Other columns record the number of certain types of editorials.

The last step, then, is to analyze the data that have been tabulated. As in other methods of research, the descriptive statistical procedures discussed in Chapter Ten are useful to summarize the data and assist the researcher in interpreting what they reveal.

A common way to interpret content analysis data is through the use of frequencies (i.e., the number of specific incidents found in the data) and the percentage and/or proportion of particular occurrences to total occurrences. You will note that we use these statistics in the analysis of social studies research articles that follows (see Tables 20.3, 20.4, and 20.5). In content analysis studies designed to explore relationships, a crossbreak table (see Chapter Ten) or chi-square analysis (see Chapter Eleven) is often used because both are appropriate to the analysis of categorical data.*

Other researchers prefer to use codes and themes as aids in organizing content and arriving at a narrative description of findings.

An Illustration of Content Analysis

In 1988, we did a content analysis of all the research studies published in *Theory and Research in Social Education (TRSE)* between the years 1979 and 1986.[5] *TRSE* is a journal devoted to the publication of social studies research. We read 46 studies contained in those issues. The following presents a breakdown by type of study reviewed.

Type of Studies Reviewed

True experiments	7 (15%)
Quasi-experiments	7 (15%)
Correlational studies	9 (19%)
Questionnaire-type surveys	9 (19%)
Interview-type surveys	6 (13%)
Ethnographies	9 (19%)
	$n = 47^a$ (100%)

[a]This totals 47 rather than 46 because the researchers in one study used two methodologies.

*In studies in which ratings or scores are used, averages, correlation coefficients, and frequency polygons are appropriate.

Table 20.3 *Clarity of Studies*

Category	Number
a. Focus clear?	46 (100%)
b. Variables clear?	
1. Initially	31 (67%)
2. Eventually	7 (15%)
3. Never	8 (17%)
c. Is treatment in intervention studies made explicit?	
1. Yes	12 (26%)
2. No	2 (4%)
3. NA (no treatment)	32 (70%)
d. Is there a hypothesis?	
1. No	18 (39%)
2. Explicitly stated	13 (28%)
3. Clearly implied	15 (33%)

Table 20.4 *Type of Sample*

Category	Number
Random selection	2 (4%)
Representation based on argument	6 (13%)
Convenience	29 (62%)
Volunteer	4 (9%)
Can't tell	6 (13%)

Note: One study used more than one type of sample. Percent is based on $n = 46$.

Both of us read every study that was published during this period that fell into one of these categories. We analyzed the studies using a coding sheet that we jointly prepared. To test our agreement concerning the meaning of the various categories, we each initially read a sample of (the same) six studies, and then met to compare our analyses. We found that we were in substantial agreement concerning what the categories meant, although it soon became apparent that we needed to add some additional subcategories as well as some totally new categories. Figure 20.4 presents the final set of categories.

We then reread the initial six studies using the revised set of categories, as well as the remaining 40 studies. We again met to compare our assessments. Although we had a number of disagreements, the great majority were simple oversights by one or the other of

1. **Type of Research**

   A. Experimental
      (1) Pre
      (2) True
      (3) Quasi
   B. Correlational
   C. Survey
   D. Interview
   E. Causal-comparative
   F. Ethnographic

2. **Justification**

   A. No mention of justification
   B. Explicit argument made with regard to worth of study
   C. Worth of study is implied
   D. Any ethical considerations overlooked?

3. **Clarity**

   A. Focus clear? (yes or no)
   B. Variables clear?
      (1) Initially
      (2) Eventually
      (3) Never
   C. Is treatment in intervention studies made explicit? (yes, no, or n.a.)
   D. Is there a hypothesis?
      (1) No
      (2) Yes: explicitly stated
      (3) Yes: clearly implied

4. **Are Key Terms Defined?**

   A. No
   B. Operationally
   C. Constitutively
   D. Clear in context of study

5. **Sample**

   A. Type
      (1) Random selection
      (2) Representation based on argument
      (3) Convenience
      (4) Volunteer
      (5) Can't tell
   B. Was sample adequately described?
      (1 = high; 5 = low)
   C. Size of sample (n)

6. **Internal Validity**

   A. Possible alternative explanations for outcomes obtained
      (1) History
      (2) Maturation
      (3) Mortality
      (4) Selection bias/subject characteristics
      (5) Pretest effect
      (6) Regression effect
      (7) Instrumentation
      (8) Attitude of subjects
   B. Threats discussed and clarified? (yes or no)
   C. Was it clear that the treatment received an adequate trial? (in intervention studies) (yes or no)
   D. Was length of time of treatment sufficient? (yes or no)

7. **Instrumentation**

   A. Reliability
      (1) Empirical check made? (yes or no)
      (2) If yes, was reliability adequate for study?
   B. Validity
      (1) Empirical check made? (yes or no)
      (2) If yes, type:
         (a) Content
         (b) Concurrent
         (c) Construct

8. **External Validity**

   A. Discussion of population generalizability
      (1) Appropriate
         (a) Explicit reference to defensible target population
         (b) Appropriate caution expressed
      (2) Inappropriate
         (a) No mention of generalizability
         (b) Explicit reference to indefensible target population
   B. Discussion of ecological generalizability
      (1) Appropriate
         (a) Explicit reference to defensible settings (subject matter, materials, physical conditions, personnel, etc.)
         (b) Appropriate caution expressed
      (2) Inappropriate
         (a) No mention of generalizability
         (b) Explicit reference to indefensible settings

9. **Were Results and Interpretations Kept Distinct?** (yes or no)

10. **Data Analysis**

    A. Descriptive statistics? (yes or no)
       (1) Correct technique? (yes or no)
       (2) Correct interpretation? (yes or no)
    B. Inferential statistics? (yes or no)
       (1) Correct technique? (yes or no)
       (2) Correct interpretation? (yes or no)

11. **Do Data Justify Conclusions?** (yes or no)

12. **Were Outcomes of Study Educationally Significant?** (yes or no)

13. **Relevance of Citations**

Figure 20.4 *Categories Used to Evaluate Social Studies Research*

Table 20.5 *Threats to Internal Validity*

Possible Alternative Explanations for Outcomes Obtained	Number
1. History	4 (9%)
2. Maturation	0 (0%)
3. Mortality	10 (22%)
4. Subject characteristics	15 (33%)
5. Pretest effect	2 (4%)
6. Regression effect	0 (0%)
7. Instrumentation	21 (46%)
8. Attitude of subjects	7 (15%)

Type	Number of Articles	Threats Discussed and Clarified?	
		Identified by Reviewers	Discussed by Authors
True experiments	7	3 (43%)	2 (29%)
Quasi-experiments	7	7 (100%)	4 (57%)
Correlational studies	9	5 (56%)	3 (33%)
Questionnaire surveys	9	3 (33%)	0 (0%)
Interview-type surveys	6	9 (67%)	1 (17%)
Ethnographies	9	9 (100%)	0 (0%)

us, and were easily resolved.* Tables 20.3 through 20.5 present some of the findings of our research.

These tables indicate that the intent of the studies was clear; that the variables were generally clear (82 percent); that the treatment in intervention studies was clear in almost all cases; and that most studies were hypothesis testing, although the latter was not always made clear. Only 17 percent of the studies could claim representative samples, and most of these required argumentation. Mortality, subject characteristics, and instrumentation threats existed in a substantial proportion of the studies. These were acknowledged and discussed by the authors in 9 of the 15 experimental or correlational studies, but rarely by the authors of any of the other types.

Using the Computer in Content Analysis

In recent years, computers have been used to offset much of the labor involved in analyzing documents.

Computer programs have for some time been a boon to quantitative research, allowing researchers to calculate quite rapidly very complex statistics. Programs to assist qualitative researchers in their analysis, however, now also exist. Many simple word-processing programs can be used for some kinds of data analysis. The "find" command, for example, can locate various passages in a document that contain key words or phrases. Thus, a researcher might ask the computer to search for all passages that contain the words "creative," or "nonconformist," or "punishment," or phrases such as "corporeal punishment" or "artistic creativity."

Notable examples of qualitative computer programs that are currently available include ATLAS.ti, QSR NUD*IST, Nvivo, and HyperResearch. These programs will identify words, phrases, or sentences, tabulate their occurrence, print and graph the tabulations, and sort and regroup words, phrases, or sentences according to how they fit a particular set of categories. Computers, of course, presume that the information of interest is in written form. Optical scanners are available that make it possible for computers to "read" documents and store the contents digitally, thus eliminating the need for data entry by hand. Should you have to do some qualitative

---

*It would have been desirable to compare our analysis with the findings of a second team as a further check on reliability, but this was not feasible.

data analysis, a few of these programs are worth taking some time to examine.

Advantages of Content Analysis

As we mentioned earlier, much of what we know is obtained, not through direct interaction with others, but through books, newspapers, and other products of human beings. A major advantage of content analysis is that it is unobtrusive. A researcher can "observe" without being observed, since the contents being analyzed are not influenced by the researcher's presence. Information that might be difficult, or even impossible, to obtain through direct observation or other means can be gained unobtrusively through analysis of textbooks and other communications, without the author or publisher being aware that it is being examined. Another advantage of content analysis is that, as we have illustrated, it is extremely useful as a means of analyzing interview and observational data.

A third advantage of content analysis is that the researcher can delve into records and documents to get some feel for the social life of an earlier time. He or she is not limited by time and space to the study of present events.

A fourth advantage accrues from the fact that the logistics of content analysis are often relatively simple and economical—with regard to both time and resources—as compared to other research methods. This is particularly true if the information is readily accessible, as in newspapers, reports, books, periodicals, and the like.

Lastly, because the data are readily available and almost always can be returned to if necessary or desired, content analysis permits replication of a study by other researchers. Even live television programs can be videotaped for repeated analysis at later times.

Disadvantages of Content Analysis

A major disadvantage of content analysis is that it is usually limited to recorded information, although the researcher may, of course, arrange the recordings, as in the use of open-ended questionnaires or projective techniques (see page 137). One would not be likely to use such recordings to study such variables as proficiency in calculus, Spanish vocabulary, or the frequency of hostile acts because they require demonstrated behaviors or skills.

The other main disadvantage is in establishing validity. Assuming that different analysts can achieve acceptable agreement in categorizing, the question remains as to the true meaning of the categories themselves. Recall the earlier discussion of this problem under "Manifest Versus Latent Content." A comparison of the results of these two methods provides some evidence of criterion-related validity, although the two measurements obviously are not completely independent. As with any measurement, additional evidence of a criterion or construct nature is important. In the absence of such evidence, the argument for content validity rests on the persuasiveness of the logic connecting each category to its intended meaning. For example, our interpretation of the data on social studies research assumes that what was clear or unclear to us would also be clear or unclear to other researchers or readers. Similarly, it assumes that most, if not all, researchers would agree as to whether definitions and particular threats to internal validity were present in a given article. While we think these are reasonable assumptions, that does not make them so.

With respect to the use of content analysis in historical research, the researcher normally has records only of what has survived or what someone thought was of sufficient importance to write down. Because each generation has a somewhat different perspective on its life and times, what was considered important at a particular time in the past may be viewed as trivial today. Conversely, what is considered important today might not even be available from the past.

Finally, sometimes there is a temptation among researchers to consider that the interpretations gleaned from a particular content analysis indicate the *causes* of a phenomenon rather than being a reflection of it. For example, portrayal of violence in the media may be considered a cause of today's violence in the streets, but a more reasonable conclusion may be that violence in both the media and in the streets reflect the attitudes of people. Certainly much work has to be done to determine the relationship between the media and human behavior. Again, some people think that reading pornographic books and magazines causes moral decay among those who read such materials. Pornography probably does affect some individuals, and it is likely that it affects different people in different ways. It is also quite likely that it does not affect other individuals at all, but exactly how people are affected, and why or why not, is unclear.

An Example of a Content Analysis Study

In the remainder of this chapter, we present a published example of content analysis, followed by a critique of its strengths and weaknesses. As we did in our critiques of other types of research studies, we use concepts introduced in earlier parts of the book in our analysis.

From: *Journal of Educational Research, 88:3* (1995): 164–171.

Student Teachers and Classroom Discipline

Michael Tulley
Lian Hwang Chiu
Indiana University, Kokomo

ABSTRACT

Participants in this study were 135 student teachers at Indiana University who sub-mitted detailed written narratives describing one effectively managed and one ineffectively managed incident involving a discipline problem. Results showed that the student teachers cited five types of discipline problems; the most frequently described involved disruption, defiance, and inattention. The student teachers used seven different strategies when at-tempting to manage these discipline problems, the most effective of which were positive reinforcement, explanation, and a change of teaching strategy. The major conclusions of the study were that (a) elementary- and secondary-level student teachers defined and man-aged discipline problems in much the same way, (b) the most effective strategies were the most "humanistic," and (c) the least effective strategies were the most "authoritarian."

Effective classroom discipline continues to be one of the most universal and troubling prob-lems faced by teachers (Charles, 1989; Edwards, 1993). Preservice teachers have consistently ranked discipline as one of their greatest sources of anxiety and uncertainty (Lindgren, 1972; Wesley & Vocke, 1992), and discipline is also a major factor in student teacher failure (Rickman & Hollowell, 1981). Despite this, student teachers identify discipline as an area in which they be-lieve they receive little preparation (Purcell & Seifert, 1982).

In studies in which student teachers and discipline have been examined, researchers gener-ally focused on the way that student teachers handle common classroom occurrences. Among the findings of such research are that (a) student teachers tend to prefer humanistic approaches to classroom management (Hall & Wahrman, 1987; Osborne & Boisvert, 1989); (b) the classroom management strategies student teachers select can be related to personality type (Halpin, 1982), university-level course work (Tingstrom, 1989), the subject being taught (Brand, 1982; Clayton, 1984; Murwin & Matt, 1990), and grade level (Jones, 1982; Sage, 1990); and (c) after their field experience, student teachers are more willing to use harsher discipline methods (Moser, 1982).

Authors of similar studies have often relied on student teachers' predictions about how they might behave in hypothetical situations, rather than on examinations of their actual classroom decisions and actions. And many of these researchers have relied on relatively simple and stan-dard survey methods to gain insight into how student teachers respond to "typical" classroom events. As such, much of this research is of somewhat limited use to teacher educators. | **Justification**

Where discipline is concerned, the goal of teacher education is to help individuals develop the expertise necessary to effectively manage a learning environment. Ultimately, individual teachers' values and versatility most influence classroom culture and climate. Of greater relevance, there-fore, is an understanding of student teachers' decisions about classroom management, within the context of what they believe constitutes a "discipline problem" in the first place.

Our purposes in this study were to investigate student teachers' perceptions about the disci-pline problems they encountered during their student teaching experience and to examine the | **Purpose**

Address correspondence to Michael Tulley, Division of Education, Indiana University, Kokomo, 2300 South Washing-ton Street, P.O. Box 9003, Kokomo, IN 46904-9003.

strategies they used—both effectively and ineffectively—when dealing with those problems. Specifically, the study attempted to answer these questions:

Clear

1. What kinds of classroom behaviors do student teachers define as discipline problems?
2. What strategies do student teachers use when dealing with these discipline problems?
3. Which strategies are effective with which discipline problems, and which are ineffective?

METHOD

Participants

The participants in this study were 135 undergraduate elementary- and secondary-level student teachers (119 women and 16 men) who were completing teacher-training programs at one of four campuses in the Indiana University (IU) system. (The IU system comprises eight campuses.) The participants were enrolled in education programs at regional campuses located in Kokomo, South Bend, Indianapolis, and Gary. Of the total, 81 participants were elementary-level, preservice teachers and 54 were secondary-level preservice teachers. Of the elementary-level student teachers, 58 (72%) were assigned to primary-level classrooms and 23 (28%) were assigned to intermediate-level classrooms. Of the secondary-level student teachers, 16 (30%) were assigned to junior high classrooms and 38 (70%) were assigned to senior high classrooms. Twenty-seven (33%) of the elementary-level student teachers were parents, as were 19 (35%) of the secondary-level student teachers. Participants ranged in age from 21 years to 48 years, with a median age of 27.8 years.

Data Collection

Justification

In this study we used the critical incident technique originally proposed by Flanagan (1954) and adapted to classroom research by Ryans (1960). Using this technique, we asked the student teachers to identify and describe specific classroom incidents considered to be examples of "discipline problems," and also to identify and describe the specific action or strategy used when attempting to manage that incident. This technique is considered superior to traditional surveys and observations because it yields in-depth, rich narratives that are usually more insightful and relevant to classroom practice. All participants were asked to submit detailed written narrative responses to two questions:

1. Think over the past month or two and recall the last time you did something especially effective in dealing with a discipline problem. What did the student(s) do? What did you do?
2. Think over the past month or two and recall the last time you did something especially ineffective in dealing with a discipline problem. What did the student(s) do? What did you do?

"Discipline problem" was not defined for the participants because their perceptions of the kinds of student behaviors that were problematic was one of the issues of concern in this study.

Data were collected during a three-semester period from fall 1990 through fall 1991, in one of two ways, depending on the campus at which student teachers were enrolled. Most participants were asked to write and submit their narratives during an on-campus seminar held during the latter portion of their student-teaching semester. Other participants received written instructions by mail, and their narratives were written independently and then returned to researchers at the completion of their student teaching.

Data Analyses

Critical incidents described by participants were subjected to content analyses typical of those used with qualitative data (Guba & Lincoln, 1981; Miles & Huberman, 1984). Specifically, the student teachers' narrative responses to the two broad questions (i.e., problems and strategies) were first examined for naturally occurring or "grounded" categories (Glaser & Strauss, 1967; Guba, 1978). Each response was then coded and placed into a category and then reviewed to ensure that each was externally distinct and internally consistent. Responses in each category were then subjected to descriptive statistical analyses.

Emergent codes

The three examples below illustrate how the anecdotal data were analyzed and coded. The first is an excerpt from a narrative contributed by a student teacher in a first-grade classroom who described an incident that was effectively handled:

> Several students were tipping their chairs and continually falling to the floor. I decided that they wanted to sit on the floor. Now, when students tip their chair, they move it back and sit 'Indian style' on the floor with their work.

Adds clarity

The discipline problem described here was coded as a "disruption" because the most salient factor about student behavior appears to be that it interrupted instructional flow. The strategy was coded as a "change of strategy" because the teacher adopted a new approach, style, or policy as a way to deal with the disruption.

The second example is an excerpt from a narrative contributed by a student teacher in a second-grade classroom who also described an incident of "disruption" that was effectively handled but, in this instance, with a strategy coded as "positive reinforcement' because of the emphasis on praise and approval:

> Justin has a real problem with self-control, especially when walking in the hall. I feel like I am constantly asking him to keep his lips together and to keep his hands together. . . . I told Justin, in front of all the children, that I needed him to show the other students how to walk appropriately down the hall. I told him I was counting on him to do a good job. It worked. I was pleased and Justin was pleased with himself. . . .

Clarifies

The third example is an excerpt from a narrative contributed by a student teacher in a high school classroom who described an incident that was ineffectively handled:

> The student was playing with items on the teachers [*sic*] desk during the class and I asked him repeatedly to stop the behavior . . . he became verbally abusive and threw the stapler onto the floor. After asking him to stop the behavior he would not do it. I told him to please step outside until he could do as I asked. At this point he jumped out of his seat and yelled. . . . I yelled back. . . . Although he went out to the hall, I lost my temper. . . . Other students were talking loudly also. I think I was trying to make an example out of him. He knew it and it backfired.

Clarifies

This incident describes student behavior that clearly could have been labeled as "disruption," but which was instead coded as "defiance," because the most salient aspects of the behavior related to an unwillingness to obey teacher directives. Although there are elements of more than one strategy described here, the strategy was eventually coded as "punishment—Type 1" because the critical elements in the teacher's behavior were her attempts to punish the student and because of the arguing and yelling that ensued as the incident escalated.

We independently coded, categorized, and tabulated all the incidents described in the student teachers' narratives. To estimate the consistency of each of our analyses, we computed the percentage of agreement by (a) tabulating the number of instances of agreement and disagreement, (b) dividing the number of instances of agreement by the total number of instances (i.e., the sum of instances of agreement and disagreement), and (c) multiplying that quotient by 100. Consistency for categorization of student teachers' definitions of discipline problems was 96% agreement between us; for categorization of the strategies student teachers used when managing discipline problems, we had 91% agreement. We resolved all disagreements by discussion until 100% agreement was reached.

Good agreement

RESULTS

But Table 1
shows 270.

Why?

A total of (254) narratives were submitted and analyzed. The 81 elementary-level student teachers submitted 151 narratives, and the 54 secondary-level student teachers submitted 103 narratives. Of these 254 narratives, 133 described incidents that were effectively managed, and 121 described incidents that were ineffectively managed. In 16 instances, narratives were either not submitted or were (unusable) (two related to effectively managed incidents, and 14 related to ineffectively managed ones).

Discipline Problems

Emergent Definition

Narratives related to discipline problems, in both effectively and ineffectively managed incidents, were eventually arranged into five categories: (a) disruption (e.g., talking, or some type of behavior that deliberately interrupts instruction), (2) defiance (disrespectful behavior, or disobedience), (c) inattention (off-task, inattentive, not doing work, out of seat), (d) aggression (fighting, pushing, name calling), and (e) miscellaneous (crying, lying, tardiness, cheating, stealing, gum chewing). The number of incidents in which a particular discipline problem was involved, which was then managed either effectively or ineffectively, are reported in Table 1. For example, 79 student teachers described an incident that involved a disruption that was then dealt with effectively; 80 student teachers described an incident involving a disruption that was dealt with ineffectively; the 159 incidents involving disruptions made up 63% of all incidents.

Effective and Ineffective Strategies

More definitions

Narratives related to effective and ineffective strategies were eventually arranged into seven categories: (a) punishment—Type 2 (detention, taking away privileges, isolation), (b) explanation (e.g., discussing correct or desired behavior with student or whole class), (c) threats and warnings (which includes not following through on a threat or policy), (d) positive reinforcement (praise, approval, reward), (e) change of strategy (raising or lowering voice, pausing, moving closer to student, devising a new teaching approach or policy), (f) punishment—Type 1 (corporal punishment, yelling at student, humiliation), and (g) no action taken (ignoring student behavior). The number of incidents in which a particular strategy was used, either effectively or ineffectively, are reported in Table 2. For example, 43 student teachers described incidents effectively managed with the use of punishment—Type 2; 38 student teachers described incidents in which the use of punishment—Type 2 was ineffective; the 81 incidents in which punishment—Type 2 was used made up 32% of all incidents.

Table 1 *Type and Frequency of Discipline Problems Involved in Effective and Ineffective Incidents*

Discipline Problem	Effective	Ineffective	Total	% (of 254)
Disruption	79	80	159	63
Defiance	33	19	52	20
Inattention	10	12	22	9
Aggression	5	4	9	4
Miscellaneous	6	6	12	5
No response	2	14	16	—
Total	135	135	270	101

Note: Percentages were rounded.

Table 2 *Type and Frequency of Strategies Used in Effective and Ineffective Incidents*

Strategy	Effective	Ineffective	Total	% (of 254)
Punishment—Type 2	43	38	81	32
Explanation	39	11	50	20
Threats/warnings	9	24	33	13
Positive reinforcement	22	2	24	9
Change of strategy	15	8	23	9
Punishment—Type 1	1	22	23	9
No action	4	16	20	8
No response	2	14	16	—
Total	135	135	270	101

Note: Percentages were rounded.

We report which strategies were used in effectively managed incidents and which were used in ineffectively managed incidents, respectively, in Tables 3 and 4. For example, elementary-level student teachers used punishment—Type 2 nine times when effectively managing incidents involving disruption, seven times when effectively managing incidents involving defiance, and so on. Secondary-level student teachers used punishment—Type 2 eleven times when effectively managing incidents involving disruption, ten times when effectively managing incidents involving defiance, and so on. Elementary-level student teachers used punishment—Type 2 thirteen times when ineffectively managing incidents involving disruption, one time when ineffectively managing incidents involving defiance, and so on (see Table 4). Secondary-level student teachers used punishment—Type 2 nine times when ineffectively managing incidents involving disruption, four times when ineffectively managing incidents involving defiance, and so on.

We also report in Tables 3 and 4 the number of times a particular strategy, was used to manage a specific discipline problem. For example, when incidents involving disruption were effectively managed, elementary-level student teachers used punishment—Type 2 nine times, explanation thirteen times, and so on (see Table 3). Secondary-level student teachers used punishment—Type 2 eleven times, explanation seven times, and so on. When incidents involving disruption were ineffectively managed, elementary-level student teachers used punishment—Type 2 thirteen times, explanation two times; and so on (see Table 4). Secondary-level student teachers used punishment—Type 2 nine times, explanation three times, and so on.

Table 5 is a summary of synthesis of data displayed in Tables 3 and 4; the ratio of effectiveness versus ineffectiveness of particular strategies used with specific discipline problems is reported. For example, when used with incidents involving disruptions, punishment—Type 2 was effective twenty times and ineffective twenty-two times; with incidents involving defiance, punishment—Type 2 was effective seventeen times, and ineffective five times, and so on.

We compared elementary- and secondary-level student teachers and list the types of discipline problems and strategies that each group described in their narratives (see Table 6). For example, of the 151 incidents described by elementary-level student teachers, 100 (66%) involved disruptions, 22 (15%) involved defiance, and so on (see Table 6). Of the 103 incidents described by secondary-level student teachers, 59 (57%) involved disruptions, 30 (29%) involved defiance, and so on. Where strategies were concerned, 41 (27%) of the incidents described by elementary-level student teachers involved punishment—Type 2, 30 (20%) involved explanation, and so on; 40 (39%) of the incidents described by secondary-level student teachers involved punishment—Type 2, 20 (20%) involved explanation, and so on.

Table 3 *Frequency of Strategies Used in Effective Incidents*

Strategy	Disruption	Defiance	Inattention	Aggression	Miscellaneous	Total
Punishment—Type 2						
Elementary	9	7	1	2	1	20
Secondary	11	10	0	1	1	23
Explanation						
Elementary	13	5	1	1	2	22
Secondary	7	5	2	1	2	17
Threats/warnings						
Elementary	2	1	2	0	0	5
Secondary	2	2	0	0	0	4
Positive reinforcement						
Elementary	15	1	2	0	0	18
Secondary	2	1	1	0	0	4
Change of strategy						
Elementary	9	1	0	0	0	10
Secondary	4	0	1	0	0	5
Punishment—Type 1						
Elementary	1	0	0	0	0	1
Secondary	0	0	0	0	0	0
No action						
Elementary	3	0	0	0	0	3
Secondary	1	0	0	0	0	1
No response						
Elementary						2
Secondary						0
Total	79	33	10	5	6	135

DISCUSSION

Three significant findings emerged from this study. First, the majority (91%) of the discipline problems that these student teachers described related to only three types of behavior: disruptions, defiance, and inattention. This finding suggests that if student teachers develop strategies for effectively managing these behaviors, many or most of their discipline problems could be solved.

By far the most frequently described discipline problems were disruptions (i.e., talking or some type of behavior that deliberately interrupts instruction); they were involved in well over half of all incidents. Disruptions were managed effectively by these student teachers as often as they were managed ineffectively, however, and the strategies that appeared to work best (i.e., more than half of the time) were explanation, positive reinforcement, and a change of strategy. The second most frequently described problem (20% of all incidents) was defiance (disrespectful behavior or disobedience), arguably one of the more difficult and delicate problems to manage, even for experienced teachers. Yet, these student teachers managed incidents of defiance effectively substantially more often than ineffectively. Here, the strategies that appeared to work best were explanation, positive reinforcement, and punishment—Type 2. The third most frequently described problem (9% of all incidents) was inattention (off task, inattentive, not doing work, out of seat), which also was managed effectively about as often as it was managed ineffectively. Here, the strategies that appeared to work best were positive reinforcement, change of strategy, and threats and warnings. Incidents involving aggression (fighting, pushing, name calling) and miscellaneous problems crying, lying, tardiness, cheating, stealing, gum chewing ac-

Were reported as managed

Table 4 *Frequency of Strategies Used in Ineffective Incidents*

Strategy	Disruption	Defiance	Inattention	Aggression	Miscellaneous	Total
Punishment—Type 2						
Elementary	13	1	3	2	2	21
Secondary	9	4	2	0	2	17
Explanation						
Elementary	2	2	3	0	1	8
Secondary	3	0	0	0	0	3
Threats/warnings						
Elementary	17	1	1	0	0	19
Secondary	4	1	0	0	0	5
Positive reinforcement						
Elementary	0	1	1	0	0	2
Secondary	0	0	0	0	0	0
Change of strategy						
Elementary	5	1	0	0	0	6
Secondary	2	0	0	0	0	2
Punishment—Type 1						
Elementary	6	1	0	2	0	9
Secondary	9	4	0	0	0	13
No action						
Elementary	5	0	1	0	1	7
Secondary	5	3	1	0	0	9
No response						
Elementary						9
Secondary						5
Total	80	19	12	4	6	135

Table 5 *Frequency of Strategies Used With Discipline Problems*

Strategy	Ratio of Effectiveness vs. Ineffectiveness				
	Disruption	Defiance	Inattention	Aggression	Miscellaneous
Punishment—Type 2	20/22	17/5	1/5	3/2	2/4
Explanation	20/5	10/2	3/3	2/0	4/1
Threats/warnings	4/21	3/2	2/1	0/0	0/0
Positive reinforcement	17/0	2/1	3/1	0/0	0/0
Change of strategy	13/7	1/1	1/0	0/0	0/0
Punishment—Type 1	1/15	0/5	0/0	0/2	0/0
No action	4/10	0/3	0/2	0/0	0/1

counted for a small portion of all incidents (4% and 5%, respectively); both were managed equally effectively and ineffectively, and explanation was the strategy that appeared to work best with both.

A second significant finding was that almost all of the incidents managed effectively involved any of four strategies, whereas three strategies were relatively ineffective. The most obvious explanation for the effectiveness or ineffectiveness of particular strategies relates to the extent to which they are either "humanistic" or "authoritarian," respectively.

Overall, positive reinforcement (i.e., praise, approval, reward) was the most effective strategy for these student teachers; a 92% success rate was achieved in instances in which it was used.

Table 6 *Elementary- and Secondary-Level Comparison: Type and Proportion of Discipline Problems and Strategies*

Variable	Elementary		Secondary	
	n	% of 151	*n*	% of 103
Discipline problem				
Disruption	100	66	59	57
Defiance	22	15	30	29
Inattention	15	10	7	7
Aggression	7	5	2	2
Miscellaneous	7	5	5	5
Strategy				
Punishment—Type 2	41	27	40	39
Explanation	30	20	20	20
Threats/warnings	24	16	9	9
Positive reinforcement	20	13	4	4
Change of strategy	16	11	7	7
Punishment—Type 1	10	7	13	13
No action	10	7	10	10

Note: Percentages were rounded.

This strategy was effective in every instance of disruption in which it was used, and it was effective more often than it was ineffective when used to curtail defiance and inattention.

The second most effective strategy was explanation (discussing correct or desired behavior with student or whole class). This strategy, which had a 78% success rate, was effective in every instance of aggression in which it was used; it was effective more often than it was ineffective when used with disruptions, defiance, and miscellaneous problems; when employed with inattention, it was effective as often as it was ineffective.

But only two

The third most effective strategy was a change of strategy (raising or lowering voice, pausing, moving closer to student, devising a new teaching approach or policy). This strategy, which had a 65% success rate, was effective in every instance in which it was used with inattention; it was more effective than ineffective when used with disruptions; and it was effective as often as it was ineffective when used with defiance.

Only one

The fourth most effective strategy was punishment—Type 2 (detention, taking away privileges, isolation). Successful 53% of the time, this strategy was more effective than ineffective when used with defiance and aggression; it was about as effective as ineffective when used with disruptions; and it was less effective than ineffective when used with inattention and miscellaneous problems.

Three to two

Among the least effective strategies was the use of threats and warnings; this strategy had a success rate of only 27% in instances in which it was used. This strategy was more effective than ineffective when used with defiance and inattention, but less effective than ineffective when used with disruptions. Also largely ineffective was the strategy of taking no action, which had a success rate of 20%. This strategy was less effective than ineffective when used with disruptions, and it was ineffective in every instance in which it was used with defiance, inattention, and miscellaneous problems. Least effective was punishment—Type 1, which had a success rate of only 4% and was ineffective in all instances in which it was used (except for one instance of disruption).

All of these percentages are based on a small number of cases.

A third significant finding was that, despite differences in the ages of the students with whom they interacted, there was much similarity in the types of discipline problems described by these student teachers and in the types of strategies they used to deal with those behaviors. Among

Right

both groups, incidents involving disruptions and defiance were, respectively, the most frequently and the second most frequently described. For both groups, incidents involving one or the other of these two behaviors made up a relatively (and similarly) large proportion of the total number of incidents described (81% of the elementary-level incidents, and 86% of the secondary-level ones). Although incidents involving other types of discipline problems were described much less frequently, the proportion of those incidents to the total number of incidents was also similar, at both the elementary and the secondary levels.

Both groups also used two strategies (punishment—Type 2 and explanation) more often than any other strategy, regardless of the type of discipline problem being dealt with. A large propor- **Right** tion of the total number of incidents described involved the use of one or the other of these two strategies (47% of the elementary-level incidents and 59% of the secondary-level incidents.)

These similarities might reflect the fact that despite their diversity (in terms of age, marital and parental status, program, and grade taught), the student teachers were nevertheless all clustered in a single geographic area, and to the extent that a prevailing midwestern point of view shapes **Limitation recognized** schooling there, all operating within similar cultural contexts. Or, these similarities could reflect the fact that all of the student teachers were receiving their training at the same university (there is a high degree of consistency among education programs across Indiana University campuses).

CONCLUSION

The participants of this study were a select group, asked to provide selected information about their individual experiences, so generalizations derived from these findings should be made carefully. Nonetheless, the anecdotal data they provided described incidents that occurred **Good** in dozens of different classrooms and schools spread across a large portion of the state of Indiana, which included urban and rural, large and small, and rich and poor settings. It is reasonable to assume, then, that these student teachers and the classrooms in which they practiced had some degree of comparability to student teachers and classrooms in general, and that the find- **Unclear to us** ings of this study therefore have a corresponding degree of relevance to teacher-education programs throughout the country.

Further study, which would examine student teachers at other universities and in even more varied classrooms, can help determine whether all student teachers face similar discipline problems and whether they can rely upon these same strategies to manage those problems effectively.

References

Brand, M. (1982). Effects of student teaching on the classroom management beliefs and skills of music student teachers. *Journal of Research in Music Education, 30:* 255–265.

Charles, C. M. (1989). *Building classroom discipline: From models to practice,* 3rd ed. New York: Longman.

Clayton, K. (1984). Relationship of role preference to teaching effectiveness during student teaching. *Home Economics Research Journal, 13:* 167–174.

Edwards, C. H. (1993). *Classroom discipline and management.* New York: Macmillan.

Flanagan, J. S. (1954). The critical incident technique. *Psychological Bulletin, 51:* 327–358.

Glaser, B. G., & Strauss, A. L. (1967). *The discovery of grounded theory.* Chicago: Aldine.

Guba, E. (1978). *Toward a methodology of naturalistic inquiry in educational evaluation* (Monograph Series, No. 8). Los Angeles: Center for the Study of Evaluation, University of California.

Guba, E., & Lincoln, Y. (1981). *Effective evaluation: Improving the usefulness of evaluation results through responsiveness and naturalistic approaches.* San Francisco: Jossey-Bass.

Hall, C. W., & Wahrman, E. (1987). *Theoretical orientations of intervention strategies and perceived acceptability.* Paper presented at the annual meeting of the National Association of School Psychologists, New Orleans, LA.

Halpin, G. (1982). Personality characteristics and self-concept of preservice teachers related to their pupil control orientation. *Journal of Experimental Education, 50:* 195–199.

Jones, D. R. (1982). The influence of length and level of student teaching on pupil control ideology. *High School Journal: 65:* 220–225.

Lindgren, H. C. (1972). *Educational psychology in the classroom* (4th ed.). New York: Wiley.

Miles, M. B., & Huberman, A. M. (1984). *Qualitative data analysis.* Beverly Hills: Sage.

Moser, C. J. (1982). Changing attitudes of student teachers on classroom discipline. *Teacher Educator, 18:* 10–15.

Murwin, S., & Matt, S. (1990). Fears prior to student teaching. *Technology Teacher, 49:* 25–26.

Osborne, J. W. & Boisvert, G. (1989). Student teachers' classroom management preferences. *Journal of Humanistic Education and Development, 28:* 45–54.

Purcell, T. D., & Seifert, B. B. (1982). A tri-state survey of student teachers. *College Student Journal, 16:* 27–29.

Rickman, L. W., & Hollowell, J. (1981). Some causes of student teacher failure. *Improving College and University Teaching, 29:* 176–179.

Ryans, D. G. (1960). *Characteristics of teachers.* Washington, DC: American Council on Education.

Sage, M. (1990). Preservice teachers' attitudes toward middle level prior to student teaching. *Action in Teacher Education, 11:* 19–23.

Tingstrom, D. H. (1989). Increasing acceptability of alternative behavioral interventions through education. *Psychology in the Schools, 26:* 188–194.

Wesley, D. A., & Vocke, D. E. (1992). *Classroom discipline and teacher education.* Paper presented at the annual meeting of the Association of Teacher Educators, Orlando, FL.

Analysis of the Study

PURPOSE/JUSTIFICATION

The purpose of the study is made clear at the end of the introduction—that is, to describe classroom behaviors seen as discipline problems by student teachers and both effective and ineffective strategies for dealing with these problems. The study is justified by citing several references attesting to the importance of discipline problems as well as by reviewing some of the research on factors related to how student teachers handle discipline problems. It is not clear how comprehensive this review is, however. More specific justification is that most prior studies have not used actual examples of classroom actions; if there are some that have, they should have been reviewed.

DEFINITIONS

It is appropriate that the key term "discipline problem" was not defined for participants, since their own definitions were part of what was investigated. We think, however, that the report would have been strengthened by a definition that emerged from the study. Although not identified as such, the five categories of "discipline problem" are defined in the "Results" section. While some of these are clear to us, others remain somewhat ambiguous, such as "disrespectful" and "deliberately interrupts." Operational definitions of these are implicit in the categorizing process. Although not a major problem, we are unclear whether the respondents' identification of "effective" and "ineffective" were the only criteria for inclusion in these categories. The examples provided add clarity.

PRIOR RESEARCH

The references cited all appear pertinent. As mentioned previously, it is unclear how comprehensive the review was. It appears that there may have been prior studies using similar methodology; if so, they should have been reviewed.

HYPOTHESES

No hypotheses are stated, which is appropriate, since the study is intended to be descriptive. If the researchers expected some strategies to be more effective with certain problems, they could have stated them as hypotheses.

SAMPLE

The sample of respondents was a convenience sample obtained from students enrolled in the teacher-training program at four Indiana University campuses. It is unclear what proportion of all enrolled students were included. Generalization beyond these campuses is not justified from the sampling method. The sample is described in terms of gender, grade-level assignments, age, and percent who were parents. Of at least equal importance to teacher characteristics is the nature of the classrooms and students from which behavioral incidents were obtained; some such information is provided. These limitations are recognized in the "Discussion" and "Conclusion" sections. The sample of incidents themselves is best viewed as a purposive sample of incidents, based on student teacher recall using specified criteria.

INSTRUMENTATION AND DATA ANALYSIS

The "instrument" consisted of a well-known technique—detailed description of specific incidents selected by respondents according to specified (and clear) criteria and based on recall over a two-month period. Typical content analysis methods were used to generate five categories into which each narrative was classified. Coder agreement was very good.

Other than coder agreement, reliability could have been checked by randomly dividing the total of 254 narratives and comparing frequencies in each category across the two subsamples, a procedure analogous to the equivalent-forms method that we discuss in Chapter Eight. Validity might have been checked by comparing category placement (latent content) with prevalence of key words or phrases in each narrative, such as "now, when they" (change of strategy); "told him to step outside" (punishment); "needed him to show" (positive reinforcement); although this is admittedly complicated because of the diversity of specific content.

Counting of incidents within each category and conversion to percentages are appropriate methods of analysis. The ratio of effectiveness to ineffectiveness of particular strategies shown in Table 5 is appropriate as long as importance is *not* attached to small differences in frequencies. To their credit, the authors do not report any inferential statistics.

INTERNAL VALIDITY

This study reports three types of relationships: (1) between type of discipline problem and strategy; (2) between type of problem, strategy and effectiveness/ineffectiveness (Table 5); and (3) between grade level and both problem type and strategy. Because (1) and (2) involve different classifications of "incidents," the only threat to internal validity is a testing threat, in that coding into one category (e.g., "disruption") might lead to subsequent coding into another (e.g., "punishment"). This could have been controlled by having one coder classify problem type and another coder classify strategies. Similarly, any bias resulting from prior knowledge as to which grade level (elementary or secondary) the incident came from could be controlled by deleting this information from the written narrative.

RESULTS AND DISCUSSION

Description of results is consistent with the data provided. We have only two criticisms. First, the frequent use of the phrases "were managed effectively" and "were managed ineffectively" is misleading because this is only true for the incidents reported and the instructions asked for one example of each—effective and ineffective. We cannot therefore conclude that these teachers managed disruption effectively as often as ineffectively. Second, too much is made of small frequencies, e.g., "this strategy (explanation) . . . was effective in every instance of aggression in which it was used." True, but there were only two instances!

The authors appropriately mention limitations on generalizing their findings, although we find the statement that there is "some degree of comparability to student teachers and classrooms in general, and that the findings of this study therefore have a corresponding degree of relevance to teacher-education programs throughout the country" highly ambiguous. We agree that replication is highly desirable.

Go back to the **Interactive and Applied Learning Tools** feature at the beginning of the chapter for a listing of interactive and applied activities. Go to the **Online Learning Center** at www.mhhe.com/fraenkel5e or your **Interactive Student CD-ROM** to take practice quizzes and receive immediate feedback, practice with key terms, review chapter content and main ideas, and find annotated Web links.

Main Points

WHAT IS CONTENT ANALYSIS?

- Content analysis is an analysis of the contents of a communication.
- Content analysis is a technique that enables researchers to study human behavior in an indirect way by analyzing communications.

APPLICATIONS OF CONTENT ANALYSIS

- Content analysis has wide applicability in educational research.
- Content analysis can give researchers insights into problems that they can test by more direct methods.
- There are several reasons to do a content analysis: to obtain descriptive information of one kind or another; to analyze observational and interview data; to test hypotheses; to check other research findings; and/or to obtain information useful in dealing with educational problems.

CATEGORIZATION IN CONTENT ANALYSIS

- Coding (categorizing) by using predetermined categories.
- Coding by use of categories that emerge as data is reviewed.

STEPS INVOLVED IN CONTENT ANALYSIS

- In doing a content analysis, researchers should always develop a rationale (a conceptual link) to explain how the data to be collected are related to their objectives.
- Important terms should at some point be defined.
- All of the sampling methods used in other kinds of educational research can be applied to content analysis. Purposive sampling, however, is the most commonly used.
- The unit of analysis—what specifically is to be analyzed—should be specified before the researcher begins an analysis.
- After precisely defining what aspects of the content are to be analyzed, the researcher needs to formulate coding categories.

CODING CATEGORIES

- Developing emergent coding categories requires a high level of familiarity with content.
- In doing a content analysis, a researcher can code either the manifest or the latent content of a communication, and sometimes both.
- The manifest content of a communication refers to the specific, clear, surface contents: the words, pictures, images, and such that are easily categorized.
- The latent content of a document refers to the meaning underlying what is contained in a communication.

RELIABILITY AND VALIDITY AS APPLIED TO CONTENT ANALYSIS

- Reliability in content analysis is commonly checked by comparing the results of two independent scorers (categorizers).
- Validity can be checked by comparing data obtained from manifest content to that obtained from latent content.

DATA ANALYSIS

- A common way to interpret content analysis data is by using frequencies (i.e., the number of specific incidents found in the data) and proportion of particular occurrences to total occurrences.
- Another method is to use coding to develop themes to facilitate synthesis.
- Computer analysis is extremely useful in coding data once categories have been determined. It can also be useful at times in developing such categories.

ADVANTAGES AND DISADVANTAGES OF CONTENT ANALYSIS

- Two major advantages of content analysis are that it is unobtrusive and it is comparatively easy to do.
- The major disadvantages of content analysis are that it is limited to the analysis of communications and it is difficult to establish validity.

Key Terms

For Discussion

1. When, if ever, might it be more appropriate to do a content analysis than to use some other kind of methodology?
2. When would it be inappropriate to use content analysis?
3. Give an example of some categories a researcher might use to analyze data in each of the following content analyses:
   a. To investigate the amount and types of humor on television.
   b. To investigate the kinds of "romantic love" represented in popular songs.
   c. To investigate the social implications of impressionistic paintings.
   d. To investigate whether civil or criminal law makes the most distinctions between men and women.
   e. To describe the assumptions made in elementary school science programs.
4. Which of the following proposed studies might lend themselves well to content analysis?
   a. Finding out how teachers and students in an inner-city high school view the implementation of a new counseling program.
   b. Finding out whether women are portrayed differently in novels today as compared to those of 30 years ago.
   c. Finding out whether a new spelling book is more effective in helping students learn to spell than one that has previously been used.
   d. Finding out if playing classical music in writing classes helps students produce more original stories.
   e. Finding out if vocabulary level is related to speaking ability.
   f. Finding out why some students have trouble learning to read.
   g. Finding out how well kindergartners play with each other in the sandbox during recess.
   h. Finding out what courses were required to graduate from high school in the year 1890
5. Which do you think would be more difficult to code, the manifest or the latent content of a movie? Why?
6. "*Never* code only the latent content of a document without also coding at least some of the manifest content." Would you agree with this statement? Why or why not?
7. In terms of difficulty, how would you compare a content analysis approach to the study of social bias on television with a survey approach? In terms of useful information?

Notes

1. G. Gerbner, et al. (1978). Cultural indicators: Violence profile no. 9. *Journal of Communication, 28:*177–207.

2. Ibid., p. 181.

3. K. Horney (1945). *Our inner conflicts.* New York: Norton.

4. John W. Creswell (2002). *Educational research: Planning, conducting, and evaluating qualitative research.* Columbus, OH: Merrill Prentice-Hall, p. 268.

5. J. R. Fraenkel and N. E. Wallen (1988). *Toward improving research in social studies education.* Boulder, CO: Social Science Consortium.

Qualitative Research Methodologies

6

Part six continues the discussion of qualitative research we began in Part Five. We concentrate here on ethnography and historical research. As we did in Parts Four and Five, we not only discuss each of these methodologies in some detail, but we also provide some examples of published studies in which the researchers used these methods. We then provide our analysis of the strengths and weaknesses of these studies.

Ethnographic Research

CHAPTER 21

Ethnographic Research

- **What Is Ethnographic Research?**
  - The Unique Value of Ethnographic Research
- **Ethnographic Concepts**
  - Topics that Lend Themselves Well to Ethnographic Research
- **Sampling in Ethnographic Research**
- **Do Ethnographic Researchers Use Hypotheses?**
- **Advantages and Disadvantages of Ethnographic Research**
- **Roger Harker and His Fifth-Grade Classroom**
- **Data Analysis in Ethnographic Research**
- **Data Collection in Ethnographic Research**
  - Field Notes
  - An Example of Field Notes

Objectives

Studying this chapter should enable you to:

- Explain *what is meant by the term "ethnographic research," and* give an example *of a research question that might be investigated in an ethnographic study.*
- Describe *briefly what each of the following concepts mean to ethnographers: "culture," "holistic outlook," "contextualization," and "multiple realities."*
- Explain *the difference between an "emic" and an "etic" perspective.*
- Name *at least three topics that would lend themselves well to ethnographic research.*
- Describe *the characteristics of the kinds of samples used in ethnographic research.*
- Explain *how ethnographers employ hypotheses in their research.*
- Describe *the two major data collection techniques used in ethnographic research.*
- Explain *what is meant by the term "field notes" and how they differ from field jottings, a field diary, and a field log.*
- Explain *what is meant by the terms "triangulation" and "contextualization."*
- Explain *what a "key event" is in ethnographic research.*
- Describe *briefly how statistics are used in ethnographic research.*
- Name *at least one advantage and one disadvantage of ethnographic research.*

Interactive and Applied Learning

After, or while reading this chapter:

🔵 Go to your Interactive Student CD-ROM to:
- Learn More About Ethnographic Research

🔵 📖 Go to your Interactive Student CD-ROM or Student Workbook to do the following activities:
- Activity 21.1: Ethnographic Research Questions
- Activity 21.2: True or False?
- Activity 21.3: Do Some Ethnographic Research

What do you intend to do for your doctoral dissertation, Sam?"

"I'm going to do an ethnography of a school principal."

"No kidding! Impressive!"

"I just talked to Elizabeth Rodriguez today—you know, the principal at Roosevelt Elementary. She's agreed to let me follow her around for the next four weeks so that I can see what she does during the day—you know, whom she meets with, where, when, what they talk about, etc."

"You're going to keep a record of this, I assume?"

"You bet! I'll carry a notebook and make notes about what I see and hear. I also have Elizabeth's permission to carry a tape recorder, and I intend to tape her conversations. And I have another idea. During two of these days, I want to videotape her as she goes about her daily routine, both in school and as she ventures out into the community."

"That's it?"

"Nope. I also intend to take a look at the school's records and the daily log she keeps. I'm planning on doing a lot of interviews, too—talk with her secretary, some of the faculty, the custodial staff, even some students. And, of course, Elizabeth herself. And if she will permit it, the members of her family. I don't plan to do the interviews until after I've finished with my observations, however."

"Boy, that sounds like a lot of work."

"No question, it is. Not to mention writing all this up. But it will be worth it. When I'm finished, I think I will be able to paint a pretty accurate picture of what the life of an elementary school principal is like."

Sam's description of what he intends to do is an example *of ethnographic research*, the subject of this chapter.

What Is Ethnographic Research?

Ethnographic research is, in many respects, the most complex of all research methods. A variety of approaches are used in an attempt to obtain as holistic a picture as possible of a particular society, group, institution, setting, or situation. The emphasis in ethnographic research is on documenting or portraying the everyday experiences of individuals by observing and interviewing them and relevant others. The key tools, in fact, in all ethnographic studies are in-depth interviewing and continual, ongoing participant observation of a situation. Researchers try to capture as much of what is going on as they can—the "whole picture," so to speak. H. R. Bernard described the process briefly, but well:

> It involves establishing rapport in a new community; learning to act so that people go about their business as usual when you show up; and removing yourself every day from cultural immersion so you can intellectualize what you've learned, put it into perspective, and write about it convincingly. If you are a successful participant observer you will know when to laugh at what your informants think is funny; and when informants laugh

at what you say, it will be because you *meant* it to be a joke.[1]

Wolcott has pointed out that ethnographic procedures require three things: a detailed description of the culture-sharing group being studied, an analysis of this group in terms of perceived themes or perspectives, and then some interpretation of the group by the researcher as to meanings and generalizations about the social life of human beings in general.[2] The final product is a *holistic cultural portrait* of the group—a pulling together by the researcher of everything he or she learned about the group in all its complexity.

Here are some titles of studies that ethnographers have conducted in education:

- "Small-Town Teacher."[3]
- "The Cultural Organization of Participation Structures in Two Classrooms of Indian Students."[4]
- "The Ethnography of Children's Play."[5]
- "Hempies and Squeaks, Truckers and Cruisers: A Participant Observer Study in a City High School."[6]
- "The Other Side of the Fence: Seeing Black and White in a Small Southern Town."[7]

Important Findings
in Ethnographic Research

Anthropologist Margaret Mead's ethnography of life in Samoa—in particular her study of the adolescence of girls—is a social science classic. In the 1920s, she spent nine months in Samoa as a participant observer, relying mostly on observation and interviews with selected informants. Her major conclusions were that adolescence in Samoa was not the stressful period it is for adolescents in the United States. She believed that this was largely because Samoans were not faced with the dilemmas that young people in the United States face and because the Samoan culture took a relaxed view toward all forms of behavior. She also concluded that the incidence of emotional disturbance was much lower in Samoa, owing to the diffusion of emotional attachments and the clear-cut rules regarding the forming of relationships.

In the preface to the sixth edition of this report (1973),* Mead pointed out that while neither U.S. nor Samoan culture has remained constant, recent visits had impressed her with the extraordinary persistence of the Samoan culture.

A subsequent ethnography done 20 years later resulted in very different conclusions that anthropologists do not attribute to the passage of time.† This discrepancy illustrates the rich and provocative nature of ethnographic research, as well as the difficulty in arriving at firm conclusions.

*M. Mead (1973). *Coming of age in Samoa,* 6th ed. New York: Morrow Hill.
†D. Freeman (1983). *Margaret Mead and Samoa—The making and unmaking of an anthropological myth.* Cambridge, MA: Harvard University Press.

- "Inside High School: The Student's Perspective."[8]
- "Boys in White: Student Culture in Medical School."[9]

THE UNIQUE VALUE
OF ETHNOGRAPHIC RESEARCH

Ethnographic research has a particular strength that makes it especially appealing to many researchers. It can reveal nuances and subtleties that other methodologies miss. An excellent example is offered by Babbie.

> If you were walking through a public park and you threw down a bunch of trash, you'd discover that your action was unacceptable to those around you. People would glare at you, grumble to each other, and perhaps someone would say something to you about it. Whatever the form, you'd be subjected to definite, negative sanctions for littering. Now here's the irony. If you were walking through that same park, came across a bunch of trash that someone else had dropped, and cleaned it up, it's likely that your action would also be unacceptable to those around you. You'd probably be subject to definite, negative sanctions for cleaning it up.
>
> Most [of my students] felt (that this notion) was absurd . . . Although we would be negatively sanctioned for littering, . . . people would be pleased with us for [cleaning up a public place]. Certainly, all my students said *they* would be pleased if someone cleaned up a public place.
>
> To settle the issue, I suggested that my students start fixing the public problems they came across in the course of their everyday activities. . . .
>
> My students picked up litter, fixed street signs, put knocked-over traffic cones back in place, cleaned and decorated communal lounges in their dorms, trimmed trees that blocked visibility at intersections, repaired public playground equipment, cleaned public restrooms, and took care of a hundred other public problems that weren't "their responsibility."
>
> Most reported feeling very uncomfortable doing whatever they did. They felt foolish, goody-goody, conspicuous. . . . In almost every case, their personal feelings of discomfort were increased by the reactions of those around them. One student was removing a damaged and long-unused newspaper box from the bus stop where it had been a problem for months when the police arrived, having been summoned by a neighbor. Another student decided to clean out a clogged storm drain on his street and found himself being yelled at by a neighbor who insisted the mess should be left for the street cleaners. Everyone who picked up litter was sneered at, laughed at, and generally put down. One young man was picking up litter scattered around a trashcan when a passerby sneered, "Clumsy!"[10]

The point of the above example, we hope, is obvious. What people think and say happens (or is likely to happen) often is not really the case. By going out into the world and observing things as they occur, we are (usually) better able to obtain a more accurate picture. This is what ethnographers try to do—study people in their natural habitat in order to "see" things that otherwise might not even be anticipated. This is a major advantage of the ethnographic approach.

Ethnographic Concepts

There are a number of concepts that guide the work of ethnographers as they go about their research in the field. Some of the most important include culture, a holistic outlook, contextualization, an emic perspective, multiple realities, thick description, member checking, and a nonjudgmental orientation. Let us give a brief description of each.

Culture. The concept of **culture** is typically defined in one of two ways. Those who focus on behavior define it as the sum of a social group's observable patterns of behavior, customs, and ways of life.[11] Those who concentrate on ideas say that it comprises the ideas, beliefs, and knowledge that characterize a particular group of people.[12] However one defines it, culture is the most important of all ethnographic concepts. In Fetterman's words, it

> helps the ethnographer to search for a logical, cohesive pattern in the myriad, often ritualistic behaviors and ideas that characterize a group. This concept becomes immediately meaningful after cross-cultural experience. Everything is new to a student first entering a different culture. Attitudes or habits that natives espouse virtually without thinking are distinct and clear to the stranger. Living in a foreign community for a long period of time enables the fieldworker to see the power of dominant ideas, values, and patterns of behavior in the way people walk, talk, dress, eat, and sleep. The longer an individual stays in a community, building rapport, and the deeper they probe into individual lives, the greater the probability of his or her learning about the sacred subtle elements of the culture: how people pray, how they feel about each other, and how they reinforce their own cultural practices to maintain the integrity of their system.[13]

The interpretation of a group's culture is considered by many researchers to be the primary contribution of ethnographic research. Cultural interpretation refers to the researcher's ability to describe what he or she sees and hears from the point of view of the members of the group. A frequently cited example is that of the difference between a "wink" and a "blink." In one sense, there is no difference between the two. How-

ever, "anyone who has ever mistaken a blink for a wink is fully aware of the significance of cultural interpretation."[14]

A Holistic Perspective. Ethnographers try to describe as much as they can about the culture of a group. Thus, they try to gain some idea of the group's history, social structure, politics, religious beliefs, symbols, customs, rituals, and environment. No single study, of course, can ever capture completely an entire culture, but ethnographic researchers do their best to see beyond the immediate scene or event occurring in a classroom, in a neighborhood, on a particular street, or in a location in order to understand the larger picture of which the particular event may be a part. As you can imagine, developing a holistic perspective demands that the ethnographer spend a great amount of time out in the field gathering many different kinds of data. Only by doing so is he or she able to develop a picture of the social or cultural whole of that which he or she is studying.

Contextualization. When a researcher contextualizes data, he or she places what was seen and heard into a larger perspective. For example, the administrators of a large urban school district in which one of the authors of this text taught were about to terminate an after-school tutoring project because of its low attendance—about 50 percent. It was suggested to them that an attendance rate of 50 percent was actually pretty good when one considered the students involved (the students encouraged to attend the tutoring sessions were those who were doing failing work in most, if not all, of their classes). This suggestion resulted in the district continuing the program, as the administrators were now able to make a more informed decision about the worth of the program. In other words, contextualization helped maintain a worthwhile program that otherwise might have been eliminated.

An Emic Perspective. An **emic perspective**—that is, an "insider's" perspective of reality—is at the heart of ethnographic research. Gaining an emic perspective is essential to understanding—and thus describing accurately—the behaviors and situations an ethnographer sees and hears. An emic perspective requires one to recognize and accept the idea of **multiple realities.** "Documenting multiple perspectives of reality in a given study is crucial to an understanding of why people think and act in the different ways they do."[15]

An **etic perspective,** on the other hand, is the external objective perspective on reality. Most ethnographic researchers try to look at their data from both these perspectives. They may start collecting data from an emic perspective, doing their best to understand the point of view of those they are studying, and then try to make sense of what they have collected in terms of a more objective, scientific analysis. In short, they try to combine an insightful and sensitive cultural interpretation with a rigorous collection and analysis of what they have seen and heard.

Thick Description. When ethnographers prepare the final report of their research, they engage in what is known as **thick description.** In essence, this involves describing what they have seen and heard—their work in the field—in great detail, frequently using extensive quotations from the participants in their study. The intent is, as mentioned earlier, to "paint a portrait" of the culture they have studied, to make it "come alive" for those who read the report.

Member Checking. As mentioned above, a major objective of ethnographic research is to represent as accurately as possible an emic perspective of reality—that is, reality as seen from the point of view of the participants in the study. One way that ethnographic researchers do this is through what is known as **member checking**—checking their presentation of the participants' perspective by having the participants review what the researchers have written as a check for accuracy and completeness. It is one of the primary strategies used in ethnographic research to validate the accuracy of the researcher's findings.

A Nonjudgmental Orientation. A **nonjudgmental orientation** requires researchers to do their best to refrain from making value judgments about unfamiliar practices. None of us, of course, can be completely neutral. But we can guard against our most obvious biases. How? By doing our best to view another group's behaviors as impartially as we can. Fetterman gives an example of how one of his biases might have been fatal:

> An experience I had with the Bedouin Arabs in the Sinai desert provides a useful example. . . . During my stay with the Bedouins, I tried not to let my bias for Western hygiene practices [show]. [M]y reaction to one of my first acquaintances, a Bedouin with a leathery face and feet, was far from neutral. . . . I admired his ability to survive and adapt in a harsh environment, moving from one water hole to the next throughout the desert. However, my personal reaction to the odor of his garments

(particularly after a camel ride) was far from impartial. He shared his jacket with me to protect me from the heat. I thanked him of course, because . . . I did not want to insult him. But I smelled like a camel for the rest of the day in the dry desert heat. I thought I didn't need the jacket because we were only a kilometer or two from our destination. . . . I learned later that without his jacket I would have suffered from sunstroke. The desert heat is so dry that perspiration evaporates almost immediately and an inexperienced traveler does not always notice when the temperature climbs above 130°F. By slowing down the evaporation rate, the jacket helped me retain water. Had I rejected the jacket and, by implication, Bedouin hygiene practices, I would have baked, and I would never have understood how much their lives revolve around water.[16]

The most serious mistake an ethnographer can make is to impose his or her own culture's standards of behavior and values onto those of another culture.

TOPICS THAT LEND THEMSELVES WELL TO ETHNOGRAPHIC RESEARCH

As we have suggested, researchers who undertake an ethnographic study want to obtain as holistic a picture of an educational setting as possible. Indeed, one of the key strengths of ethnographic research is the comprehensiveness of perspective it provides. Because the researcher goes directly to the situation or setting that he or she wishes to study, deeper and more complete understanding becomes possible. As a result, ethnographic research is particularly suitable for topics such as the following:

- Those that by their very nature defy simple quantification (for example, the interaction of students and teachers in classroom discussions).
- Those that can best be understood in a natural (as opposed to an artificial) setting (for example, the behavior of students at a school event).
- Those that involve the study of individual or group activities over time (such as the changes that occur in the attitudes of at-risk students as they participate in a specially designed, year-long, reading program).
- Those involving the study of the roles that educators play, and the behaviors associated with those roles (for example, the behavior of classroom teachers, students, counselors, administrators, coaches, staff, and other school personnel as they fulfill their various roles and how such behavior changes over time).
- Those that involve the study of the activities and behavior of groups as a unit (such as classes, athletic

teams, subject matter departments, administrative units, work teams, etc.).

• Those involving the study of formal organizations in their totality (for example, schools, school districts, and so forth).

Sampling in Ethnographic Research

Since ethnographers attempt to observe everything within the setting or situation they are observing, in a sense they do not sample at all. But as we have mentioned before, no researcher can observe everything. To the extent that what is observed is only a portion of what might be observed, what a researcher observes is, therefore, a de facto sample of all the possible observations that might be made.

Also, the samples of persons studied by ethnographers are typically small (often only a few individuals, or a single class) and do not permit generalization to a larger population. Many ethnographers, in fact, state right at the outset of a study that they have no intention of generalizing the results of their study. What they are after, they point out, is a more complete understanding of a particular situation. The applicability of their findings can best be determined by replication of their work in other settings or situations by other researchers.

Do Ethnographic Researchers Use Hypotheses?

Ethnographic researchers seldom initiate their research with precise hypotheses that they have formulated ahead of time. Rather, they attempt to understand an ongoing situation or set of activities that cannot be predicted in advance. They observe for a period of time, formulate some initial hypotheses that suggest to them additional kinds of observations that may lead them to revise their initial conclusions, and so on. Ethnographic research, perhaps more so than any other kind of research, relies on both observation and interviewing that is continual and sustained over time.

An example of a question that might be investigated through ethnographic research would be the following: "What is life like in an inner-city high school?" The researcher's goal would be to document or portray the daily, ongoing experiences of the teachers, students, administrators, and staff in such a school. The school would be regularly visited over a considerable length of time (a year would not be uncommon). Classrooms would be observed on a regular basis, and an attempt made to describe, as fully and as richly as possible, what exists and what happens in those classrooms. Several of the teachers, the students, the administrators, and the support staff would be interviewed in depth.

Descriptions (a better word might be "portrayals") might depict the social atmosphere of the school; the intellectual and emotional experiences of students; the manner in which administrators and teachers (and staff and students) act toward and react to others of different ethnic groups, sexes, or abilities; how the "rules" of the school (and the classroom) are learned, modified, and enforced; the kinds of concerns teachers (and students) have; the views students have of the school, and how these compare with the views of the administration and the faculty; and so forth.

The data to be collected might include detailed prose descriptions written out on writing tablets by the researcher-observer; audiotapes of pupil-student, administrator-student, and administrator-faculty conferences; videotapes of classroom discussions and faculty meetings; examples of teacher lesson plans and student work; sociograms depicting "power" relationships that exist in a classroom; flowcharts illustrating the direction and frequency of certain types of comments (for example, the kinds of questions asked by teachers and students of one another, and the responses that different kinds produce); and anything else the researcher thinks would provide insights into what goes on in this school. Notice that in this instance, hypotheses were not formulated at the beginning of the study.

In short, then, the goal of researchers engaging in ethnographic research is to "paint a portrait" of a school or a classroom (or any other educational setting) in as thorough, accurate, and vivid manner as possible so that others can also truly "see" that school or that classroom and its participants and what they do. In fact, it can be viewed as an attempt to determine how a group gives meaning to its activities. Many believe that the ethnographic approach offers a richness of description that is especially fruitful for understanding education.

Data Collection in Ethnographic Research

The two major means of data collection in ethnographic research are through participant observation and interviewing. **Interviewing,** in fact, is the most important tool that ethnographers use. Through interviews, the researcher is able to put into a larger context that which he or she has seen, heard, or experienced. As we described in Chapter Nineteen, interviews come in many forms: structured, semi-structured, informal, and retrospective. We won't expand on the discussion here, except to say that informal interviews are the most common. To the inexperienced, informal interviews may seem to be the easiest to do, as they require neither any particular type of question nor any particular sequence in which questions must be asked. The interviewer can pretty much follow the participant's interests. Often they seem to be no more than a casual conversation. Actually, however, they are quite difficult to do well. The researcher must maintain a comfortable manner and establish a friendly situation, yet still attempt to learn about another individual's life in a fairly systematic fashion. This is not an easy thing to do. Experienced interviewers, therefore, begin with nonthreatening questions posed in a conversational manner before they ask highly personal questions that involve sensitive topics.

The other major technique that ethnographers use is **participant observation,** which we also discussed in some detail in Chapter Nineteen. Participant observation is crucial to effective fieldwork. As Fetterman suggests, participant observation "combines participation in the lives of the people under study with maintenance of a professional distance that allows adequate observation and recording of data."[17] An important aspect of participant observation is that it requires immersion in a culture. Typically, the researcher lives and works in the community of interest for six months to a year or even longer to internalize the basic beliefs, fears, hopes, and expectations of the people under study. In educational research, participant observation, however, is often noncontinuous and spread out over a long, extended period of time. Fetterman gives an example:

> In two ethnographic studies, of dropouts and gifted children, I visited the programs for only a few weeks every couple of months over a three-year period. The visits were intensive and included classroom observation, nonstop informal interviews, occasional substitute teaching, interaction with community members, and the use of various other research techniques, including long-distance phone calls, dinner with students' families, and time spent hanging out in the hallways and parking lot with students cutting classes.[18]

FIELD NOTES

A major check on the accuracy of an ethnographer's observations lies in the quality of his or her **field notes.** To

place an ethnographic report in perspective, interested readers need to know as much as possible about the ideas and views of the researcher. That is why the researcher's field notes are so important. Unfortunately, this remains a major problem in the reporting of much ethnographic research, in that the readers of ethnographic reports seldom, if ever, have access to the researcher's field notes. Rarely do ethnographers tell us how their information was collected, and hence it often is difficult to determine the reliability of the researcher's observations.

Field notes are just what their name implies—the notes researchers take in the field. In educational research, this usually means the detailed notes researchers take in the educational setting (classroom or school) as they observe what is going on or as they interview their informants. They are the researchers' written account of what they hear, see, experience, and think in the course of collecting and reflecting on their data.[19]

Bernard suggests that field notes be distinguished from three other types of writing: field jottings, a field diary, and a field log.[20]

Field jottings refer to quick notes about something the researcher wants to write more about later. They provide the stimulus to help researchers recall a lot of details they do not have time to write down during an observation or an interview.

A **field diary** is, in effect, a personal statement of the researcher's feelings, opinions, and perceptions about others with whom the researcher comes in contact during the course of his or her work. It provides a place where researchers can "let their hair down," so to speak—an outlet for writing down things that the researcher does not want to become part of the public record. Here is an example of part of a page from such a diary of one of the authors of this book, written during a semester-long observation of a social studies class in a suburban high school.

Monday, 11/5. Cold, very rainy day. Makes me feel sort of depressed. Phil, Felix, Alicia, Robert, and Susan came into classroom early today to discuss yesterday's assignment. Susan is looking more disheveled than usual today—seems preoccupied while others are discussing ways to prepare the group report. She doesn't speak to me, although all others say hello. I regret my failure to support her idea during yesterday's discussion when she asked me to. Hope that it will not result in her refusing to be interviewed.

Tuesday, 11/13. Susan and other members of committee supposed to meet me in library before school today for help with their report. Nobody showed. Feel that I've done something to turn these kids off, especially Susan. Makes me angry toward her, as this will now be the third time that she has missed a meeting with me. Only first time for the others. Perhaps she has more influence on them than I thought? I don't feel I am getting anywhere in understanding her, or why she has such influence on so many of the other kids.

Thursday, 11/29. Wow! Mrs. R. (teacher) had extremely good discussion today. Seems like entire class participated (note: check discussion tally sheet to corroborate). I think secret is to start off with something that they perceive as interesting. Why is it that sometimes they are so—so good! so involved in ideas and thinking and other times so apathetic? I can't figure it out. . . .

Field work is often an intense, emotionally draining experience, and a diary can serve as a way for the researcher to let out his or her feelings, yet still keep them private.

A **field log** is a sort of running account of how researchers plan to spend their time compared to how they actually spend it. It is, in effect, the researcher's plan for collecting his or her data systematically. A field log consists of books of blank, lined paper. Each day in the field is represented by two pages of the log. On the left page, the researcher lists what he or she plans to do that day—where to go, who to interview, what to observe, and so on. On the right side, the researcher lists what he or she *actually* did that day. As the study progresses, and things come to mind that the researcher wants to know, the log provides a place for them to be scheduled. Bernard gives an example of how such a log is used.

> Suppose you're studying a local educational system. It's April 5 and you are talking with an informant called MJR. She tells you that since the military government took over, children have to study politics for two hours every day, and she doesn't like it. Write a note to yourself in your log to ask other mothers about this issue, and to interview the school principal.
>
>   Later on, when you are writing up your notes, you may decide not to interview the principal until after you have accumulated more data about how mothers in the community feel about the new curriculum. On the left-hand page for April 23 you note: "target date for interview with school principal." On the left-hand page of April 10 you note "make appointment for interview on 23rd with school principal." For April 6 you note "need more interviews with mothers about new curriculum."[21]

The value of maintaining a log is that it forces the researcher to think hard about the questions he or she truly wants answered, the procedures to be followed, and the data really needed. Taking field notes is an art in itself. We can give only a brief introduction here, but the points presented below should give you some idea of the importance and complexity of the task.

Bogdan and Biklen state that field notes consist of two kinds of materials—descriptive and reflective.[22] **Descriptive field notes** attempt to describe the setting, the people, and what they do according to what the researcher observes. They include the following:

- Portraits of the subjects—their physical appearance, mannerisms, gestures, how they act, talk, and so on.
- Reconstruction of dialogue—conversations between subjects, as well as what they say to the researcher. Unique or particularly revealing statements should be quoted.
- Description of the physical setting—a quick sketch of the room arrangements, placement of materials, and so on.
- Accounts of particular events—who was involved, when, where, and how.
- Depiction of activities—a detailed description of what happened, along with the order in which it happened.
- The observer's behavior—the researcher's actions, dress, conversations with participants, reactions, and so on.

Reflective field notes present more of what the researcher himself or herself is thinking *about* as he or she observes. These include the following:

- Reflections on analysis—the researcher's speculations about what he or she is learning, ideas that are developing, patterns or connections seen, and so on.
- Reflections on method—procedures and materials the researcher is using in the study, comments about the design of the study, problems that are arising, and so on.
- Reflections on ethical dilemmas and conflicts—such as any concerns that arise over responsibilities to subjects or value conflicts.
- Reflections on the observer's frame of mind—such as on what the researcher is thinking as the study progresses (his or her attitudes, opinions, and beliefs) and how these might be affecting the study.
- Points of clarification —notes to the researcher about things that need to be clarified, checked later, etc.

In no other form of research is the actual doing of the study—the process itself—considered as consciously and deliberately as it is in ethnographic research. The reflective aspect of field notes is the researcher's way of attempting to control for the danger of observer effect that we mentioned in Chapter Nineteen, and to remind us that research, to be done well, requires ongoing evaluation and judgment.

AN EXAMPLE OF FIELD NOTES: MARGE'S ROOM[23]

Date: March 24, 1980
Joe McCloud
11:00 A.M. to 12:30 P.M.
Westwood High
6th Set of Notes

The Fourth-Period Class in Marge's Room

I arrived at Westwood High at five minutes to eleven, at the time Marge told me her fourth period started. I was dressed as usual: sport shirt, chino pants, and Woolrich parka. The fourth period is the only time during the day when all the students who are in the "neurologically impaired/learning disability" program, better known as "Marge's program," come together. During the other periods, certain students in the program, two or three or four at most, come to her room for help with the work they are getting in other regular high school classes.

It was a warm, fortyish, promise of a spring day. There was a police patrol wagon, the kind that has benches in the back that are used for large busts, parked in the back of the big parking lot that is in front of the school. No one was sitting in it and I never heard its reason for being there. In the circular drive in front of the school was parked a United States Army car. It had insignias on the side and was a khaki color. As I walked from my car, a balding fortyish man in an Army uniform came out of the building and went to the car and sat down. Four boys and a girl also walked out of the school. All were white. They had on old dungarees and colored stenciled t-shirts with spring jackets over them. One of the boys, the tallest of the four, called out, "oink, oink, oink." This was done as he sighted the police vehicle in the back.

> *O.C.:* This was strange to me in that I didn't think that the kids were into "the police as pigs." Somehow I associated that with another time, the early 1970s. I'm going to have to come to grips with the assumptions I have

about high school due to my own experience. Sometimes I feel like Westwood is entirely different from my high school and yet this police car incident reminded me of mine.

I walked into Marge's class and she was standing in front of the room with more people than I had ever seen in the room save for her homeroom, which is right after second period. She looked like she was talking to the class or was just about to start. She was dressed as she had been on my other visits—clean, neat, well-dressed but casual. Today she had on a striped blazer, a white blouse and dark slacks. She looked up at me, smiled and said: "Oh, I have a lot more people here now than the last time."

> *O.C.:* This was in reference to my other visits during other periods where there are only a few students. She seems self-conscious about having such a small group of students to be responsible for. Perhaps she compares herself with the regular teachers who have classes of thirty or so.

There were two women in their late twenties sitting in the room. There was only one chair left. Marge said to me something like: "We have two visitors from the central office today. One is a vocational counselor and the other is a physical therapist," but I don't remember if those were the words. I felt embarrassed coming in late. I sat down in the only chair available, next to one of the women from the central office. They had on skirts and carried their pocketbooks, much more dressed up than the teachers I've seen. They sat there and observed.

(The class seating arrangement is on the next page.)
. . . Marge walked about near her desk during her talk, which she started by saying to the class: "Now remember, tomorrow is a fieldtrip to the Rollway Company. We all meet in the usual place, by the bus, in front of the main entrance at 8:30. Mrs. Sharp wanted me to tell you that the tour of Rollway is not specifically for you. It's not like the trip to G.M. They took you to places where you were likely to be able to get jobs. Here, it's just a general tour that everybody goes on. Many of the jobs that you will see are not for you. Some are just for people with engineering degrees. You'd better wear comfortable shoes because you may be walking for two or three hours." Maxine and Mark said: "Ooh," in protest to the walking.

She paused and said in a demanding voice: "OK, any questions? You are all going to be there. (Pause) I want you to take a piece of paper and write down some

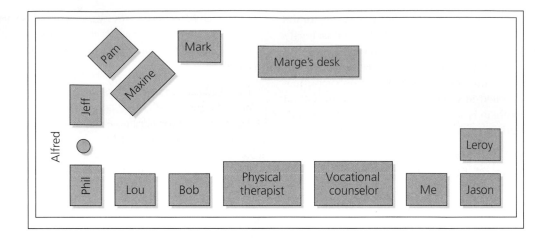

questions so you have things to ask at the plant." She began passing out paper and at this point Jason, who was sitting next to me, made a tutting sound of disgust and said: "We got to do this?" Marge said: "I know this is too easy for you, Jason." This was said in a sarcastic way but not like a strong putdown.

O.C.: It was like sarcasm between two people who know each other well. Marge has known many of these kids for a few years. I have to explore the implications of that for her relations with them.

Marge continued: "OK, what are some of the questions you are going to ask?" Jason yelled out "Insurance," and Marge said: "I was asking Maxine not Jason." This was said matter of factly without anger toward Jason. Maxine said: "Hours—the hours you work, the wages." Somebody else yelled out: "Benefits." Marge wrote these things on the board. She got to Phil who was sitting there next to Jeff. I believe she skipped over Jeff. Mr. Armstrong was standing right next to Phil. She said: "Have you got one?" Phil said: "I can't think of one." She said: "Honestly Phil. Wake up." Then she went to Joe, the white boy. Joe and Jeff are the only white boys I've seen in the program. The two girls are white. He said: "I can't think of any."

She got to Jason and asked him if he could think of anything else. He said: "Yeah, you could ask 'em how many of the products they made each year." Marge said: "Yes, you could ask about production. How about Leroy, do you have any ideas Leroy?" He said: "No." . . . Jason said out loud but not yelling: "How much schooling you need to get it." Marge kept listing them.

O.C.: Marge was quite animated. If I hadn't seen her like this before I would think she was putting on a show for the people from central office. . . .

. . . I looked around the room, noting the dress on some of the students. Maxine had on a black t-shirt that had some iron-on lettering on it. It was a very well-done iron-on and the shirt looked expensive. She had on Levi jeans and Nike jogging sneakers. Mark is about 5′9″or 5′10″. He had on a long sleeve jersey with an alligator on the front, very stylish but his pants were wrinkled and he had on old muddy black basketball sneakers with both laces broken, one in two places. Pam had on a lilac-colored velour sweater over a button-down striped shirt. Her hair looked very well-kept and looked like she had had it styled at an expensive hair place. Jeff sat next to her in his wheelchair. He had one foot up without a shoe on it as if it were sprained. . . .

Phil had on a beige sweater over a white shirt and dark pants and low-cut basketball sneakers. The sneakers were red and were dirty. He had a dirt ring around the collar. He is the least well-dressed of the crowd. . . .

Jim is probably 5′9″ or 5′10″. He had on a red pullover. Jason had on a black golf cap and a beige spring jacket over a university t-shirt. He had on dark dress pants and a red university t-shirt with a v-neck. It was faded from being washed. Jason's eyes were noticeably red.

O.C.: Two of the kids told me that Westwood High was a fashion show. I have a difficult time figuring out what's in fashion. Jason used that expression. He seems to me to be the most clothes-conscious. . . .

I don't know what got this started but she started talking about the social background of the kids in the class. She said: "Pam lives around here right up there so she's from a professional family. Now, Maxine, that's different. She lives on the east side. She is one of six kids and her father isn't that rich. As a matter of fact, he's in maintenance, taking charge of cleaning crews.

Now, Jeff, he lives on Dogwood. He's middle class." I asked about Lou. She said: "Pour Lou, talk about being neurologically impaired. I don't know what to do about that guy. Now he has a sister who graduated two years ago. He worries me more than anybody. I don't know what is going to become of him. He is so slow. I don't know any job that he could do. His father came in and he looks just like him. What are you going to tell him? What is he going to be able to do? What is he going to do? Wash airplanes? I talked to the vocational counselor. She said that there were jobs in airports washing airplanes. I mean, how is he going to wash an airplane? How about sweeping out the hangars? Maybe he could do that. The mother is something else. His mother thinks that Lou is her punishment. Can you imagine an attitude like that? I was just wondering what could she have done to think that she deserved Lou?

"Now Luca Meta, he is upper class all the way. Leroy, there's your low end of the spectrum. I don't know how many kids they have but they have a lot. His mother just had a kidney removed. Everybody knows he is on parole. Matter of fact, whenever there is any stealing in the school, they look at him. He used to go to gym and every time he went, something was stolen. Now they don't let him go to gym anymore. His parole officer was down. He won't be here next year.". . .

. . . She said: "By the way, I was talking and maybe you overheard me about what we need is a competency-based program here. I have already finished a competency-based program if they ever took it. It is silly to have kids spend four years sitting here, when it makes no sense in terms of them. They ought to be out working. If they're not going to graduate, what they ought to have is some living skills like what we did with writing the checks. People aren't going to teach them that out in the world so they could do that. Once they had enough skills, living skills, to make it on their own then they ought to go out. There is no sense to this." . . .

We left the room. Alfred and Marge walked up the empty hall with me. I asked her how the kids felt about being in this class. She said: "Well, it varies. It really bothers Pam. Like she failed history and she has to go to summer school. The reason she failed it was she wouldn't tell them that she was in this program so she didn't get any extra help and then she failed." Marge walked me to the door. Alfred dropped off at the teachers' room.

On the way to the door she said: "Remember that boy I told you about who's going to be in there? The dentist's son, the Swenson boy? Well, I have been hearing stories about him. I come to find out that he is really E.M.H. (Educable Mentally Handicapped) and a hyper-

active kid. I really am going to have my hands full with him. If there is twenty in the program next year, I really am going to need another aide." I said good-bye and walked to my car.

Data Analysis in Ethnographic Research

Analysis is one of the most interesting aspects of ethnographic research. It begins from the first moment a researcher selects a problem to study and continues until the final report is written. Many techniques, including content analysis (see Chapter 20) are involved in analyzing ethnographic data. Some of the more important include triangulation, searching for patterns, identifying key events, preparing visual representations, using statistics, and crystallization. What follows is a brief description of each.

Triangulation. **Triangulation** is fundamental in ethnographic research. Essentially, it establishes the validity of an ethnographer's observations. It involves checking what one hears and sees by comparing one's sources of information—do they agree? Here's an example: A researcher might compare a student's oral statements that he was a "good" student with a written transcript of his grades, his teacher's comments in this regard, and, perhaps, some unsolicited remarks from his fellow students. Triangulation here could verify—or not—the student's self-assessment.

Triangulation can work with any subject, in any setting, and at any level (see Figure 21.1). It improves the quality of the data that are collected and the accuracy of the researcher's interpretations. It can occur naturally, even in informal conversation. Consider this example:

A prominent superintendent, managing one of the largest districts in the nation, had just finished explaining why school size made no difference in education. He said that he had one 1500-pupil school and one 5000-pupil school in his district that he was particularly proud of, and that the school size had no effect on school spirit, the educative process, or his ability to manage. He also explained that he had to build two or three new schools next year, either three small schools or one small school and one large one. A colleague interrupted to ask which he preferred. The superintendent replied, "Small ones, of course; they are much easier to handle." He had betrayed himself in one phrase. Although the administrative party line was that size made no difference—management is

Figure 21.1
Triangulation and Politics

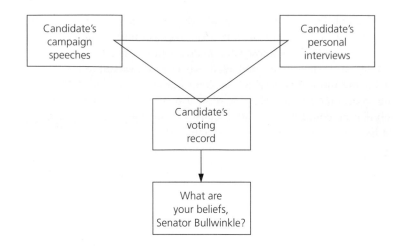

management no matter how big or small the unit—this superintendent revealed a very different personal opinion in response to a casual question.[24]

Patterns. Those who do ethnographic research look for **patterns** in the ways that people think and behave. They offer a means of checking ethnographic reliability when they reveal consistencies in what people say and what they do. Typically, researchers start with a large mass of undifferentiated information and then, by comparing and contrasting what they collected, sort this information until a discernible line of thought or pattern of behavior emerges. They then observe and listen some more to see whether the new observations correspond to what they saw and heard before. This then requires further sifting and sorting until the researchers are satisfied that what they are describing matches what was observed.

Key Events. **Key events** occur in every social group and provide data that ethnographic researchers can use to describe and analyze an entire culture. They convey a tremendous amount of information. They provide a "lens through which to view a culture."[25] Examples might include the introduction of computers in an elementary school; a fistfight between two girls during a high school basketball game; the response of a group of recovery room nurses to a medical emergency; a fire in a crowded apartment building; the introduction of a new teaching method in a social studies classroom; or the return of a popular professor from sabbatical leave. Such events are especially useful for analysis, as they not only help the researcher understand the group he or she is studying, but they also help the researcher explain the culture of the group to others.

Visual Representations. These include such things as *maps* (e.g., of a classroom or school); *flowcharts* (e.g., of who says what to whom during a classroom discussion); *organizational charts* (e.g., of how a school library is organized); *sociograms* (e.g., of which students receive the most invitations to participate as a member of a classroom research team; *matrices* (e.g., a chart to compare and cross-reference the various categories that exist in a creative arts department in a university, such as music, dance, theatre, painting, and the like). The very process of preparing a visual representation often can help a researcher crystallize his or her understanding of an area, a system, a location, or even an interaction. Visual representations are very useful tools in ethnographic research.

Statistics. Although you might not expect it, ethnographers often do use statistics in their work. Usually, however, they use nonparametric techniques (see Chapter 11), such as a chi-square test (see Appendix D) more often than parametric ones. Typically, they are more likely to report frequencies than scores. They do use parametric statistics when they have large samples, however.

Nevertheless, the use of statistics in ethnographic research presents a number of problems. Meeting the assumptions that many inferential tests require (e.g., that the sample is random) often is virtually impossible. Typically, ethnographic studies use small samples and purposive samples. On the other hand, descriptive statistics—means and medians—can at times be used to summarize the frequency of actions or events and more and more often are being found in ethnographic reports.

Crystallization. Ethnographers try to pull together their thoughts at various stages throughout their research. Sometimes this results in only a summing up of information, but other times it results in a genuine insight. "Every study has classic moments when everything falls into place. After months of thought and immersion in the culture, a special configuration gels. All the subtopics, miniexperiments, layers of triangulated effort, key events, and patterns of behavior form a coherent and often cogent picture of what is happening."[26] Nothing is more exciting to an ethnographer than when this happens.

The important thing to realize about the analysis of ethnographic data is that there is no single stage or time when it occurs. Multiple analyses and multiple forms are essential. Often it is cyclical—data are collected, thought about, more data are collected, patterns are looked for, more data are collected, new patterns are looked for, matrices and then more matrices are developed, and on and on. Data analysis in ethnography is ongoing, from start to finish.

Roger Harker and His Fifth-Grade Classroom

Let us look, then, at an example of ethnographic research. What follows is a short description, by the researcher, of an ethnographic study of a fifth-grade classroom.

> I [the researcher] worked in depth with Roger Harker for six months. I did an ethnography of his classroom and the interaction between him and his pupils. This young man had taught for three years in the elementary school. He volunteered for the study in order, he said, "to improve my professional competence."
>
> My collection of data fell into the following categories: (1) personal, autobiographical, and psychological data on the teacher; (2) ratings of him by his principal and other superiors in the superintendent's office; (3) his own self-estimates on the same points; (4) observations of his classroom, emphasizing interaction with children; (5) interviews with each child and the elicitation of ratings of the teacher on many different dimensions, both formally and informally; (6) his ratings and estimates for each child in his classroom, including estimates of popularity with peers, academic performance and capacity, personal adjustment, home background, and liking for him; (7) sociometric data from the children about each

> other; and (8) interviews with each person (superintendent, principal, supervisors, children) who supplied ratings of him.
>
> I also participated in the life of the school to the extent possible, accompanying the teacher where I could and "melting" into the classroom as much as feasible. I was always there, but I had no authority and assumed none. I became a friend and confidant to the children.
>
> This teacher was regarded by his superiors as most promising—"clear and well-organized," "sensitive to children's needs," "fair and just to all of the children," "knowing his subject areas well." I was not able to elicit with either ratings scales or in interviews any criticisms or negative evaluations. There were very few suggestions for change—and these were all in the area of subject matter and curriculum.
>
> Roger Harker described himself as "fair and just to all my pupils," as making "fair decisions," and as "playing no favorites." This was a particular point of pride with him.
>
> His classroom was made up of children from a broad social stratum—upper-middle, middle, and lower classes—and the children represented Mexican-American, Anglo-European, and Japanese-American ethnic groups. I was particularly attentive to the relationships between the teacher and children from these various groups.
>
> One could go into much detail, but a few items will suffice since they all point in the same direction, and that direction challenges both his perceptions of his own behavior and those of his superiors. He ranked highest on all dimensions, including personal and academic factors, those children who were most like himself—Anglo, middle to upper-middle social class, and, like him, ambitious (achievement-oriented). He also estimated that these children were the most popular with their peers and were the leaders of the classroom group. His knowledge about the individual children, elicited without recourse to files or notes, was distributed in the same way. He knew significantly more about the children culturally like himself (on items concerned with home background as well as academic performance) and least about those culturally most different.
>
> The children had quite different views of the situation. Some children described him as not always so "fair and just," as "having special pets," as not being easy to go to with their problems. On sociometric "maps" of the classroom showing which children wanted to spend time with other specific children, or work with them, sit near them, invite them to a party or a show, etc., the most popular

children were not at all those the teacher rated highest. And his negative ratings proved to be equally inaccurate. Children he rated as isolated or badly adjusted socially, most of whom were non-Anglo or non-middle-class, more often than not turned out to be "stars of attraction" from the point of view of the children.

Observations of his classroom behavior supported the data collected by other means. He most frequently called on, touched, helped, and looked directly at the children culturally like himself. He was never mean or cruel to the other children. It was almost as though they weren't there. His interaction with the children of Anglo-European ethnicity and middle and upper-middle social class background was more frequent than with the other children, and the quality of the interaction appeared to be differentiated in the same way.

This young man, with the best of intentions, was confirming the negative hypotheses and predictions (as well as the positive ones) already made within the social system. He was informing Anglo middle-class children that they were capable, had bright futures, were socially acceptable, and were worth a lot of trouble. He was also informing non-Anglo children that they were less cabable, less socially acceptable, less worth the trouble. He was defeating his own declared educational goals.

This young teacher did not know that he was discriminating. He was rated very positively by his superiors on all counts, including being "fair and just to all the children." Apparently they were as blind to his discrimination as he was. The school system supported him and his classroom behavior without questioning or criticizing him. And the dominant social structure of the community supported the school.[27]

Notice several several things about this description

- The study took place in a naturalistic setting—in the classroom and school of Roger Harker.
- The researcher did not try to manipulate the situation in any way.
- There was no comparison of methods or treatments (as is often the case in experimental or causal-comparative research).
- The study involved only a single classroom (an *n* of one).
- The researcher was a participant observer, participating "in the life of the school to the extent possible."
- The researcher used several different kinds of instruments to collect his data.
- The researcher tried to present a holistic description of this teacher's fifth-grade classroom.

- The study revealed much that would have been missed by researchers using other methodologies.
- No attempt was made to generalize the researcher's findings to other settings or situations. The "external validity" of the study, in other words, was very limited.
- There is no way, unfortunately, to check the validity of the data or the researcher's interpretations (unless another researcher had independently observed the same classroom).

Advantages and Disadvantages of Ethnographic Research

Ethnographic research has a number of unique strengths, but also several weaknesses. A key strength is that it provides the researcher with a much more comprehensive perspective than do other forms of educational research. By observing the actual behavior of individuals in their natural settings, one may gain a much deeper and richer understanding of such behavior. Ethnographic research also lends itself well to research topics that are not easily quantified. The thoughts of teachers and students, ideas, and other nuances of behavior that might escape researchers using other methodologies can often be detected by ethnographic researchers.

Furthermore, ethnographic research is particularly appropriate to behaviors that are best understood by observing them within their natural settings. Other types of research can measure attitudes and behaviors in somewhat artificial settings, but they frequently do not lend themselves well to naturalistic settings. The "dynamics" of a faculty meeting, or the "interaction" between students and teacher in a classroom, for example, can probably best be studied through ethnographic investigation. Finally, ethnographic research is especially suited to studying group behavior over time. Thus, to understand as fully as possible the "life" of an inner-city school over a year-long period, an ethnographic approach may well be the most appropriate methodology for a researcher to use.

Ethnographic research, like all research, however, is not without its limitations. It is highly dependent on the particular researcher's observations and interpretations, and since numerical data are rarely provided, there is usually no way to check the validity of the researcher's conclusions. As a result, observer bias is almost impossible to eliminate. Because usually only a single situation (such as one classroom or one school) is observed, generalizability is almost nonexistent, except when it is possible to replicate the study in other settings or situations by other researchers. Because the researcher usually begins his or her observations without a specific hypothesis to confirm or deny, terms may not be defined, and hence the specific variables or relationships being investigated (if any) may remain unclear.

Because of the inevitable ambiguity that accompanies this method, preplanning and review by others are much less useful than in quantitative studies. While it is true that no study is ever carried out precisely as planned, potential pitfalls are more easily identified and corrected in other methodologies. For this reason, we believe ethnographic research to be a very difficult type of research to do well. It follows that beginning researchers using this method should receive close supervision.

An Example of Ethnographic Research

In the remainder of this chapter, we present a published example of ethnographic research, followed by a critique of its strengths and weaknesses. As we did in our critiques of the different types of research studies we analyzed in other chapters, we use concepts introduced in earlier parts of the book in our analysis.

From *Urban Education*, 33, 218–242. Copyright © 1998 by Corwin Press, Inc. Reprinted with permission of Corwin Press, Inc.

Dumping Ground or Effective Alternative? Dropout-Prevention Programs in Urban Schools

Cori Groth
University of Utah

Abstract

Focusing on students' perspectives, this article examines whether an urban dropout prevention program offers students effective alternatives to regular classes or if, instead, the program is simply a dumping ground for unwanted students. Findings generated from interviews and observations suggest both. Although the analysis of the students' perceptions indicates that the program helps students to remain in school and acquire credits, the program does little to help students create and apply practical knowledge in their everyday lives. Nor does the program help students to acquire the skills either for fitting into the dominant culture or for surviving as resisters of that culture. A discussion of policy implications is provided along with suggestions for future research.

Justification

Dropping out of high school reportedly has negative effects for both individuals and society. Dropouts tend to have lower-paying jobs, lower employment rates, and generally lower standards of living (Catterall, 1985). Similarly, dropping out leads to social costs in the form of increased crime rates, increased dispensation of welfare and unemployment subsidies, increased health care costs, and lowered tax revenues for the state (Catterall, 1985; Levin, 1972).

The failure of mainstream public schools to respond to the issues of an increasingly pluralistic context and the resulting problems of students who leave the educational system early have moved educators to provide alternatives to regular schools. A variety of programs have

Need more detail

been designed to remedy the dropout problem. Despite the proliferation of such programs[1] (Reilly & Reilly, 1983), few researchers have studied the interactional dynamics between students and teachers to determine the effectiveness of the programs. In this article, I address these issues

Purpose?

by examining one dropout-prevention program to understand how interaction between students and faculty is defined and how these interactions relate to behavior associated with either staying in or leaving school.

Most researchers studying the dropout problem have focused primarily on the at-risk students' characteristics, while neglecting their experiences (Fine, 1991; Kelly, 1993). Understanding the students' experience is crucial for a critical analysis of educators' decisions to adopt re-

Justification

medial dropout-prevention programs. Without critically analyzing the experiences of students in these programs, educators may perpetuate the patterns that influence students to drop out and, therefore, they will merely replicate the dysfunctional system that consistently loses about one out of four of its students (Catterall, 1985; LeCompte, 1987).

THE "MISFITS"

Often labeled as dropout-prevention programs or continuation schools, these programs have been created to extend the promise of education to students who have not fit into the mainstream public schools (Kelly, 1996). In discussing the response of educators to at-risk populations, Kelly (1996) suggests that options provided to potential or present dropouts should respond to two issues:

(1) students' need for flexibility and personalization, with the stated aim of "dropout prevention and recovery," and (2) mainstream comprehensive high schools' need for mechanisms to isolate students identified as discipline problems and to provide specialized services efficiently. (p. 118)

Kelly is pessimistic about these second-chance programs, particularly because they do not address the larger structures both inside and outside the educational system (e.g., job programs, more and better funding for child care, funded access to contraception and abortion services, balanced housing development, social and health services) that currently replicate the traditional sorting process (1996, p. 119).

Schools have long been criticized for their normative culture, which may be the source of student alienation and consequent disengagement, particularly for students who do not conform to mainstream standards of a typical student. Dei (1996) states:

> School "culture" embraces a unique set of core norms and values, well-defined hierarchies of authority, and definitions of what is knowledge, what is good pedagogy, and how students are best assessed and rewarded. Conventional norms about schooling rest on assimilationist assumptions. (p. 177)

Definition?

This educational culture becomes problematic as schools serve increasingly diverse populations. Furthermore, this issue of diversity is especially relevant to the study of dropout prevention because of the disproportionate numbers of minority youth and those from lower socioeconomic status groups being served by alternative programs. To avoid a common pitfall of much research on dropout prevention, I find it critical not to view dropping out of school as a pathological and individual problem (Dei, 1996). Student alienation and disengagement from school most certainly affects individuals, yet the sources of alienation and disengagement may be quite structural. In fact, Fine (1991) and Dei (1996) suggest that students disengaging from school are social actors, critiquing the "very foundations of schooling in our society" (Dei. 1996, p. 184). Students in alternative dropout-prevention programs may offer the kind of marginal voice that illuminates structural characteristics of systems that otherwise may be difficult to see.

Assumption

EDUCATIONAL SOLUTIONS TO THE DROPOUT PROBLEM

Dropout-prevention programs provide one strategy for addressing the dropout problem. As noted above, these programs provide alternative settings where students can obtain credits toward a high-school diploma. The growing popularity of such programs also addresses educators' concern for accommodating an increasingly diverse student population (Ascher, 1982; Catterall & Stern, 1986; Collins, 1987; Deal & Nolan, 1978; Duke & Perry, 1978; Franklin, 1992; Gold & Mann, 1982; Wehlage, Rutter, Smith, Lesko, & Fernandez, 1989).

Despite the increasing popularity of dropout-prevention programs and other alternative programs, only a handful of researchers have addressed the issue. Research on alternative education is described by Franklin (1992) as "generally terrible." Compared to the copious attention paid to high-school dropouts, the attention researchers give to studying dropout prevention and alternative education programs is inadequate.

Need more detail

As a result, in part, of increasing governmental pressure to perform, educators are interested in retaining and providing options for their students, particularly racial and ethnic minorities. Providing alternative programs, however, does not completely solve the problem. Researchers criticize alternative programs on several fronts. They claim the programs serve as dumping grounds for unwanted behavior problem students, especially minority students. Enrollment in alternative programs can stigmatize students. Gold and Mann (1982) state:

> Youth may be made to feel that they are different in a derogatory sense by having been sent to a special school for "bad kids." A substantial number of administrators,

Prior research

teachers, and students did hold negative opinions about the alternative programs and the young people who went there. (p. 311)

Findings or opinion?

Researchers (suggest that) placing students in dropout-prevention programs may be an extreme version of the tracking system, in which administrators disproportionately and continually place low-achieving, low socioeconomic status (SES), and minority students in lower academic level or vocational courses (Kelly, 1993). The same types of students occupying lower academic level and vocational courses also occupy dropout-prevention programs. Researchers also (claim) that dropout-prevention programs require only minimal scholastic standards. They say these programs have been criticized because "students earn scholastic credits with less effort, that they receive passing grades for below-standard work, and that they are privileged to break ordinary school rules" (Gold & Mann, 1982, p. 315).

Educators face the difficult task of providing effective alternatives for students that would give them access to the rewards a diploma supposedly offers. They attempt to create alternative programs by adapting policies and offering curriculum that will satisfy the students' needs, while maintaining conformity to the existing practices of the educational system. They have not agreed, however, on the ways to do this. This is a very tough job but one that needs examination.

METHODS

Method

The design of this project is exploratory and interpretive in nature. Assuming an interactionist perspective, I placed primary emphasis on the students' definitions of their own situation in school, as well as their past experiences. This theoretical framework calls for a participant-observational approach to data collection, which involves "being unusually thorough and reflective in noticing and describing everyday events in the field setting, and in attempting to identify the significance of actions in the events from the various points of view of the actors themselves" (Erickson, 1986, p. 121).

Data collection

Using this type of participant-observational approach, I attempted to capture the assertions students made about their experiences and to understand their point of view by recording interviews with students, making weekly and daily site visits to the school, observing participants in the program in their everyday setting, and taking extensive field notes of all the conversations and dynamics in the classroom. Data were collected during the 1994–1995 school year.

Procedures

During site visits, I observed students doing their work, and I engaged in conversations with them throughout the visit. In addition, I participated in bi-weekly focus group meetings conducted by the school counselor who was working with the Advanced Achievement Academy (AAA)[2] program coordinator. These focus group meetings provided an excellent opportunity for me to obtain information about the students' personal lives as well as their perceptions of themselves in the larger school system.

Useful clarification

Finally, I conducted in-class interviews with the students. During each interview, students were asked to discuss the following issues: their experiences in AAA, how experiences in AAA differed from those in regular classes, their work on computers, their relationships with the teachers in AAA, how their relationship with the faculty in AAA differed from relationships with faculty in regular classes, their perceptions of what others think of AAA, the reasons they enrolled in AAA, their options for getting a diploma, how they knew about these options, their plans after graduation, what they think about school, and what they perceive as the things that limit them. These interviews were tape recorded and transcribed.

Setting: Dropout-Prevention Program

The dropout-prevention program I studied, AAA, is located on the perimeter of a high-school campus in a southwestern metropolitan city. Established 4 years ago, the program offers computer-assisted instruction. The students in AAA have either dropped out of school or were in the process of dropping out at the time of enrollment in the program. Students in the program receive credit for completing work on computer-assisted tutorials that are the equivalent of one regular semester course. The students participate in a focus group twice a week, in which a counselor leads them in discussions related to their personal lives and school or community issues. A teacher is present in the classroom at all times, and a teacher's aide is there twice a week. Enrollment in this program is limited to 1 year, although some exceptions are made based on personal extenuating circumstances.

Program description

The program director selects students for the program from a waiting list based on <u>who the director thinks will benefit most from the program</u>. Students are not recruited or placed in AAA by counselors or other administrators: <u>rather, they must actively seek enrollment in the program on their own</u>. Because of these policies, administrators of AAA are in an unusually good position to help students get back on track and start earning credits for several reasons. First, the students who request enrollment already have reached a critical point at which they decided they did not want to be dropouts or remain dropouts. Second, the students have adopted a proactive strategy in trying to improve their academic standing.

Student selection

Participants

During the course of my investigation, 25 students (4 Hispanic females, 6 Hispanic males, 1 Native American female, 9 White females, and 5 White males) were enrolled in AAA. The average enrollment was approximately 20 to 22 students, dropping to 15 students at one point. Students ranged in age from 16 to 18. The program director tries to reflect the school's dropout population within the program population by matching the percentage of ethnic and racial distribution of the school in the program.

Sample

The students come from a wide range of ethnic and class backgrounds and have dramatically different experiences with school. Many of the students have one or more parents who did not graduate from high school, whereas others have parents who have postsecondary degrees. Students have a variety of obligations outside school life, such as working several jobs or raising children. Despite such varied backgrounds, the most common reason given for enrolling in the program is lack of credits.

Useful description

Findings

The formally stated goal of AAA is that the program helps students stay in school and eventually graduate. The implicit assumption of AAA, however, is that the program acts as a safety net for students who otherwise would drop out of school altogether. The program is the administrators' attempt to temper the problem of dropouts. They do not attempt to retain all students at risk of dropping out nor do they actively seek students to enroll in the program. Instead, the responsibility for enrolling in the program is left to the students.

This has several effects. First, (because) the students enrolled in AAA take measures to pursue their education, they treat the program as a privilege. For most students, this program is their last chance for obtaining a diploma or for acquiring credits toward a diploma. (For these reasons) students as well as faculty treat students' participation in the program differently than they treat participation in regular classes. The following findings explore the various components of the attitudes of students in AAA toward these two different environments. The names presented here are changed to maintain the anonymity of the students in the program.

Cause/Effect

Contrasting Features of the Dropout Program and Regular Classes

As I learned more about the situation in the dropout-prevention program, I found that several concepts reflected the experiences of the students. These concepts, divided into five categories, constitute the components of the educational experience that contrast between the dropout program and comprehensive school or regular classes. The categories are as follows:

Emergent categories

1. The pursuit of credits and diplomas,
2. The relationships between students and teachers (and administrators),
3. The construction of time frames,
4. Classroom management and work context, and
5. The effects of rules and policies.

These concepts relate to various features of the students' everyday life experiences. The dividing lines drawn among these categories, however, are not necessarily sharply defined. I discuss these categories by pointing out the differences in students' perceptions of their past experiences with regular classes and their present experience in AAA. The following discussion describes these five categories.

Credits and Diploma Pursuit

Findings

In the dropout-prevention program, students do all their work on computers. This computer-assisted instruction seems to be analogous to the use of Automated Teller Machines (ATMs), which expedite the process of getting cash. When I asked students to describe the program to me, I was told repeatedly, "You can get credits quicker." The dropout-prevention program thus is like an "ATM for diplomas." This is an especially salient notion, considering the exclusive use of computer-assisted instruction, testing, and grading. The following examples illustrate the relative ease and speed with which students acquire credits.

I'm not a rocket scientist, but it's pretty easy. It's just manipulation; just push the buttons. (Brad, interview, 12/1/94)

Good examples

You get to work at your own pace. You can work faster than in regular school. (Tammy, interview, 11/29/94)

I like how you can earn credits faster in here. You can earn a lot of credits in a semester if you want to. (Anthony, field notes, 10/4/94)

Interpretation

The technological advances and changes, particularly the use of computers in the classroom, affect the way students view their own education. Students actually are using the computers to *withdraw* an education, just as bank customers use computers to *withdraw* their money. In essence, the students are the clients (consumers), and the teachers are the bank tellers (facilitators) who simply monitor a computer-human interaction. This phenomenon is similar to the concepts discussed by Ritzer in *The McDonaldization of Society* (1993), in which he suggests that organizational systems are designed to exert the maximum amount of efficiency, calculability, predictability, and control as possible, invading every aspect of society, including education. Ritzer argues that the "replacement of human with nonhuman technology is very often motivated by a desire for greater control" and for lower costs for capitalism, aimed primarily at people because they are most often the hardest to control (p. 100).

Results or interpretation?

The students see themselves as gaining control when pursuing a diploma in AAA, because they set the pace of their learning and they minimize distractions. In contrast, a full seven-period class schedule is quite complicated. Students limit these complications by focusing their attention on obtaining one class credit at a time.

Findings

Every student, except one, said he or she definitely wanted to get a high-school diploma. When asked how a diploma would help them, however, few students stated clear reasons. Rather, the students saw getting a diploma as an accomplishment to strive for, a goal, "you just need it." This demonstration of high ambitions, but with little indication of the rewards education offers, is common. Anthony, a Hispanic male, is a transfer student from Southern California, where he was heavily involved in gangs. His parents relocated with the hope that Anthony might graduate from high school—the first from his family.

> CG: So why do you want to get a diploma?
>
> Anthony: Because it's good to have a diploma. You know, you gotta go a step forward than a step behind. It's good I guess.
>
> CG: What do you think it will help you with?
>
> Anthony: I don't know if it will help but, like, it's a goal that I have. It's something I want, not something that somebody wants for me. It's what I want. (interview, 1/20/95)

Good examples

Another example of this contradiction between student aspirations and potential benefits of educational achievement is illustrated by Tammy, a White female who works part-time at a local drugstore, and recently has been hospitalized for methamphetamine addiction and multiple eating disorders.

> My mom was like, "Tammy, if you don't want to go to school, I'll go down there and withdraw you from school. You won't ever have to go. You can go out and find a full-time job at McDonald's or something. You're never going to get an office job." (Tammy, interview, 11/29/94)

Tammy's and her mother's association of having a high-school diploma with being able to have an "office job" indicates the recognition of the marked distinction between the employment opportunities of high-school dropouts and graduates.

The students' vague descriptions of what a diploma represents seem to express the general division between the knowledge obtained or created in the classroom and the piece of paper symbolizing that knowledge. This division emphasizes quantity over quality. I rarely heard students talk about what they were actually learning. In contrast, I repeatedly heard students talk about the amount of credits they were earning. This attitude toward learning seems to occur in both the regular classes and the alternative program.

Results

Student/Teacher Relationships

The students in AAA often discussed problems with past teachers. For example, Lisa, a White female, is one of the more vocal members of the program. She comes from a middle-class background, with both parents in the household and both college educated.

Results

During a group discussion with the counselor, students were airing their grievances about a particular assessment practice at the school. This conversation led to general complaints of teachers and policies.

> A Black teacher told a student, "I can understand why you don't understand this, because you come from a lower class." This is exactly what the teacher told a student, and I was offended by this statement. (Lisa, field notes, 11/3/94)

Although Lisa does not come from a "lower class," it was apparent from my interaction with her that she is well aware of the differential treatment "lower-class" students receive from teachers, administrators, and students. It is possible that her awareness of this unequal treatment has, in part, developed from her own marginalized status in the dropout program.

Deborah, a Hispanic female, provides another example of problematic student-teacher relationships.

> I remember one teacher who said, "You're never going to graduate. You're no good." Right in front of my class. That made me feel really bad. I just didn't care. (interview, 2/24/95)

Good examples

Deborah has experienced ongoing conflict with teachers regarding her parental and minority status. Deborah has two children and has had difficulties finding child care for them. Some days, she will bring her youngest to class with her when he has a cold because her day care does not accept children with illnesses.

The last example of problematic student-teacher relationships comes from another female student who seems to be marginalized by her status, not as a Hispanic or mother, but rather as the object of stigmatizing labels. (She told me that she has been called a "druggie" and a "slut" for her association with current and past boyfriends.)

During a group discussion with the counselor, students were offering their opinions about who they thought were bad teachers in the high school. Denise pointed out the power differential between students and teachers.

> If you don't get along with a teacher, it's more of a problem for the student, because the teachers are the ones giving out the credit. (field notes, 11/21/94)

Only one example

Students recognize the hierarchical relationship between themselves and the adults within the school, but they do not always submit to the adult authority. Rather, students actively resist. The following example demonstrates the role of student as social critic.

During a group discussion, the counselor explained to the class that Jill's teacher from the high school came to her complaining that Jill had not been in class, after telling the teacher she would be there. Jill replied to the counselor that she had told the teacher she would *try* to be there if she could.

> She (the teacher) gets an attitude with me, so I'm going to get one with her. (field notes, 11/29/94)

In this situation, Jill, a Hispanic female, does not submit to the teacher's authority; instead, she maintains her autonomy by determining for herself when she will attend class. Furthermore, she uses her own language (getting an "attitude") to negate the legitimacy of the teacher's authority. Jill, like Deborah, is a mother, for whom negotiating day care and educational activities is problematic. Unlike Deborah, Jill has more educated parents, from middle-class backgrounds, who can provide additional support as well as advocate for their daughter. This seems to mediate the difficulties of the student-teacher relationships for Jill.

Furthermore, Jill does not exhibit the same type of animosity toward adults in AAA as she does in regular classes. She told me that she has gotten to know the teacher in AAA better than any of the teachers in regular school. When I asked her how this type of relationship changes things for her, she replied, "It probably makes you act better. You're a better student." This sentiment was common among students in AAA.

Student-teacher relationships in AAA were quite informal. The adult faculty included the primary teacher, a teaching aide, the program director, and the counselor. The teacher did not lead any students in lessons; instead, he monitored students' work on the computer and assisted students when they had questions about the programs. I noticed immediately that students in AAA appear to get along well with the main instructor. He has a casual personable style, sharing much of his private life with the students, as well as showing interest in theirs.

> You all know I'm a little different than a normal teacher. I don't have a problem with these things [bringing pagers or Walkman-type sound systems to school]. I cover for you guys a lot, believe it or not. (Mr. Brown, field notes, 12/6/94)

Aside from his personal relationships with each student and the informal counseling he gives them, his primary role as a teacher is to monitor the students' progress through the tutorials, helping them where needed. He also manages classroom policies, such as coming to class on time, making up missed days or hours, announcing work breaks, and running the computer programs. These tasks are not typical of the duties in regular classes, where the teachers traditionally have prepared lectures or exercises with which they lead a group.

In AAA, the role of the teacher is more that of a coach or a guide, with the passing of information done by the computers. The students define their relationship with the teacher in very positive terms, unlike in the regular classes. The following is an example of students' perceptions of student-teacher interaction that occurs in the class.

> Well he's doing a good job, but it's, I mean, he loves it. He told us he loved us. He's a good guy . . . He's not got, every hour another 30 students. He's got a better relationship because he sees us all the time. (Don, interview, 12/6/94)

This type of student perception of the teacher eliminates many of the conflicts that the students complained of when they were in regular classes.

Cause/Effect

Time Frame Constructions

Semesters, and the school year they constitute, are socially constructed time frames, historically designed to accommodate families who needed their children to work during the harvest season. Problems arise when the beginning and end of a semester do not coincide with the students' personal activities or events, such as traveling, working, moving from another city, or having a child.

If students cannot start school at the beginning of the semester, they often must skip the entire semester or take night school classes. For example, Jose, a Hispanic male, had spent the summer out of town at a state-run ranch for juvenile offenders. When asked why he enrolled in AAA, Jose explained that the reason was that he was not allowed to enroll in school 2 weeks late, not because of lack of credits.

> The reason I'm in AAA is because I was in . . . [the ranch], and when I came back my parents wanted me to finish school. And, so they brought me back. But, when they brought me back, they [the administrators] told me it was too late. I either had to wait until another semester or go to night school. I didn't want to go to night school and I didn't want to wait until another semester. And, so they told me to go talk to Mr. Smith [the program director of AAA]. (interview, 1/23/95)

This student continued to tell me that because he enrolled in AAA, he could stay in school and eventually graduate early. This prospect was appealing to him, considering that he and his girlfriend recently had a child. He could now pursue his goal of finding a full-time job to support his new family.

In contrast to the rigid time frames of semester courses in regular classes, students are not strictly bound by time frames in the alternative program. Courses are not set up on a semester basis; rather, students can enter the program at any time during regular semester time frames and complete courses at their own pace. The length of time it takes to complete a course is determined by the amount of time and effort they contribute. Students therefore set their own time frames. The only restriction is a 1-year maximum enrollment in the program, after which students either graduate or enter regular classes again.

Negotiating behavior in accordance with these time frames often is difficult when extenuating circumstances prohibit or merely hinder students from complying with policies. For example, Belinda, a White female, is severely limited medically as a result of diabetes, and she is able to attend classes only sporadically, when she feels well enough. If she were to remain in regular classes, she would be expelled within the first few weeks of the semester because of the rule limiting students to 11 absences. She defines herself as a productive student, yet because of her medical condition, she is restricted from participating in an education she would otherwise value greatly. She says AAA has helped her to pursue her goal of graduating from high school and going to college. She also has the advantage of parents, both college educated, who can assist her in negotiating with teachers and administrators.

Daily time frames constructed in the school are also sites of negotiation. AAA minimizes the problems for most students, including those with jobs and children, because it condenses all the school time into 4 hours, compared to 7 hours in regular classes. I was surprised when I overheard students asking the teacher if he would come early in the mornings or on Saturdays so they could spend time on the computer. When asked, none of the students said they would change anything about the times classes are held in AAA. All the working students told me their job schedules worked well with the class schedules. Similarly, the parents in the program have to leave their children in a day care for only 4 hours rather than 7.

Classroom Management

An issue relating to the work context in AAA is the construction or power relations between the actors in the setting. The purported goal of the alternative program is to provide an opportunity for students to get credits in a different manner from that offered in mainstream classes. The staff assumes that the alternative is better because students are self-directed and have freedom to work at their own pace. Because of this, students in AAA have more positive perceptions of the student-teacher relationship than do those in regular classes.

Cause/Effect

> You work at your own pace. Brown doesn't tell you you have to get this work done at this time. It's like you decide how much work you want to do. (Brad, interview 12/1/94)

Cause/Effect

Because of the computer-assisted instruction and self-directed strategy, students do not feel as though they are being judged or treated unfairly by a teacher, as they did in regular classes. In AAA, however, students cannot always expect to be self-directed. This often leads to students being treated in similar ways as in the traditional classrooms. Classroom management by the teacher sometimes conflicts with the autonomy of the students. For example, on several occasions, I overheard the teacher telling students that if the talking continues, he would write them up (a disciplinary measure). This was especially perplexing because the teacher also had told the students recently that he wanted them to use teamwork to solve problems and find answers to questions about their work on the tutorials. Contradicting situations such as these illustrate the malleable power relations within classroom hierarchies, which are usually characterized by the teacher's control over students.[3]

Data

One student demonstrated a technique for managing such ambiguous situations. Jill knows that the teacher usually allows students to talk quietly among themselves. After she was told by the teacher not to talk, she turned to me and said, "Mr. Brown is in a bad mood today." She did not accept the teacher's immediate statement to be quiet; rather, she accepted this as merely a temporary situation, one that would change once the teacher got in a "better mood." Deciding how to act so as to be successful in finding their way through the educational maze becomes a complex, if not difficult, task, especially for students who do not normally conform to the narrow standards of acceptable behavior.

Good example

Interpretation

Effects of Rules and Policies

Interpretation

The policies of the high school and the procedures within AAA promote a working-class ideology. This is illustrated best by the procedure of the timecards for students, on which the teacher keeps track of the exact time students arrive and leave class. The interesting feature of using time cards in the classroom is that it reflects the atmosphere in low-paying jobs, such as manufacturing or service-industry jobs (Anyon, 1980; Bowles & Gintis, 1976). Students in AAA focus more on the amount of time they put into their work than they do on the quality of time

Other evidence?

they put into their work. Perhaps educators have the same low expectations for dropouts or potential dropouts as working-class employers have for their employees.[4] If students think teachers have low expectations of them, they might produce lower-quality of work and consequently "get by" without doing the kind of work they are capable of doing.

The emphasis on attendance was discussed frequently among the students, whom I saw regularly looking at the posted times on the dry erase board. The board indicated which students were falling behind in their hours. Furthermore, the teacher asks students to telephone him if they are going to be absent, rather than simply bringing an excuse note when they return.

In a conversation during their 10-minute break, several students expressed their awareness of the school's strict attendance policies (both in regular classes and in AAA). This was illustrated by their surprise at my description of large college courses.

Anthony: How do they take roll?
CG: They don't.
Anthony: You mean they can come when they want? They don't have to show up? Ah, but they paid for it, so they want to go. (field notes, 12/6/94)

It seemed that Anthony realized as he was speaking that students are not obligated to attend school for the same reasons in college as they are in high school.

Disparate attendance policies point to a subtle difference in students' perceptions of attendance in AAA compared to regular classes. Based on self-reports, the students in AAA have a much higher attendance rate than they did in regular classes. Students repeatedly told me stories of skipping regular classes with little concern for the consequences, despite the rule that students can miss only 11 days of a class before being dismissed for the semester. Conversely, students in AAA place a great deal of importance on coming to class, and especially on making up missed hours, because they have no other options if removed from AAA. In a discussion of students' attendance deficits, Jennie and Jill, both Hispanic females with children, expressed their concern for a close friend, Deborah, who is dealing with some personal problems (breaking up with a drug-addicted boyfriend, being kicked out of her home, and finding child care for her children). Jennie and Jill are concerned that Deborah is getting behind in her work and have a more general concern about other students making it through the AAA program.

Jennie and Jill felt that people who really care will come after lunch to make up their hours: "Deborah just doesn't care. " They gave Anthony as an example of someone who is really dedicated. "He is in here every day after lunch" (field notes, 10/18/94).   *Good example*

The students stress the importance of individual responsibility when explaining behavior, another attitude distinct from their explanations of regular classes. This theme (was common) in the students' explanations of their failure to follow school policy, or for "messing up." "In the case of drop-outs, since individualism means that everyone has an equal chance to succeed irrespective of their personal or family circumstances, failure can only be attributed to deficiencies in the individual" (Stevenson & Ellsworth, 1993, p. 270). The students implicitly define the rules as "right" and the people not following the rules as "wrong."   *Results*

Banking Education

Regarding the education of illiterates in Latin America, Paulo Freire said that "education is suffering from narration sickness" (1993, p. 52). Furthermore,

The teacher talks about reality as if it were motionless, static, compartmentalized, and predictable. Or else he expounds on a topic completely alien to the existential experience of the students. His task is to "fill" the students with the contents of his narration—contents which are detached from reality, disconnected from the totality that engendered them and could find them significant. (Freire, 1993, p. 52)

These characteristics of education seem to describe not only education in Third World countries but also the experiences of the students I encountered in AAA.

Interpretation

The founders of comprehensive education envisioned public schools as places where the "skills of democracy can be practiced, debated, and analyzed" (Giroux, 1988, p. 114). Education in AAA is nothing like this vision. Students are expected to passively absorb information they receive via computer programs, which act as the teachers. Students, therefore, do not play an active role in the production of knowledge; rather, they comply with the ideological assumption that knowledge is not necessarily created but transferred from one source to another. This assumption arises from the conservative notion of education in which knowledge is a "storehouse of artifacts" (Giroux, 1988). Somewhere, a computer programmer inputs a specified body of knowledge that allegedly includes the basic core of information that high-school students should know. The students then unquestioningly accept this information as "true."

The knowledge students obtain in this setting is structured more by the goals of maintaining order, minimizing complications, and maximizing efficiency. Giroux (1988) states:

> Student voice and experience is reduced to the immediacy of its performance and exists as something to be measured, administered, registered, and controlled. Its distinctiveness, its disjunctions, its lived quality are all dissolved under an ideology of control and management. In the name of efficiency, the resources and wealth of student life histories are generally ignored. (p. 122)

The lack of student participation in the construction of knowledge in AAA is evidenced by students' descriptions of the work they do: "I mean there's times I get bored with it because you get the same chair, the same screen, the same stuff every day."

The elimination of distractions and complicated interactions makes the experience simpler; however, students also complain that this lack of interaction is frustrating and boring. Students in AAA do not actively engage in the production of knowledge by discussing and critically thinking about ideas. By controlling the pace of learning and the amount of effort exerted, the students feel empowered. One student says, "I'm learning more in here, because this way I don't really have a choice. You can't just get up and walk out. I mean I could, but I don't want to, because nobody is telling me what to do."

Although the students do not participate in knowledge production, they have resisted the status quo by leaving the mainstream classes and enrolling in an alternative educational setting. By disengaging from regular classes, they act as nonconformists, as social critics (Fine, 1991). They acquire a sense of ownership over their education, which also engenders a sense of power over their own lives. They have positive attitudes toward the program and "stick with it" because they feel, ironically, privileged for being able to participate in the program. They appreciate this second chance.

CONCLUSIONS

Not clear to us

The designers of AAA seem to have created an effective alternative for helping at-risk students remain in school and acquire credits toward a high-school diploma. According to the students, the program is a successful alternative. The students suggested both implicitly and explicitly that without AAA, they would not be in school. The program, however, does little to help students create and apply practical knowledge in their everyday lives, nor does it help students to acquire the skills for either fitting into the dominant culture or surviving as resisters of that culture. Furthermore, because the program is voluntary and has a limited enrollment, it is not catching every student who drops out. In these respects, it may be viewed as a dumping ground.

Students enrolling in programs such as AAA often have problems interacting with others in the conventional setting (Gold & Mann, 1982). These problems may stem from, among other reasons, lack of skill at negotiating with teachers or lack of compliance with the rules of the classroom. If educators provide an alternative setting for students lacking the social skills *to get by* in regular classes, then it seems counterproductive to place these students in a setting where they will not learn how to improve those skills. In essence, these programs act as holding tanks for those who do not "fit in" so that conflict is reduced in mainstream classes.   } True of sample?

Many alternative programs, particularly dropout-prevention programs, purport to offer students true alternatives to traditional classes or schools. To provide useful information to educators and researchers for adapting programs or creating new ones to better serve students, it would be beneficial to know whether a program is truly an alternative or just a modification of the traditional format. Students in AAA define the program as markedly different from regular classes, primarily because of the breakdown of power relations between teachers and students. In contrast, the students describe the learning process in AAA and regular classes similarly—the focus is on credits and the passive absorption of information.

Educators and administrators of urban youth face a variety of challenges in developing genuine educational alternatives. The larger problem stems from structural issues rather than individual student issues (i.e., current economic structures in a postindustrial era limiting the job, health, and housing opportunities of urban youth).

> While many view schools and education as the keys to solving the problems of drugs, crime, poverty, and the myriad of urban ills, the opposite is more the reality: The success of urban schools is dependent upon our nation's health, criminal justice, economic, and other systems. (Raffel, Boyd, Briggs, Eubanks, & Fernandez, 1992, p. 264)

We must assume, nevertheless, that schools can make a difference for urban youth.

Based on my interaction with administrators and teachers involved with one alternative program, it appears that educators are limited in the types of alternatives they can provide by their own lack of vision. We commonly hear complaints about district regulations or other entities governing curriculum, staffing, and other matters (see Raffel et al., 1992). Without changing the educational strategies, however, we can expect the same outcomes. In other words, if we do not alter the current practices, or at least offer students true alternatives, students will be alienated, disengage from schools, and drop out at the same rates, or more so. In discussing the reform of urban education, Lytle (1990) calls for a rethinking of educational practices that currently do not seem to be working for a growing number of youth.   } Need data

> Even the most vocal of the advocates [of urban school reform] accept urban schools in their present form; improvement is considered a matter of modifying staffing, policy, and resource allocation practices. None of the advocates entertains the possibility that urban schools as currently organized might be inappropriate for educating disadvantaged students. (p. 219)

Along these same lines, providing alternative programs such as AAA seems to be a band-aid approach to "solving the dropout problem." Although it does appear successful at retaining students and aiding them in acquiring credits, it is unclear whether it can give students the educational experiences needed to successfully cope with their problematic circumstances.   } We agree

To understand better the challenges of creating true alternatives, we could greatly benefit from research that examines the way alternative programs within school systems initially get created. Unfortunately, research in this area is inadequate. Furthermore, because I focused narrowly on student perceptions of their situation, I did not gather any substantial data on administrators' perceptions. Acquiring administrators' views may aid in understanding administrators' intentions and, thus, the dynamics of working within a set of policies. Without critical analysis of school policies, little is done to promote the best possible environment for students to learn and become contributing members of society.   Suggestions for future research

Recognizes limitations

> Regarding the usefulness of my findings, I think several issues are important. First, data obtained for my analysis and interpretation came from a sample of 25 students and a few faculty members. A better understanding of the situation could be obtained by gathering more information from family members and from other students and teachers in regular classes, or by investigating other programs in other schools. Second, such a small sample and a single-case study limit the generalizability of the results.

Finally, studying the longitudinal effects of participating in programs such as AAA could greatly inform this discussion. Longitudinal data would enable a better understanding of the degree to which students find the knowledge they gain in a program practical, and of whether the students continue to experience the success, both academic and personal, they described having in AAA.

Research on high-school dropouts and the programs designed to help this population need more attention. This project demonstrates the need to examine not only the characteristics of students at risk of dropping out but also the perceptions and experiences of students and faculty. The interaction among actors in public schools provides invaluable information for understanding the problems within public schools, and it should not be overlooked.

Notes

1. Preventing students from dropping out becomes increasingly salient at the high school level because of the increased visibility of the problems resulting from leaving school early (Natriello, 1996). These programs, therefore, are aimed primarily at secondary students.

2. I have changed the name of this program to maintain anonymity for the subjects of this study.

3. Ritzer (1993) discusses this notion of control in educational settings. He states:

> Not only are students taught to be obedient to authority, but also to be receptive to the rationalized procedures of rote learning and objective testing. More important, spontaneity and creativity tend not be rewarded, and may even be discouraged, leading to what one expert calls "education for docility." (p. 115)

4. This type of treatment may be occurring in the regular classes of the high school as well, but without extending this project to examine those settings, it is impossible to determine.

References

Anyon, J. (1980). Social class and the hidden curriculum of work. *Journal of Education, 162*:67–92.

Ascher, C. (1982). ERIC/CUE: Alternative schools—some answers and questions. *The Urban Review, 14*:65–69.

Bowles, S., & Gintis, H. (1976). *Schooling in capitalist America: Education and the contradictions of economic life.* New York: Basic Books.

Catterall, J. S. (1985). *A process model of dropping out of school: Implications for research and policy in an era of raised academic standards* (Grant No. OERIG860003). Los Angeles: University of California, Los Angeles, Center for the Study of Evaluation. (ERIC Document Reproduction Service No. ED 271 837)

Catterall, J. S., & Stern, D. (1986). The effects of alternative school programs on high school completion and labor market outcomes. *Educational Evaluation and Policy Analysis, 8*:77–86.

Collins, R. L. (1987). Parents' views of alternative public school programs: Implications for the use of alternative programs to reduce school dropout rates. *Education and Urban Society, 19*:290–302.

Deal, T. E., & Nolan, R. R. (1978). Alternative schools: A conceptual map. *School Review, 87*(1):29–49.

Dei, G. J. S. (1996). Black youth and fading out of school. In D. Kelly & J. Gaskell (eds.), *Debating dropouts: Critical policy and research perspectives on school leaving* (pp. 173–189). New York: Teachers College Record.

Duke, D. L., & Perry, C. (1978). Can alternative schools succeed where Benjamin Spock, Spiro Agnew, and B. F. Skinner have failed? *Adolescence, 13*:375–392.

Erickson, F. (1986). Qualitative methods in research on teaching. In M. C. Wittrock (Ed.). *Handbook of research on teaching* (3rd ed., pp. 119–161). New York: Macmillan.

Fine, M. (1991). *Framing dropouts: Notes on the politics of an urban public high school.* Albany: State University of New York Press.

Franklin, C. (1992). Alternative school programs for at-risk youth. *Social Work in Education. 14*:239–251.

Freire, P. (1993). *Pedagogy of the oppressed.* New York: Continuum.

Giroux, H. A. (1988). *Schooling and the struggle for public life.* Minneapolis: University of Minnesota Press.

Gold, M., & Mann, D. W. (1982). Alternative schools for troublesome secondary students. *The Urban Review, 14*:305–316.

Kelly, D. M. (1993). *Last chance high: How girls and boys drop in and out of alternative schools.* New Haven, CT: Yale University Press.

Kelly, D. (1996). "Choosing" the alternative: Conflicting missions and constrained choice in a dropout prevention program. In D. Kelly & J. Gaskell (Eds.), *Debating dropouts: Critical policy and research perspectives on school leaving* (pp. 101–122). New York: Teachers College Record.

LeCompte, M. D. (1987). The cultural context of dropping out: Why remedial programs fail to solve the problem. *Education and Urban Society, 19*(3):232–249.

Levin, H. M. (1972). *The costs to the nation of inadequate education.* Washington, DC: U.S. Senate Select Committee on Equal Education Opportunity.

Lytle, J. H. (1990). Reforming urban education: A review of recent reports and legislation. *The Urban Review, 22*(3):199–220.

Natriello, G. (1996). Evaluation processes and student disengagement from high school. *Sociology of Education and Socialization, 11*:147–172.

Raffel, J. A., Boyd, W. L., Briggs, V. M., Eubanks, E. E., & Fernandez, R. (1992). Policy dilemmas in urban education: Addressing the needs of poor, at-risk children. *Journal of Urban Affairs, 14*(3–4):263–289.

Reilly, D. H., & Reilly, J. L. (1983). Alternative schools: Issues and directions. *Journal of Instructional Psychology, 10*(2):89–98.

Ritzer, G. (1993). *The McDonaldization of society.* Thousand Oaks, CA: Pine Forge.

Stevenson, R. B., & Ellsworth, J. (1993). Dropouts and the silencing of critical voices. In L. Weis & M. Fine (Eds.), *Beyond silenced voices: Class, race, and gender in United States schools* (pp. 259–271). New York: State University of New York Press.

Wehlage, G. G., Rutter, R. A., Smith, G. A., Lesko, N., & Fernandez, R. R. (1989). *Reducing the risk: Schools as communities of support.* London: Falmer.

Analysis of the Study

PURPOSE

The purpose is not clearly stated. By inference, it is to clarify whether urban dropout prevention programs are effective alternatives to regular classes or simply "dumping grounds for unwanted students."

JUSTIFICATION

The justification is extensive and usually documented. Points include: negative effects of dropping out, the need for and variety of alternative programs, the impact of the broader society, the paucity and poor quality of previous research, the tendency to blame the students, increasing diversity of students, and the allegation that the programs are "dumping grounds." With regard to ethical issues, we see no problems of risk. Presumably, confidentiality was maintained. It would be helpful to know what participants were told regarding the purpose of the study and potential uses of the findings. The author's values are evident as are 'social consequences'. We think these are generally clear to the reader.

DEFINITIONS

No definitions are provided. The term "dropout" is probably sufficiently understood, though there are variations in usage. In this study it apparently was taken to mean "students who have either dropped out of school or were in the process of dropping out at the time of the enrollment in the program." Other key terms, some emerging during the study, as is common in such studies are: "effective alternative," "problematic student-teacher relationship," "negotiating behavior," "banking education," and "practical knowledge." Although these may be clear from the discussion and examples, definitions would help.

PRIOR RESEARCH

Most prior research is included as justification or discussion. The work of the "few researchers (who) have studied the interactional dynamics between students and teachers to determine the effectiveness of the programs" should have been reported.

HYPOTHESES

As is typical in ethnographic research, no hypotheses are stated, at the outset nor do any emerge during the study. The tenor of the report, particularly the first three introductory sections, suggests that a hypothesis could have been stated as: dropout programs are more like dumping grounds than effective alternatives to regular classes.

SAMPLING

The purposive sample consisted of 25 students and their teacher, aide, counselor, and program director in a particular alternative program. Age and ethnicity of students are given. Students in the program must have actively sought entry and were selected from a waiting list based on potential benefit to them and to match the ethnic characteristics of the school.

INSTRUMENTATION

The author states that "participant observation" was the method, though it is not always clear how participation occurred. The primary source of information used in relation to the findings is individual interviews. No evidence on reliability and validity is presented, though it appears that checking information across different sources (triangulation) was possible. The topics addressed in the interviews are provided.

PROCEDURES/INTERNAL VALIDITY

Little procedural detail is given beyond "weekly and daily" (?) site visits (how many?), observing everyday activities, attending biweekly "focus group" meetings led by the counselor, and individual recorded interviews. The program studied is described as entirely computer work. Description of class activities and the role of the teacher are provided.

Internal validity is largely irrelevant because relationships were not directly studied. Some, however, are included in the findings section and must be considered in the absence of clear-cut controls or data. All are subject to possible threats due to data collector characteristics and/or bias, subject characteristics (e.g., self-insight), and subject attitude.

DATA ANALYSIS

As is common in ethnographic research, no formal analysis was done; instead a narrative is provided with examples. Organization under five categories is helpful. More quantification, as is done with respect to "wanting a diploma" (all but one), would be helpful. For example, how many of the 25 students felt they were treated fairly?

RESULTS/DISCUSSION

Results are presented as "findings" supported in part by examples, in part by assertions such as "most students," and partly by reference to other writers. It is virtually impossible to distinguish results from interpretation. Use of examples is often helpful in clarification, but the reader must trust that the findings accurately reflect the information. In some cases, interpretation goes far beyond the data, and this may not be clear to the reader. For example, although we agree that "banking education" is contrary to the goals of comprehensive education and that this program cannot prepare students for everyday life, these opinions do not follow closely from the information provided and, in our opinion, require better argumentation.

Some findings describe cause-and-effect relationships and often are open to question. Examples are: "*because* the students enrolled in AAA take measures to pursue their education, they treat the program as a privilege"; "if educators provide an alternative setting for students lacking the social skills to get by in regular classes [not, we think, demonstrated for these students], then it seems counterproductive to place these students in a setting where they *will not* learn how to improve these skills"; the conclusion that the policies of the high school and the procedures within AAA promote a working-class ideology" is supported only by evidence on use of time cards.

This study illustrates both the richness of such research and the difficulty in arriving at clear-cut conclusions. The author properly recognizes limitations due to sampling and scope of data gathering and recommends a longitudinal approach to future research. We would add that the study also suggests many topics for more direct investigation.

Go back to the **Interactive and Applied Learning Tools** feature at the beginning of the chapter for a listing of interactive and applied activities. Go to the **Online Learning Center** at www.mhhe.com/fraenkel5e or your **Interactive Student CD-ROM** to take practice quizzes and receive immediate feedback, practice with key terms, review chapter content and main ideas, and find annotated Web links.

Main Points

THE NATURE AND VALUE OF ETHNOGRAPHIC RESEARCH

- Ethnographic research is particularly appropriate for behaviors that are best understood by observing them within their natural settings.
- The key techniques in all ethnographic studies are in-depth interviewing and highly detailed, almost continual, ongoing participant observation of a situation.
- A key strength of ethnographic research is that it provides the researcher with a much more comprehensive perspective than do other forms of educational research.

ETHNOGRAPHIC CONCEPTS

- Important concepts in ethnographic research include *culture, holistic outlook, thick description contextualization, a nonjudgmental orientation, emic perspective, member checking,* and *multiple realities.*

TOPICS THAT LEND THEMSELVES WELL TO ETHNOGRAPHIC RESEARCH

- These include topics that defy simple quantification; those that can best be understood in a natural setting; those that involve studying individual or group activities over time; those that involve studying the roles that individuals play and the behaviors associated with those roles; those that involve studying the activities and behaviors of groups as a unit; and those that involve studying formal organizations in their totality.

SAMPLING IN ETHNOGRAPHIC RESEARCH

- The sample in ethnographic studies is almost always purposive.
- The data obtained from ethnographic research samples rarely, if ever, permit generalization to a population.

THE USE OF HYPOTHESES IN ETHNOGRAPHIC RESEARCH

- Ethnographic researchers seldom formulate precise hypotheses ahead of time. Rather, they develop them as their study emerges.

DATA COLLECTION AND ANALYSIS IN ETHNOGRAPHIC RESEARCH

- The two major means of data collection in ethnographic research are participant observation and detailed interviewing.
- Researchers use a variety of instruments in ethnographic studies to collect data and to check validity. This is frequently referred to as "triangulation."
- Analysis consists of continual reworking of data with emphasis on patterns, key events, and use of visual representations in addition to interviews and observations.

FIELDWORK

- Field notes are the notes a researcher in an ethnographic study takes in the field. They include both descriptive field notes (what he or she sees and hears) and reflective field notes (what he or she thinks about what has been observed).
- "Field jottings" refer to quick notes about something the researcher wants to write more about later.
- A field diary is a personal statement of the researcher's feelings and opinions about the people and situations he or she is observing.
- A field log is a sort of running account of how the researcher plans to spend his or her time compared to how he or she actually spends it.

ADVANTAGES AND DISADVANTAGES OF ETHNOGRAPHIC RESEARCH

- A key strength of ethnographic research is that it provides a much more comprehensive perspective than other forms of educational research. It lends itself well to topics that are not easily quantified. Also, it is particularly appropriate to studying behaviors best understood in their natural settings.
- Like all research, ethnographic research also has its limitations. It is highly dependent on the particular researcher's observations. Furthermore, some observer bias is almost impossible to eliminate. Lastly, generalization is practically nonexistent.

Key Terms

1. A major criticism of ethnographic research is that there is no way for the researcher to be totally objective about what he or she observes. Would you agree? What might an ethnographer say to rebut this charge?

2. Ethnographic studies are rarely replicated. Why do you suppose this is so? Might they be? If so, how?

3. What would you say is the most difficult aspect of ethnographic research? Why?

4. What do you think is the biggest advantage of ethnographic research? The biggest disadvantage? Explain your thinking.

5. Would you be willing to be a participant in an ethnographic study? Why or why not?

6. Supporters of qualitative research say that it can do something that no other type of research can do. If true, what might this be? Would this be especially true of ethnography?

7. Are there any kinds of information that other types of research can provide *better* than ethnographic research? If so, what might they be?

8. How would you compare ethnographic research to the other types of research we have discussed in this book in terms of difficulty? Explain your reasoning.

1. H. R. Bernard (1994). *Research methods in cultural anthropology,* 2nd ed. Beverly Hills, CA: Sage, p. 137.

2. H. F. Wolcott (1966). Quoted in J. R. Creswell (2002). *Educational research: Planning, conducting, and evaluating qualitative and quantitativ research.* Columbus, OH: Merrill Prentice-Hall, p. 60.

3. G. McPherson (1972). *Small-town teacher.* Cambridge, MA: Harvard University.

4. F. Erickson and G. Mohatt (1982). Cultural organization of participation structures in two classrooms of Indian students. In G. Spindler (1982). *Doing the ethnography of schooling.* New York: Holt, Rinehart & Winston, pp. 132–175.

5. C. R. Finnan (1982). The ethnography of children's play. In G. Spindler, op. cit., pp. 356–380.

6. S. B. Palonsky (1975). Hempies and squeaks, truckers and cruisers: A participant observer study in a city high school. *Educational Administration Quarterly, 11*(2): 86–103.

7. C. Ellis (1995) The other side of the fence: Seeing black and white in a small southern town. *Qualitative Inquiry, 1*(2): 147–167.

8. P. A. Cusick (1973). *Inside high school: The student's perspective.* New York: Holt, Rinehart & Winston.

9. H. S. Becker, B. Greer, E. C. Hughes, and A. Strauss (1961). *Boys in white: Student culture in medical school.* Chicago: University of Chicago Press.

10. E. Babbie (1998). *The practice of social research,* 8th ed. Belmont, CA: Wadsworth, pp. 241–242.

11. M. Harris (1968). *The rise of anthropological theory.* New York: Thomas Y. Crowell, p. 16.

12. David M. Fetterman (1989). *Ethnography: Step by step.* Thousand Oaks, CA: Sage, p. 27.

13. Ibid.

14. Ibid., p. 28.

15. Ibid., p. 31.

16. Ibid., p. 33.

17. Ibid., p. 45.

18. Ibid., pp. 46–47.

19. For a good description of field notes, see Chapter Four in R. C. Bogdan and S. K. Biklen (1998). *Qualitative research in education: An introduction to theory and practice,* 3rd ed. Boston: Allyn & Bacon.

20. Bernard, op. cit., pp. 181–186.

21. Bernard, op. cit., p. 185.

22. Bogdan and Bicklen, op. cit., p. 121.

23. Ibid., excerpted from pp. 109–120.

24. Fetterman, op. cit., pp. 91–92.

25. Ibid., p. 93.

26. Ibid., p. 101.

27. From the Familiar to the Strange and Back Again. In G. Spindler, op. cit.

Historical Research

CHAPTER 22

Historical Research

What Is Historical Research?

The Purposes of Historical Research
What Kinds of Questions Are
Pursued Through Historical Research?

Steps Involved in Historical Research

Defining the Problem
Locating Relevant Sources
Summarizing Information
Obtained from Historical Sources
Evaluating Historical Sources

Data Analysis in Historical Research

Advantages and Disadvantages of Historical Research

Generalization in Historical Research

Objectives

Studying this chapter should enable you to:

- Describe *briefly what historical research involves.*
- State *three purposes of historical research.*
- Give some examples *of the kinds of questions investigated in historical research.*
- Name *and describe briefly the major steps involved in historical research.*
- Give some examples *of historical sources.*
- Distinguish *between primary and secondary sources.*
- Distinguish *between external and internal criticism.*
- Discuss *when generalization in historical research is appropriate.*
- Locate *examples of published historical studies and* critique *some of the strengths and weaknesses of these studies.*
- Recognize *an example of a historical study when you come across one in the literature.*

Interactive and Applied Learning

After, or while, reading this chapter:

Go to your Interactive Student CD-ROM to:
- Learn More About Primary vs. Secondary Sources

Go to your Interactive Student CD-ROM or Student Workbook to do the following activities:
- Activity 22.1: Historical Research Questions
- Activity 22.2: Primary or Secondary Source?
- Activity 22.3: What Kind of Historical Source?
- Activity 22.4: True or False?

Hey Becky!"

"Hey, Brent, where ya' been?"

"Library. Trying to come up with a topic for my research study."

"How's it going?"

"Pretty good. I think I have an idea. You know, they want to introduce this new reading program—sort of a modified "look-say" approach—in some of the elementary schools in our district next year, but I sort of have my doubts about it."

"How come?"

"Well, the administration keeps praising it to the skies, but I haven't seen any evidence that it will work any better than the program we now use. Plus it's pretty expensive. I'm on the curriculum advisory council, you know, and I'd like to find out whether it's as effective as they say before we recommend spending a lot of money to buy all of the program materials. So . . ."

"Hey. Sounds like you've found your topic. Some kind of study of the program's past effectiveness (or lack thereof) might be just the ticket, eh?"

"Right! A little historical research is called for here, I think."

We agree. Brent might indeed do a historical study, or perhaps locate one that has already been done. What this involves is what this chapter is about.

What Is Historical Research?

Historical research takes a somewhat different tack than much of the other research we have described. There is, of course, no manipulation or control of variables like there is in experimental research, but more particularly, it is unique in that it focuses primarily on the *past*. As we mentioned in Chapter One, some aspect of the past is studied, by perusing documents of the period, by examining relics, or by interviewing individuals who lived during the time. An attempt is then made to reconstruct what happened during that time as completely and as accurately as possible, and (usually) to explain why it happened—although this can never be fully accomplished, since information from and about the past is always incomplete. Historical research, then, is the systematic collection and evaluation of data to describe, explain, and thereby understand actions or events that occurred sometime in the past.

THE PURPOSES OF HISTORICAL RESEARCH

Educational researchers undertake historical studies for a variety of reasons:

1. To make people aware of what has happened in the past so they may learn from past failures and successes. A researcher might be interested, for example, in investigating why a particular curriculum modification (such as a new "inquiry-oriented" Eng-

lish curriculum) succeeded in some school districts but not in others.

2. To learn how things were done in the past to see if they might be applicable to present-day problems and concerns. Rather than "reinventing the wheel," for example, it often may be wiser to look to the past to see if a proposed innovation has not been tried before. Sometimes an idea proposed as "a radical innovation" is not all that new. Along this line, the "review of literature" that we discussed in detail in Chapter Five, which is done as a part of many other kinds of studies, is a kind of historical research. Often a review of the literature will show that what we think is new has been done before (and surprisingly many times!).

3. To assist in prediction. If a particular idea or approach has been tried before, even under somewhat different circumstances, past results may offer policymakers some ideas about how present plans may turn out. Thus, if "language laboratories" have been found effective (or the reverse) in certain school districts in the past, a district contemplating their use would have evidence upon which to base its own decisions.

4. To test hypotheses concerning relationships or trends. Many inexperienced researchers tend to think of historical research as purely descriptive in nature. When well-designed and carefully executed, however, historical research can lead to the confirmation

or rejection of relational hypotheses as well. Here are some examples of hypotheses that would lend themselves to historical research:

a. In the early 1900s, most female teachers came from the upper middle class, but most male teachers did not.

b. Curriculum changes that did not involve extensive planning and participation by the teachers involved usually failed.

c. Nineteenth-century social studies textbooks show increasing reference to the contributions of women to the culture of the United States from 1800 to 1900.

d. Secondary school teachers have enjoyed greater prestige than elementary school teachers since 1940.

Many other hypotheses are possible, of course; the ones above are intended to illustrate only that historical research can lend itself to hypothesis-testing studies.

5. To understand present educational practices and policies more fully. Many current practices in education are by no means new. Inquiry teaching, character education, open classrooms, an emphasis on "basics," Socratic teaching, the use of case studies, individualized instruction, team teaching, and teaching "laboratories" are but a few of many ideas that reappear from time to time as "the" salvation for education.

WHAT KINDS OF QUESTIONS ARE PURSUED THROUGH HISTORICAL RESEARCH?

Although historical research focuses on the past, the types of questions that lend themselves to historical research are quite varied. Here are some examples:

- How were students educated in the South during the Civil War?
- How many bills dealing with education were passed during the presidency of Lyndon B. Johnson, and what was the major intent of those bills?
- What was instruction like in a typical fourth-grade classroom 100 years ago?
- How have working conditions for teachers changed since 1900?
- What were the major discipline problems in schools in 1940 as compared to today?
- What educational issues has the general public perceived to be most important during the last 20 years?

- How have the ideas of John Dewey influenced present-day educational practices?
- How have feminists contributed to education?
- How have minorities (or the physically impaired) been treated in our public schools during the twentieth century?
- How were the policies and practices of school administrators in the early years of this century different from those today?
- What has been the role of the federal government in education?

Steps Involved in Historical Research

There are four essential steps involved in doing a historical study in education. These include defining the problem or question to be investigated (including the formulation of hypotheses if appropriate); locating relevant sources of historical information; summarizing and evaluating the information obtained from these sources; and presenting and interpreting this information as it relates to the problem or question that originated the study.

DEFINING THE PROBLEM

In the simplest sense, the purpose of a historical study in education is to describe clearly and accurately some aspect of the past as it related to education and/or schooling. As we mentioned previously, however, historical researchers aim to do more than just describe; they want to go beyond description to clarify and explain, and sometimes to correct (as when a researcher finds previous accounts of an action or event to be in error).

Historical research problems, therefore, are identified in much the same way as are problems studied through other types of research. Like any research problem, they should be clearly and concisely stated, be manageable, have a defensible rationale, and (if appropriate) investigate a hypothesized relationship among variables. A concern somewhat unique to historical research is that a problem may be selected for study for which insufficient data are available. Often important data of interest (certain kinds of documents, such as diaries or maps, from a particular period) simply cannot be located in historical research. This is particularly true the further back in the past an investigator looks. As a result, it is better to study in depth a well-defined problem that is perhaps more narrow than one would like than to pursue a more broadly stated problem that cannot be sharply defined, or fully resolved. As with all research, the nature of the problem or hypothesis guides the study; if it is well-defined, the investigator is off to a good start.

Some examples of historical studies that have been published are as follows:

- "The Schooling Process in First Grade: Two Samples a Decade Apart"[1]
- "Teacher Survival Rate in St. Louis, 1969–1982"[2]
- Women Teachers on the Frontier[3]
- "Origins of the Modern Social Studies"[4]
- "Missing the Mark: Intelligence Testing in Los Angeles Public Schools, 1922–1932"[5]
- "The Responses of American Indian Children to Presbyterian Schooling in the Nineteenth Century: An Analysis Through Missionary Sources"[6]
- "The 1960s and the Transformation of Campus Cultures"[7]
- "Emma Willard: Pioneer in Social Studies Education"[8]
- "Inquiry into Educational Administration: The Last 25 Years and the Next"[9]
- "Bertrand Russell and Education in World Citizenship"[10]
- "The Decline in Age at Leaving Home, 1920–1979"[11]

LOCATING RELEVANT SOURCES

Categories of Sources. Once a researcher has decided on the problem or question he or she wishes to investigate, the search for sources begins. Just about everything that has been written down in some form or other, and virtually every object imaginable, is a potential source for historical research. In general, however, historical source material can be grouped into four basic categories: documents, numerical records, oral statements and records, and relics.

1. **Documents:** Documents are written or printed materials that have been produced in some form or another—annual reports, artwork, bills, books, cartoons, circulars, court records, diaries, diplomas, legal records, newspapers, magazines, notebooks, school yearbooks, memos, tests, and so on. They may be handwritten, printed, typewritten, drawn, or sketched; they may be published or unpublished; they may be intended for private or public consumption; they may be original works or copies. In short, "documents" refers to any kind of information that exists in some type of written or printed form.

2. **Numerical records:** Numerical records can be considered either as a separate type of source in and of themselves or as a subcategory of documents. Such records include any type of numerical data in printed form: test scores, attendance figures, census reports, school budgets, and the like. In recent years, historical researchers are making increasing use of computers to analyze the vast amounts of numerical data that are available to them.

3. **Oral statements:** Another valuable source of information for the historical researcher lies in the statements people make orally. Stories, myths, tales, legends, chants, songs, and other forms of oral expression have been used by people down through the ages to leave a record for future generations. But historians can also conduct *oral interviews* with people who were a part of or witnessed past events. This is a special form of historical research, called *oral history,* which is currently undergoing somewhat of a renaissance.

4. **Relics:** The fourth type of historical source is the relic. A *relic* is any object whose physical or visual characteristics can provide some information about the past. Examples include furniture, artwork, clothing, buildings, monuments, or equipment.

Following are different examples of historical sources.

- A primer used in a seventeenth-century schoolroom.
- A diary kept by a woman teacher on the Ohio frontier in the 1800s.
- The written arguments for and against a new school bond issue as published in a newspaper at a particular time.
- A 1958 junior high school yearbook.
- Samples of clothing worn by students in the early nineteenth century in rural Georgia.
- High school graduation diplomas from the 1920s.
- A written memo from a school superintendent to his faculty.
- Attendance records from two different school districts over a 40-year period.
- Essays written by elementary school children during the Civil War.

- Test scores attained by students in various states at different times.
- The architectural plans for a school to be organized around flexible scheduling.
- A taped oral interview with a secretary of education who served in the administrations of three different presidents of the United States.

Primary Versus Secondary Sources. As in all research, it is important to distinguish between primary and secondary sources. A **primary source** is one prepared by an individual who was a participant in or a direct witness to the event being described. An eyewitness account of the opening of a new school would be an example, as would the reporting of the results of an experiment carried out directly by a researcher. Other examples of primary source material are as follows:

- A nineteenth-century teacher's account of what it was like to live with a frontier family.
- A transcript of an oral interview conducted in the 1960s with the superintendent of a large urban school district concerning the problems his district faces.
- Essays written during World War II by students in response to the question, "What do you like most and least about school?"
- Songs composed by members of a high school glee club in the 1930s.
- Minutes of a school board meeting in 1878, taken by the secretary of the board.
- A paid consultant's written evaluation of a new French curriculum adopted in 1985 by a particular school district.
- A photograph of an eighth-grade graduating class in 1930.
- Letters written between an American student and a Japanese student describing their school experiences during the Korean conflict.

A **secondary source,** on the other hand, is a document prepared by an individual who was not a direct witness to an event, but who obtained his or her description of the event from someone else. They are "one step removed," so to speak, from the event. A newspaper editorial commenting on a recent teachers' strike would be an example. Other examples of secondary source material are as follows:

- An encyclopedia entry describing various types of educational research conducted over a 10-year period.

- A magazine article summarizing Aristotle's views on education.
- A newspaper account of a school board meeting based on oral interviews with members of the board.
- A book describing schooling in the New England colonies during the 1700s.
- A parent's description of a conversation (at which she was not present) between her son and his teacher.
- A student's report to her counselor of why her teacher said she was being suspended from school.
- A textbook (including this one) on educational research.

Whenever possible, historians (like other researchers) want to use primary rather than secondary sources. Can you see why?* Unfortunately, primary sources are admittedly more difficult to acquire, especially the further back in time a researcher searches. Secondary sources are of necessity, therefore, used quite extensively in historical research. If it is at all possible, however, the use of primary sources is preferred.

SUMMARIZING INFORMATION OBTAINED FROM HISTORICAL SOURCES

The process of reviewing and extracting data from historical sources is essentially the one described in Chapter Five—determining the relevancy of the particular material to the question or problem being investigated; recording the full bibliographic data of the source; organizing the data one collects under categories related to the problem being studied; and summarizing pertinent information (important facts, quotations, and questions) on note cards (see Chapter Five).

For an example of organizing data, consider a study investigating the daily activities that occurred in nineteenth-century elementary schoolrooms. A researcher might organize his or her facts under such categories as "subjects taught," "learning activities," "play activities," and "class rules."

Reading and summarizing historical data is rarely, if ever, a neat, orderly sequence of steps to be followed, however. Often reading and writing are interspersed. Edward J. Carr, a noted historian, provides the following description of how historians engage in research:

---

*When a researcher must rely on secondary data sources, he or she increases the chance of the data being less detailed and/or less accurate. The accuracy of what is being reported also becomes more difficult to check.

[A common] assumption [among lay people] appears to be that the historian divides his work into two sharply distinguishable phases or periods. First, he spends a long preliminary period reading his sources and filling his notebooks with facts; then, when this is over he puts away his sources, takes out his notebooks, and writes his book from beginning to end. This is to me an unconvincing and unplausible picture. For myself, as soon as I have got going on a few of what I take to be the capital sources, the itch becomes too strong and I begin to write—not necessarily at the beginning, but somewhere, anywhere. Thereafter, reading and writing go on simultaneously. The writing is added to, subtracted from, reshaped, and cancelled, as I go on reading. The reading is guided and directed and made fruitful by the writing; the more I write, the more I know what I am looking for, the better I understand the significance and relevance of what I find.[12]

EVALUATING HISTORICAL SOURCES

Perhaps more so than in any other form of research, the historical researcher must adopt a critical attitude toward any and all sources he or she reviews. A researcher can never be sure about the genuineness and accuracy of historical sources. A memo may have been written by someone other than the person whose signature one finds on it. A letter may refer to events that did not occur, or that occurred at a different time or in a different place. A document may have been forged or information deliberately falsified. Key questions for any historical researcher are:

- Was this document really written by the supposed author (i.e., is it *genuine*)?
- Is the information contained in this document true (i.e., is it *accurate*)?

The first question refers to what is known as *external criticism,* the second to what is known as *internal criticism.*

External Criticism. **External criticism** refers to the genuineness of any and all documents the researcher uses. Researchers engaged in historical research want to know whether or not the documents they find were really prepared by the (supposed) author(s) of the document. Obviously, falsified documents can (and sometimes do) lead to erroneous conclusions. Several questions come to mind in evaluating the genuineness of a historical source.

- *Who* wrote this document? Was the author living at that time? Some historical documents have been shown to be *forgeries*. An article supposedly written by, say, Martin Luther King, Jr., might actually have been prepared by someone wishing to tarnish his reputation.
- *For what purpose* was the document written? For whom was it intended? And why? (Toward whom was a memo from a school superintendent directed? What was the intent of the memo?)
- *When* was the document written? Is the date on the document accurate? Could the details described have actually happened during this time? (Sometimes people write the date of the previous year on correspondence in the first days of a new year.)
- *Where* was the document written? Could the details described have occurred in this location? (A description of an inner-city school supposedly written by a teacher in Fremont, Nebraska, might well be viewed with caution.)
- *Under what conditions* was the document written? Is there any possibility that what was written might have been directly or subtly coerced? (A description of a particular school's curriculum and administration prepared by a committee of nontenured teachers might give quite a different view than one written by those who have tenure.)
- Do *different forms or versions* of the document exist? (Sometimes two versions of a letter are found with nearly identical wording and only slight differences in handwriting, suggesting that one may be a forgery.)

The important thing to remember with regard to external criticism is that researchers should do their best to ensure that the documents they are using are genuine. The above questions (and others like them) are directed toward this end.

Internal Criticism. Once researchers have satisfied themselves that a source document is genuine, they need to determine if the *contents* of the document are *accurate*. This involves what is known as **internal criticism.** Both the accuracy of the information contained in a document and the truthfulness of the author need to be evaluated. Whereas external criticism has to do with the nature or authenticity of the document itself, internal criticism has to do with what the document says. Is it likely that what the author says happened really did happen? Would people at that time have behaved as

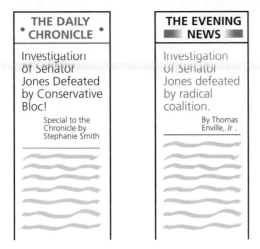

THE DAILY CHRONICLE

Investigation of Senator Jones Defeated by Conservative Bloc!

Special to the Chronicle by Stephanie Smith

THE EVENING NEWS

Investigation of Senator Jones defeated by radical coalition.

By Thomas Enville, Jr.

Figure 22.1 *What Really Happened?*

they are portrayed? Could events have occurred this way? Are the data presented (attendance records, budget figures, test scores, and so on) reasonable? Note, however, that researchers should not dismiss a statement as inaccurate just because it is unlikely—unlikely events do occur. What researchers must determine is whether a particular event *might* have occurred, even if it is unlikely. As with external criticism, several questions need to be asked in attempting to evaluate the accuracy of a document and the truthfulness of its author. See Figure 22.1.

1. *With regard to the author of the document:*
   - Was the author *present* at the event he or she is describing? In other words, is the document a primary or a secondary source? As we mentioned before, primary sources are preferred over secondary sources because they usually (though not always) are considered to be more accurate.
   - Was the author a *participant* in *or* an *observer* of the event? In general, we might expect an observer to present a more detached and comprehensive view of an event than a participant. Eyewitnesses do differ in their accounts of the same event, however, and hence the statements of an observer are not necessarily more accurate than those of a participant.
   - Was the author *competent* to describe the event? This refers to the qualifications of the author. Was he or she an expert on whatever is being described or discussed? An interested observer? A "passer-by"?
   - Was the author *emotionally involved* in the event? The wife of a fired teacher, for example, might

well give a distorted view of the teacher's contributions to the profession.
   - Did the author have any *vested interest* in the outcomes of the event? Might he or she have an ax of some sort to grind, for example, or possibly be biased in some way? A student who continually was in disagreement with his teacher, for example, might tend to describe the teacher more negatively than would the teacher's colleagues.

2. *With regard to the contents of the document:*
   - Do the contents make *sense* (i.e., given the nature of the events described, does it seem reasonable that they could have happened as portrayed)?
   - Could the event described have occurred *at that time?* For example, a researcher might justifiably be suspicious of a document describing a World War II battle that took place in 1946.
   - Would people have behaved as described? A major danger here is what is known as *presentism—* ascribing present-day beliefs, values, and ideas to people who lived at another time. A somewhat related problem is that of *historical hindsight.* Just because we know how an event came out does not mean that people who lived before or during the occurrence of an event believed an outcome would turn out the way it did.
   - Does the language of the document suggest a *bias* of any sort? Is it emotionally charged, intemperate, or otherwise slanted in a particular way? Might the ethnicity, gender, religion, political party, socioeconomic status, or position of the author suggest a particular orientation? For example, a teacher's account of a school board meeting in which a pay raise was voted down might differ from one of the board member's accounts.
   - Do *other versions* of the event exist? Do they present a different description or interpretation of what happened? But note that just because the majority of observers of an event agree about what happened, this does not mean they are necessarily always right. On more than one occasion, a minority view has proved to be correct.

Data Analysis in Historical Research

As is the case with other types of qualitative research, historical researchers must find ways to make

Should Historians Influence Policy?

A recurring controversy in the history of education involves the relationship of history to educational policy. Here is what one scholar recently had to say about the issue: "For historians of education, is political relevance achieved at the expense of academic respectability? Should educational historians involve themselves in discussions of policy and, if so, how?"* David Tyack, a noted historian, replied as follows: "Do historians have anything to contribute to educational policy? Many think not, including some educational historians

who fear that 'presentism' will corrupt the disinterestedness of the scholar. That may be, but there is a problem: Everybody uses some kind of history, if only personal memory, in making sense of the world. The question is not whether to use history in policy-making, but whether that history is going to be as accurate as possible. Historians surely do not have policy genes. They do have special knowledge, however, that might prove useful. In educational reform, for example, there is a whole storehouse of experiments to explore for a sense of what works and does not and why. Luckily, it is cheap to learn from those experiments and they don't harm living people."† (We assume this quote refers to naturally occurring "experiments," rather than true experiments.)

What do you think? Should educational historians involve themselves in discussions of policy?

*K. Mahoney (2000). New times, new questions. *Educational Researcher, 29:* 18–19.

†D. Tyack (2000). Reflections on histories of U.S. education. *Educational Researcher, 29:*19–20.

---

sense out of what is usually a very large amount of data and then synthesize it into a meaningful narrative of their own. Some prefer to operate from a theoretical model that helps them to organize the information they have collected and may even suggest categories for a content analysis. Others prefer to immerse themselves in their information until patterns or themes suggest themselves. A coding system may be useful in doing so. Recently, some historians have used quantitative data, such as crime and unemployment rates, to validate interpretations derived from documents.[13]

Generalization in Historical Research

Can researchers engaged in historical research generalize from their findings? It depends. As perhaps is obvious to you, historical researchers are rarely, if ever, able to study an entire population of individuals or events. They usually have little choice but to study a sample of the phenomena of interest. And the sample studied is determined by the historical sources that remain from the past. This is a particular problem for the historian, because almost always certain documents, relics, and other sources are missing, have been lost, or otherwise cannot be found. Those sources that are available per-

haps are not representative of all the possible sources that did exist.

Suppose, for example, that a researcher is interested in understanding how social studies was taught in high schools in the late 1800s. She is limited to studying whatever sources remain from that time. The researcher may locate several textbooks of the period, plus assignment books, lesson plans, tests, letters and other correspondence written by teachers, and their diaries, all from this period. On the basis of a careful review of this source material, the researcher draws some conclusions about the nature of social studies teaching at that time. The researcher needs to take care to remember, however, that all of these are written sources—and they may reflect quite a different view from that held by people who were not inclined to write down their thoughts, ideas, or assignments. What might the researcher do? As with all research, the validity of any generalizations that are drawn can be strengthened by increasing the size and diversity of the sample of data on which the generalizations are based. For those historical studies that involve the study of quantitative records, the computer has made it possible, in many instances, for a researcher to draw a representative sample of data from large groups of students, teachers, and others who are represented in school records, test scores, census reports, and other documents.

Important Findings in Historical Research

Perhaps the best-known example of historical research that is pertinent to education is a series of studies begun in 1934 by the German sociologist Max Weber, who offered the theory that religion was a major cause of social behavior and, in particular, of economic capitalism.* A more recent example of such studies is that of Robert N. Bellah, who exam-

ined historical documents pertaining to Japanese religion during the late 1800s and early 1900s.[†] He concluded that several emergent religious beliefs, including the desirability of hard work and the acceptance of being a businessman, heretofore a low-status role, were instrumental in setting the stage for the growth of capitalism in Japan. These conclusions paralleled those of Weber's earlier studies of Calvinism in Europe. Weber also concluded that capitalism failed to develop in the early societies of China, Israel, and India because none of their religious doctrines supported the essential capitalist idea of accumulation and reinvestment of wealth as a sign of worthiness.

*M. Weber (1958). *The Protestant ethic and the spirit of capitalism.* Translated by T. Parsons. New York: Charles Scribner and Sons.

[†]R. N. Bellah (1967). Research chronicle: Tokugawa religion. In P. E. Hammond (Ed.), *Sociologists at work.* Garden City, NY: Anchor Books, pp. 164–185.

Advantages and Disadvantages of Historical Research

The principal advantage of historical research is that it permits investigation of topics and questions that can be studied in no other way. It is the only research method that can study evidence from the past in relation to questions such as those presented earlier in the chapter. In addition, historical research can make use of more different kinds of evidence than most other methods (with the possible exceptions of ethnographic and case-study research). It thus provides an alternative and perhaps richer source of information on certain topics that can also be studied with other methodologies. A researcher might, for example, wish to investigate the hypothesis that "curriculum changes that did not involve extensive planning and participation by the teachers involved usually fail(ed)" by collecting interview or observational data on groups of teachers who (1) have and (2) have not participated in developing curricular changes (a causal-comparative study), or by arranging for variations in teacher participation (an experimental study). The question might also be studied, however, by examining documents prepared over the past 50 years by disseminators of new curricula (their reports), by teachers (their diaries), and so forth.

A disadvantage of historical research is that the measures used in other methods to control for threats to internal validity are simply not possible in a historical study. Limitations imposed by the nature of the sample of documents and the instrumentation process (content analysis) are likely to be severe. Researchers cannot ensure representativeness of the sample, nor can they (usually) check the reliability and validity of the inferences made from the data available. Depending on the question studied, all or many of the threats to internal validity we discussed in Chapter Nine are likely to exist. The possibility of bias due to researcher characteristics (in data collection and analysis) is always present. The possibility that any observed relationships are due to a subject characteristics (the individuals on whom information exists), implementation, history, maturation, attitude, or location threat also is always present. Although any particular threat depends on the nature of a particular study, methods for its control are unfortunately unavailable to the researcher. Because so much depends on the skill and integrity of the researcher—since methodological controls are unavailable—we believe that historical research is among the most difficult of all types of research to conduct (Figure 22.2).

Doing historical research requires much more than digging up good material; done properly it can demand a broader array of skills than other methods. The historian may find she needs some of the skills of a linguist, chemist or archaeologist. Further, since history is admittedly highly interpretive in a global sense, knowledge of psychology, anthropology, and other disciplines may also be required.

Figure 22.2 *Historical Research Is Not as Easy as You May Think!*

An Example of Historical Research

In the remainder of this chapter, we present a published example of historical research, followed by a critique of its strengths and weaknesses. As we did in our critiques of the different types of research studies we analyzed in other chapters, we use several of the concepts introduced in earlier parts of the book in our analysis.

*The Journal of Psychohistory, 28:*1 (Summer 2000): 62–71.

Lydia Ann Stow: Self-actualization in a Period of Transition

Vivian C. Fox
Worcester State College

This paper is concerned with a crucial period of self-actualization in the life of Lydia Ann Stow (1823–1904), an early nineteenth century Massachusetts woman who illustrates the interactions between adolescent development and the dynamics of reforms in education and feminism. The term "self-actualization" is adopted from Frederic L. Bender, who defines this Marxian concept as "the development of one's talents and abilities and, the pursuit of one's life interests in and through one's work."[1] Although self-actualization appears to be a highly individualized process, it always occurs in a larger social context. It is crucial to emphasize this in Lydia Stow's case since the most relevant context for her self-actualization was highly transitional in two important respects, namely, the development of educational theory and practice, and the evolution in the status of women.

Definition

Purpose?

The major source for describing Stow's self-actualization is the set of four Journals which she kept during the period of her training in Massachusetts as a professional teacher at the Lexington Normal School, and for about two years thereafter (July 8, 1839–February 23, 1843).[2]

Primary source

In this paper I undertake a brief description of the contextual events before proceeding to an analysis of the Journals. I would like to start with school reform.

SCHOOL REFORM

The process of school reform *that played such an important role* in Lydia's life was itself a reflection of a panoply of post-Revolution concerns. To some, the advent of technology was altering New England's predominantly rural work patterns through the construction of factories and railroads. Cities were growing larger, more varied, and increasingly sinister with vast numbers of immigrant-strangers, prostitutes and salesmen of magical drug products. The new arrivals were, moreover, largely untrained, uneducated and non-Anglo-Saxon men who appeared quickly to acquire political power at the ballot box. In view of these cascading changes, many wondered whether the glorious achievements of the Revolution could be maintained.[3]

Independent variable

To some, the appropriate response to these issues was in the direction of ensuring an educated citizenry. Leaders in this movement emerged in the Northeast, particularly in Massachusetts. Such Massachusetts men as Horace Mann, James G. Carter, Edward Everett, Edmund Dwight, Cyrus Peirce, and Henry Barnard who was from New York, supported the idea that a key to confronting post-Revolutionary challenges was in the field of educational reform.[4]

James G. Carter, for example, while Chairman of the Committee on Education of the Massachusetts House of Representatives, successfully established himself as the architect of an educational renaissance that included creation of a state-wide Board of Education. Horace Mann was appointed in 1837 as the first Secretary of the Board.[5]

Background

Mann immediately launched a crusade, which continued during his twelve years of incumbency, from which his ideas spread throughout the nation. His accomplishments included a proliferation of the common schools, an expansion of their curriculum, and the training of teachers in new approaches to teaching which encompassed a new philosophy of learning and moral discipline.[6]

He accepted the Republican view, moreover, that popular education was necessary for the intellectual and monetary enhancement of citizens which would contribute to the general well-being of the Republic. His beliefs emphasized that the new Republic required a high standard of morality in order to eliminate, as he put it, "the long catalogue of human ills."[7]

Reference needed

Central to achieving educational reform and progress was the provision of professional training for school teachers. Prior to this time, little or no training was required and persons with a minimal amount of education could take charge of classrooms.

Many of the ideas of Mann and his colleagues were obtained from Europe, especially from Prussia. Unlike its European counterparts, however, professional teacher training in what were called the Normal Schools (a title derived from the French École Normale) was open to females. In 1838 Massachusetts adopted a law authorizing the establishment of three Normal Schools. The first appeared in Lexington in 1839, and in accordance with the statute it was open only to females. The other two, in Barre and Bridgewater in 1840, were co-educational. Lydia was a member of the first class to enroll in Lexington.

Speaking for many reformers, Horace Mann emphasized the importance of employing female teachers.

Primary source

> Education . . . is woman's work. . . Let woman, then be educated to the highest practicable point; not only because it is her right, but because it is essential to the world's progress. Let her voice be a familiar voice in the schools and the academies, and in halls of learning and science.[8]

Mann was not, of course, the first to recognize appropriate roles for women in the educational enterprise. By the last part of the eighteenth century, for example, New England clergymen, struck by the greater church attendance of women, intoned that females were purer and more delicate than men, and advocated greater exposure to education for them as caretakers of the very young.[9] From the latter part of the eighteenth century, then, sons as well as daughters came to be under the pedagogy of their mothers, unlike in the prior period when fathers became responsible for the education of boys when they reached the age of seven. The assumption that women had special moral strengths—that they were "angels in the house"—gave them important credentials for both domestic and professional teaching roles.[10]

The call for women's education grew stronger as post-Revolutionary ideology expressed the sentiment that in a Republic, school education must become available to all citizens, both male and female. Boston, for example, allowed girls to be educated in its grammar school in 1789; and Dedham, Lydia's hometown, had already anticipated this as early as the 1750s. In a highly unusual development, one Mary Green was so successful a teacher that she was added to the permanent Dedham teaching staff.[11]

We agree.

Clearly, when Lydia enrolled at Lexington she was riding the crest of unique educational opportunities. As detailed in the next section, this enhanced status of women as educators of the young was also strongly strengthened by demographic and economic conditions of the time.

Now I want to discuss the matter of gender reform.

GENDER REFORM

At the same time that Mann and the other reformers were reconstructing the field of education so as to create new opportunities for women, their legal, social and economic circumstances generally were, paradoxically, much against the enhancement of their status. New England continued to follow common law and Christian traditions. These acknowledged the husband to be the head of the household who controlled the landed and personal property of the wife, as well as the wages she might earn. Although white women were legally considered citizens, they were prohibited from most public activities. They could not vote, sit on juries, execute wills, or serve as guardians of their children upon the death of their husbands; and most professions were not open to them.[12]

Secondary source

But there were currents of change as well, and nothing illustrated this better than the (opportunities presented to Lydia.) In addition to teaching, the newly created New England textile factories welcomed women, as did many of the developing reform movements such as temperance, abolition, and child welfare. Women such as Harriet Beecher Stowe and Louisa May Alcott entered the ranks of professional writers.[13]   *Independent variable*

Much of this might be explained by demography. From about the end of the eighteenth century, New England generally and Massachusetts in particular experienced an imbalance in the demographic ratio of the sexes in favor of women. This presented the question of how some of these "surplus women," as they were called, would be supported.[14] The problem was further exacerbated by the many new work opportunities for men, such as those that opened in the west and were created by the industrial revolution. An appropriate response to the shortage of male workers was to provide the new opportunities for working class women that have already been noted.[15]   *Hypothetical speculation*

But there were other less tangible forces at work as well that contributed to the gender evolution that Lydia found herself in. A number of women sensed that they were experiencing a shift in their fortunes. Lucy Larcom, for example, a Massachusetts factory worker during Lydia's time, expressed such a view in her autobiography.

> [In] the olden times it was seldom said to little girls, as it always has been to boys, that they ought to have some definite plan, while they were children, what to be and do when they were grown up . . . But when I was growing up, we were often told that it was our duty to develop any talent one might possess, or at least to learn how to do some one thing which the world needed, or which would make it a pleasanter world.[16]   *Primary source*

Although when Lydia enrolled at Lexington, legal changes in the status of women were still in the future, the social ecology of women was certainly different from what it had been traditionally. (Self-actualization) was a possibility.   *Interpretation*
      Dependent variable

LYDIA'S SELF-ACTUALIZATION

I have already mentioned that Lydia's four Journals are the primary source for conclusions concerning self-actualization. The first two of these chronologically were written while she was in residence at Lexington. The latter two were penned after she returned to Dedham having been graduated from Lexington.

The Journals were not a personal indulgence. Keeping them was a daily requirement for all pupils, containing a summary of the day's lectures and reading. Lydia's Journals appear to be unique in their inclusion of personal remarks concerning her responses to the lectures and reading, and evaluations of her own abilities and activities.[17] It was a weekly requirement that the Journals be turned in to the Principal, Cyrus Peirce, who would return them with his comments.   *Argues for validity*

The four Journals as a whole reveal that the time she spent at Lexington was crucial to the self-actualization Lydia achieved. She came to regard herself as a professional teacher capable of expressing herself fully, able to love her pupils, having the capacity to evaluate teaching performances of herself and others, and contributing to the moral progress of the larger community.   *Interpretation*

The outward manifestations of this self-actualization included her election as the first woman to the Board of Education of the city of Fall River. It was there that she married, lived with her husband and raised a child. It was also the city where she established a sewing school for young women, to insure that they could earn a wage; where she became a member of the Women's Suffrage League of Fall River; and where she began her work in the anti-slavery movement and the underground railroad, often placing herself at personal risk. Her work in the abolitionist movement led her to entertain such leaders as William Garrison, William Douglas, Sojourner Truth, and Wendell Phillips.[18]   *Justification?*

Interpretation

One would never expect such accomplishments from a reading of her first two Journals. Significant self-actualization did not appear a promising outcome, especially in the complexities of her family background. There was much to provide an anxiety about accomplishment. Death had been a pervasive presence in her family. Her father died when she was one year old and her mother when she was eleven. With the additional deaths of six siblings, only Lydia and her older sister survived from the nuclear family. After the age of eleven, then, she was dependent upon

Interpretation

the care of her kin.[19] It would not be surprising if the pervasiveness of such primary loss surrounded her with uncertainty about any accomplishment, and induced compliant behavior to those willing to become responsible for her well-being. Some of this vulnerability, however, was likely to have been offset by the warmth and support of her kin.

As a child in Dedham, she lived with a grandmother and an aunt. In the same town or nearby vicinity, her last two Journals reveal a rich kin group: it is possible to count two grandmothers, eight aunts, six uncles, and numerous cousins. Among the women there were at least three

Interpretation

teachers, one of them her sister, but only Lydia received professional training. In her last two Journals she portrays her family as close, continuously interactive, and as kin who supported one another in illnesses as well as in celebrations. With her aunts and friends she attended lectures and studied French and took singing lessons.[20] Thus, despite the many deaths in her immediate family, the Journals reveal a young woman who did not feel abandoned nor did she act depressed.

Interpretation

On the other hand, and most strikingly, while she undertook many challenges during her training at the Normal School, she invariably expressed doubts as to whether she could perform them

Interpretation

adequately. The experience at Lexington, however, made all the difference in developing the strengths that were manifested in the rest of her life. It also helped her to assuage her pervasive lack of confidence.

Independent variable

The core of the Lexington experience was Cyrus Peirce.[21] His influence on Lydia was most singular. He belonged to a generation of school reformers who stressed moral development as a central goal of education, a belief that included the fusion of mental discipline and Christian ideals that had already been a key part of Lydia's upbringing.[22] His extraordinary teaching ability attracted the admiration of Horace Mann, who engaged him as Principal and then visited the school in its first weeks of operation. Mann recorded:

Primary source

> Highly as I had appreciated his talent, he surpassed the ideas I had formed of his ability to teach, and in the prerequisite of all successful teaching, the power of winning the confidence of his pupils. This surpassed what I had ever seen before in any school. The exercises were conducted in the most thorough manner: the principle being stated, and then applied to various combinations of facts, however, different, to find the principle which underlies them all . . .[23]

Peirce's abilities were not lost on Lydia, who developed an emotional and personal response to his work. Her first Journal reveals that her reaction was one of great remorse whenever she or any of her classmates caused him distress. "There is" she wrote, informing him about her feel-

Supportive example

ings in the Journal he would read, "nothing that more affects my happiness than this . . . to cause him [underlined in original] unhappiness who has been so forbearing and patient with us."[24]

Interpretation

Whenever such episodes happened, Stow increased her effort to improve herself and to be perfect if she could. This was a serious challenge for Lydia, who questioned her performance in almost everything she did as previously mentioned. She complained, for example, that she could

Example

not achieve a "balance between impulses and belief"[25] when she would finish eating toffee or something else sweet, or when she chatted with her fellow pupils against the commands of her principal.[26]

Interpretation

More seriously, she questioned her own intelligence, using the language of phrenology, a pseudo-psychological science which demonstrated a person's talent based upon the bumps or organs, or lack thereof, on her head. She expressed her frustration when studying algebra with: "Oh how I wish my organ of calculation was large."[27] Peirce would have none of it. He directly challenged the prevailing view that women were incapable of studying mathematics. Some people, he wrote,

> have doubted if girls should be taught this branch, and indeed, some have questioned the propriety of educating women for this study! Benevolent spirit indeed. The appropriateness of this study for women, how could it be asked? She fills and ought to fill those stations where this branch is requisite. The discipline of the mind which this branch affords is important to the educator.[28]

Example

Her self-deprecation and doubts were ubiquitous in the first two Journals. Composition exercises did not escape. "Composition I almost despise [but] I must begin now and do the best I can which is always poor."[29] Peirce's response was simply to write in large capital letters across her Journal, "DESPISE !!". But this expression of disgust was unusual. Normally, he complimented this often anxious and over-critical pupil. These compliments were well deserved; for despite her own doubts, an examination of her Journals in comparison with those of her classmates reveals their superiority in terms of comprehensiveness, understanding and clarity. There may be one exception in the Journals of a Mary Swift, although these were devoid of the personal comments found so often in Lydia's Journals.[30]

Interpretation

Example

Peirce's impact on Lydia may be inferred from a survey of the goals of his interactions with the Lexington pupils. The most prominent of these were (1) to inculcate new teaching methodologies; (2) to challenge the prevailing stereotypes about the nature of women's intelligence; (3) to inspire them in the belief that women, compared to men, possessed at least equal intellectual capabilities and in the case of teaching skills, that they were superior. Peirce also shared Horace Mann's oft-expressed belief in the moral superiority of women.[31]

Given the relationship of affection and respect that existed between Lydia and her mentor, it would not be surprising if many of her initial feelings of inadequacy and inferiority did not begin to be displaced as she entered the practice of professional teaching. Her later Journals reveal a confidence in critically assessing the techniques of fellow teachers, both male and female, whose classrooms she visited. More importantly, she developed an independence from the influence of Peirce, recognizing that some circumstances required a deviation from his teachings. Use of the ferule, for example, she found to be occasionally necessary when confronted by an oversized class of undisciplined young men, even though Peirce had been inexorably opposed to the practice.[32]

Interpretation

Interpretation

Quote would help here

In a later teaching position in Fall River, she found great joy, however, in developing the kind of relationship with her pupils that Peirce had strongly emphasized and she herself wanted to have. She wrote of this achievement: "My scholars are very tractable. I am becoming more attached to them as the weeks glide on and may the love strengthen day by day during our connection."[33] It was in this experience that Lydia fulfilled the promise of the Normal School reform.

Good example

CONCLUSION

It is possible to conclude that Lydia's self-actualization in the field of professional teaching, and as a concerned and active citizen, flows from diverse sources: those available because of the historical environmental circumstances as well as from her own childhood experiences. Her own efforts to achieve success were of major importance as well, particularly her choice to undertake the new professional training even though members of her own family demonstrated that it was not necessary to becoming a teacher. Even as she doubted her ability to meet the school's standards, she persisted in seeking self-improvement. At this point fortune joined her fate with the efforts of Cyrus Peirce who was, at a time and at a place that was right for Lydia, crusading for

Interpretation

Interpretation

the recruitment of women like Lydia to the teaching profession, and providing inspiration for females to strengthen their capacities to take an active part in the world's affairs. Peirce's mentorship to Lydia, a talented, disciplined, but anxious adolescent, provided her with intellectual tools, a moral and probably emotional guardianship, and an unswerving faith in the abilities of her sex. It was with these gifts that Lydia Ann Stow underwent the process of self-actualization. She developed her talents, and she pursued her life's interests which were to make moral contributions to her world.

Notes

Secondary source

1. Frederic L. Bender, editor, *Karl Marx, The Communist Manifesto* (New York, 1988): 21. According to Bender, Marx believed this important process could not be achieved under capitalism—where the worker experiences alienation from her work.

Primary source

2. See the unpublished four volume *Journal of Lydia Ann Stow* held at Framingham State College at Framington, Massachusetts. Framingham is a successor to the Lexington Normal School. I would like to extend my appreciation to the library staff for their assistance, especially to the archivist Sally Phillips, who was so helpful when I first began my research.

Secondary source

3. Several historians attribute this anxiety to the advance of commerce. See e.g., Charles Sellersk, *The Market Revolution: Jacksonian America, 1815–1840 (New York, 1991).* For a more optimistc description of the period, see Daniel Feller, *The Jacksonian Promise: 1815–1846* (Baltimore, 1995).

Secondary source

4. See, for example, Paul H. Mattingly, *The Classless Profession: American Schoolmen in the Nineteenth Century* (New York: New York University Press, 1975).

Secondary source

5. Lawrence A. Cremin, *American Education: The National Experience, 1783–1876* (New York, 1980): 136; Arthur O. Norton, *The First Normal School in America: The Journals of Cyrus Peirce and Mary Swift* (Cambridge: Harvard University Press, 1926), Introduction.

6. Ibid, Cremin.

7. Horace Mann, *Common School Journal,* III (1841) 15, in Cremin, p. 137.

Primary source

8. Horace Mann, "A Few Thoughts on the Powers and Duties of Women," in *Lectures on Various Subjects* (New York, 1864) in Cremin, p. 143.

Secondary source

9. Winston E. Langley and Vivian C. Fox, *Women's Rights in the United States: A Documentary History,* Parts I and II (Greenwood, 1994); Paula Baker, "The Domestication of Politics: Women and the American Political Society, 1780–1920." *The American Historical Review,* 89:3, June, 1984: 620–647; Nancy Cott, *The Bonds of Womanhood: Woman's Sphere in New England* (New Haven, Yale University Press, 1977).

10. Ibid, Cott; see also Linda K. Kerber, *Women of the Republic.*

Secondary source

11. Thomas Woody, *The History of Women's Education in The United States,* Vol. I (New York: The Science Press, 1929); Carlos Slafter, *A Record of Education: The Schools and Teachers of Dedham, Massachusetts, 1644–1904* (Dedham Transcript 1952):45.

Secondary source

12. See Langley and Fox, *Women's Rights,* especially parts I and II.

Secondary source

13. Geraldine Jonich Clifford, "Home and School in 19th Century America: Some Personal History Reports From the United States," *History of Education Quarterly,* 18:1 (Spring, 1978): 3–4.

Secondary source

14. Maris A. Vinovskis, *Fertility in Massachusetts from the Revolution to the Civil War* (New York: Academic Press, 1981): 221. Horace Mann said that in 1839 there were far many more female teachers than male teachers. See Mary Swift's Journals in Norton, *The First Normal School,* footnote 14.

Secondary source

15. Barbara Myer Wertheimer, *We Were There: The Story of Working Women in America* (New York: Pantheon Books, 1961): Claudi Goldin, "The Economic Status of Women in the Early Republic: Quantitative Evidence," *Journal of Interdisciplinary History*, XVI:3 (Winter, 1986):375–404.

Primary source

16. Lucy Larcom, *A New England Childhood.*

Primary source

17. Lydia reveals that it was Professor Newman, principal of Barre Normal School, who introduced her to the high standards of journal-keeping she would maintain. She said, "He gave us some useful tips regarding the importance of writing abstracts of lectures, lessons or anything else we might hear." She recorded this in Volume IV, p. 16 of her Journals. Her summaries of lectures and of the books she read were remarkable especially in contrast to her classmates. Except for Mary Swift, all the other Journals from Lexington do not compare in quality or length with that of Stow's.

Primary source

18. Most of this information was obtained from her obituary in the *Fall River Evening News* written on Friday, August 16, 1904. Lydia was 81 years old when she died.

Primary source

19. Don Gleason Hill, editor, *The Record of Baptisms, Marriages and Deaths and Admission to the Church, 1638–1845* (Dedham, 1888):288. This record of the First Parish Church is listed as Dedham Cemetery Epitaphs. In the

registry of Probate, Norfolk County, NP 17508, Lydia's father, Timothy Stow, Jr., is listed as a "Hoosewright" or "Housewright." The O.E.D. defines these as housebuilders.

20. These impressions are to be gleaned from her last two Journals when she was living at home. However, while at school Lydia wrote about her feelings regarding her home. "There [meaning home] is the true City of Refuge. Where are we to turn when it is shut from us or changed?" It is interesting to note that Lydia is expressing two feelings: one that she is lucky to have that true refuge, but also, secondly she exhibits an awareness of the plight one would have without it. Probably this is because she is an orphan and probably contemplated what would happen if she were not cared for by her relatives. Journal II, p. 72. *Primary source*

21. For Peirce's background, see Norton, Introduction, *The First State Normal School.* Secondary source

22. For an interesting interpretation of the personality fostered by the Congregationalist religion, see Philip Greven, *The Protestant Temperament: Patterns of Child-Rearing, Religious Experience, and the Self in Early America* (New York, 1977):152–179. Of course reading Lydia's Journals also provides one with the most detailed view of her religious and moral ideas. Secondary source

23. See Norton, Introduction, *The First State Normal School.* Secondary source

24. Stow, Journals, no. 1, p. 25.

25. Ibid., p. 180. See also ibid at 217 and 241 for further examples of this belief.

26. Ibid., p. 217, 241.

27. Ibid., p. 25.

28. Journals vol. II, p. 16.

29. Ibid., p. 56.

30. See Mary Swift's published Journal in Norton, *The First State Normal School.* Primary source

31. For Peirce's views see Lydia's Journals and Norton, which contains the Journals of Mary Swift and of Cyrus Peirce. From them it is very clear that Peirce believed women to have many talents including a highly developed moral capacity. For Horace Mann, see his published lectures entitled, *A Few Thoughts on the Powers and Duties of Woman, Two Lectures* (Syracuse, Hall, Mills and Co., 1853). Primary source

32. Journals vol. IV, p. 41.

33. Ibid., p. 86.

Analysis of the Study

PURPOSE/JUSTIFICATION

We do not find a clear statement of purpose. In part because of the publication in which the study appears, *The Journal of Psychohistory,* we think the purpose could have been stated as, for example: "To enhance our understanding of the ways in which societal conditions and personal characteristics interact in producing valued qualities such as 'self-actualization.'" The justification implied in the introduction is that the life of Lydia Stow is important to understand; this is elaborated later under "gender reform."

DEFINITIONS

A clear definition of "self-actualization" is given in the introduction. This is particularly important because not all definitions of this term include "pursuit of one's life interests in and through one's work." Other terms such as "self-improvement" and "concerned and active citizen" are probably clear enough in context.

HYPOTHESES

None are stated. The "interaction" hypothesis is clearly implied; it appears likely that it conceptually preceded analysis of information.

SAMPLE

The sampling issue is quite different in historical research as compared with other types of research. There typically is no population of persons to be sampled. It could be argued that a population of events exists, but if so, they are likely to be so different that selection among them makes more sense if done purposefully, in other words, a purposive sample. In this study, a population of persons could have been specified, though it's not clear what its characteristics would be. Perhaps "nineteenth-century women who made a significant impact on education." A sample of such women would greatly increase the generalizability of findings but would, presumably, involve major problems in locating suitable source material.

INSTRUMENTATION

There is no instrumentation in the sense that we discuss it in this text. The "instrument" in this case is the researcher's talent for locating, evaluating, and analyzing

pertinent sources. The concept of reliability usually has little relevance to historical data, because each item is not meaningfully considered to be a sample across either content or time. In this study, however, comparison of journal statements pertaining to the same topic (e.g., self-confidence) could be made across the early two journals and, again, across the later two. These comparisons would give an indication of the consistency of these statements.

Validity, on the other hand, is paramount. It is addressed by evaluating sources and by comparing different sources regarding the same specifics. In this study, data are from two types of source. Secondary sources are used extensively in the sections on school reform and gender reform. The source of information about Stow is a primary one, her four journals. Some of the secondary sources could, it seems, have been used as cross-checks for validity, but this apparently was not done. The validity of the author's summaries of this information is supported, in some instances, by quotations from the journals and from other primary sources.

External criticism does not appear to be an issue with respect to the journals or, presumably, other references. The question of internal criticism is somewhat difficult to deal with, because the journals must be evaluated in terms of the writer's feelings and perceptions rather than events. Here, we are highly dependent on the researcher's summaries.

PROCEDURES/INTERNAL VALIDITY

There is little to be said about procedures except that some discussion of the plans that the researcher developed and followed for analyzing the documents, particularly the journals, would be useful, especially so that readers could evaluate the presumed selection of content. Historical research is always subject to the allegation that the researcher has selected content based on personal bias. Internal validity concerns are justified regarding this research because of the intent to study the relationships among societal conditions, prior personal qualities, and personal development. In addition to data collector (researcher) bias, other major threats include history (other events) and maturation. There is no way to control for these threats in historical research.

DATA ANALYSIS

Data analysis procedures, as we have explained them in this book, are not used in this study, nor do we see how most of them could be. Use of the content analysis methods in Chapter 20 would serve to organize the information. Category-by-category tabulation of frequency of similar statements might have clarified interpretations.

RESULTS AND DISCUSSION

Though we advocate keeping the results of a study separate from the discussion of them, such separation is extremely difficult in historical research. The question here is whether the information (data) provided justifies the author's interpretations and conclusions. Though not proven, we think the well-documented summaries of school and gender reforms during Stow's young adulthood are persuasive. With respect to changes in Stow over a four-year period (ages 17 to 21), we are very dependent upon the author's highly inferential psychological interpretations. Though we find them plausible (e.g., interpretation of Stow's factual family history), more quotations from the journals would strengthen such interpretations, most importantly that her confidence and independence increased greatly during this time. Several are provided from the early journals but none from the later ones.

The assertion that "Even as she doubted her ability to meet the school's standards, she persisted in seeking self-improvement" is reflected in quotations. We must assume, however, that they are typical of both Stow's statements and her feelings. Similarly, the influence of Peirce, in turn reflecting social changes, seems persuasive, but, again, we must assume that the examples are representative. We think there is a clear implication that societal changes, family support, personal persistence, and the influence of Peirce were all necessary to Stow's self-actualization. While this is plausible, it is not demonstrated by the study.

Go back to the **Interactive and Applied Learning Tools** feature at the beginning of the chapter for a listing of interactive and applied activities. **Go to the Online Learning Center** at www.mhhe.com/fraenkel5e or your **Interactive Student CD-ROM** to take practice quizzes and receive immediate feedback, practice with key terms, review chapter content and main ideas, and find annotated Web links.

Main Points

THE NATURE OF HISTORICAL RESEARCH

- The unique characteristic of historical research is that it focuses exclusively on the past.

PURPOSES OF HISTORICAL RESEARCH

- Educational researchers conduct historical studies for a variety of reasons, but perhaps the most frequently cited is to help people learn from past failures and successes.
- When well-designed and carefully executed, historical research may lead to the confirmation or rejection of relational hypotheses.

STEPS IN HISTORICAL RESEARCH

- There are four essential steps involved in doing a historical study. These include defining the problem or hypothesis to be investigated; searching for relevant source material; summarizing and evaluating the sources the researcher is able to locate; interpreting the evidence obtained and then drawing conclusions about the problem or hypothesis.

HISTORICAL SOURCES

- Most historical source material can be grouped into four basic categories: documents, numerical records, oral statements, and relics.

- Documents are written or printed materials that have been produced in one form or another sometime in the past.
- Numerical records include any type of numerical data in printed or handwritten form.
- Oral statements include any form of statement spoken by someone.
- Relics are any objects whose physical or visual characteristics can provide some information about the past.
- A primary source is one prepared by an individual who was a participant in, or a direct witness to, the event that is being described.
- A secondary source is a document prepared by an individual who was not a direct witness to an event, but who obtained his or her description of the event from someone else.

EVALUATION OF HISTORICAL SOURCE MATERIAL

- Content analysis is a primary method of data analysis in historical research.
- External criticism refers to the genuineness of the documents a researcher uses in a historical study.
- Internal criticism refers to the accuracy of the contents of a document. Whereas external criticism has to do with the authenticity of a document, internal criticism has to do with what the document says.

GENERALIZATION IN HISTORICAL RESEARCH

- As in all research, researchers who conduct historical studies should exercise caution in generalizing from small or nonrepresentative samples.

ADVANTAGES AND DISADVANTAGES OF HISTORICAL RESEARCH

- The main advantage of historical research is that it permits the investigation of topics that could be studied in no other way. It is the only research method that can study evidence from the past.
- A disadvantage is that controlling for many of the threats to internal validity is not possible in historical research. Many of the threats to internal validity discussed in Chapter Nine are likely to exist in historical studies.

Key Terms

Documents 550	Internal criticism 552	Primary source 551
External criticism 552	Numerical records 550	Relic 550
Generalization 554	Oral statements 550	Secondary source 551
Historical research 548		

For Discussion

1. A researcher wishes to investigate changes in high school graduation requirements since 1900. Pose a possible hypothesis the researcher might investigate. What sources might he or she consult?
2. Which of the following would constitute examples of a primary historical source? (Assume they are genuine.)
   a. An article on intelligence testing written by a school psychologist.
   b. The *Encyclopedia of Educational Research.*
   c. A final examination booklet.

    d. A spelling primer used in a midwestern school in 1840.

    e. A bulletin from a school principal.

    f. An eighteenth-century school desk.

    g. A 1969 newspaper announcing the landing of men on the moon.

    h. A menu from a school cafeteria.

3. Why might a researcher be cautious or suspicious about each of the following sources?

    a. A typewriter imprinted with the name "Christopher Columbus."

    b. A letter from Franklin D. Roosevelt endorsing John F. Kennedy for the presidency of the United States.

    c. A "Letter to the Editor" from an eighth-grade student complaining about the adequacy of the school's advanced mathematics program.

    d. A typed report of an interview with a recently fired teacher describing the teacher's complaints against the school district.

    e. A 1920 high school diploma indicating a student had graduated from the tenth grade.

    f. A high school teacher's attendance book indicating no absences by any member of her class during the entire year of 1942.

    g. A photograph of an elementary school classroom in 1800.

4. How would you compare historical research to the other methodologies we have discussed in this book—harder or easier to do? Why?

5. "Researchers cannot ensure representativeness of the sample" in historical research. Why not?

Notes

1. D. R. Entwisele et al. (1986). The schooling process in first grade: Two samples a decade apart. *American Educational Research Journal, 23*(4):587–613.

2. J. H. Mark and B. D. Anderson (1985). Teacher survival rates in St. Louis, 1969–1982. *American Educational Research Journal, 22*(2):413–422.

3. P. W. Kaufman (1985). *Women teachers on the frontier.* New Haven, CT: Yale University Press.

4. M. Lybarger (1983). Origins of the modern social studies. *History of Education Quarterly, 23*(4):445–468.

5. J. R. Rafferty (1988). Missing the mark: Intelligence testing in Los Angeles public schools, 1922–1932. *History of Education Quarterly, 28*(1):73–93.

6. M. C. Coleman (1987). The responses of American Indian children to Presbyterian schooling in the nineteenth century: An analysis through missionary sources. *History of Education Quarterly, 27*(4):473–498.

7. H. L. Horowitz (1986). The 1960s and the transformation of campus cultures. *History of Education Quarterly, 26*(1):1–38.

8. M. R. Nelson (1987). Emma Willard: Pioneer in social studies education. *Theory and Research in Social Education, 15*(4):245–256.

9. D. J. Willower (1987). Inquiry into educational administration: The last 25 years and the next. *Journal of Educational Administration, 15*(1):12–28.

10. S. D. Jespersen (1987). Bertrand Russell and education in world citizenship. *Journal of Social Studies Research, 11*(1):1–6.

11. F. K. Goldscheider and C. LeBourdars (1986). The decline in age at leaving home, 1920–1979. *Sociology and Social Research: An International Journal, 70*(2):143–145.

12. E. J. Carr (1967). *What Is history?* New York: Random House, pp. 32–33.

13. L. Isaac and L. Griffin (1989). Ahistoricism in time-series analyses of historical process: Critique, Redirection, and Illustrations from U.S. labor history." *American Sociological Review, 54:* 873–90.

Research by Practitioners

7

Part Seven presents a discussion of action research. Both similar to
and different from the more formal methodologies discussed earlier,
action research has of late shown increasing popularity. We discuss
this methodology in some detail and present several examples of how
action research studies might actually be carried out in schools.
Lastly, we present a published example of action research, followed
by our analysis of its strengths and weaknesses.

Action Research

CHAPTER 23

Action Research

What Is Action Research?

Basic Assumptions
Underlying Action Research

Types of Action Research

Practical Action Research
Participatory Action Research
Levels of Participation

The Advantages of Action Research

Similarities and Differences Between Action Research and Formal Quantitative and Qualitative Research

Sampling in
Action Research
Internal Validity in
Action Research
Action Research and External Validity

Steps in Action Research

Identifying the Research Question
Gathering the Necessary Information
Analyzing and Interpreting
the Information
Developing an Action Plan

Objectives

Studyng this chapter should enable you to:

- Explain *the term "action research."*
- Describe *the assumptions that underlie action research.*
- Explain *the purpose of action research.*
- Describe *the four steps involved in action research.*
- Describe *some of the advantages of action research.*
- Describe *some of the similarities and differences between action research and formal quantitative and qualitative research.*
- Describe *the difference between practical and participatory action research.*
- Suggest *some ways that other kinds of research methodologies might be used in action research.*
- Name *some of the threats to internal validity that exist in action research studies.*
- Describe *the kinds of sampling used in action research.*
- Explain *why action research studies are weak in external validity.*
- Recognize *an example of action research when you come across it in the educational literature.*

Interactive and Applied Learning

After, or while reading this chapter:

Go to your Interactive Student CD-ROM to:
- Learn More About the Role of Researchers in Action Research

Go to your Interactive Student CD-ROM or Student Workbook to do the following activities:
- Activity 23.1: Action Research Questions
- Activity 23.2: True or False?

Robert Jackson is in his second year of teaching at an elementary school in Sarasota, Florida. Recently, he has been more and more bothered by a considerable amount of disruptive behavior in his fifth-grade class. The boys in the class are particularly troublesome. Many take a long time to settle in their seats after the afternoon recess, have trouble paying attention when he is giving instruction, and often punch out at other students for apparently no reason. The girls in the class never seem to stop talking. Robert is becoming very concerned, as a lot of valuable class time is taken up by his so-far-unsuccessful attempts to deal with these problems. Of special concern is that he feels his students are learning only a small amount of what they could were he able to maintain a more orderly class.

What might Mr. Jackson do in this situation? Action research, the subject of this chapter, is an ideal methodology that he might employ.

What Is Action Research?

Action research is research conducted by one or more individuals or groups for the purpose of solving a problem or obtaining information in order to inform local practice. Those involved in action research generally want to solve some kind of day-to-day immediate problem, such as how to decrease absenteeism or incidents of vandalism among the student body, motivate apathetic students, figure out ways to use technology to improve the teaching of mathematics, or increase funding.

There are many kinds of questions that lend themselves to action research in schools. What kinds of methods, for example, work best with what kinds of students? How can teachers encourage students to think about important issues? How can content, teaching strategies, and learning activities be varied to help students of differing ages, gender, ethnicity, and ability to learn more effectively? How can subject matter be presented so as to maximize understanding? What can teachers and administrators do to increase the interest of students in schooling? What can counselors do? What can other educational professionals do? How can parents become more involved?

Classroom teachers, counselors, supervisors, and administrators can help provide some answers to these (and other) important questions by engaging in action research. Such studies, taken individually, are seriously limited in *generalizability*. If, however, several teachers in different schools within the same district, for example, were to investigate the same question in their classrooms (thereby *replicating* the research of their peers), they could create a base of ideas that could generalize to policy or practice.

Action research often does not require complete mastery of the major types of research we have described in previous chapters. The steps involved in action research are actually pretty straightforward. The important thing to remember is that such studies are rooted in the interests and needs of practitioners.

BASIC ASSUMPTIONS UNDERLYING ACTION RESEARCH

A number of assumptions underlie action research. Those who do action research assume that those involved, either singly or in groups, are informed individuals who are capable of identifying problems that need to be solved and of determining how to go about solving them. It is also assumed that those involved are seriously committed to improving their performance and that they want continuously and systematically to reflect on such performance. Further, it is assumed that teachers and others involved in the schools *want* to engage in research systematically—to identify problems, decide on investigative procedures, determine data collection techniques, analyze and interpret data, and develop plans of action to deal with problems. Lastly, it is assumed that those intending to carry out the research have the authority to undertake the necessary procedures and implement recommendations. These assumptions are described a bit further and exemplified in Table 23.1.

Types of Action Research

Mills has identified two main types of action research, although variations and combinations of the two are possible.[1]

Table 23.1 *Basic Assumptions Underlying Action Research*

Assumption	Example
Teachers and other education professionals have the authority to make decisions.	A team of teachers, after discussions with the school administration, decide to meet weekly to revise the mathematics curriculum to make it more relevant to low-achieving students.
Teachers and other education professionals want to improve their practice.	A group of teachers decide to observe each other on a weekly basis and then discuss ways to improve their teaching.
Teachers and other education professionals are committed to continual professional development.	The entire staff—administration, teachers, counselors, and clerical staff—of an elementary school go on a retreat to plan ways to improve the attendance and discipline policies for the school.
Teachers and other education professionals will and can engage in systematic research.	Following up on the example just listed above, the staff decides to collect data by reviewing the attendance records of chronic absentees over the past year, to interview a random sample of attendees and absentees to determine why they differ, to hold a series of after-school roundtable sessions between discipline-prone students and faculty to identify problems and discuss ways to resolve issues of contention, and to establish a mentoring system in which selected students can serve as counselors to students needing help with their assigned work.

PRACTICAL ACTION RESEARCH

Practical action research is intended to address a specific problem within a classroom, school, or other "community." It can be carried out in a variety of settings, such as educational, social service, or business. Its primary purpose is to improve practice in the short term as well as to inform larger issues. It can be carried out by individuals, teams, or even larger groups, provided the focus remains clear and specific. To be maximally successful, practical action research should result in an *action plan* that, ideally, will be implemented and further evaluated.

PARTICIPATORY ACTION RESEARCH

Participatory action research, while sharing the focus on a specific local issue and on using the findings to implement action, differs in important ways from practical action research. The first difference is that it has two additional purposes: to empower individuals and groups to improve their lives and to bring about social change at some level—school, community, or society. Accordingly, it deliberately involves a sizable group of people representing diverse experiences and viewpoints, all of whom are focused on the same problem. The intent is to have intensive involvement of all these **stakeholders,** who function as equal partners (see Figure 23.1).

The latter requires that the stakeholders, although they may not all be involved at the outset, become active early in the process and jointly plan the study. This includes not only clarifying purposes but also agreeing on other aspects, including data collection and analysis, interpretation of data, and resulting actions. For this reason, participatory action research is often referred to as "collaborative" research. In its "pure" form, participatory action research is

a collaborative approach to research that provides people with the means to take systematic action in an effort to resolve specific problems. [It] encourages consensual, democratic, and participatory strategies to encourage people to examine reflectively problems affecting them . . . Further, it encourages people to formulate accounts and explanations of their situation, and to develop plans that may resolve these problems.[7]

Sometimes a trained researcher identifies a problem and brings it to the attention of the stakeholders. But it

Figure 23.1
Stakeholders

Figure 23.2 *The Role of the "Expert" in Action Research*

is essential that the researcher realize that the problem to be studied must be a problem that is important *to the stakeholders,* and not simply of interest to the researcher. The researcher and the stakeholders *jointly* formulate the research problem (often through brainstorming or by conducting focus groups). This approach contrasts with many of the more traditional investigations, in which the researchers formulate the problem by themselves (see Figure 23.2). Berg describes the trained researcher's role as follows:

> The formally trained researcher stands with and alongside the community or group under study, not outside as an objective observer or external consultant. The researcher contributes expertise when needed as a participant in the process. The researcher collaborates with

local practitioners as well as stakeholders in the group or community. Other participants contribute their physical and/or intellectual resources to the research process. The researcher is a partner with the study population; thus, this type of research is considerably more value-laden than other more traditional roles and endeavors.[3]

LEVELS OF PARTICIPATION

In part because of the influence of participatory action research, more attention has been paid in recent years to the role of individuals who participate in research projects. Historically, in most educational and other research, the subjects in a study simply provided data—by being tested, observed, interviewed, and so forth. They received little or no benefit other than a "thank you" (and sometimes not even that). The benefits of the study accrued to the researcher and (presumably) to the society as a whole.

Such use of individuals raises questions of ethics, even though there may be no risk, deception, or issues of confidentiality involved. Consequently, more effort has been directed toward at least informing the **participants** in a study as to the purposes of the study. This may, however, create a threat to the internal validity of the study or the validity of the data. Participants may, in some cases, be provided the results of the study and, perhaps, be asked to review them. There is, in fact, a continuum of participation (see Figure 23.3). Higher levels of involvement may include helping in instrument development, data collection, and data analysis; participating in data interpretation; making recommendations for further research; actively participating in designing the study; formulating the problem of concern;

even initiating the research effort. In addition to degree of participation, the nature of the participation varies with participant interest and background. It would be unusual, for example, for elementary students to participate at or beyond level three. Similarly, the stakeholders in participatory action research are unlikely to be involved at all levels.

Steps in Action Research

Action research involves four basic stages: (1) identifying the research problem or question, (2) obtaining the necessary information to answer the question(s), (3) analyzing and interpreting the information that has been gathered, and (4) developing a plan of action. Let us discuss each of these stages in a bit more detail.

IDENTIFYING THE RESEARCH QUESTION

The first stage in action research is clarifying the problem of concern. An individual or group needs to carefully examine the situation and identify the problem. Action research is most appropriate when teachers or others involved in education wish to make something better, improve their practice, deal with a troublesome issue, or correct something that is not working.

An important thing to remember is that for an action research project to be successful, it must be manageable. Thus, large scale, complex issues are probably best left to professional researchers. Action research projects are (usually) quite narrow in scope. However, if a group of teachers, students, administrators, and so on have decided to work together on some type of long-term project, the research can be more extensive. Thus, a problem like "What might be a better way to teach fractions?" is more suitable than "Is inquiry teaching more appropriate than more traditional type teaching?" While quite important, the latter is too broad for easy resolution with a single classroom or teacher.

GATHERING THE NECESSARY INFORMATION

Once a problem has been identified, the next step is to decide what sorts of data are needed and how to collect such. Any of the methodologies we have described earlier in this book can be used (although usually in a somewhat simplified and less sophisticated form)

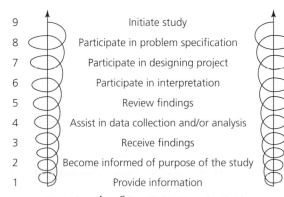

9   Initiate study

8   Participate in problem specification

7   Participate in designing project

6   Participate in interpretation

5   Review findings

4   Assist in data collection and/or analysis

3   Receive findings

2   Become informed of purpose of the study

1   Provide information

Figure 23.3 *Levels of Participation in Action Research*

How Much Should Participants Be Involved in Research?

The active involvement of subjects in all aspects of planning and carrying out research has been advocated on the grounds that participants not only have a right to influence the direction and procedures of a study, but also that they can make major contributions to the research effort itself. Questions have been raised, however, as to whether participation by individuals with only a limited background in research may result in errors and/or bias in the findings and perhaps be subverted to political ends,*,† and that community participants often could be exploited.‡

*A. Bowes. (1996). Evaluating an empowering research strategy: Reflections on action research with South Asian women. *Sociological Research Online 1*. Available at http//kennedy.soc.survey.ac.uk. sosresonline/1/1contents.html.

†S. Nyoni. (1991). People power in Zimbabwe. In O. Fals-Border and M. A. Rahmar (Eds.). *Action and knowledge: Breaking the monopoly with participatory action research.* New York: Apex, pp. 109–120.

‡Hall, B. (1992). "From margins to center? The development and purpose of participatory research," *American Sociologist, 23,* pp. 15–28.

Sclove contends that policy boards such as the National Science Board should include nonexpert members as a way to democratize science and enhance public support for research—as has been done for years in other countries.§ Others argue that the active involvement of participants can lead to social change as "community members become self-sufficient researchers and activists."‖ Some, however, see a danger in mixing research and activism. Stoecker has explored three major, and controversial, roles that the academic expert might play in participant research: the initiator, the consultant, and the collaborator, each appropriate to different community needs.#

What do you think? To what extent should the participants in a study have a say in the planning and execution of the study?

§Sclove, R. E. (1998). "Better approaches to science policy." Editorial and Letters, *Science, 279* (February): p. 1283.

‖R. Stoecker (1999). Are academics irrelevant? Roles for scholars in participatory research. *American Behavioral Scientist, 42* (5): 842.

#Ibid., pp. 840–854.

in action research. Experiments, surveys, causal-comparative studies, observations, interviews, analysis of documents, ethnographies—all are possible methodologies to consider. (We will present some examples of how these might be used later in the chapter).

Teachers can be either active participants (e.g., observing the computer strategies used by one's students while instructing them in computer usage) or nonparticipants (e.g., observing how students interact with one another during classroom study time). Whichever role is chosen, it is a good idea to record as much as possible during the observations—in short, to take *field notes* to describe what was seen and heard.

In addition to observing, a second major category of data collection involves the use of *interviews* of students or other individuals from whom information is desired. Data collected through observations often can suggest questions to be followed up through interviews or the administration of *questionnaires.* In fact, administering questionnaires and interviewing the participants in a study can be a valid and productive way to assess the accuracy of observations. As is true of other aspects

of action research, interviews tend to be less formal and often a bit more unstructured than in more formal research studies.

A third category of data collection involves the examination and *analysis of documents.* This method is perhaps the least time consuming of the three and the easiest to commence. Attendance records, minutes of faculty meetings, counselor records, school newspaper accounts, student journals, lesson plans, administrative logs, suspension lists, detention records, seating charts, photographs of class and school activities, student portfolios—all are grist for the action researcher's mill.

Action research allows for the use of all of the types of instruments discussed in Chapter Seven—questionnaires, interview schedules, checklists, rating scales, attitudinal measures, and so forth. However, often the teachers, administrators, or counselors involved (sometimes even students) develop their own instrument(s) in order to make them locally appropriate. And they are usually shorter, simpler, and less formal than the instruments used in more traditional research studies.

Some action research uses more than one instrument or other forms of *triangulation* (see p. 463). Thus, asking students to respond to carefully prepared interview questions might be supplemented by video recordings; data obtained through the use of observational checklists might be checked against audio recordings of classroom discussions, and so forth. What method(s) to use is dictated, as in any research investigation, by the nature of the research question.

Action researchers must avoid collecting merely anecdotal data—that is, just the opinions of people as to how the problem might be addressed. Although anecdotal data are often valuable, we believe strongly that more substantive evidence of some sort (e.g., audio tape recordings, videotapes, observations, written replies to questionnaires, and so forth) should be obtained.

ANALYZING AND INTERPRETING THE INFORMATION

This stage focuses on analyzing and interpreting the data gathered in stage two. After being collected and summarized, the data need to be analyzed so that the participants can decide what the data reveal. However, analysis of action research data is usually much less complex and detailed than other forms of research.

What is important at this stage is that the data be examined in relation to resolving the research question or problem for which the research was conducted. With regard to participatory action research, Stringer suggests a number of questions that can provide a guiding procedure for analyzing the gathered data.

> The first question, *why,* establishes a general focus for the investigation, reminding everyone what the purpose of the study originally was. The remaining questions—*what, how, who, where,* and *when*—enable participants to identify associated influences. The intent is to better understand the data in context of the setting or situation. *What* and *how* questions help to establish the problems and issues: What is going on that bothers people? How do these problems or issues intrude upon the lives of the people or the group? *Who, where,* and *when* questions focus on specific actions, events, and activities that relate to the problems or issues at hand. The purpose here is not for participants to make quality judgments about these elements; rather, it is to assess the data and clarify information that has been gathered. Additionally, . . . this process provides a means for participants to reflect on things that they have themselves discussed (captured in the data) or that other participants have mentioned.[4]

When analyzing and interpreting data gathered in participatory action research, it is important that the participants try to reflect the perceptions of *all* the stakeholders involved in the study. Hence, they should work collaboratively to create descriptions of what the data reveal. Furthermore, the participants must make every effort to keep all of the stakeholders informed of what is going on during the data-gathering stage and to provide opportunities for everyone involved to read accounts of what is happening as they are prepared (not simply after the study is completed). This permits all of the stakeholders to give their input continuously as the study progresses (see Figure 23.4).

DEVELOPING AN ACTION PLAN

Fulfilling the intent of an action research study requires creating a plan to implement changes based on the findings. While it is desirable that a formal document be prepared, it is not essential; what is essential is that the study, at the very least, indicate clear directions for further work on the original problem or concern.

Similarities and Differences Between Action Research and Formal Quantitative and Qualitative Research

Action research is different in many ways from more formal quantitative and qualitative research, but it also has a number of similarities. Both are shown in Table 23.2.

SAMPLING IN ACTION RESEARCH

Action research problems almost always focus on only a particular group of individuals (a teacher's class, some of a counselor's clients, an administrator's faculty), and hence the sample and population are identical. Random sampling is often difficult in schools, but this is not as critical as it would be in more traditional research endeavors, because generalizing is not necessarily likely nor desired.

INTERNAL VALIDITY IN ACTION RESEARCH

Action research studies are subject to all of the threats to internal validity we described in Chapter Nine, although in differing degrees. Such studies suffer particularly from

Figure 23.4
Participation in Action Research

Table 23.2 *Similarities and Differences Between Action Research and Formal Quantitative and Qualitative Research*

Action Research	Formal Research
Systematic inquiry.	Systematic inquiry.
Goal is to solve problems of local concern.	Goal is to develop and test theories and to produce knowledge generalizable to wide population.
Little formal training required to conduct such studies.	Considerable training required to conduct such studies.
Intent is to identify and correct problems of local concern.	Intent is to investigate larger issues.
Carried out by teacher or other local education professional.	Carried out by researcher who is not usually involved in local situation.
Uses primarily teacher-developed instruments.	Uses primarily professionally-developed instruments.
Less rigorous.	More rigorous.
Usually value-based.	Frequently value-neutral.
Purposive samples selected.	Random samples (if possible) preferred.
Selective opinions of researcher often considered as data.	Selective opinions of researcher never considered as data.
Generalizability is very limited.	Generalizability often appropriate.

the possibility of data-collector bias, because the data collector is well aware of the intent of the study. He or she must take care not to overlook results or responses he or she does not want to see. Implementation and attitudinal effects are also a strong possibility, as either implementers or data collectors can, unwittingly, distort the results of a study.

ACTION RESEARCH AND EXTERNAL VALIDITY: ONCE AGAIN, THE IMPORTANCE OF REPLICATION

As is true of single-subject experimental studies, action research studies are weak when it comes to external validity—generalizability. One cannot recommend using a practice found to be effective in only one classroom!

Thus, action research studies that show a particular practice to be effective, or reveal certain types of attitudes, or encourage particular kinds of changes need to be replicated if their results are to be generalized to other individuals, settings, and situations.

The Advantages of Action Research

We can think of at least five advantages of doing action research. First, it can be done by almost any professional, in any type of school, at any grade level, to investigate just about any kind of problem. It can be carried out by an individual teacher in his or her classroom. It can be done by a group of teachers and/or parents, by a school principal or counselor, or by a school administrator at the district level.

Second, action research can improve educational practice. It helps teachers, counselors, and administrators become more competent professionals. Not only can it help them to become more competent and effective in what they do, but also it can help them be better able to understand and apply the research findings of others. By doing action research *themselves,* teachers and other education professionals can not only improve their skills, they can also improve their ability to read, interpret, and critique more formal research when appropriate.

Third, when teachers or other professionals design and carry out their own action research, they can develop more effective ways to practice their craft. This can lead them to read more formal research reports about similar practices with greater understanding as to how the results of such studies might apply to their own situations. More importantly, such research can serve as a rich source of ideas about how to modify and perhaps enrich one's own strategies and techniques.

Fourth, action research can help teachers identify problems and issues systematically. Learning how to do action research requires that individuals define a problem precisely (often operationally), identify and try out alternative ways to deal with the problem, evaluate these ways, and then share what they have learned with their peers. In effect, action research "shows practitioners that it is possible to break out of the rut of institutionalized, taken-for-granted routines and to develop hope that seemingly intractable problems in the workplace can be solved."[5]

Last, action research can build up a small community of research-oriented individuals within the school itself. Action research, when systematically undertaken, can involve several individuals working together to solve a problem or issue of mutual concern. This can help reduce the feeling of isolation that many teachers, counselors, and administrators experience as they go about their daily tasks within the school. One of the current authors, before becoming a university professor, taught high school social studies. During his first year of teaching, he was assigned a class of particularly difficult students. Some of the other teachers in the school had been working systematically as part of an action research project to test and evaluate various strategies for dealing with such students. They shared what they had learned (through their own action research). Their support and sharing of information proved invaluable to a somewhat overwhelmed beginner.

Some Hypothetical Examples of Practical Action Research

Almost all of the methodologies described in the other chapters in this book can be adapted (in a less formal and sophisticated form) by teachers and other education professionals in the schools to investigate problems and questions of interest. Although we use school-based settings for the examples that follow, it takes only a little imagination to conceptualize how action research can be used elsewhere (e.g., mental health institutions, volunteer organizations, community service agencies). We now present some examples of what could be done.

INVESTIGATING THE TEACHING OF SCIENCE CONCEPTS BY MEANS OF A COMPARISON-GROUP EXPERIMENT

Ms. Gonzales, a fifth-grade teacher, is interested in the following question:

- Does using drama improve understanding of basic science concepts in fifth-graders?

How might Ms. Gonzales proceed?

Although it could be investigated in a number of ways, this question lends itself particularly well to a comparison-group experiment. Ms. Gonzales could randomly assign students to classes in which some teachers use dramatics and some teachers do not. She

An Important Example of Action Research

The early 1990s provide an example of effective participatory action research. When a new powerhouse for the Bonneville Dam was to be built in the center of the town of North Bonneville WA, all 470 residents faced eviction, relocation, and the probable demise of their town. Citizens rallied around the goal of relocating as an existing town and where they chose. To do so, they had to oppose the U.S. Army Corps of Engineers. With help from faculty and students at the University of Washington and Evergreen State College, a broad-based citizen group undertook research to inform themselves in detail about the assets and characteristics of their town as well as the details of community planning and the political process. College students lived and worked in the town as they gathered data through documents, informal discussions, and workshops accompanied by ongoing feedback and discussion with all sectors of the community. The town council provided financial and logistical support. Citizens became increasingly involved in providing information and in political action. In the end, they not only attained their goal but succeeded in having their design for their 'new' town replace the one proposed by the Corps of Engineers.*

*Fischer, F. (2000). *Citizens, experts and the environment: The politics of local knowledge.* Durham and London: Duke University Press, pp. 268–272.

could compare the effects of these contrasting methods by testing the conceptual knowledge of the students in these classes at specified intervals with a test designed to measure conceptual understanding. The average score of the different classes on the test (the dependent variable) would give Ms. Gonzales some idea of the effectiveness of the methods being compared.

Of course, Ms. Gonzales wants to have as much control as possible over the assignment of individuals to the various treatment groups. In most schools, the random assignment of students to treatment groups (classes) would be very difficult to accomplish. Should this be the case, comparison still would be possible using a quasi-experimental design. Ms. Gonzales might, for example, compare student achievement in two or more *intact* classes in which some teachers agree to use the drama approach. Because the students in these classes would not have been assigned randomly, the design could not be considered a true experiment; but if the differences between the classes in terms of what is being measured are quite large, and if students have been matched on pertinent variables (including a pretest of conceptual understanding), the results could still be useful with regard to how the two methods compare.

We would be concerned that the classes might differ with regard to important variables that could affect the outcome of the study. If Ms. Gonzales is the data collector, she could unintentionally favor one group when she administers the instrument(s).

Ms. Gonzales should attempt to control for all extraneous variables (student ability level, age, instructional time, teacher characteristics, and so on) that might affect the outcome under investigation. Several control procedures were described in Chapter Nine: teaching during the same or closely connected periods of time, using equally experienced teachers for both methods, matching students on ability and gender, having someone else administer the instrument(s), and so forth.

Ms. Gonzales might decide to use the causal-comparative method if some classes are *already* being taught by teachers using the drama approach.

STUDYING THE EFFECTS OF TIME-OUT ON A STUDENT'S DISRUPTIVE BEHAVIOR BY MEANS OF A SINGLE-SUBJECT EXPERIMENT

Ms. Wong, a third-grade teacher, finds her class continually interrupted by a student who can't seem to keep quiet. Distressed, she asks herself what she can do to control this student, and wonders if some kind of "time-out" activity might work. Accordingly, she asks:

- Would brief periods of removal from the class decrease the frequency of this student's disruptive behavior?

What might Ms. Wong do to get an answer to her question?

This sort of question can best be answered by means of a single-subject A-B-A-B design. First, Ms. Wong needs to establish a baseline of the student's disruptive behavior. Hence, she should observe the student carefully over a period of several days, charting the frequency of the disruptive behavior. Once she has established a stable pattern of the student's behavior, she should introduce the treatment—in this instance, "time-out," or placing the student outside the classroom for a brief period of time—for several days and observe the frequency of the student's disruptive behavior after the treatment periods. She then should repeat the cycle. Ideally, the student's disruptive behavior will decrease and Ms. Wong will no longer need to use a "time-out" period with this student.

The main problem for Ms. Wong is being able to observe and chart the student's behavior during the time-out period and yet still teach the other students in her class. She may also have difficulty making sure the treatment (time-out) works as intended (e.g., that the student is not wandering the halls). Both of these problems would be greatly diminished if she has a teacher's aide to assist with these concerns.

DETERMINING WHAT STUDENTS LIKE ABOUT SCHOOL BY MEANS OF A SURVEY

Mr. Abramson, a high school guidance counselor, is not interested in comparing instructional methods. He is interested in how students feel about school in general. Accordingly, he asks the following questions:

- What do students like about their classes? What do they dislike? Why?
- What types of subjects are liked the best or least?
- How do the feelings of students of different ages, sexes, and ethnicities in our school compare?

What might Mr. Abramson do to get some answers?

These sorts of questions can best be answered by a survey that measures student attitudes toward their classes. Mr. Abramson will need to prepare a questionnaire, taking time to ensure that the questions he intends to ask are directed toward the information he wants to obtain. Next, he should have some other members of the faculty look over the questions and identify any they feel will be misleading or ambiguous.

There are two difficulties involved in such a survey. First, Mr. Abramson must ensure that the questions to be answered are clear and not misleading. He can accomplish this, to a fair extent, by using objective or closed-ended questions, ensuring that they all pertain to the topic under investigation, and then further eliminating ambiguity by pilot-testing a draft of the questionnaire with a small group of students. Second, Mr. Abramson must be sure that a sufficient number of questionnaires are completed and returned so that meaningful analyses can be made. He can improve this rate of return by giving the questionnaire to students to complete when they are all in one place. Once he collects the completed questionnaires, he should tally the responses and see what he's got.

The big advantage of questionnaire research is that it has the potential to provide a lot of information from quite a large sample of individuals. If more details about particular questions are desired, Mr. Abramson can also conduct personal interviews with students. As we have mentioned before, the advantage here is that Mr. Abramson can ask open-ended questions (those giving the respondent maximum freedom of response) with more confidence, and pursue particular questions of special interest or value in depth. He would also be able to ask follow-up questions and explain any items that students find unclear.

One problem here may be that some students may not understand the questions, or they may not return their questionnaire. Mr. Abramson has an advantage over many survey researchers in that he can probably ensure a high rate of return by administering his questionnaire directly to students in their classrooms. He must be careful to give directions that facilitate an honest and serious set of answers and to ensure the anonymity of the respondents. Although it is difficult, he also should try to get data on both reliability (perhaps by giving the questionnaire to a subsample a second time after an appropriate time interval—say, two weeks) and validity (perhaps by selecting a subsample that is interviewed immediately after they individually fill out the questionnaire). Checking reliability and validity requires sacrificing anonymity for those students in the subsample, since he must be able to identify individual questionnaires.

CHECKING FOR BIAS IN ENGLISH ANTHOLOGIES BY MEANS OF A CONTENT ANALYSIS

Ms. Hallowitz, an eighth-grade English teacher, is concerned about the accuracy of the images or concepts that are presented to her students in their literature anthologies. She asks the following questions.

- Is the content presented in the literature anthologies in our district biased in any way? If so, how?

What might Ms. Hallowitz do to get answers?

To investigate these questions, *content analysis* (Chapter Twenty) is called for. Ms. Hallowitz decides to look particularly at the images of heroes that are presented in the literature anthologies used in the district.

First, she needs to select the sample of anthologies to be analyzed—that is, to determine which texts she will peruse. (She restricts herself to only the current texts available for use in the district.) She then needs to think about the specific categories she wants to look at. Let us assume she decides to analyze the physical, emotional, social, and mental characteristics of heroes that are presented. She could then break these categories down into smaller coding units such as those shown below.

Physical	Emotional	Social	Mental
Weight	Friendly	Ethnicity	Wise
Height	Aloof	Dress	Funny
Age	Hostile	Occupation	Intelligent
Body type	Uninvolved	Status	Superhuman
.	.	.	.
.	.	.	.
.	.	.	.

Ms. Hallowitz can prepare a coding sheet to tally the data in each of the categories that she identifies in each anthology she studies. She can also readily compare among categories to determine, for example, whether white men are portrayed as "white-collar" workers and nonwhite people are portrayed as "blue-collar" workers.

A major advantage of content analysis is that it is unobtrusive. Ms. Hallowitz can "observe" without being observed, since the contents being analyzed are not influenced by her presence. Information that she might find difficult or even impossible to obtain through direct observation or other means can be gained through a content analysis of the sort sketched above.

A second advantage is that content analysis is fairly easy for others to replicate. Lastly the information that is obtained through content analysis can be very helpful in planning for further instruction. Data of the type sought by Ms. Hallowitz can suggest additional information that students may need to gain a more accurate and complete picture of the world they live in, the factors and forces that exist within it, and how these factors and forces impinge on people's lives.

Ms. Hallowitz's major problem lies in being able to specify clearly the categories that will suit her questions. If, for example, nonwhite males are less often portrayed as "professionals," does this indicate bias in the materials or does it reflect reality (or both)? She should try to identify all the anthologies being used in her district and then either analyze each one or select a random sample.

Ms. Hallowitz could, of course, survey teacher and/or student opinions about bias, but that would answer a different question.

PREDICTING WHICH KINDS OF STUDENTS ARE LIKELY TO HAVE TROUBLE LEARNING ALGEBRA BY MEANS OF A CORRELATIONAL STUDY

Let's turn to mathematics for our next example. Mr. Thompson, an algebra teacher, is bothered by the fact that some of his students have difficulty learning algebra while other students learn it with ease. As a result, he asks:

- How can I predict which sorts of individuals are likely to have trouble learning algebra?

What might Mr. Thompson do to investigate this question?

If Mr. Thompson could make fairly accurate predictions in this regard, he might be able to suggest some corrective measures that he or other teachers could use to help students so that large numbers of "math-haters" are not produced. In this instance, *correlational analysis* would be appropriate. Mr. Thompson could use a variety of measures to collect different sorts of data on his students: their performance on a number of "readiness" tasks related to algebra learning (e.g., calculating, story problems); other variables that might be related to success in algebra (anxiety about math, critical thinking ability); familiarity with specific concepts ("constant," "variable," "distributed"); and any other variables that might conceivably point out how those students who do better in algebra differ from those who do more poorly.

The information obtained from such research can help Mr. Thompson predict more accurately which students will have learning difficulties in algebra and should suggest some techniques for him to try in order to help students learn.

The main problem for Mr. Thompson is likely to be getting adequate measurements on the different variables he wishes to study. Some information should be available from school records; other variables will probably require special instrumentation. (He must remember that this information must apply to students *before* they take the algebra class, not during or after.)

Mr. Thompson must, of course, have an adequately reliable and valid way to measure proficiency in algebra. He must also try to avoid incomplete data (i.e., missing scores for some students on some measures).

COMPARING TWO WAYS OF TEACHING CHEMISTRY BY MEANS OF A CAUSAL-COMPARATIVE STUDY

Ms. Perea, a first-year chemistry teacher, is interested in discovering whether students in past classes achieved more in, and felt better about, chemistry when they were taught by a teacher who used "inquiry science" materials. Accordingly, she asks the following question:

- How has the achievement of those students who have been taught with inquiry science materials compared with that of students who have been taught with traditional materials?

What might Ms. Perea do to get some answers to her question?

If this question were to be investigated experimentally, two groups of students would have to be formed, and then each group taught differently by the teachers involved (one teacher using a standard text, let's say, and the other using the inquiry-oriented materials). The achievement and attitude of the two groups could then be compared by means of one or more assessment devices.

To test this question using a *causal-comparative design,* however, Ms. Perea must find a group of students who *already* have been exposed to the inquiry science materials and then compare their achievement with that of another group taught with the standard text. Do the two groups differ in their achievement and attitude toward chemistry? Suppose they do. Can Ms. Perea then conclude with confidence that the difference in materials produced the difference in achievement and/or attitude? Alas, no, for other variables may be the "cause." To the extent that she can rule out such alternative explanations, she can have some confidence that the inquiry materials are at least one factor in causing the difference between groups.

Ms. Perea's main problems are in getting a good measure of achievement and in controlling extraneous variables. The latter is likely to be difficult, since she needs to have access to prior classes in order to get the relevant information (such as student ability and teacher experience). She might locate classes that were as similar as possible with regard to extraneous variables that might affect results.

Unless she has a special reason for wanting to study previous classes, Ms. Perea might be advised to compare methods that are being used currently. She might be able to use a quasi-experimental approach (by assigning teachers to methods and controlling the way in which the methods are carried out). If not, her causal-comparative approach would permit easier control of extraneous variables if current classes were used.

FINDING OUT HOW MUSIC TEACHERS TEACH BY MEANS OF AN ETHNOGRAPHIC STUDY

Mr. Adams, the director of curriculum in an elementary school district, is interested in knowing more about how the district's music teachers teach their subject. Accordingly, he asks:

- What do our music teachers do as they go about their daily routine—in what kinds of activities do they engage?
- What are the explicit and implicit rules of the game in music classes that seem to help or hinder the process of learning?

What can Mr. Adams do to get some answers?

To gain some insight into these questions, Mr. Adams could choose to carry out an *ethnography* (Chapter Twenty-One). He could try to document or portray the activities that go on in a music teacher's classes as the teacher goes about his or her daily routine. Ideally, Mr. Adams should focus on only one classroom (or a small number of them at most) and plan to observe the teacher and students in that classroom on as regular a basis as possible (perhaps once a week for one semester). He should attempt to describe, as fully and as richly as possible, what he sees going on.

The data to be collected might include interviews with the teacher and students, detailed prose descriptions of classroom routines, audiotapes of teacher-student conferences, videotapes of classroom discussions, examples of teacher lesson plans and student work, and flowcharts that illustrate the direction and frequency of certain types of comments (e.g., the kinds of questions that teacher and students ask of one another, and the responses that different kinds of questions produce).

Ethnographic research can lend itself well to a detailed study of individuals as well as classrooms. Sometimes much can be learned from studying just one individual. For example, some students learn how to play a musical instrument very easily. In hopes of gaining insight into why this is the case, Mr. Adams might observe and interview one such student on a regular basis to see if there are any noticeable patterns or regularities in the student's behavior. Teachers and counselors, as well as the student, might be interviewed in depth. Mr. Adams might also conduct a similar series of observations and

Figure 23.5 *Action Research: A Matter of Definition*

interviews with a student who finds learning how to play an instrument very difficult, to see what differences can be identified. As in the study of a whole classroom, as much information as possible (study style, attitudes toward music, approach to the subject, behavior in class) would be collected. The hope here is that through the study of an individual, insights can be gained that will help the teacher with similar students in the future.

In short, then, Mr. Adams's goal should be to "paint a portrait" of a music classroom (or an individual teacher or student in such a classroom) in as thorough and accurate a manner as possible so that others can also "see" that classroom and its participants, and what they do.*

---

*Although it may appear that ethnographic research is relatively easy to do, it is, in fact, extremely difficult to do well. If you wish to learn more about this method, consult one or more of the following references: H. B. Bernard (2000). *Social research methods.* Thousand Oaks, CA: Sage Publications; J. P. Goetz and M. D. LeCompte (1993). *Ethnography and qualitative design in educational research,* 2nd ed. San Diego, CA: Academic Press; Y. S. Lincoln and E. G. Guba (1985). *Naturalistic inquiry.* Newbury Park, CA: Sage Publications; D. F. Lancy (2001). *Studying Children and Schools: Qualitative research traditions.* Prospect Heights, IL: Waveland Press; D. M. Fetterman (1989). *Ethnography: Step by Step.* Thousand Oaks, CA: Sage; R. C. Bogdan and S. K. Biklen (1998). *Qualitative research in education: An introduction to theory and methods,* 3rd ed. Boston: Allyn & Bacon.

One of the difficulties in conducting an ethnographic study is that relatively little advice can be given beforehand. The primary pitfall is allowing personal views to influence the information obtained and its interpretation.

Mr. Adams could elect to use a more structured observation system and a structured interview. This would reduce the subjectivity of his data, but it might also detract from the richness of what he reports. We believe that an ethnographic study should be done only under the guidance of someone with prior training and experience in using this methodology.

An Example of Action Research

At this point, we want to present a real-life example of how even one of the most difficult types of research to do in schools (a quasi-experiment) can be carried out in the context of ongoing school activities and responsibilities. The following study was carried out by one of our students, Darlene DeMaria, in her special class for learning-disabled students in a public elementary school near San Francisco, California.[6] Ms. DeMaria hypothesized that male learning-disabled students in elementary schools who receive a systematic program

Things to Consider When Doing In-School Research

- Check the clarity of purpose and definitions with others.
- Give attention to obtaining and describing your sample in a way that is clear to others and, it is hoped, permits generalization of results.
- If appropriate, use existing instruments; if it is necessary to develop your own, remember the guidelines presented in Chapter Seven.

- Make an effort to check the reliability and validity of your measures.
- Give thought to each of the threats to internal validity. Take steps to reduce these threats as much as possible.
- Use statistics where appropriate to clarify data. Use inferential statistics only when justified—or as rough guides.
- Be clear about the population to which you are entitled to generalize. It may be only those you actually include in your study (i.e., your sample). It may be that you can provide a rationale for broader generalization.

of relaxation exercises would show a greater reduction in off-task behaviors than students who do not receive such a program of exercise.

Using an adaptation of an existing instrument, Ms. DeMaria selected 25 items (behaviors) from a 60-item scale previously designed to assess attention deficit. The 25 items selected were those most directly related to off-task behavior. Each item was rated from 0 to 4 on the basis of prior observation of the student, with a rating of 0 indicating that the behavior had never been observed and a rating of 4 indicating that the behavior had been observed so frequently as to seriously interfere with learning.

Three weeks after school began Ms. DeMaria and her aide independently filled out the rating scale for each of the 18 students. The scores provided the basis for assessing improvement and for matching two groups prior to intervention.

Because the students were assigned to the Resource Room (where Ms. DeMaria taught) approximately one hour a day in groups of two to four, and their schedules had been set previously, random assignment was not possible. It was, however, possible to match students across groups on grade level and (roughly) on initial ratings of off-task behavior. The class included students in grades 1 through 6. Students selected to be in the experimental group received the relaxation program on a daily basis for four weeks (Phase I), after which both Ms. DeMaria and her aide again independently rated all 18 students. Comparison of the groups at this time provided the first test of the hypothesis. Next, the relaxation program was continued for the original experimental group and *begun* for the comparison group for another four weeks (Phase II), permitting additional comparison of groups and resolving the ethical question of excluding one group from a potentially beneficial

experience. At the end of this time, all students were again rated independently by Ms. DeMaria and her aide. The experimental design is shown in Figure 23.6.

The results showed that after Phase I the experimental group showed deterioration (*more* off-task behavior—contrary to the hypothesis), whereas the comparison group showed little change. At the end of Phase II, the scores for both groups remained about the same as at the end of Phase I. Further analysis of the various subgroups (each instructed during a different time period) showed that little change occurred in the groups that received only four weeks of training. Of the three subgroups that received eight weeks of training, two showed a substantial *decrease* in off-task behavior and one showed a marked *increase*. The explanation for the latter appears clear. One student who was placed in the Resource Room program just prior to the onset of relaxation training had an increasingly disruptive effect on the other members of his subgroup, an influence that the training was not powerful enough to counteract.

This study demonstrates how research on important questions can be conducted in real-life situations in schools and can lead to useful, although tentative, implications for practice.

Like any study, this one has several limitations. The first is that agreement between Ms. DeMaria and her

			Phase I		Phase II	
Group I	O	M	X_1	O	X_1	O
Group II	O	M		O	X_1	O

Figure 23.6 *Experimental Design for the DeMaria Study*

aide on the pretest was insufficient and required further discussion and reconciliation of differences, thus making the pretest scores somewhat suspect. Agreement, however, was satisfactory (an r above .80) for the posttests.

A second limitation is that the comparison groups could not be precisely matched on the pretest, since the control group had more students at both extremes. Although neither group initially showed more off-task behavior overall, this difference as well as other uncontrolled differences in subject characteristics could conceivably explain the different outcomes for the two groups. Further, the fact that the implementer (Ms. De-Maria) was one of the raters could certainly have influenced the ratings. That this did not happen is suggested by the fact that Ms. DeMaria's Phase II scores for the original experimental group were in fact higher (contrary to her hypothesis) than in Phase I. Evidence of retest reliability of scores could not be obtained during the time available for the study. Evidence for validity rests on the agreement between independent judges. Generalization beyond this one group of students and one teacher (Ms. DeMaria) clearly is not justified. The analysis of subgroups, although enlightening, is after the fact, and hence the results are highly tentative.

Despite these limitations, the study does suggest that the relaxation program may have value for at least some students if it is carried out long enough. One or more other teachers should be encouraged to replicate the study. An additional benefit was that the study clarified, for the teacher, the dynamics of each of the subgroups in her class.

Classroom teachers and other professionals can (and should, we would argue) conduct studies like the one we have summarized. As mentioned earlier, there is much in education about which we know little. Many questions remain unanswered; much information is needed. Classroom teachers, counselors, and administrators can help to provide this information. We hope you will be one of those who do.

A Published Example of Action Research

To conclude this chapter, we present a published example of action research, followed by a critique of its strengths and weaknesses. As we did in our critiques of other types of research studies, we use concepts introduced in earlier parts of the book in our analysis.

Journal of Research in Childhood Education, 14:2 (2000): 232–238. Copyright 2000 by the Association for Childhood Education International.

What Do You Mean "Think Before I Act"?: Conflict Resolution with Choices

Lonisa Browning
Barbara Davis
Virginia Resta
Southwest Texas State University, San Marcos

Abstract.

Twenty 1st-grade students participated in an eight-week action research study. Students participated in class meetings where they discussed problem-solving solutions, particularly positive forms of conflict resolution. The "Wheel of Choice" provided the students with the choices for solutions that included 1) make an apology, 2) tell the other person to stop, 3) walk away, and 4) give an "I" message. Data was collected through 1) student pre- and post-surveys, 2) student conflict-resolution journals, 3) behavior tally sheets, 4) observational notes, and 5) teacher reflective journal. Pre- and post-surveys indicated that the students developed more positive strategies for solving conflicts. The student conflict-resolution journals demonstrated that students were able to write down positive forms of conflict resolution after thinking about the problem. Analysis of the tally sheets indicated that (physical and verbal) aggression decreased from the first week (22 incidents) to the eighth week (4 incidents) of the study. The teacher reflection journal and observational notes also documented that students used the "Wheel of Choice" when given the opportunity and time to think about the problem.

verbal only

"Stop laughing at me," yelled Michael (all names are pseudonyms) as he shoved a classmate with full force into the bulletin board. His forehead was creased with lines, his eyes glared, and his mouth was one straight line. Michael's clenched fists and stiff body showed me (the first author) that he was not in the mood to talk about the problem. During my first year of teaching 1st grade, I confronted incidents like these on a daily basis. My students did not seem to have the necessary skills to successfully solve conflicts with their peers. Like Michael, their first reaction was usually to hit, shove, push, and/or yell.

As a teacher, I wanted to guide my students into solving conflicts productively. Most of my students witnessed verbal and physical aggression in their neighborhoods and homes, so they emulated that model as solutions to their problems. Therefore, helping my students learn positive methods of resolving conflicts became the focus of an action research project I conducted in my classroom during that first year of teaching.

The students in my 1st-grade class live in a world where violence, both gang and domestic, is commonplace. The majority of the students come from low-income, minority families. Many of them live in multi-family homes. They frequently move from home to home. These children act out what they see in their environment (e.g., hitting, yelling, fighting). Each week, I had to complete numerous referrals to the office for children who solved conflicts in physically or verbally aggressive ways.

Sample description

The research question I developed to focus my investigation was, "Will physically and verbally aggressive students solve conflicts in a constructive manner if provided models of pro-social alternative solutions?" I wanted my young students to 1) decrease the use of physical and

Research question

Purpose

verbal aggression to solve conflicts, 2) increase the use of positive solutions, and 3) be able to verbalize the problem, their feelings, and a constructive solution. Ultimately, I wanted the children to become prepared for society-at-large by learning and using constructive forms of conflict management.

Prior research

Numerous researchers have studied the effects of pro-social behavior and social skills on young children. Children are very egocentric (i.e., they see the world from their own perspective). They focus on an aspect of a situation that is important to them (Bailey, 1994). Adults play an important role in helping children develop pro-social attitudes and behaviors. Children live what they learn (Nelsen, Lott, & Glenn, 1997; Wittmer & Honig, 1994). A major reason that children fight is that the adults in their lives have not taught them other options for resolving conflicts (Nelsen, Duffy, Escobar, Ortolano, & Owen-Sohocki, 1996). Adults need to teach children to express their feelings and to understand others' feelings. Children also need to be able to think through a problem step-by-step and to develop alternative solutions. If teachers take time to encourage, facilitate, and teach pro-social behaviors, children's pro-social interactions increase and aggression decreases (Wittmer & Honig, 1994).

Prior resåearch

Bailey (1994) states that children need to take responsibility for conflict resolution, which turns the problem over to the students a little at a time. Students develop problem-solving skills by finding resolution ideas that work (Bailey, 1994; Sloane, 1998). Students become effective problem-solvers when teachers take the time to train students in problem-solving and give them opportunities to practice these skills (Nelsen, Lott, & Glenn, 1997). When teacher intervention is not necessary, students should be able to follow the conflict resolution steps, which include: 1) defining the problem, 2) generating solutions, 3) reaching agreements, 4) implementing solutions, and 5) evaluating whether or not the problem was solved (Sloane, 1998). Using these problem-solving steps and taking responsibility for their actions can help students learn to listen, understand other perspectives, recognize problems, and look for alternative solutions (Bailey, 1994).

Prior research

Class meetings, as defined by Nelsen, Lott, and Glenn in *Positive Discipline in the Classroom* (1997), provide a designated time (e.g., 20 to 30 minutes) during the school day when students form a circle to discuss classroom issues and problems. Class meetings provide an opportunity for students to practice using pro-social skills by making decisions and solving problems together. They also help students develop a sense of value and belonging by allowing them to share concerns, anxieties, frustration, and celebrations. Through class meetings, students are able to express concerns and solve conflicts in a non-threatening environment. By developing solutions that are related, respectful, and reasonable, students learn skills that enable them to solve problems when they occur. The goal of class meetings is to help students learn skills they can use every day of their lives (McEwan, Gathercoal, Donahue, Greenfield, & Strangio, 1998; Nelsen, Lott, & Glenn, 1997).

METHODS AND PROCEDURES

Sample

This action research project was conducted in my 1st-grade classroom at an elementary school located in the southwestern United States. Ninety-five percent of the students at this prekindergarten through 5th-grade campus represent minority populations; the majority come from low-socioeconomic backgrounds. My 1st-grade class consisted of 20 students (12 boys and 8 girls). One-fourth of the class was African American, approximately three-fourths were Hispanic, and one child was Caucasian. This eight-week project was implemented during the second semester of the school year.

Method

At the beginning of the school year, I introduced the class meeting format outlined by Nelsen et al. (1997). The format consists of 1) forming a circle, 2) giving compliments and appreciations, 3) following up on prior solutions, 4) discussing agenda items (e.g., sharing prob-

WHEEL OF CHOICE

lems/concerns, problem-solving solutions), and 5) discussing future plans (e.g., field trips, parties, projects).

One aspect of Nelsen's "Positive Discipline" procedures that I introduced to my students was the use of the "Wheel of Choice" (see Sample A). The "Wheel of Choice" provides several alternative choices for solving disagreements. Some of the strategies on the "Wheel of Choice" include 1) make an apology, 2) tell the person to stop, 3) walk away, and 4) give an "I" message. Each step of the "Wheel of Choice" was introduced through role play (by myself and the students) and discussion. A large "Wheel of Choice" poster, which included pictures depicting the problem-solving strategies (to assist emergent readers), was hung on the classroom door for the children to refer to whenever a conflict arose. By implementing the "Wheel of Choice," I hoped to engage my students in positive forms of conflict resolution by giving them choices for solutions.

Data Collection

Both quantitative and qualitative data were collected during this study. While data was collected on all of the class, I targeted (five students) to observe more closely during the project. These students were selected because I had observed them having difficulty with problem solving throughout the first semester. Their first reaction in times of conflict was to act out, either physically or verbally (e.g., hitting, pushing, fighting, yelling, or tattling). As the targets of my study, I hoped to find that, during times of anger, these five students would change their negative behavior to constructive problem-solving.

In the following sections, I will describe the various methods of data collection. These included 1) student pre- and post-surveys, 2) student conflict-resolution journals, 3) behavior tally sheets, 4) observational notes, and 5) teacher reflective journal.

Purposive subsample

Sample B *Student Survey*
_____

Name: _____ Date: _____

1. When you get mad at a friend you . . .
   a. hit your friend
   b. yell at your friend
   c. tell an adult
   d. tell your friend how you feel
2. When I have a fight, I fix it myself.
   a. yes
   b. no
3. Draw a picture of one time you had a fight with a friend. (The teacher will write the child's dictated responses.)
4. Draw a picture of how you solved that problem. (The teacher will write the child's dictated responses.)

Reliability? Validity?

Student surveys. Surveys were collected to determine how students viewed their own problem-solving strategies (see Sample B). I read the survey questions to the students and asked them to circle the answers they felt were appropriate. For questions 3 and 4, the students drew pictures and then dictated their responses to me. These surveys were administered at the beginning and end of the study to determine the students' progress in developing skills in conflict resolution.

Cognitive, not behavioral

Possible validity checks

Conflict-resolution journals. Data also were collected from student conflict-resolution journals. Following a conflict, students wrote about what happened in their journals. They addressed the following three questions in their journals: 1) What was the problem? 2) How did you solve it? and 3) What is another way to solve it? The purpose of the journals was to help the students remember what happened so they could discuss it with me later.

Recall of behavior

Tally sheets. A behavior tally sheet was used to collect data on the number of times the targeted students exhibited physical and verbal aggression. I also moved on the tally sheets to record how often students used the "Wheel of Choice" to solve problems. By each tally mark, I wrote the first letter of the student's name and what he/she did. At the end of each week, I added up the tally marks.

Behavioral measure

Observational notes. During the class meetings, I kept observational notes in a spiral-bound notebook of the meeting's agenda. After the "Wheel of Choice" had been introduced as a conflict-resolution strategy, I analyzed the class meeting agenda notes each week during the project to see if the students were using the strategies to solve conflicts as a group. The agenda notes included the problem or concern of an individual child and the list of solutions the students developed collaboratively during the class meeting. In my analysis, I was looking to see if the types of resolutions students suggested were changing from punitive measures—such as "go to DIL" (in-school suspension), "take them to the principal," "go to time out," or "move their clothespin to red" (on a classroom disciplinary color-change chart)—to more positive solutions.

Behavioral evidence of cognitive change only

Teacher journal. I also kept a teacher reflective journal during this project, in which, each week, I wrote about the occurrences in my classroom. The following questions were addressed: Were the students having many conflicts? Were they using the "Wheel of Choice"? Was there any particular student who was having more trouble than others? As I kept this journal, I looked for trends in students' behavior and among the conflict-resolution suggestions they chose to use.

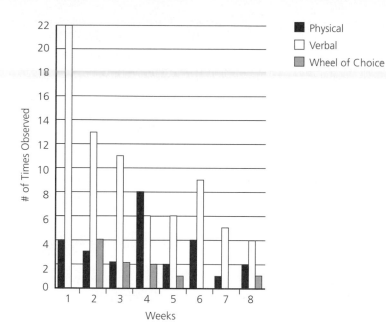

Figure 1 — legend:
- ■ Physical
- □ Verbal
- ▨ Wheel of Choice

Y-axis: # of Times Observed (0 to 22)
X-axis: Weeks (1 to 8)

Figure 1 *Types of Conflict-Resolution Strategies Used by Target Students (N-5)*

Title is wrong; the tally sheets record aggression, not strategies.

Analysis of Data and Findings

As shown in Figure 1, an analysis of the tally sheets indicates that incidences of physical and verbal aggression decreased from the first to the eighth week of the study. At the beginning of the study, verbal aggression was the method most frequently used to resolve a conflict. The total number of verbally aggressive incidences recorded for week one was 22, as compared to only 4 incidences during week eight. Physical agression decreased the first three weeks, but then increased dramatically during week four (from 4 times to 8 times). After seeing this increase, I analyzed the names on the tally sheet to see which student(s) were solving conflicts in this way. The same student had used this strategy for all eight conflicts. Although it fluctuated, the number of physically aggressive acts did decrease from the beginning to the end of the study.

Targeted subsample only

Clear results for verbal; less so for physical

While the number of incidences of physical and verbal aggression did decrease by the end of the study, the tally sheets did not indicate that students used strategies from the "Wheel of Choice" during the "heat" of a conflict. The most frequent use of the "Wheel of Choice" strategies occurred during the second week, after the strategies had been introduced. Thereafter, the use of these strategies tapered off and began showing up again at the conclusion of the study. This finding suggests that students need to be reminded to refer to the "Wheel of Choice" when conflicts arise.

Interpretation

Results of the comparison of pre- and post-surveys indicate that my students were developing the skills to use more positive strategies for solving conflicts. The ⟨majority⟩ of the responses on the pre-surveys indicate that the students' first reaction to conflict was to act out of anger rather than to stop and think about the problem. The post-surveys, however, ⟨suggest that⟩ once students were given the chance to analyze the situation and think about how to solve it, they were able to generate more positive alternatives. For example, as demonstrated in Figure 2, when Karen had a conflict with Lisa, her initial reaction was to laugh at her and push her. Karen then thought about the problem and ⟨solved the disagreement⟩ in a more productive fashion. This action suggests that Karen was able to use what she had learned from the "Wheel of Choice," as well as from the class meetings.

f = ?

f = ?

Recall of behavior

Figure 2 *Karen's Post-Survey*

3. Draw a picture of one time you had a fight with a friend. (Teacher will dictate.)

He made me want to fight w/ him.
He made me mad because I was writing something and he took it (my crayon, away from me.

4. Draw a picture of how you solved that problem. (Teacher will dictate.)

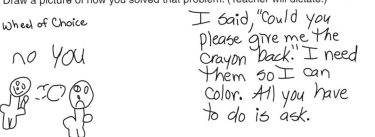

I said, "Could you please give me the crayon back." I need them so I can color. All you have to do is ask.

And use?

The conflict-resolution journals were used to guide students into thinking about the problem and the solution they chose to use. Through the journals, I was able to see what type of conflict-resolution strategies were being used (e.g., if students were able to think of alternative choices for conflict management). I was also able to see which students had the most difficulty when conflicts arose. The journal notes reflect that students were able to write positive forms of conflict resolution down after thinking about the problem. These solutions were usually based on the choices from the "Wheel of Choice." . . .

By whom?

Good detail

Did they do it?

I analyzed the content of my reflective journal and observational notes by color-coding response patterns. I was looking for trends in types of conflict resolutions used. I also wanted to see which students were successful at using the "Wheel of Choice" and which students needed more assistance. My journal was a kaleidoscope of colors. The first few entries showed only physical and verbal aggression. The "Wheel of Choice" was used at least once a day for one or two days. By the middle of the project, I had recorded that the "Wheel of Choice" poster was being used more by students, especially during class meetings. For example, the solutions my students began suggesting during class meetings included 1) tell the person to stop, 2) tell him or her how you feel, 3) walk away, and 4) ignore it. My students also learned how to ask someone else for help (e.g., counselor, teacher, other students) if any of these solutions did not work. Being given the opportunity to discuss problems and develop solutions as a group helped my young students become more effective problem solvers. Through my journal, I found that my students were capable of using the "Wheel of Choice" when given the opportunity and time to think about the problem.

Good example

Behavioral or cognitive?

Based on the notes in my reflective journal and the observational data, I selected one target student who appeared to be having more difficulty than others when solving conflicts. Michael's initial response was to hit, shove, or yell "Stop!" I took observational notes on Michael as he interacted with others in the class to see when he had the most difficulty. From the color-coding of physical and verbal aggression and by comparing the conflicts in the observational notes and the student journals, I saw that Michael clearly had more difficulty with conflict when he was individually engrossed in an activity and another child disturbed him. For instance, one day while Michael was reading, Tim bumped him. Michael's initial reaction was to hit Tim on the arm and yell, "You did that!" He then went back to his work, almost unaware of Tim's feelings. What I noticed from my notes was that when Michael had time to consider the choices for conflict resolution, he would make a positive choice. This was especially obvious in his conflict-resolution journal, where he wrote "Wheel of Choice" solutions for all of his problems.

CONCLUSIONS

Through this research, I learned that students need time and practice to change negative conflict management habits. While their first reaction may be to resort to physical or verbal aggression, when given appropriate models and time to think about alternative solutions, even young children can learn to be effective problem solvers.

Behavioral or cognitive habits?

Young children are eager to imitate the adults in their environment. Children roleplay what they observe the adult models in their lives doing. My class came to me with a background of violence and of using negative forms of conflict resolution. I could not take away the students' environment or negative role models, but I could teach them better ways of handling anger, frustration, and differences of opinion.

Although my students did not initially solve conflicts in a productive manner, I knew they understood the role of problem-solving as a group. At the end of the year, I asked the students why we solved problems as a group during class meetings. The success of my action research project became apparent when Lisa said, "When we solve problems together we have more than one idea. If one doesn't work, we have more to try. If we tried to solve problems by ourselves, there would be only one thing to do." By implementing class meetings and the "Wheel of Choice," my students were given additional resources to assist them in developing constructive social skills.

Cognitive, not behavioral

We agree.

I believe my students are on the road to becoming successful problem solvers, both at school and beyond. Most important, they need continued opportunities to practice using constructive problem-solving strategies in a supportive environment in order to further develop the skill of thinking before they act.

References

Bailey, B. (1994). *There's gotta be a better way: Discipline that works.* Oviedo, FL: Loving Guidance.

McEwan, B., Gathercoal, P., Donahue, M., Greenfield, L., & Strangio, A. M. (1998, April). *Empowering students to take control of their own decisions: The synthesis of judicious discipline, class meetings, and issues of resiliency.* Paper presented at the annual meeting of the American Educational Research Association, San Diego, CA.

Nelsen, J., Duffy, R., Escobar, L., Ortolano, K., Owen-Sohocki, D. (1996). *Positive discipline: A teacher's A–Z guide.* Rocklin, CA: Prima Publishing and Communications.

Nelsen, J., & Lott, L. (1997). *Positive discipline in the classroom: Teacher's guide.* Orem, UT: Empowering People Books, Tapes, & Videos.

Nelsen, J., Lott, L., & Glenn, H. S. (1997). *Positive discipline in the classroom.* Rocklin, CA: Prima Publishing.

Sloane, M. W. (1998). Scoring conflict-resolution goals. *Kappa Delta Pi Record, 35:*21–23.

Wittmer, D. S., & Honig, A. S. (1994). Encouraging positive attitudes and behavior in young children. *Young Children, 49:*4–12.

Analysis of the Study

PURPOSE/JUSTIFICATION

The purpose is stated in the fourth paragraph in terms of desired changes in behavior of a current class, and presumably of future classes: "Ultimately, I wanted the children to become prepared for society-at-large by learning and using constructive forms of conflict management." This is an excellent example of purpose in action research. Extensive justification is provided including both the existing problem and pertinent research. There appear to be no problems regarding risk, deception, or confidentiality.

DEFINITIONS

Definitions are not provided. Although key terms may seem obvious and are somewhat clarified by examples, we think definition of "physical and verbal aggression," "positive solutions," "constructive solution," and "conflict" would be helpful.

PRIOR RESEARCH

Numerous relevant references are provided, both as background and on the specific intervention. It is not clear whether they are comprehensive or representative but this is less of a problem in action research.

HYPOTHESES

A directional hypothesis is clearly implied, i.e., that students, subsequent to intervention, will show decreased physical and verbal aggression, be better able to verbalize conflicts and feelings and implement more constructive solutions to conflict.

SAMPLE

As is to be expected in action research, the authors give no indication of intending to generalize beyond their sample, in which case the sample is the population. If generalization is intended, theirs is a convenience sample. The sample of 20 first-graders is described in terms of gender, ethnicity, general location, and socioeconomic status. Five of these, selected as needing the most help, provided the data on aggression.

INSTRUMENTATION

The five instruments are, in general, adequately described. We must assume that dictated responses to the survey were done individually. Reliability and validity are not addressed; they are as important in action research as in other types. While requiring more time and effort, it might have been possible to do the student survey twice at pre- and posttesting, with an interval of a few days. A scoring system could easily have been developed based on frequencies and used to check reliability. Similarly, across-time comparisons could, we think, have been made with conflict-resolution journal entries, tally sheets, observational notes and, perhaps, teacher journal entries. Validity checks could consist of comparison across instruments (by individual or group) on common items such as "use of aggression to solve the problem."

PROCEDURES/INTERNAL VALIDITY

Procedures are generally well described and include a reference for more detail on the intervention. We think a reader is given enough detail to permit replication, if desired. A part of the intervention, class meetings, was begun at the beginning of the school year; the focus on conflict resolution, including use of the "Wheel of Choice," was carried out for eight weeks during the second semester. It is implied that this was implemented for 20 to 30 minutes (daily?). This study used a one-group pretest-posttest experimental design. As such, it is subject to almost all of the threats to internal validity we discussed in Chapter Nine. That is, subject characteristics (those not addressed by the pretest, such as ability level, family composition, and direct exposure to abuse), location, researcher bias, history, maturation, attitudinal, and implementation are all possible alternative explanations for outcomes. It can be argued that, because the primary purpose was (we think) to affect the students in the study, it doesn't matter whether the intervention itself was responsible for positive changes, or was perhaps due to the teacher's skill in working with children. It does matter, however, in assessing the intervention.

DATA ANALYSIS

The descriptive procedures used, including the bar graph, are appropriate. Scores based on frequency of occurrence for each individual and subsequent graphing would have provided more information. Frequencies, rather than terms such as "the majority" and "tapered off," should have been reported more often throughout, particularly in pre/post comparisons. The examples provide useful clarification.

RESULTS/INTERPRETATION/DISCUSSION

Although results and interpretation are intermixed, the distinction is, we think, usually clear. The written results are, in general, supported by the data, though more detail, as noted above, would have strengthened the study. Results and their interpretation seem appropriate with one exception; the distinction between cognitive tools and behavior is not consistently maintained. The behavior of "verbal ag-

gression" clearly decreased for the five targeted students; physical aggression did not, perhaps largely due to one student (Michael). For the class as a whole, the extent to which the "teacher journal" results reflect actual behavioral resolution of conflicts is not clear. The student survey, conflict-resolution journals, and observational notes apparently pertain mainly to individual or group intellectual use of tools, which is different from actual behavior.

We think this study is a good example of action research. It seems clear that the class and teacher benefited from carrying out the study. There is evidence that the students learned the intervention content; less that they used it. Replication of the study by other teachers in the same locale or elsewhere would be valuable to them, we think, and, if combined, would be useful in evaluating the intervention.

Go back to the **Interactive and Applied Learning Tools** feature at the beginning of the chapter for a listing of interactive and applied activities. Go to the **Online Learning Center** at www.mhhe.com/fraenkel5e or your **Interactive Student CD-ROM** to take practice quizzes and receive immediate feedback, practice with key terms, review chapter content and main ideas, and find annotated Web links.

Main Points

THE NATURE OF ACTION RESEARCH

- Action research is research conducted by a teacher, administrator, or other education professional to solve a problem at the local level.
- Each of the specific methods of research can be used in action research studies, although on a smaller scale.
- A given research question may often be investigated by any one of several methods.
- Some methods are more appropriate to a particular research question and/or setting than other methods.

ASSUMPTIONS UNDERLYING ACTION RESEARCH

- Several assumptions underly action research studies. These are that the participants have the authority to make decisions, want to improve their practice, are committed to continual professional development, and will engage in systematic inquiry.

TYPES OF ACTION RESEARCH

- Practical action research addresses a specific local problem.
- Participatory action research in addition attempts to empower participants or bring about social change.

LEVEL OF PARTICIPATION IN ACTION RESEARCH

- Participation can vary from information giving to greater and greater involvement in aspects of the study.

STEPS IN ACTION RESEARCH

- There are four. These include identifying the research question or problem, gathering the necessary data, analyzing and interpreting the data, sharing the results with the participants, and developing an action plan.
- In participatory research, every effort is made to involve all those who have a vested interest in the outcomes of the study—the stakeholders.

ADVANTAGES OF ACTION RESEARCH

- There are at least five. It can be done by just about anyone, in any type of school or other institution, to investigate just about any kind of problem or issue. It can help to improve educational practice. It can help education and other professionals to improve their craft. It can help them learn to identify problems systematically; and it can build up a small community of research-oriented individuals at the local level.
- Action research has both similarities to, and differences from, formal quantitative and qualitative research.

SAMPLING IN ACTION RESEARCH

- Action researchers are most likely to choose a purposive sample.

THREATS TO THE INTERNAL VALIDITY OF ACTION RESEARCH

- Action research studies suffer especially from the possibility of data-collector bias, implementation, and attitudinal threats. Most others can be controlled to a considerable degree.

EXTERNAL VALIDITY AND ACTION RESEARCH

- Action research studies are weak in external validity.
- Replication is, of necessity, therefore, essential in these studies.

Key Terms

Action research 572

Practical action
  research 573

Participant 575

Stakeholder 573

Participatory action
  research 573

For Discussion

1. Are there any kinds of questions that could *not* be investigated by means of an action research study? If you think so, give an example.
2. Do you think the assumptions that underlie action research are true? Explain your reasoning. Are any of them questionable?
3. Which of the four stages of action research would be the hardest to carry out? Why?
4. "The important thing in action research is *not* to rely on collecting merely anecdotal data." Would you agree? Why would this be insufficient (if it would be)?
5. All of the participants—the stakeholders—in an action research study must be involved in the entire research process. Why not also require this in formal qualitative and quantitative studies?
6. What do you think is the major advantage of action research? The major disadvantage?

7. Which methodologies, other than the ones discussed, might be used in each of the hypothetical examples in this chapter?

8. What other methods might have been used in the DeMaria study? Which, if any, would you recommend? Why?

1. G. E. Mills (2000). *Action research: A guide for the teacher researcher.* Upper Saddle River, NJ: Merrill.

2. Ibid., p. 6.

3. B. L. Berg (2001). *Qualitative methods for the social sciences.* Boston: Allyn & Bacon, p. 180.

4. E. T. Stringer (1999). Action research, 2nd ed. Thousand Oaks, CA: Sage. Cited in Berg, op. cit., p. 183.

5. Berg, op. cit., p. 182.

6. D. DeMaria (1990). *A study of the effect of relaxation exercises on a class of learning-disabled students.* Master's thesis. San Francisco State University, San Francisco, CA.

Notes

Writing Research Proposals and Reports

Part Eight discusses how to prepare a research proposal or report.

We describe the major sections of such proposals and reports and

then describe some sections that are unique to reports. We conclude

with an example of a student's research proposal, followed by our

analysis of it.

Preparing Research Proposals and Reports

Preparing Research Proposals and Reports

- **What Is the Purpose of a Research Proposal?**

- **The Major Sections of a Research Proposal or Report**
  - Problem to Be Investigated
  - Background and Review of Related Literature
  - Procedures
  - Budget
  - General Comments

- **Sections Unique to Research Reports**
  - Results/Findings
  - Discussion
  - An Outline of a Research Report

- **A Sample Research Proposal**

Objectives

Studyng this chapter should enable you to:

- Describe *briefly the main sections of a research proposal and a research report.*
- Describe *the major difference between a research proposal and a research report.*
- Write *a research proposal.*
- Understand *and critique a typical research report or proposal.*

Interactive and Applied Learning

Go to your Interactive Student CD-ROM or Student Workbook to do the following activities:
- Activity 24.1: Put Them in Order

By now we hope you have learned many of the concepts and procedures involved in educational research. You may, in fact, have done considerable thinking about a research study of your own. To help you further, we discuss in this chapter the major components involved in proposal and report writing. A research proposal is nothing more than a written plan for conducting a research study. It is a generally accepted and commonly required prerequisite for carrying out a research investigation.

What Is the Purpose of a Research Proposal?

A **research proposal** communicates the intentions of the researcher—the purpose of his or her intended study and its importance, together with a step-by-step plan for conducting the study. Problems are identified, questions or hypotheses are stated, variables are identified, and terms are defined. The subjects to be included in the sample, the instrument(s) to be used, the research design, the procedures to be followed, how the data will be analyzed—all are spelled out in some detail, and at least a partial review of previous related research is included. Such a written plan is highly desirable, since it allows interested others to evaluate the worth of a proposed study and to make suggestions for improvement.

A research proposal, then, is a written plan for a study. It spells out in detail what the researcher intends to do. It permits others to learn about the intended research and to offer suggestions for improving the study. It helps the researcher clarify what needs to be done and avoid unintentional pitfalls or unknown problems. A **research report** follows much the same format as a proposal, with two main differences: (1) it states what *was* done rather than what *will be* done (some alterations are almost inevitable), and (2) it includes the actual results of the study, along with a discussion of them.

This chapter describes what is expected in each section of a research proposal or report. It also discusses what is appropriate to include in the results and discussion sections of a research report. We highlight what we have found to be the most common mistakes made by beginning researchers in preparing research proposals. Finally, we present an example of a research proposal prepared by one of our students and comment on its strengths and weaknesses.

The Major Sections of a Research Proposal or Report

PROBLEM TO BE INVESTIGATED

There are usually four topics addressed in this section: (1) the purpose of the study, including the researcher's assumptions; (2) the justification for the study; (3) the research question and/or hypotheses, including the variables to be investigated; and (4) the definition of terms.

Purpose of the Study. Usually the first section in the proposal or report, the **purpose** states succinctly what the researcher proposes to investigate. The purpose should be a concise statement, providing a framework to which details are added later. Generally speaking, any study should seek to clarify some aspect of the field of interest that is considered important, thereby contributing both to overall knowledge and to current practice. Here are some examples of statements of purpose in research reports taken from the literature.

- The purpose of this study was to identify and describe the bedtime routines and self-reported nocturnal sleep patterns of women over age 65 and to determine the differences and relationships between these routines and patterns according to whether or not the subject was institutionalized.[1]
- The purpose of this study was to explore how young adolescents portray the ideal person in drawing and in response to a survey.[2]
- This study attempts to identify some of the processes mediating self-fulfilling prophecies in the classroom.[3]

The researcher should articulate any *assumptions* that are basic to the study. For example:

- It is assumed that, if found effective, the methods studied could be adopted by many teachers without special training.
- It is assumed that the descriptive information on family interaction that is provided by this study, if disseminated, will have an influence on family functioning.
- It is assumed that predictive information from this study would be used by counselors in advising students.

Justification for the Study. In the **justification**, researchers must make clear why this particular subject is important to investigate. They must present an argument for the "worth" of the study, so to speak. For example, if a researcher intends to study a particular method for modifying student attitudes toward government, he or she must make the case that such a study is important—that people are, or should be, concerned about it. The researcher must also make clear why he or she chooses to investigate the particular method. In many such proposals, there is the implication that current methods are not good enough; this should be made explicit, however.

A good justification should also include any specific implications that follow if relationships are identified. In an intervention study, for example, if the method being studied appears to be successful, changes in preservice or in-service training for teachers may be necessary; money may need to be spent in different ways; materials and other resources may need to be used differently, and so on. In survey studies, strong opinions on certain issues (such as peer opinions about drug use) may have implications for teachers, counselors, parents, and others. Relationships found in correlational or causal-comparative studies may justify predictive uses. Also, results of correlational or ethnographic studies may suggest possibilities for subsequent experimental studies. These should be discussed.

Here is an example of a justification. It is taken from a report of a study investigating the relationship between narrative and historical understanding in a literature-based sixth-grade history program.

> Recent research on the development of historical understanding has focused on secondary students. For several decades research has rested on the premise that historical understanding is demonstrated in the ability to analyze and interpret passages of history—or at least passages containing historical names, dates, and events. The results have indicated that if historical understanding develops at all, it does not appear until late adolescence (Hallam, 1970, 1979; Peel, 1967). From the perspective of those who work with younger children, however, this approach reflects an incomplete view of historical understanding.
>
> The inference often drawn from the research is that young children cannot understand history; therefore history should not be part of their curriculum. Certainly, surveys have shown that young children do not indicate much interest in history as a school subject. Yet teachers and parents know that children evince interest in the old days, in historical events or characters, and in descriptions of everyday life in historic times, such as Laura Ingalls Wilder's *Little House* books (e.g., 1953). Children respond to history long before they are capable of handling current tests of historical understanding. The

research, however, has not taken historical response into account in the development of mature understanding.

> The research on children's response to literature provides some guidelines for examining historical response. Research by Applebee (1978), Favat (1977), and Schlager (1975) suggests that aspects of response are developmental. Other scholars (Britton, 1978; Egan, 1983; Rosenblatt, 1938) extend that suggestion to historical understanding, arguing that early, personal responses to history—especially history embedded in narrative—are precursors to more mature and objective historical understanding.
>
> Little has been done to study the form of such early historical response. Kennedy's (1983) study examined the relationship between information-processing capacity and historical understanding, but concentrated on adolescents. Reviews of research on historical understanding also fail to uncover studies of early response. There is nothing describing how children respond to historical material in a regular classroom setting. How do children respond on their own, or in contact with peers? What forms of history elicit the strongest responses? How do children express interest in historical material? Does the classroom context influence responses? What teacher behaviors inhibit or encourage response?
>
> These are important questions for the elementary teacher faced with a social studies curriculum that continues to emphasize history, as well as for the theorist interested in the development of historical understanding. Yet these questions cannot easily be answered by traditional empirical models. Research needs to be extended to include focus on the range of evidence available through naturalistic inquiry.

Using Naturalistic Inquiry to Study Historical Response

Classroom observation suggests that narrative is a potent spur to historical interest. Teachers note the interest exhibited by students in such historical stories as *The Diary of Anne Frank* (Frank, 1952) and *Little House on the Prairie* (Wilder, 1953) and in the oral tradition of family history (Huck, 1981). Research in discourse analysis and schema theory suggests that narrative may help children make sense of history. White and Gagne (1976), for instance, found that connected discourse leads to better memory for meaning. Such discourse provides a framework that improves recall and helps children recognize important features in a text (Kintsch, Kozminsky, Streby, McKoon & Keenan, 1975). DeVilliers (1974) and Levin (1970) found that readers processed words in connected discourse more deeply than when the same words appeared in sentences or lists. Cullinan, Harwood, and Galda (1983) suggest that readers may be better able to remember things in narratives where the "connected discourse allows the reader to organize and interrelate elements in the text" (p. 31).

One way to help children understand history, then, may be to use the connected discourse of literature. Such an approach also allows the researcher to focus on response as the ongoing construction of meaning as children encounter history in literature. The following study investigated children's responses to a literature-based approach to history.[4]

Key Questions to Ask Yourself at This Point:
1. Have I identified the specific research problem I wish to investigate?
2. Have I indicated what I intend to do about this problem?
3. Have I put forth an argument as to why this problem is worthy of investigation?
4. Have I made my assumptions explicit?

Research Questions or Hypothesis. The particular **question** to be investigated should be stated next. This is usually, but not always, a more specific form of the problem in question form. As you will recall, we, along with many other researchers, favor **hypotheses** for reasons of clarity and as a research strategy. If a researcher has a hypothesis in mind, it should be stated as clearly and as concisely as possible. It is unnecessarily frustrating for a reader to have to infer what a researcher's hypothesis or hypotheses might be. (See Chapter Two for several examples of typical research questions and hypotheses in education.)

Key Questions to Ask Yourself at This Point:
5. Have I asked the specific research question I wish to pursue?
6. Do I have a hypothesis in mind? If so, have I expressed it?
7. Do I intend to investigate a relationship? If so, have I indicated the variables I think may be related?

Definitions. All key terms should be defined. In a hypothesis-testing study, these are primarily the terms that describe the variables of the study. The researcher's task is to make his or her definitions as clear as possible. If previous definitions found in the literature are clear to all concerned, well and good. Often, however, they need

to be modified to fit the present study. It is often helpful to formulate operational definitions as a way of clarifying terms or phrases. While it is probably impossible to eliminate all ambiguity from definitions, the clearer the terms used in a study are—to both the researcher and others—the fewer difficulties will be encountered in subsequent planning and conducting of the study. (See Chapter Two for examples of different ways to define key terms in a research investigation.)

Key Question to Ask Yourself at This Point:
8. Have I defined all key terms clearly (and, if possible, operationally)?

BACKGROUND AND REVIEW OF RELATED LITERATURE

In a research report, this may be a lengthy section, especially in a master's thesis or a doctoral dissertation. In a research proposal, it is a partial summary of previous work related to the hypothesis or focus of the study. The researcher is trying to show here that he or she is familiar with the major trends in previous research and opinion on the topic and understands their relevance to the study being planned. This review may include theoretical conceptions, directly related studies, and studies that provide additional perspectives on the research question. In our experience, the major weakness of many literature reviews is that they cite references (often many references) without indicating their relevance or implications for the planned study. (See Chapter Five for details on literature reviews). A portion of a literature review follows. It is taken from a study investigating the relationship between kindergarten teachers' theoretical orientation toward reading and student outcomes of children with different initial reading abilities.

> The *whole language* approach to teaching reading has captured the attention of many teachers and teacher educators over the past 20 years. It . . . asserts that children learn language most effectively at their own developmental pace through social interaction in language-rich environments and through exposure to quality literature. This approach is often contrasted with a phonics-oriented strategy in which children receive formal instruction emphasizing sound-symbol correspondence. . . . Stahl and Miller (1989) and Stahl, McKenna, and Pagnucco (1994) conducted meta-analyses of studies conducted in kindergarten and first-grade classrooms comparing the relative impact of whole language and traditional

approaches to reading instruction. Both meta-analyses yielded the general conclusion that the overall impact of the two approaches was "essentially similar" (Stahl et al., 1994, p. 175), a position disputed by Schickedanz (1990) and McGee and Lomax (1990).

In reviewing the whole language/phonics debate, and the inability of researchers to reach similar conclusions after reviewing the same studies, several problematic areas emerge. First, the meaning of the term *whole language* and a set of distinctive classroom practices representing its operationalization are difficult to specify (Stahl & Miller, 1989). This is exacerbated by the fact that some proponents conceive of whole language as a philosophy rather than an explicitly defined instructional methodology (Edelsky, 1990; Goodman, 1986; McKenna, Robinson, & Miller, 1990; Newman, 1985; Rich, 1985). Second, many—if not most—teachers are eclectic in their approach to reading instruction, and pure contrasts between whole language- and phonics-oriented instruction are generally difficult to find in naturally occurring, unmanipulated classroom environments (Slaughter, 1988). Third, with the exception of Fisher and Hiebert (1990), relatively little research has documented differences in the instructional behavior and practices of teachers subscribing to whole language versus traditional approaches to early reading instruction (Feng & Etheridge, 1993; Lehman, Allen, & Freeman, 1990; Stahl et al., 1994). Finally, "relatively few studies" (Stahl et al., 1994, p. 175) comparing whole language and traditional reading instruction have used standardized achievement measures or included large numbers of students (e.g., Watson, Crenshaw, & King, 1984). . . .

A number of researchers have examined the impact of whole language approaches to reading development for students considered educationally at risk. Stahl and Miller (1989) concluded that "whole language/language experience approaches . . . produce weaker effects with populations labeled specifically as disadvantaged" (p. 87). This conclusion is supported by the research of Gersten, Darch, and Gleason, (1988) who reported positive effects for at-risk (economically disadvantaged) children of a direct instruction kindergarten classroom, based largely on traditional, phonics-oriented principles. However, a number of recent studies (Milligan & Berg, 1992; Otto, 1993; Pinnell, Lyons, DeFord, Bryk, & Seltzer, 1994; Sulzby, Branz, & Buhle, 1993) present evidence consistent with Kasten and Clarke's (1989) argument that whole language-based reading instruction should be especially beneficial for disadvantaged children. . . .

Otto (1993) and Sulzby et al. (1993) presented evidence suggesting that storybook reading, generally associated with developmentally sensitive, whole language approaches to reading instruction, was helpful in increasing the emergent reading ability of inner-city kindergartners (Otto, 1993; Sulzby et al., 1993) and first graders (Sulzby et al., 1993). However, neither of these studies used control groups, either of children not seen as at-risk or of children receiving more traditional instruction in the same schools. Purcell-Gates, McIntyre, and Freppon (1995) reported that children in well-implemented whole language classes showed significantly greater growth in their knowledge of written language and more extensive breadth of knowledge of written linguistic features than their peers in skills-based kindergarten classes. Putnam (1990) found that inner-city kindergarten students in a "Literate Environment" classroom gained more in vocabulary and syntactic complexity than students in "Traditional" or "IBM Write to Read" classrooms.

Finally, research by Pinnell et al. (1994) found that "Reading Recovery," a tutoring program for educationally disadvantaged children, was more effective in improving the reading efficacy of high-risk first graders than a similar program (called "Reading Success") provided by teachers who were more traditional (phonics- or skills-oriented) compared to the "Reading Recovery" teachers. However, given that the "Reading Recovery" and the "Reading Success" teachers also differed in a number of other ways (previous experience and training, training time schedule, training activities), it is impossible to tease out the effects of the teachers' theoretical orientations toward reading.[5]

Key Questions to Ask Yourself at This Point:

9. Have I surveyed and described relevant studies related to the problem?
10. Have I surveyed existing expert opinion on the problem?
11. Have I summarized the existing state of opinion and research on the problem?

PROCEDURES

The **procedures** section includes discussions of: (1) research design, (2) sample, (3) instrumentation, (4) procedural detail, (5) internal validity, and (6) data analysis.

Research Design. In experimental or correlational studies, the **research design** can be described using the symbols presented in Chapters Thirteen or Fifteen. In causal-comparative studies, the research design should be described using the symbols presented in Chapter Sixteen. The particular research design to be used in the study and its application to the study should be identified. In most studies, the basic design is fairly clear-cut and fits one of the models we presented in Chapters Thirteen to Seventeen and in Chapters Twenty to Twenty-Two.

Sample. In a proposal, a researcher should indicate in considerable detail how he or she will obtain the subjects—the *sample*—for the study. If generalization is intended, a *random sample* should be used. If a *convenience sample* must be used, relevant *demographics* (gender, ethnicity, occupation, IQ, and so on) of the sample should be described. Lastly, the legitimate population to which the results of the study may be generalized should be indicated. (See Chapter Six for details on sampling.)

Here is an example of a description of a convenience sample. It was taken from the report of a study designed to investigate the effects of behavior modification on the classroom behavior of first- and third-graders.

> Thirty grade 1 (mean age = 7 years, 1 month) and 25 grade 3 children (mean age = 9 years, 3 months) were identified by their classroom teachers as exhibiting inappropriate classroom behavior, receiving no special services, and having intelligence quotients between 85 and 115. These children represented 23% of the grade 1 children in a large elementary school in the southeastern United States and 21% of the grade 3 children in the same school. All participants were from regular classrooms; none were receiving special educational services. Fifteen grade 1 subjects were assigned randomly to the experimental treatment and 15 to the control condition; 25 grade 3 subjects were assigned randomly to each of the two conditions, with the experimental treatment receiving 13 and control, 12. The experimental group included 22 boys, 6 girls; 11 black children, 17 white children; 14 of low socioeconomic status, 14 of middle to high socioeconomic status. The control group was composed of 15 boys, 12 girls; 15 black children, 12 white children; 7 of low socioeconomic status, 20 of middle to high socioeconomic status. No attrition occurred during this study.[6]

Key Questions to Ask Yourself at This Point:
12. Have I described my sampling plan?
13. Have I described the relevant characteristics of my sample in detail?
14. Have I identified the population to which the results of the study may legitimately be generalized?

Instrumentation. Whenever possible, existing instruments should be used in a study, since construction of even the most straightforward test or questionnaire is often a very time-consuming and difficult task. The use of an existing instrument, however, is not justified unless sufficiently reliable and valid results can be obtained for the researcher's purpose. Too many studies are done with instruments that are merely convenient or well known. Usage is a poor criterion of quality, as shown by the continuing popularity of some widely used achievement tests despite years of scathing professional criticism. (See Chapter Seven for examples of the many types of instruments that educational researchers can use.)

In the event that appropriate instruments are not available, the procedures to be followed in developing the instruments to be used in the study should be described with attention to how validity and reliability will (presumably) be enhanced. At least some sample items from the instruments should be included in the proposal.

Even with instruments for which reliability and validity of scores are supported by impressive evidence, there is no guarantee that these instruments will function in the same way in the study itself. Differences in subjects and conditions may make previous estimates of validity and reliability inapplicable to the current context. Further, validity always depends on the intent and interpretation of the researcher. For all these reasons, the reliability and validity of the scores obtained from all instruments should be checked as a part of every study, preferably before the study begins.

It is almost always feasible to check internal consistency reliability since no additional data are required. Checking reliability of scores over time *(stability)* is more difficult since an additional administration of the instrument is required. Even when feasible, repetition of exactly the same instrument may be questionable, since individuals may alter their responses as a result of taking the instrument the first time.* Asking respondents to reply to a questionnaire or an interview a second time is often difficult, since it seems rather foolish to them. Nonetheless, ingenuity and the effort required to develop a parallel form of the instrument(s) can often overcome these obstacles.†

---

*For example, they may look up the answers.
†A compromise is to divide the existing instrument into two halves (as in the split-half procedure) and administer each half with a time interval between administrations.

The most straightforward way to check validity is to use a second instrument to measure the same variable. Often, this is not as difficult as it may seem, given the variety of types of instruments that are available (see Chapter Seven). Frequently, the judgment of knowledgeable persons (teachers, counselors, parents, and friends, for instance), expressed as ratings or as a ranking of the members of a group, can serve as the second instrument. Sometimes a useful means of validating the responses to attitude, opinion, or personality (such as self-esteem) scales filled out by subjects is to have a person who knows each subject well fill out the same scale (as it applies to the subject), and then check to see how well the ratings correspond. A final point is that reliability and validity data need not be obtained for the entire sample, although this is preferable. It is better to obtain such data for only a portion of the sample (or even for a separate, although comparable, sample) than to obtain no data at all. (For a more detailed discussion of reliability and validity, see Chapter Eight.)

In some studies, especially historical and qualitative ones, there may be no formal instrument like a test or a rating scale involved. In such studies, the researcher is often the "instrument" for obtaining data. Even so, ways of maximizing and checking on validity and reliability should be set forth in the proposal, and described later in the report.

Key Questions to Ask Yourself at This Point:
15. Have I described the instruments to be used?
16. Have I indicated their relevance to the present study?
17. Have I stated how I will check the reliability of scores obtained from all instruments?
18. Have I stated how I will check the validity of scores obtained from all instrument(s)?

Procedural Details. Next, the procedures to be followed in the study—what will be done, as well as when, where, and how—should be described in detail. In intervention studies in particular, additional details are usually needed on the nature of the intervention and on the means of introducing the method or treatment. Keep in mind that the goal here is that of making replication of the study possible; another researcher should, on the basis of the information provided in this section, be able to repeat the study in exactly the same way as the original researcher. Certain procedures may change as the study is carried out, it is true, but a proposal should nonetheless have this level of clarity as its goal.

The researcher should also make clear how the information collected will be used to answer the original question or to test the original hypothesis.

Key Question to Ask Yourself at This Point:
19. Have I fully described the procedures to be followed in the study—what will be done, where, when, and how?

Internal Validity. At this point, the essential planning for a study should be nearly completed. It is now necessary for the researcher to examine the proposed methodology for the presence of any feasible alternative explanations for the results should the study's hypothesis be supported (or should nonhypothesized relationships be identified). We suggest that each of the threats to internal validity discussed in Chapter Nine be reviewed to see if any might apply to the proposed study. Should any troublesome areas be found, they should be mentioned and their likelihood discussed. The researcher should describe what he or she would do to eliminate or minimize them. Such an analysis often results in substantial changes in, or additions to, the methodology of the study; if this occurs, realize that it is better to become aware of the need for such changes at this stage than after the study is completed.

Key Questions to Ask Yourself at This Point:
20. Have I discussed any feasible alternative explanations that might exist for the results of the study?
21. Have I discussed how I will deal with these alternative explanations?

Data Analysis. The researcher then should indicate how the data to be collected will be organized (see Chapter Seven), and analyzed (see Chapters Ten, Eleven, and Twelve).

Key Questions to Ask Yourself at This Point:
22. Have I described how I will organize the data I will collect?
23. Have I described how I will analyze the data, including statistical procedures that will be used, and why these procedures are appropriate?

BUDGET

Research proposals are often submitted to government or private funding institutions in hopes of obtaining financial support. Such institutions almost always require submission of a tentative **budget** along with the proposal. Needless to say, the amount of money involved in a research proposal can have a considerable impact on whether or not it is funded. Thus, great care should be given to preparing the budget. Budgets usually include such items as salaries, materials, equipment costs, secretarial and other assistance, expenses (such as travel and postage), and overhead.

GENERAL COMMENTS

One other comment may not seem necessary, but in our experience it is. Remember that all sections of a proposal must be consistent. It is not uncommon to read a proposal in which each section by itself is quite acceptable but some sections contradict others. The terms used in a study, for example, must be used throughout as originally defined. Any hypotheses must be consistent with the research question. Instrumentation must be consistent with, or appropriate for, the research question, the hypotheses, and the procedures for data collection. The method of obtaining the sample must be appropriate for the instruments that will be used and for the means of dealing with alternative explanations for the results, and so forth.

Sections Unique to Research Reports

RESULTS/FINDINGS

As discussed previously, the **results** of a study can be presented only in a research report; ordinarily there are no results in a proposal (unless results of some exploratory research or a pilot study are included as part of the background of the proposal). A report of the results, sometimes called the **findings,** is included near the end of the report. The findings of the study constitute the results of the researcher's analysis of his or her data—that is, what the collected data reveal. In comparison-group studies, the means and standard deviation for each group on the posttest measure(s) usually are reported. In correlational studies, correlation coefficients and scatterplots are reported. In survey studies, percentages of responses to the questions asked, crossbreak tables, contingency coefficients, etc., are given. (For examples of findings, see the published research reports presented in Chapters Thirteen through Seventeen and Twenty to Twenty-Three.)

DISCUSSION

The discussion section of a report presents the author's interpretation of what the results imply for theory and/or practice. This includes, in hypothesis-testing studies, an assessment of the extent to which the hypothesis was supported.

In the discussion section, researchers place their results in a broader context. Here they recapitulate any difficulties that were encountered, make note of the limitations of the study, and suggest further, related studies that might be done.

To the extent possible, we believe the results and discussion sections of a study should be kept distinct from each other. A discussion section will typically go considerably beyond the data in attempting to place the findings in a broader perspective. It is important that the reader not be misled into thinking that the investigator has obtained evidence for something that is only speculation. To put it differently, there should be no room for disagreement regarding the statements in the results section of the report. The statements should follow clearly and directly from the data that were obtained. There may be much argumentation and disagreement about the broader interpretation of these results, however.

Let us consider the results of a study on teacher personality and classroom behavior. As hypothesized in that study, correlations of .40 to .50 were found between a test of control need on the part of the teacher and (1) the extent of controlling behavior in the classroom as observed and (2) ratings by interviewers as "less comfortable with self" and "having more rigid attitudes of right and wrong." (See page 171.) These were the results of the study and should clearly be identified as such in a report. In the discussion section, however, these findings might be placed in a variety of controversial perspectives. Thus, one investigator might propose that the study provides support for selection of prospective teachers, arguing that anyone scoring high in control need should be excluded from a training program on the grounds that this characteristic and the classroom behavior it appears to predict are undesirable in teachers. In contrast, another investigator might interpret the results to support the desirability of attracting people with higher control need into teaching. This investigator might argue that, at least in inner-city schools, teachers scoring higher in control need are likely to have more business-like classrooms.

Clearly, both of these interpretations go far beyond the results of the particular study. There is no reason the investigator should not make such an interpretation, provided that it is clearly identified as such and does not give the impression that the results of the study provide direct evidence in support of the interpretation. Many times a researcher will sharply differentiate between results and interpretation by placing them in different sections of a report and labeling them accordingly. At other times a researcher may intermix the two, making it difficult for the reader to distinguish the results of the study from the researcher's interpretations. (For examples of discussions, see any of the published research reports presented in Chapters Thirteen through Twenty-Three.)

Suggestions for Further Research. Normally, this is the final section of a report. Based on the findings of the present study, the researcher suggests some related and follow-up studies that might be conducted in the future to advance knowledge in the field.

AN OUTLINE OF A RESEARCH REPORT

Figure 24.1 shows an outline of a research report. Although the topics listed are generally agreed to within the research community, the particular sequence may vary in different studies. This is partly because of different preferences among researchers and partly because the headings and organization of the outline will be somewhat different for different research methodologies. This outline may also be used for a research proposal, in which case sections IV and V would be omitted (and the future tense used throughout). Also, a budget might be added.

A Sample Research Proposal

The research proposal that follows was prepared by a student in one of our classes and is a good example of a beginning effort. Such a proposal will normally go through further revision based on the comments of faculty and others, but this will give you some idea of what a completed proposal by a student looks like. We comment on both its strengths and weaknesses in the margins.

Note that this proposal does not follow the organization recommended in Figure 24.1 exactly. It does, however, contain all of the major components previously discussed. It also includes a report of a pilot study. A **pilot study** is a small-scale trial of the proposed procedures. Its purpose is to detect any problems so that they can be remedied before the study proper is carried out.

Figure 24.1

Organization of a Research Report

Introductory section
    Title Page
    Table of Contents
    List of Figures
    List of Tables
Main Body
  I. Problem to be investigated
    A. Purpose of the study (including assumptions)
    B. Justification of the study
    C. Research question and hypotheses
    D. Definition of terms
    E. Brief overview of study
  II. Background and review of related literature
    A. Theory, if appropriate
    B. Studies directly related
    C. Studies tangentially related
 III. Procedures
    A. Description of the research design
    B. Description of the sample
    C. Description of instruments used (scoring procedures; reliability; validity).
    D. Explanation of the procedures followed (the what, when, where, and how of the study)
    E. Discussion of internal validity
    F. Discussion of external validity
    G. Description and justification of the statistical techniques or other methods of analysis used
 IV. Findings
    Description of findings pertinent to each of the research hypotheses or questions
  V. Summary and conclusions
    A. Brief summary of the research question being investigated, the procedures employed, and the results obtained
    B. Discussion of the implications of the findings—their meaning and significance
    C. Limitations—unresolved problems and weaknesses
    D. Suggestions for further research
References (Bibliography)
Appendixes

THE EFFECTS OF INDIVIDUALIZED READING
UPON STUDENT MOTIVATION IN GRADE FOUR

Nadine DeLuca*

Purpose

Requires documentation.

The general purpose of this research is to add to the existing knowledge about reading methods. Many educators have become dissatisfied with general reading programs in which teacher-directed group instruction means boredom and delay for quick students and embarrassment and lack of motivation for others. Although there has been a great deal of writing in favor of an individualized reading approach which is supposedly a highly-motivating method of teaching reading, sufficient data has not been presented to make the argument for or against individualized reading programs decisive. With the data supplied by this study (and future ones), soon schools will be (free) to make the choice between implementing an individualized reading program or retaining a basal reading method.

Demonstrates importance of study.

Indicates implications if hypothesis is supported.

Replace with "better able"

Definitions

Could be more specific to this study. An operational definition would help.

Motivation: Motivation is inciting and sustaining action in an organism. The motivation to learn could be thought of as being derived from a combination of several more basic needs such as the need to achieve, to explore, to satisfy curiosity.

"Motivation to read" is really the variable.

Individualization: (Individualization is characteristic of an individualized reading program.) Individualized reading has as its basis the concepts of seeking, self-selection, and pacing. An individualized reading program has the following characteristics:

You should delete this.

1. Literature books for children predominate.
2. Each child makes personal choices with regard to his reading materials.
3. Each child reads at his own rate and sets his own pace of accomplishment.
4. Each child confers with the teacher about what he has read and the progress he has made.
5. Each child carries his reading into some form of summarizing activity.
6. Some kind of record is kept by the teacher and/or the student.

Good—clear and specific.

*Used by permission of the author.

7. Children work in groups for an immediate learning purpose and leave group when the purpose is accomplished.

8. Word recognition and related skills are taught and vocabulary is accumulated in a natural way at the point of each child's need.

Prior Research

Abbott, J. L., "Fifteen Reasons Why Personalized Reading Instruction Doesn't Work." Elementary English (January, 1972), 44:33–36.

ok.

This article refutes many of the usual arguments against individualized reading instruction. It lists those customary arguments then proceeds to explain why the objections are not valid ones.

It explains how such a program can be implemented by an ordinary classroom teacher in order to show the fallacy in the complaint that individualizing is impractical. Another fallacy involves the argument that unless a traditional basal reading program is used, children do not gain all the necessary reading skills.

Barbe, Walter B., Educator's Guide to Personalized Reading Instruction. Englewood Cliffs, New Jersey: Prentice-Hall, Inc., 1961.

ok.

Mr. Barbe outlines a complete individualized reading program. He explains the necessity of keeping records of children's reading. The book includes samples of book-summarizing activities as well as many checklists to ensure proper and complete skill development for reading.

Hunt, Lyman C., Jr., "Effect of Self-selection, Interest, and Motivation upon Independent, Instructional and Frustrational Levels." Reading Teacher (November, 1970), 24:146–151.

Dr. Hunt explains how self-selection, interest, and motivation (some of the basic principles behind individualized reading), when used in a reading program, result in greater reading achievement.

Miel, Alice, Ed., Individualizing Reading Practices. New York: Bureau of Publications, Teachers College, Columbia University, 1959.

Veatch, Jeanette, Reading in the Elementary School. New York: The Roland Press Co., 1966.

West, Roland, <u>Individualized Reading Instruction.</u> Port Washington, New York: Kennikat Press, 1964.

This is not really a literature review, although it is a good beginning at preparing one. Additional material needs to be added and summarized to justify the study.

The three books listed above all provide examples of various individualized reading programs actually being used by different teachers. (The definitions and items on the rating scale were derived from these three books.)

Good—shows relevance to present study.

Hypothesis

The greater the degree of individualization in a reading program, the higher will be the students' motivation.

Variables are clear. Hypothesis is directional.

Population

Right.

An ideal population would be all fourth graders in the United States. Because of different teacher-qualification requirements, different laws, and different teaching programs, though, such a generalization may not be justifiable. One that might be justifiable would be a population of all fourth-grade classrooms in the San Francisco-Bay Area.

Sampling

Good sampling plan.

The study will be conducted in fourth-grade classrooms in the San Francisco-Bay Area, including inner-city, rural, and suburban schools. The sample will include at least one hundred classrooms. Ideally, the sampling will be done randomly by identifying all fourth-grade classrooms for the population described and using random numbers to select the sample classrooms. As this would require excessive amounts of time, this sampling might need to be modified

Add random!

by taking a sample of schools in the area, identifying all fourth-grade classrooms in these schools only, then taking a random sample from these classrooms.

Two-stage sampling.

Instrumentation

Appears to have good content validity. Items are consistent with definition.

Instrumentation will include a rating scale to be used to rate the degree of individualization in the reading program in each classroom. A sample (rating scale) is shown below. Those items on the left indicate characteristics of classrooms with little individualization.

Reliability: The ratings of the two observers who are observing separately but at the same time in the same room will be compared to see how closely the ratings agree. The rating scale will be repeated for each classroom on at least three different days.

Should state how data on different days will be used. It can be used to check stability.

Three days may not be sufficient to get reliable scores.

Would parents be qualified to judge this?

Validity: Certain items on the student questionnaire (to be discussed in the next section) will be compared with the ratings on the rating scale to determine if there is a correlation between the degree of individualization apparently observed and the degree indicated by students' responses. In the same manner, responses to questions asked of teachers and parents can be used to indicate whether the rating scale is a true measure of the degree of individualization.

Good.

Can't use the same item for both variables

Another means of instrumentation to be used is a student questionnaire. A sample questionnaire is included. The following questions have as their purpose to determine the degree of motivation by asking how many books read and how the child indicates what he feels about reading: questions numbered 1, ④, 5, 6, 7, 9, 10, 11, 12, and 13. Questions 2, 3, ④, and 8 have as their purpose to help determine the validity of the items on the rating scale. Questions 14 and 15 are included to determine the students' attitudes toward the questionnaire to help determine if their attitudes are possible sources of bias for the study. Questions 8 and 9 have an additional purpose which is to add knowledge about the <u>novelty</u> of the reading situation in which the child now finds himself. This may be used to determine if there is a relationship between the novelty of the situation and the degree of motivation.

Most items appear to have logical validity, but the lack of definition of motivation to read makes it difficult to judge.

Good.

Good idea but may be too few items to give a reliable index.

Good idea but may not be enough items to give a reliable index.

But why? To control novelty as an extraneous variable?

RATING SCALE

1. Basal readers or programmed readers predominate in room.	1 2 3 4 5	There is an obvious center in the room containing at least five library books per child.
2. Teacher teaches class as a group.	1 2 3 4 5	Teacher works with individuals or small groups.
3. Children are all reading from the same book series.	1 2 3 4 5	Children are reading various materials at different levels.
4. Teacher initiates activities.	1 2 3 4 5	Student initiates activities.
5. No reading records are in evidence.	1 2 3 4 5	Children or teacher are observed to be making notes or keeping records of books read.

RATING SCALE

6. There is no evidence of book summarizing activities in the room.

1 2 3 4 5

There is evidence of book summarizing activities around room (e.g., student-made book jackets, paintings, drawings, models of scenes or characters from books, class list of books read, bulletin board displays about books read . . .).

7. Classroom is arranged with desks in rows and no provision for a special reading area.

1 2 3 4 5

Classroom is arranged with a reading area so that children have opportunities to find quiet places to read silently.

8. There is no conference area in the room for the teacher to work with children individually.

1 2 3 4 5

There is a conference area set apart from the rest of the class where the teacher works with children individually.

9. Children are doing the same activities at the same time.

1 2 3 4 5

Children are doing different activities from their classmates.

10. Teacher tells children what they are to read during class.

1 2 3 4 5

Children choose their own reading materials.

11. Children read aloud in turn to teacher as part of a group using the same reading textbook.

1 2 3 4 5

Children read silently at their desks or in a reading area or orally to the teacher on an individual basis.

Student Questionnaire

Age _____ Grade _____ Father's work _____

Mother's work _____

} Is your intent here to get at socioeconomic level?

Appears valid. 1. How many books have you read in the last month? _____

2. Do you choose the books you read by yourself? _____

Appears valid. If not, who does choose them for you? _____

Some indication of the scoring system should be given. Open-ended questions must rely on logical analysis of responses. You could use examples from your pilot study.

Appears valid.

3. Do you keep a record of what books you have read? _____

   Does your teacher? _____

Appears valid.

4. What different kinds of reading materials have you read this year?

Questionable validity.

5. Do you feel you are learning very much in reading this year? _____

   Why or why not? _____

6. Complete these sentences:

How scored?

   Books _____

   Reading _____

Appears valid.

7. Do you enjoy reading time? _____

Appear valid as indications of novelty. Generally not a good idea to have one item (9) dependent on another item (8).

8. Have you ever been taught reading a different way? _____

   When? _____ How was it different? _____

9. Which way of learning to read do you like better? _____

   _____ Why? _____

Appears valid.

10. If you couldn't come to reading class for some reason, would you be disappointed? _____ Why? _____

Appears valid.

11. Is this classroom a happy place for you during reading time? _____

Questionable validity.

12. Do most of the children in your classroom enjoy reading?

   _____

Appears valid.

13. How much of your spare time at home do you spend reading just for fun? _____

Good idea.

{

14. Did you like answering these questions or would you have preferred not to? _____

15. Were any of the questions confusing? _____

   If so, which ones? _____

   How were they confusing? _____

Student Questionnaire:

Reliability: An attempt will be made to control item reliability by asking the same question in different ways and comparing the answers.

Which items will be compared?

Validity: Validity may be questionable to some degree since school children may be reluctant to report anything bad about their teachers or the school. Observers will be reminded to establish rapport with children as much as possible before administering questionnaires and to assure them that the purpose of the questions does not affect them or their school in any way.

Good point.

Good idea.

Why do you want this information?

A teacher questionnaire will also be administered. A sample questionnaire is included. Some of the questions are intended to indicate if the approach being used by the teacher is new to her and what her attitude is toward the method. These questions are numbered 1, 2, 3, and 4. Question 5 is supposed to indicate how available reading materials are so that this can be compared to the degree of student motivation. Questions 6 and 8 will provide validity checks for the rating scale. Question 7 will help in determining a relationship between socioeconomic levels and student motivation.

Why? How is this related to your hypothesis?

May be too few items to give reliable index.

Good.

Reliability: Reliability should not be too great a problem with this instrument since most questions are of a factual nature.

Incorrect. It is the reliability of information that counts. Persons may or may not be consistent in giving factual information. It does seem likely that these questions would provide reliable data.

Validity: There may be a question as to validity depending upon how the questions are asked (if they are used in a structured interview). The way they are asked may affect the answers. An attempt has been made to state the questions so that the teacher does not realize what the purposes of this study are and so prejudice her answers.

Good.

Why include? As a means of controlling "experience"?

Teacher Questionnaire

1. How long have you been teaching? _____

Why? To assess novelty?

2. How long have you taught using the reading approach you are now using? _____

Why?

3. What other approaches have you used? _____

Why?

4. If you could use any reading approach you liked, which would you use?

_____

Why? _____

Under procedures, you explain that items 1–5 and 7 are intended as attempts to control extraneous variables. This is a very good idea, but the purpose should be made clear earlier (in this section).

Why? 5. In what manner do you obtain reading materials? _____

_____

Where did you get most of those you now use? _____

_____

Appears valid for individualization. 6. How often are the children grouped for reading? _____

_____

7. From what neighborhood or area do most of the children in this class come?

To assess socio-economic status.

_____

Appears valid for individualization. 8. How do you decide when and how word recognition skills and vocabulary are taught to each child? _____

_____

Good idea. Parents should be able to judge "motivation to read."   If it were feasible, an excellent instrument would be a parent questionnaire. The purpose of it would be to determine how much the child reads at home, his general attitude toward reading, and any changes in his attitude the parent has noticed.

Procedures

Identify the research method to be used.   Since the sample of one hundred classrooms is large and each classroom will need to be visited at least three times for thirty minutes to one hour during each visit on different weeks, quite a large team of observers—probably around twenty—will be needed. They will work in pairs observing independently. They will spend about one-half hour each visit on the rating scale. The visits should take place between Monday and Thursday, since activities and attitudes are often different on Fridays. The investigation will not begin until *Good idea.* after school has been in session for at least six weeks so that all programs have had sufficient time to function smoothly.

Good.   Control of extraneous variables: Sources of extraneous variables might include that teachers using individualized reading might be the more skillful and innovative teachers. Also, in cases where the individualized reading program is a new one, teacher enthusiasm for the *Good.* new program might carry over to students. In this case it might be the novelty of the approach and teacher enthusiasm rather than the program itself that is motivating. An attempt will be made to deter-

This section does a good job of identifying and attempting to control variables likely to be detrimental to internal validity.

mine if there is a relationship between novelty and teacher enthusi- *Good.*
asm and student motivation by correlating the results of the teacher
questionnaire (showing newness of program and teacher preference *OK but could be clearer. Better to use term "relationship," since we aren't sure about causality, which is implied by the word "influence."*
of program), indications from questions on student questionnaire, and
statistics on motivation in a scatterplot. The (influence) of student
socioeconomic levels on motivation will be determined by comparing
the answers to the question on the teacher questionnaire concerning
You should delete this. what area or neighborhood children live in, the question on parental
occupations on the student questionnaire with student motivation. The *Good.*
amount and availability of materials may (influence) motivation also. *Good but how will information be scored?*
This (influence) will be determined by the answers of teachers concern-
Isn't it likely that all classrooms would be affected the same? Further, it seems unlikely that your second variable (individualization) would be affected. If so, it's no problem so far as internal validity is concerned. ing where and how they get materials. *relate to*

The presence of observers in the classroom may cause distraction
and influence the degree of motivation. By having observers repeat
procedures three or more times, later observations may prove to be *Will you use all of the observations?*
nearly without this procedure bias. By keeping observers in the dark
about the purpose of the study, it is hopeful that will control as much
bias in their observations and question-asking as possible. *Good idea. However, since they both observe (individualization) and administer your questionnaire (motivation) they may well figure out the hypothesis. If there is concern that this "awareness" could influence their ratings and/or administration of the questionnaire, it would be preferable to have each instrument administered by different persons.*

<u>Data Analysis</u>

Observations on the rating scale and answers on the questionnaires will be given number ratings according to the degree of individualization and amount of motivation respectively. The average of
the total ratings will then be averaged for the two observers on the
rating scale, and the average of the total ratings will be averaged
Delete. This is incorrect. Do you see why? for the questionnaires in each classroom to be used on a scatterplot
to show the relationship between motivation and individualization (in)
(each classroom.) Results of the teacher questionnaire will be com-
pared similarly with motivation on the scatterplot. The correlation *But teacher questions lack content validity as indicators of "motivation." Items 6 and 8 can check "individualization," however.*
will be used to further indicate relationships.

PILOT STUDY

<u>Procedure</u>

The pilot study was conducted in three primary grade schools in
San Francisco. The principals of each school were contacted and were
asked if one or two reading classes could be observed by the investigator for an hour or less. The principals chose the classrooms observed. About forty-five minutes was spent in each of four third-
grade classrooms. No fourth grades were available in these schools.

Room	Individualization	Motivation
#1	1.4	1.3
#2	2.1	1.6
#3	3.0	1.8
#4	3.2	1.7

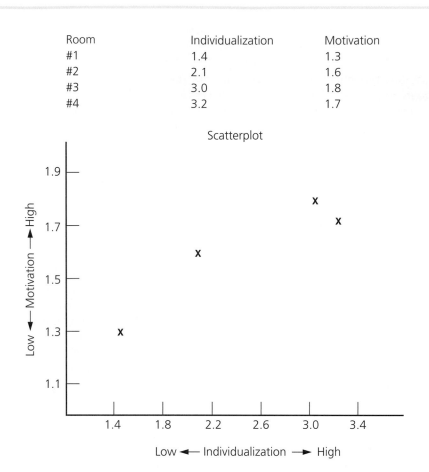

Scatterplot

The instruments administered were the student questionnaire and the rating scale.

Both the questionnaire and rating scale were coded by school and by classroom so that the variables for each classroom might be compared. The ratings on the rating scale for each classroom were added together then averaged. Answers on items for the questionnaire were rated "1" for answers indicating low motivation and "2" for answers indicating high motivation. (Note: Some items had as their purpose to test validity of rating scale or to provide data concerning possible biases, so these items were not rated.) Determining whether answers indicated high or low motivation created no problem except on Item #1. It was decided that fewer than eight books (two books per week) read in the past month indicated low motivation, while more indicated high motivation. The ratings for these questions were then added and averaged. Then these averaged numbers for all the questionnaires in each classroom were averaged. The results were as follows:

Although this pilot study could not possibly be said to uphold or disprove the hypothesis, we might venture to say that if the actual study were to yield results similar to those shown on the graph, there would be a strong correlation (estimate: $r = .90$) between individualization and motivation. This correlation is much too high to be attributed to chance with a random sample of 100 classrooms. If these were the results of the study described in the research proposal, the hypothesis would seem to be upheld.

Indications

Good observation. Unfortunately, I was unable to conduct the pilot study in any fourth-grade classrooms which immediately throws doubt upon the validity of the results. In administering the student questionnaire, I discovered that many of the third-graders had difficulty understanding the questions. Therefore, the questioning took the form of individual structured interviews. Whether or not this difficulty would hold for fourth-graders, too, would need to be determined by conducting a more extensive pilot study in fourth-grade classrooms. *Right.*

It was also discovered that Item #7 in the rating scale was difficult to rate. Perhaps it should be divided into two separate items—one concerning desk arrangement and one on the presence of a reading area—and worded more clearly. *Right.*

Item #8 on the student questionnaire seemed to provide some problems for children. Third-graders, at least, didn't seem to understand the intent of the question. There is also some uncertainty as to whether the answers on Item #15 reflected the students' true feelings. Since it was administered orally, students were probably reluctant to answer negatively about the test to the administrator of the test. Again, a more extensive pilot study would be helpful in determining if these indications are typical. *Right.*

Although the results of the pilot study are not very valid due to its size and the circumstances, its value lies in the knowledge gained concerning specific items in the instruments and problems that can be anticipated for observers or participants in similar studies.

Go back to the **Interactive and Applied Learning Tools** feature at the beginning of the chapter for a listing of interactive and applied activities. Go to the **Online Learning Center** at www.mhhe.com/fraenkel5e or your **Interactive Student CD-ROM** to take practice quizzes and receive immediate feedback, practice with key terms, review chapter content and main ideas, and find annotated Web links.

Main Points

RESEARCH PROPOSAL VERSUS RESEARCH REPORT

- A research proposal communicates a researcher's plan for a study.
- A research report communicates what was actually done in a study, and what resulted.

MAJOR SECTIONS OF A RESEARCH PROPOSAL OR REPORT

- The main body is the largest section of a proposal or a report and generally includes the problem to be investigated (including the statement of the problem or question, the research hypotheses and variables, and the definition of terms); the review of the literature; the procedures (including a description of the sample, the instruments to be used, the research design, and the procedures to be followed; an identification of threats to internal validity; and a description and a justification of the statistical procedures used); and (in a proposal) a budget of expected costs.
- All sections of a research proposal or a research report should be consistent with one another.

SECTIONS UNIQUE TO RESEARCH REPORTS

- The essential difference between a research proposal and a research report is that a research report states what was done rather than what will be done and includes the actual results of the study. Thus, in a report, a description of the findings pertinent to each of the research hypotheses or questions is presented, along with a discussion by the researcher of what the findings of the study imply for overall knowledge and current practice.
- Normally, the final section of a report is the offering of some suggestions for further research.

For Review

1. Review the problem sheets that you have completed to see how they correspond to the suggestions made in this chapter.
2. Review any or all of the critiques of studies included in the chapters on quantitative and qualitative research to see how they correspond to the suggestions made in this chapter.

Key Terms

Budget 607	Justification 602	Research hypothesis 604
Data analysis 607	Literature review 604	Research proposal 602
Definitions 604	Pilot study 609	Research question 604
External validity 610	Procedures 605	Research report 602
Findings 608	Purpose of a study 602	Results 608
Instrumentation 606	Research design 605	Sample 606
Internal validity 607		

1. To what extent should a researcher allow his or her personal writing style to influ-ence the headings and organizational sequence in a research proposal (assuming that there is no mandatory format prescribed, by, for example, a funding agency)?

2. To what common function do the problem statement, the research question, and the hypotheses all contribute? In what ways are they different?

3. When instructors of introductory research courses evaluate research proposals of students, they sometimes find logical inconsistencies among the various parts. What do you think are the most commonly found inconsistencies?

4. Why is it especially important in a study involving a convenience sample to provide a detailed description of the characteristics of the sample in the research report? Would this be necessary for a random sample as well? Explain.

5. Why is it important for a researcher to discuss threats to internal validity in (*a*) a re-search proposal and (*b*) a research report?

6. Oftentimes researchers do *not* describe their samples in detail in research reports. Why do you suppose this is so?

For Discussion

1. J. E. Johnson (1988). Bedtime routines: Do they influence the sleep of elderly women? *Journal of Applied Gerontology, 7:*97–110.

2. D. A. Stiles, J. L. Gibbons, and J. Schnellman (1987). The smiling sunbather and the chivalrous football player: Young adolescents' images of the ideal woman and man. *Journal of Early Adolescence, 7:*411–427.

3. L. M. Coleman, L. Jussim, and J. Abraham (1987). Students' reactions to teachers' evaluations: The unique impact of negative feedback. *Journal of Applied Social Psychology, 17:*1051–1070.

4. L. S. Levstik (1986). The relationship between historical response and narrative in a sixth-grade class-room. *Theory and Research in Social Education, 14*(1):1–19. Reprinted with permission of the National Council for the Social Studies and the author.

5. C. H. Sacks and J. R. Mergendoller (1997, Winter). The relationship between teachers' theoretical orien-tation toward reading and student outcomes in kindergarten children with different initial reading abilities. *American Educational Research Journal, 34*(4):722–723.

6. B. H. Manning (1988). Application of cognitive behavior modification: First and third graders' self-management of classroom behaviors. *American Educational Research Journal, 25*(2):194.

Notes

Appendixes

Portion of a Table of Random Numbers

(a)	(b)	(c)	(d)	(e)	(f)	(g)	(h)	(i)
83579	52978	49372	01577	62244	99947	76797	83365	01172
51262	63969	56664	09946	78523	11984	54415	37641	07889
05033	82862	53894	93440	24273	51621	04425	69084	54671
02490	75667	67349	68029	00816	38027	91829	22524	68403
51921	92986	09541	58867	09215	97495	04766	06763	86341
31822	36187	57320	31877	91945	05078	76579	36364	59326
40052	03394	79705	51593	29666	35193	85349	32757	04243
35787	11263	95893	90361	89136	44024	92018	48831	82072
10454	43051	22114	54648	40380	72727	06963	14497	11506
09985	08854	74599	79240	80442	59447	83938	23467	40413
57228	04256	76666	95735	40823	82351	95202	87848	85275
04688	70407	89116	52789	47972	89447	15473	04439	18255
30583	58010	55623	94680	16836	63488	36535	67533	12972
73148	81884	16675	01089	81893	24114	30561	02549	64618
72280	99756	57467	20870	16403	43892	10905	57466	39194
78687	43717	38608	31741	07852	69138	58506	73982	30791
86888	98939	58315	39570	73566	24282	48561	60536	35885
29997	40384	81495	70526	28454	43466	81123	06094	30429
21117	13086	01433	86098	13543	33601	09775	13204	70934
50925	78963	28625	89395	81208	90784	73141	67076	58986
63196	86512	67980	97084	36547	99414	39246	68880	79787
54769	30950	75436	59398	77292	17629	21087	08223	97794
69625	49952	65892	02302	50086	48199	21762	84309	53808
94464	86584	34365	83368	87733	93495	50205	94569	29484
52308	20863	05546	81939	96643	07580	28322	22357	59502

Portion of a Table of Random Numbers (*Continued*)

(a)	(b)	(c)	(d)	(e)	(f)	(g)	(h)	(i)
32519	79304	87539	28173	62834	15517	72971	15491	79606
29867	27299	98117	69489	88658	31893	93350	01852	86381
13552	60056	53109	58862	88922	41304	44097	58305	10642
73221	81473	75249	88070	22216	27694	54446	68163	34946
41963	16813	31572	04216	49989	78229	26458	89582	82020
81594	04548	95299	26418	15482	16441	60274	00237	03741
27663	33479	22470	57066	31844	73184	48399	05209	17794
07436	23844	45310	46621	78866	30002	91855	14029	84701
53884	59886	40262	38528	28753	14814	71508	91444	94335
45080	08221	30911	87535	66101	95153	36999	60707	10947
42238	98478	80953	25277	28869	69513	93372	98587	64229
49834	43447	29857	75567	85500	24229	23099	96924	23432
38220	82174	85412	66247	80642	45181	28732	76690	06005
61079	97636	62444	07315	78216	75279	75403	49513	16863
73503	47241	61985	91537	25843	89751	63485	34927	11334
18326	96584	45568	32027	97405	06282	75452	26667	46959
89596	26372	01227	23787	33607	69714	28725	43442	19512
45851	81369	08307	58640	14287	10100	43278	55266	46802
87906	42482	50010	31486	23801	08599	32842	47918	40894
24053	02256	03743	26642	03224	93886	57367	78910	38915
20525	69314	34939	70653	40414	94127	99934	35025	50342
30315	62283	53097	99244	08033	97879	92921	68432	68168
69240	41181	08462	99916	88851	43382	28262	10582	25126
59159	99994	25434	73285	54482	91218	49955	01232	55104
33137	42409	49785	02790	98720	89495	00135	27861	39832

Selected Values from a Normal Curve Table

Column A lists the *z*-score values. Column B provides the proportion of area between the mean and the *z*-score value.

Column C provides the proportion of area beyond the *z* score.

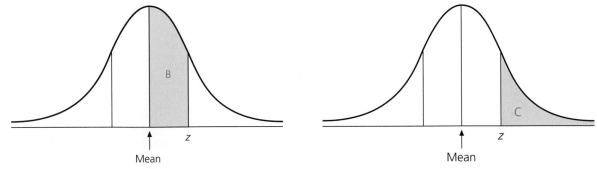

Note: Because the normal distribution is symmetrical, areas for negative *z* scores are the same as those for positive *z* scores.

(A) z	(B) Area Between Mean and z	(C) Area Beyond z	(A) z	(B) Area Between Mean and z	(C) Area Beyond z
0.00	.0000	.5000	2.10	.4821	.0179
0.10	.0398	.4602	2.20	.4861	.0139
0.20	.0793	.4207	2.30	.4893	.0107
0.30	.1179	.3821	2.40	.4918	.0082
0.40	.1554	.3446	2.50	.4938	.0062
0.50	.1915	.3085	2.58	.4951	.0049
0.60	.2257	.2743	2.60	.4953	.0047
0.70	.2580	.2420	2.70	.4965	.0035
0.80	.2881	.2119	2.80	.4974	.0026
0.90	.3159	.1841	2.90	.4981	.0019
1.00	.3413	.1587	3.00	.4987	.0013
1.10	.3643	.1357	3.10	.4990	.0010
1.20	.3849	.1151	3.20	.4993	.0007
1.30	.4032	.0968	3.30	.4995	.0005
1.40	.4192	.0808	3.40	.4997	.0003
1.50	.4332	.0668	3.50	.4998	.0002
1.65	.4505	.0495	3.60	.4998	.0002
1.70	.4554	.0446	3.70	.4999	.0001
1.80	.4641	.0359	3.80	.49993	.00007
1.90	.4713	.0287	3.90	.49995	.00005
1.96	.4750	.0250	4.00	.49997	.00003
2.00	.4772	.0228			

From table II of R. A. Fisher and F. Yates. *Statistical tables for biological, agricultural, and medical research*. London: Longman Group Ltd. (previously published by Oliver & Boyd Ltd., Edinburgh). Reprinted by permission of the authors and publishers.

Chi-Square Distribution

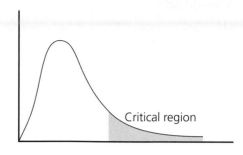

Critical region

The table entries are critical values of χ^2.

Degrees of Freedom (*df*)	Proportion in Critical Region				
	0.10	0.05	0.025	0.01	0.005
1	2.71	3.84	5.02	6.63	7.88
2	4.61	5.99	7.38	9.21	10.60
3	6.25	7.81	9.35	11.34	12.84
4	7.78	9.49	11.14	13.28	14.86
5	9.24	11.07	12.83	15.09	16.75
6	10.64	12.59	14.45	16.81	18.55
7	12.02	14.07	16.01	18.48	20.28
8	13.36	15.51	17.53	20.09	21.96
9	14.68	16.92	19.02	21.67	23.59
10	15.99	18.31	20.48	23.21	25.19
11	17.28	19.68	21.92	24.72	26.76
12	18.55	21.03	23.34	26.22	28.30
13	19.81	22.36	24.74	27.69	29.82
14	21.06	23.68	26.12	29.14	31.32
15	22.31	25.00	27.49	30.58	32.80
16	23.54	26.30	28.85	32.00	34.27
17	24.77	27.59	30.19	33.41	35.72
18	25.99	28.87	31.53	34.81	37.16
19	27.20	30.14	32.85	36.19	38.58
20	28.41	31.41	34.17	37.57	40.00
21	29.62	32.67	35.48	38.93	41.40
22	30.81	33.92	36.78	40.29	42.80
23	32.01	35.17	38.08	41.64	44.18
24	33.20	36.42	39.36	42.98	45.56
25	34.38	37.65	40.65	44.31	46.93
26	35.56	38.89	41.92	45.64	48.29
27	36.74	40.11	43.19	46.96	49.64
28	37.92	41.34	44.46	48.28	50.99
29	39.09	42.56	45.72	49.59	52.34
30	40.26	43.77	46.98	50.89	53.67
40	51.81	55.76	59.34	63.69	66.77
50	63.17	67.50	71.42	76.15	79.49
60	74.40	79.08	83.30	88.38	91.95
70	85.53	90.53	95.02	100.42	104.22
80	96.58	101.88	106.63	112.33	116.32
90	107.56	113.14	118.14	124.12	128.30
100	118.50	124.34	129.56	135.81	140.17

From Table VII (abridged) of R. A. Fisher and F. Yates. *Statistical tables for biological, agricultural, and medical research.* London: Longman Group Ltd. (previously published by Oliver & Boyd Ltd., Edinburgh). Reprinted by permission of the authors and publishers.

Illustration of Statistical Procedures

In this appendix, we illustrate the recommendations made in Chapter Twelve, "Statistics in Perspective." We present a hypothetical example that illustrates each of the three major types of analyses presented in the chapter. We carry out the calculations in detail and then interpret the results.

EXAMPLE I—COMPARING GROUPS: QUANTITATIVE DATA

Imagine that we have two groups of eighth-grade students, 60 in each group, who receive different methods of social studies instruction for one semester. The teacher of one group uses an inquiry method of instruction, while the teacher of the other group uses the lecture method. The researcher's hypothesis is that the inquiry method will result in greater improvement than the lecture method in explaining skills as measured by the "Test of Ability to Explain" (see pp. 161–162) in Chapter Eight. Each student is tested at the beginning and at the end of the semester. The test consists of 40 items; the range of scores on the pretest is from 3 to 32, or 29 points. A gain score (posttest–pretest) is obtained. These gain scores are shown in the frequency distributions in Table D.1 and the frequency polygons in Figure D.1.

These polygons indicate that a comparison of means is appropriate. Why?* The mean of the inquiry group is 5.6 compared to the mean of 4.4 for the lecture group. The difference between means is 1.2. In this instance, a comparison with the means of known groups is not possible, since such data are not available. A calculation of effect size results in an ES of .44, somewhat below the .50 that most researchers recommend for significance. Inspection of Figure D.1, however, suggests that the difference between the means of the two groups should not

*The polygons are nearly symmetrical without extreme scores at either end.

Table D.1 *Gain Scores on Test of Ability to Explain: Inquiry and Lecture Groups*

Gain Scores[a]	Inquiry		Lecture	
	Frequency	Cumulative Frequency	Frequency	Cumulative Frequency
11	1	60	0	60
10	3	59	2	60
9	5	56	3	58
8	7	51	4	55
7	9	44	4	51
6	9	35	7	47
5	6	26	9	40
4	6	20	8	31
3	5	14	7	23
2	4	9	6	16
1	2	5	4	10
0	3	3	5	6
−1	0	0	1	1

[a]A negative score indicates the pretest was higher than the posttest.

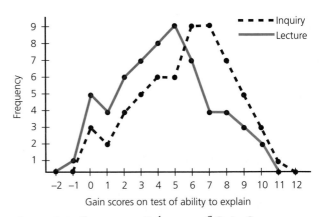

Figure D.1 *Frequency Polygons of Gain Scores on Test of Ability to Explain: Inquiry and Lecture Groups*

A negative score indicates the pretest was higher than the posttest.

Table D.2 *Calculations from Table D.1*

	Inquiry Group					Lecture Group				
Gain Score	f[a]	fX[b]	$X - \bar{X}$[c]	$(X - \bar{X})^2$[d]	$f(X - \bar{X})^2$[e]	Gain Score	f	fX	$X - \bar{X}$	$(X - \bar{X})^2$	$f(X - \bar{X})^2$
11	1	11	5.4	29.2	29.2	11	0	0	6.6	43.6	0.0
10	3	30	4.4	19.4	58.2	10	2	20	5.6	31.4	62.8
9	5	45	3.4	11.6	58.0	9	3	27	4.6	21.2	63.6
8	7	56	2.4	5.8	40.6	8	4	32	3.6	13.0	52.0
7	9	63	1.4	2.0	18.0	7	4	28	2.6	6.8	27.2
6	9	54	0.4	0.2	1.8	6	7	42	1.6	2.6	18.2
5	6	30	−0.6	0.4	2.4	5	9	45	0.6	0.4	3.6
4	6	24	−1.6	2.6	15.6	4	8	32	−0.4	0.2	1.6
3	5	15	−2.6	6.8	34.0	3	7	21	−1.4	2.0	14.0
2	4	8	−3.6	13.0	52.0	2	6	12	−2.4	5.8	34.8
1	2	2	−4.6	21.2	42.4	1	4	4	−3.4	11.6	46.4
0	3	0	−5.6	31.4	94.2	0	5	0	−4.4	19.4	97.0
−1	0	0	−6.6	43.6	0.0	−1	1	−1	−5.4	29.2	29.2
−2	0	0	−7.6	57.8	0.0	−2	0	0	−6.4	41.0	0.0
Total	$\Sigma = 338$				$\Sigma = 446.4$		$\Sigma = 262$				$\Sigma = 450.4$

$$\bar{X}_1 = \frac{\Sigma fX}{n} = \frac{338}{60} = 5.6 \qquad\qquad \bar{X}_2 = \frac{\Sigma fX}{n} = \frac{262}{60} = 4.4$$

$$SD_1 = \sqrt{\frac{f(X - \bar{X})^2}{n}} = \sqrt{\frac{446.4}{60}} = \sqrt{7.4} = 2.7 \qquad SD_2 = \sqrt{\frac{f(X - \bar{X})^2}{n}} = \sqrt{\frac{450.4}{60}} = \sqrt{7.5} = 2.7$$

$$SEM_1 = \frac{SD}{\sqrt{n-1}} = \frac{2.7}{\sqrt{59}} = \frac{2.7}{7.7} = .35 \qquad SEM_2 = \frac{SD}{\sqrt{n-1}} = \frac{2.7}{\sqrt{59}} = \frac{2.7}{7.7} = .35$$

$$SED = \sqrt{(SEM_1)^2 + (SEM_2)^2} = \sqrt{.35^2 + .35^2} = \sqrt{.12 + .12} = \sqrt{.24} = .49$$

$$t = \frac{\bar{X}_1 - \bar{X}_2}{SED} = \frac{1.2}{.49} = 2.45 \qquad p < .05$$

$$ES(\Delta) = \frac{\bar{X}_1 - \bar{X}_2}{SD_2} = \frac{1.2}{2.4} = .44$$

[a]f = frequency
[b]fX = frequency × score
[c]$X - \bar{X}$ = score − mean
[d]$(X - \bar{X})^2$ = (score − mean)^2
[e]$f(X - \bar{X})^2$ = frequency × (score − mean)^2

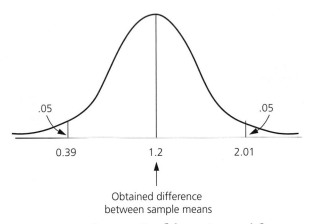

Figure D.2 *90 Percent Confidence Interval for a Difference of 1.2 Between Sample Means*

be discounted. Table D.1 and Figure D.1 show that the number of students gaining 7 or more points is 25 in the inquiry group and 13 (about half as many) in the lecture group. A gain of 7 points on a 40-item test can be considered substantial, even more so when it is recalled that the range was 29 points (3–32) on the pretest. If a gain of 8 points is used, the numbers are 16 in the inquiry group and 9 in the lecture group. If a gain of 6 points is used, the numbers become 34 and 20. We would argue that these discrepancies are large enough, in context, to recommend the inquiry method over the lecture method.

The use of an inference technique (a *t*-test for independent means) indicates that $p < .05$ in one tail (Table D.2).[†] This leads the researcher to conclude that the observed difference between means of 1.2 points probably is not due to the particular samples used. Whether this probability can be taken as exact depends primarily on whether the samples were randomly selected. The 90 percent confidence interval is shown in Figure D.2.[*] Notice that a difference of zero between the population means is not within the confidence interval.

[†]A directional hypothesis indicates use of a one-tailed test (see p. 238).

[*]1.65 SED gives .05 in one tail of the normal curve. 1.65 (SED) = 1.65 (.49) = .81. 1.2 ± .81 equals .39 to 2.01. This is the 90 percent confidence interval. Use of 1.65 rather than 1.96 is justified because the researcher's hypothesis is concerned *only* with a *positive* gain (a one-tailed test). The 95 percent or any other confidence interval could, of course, have been used.

EXAMPLE II—RELATING VARIABLES WITHIN A GROUP: QUANTITATIVE DATA

Suppose a researcher wishes to test the hypothesis that, among counseling clients, improvement in marital satisfaction after six months of counseling is related to self-esteem at the beginning of counseling. In other words, people with higher self-esteem would be expected to show more improvement in marital satisfaction after undergoing therapy for a period of six months than people with lower self-esteem. The researcher obtains a group of 30 clients, each of whom takes a self-esteem inventory and a marital satisfaction inventory prior to counseling. The marital satisfaction inventory is taken again at the end of six months of counseling. The data are shown in Table D.3.

The calculations shown in Table D.3 are not as hard as they look. Here are the steps that we followed to obtain $r = .42$.

1. Multiply n by ΣXY: 30(7023) = 210,690
2. Multiply ΣX by ΣY: (1007)(192) = 193,344
3. Subtract step 2 from step 1: 210,690 − 193,344 = 17,346
4. Multiply n by ΣX^2: 30(35,507) = 1,065,210
5. Square ΣX: $(1007)^2$ = 1,014,049
6. Subtract step 5 from step 4: 1,065,210 − 1,014,049 = 51,161
7. Multiply n by ΣY^2: 30(2354) = 70,620
8. Square ΣY: $(192)^2$ = 36,864
9. Subtract step 8 from step 7: 70,620 − 36,864 = 33,753
10. Multiply step 6 by step 9: (51,161)(33,753) = 1,725,837,233
11. Take the square root of step 10: $\sqrt{1,725,837,233}$ = 41,543
12. Divide step 3 by step 11: 17,346/41,543 = .42

Using the data presented in Table D.3, the researcher plots a scatterplot and finds that it reveals two things. First, there is a tendency for individuals with higher initial self-esteem scores to show greater improvement in marital satisfaction than those with lower initial self-esteem scores. Second, it also shows that the relationship is more correctly described as curvilinear—that is, clients with low *or* high self-esteem show less improvement than those with a moderate level of self-esteem (remember, these data are fictional). Pearson *r* equals .42. The value of eta obtained for these same data is .82, indicating a substantial degree of relationship between

Table D.3 *Self-Esteem Scores and Gains in Marital Satisfaction*

Client	Self-Esteem Score before Counseling (X)	X^2	Gain in Marital Satisfaction after Counseling (Y)	Y^2	XY
1	20	400	−4	16	−80
2	21	441	−2	4	−42
3	22	484	−7	49	−154
4	24	576	1	1	24
5	24	576	4	16	96
6	25	625	5	25	125
7	26	676	−1	1	−26
8	27	729	8	64	216
9	29	841	2	4	58
10	28	784	5	25	140
11	30	900	5	25	150
12	30	900	14	196	420
13	32	1024	7	49	219
14	33	1089	15	225	495
15	35	1225	6	36	210
16	35	1225	16	256	560
17	36	1269	11	121	396
18	37	1396	14	196	518
19	36	1296	18	324	648
20	38	1444	9	81	342
21	39	1527	14	196	546
22	39	1527	15	225	585
23	40	1600	4	16	160
24	41	1681	8	64	328
25	42	1764	0	0	0
26	43	1849	3	9	129
27	43	1849	5	25	215
28	43	1849	8	64	344
29	44	1936	4	16	176
30	45	2025	5	25	225
Total (Σ)	Σ = 1007	Σ = 35,507	Σ = 192	Σ = 2354	Σ = 7023

$$r = \frac{n\Sigma XY - \Sigma X \Sigma Y}{\sqrt{[n\Sigma X^2 - (\Sigma X)^2][n\Sigma Y^2 - (\Sigma Y^2)]}} = \frac{30(7023) - (1007)(192)}{\sqrt{[30(3507) - (1007)^2][30(2354) - (192)^2]}}$$

$$= \frac{210690 - 193344}{\sqrt{(1065210 - 1014049)(70620 - 36864)}} = \frac{17346}{\sqrt{(51161)(33753)}}$$

$$= \frac{17346}{\sqrt{1725837233}} = \frac{17346}{41543} = .42$$

Figure D.3 *Scatterplot Illustrating the Relationship Between Initial Self-Esteem and Gain in Marital Satisfaction Among Counseling Clients*

the two variables. We have not shown the calculations for eta since they are somewhat more complicated than those for *r*. The relationship is illustrated by the smoothed curve shown in Figure D.3.

The researcher calculates the appropriate inference statistic (a *t*-test for *r*), as shown, to determine whether *r* = .42 is significant.

Standard error of $r = \text{SE}_r = \dfrac{1}{\sqrt{n-1}}$

$$= \frac{1}{\sqrt{29}} = .185$$

$$t_r = \frac{r - .00}{\text{SE}_r} = \frac{.42 - .00}{.185}$$

$$= 2.3;\ p < .01$$

As you can see, it results in an obtained value of 2.3 and a probability of $p < .01$, using a one-tailed test. A one-tailed test is appropriate for *r* if the direction of the relationship was predicted before examining the data. The probability associated with eta would (presumably) be obtained using a two-tailed test (unless the researcher predicted the shape of the curve from Figure D.3 before examining the data). An eta of .82 is also statistically significant at $p = .01$, indicating that the relationship is unlikely to be due to the particular sample studied. Whether or not these probabilities are correct depends

on whether or not the sample was randomly selected. The 95 percent confidence interval around the obtained value for *r* is shown in Figure D.4.

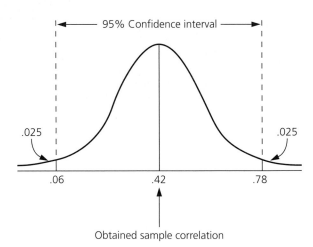

Figure D.4 *95 Percent Confidence Interval for* $r = .42$

EXAMPLE III—COMPARING GROUPS: CATEGORICAL DATA

Let us return to Tables 12.3 and 12.4 in Chapter Twelve to illustrate the major recommendations for analyzing categorical data. We shall consider Table 12.3 first.

Because there are 50 teachers, or 25 percent, of the total of 200 teachers at each grade level (4–7), we would expect that there would be 25 percent of the total number of male teachers and 25 percent of the total number of female teachers at *each* grade level as well. Out of the total of 200 teachers, 80 are male and 120 are female. Hence, the expected frequency for male teachers at each of the grade levels would be 20 (25 percent of 80), and for female teachers 30 (25 percent of 120). These expected frequencies are shown in parentheses in Table D.4. We then calculate the contingency coefficient, which equals .28.

By referring to Table 11.1 in Chapter Eleven, we estimate that the upper limit for a 2 by 4 table (which we have here) is approximately .80. Accordingly, a contingency coefficient of .28 indicates only a slight degree of relationship. As a result, we would not recommend testing for significance. Were we to do so, however, we would find by looking in a chi-square probability table that three degrees of freedom requires a chi-square value of 7.82 to be considered significant at the .05 level. Our obtained value for chi-square was 16.66, indicating that the small relationship we have discovered probably does exist in the population from which the sample was drawn.* This is a good example of the difference between statistical and practical significance. Our obtained correlation of .28 is statistically significant, but practically insignificant. A correlation of .28 would be considered by most researchers as having little practical importance.

If we carry out the same analysis for Table 12.4, the resulting contingency coefficient is .10. Such a correlation is, for all practical purposes, meaningless, but should we (for some reason) wish to see if it was statistically significant, we would find that it is not significant at the .05 level (the chi-square value = 1.98, far below the 7.82 needed for significance).

Table D.4 *Crossbreak Table Showing Teacher Gender and Grade Level with Expected Frequencies Added (Data from Table 12.3)*

	Grade 4	Grade 5	Grade 6	Grade 7	Total
Male	10 (20)	20 (20)	20 (20)	30 (20)	80
Female	40 (30)	30 (30)	30 (30)	20 (30)	120
Total	50	50	50	50	200

*Assuming the sample is random.

Again, the calculations from Table D.4 are not difficult. Here are the steps we followed:

1. For the first cell above (Grade 4-male), subtract E from O: $= 10 - 20 = -10$
2. Square the result: $(O - E)^2 = (-10)^2 = 100$
3. Divide the result by E:

$$\Sigma \frac{(O - E)^2}{E} = \frac{100}{20} = 5.00$$

4. Repeat this process for each cell (Be sure that you include *all* cells.)

O	E	$O - E$	$(O - E)^2$	$\dfrac{(O - E)^2}{E}$	
10	20	−10	100	100/20	= 5.00
40	30	10	100	100/30	= 3.33
20	20	0	0	0	= 0
30	30	0	0	0	= 0
20	20	0	0	0	= 0
30	30	0	0	0	= 0
30	20	10	100	100/20	= 5.00
20	30	−10	100	100/30	= 3.33

5. Add the results of all cells:

$$5.00 + 3.33 + 5.00 + 3.33 = 16.66 = \chi^2$$

6. To calculate the contingency coefficient, we used the formula:

$$C = \sqrt{\frac{\chi^2}{\chi^2 + n}} = \sqrt{\frac{16.66}{16.66 + 200}} = .28$$

EXAMPLE IV—DETERMINING THE STANDARD ERROR OF MEASUREMENT

For many IQ tests, the standard error of measurement over a one-year period and with different specific content is about five points. Over a 10-year period, it is about eight points. This means that a score fluctuates considerably more the longer the time between measurements. Thus, a person scoring 110 can expect to have a score between 100 and 120 one year later; five years later, the score can be expected to be between 94 and 126 (see Figure D.5). Note that we doubled the standard errors of measurement in computing the ranges within which the second score is expected to fall. This was done so we could be 95 percent sure that our reasoning was correct.

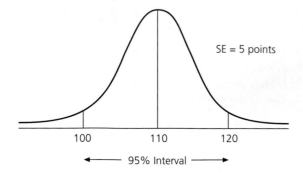

SE = 5 points

100   110   120

◄——— 95% Interval ———►

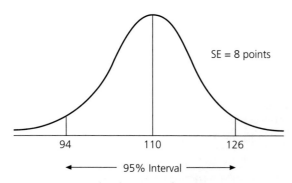

SE = 8 points

94   110   126

◄——— 95% Interval ———►

Figure D.5 *Standard Error of Measurement*

The formula for the standard error of measurement is $SD\sqrt{1 - r_{11}}$ where SD = the standard deviation of scores and r_{11} = the reliability coefficient appropriate to the conditions that vary. In the above example, the standard error (SEMeas) of 5 in the first example was obtained as follows:

$$SD = 16, \; r_{11} = .90$$

$$SEM = 16\sqrt{1 - .90} = 16\sqrt{.10} = 16(.32) = 5.1$$

Glossary

A-B design A single-subject experimental design in which measurements are repeatedly made until stability is presumably established (baseline), after which treatment is introduced and an appropriate number of measurements are made.

A-B-A design Same as the A-B design except a second baseline is added.

A-B-A-B design Same as an A-B-A design, except that a second treatment is added.

A-B-C-B design Same as A-B-A-B design except that the second baseline phase is replaced by a modified treatment phase.

abstract A summary of a study that describes its most important aspects, including major results and conclusions.

accessible population The population from which the researcher can realistically select subjects for a sample, and to which the researcher is entitled to generalize findings.

achievement test An instrument used to measure the proficiency level of individuals in given areas of knowledge or skill.

action plan A plan to implement change as a result of an action research study.

action research A type of research focused on a specific local problem and resulting in an action plan to address the problem.

age-equivalent score A score that indicates the age level for which a particular performance (score) is typical.

alpha coefficient See **Cronbach alpha.**

analysis of covariance (ANCOVA) A statistical technique for equating groups on one or more variables when testing for statistical significance; it adjusts scores on a dependent variable for initial differences on other variables, such as pretest performance or IQ.

analysis of variance (ANOVA) A statistical technique for determining the statistical significance of differences among means; it can be used with two or more groups.

aptitude test An ability test used to predict performance in a future situation.

associational research/study A general type of research in which a researcher looks for relationships having predictive and/or explanatory power. Both correlational and causal-comparative studies are examples.

assumption Any important assertion presumed to be true but not actually verified; major assumptions should be described in one of the first sections of a research proposal or report.

average A number representing the typical score attained by a group of subjects. See **measures of central tendency.**

B-A-B design The same as an A-B-A-B design, except that the initial baseline phase is omitted.

background questions Questions asked by an interviewer or on a questionnaire to obtain information about a respondent's background (age, occupation, etc.).

bar graph A graphic way of illustrating differences.

baseline The graphic record of measurements taken prior to introducing an intervention in a time-series design.

behavior questions See **experience questions.**

bias See **researcher bias.**

biography/biographical study A form of qualitative research in which the researcher works with the individual to clarify important life experiences.

case study A form of qualitative research in which a single individual or example is studied through extensive data collection.

categorical data/variables Data (variables) that differ only in kind, not in amount or degree.

causal-comparative research Research to explore the cause for, or consequences of, existing differences in groups of individuals; also referred to as ex post facto research.

census An attempt to acquire data from every member of a population.

Chaos theory A theory and methodology of science that emphasizes the rarity of general laws, the need for very large data bases, and the importance of studying exceptions to overall patterns.

chi square (χ^2) A nonparametric test of statistical significance appropriate when the data are in the form of frequency counts; it compares frequencies actually observed in a study with expected frequencies to see whether they are significantly different.

closed-ended question A question and a list of alternative responses from which the respondent selects; also referred to as a closed-form item.

cluster sampling/cluster random sampling The selection of groups of individuals, called clusters, rather than single individuals. All individuals in a cluster are included in the sample; the clusters are preferably selected randomly from the larger population of clusters.

coding The specification of categories in content analysis research. It may be done ahead of time or emerge from familiarity with the raw data.

coefficient of determination (r^2) The square of the correlation coefficient. It indicates the proportion of variance common to two variables.

cohort study A design (in survey research) in which a particular population is studied over time by taking different random samples at various points in time. The population remains conceptually the same, but individuals change (for example, graduates of San Francisco State University surveyed 10, 20, and 30 years after graduation).

collective case study One that studies multiple cases at the same time.

comparison group The group in a research study that receives a different treatment from that of the experimental group.

concurrent validity (evidence of) The degree to which the scores on an instrument are related to the scores on another instrument administered at the same time, or to some other criterion available at the same time.

confidence interval An interval used to estimate a parameter that is constructed in such a way that the interval has a predetermined probability of including the parameter.

confirming sample In qualitative research, a sample selected to validate or extend previous findings.

constant A characteristic that has the same value for all individuals.

constitutive definition The explanation of the meaning of a term by using other words to describe what is meant.

construct-related validity (evidence of) The degree to which an instrument measures an intended hypothetical psychological construct, or nonobservable trait.

content analysis A method of studying human behavior indirectly by analyzing communications, usually through a process of categorization.

content-related validity (evidence of) The degree to which an instrument logically appears to measure an intended variable; it is determined by expert judgment.

contextualization Placing information/data into a larger perspective, especially in ethnography.

contingency coefficient An index of relationship derived from a crossbreak table.

contingency question A question whose answer depends on the answer to a prior question.

contingency table See **crossbreak table.**

control Efforts on the part of the researcher to remove the effects of any variable other than the independent variable that might affect performance on a dependent variable.

control group The group in a research study that is treated "as usual."

convenience sample A sample that is easily accessible.

correlation coefficient (r) A decimal number between .00 and ±1.00 that indicates the degree to which two quantitative variables are related.

correlational research Research that involves collecting data in order to determine the degree to which a relationship exists between two or more variables.

counterbalanced design An experimental design in which all groups receive all treatments. Each group receives the treatments in a different order, and all groups are posttested after each treatment.

criterion variable The variable that is predicted in a prediction study; also any variable used to assess the criterion-related validity of an instrument.

criterion-referenced instrument An instrument that specifies a particular goal, or criterion, for students to achieve.

criterion-related validity (evidence of) The degree to which performance on an instrument is related to performance on other instruments intended to measure the same variable, or to other variables logically related to the variable being measured.

critical researchers Researchers who raise philosophical and ethical questions about the way educational research is conducted.

critical sample In qualitative research, a sample considered to be enlightening because it is unusual.

Cronbach alpha (α) An internal consistency or reliability coefficient for an instrument requiring only one test administration.

crossbreak table A table that shows all combinations of two or more categorical variables and portrays the relationship (if any) between the variables.

cross-sectional survey A survey in which data are collected at one point in time from a predetermined population or populations.

cross-validation Validation of a prediction equation with at least one group other than the group on which it was based.

crystallization Occasions, especially in ethnography, when different kinds of data "fall into place" to make a coherent picture.

culture The sum of a social group's observable patterns of behavior and/or their customs, beliefs, and knowledge.

curvilinear relationship A relationship shown in a scatterplot in which the line that best fits the points is not straight.

data Any information obtained about a sample or a population.

data analysis The process of simplifying data in order to make it comprehensible.

data-collector bias Unintentional bias on the part of data collectors that may create a threat to the internal validity of a study.

degrees of freedom A number indicating how many instances out of a given number of instances are "free to vary"—that is, not predetermined.

demographic questions See **background questions.**

demographics Characteristics of a sample or population (e.g., age, ethnicity, education).

dependent variable A variable affected or expected to be affected by the independent variable; also called "criterion" or "outcome variable."

derived score A score obtained from a raw score in order to aid in interpretation. Derived scores provide a quantitative measure of each student's performance relative to a comparison group.

descriptive field notes The researchers' attempt to record what they observe completely and objectively.

descriptive research/study Research to describe existing conditions without analyzing relationships among variables.

descriptive statistics Data analysis techniques enabling the researcher to meaningfully describe data with numerical indices or in graphic form.

descriptors Terms used to locate sources during a computer search of the literature.

design See **research design.**

directional hypothesis A relational hypothesis stated in such a manner that a direction, often indicated by "greater than" or "less than," is hypothesized for the results.

discriminant function analysis A statistical procedure for predicting group membership (a categorical variable) from two or more quantitative variables.

discussion (of a study) A review of the results including limitations of a study, placing the findings in a broader perspective.

distribution/distribution curves The real or theoretical frequency distribution of a set of scores.

document Any written or printed material.

ecological generalizability The degree to which results can be generalized to environments and conditions outside the research setting.

effect size (ES) An index used to indicate the magnitude of an obtained result or relationship.

emic perspective The view of reality of a cultural "insider," especially in ethnography.

empirical Based on observable evidence.

equivalent forms Two tests identical in every way except for the actual items included.

equivalent-forms method A method to obtain a reliability coefficient; a way of checking consistency by correlating scores on equivalent forms of an instrument. It is also referred to as alternate-forms reliability.

errors of measurement Inconsistency of individual scores on the same instrument.

eta (η) An index that indicates the degree of a curvilinear relationship.

ethnography/ethnographic research The collection of data on many variables over an extended period of time in a naturalistic setting, usually using observation and interviews.

etic perspective The "outsider" or "objective" view of a culture's reality, especially in ethnography.

experience questions Questions a researcher asks to find out what sorts of things an individual is doing or has done.

experiment A research study in which one or more independent variables is/are systematically varied by the researcher to determine the effects of this variation.

experimental group The group in a research study that receives the treatment (or method) of special interest in the study.

experimental research Research in which at least one independent variable is manipulated, other relevant variables are controlled, and the effect on one or more dependent variables is observed.

experimental variable The variable that is manipulated (systematically altered) in an intervention study by the researcher.

explanatory mixed method design A study in which quantitative data are collected first and further clarified with qualitative data.

exploratory mixed method design A study in which qualitative data are collected first and findings tested with subsequent quantitative data.

external audit An individual outside the study is asked to review the methods and interpretations of a qualitative study.

external criticism Evaluation of the genuineness of a document in historical research.

external validity The degree to which results are generalizable, or applicable, to groups and environments outside the research setting.

extraneous event(s) See **history threat.**

extraneous variable A variable that makes possible an alternative explanation of results; an uncontrolled variable.

factor analysis A statistical method for reducing a set of variables to a smaller number of factors.

factorial design An experimental design that involves two or more independent variables (at least one of which is manipulated) in order to study the effects of the variables individually, and in interaction with each other, upon a dependent variable.

feelings questions Questions researchers ask to find out how people feel about things.

field diary A personal statement of a researcher's opinions about people and events he or she comes in contact with during research.

field jottings Quick notes taken by an ethnographer.

field log A running account of how an ethnographer plans to, and actually does, spend his or her time in the field.

field notes The notes researchers take about what they observe and think about in the field.

findings See **results (of a study).**

focus group interview An interview conducted with a group in which respondents hear the views of each other.

follow-up study A study conducted to determine the characteristics of a group after some period of time.

foreshadowed problems The problem or topic that serves, in a general way, as the focus for a qualitative inquiry.

frequency distribution A tabular method of showing all of the scores obtained by a group of individuals.

frequency polygon A graphic method of showing all of the scores obtained by a group of individuals.

Friedman two-way analysis of variance A nonparametric inferential statistic used to compare two or more groups that are not independent.

gain score The difference between the pretest and posttest scores of a measure.

general references Sources that researchers use to identify more specific references (e.g., indexes, abstracts).

generalizing See **ecological generalizability; population generalizability.**

grade equivalent score A score that indicates the grade level for which a particular performance (score) is typical.

grounded theory A form of qualitative research that derives interpretations inductively from raw data with continual interplay between data and emerging interpretations.

Hawthorne effect A positive effect of an intervention resulting from the subjects' knowledge that they are involved in a study or their feeling that they are in some way receiving "special" attention.

histogram A graphic representation, consisting of rectangles, of the scores in a distribution; the height of each rectangle indicates the frequency of each score, or group of scores.

historical research The systematic collection and objective evaluation of data related to past occurrences to examine causes, effects, or trends of those events that may help explain present events and anticipate future events.

history threat The possibility that results are due to an event that is not part of an intervention, but which may affect performance on the dependent variable, thereby affecting internal validity.

holistic perspective The attempt to incorporate all aspects of a culture into an ethnographic interpretation.

homogeneous sample In qualitative research, a sample selected in which all members are similar with respect to one or more characteristics.

hypothesis A tentative, testable assertion regarding the occurrence of certain behaviors, phenomena, or events; a prediction of study outcomes.

implementation threat The possibility that results are due to variations in the implementation of the treatment in an intervention study, thereby affecting internal validity.

independent variable A variable that affects (or is presumed to affect) the dependent variable under study and is included in the research design so that its effect can be determined; sometimes called the "experimental" or "treatment" variable.

inferential statistics Data analysis techniques for determining how likely it is that results based on a sample or samples are similar to results that would have been obtained for the entire population.

informal interviews Less-structured forms of interview, usually conducted by qualitative researchers. They do not involve any specific type or sequence of questioning, but resemble more the give and take of a casual conversation.

instrument Any device for systematically collecting data, such as a test, a questionnaire, or an interview schedule.

instrument decay Changes in instrumentation over time that may affect the internal validity of a study.

instrumental case study One that focuses on a particular individual or situation with little effort to generalize.

instrumentation Instruments and procedures used in collecting data in a study.

instrumentation threat The possibility that results are due to variations in the way data are collected, thereby affecting internal validity.

interaction An effect created by unique combinations of two or more independent variables; systematically evaluated in a factorial design.

interjudge reliability The consistency of two (or more) independent scorers, raters, or observers.

internal-consistency methods Procedures for estimating reliability of scores using only one administration of the instrument.

internal criticism Determining whether the contents of a document are accurate.

internal validity The degree to which observed differences on the dependent variable are directly related to the independent variable, not to some other (uncontrolled) variable.

interval scale A measurement scale that, in addition to ordering scores from high to low, also establishes a uniform unit in the scale so that any equal distance between two scores is of equal magnitude.

intervening variable A variable that intervenes, or changes the relationship, between an independent variable and a dependent variable.

intervention A specified treatment or method that is intended to modify one or more dependent variables.

intervention study/research A general type of research in which variables are manipulated in order to study the effect on one or more dependent variables.

interview A form of data collection in which individuals or groups are questioned orally.

intrinsic case study One that attempts to generalize beyond the particular case.

item validity The degree to which each of the items in an instrument measures the intended variable.

justification (of a study) A rationale statement in which a researcher indicates why the study is important to conduct; includes implications for theory and/or practice.

key actors See **key informants.**

key informants Individuals identified as expert sources of information, especially in qualitative research.

knowledge questions Questions interviewers ask to find out what factual information a respondent possesses about a particular topic.

Kruskal-Wallis one-way analysis of variance A nonparametric inferential statistic used to compare two or more independent groups for statistical significance of differences.

Kuder-Richardson approaches Procedures for determining an estimate of the internal consistency reliability of a test or other instrument from a single administration of the test without splitting the test into halves.

latent content The underlying meaning of a communication.

level of confidence The probability associated with a confidence interval; the probability that the interval will contain the corresponding parameter. Commonly used confidence levels in educational research are the 95 and 99 percent confidence levels.

level of significance The probability that a discrepancy between a sample statistic and a specified population parameter is due to sampling error, or chance. Commonly used significance levels in educational research are .05 and .01.

Likert scale A self-reporting instrument in which an individual responds to a series of statements by indicating the extent of agreement. Each choice is given a numerical value, and the total score is presumed to indicate the attitude or belief in question.

limitation An aspect of a study that the researcher knows may influence the results or generalizability of the results, but over which he or she has no control.

linear relationship A relationship in which an increase (or decrease) in one variable is associated with a corresponding increase (or decrease) in another variable.

literature review The systematic identification, location, and analysis of documents containing information related to a research problem.

location threat The possibility that results are due to characteristics of the setting or location in which a study is conducted, thereby producing a threat to internal validity.

longitudinal survey A study in which information is collected at different points in time in order to study changes over time (usually of considerable length, such as several months or years).

manifest content The obvious meaning of a communication.

manipulated variable See **experimental variable.**

Mann-Whitney U test A nonparametric inferential statistic used to determine whether two uncorrelated groups differ significantly.

matching design A technique for equating groups on one or more variables, resulting in each member of one group having a direct counterpart in another group.

maturation threat The possibility that results are due to changes that occur in subjects as a direct result of the passage of time and that may affect their performance on the dependent variable, thereby affecting internal validity.

maximal variation sample In qualitative research, a sample selected in order to represent diversity in one or more characteristics.

mean/arithmetic mean ($\bar{X}$) The sum of the scores in a distribution divided by the number of scores in the distribution; the most commonly used measure of central tendency.

measures of central tendency Indices representing the average or typical score attained by a group of subjects; the most commonly used in educational research are the *mean* and the *median.*

measures of variability Indices indicating how spread out the scores are in a distribution. Those most commonly used in educational research are the *range, standard deviation,* and *variance.*

mechanical matching A process of pairing two persons whose scores on one or more variables are similar.

median That point in a distribution having 50 percent of the scores above it and 50 percent of the scores below it.

member checking Participants in a qualitative study are asked to check the accuracy of the research report.

meta-analysis A statistical procedure for combining the results of several studies on the same topic.

mixed method design A study combining quantitative and qualitative methods.

mode The score that occurs most frequently in a distribution of scores.

moderator variable A variable that may or may not be controlled but has an effect on the research situation.

mortality threat The possibility that results are due to the fact that subjects who are for whatever reason "lost" to a study may differ from those who remain so that their absence has an important effect on the results of the study.

multiple-baseline design A single-subject experimental design in which baseline data are collected on several behaviors for one subject, after which the treatment is applied sequentially over a period of time to each behavior one at a time until all behaviors are under treatment. Also used to collect data on different subjects with regard to a single behavior, or to assess a subject's behavior in different settings.

multiple correlation (R) A numerical index describing the relationship between predicted and actual scores using multiple regression. The correlation between a criterion and the "best combination" of predictors.

multiple perspectives The recognition and acceptance of multiple views of reality, especially in ethnography.

multiple regression A technique using a prediction equation with two or more variables in combination to predict a criterion ($y = a + b_1 X_1 + b_2 X_2 + b_3 X_3 \ldots$).

multiple-treatment interference The carryover or delayed effects of prior experimental treatments when individuals receive two or more experimental treatments in succession.

multivariate analysis of covariance (MANCOVA) An extension of analysis of covariance that incorporates two or more dependent variables in the same analysis.

multivariate analysis of variance (MANOVA) An extension of analysis of variance that incorporates two or more dependent variables in the same analysis.

naturalistic observation Observation in which the observer controls or manipulates nothing, and tries not to affect the observed situation in any way.

negatively skewed distribution A distribution in which there are more extreme scores at the lower end than at the upper, or higher, end.

nominal scale A measurement scale that classifies elements into two or more categories, the numbers indicating that the elements are different, but not according to order or magnitude.

nondirectional hypothesis A prediction that a relationship exists without specifying its exact nature.

nonequivalent control group design An experimental design involving at least two groups, both of which may be pretested; one group receives the experimental treatment, and both groups are posttested. Individuals are not randomly assigned to treatments.

nonparametric technique A test of statistical significance appropriate when the data represent an ordinal or nominal scale, or when assumptions required for parametric tests cannot be met.

nonparticipant observation Observation in which the observer is not directly involved in the situation to be observed.

nonrandom sample/sampling The selection of a sample in which every member of the population does *not* have an equal chance of being selected.

norm group The sample group used to develop norms for an instrument.

normal curve A graphic illustration of a normal distribution. See **normal distribution.**

normal distribution A theoretical "bell-shaped" distribution having a wide application to both descriptive and inferential statistics. It is known or thought to portray many human characteristics in "typical" populations.

norm-referenced instrument An instrument that permits comparison of an individual score to the scores of a group of individuals on that same instrument.

norms Descriptive statistics that summarize the test performance of a reference group of individuals and permit meaningful comparison of individuals to the group.

null hypothesis A statement that any difference between obtained sample statistics and specified population parameters is due to sampling error, or "chance."

objectivity A lack of bias or prejudice.

observational data Data obtained through direct observation.

observer bias The possibility that an observer does not observe objectively and accurately, thus producing invalid observations and a threat to the internal validity of a study.

observer effect The impact of an observer's presence on the behavior observed.

observer expectations The effect that an observer's prior information can have on observational data.

one-group pretest-posttest design A weak experimental design involving one group that is pretested, exposed to a treatment, then posttested.

one-shot case study design A weak experimental design involving one group that is exposed to a treatment and then posttested.

one-tailed test (of statistical significance) The use of only one tail of the sampling distribution of a statistic—used when a directional hypothesis is stated.

open-ended question A question giving the responder complete freedom of response.

operational definition Defining a term by stating the actions, processes, or operations used to measure or identify examples of it.

opinion questions Questions a researcher asks to find out what people think about a topic.

opportunistic sample In qualitative research, a sample chosen to take advantage of conditions that arise during a study.

ordinal scale A measurement scale that ranks individuals in terms of the degree to which they possess a characteristic of interest.

outcome variable See **dependent variable.**

outlier Score or other observation that deviates or falls considerably outside most of the other scores or observations in a distribution or pattern.

panel study A longitudinal design (in survey research) in which the same random sample is measured at different points in time.

parameter A numerical index describing a characteristic of a population.

parametric technique A test of significance appropriate when the data represent an interval or ratio scale of measurement and other specific assumptions have been met.

partial correlation A method of controlling the subject characteristics threat in correlational research by statistically holding one or more variables constant.

participant observation Observation in which the observer actually becomes a participant in the situation to be observed.

participants Individuals whose involvement in a study can range from providing data to initiating and designing the study.

participatory action research Action research intended not only to address a local problem but also to empower individuals and to bring about social change.

path analysis A type of sophisticated analysis investigating causal connections among correlated variables.

Pearson r An index of correlation appropriate when the data represent either interval or ratio scales; it takes into account each pair of scores and produces a coefficient between 0.00 and either $\pm$ 1.00.

percentile rank An index of relative position indicating the percentage of scores that fall at or below a given score.

phenomenology/phenomenological research A form of qualitative research in which the researcher attempts to identify commonalities in the perceptions of several individuals regarding a particular phenomenon.

pie chart A graphic method of displaying the breakdown of data into categories.

pilot study A small-scale study administered before conducting an actual study—its purpose is to reveal defects in the research plan.

population The group to which the researcher would like the results of a study to be generalizable; it includes *all* individuals with certain specified characteristics.

population generalizability The extent to which the results obtained from a sample are generalizable to a larger group.

portraiture A form of qualitative research in which the researcher and the individual being portrayed work together to define meaning.

positively skewed distribution A distribution in which there are more extreme scores at the upper, or higher, end than at the lower end.

positivism A philosophic viewpoint emphasizing an "objective" reality that includes universal laws governing all things including human behavior.

posttest-only control group design An experimental design involving at least two randomly formed groups; one group receives a treatment, and both groups are posttested.

power of a statistical test The probability that the null hypothesis will be rejected when there is a difference in the populations; the ability of a test to avoid a Type II error.

practical action research Action research intended to address a specific local problem.

practical significance A difference large enough to have some practical effect. Contrast with **statistical significance,** which may be so small as to have no practical consequences.

prediction The estimation of scores on one variable from information about one or more other variables.

prediction equation A mathematical equation used in a prediction study.

prediction study An attempt to determine variables that are related to a criterion variable.

predictive validity (evidence of) The degree to which scores on an instrument predict characteristics of individuals in a future situation.

predictor variable(s) The variable(s) from which projections are made in a prediction study.

pretest-posttest control group design An experimental design that involves at least two groups; both groups are pretested, one group receives a treatment, and both groups are posttested. For effective control of extraneous variables, the groups should be randomly formed.

pretest-treatment interaction The possibility that subjects may respond or react differently to a treatment because they have been pretested, thereby creating a threat to internal validity.

primary source Firsthand information, such as the testimony of an eyewitness, an original document, a relic, or a description of a study written by the person who conducted it.

probability The relative frequency with which a particular event occurs among all events of interest.

problem statement A statement that indicates the specific purpose of the research, the variables of interest to the researcher, and any specific relationship between those variables that is to be, or was, investigated; includes description of background and rationale (justification) for the study.

procedures A detailed description by the researcher of what was (or will be) done in carrying out a study.

projective device An instrument that includes vague stimuli that subjects are asked to interpret. There are no correct answers or replies.

purpose (of a study) A specific statement by a researcher of what he or she intends to accomplish.

purposive sample A nonrandom sample selected because prior knowledge suggests it is representative, or because those selected have the needed information.

qualitative research/study Research in which the investigator attempts to study naturally occurring phenomena in all their complexity.

qualitative variable A variable that is conceptualized and analyzed as distinct categories, with no continuum implied.

quantitative data Data that differ in amount or degree, along a continuum from less to more.

quantitative research Research in which the investigator attempts to clarify phenomena through carefully designed and controlled data collection and analysis.

quantitative variable A variable that is conceptualized and analyzed along a continuum. It differs in amount or degree.

quasi-experimental design A type of experimental design in which the researcher does not use random assignment of subjects to groups.

random assignment The process of assigning individuals or groups randomly to different treatment conditions.

random numbers, table of A table of numbers that provides the best means of random selection or random assignment.

random sample A sample selected in such a way that every member of the population has an equal chance of being selected.

random selection sampling The process of selecting a random sample.

range The difference between the highest and lowest scores in a distribution; measure of variability.

ratio scale A measurement scale that, in addition to being an interval scale, also has an absolute zero in the scale.

raw score The score attained by an individual on the items on a test or other instrument.

reflective field notes A record of the observer's thoughts and reflections during and after observation.

regressed gain score A score indicating amount of change that is determined by the correlation between scores on a posttest and a pretest (and/or other scores). It provides more stable information than a simple posttest-pretest difference.

regression line The line of best fit for a set of scores plotted on coordinate axes (on a scatterplot).

regression threat The possibility that results are due to a tendency for groups, selected on the basis of extreme scores, to regress toward a more average score on subsequent measurements, regardless of the experimental treatment.

relationship study A study investigating relationships among two or more variables, one of which may be a treatment (method) variable.

reliability The degree to which scores obtained with an instrument are consistent measures of whatever the instrument measures.

reliability coefficient An index of the consistency of scores on the same instrument. There are several methods of computing a reliability coefficient, depending on the type of consistency and characteristics of the instrument.

relic Any object whose physical characteristics provide information about the past.

replication Refers to conducting a study again; the second study may be a repetition of the original study, using different subjects, or may change specified aspects of the study.

representativeness The extent to which a sample is identical (in all characteristics) to the intended population.

research The formal, systematic application of scholarship, disciplined inquiry, and most often the scientific method to the study of problems.

research bias See **threat to internal validity.**

research design The overall plan for collecting data in order to answer the research question. Also the specific data analysis techniques or methods that the researcher intends to use.

research hypothesis A prediction of study outcomes. Often a statement of the expected relationship between two or more variables.

research proposal A detailed description of a proposed study designed to investigate a given problem.

research report A description of how a study was conducted, including results and conclusions.

researcher bias A situation in which the researcher's hopes or expectations concerning the outcomes of the study actually contribute to producing various outcomes, thereby creating a threat to internal validity.

results (of a study) A statement that explains what is shown by analysis of the data collected; includes tables and graphs when appropriate.

retrospective interview A form of interview in which the researcher tries to get a respondent to reconstruct past experiences.

sample The group on which information is obtained.

sampling The process of selecting a number of individuals (a sample) from a population, preferably in such a way that the individuals are representative of the larger group from which they were selected.

sampling distribution The theoretical distribution of all possible values of a statistic from all possible samples of a given size selected from a population.

sampling error Expected, chance variation in sample statistics that occurs when successive samples are selected from a population.

sampling interval The distance in a list between individuals chosen when sampling systematically.

sampling ratio The proportion of individuals in the population that are selected for the sample in systematic sampling.

scatterplot The plot of points determined by the cross-tabulation of scores on coordinate axes; used to represent and illustrate the relationship between two quantitative variables.

scientific method A way of knowing that is characterized by the public nature of its procedures and conclusions and by rigorous testing of conclusions.

search terms See **descriptors.**

secondary source Secondhand information, such as a description of historical events by someone not present when the event occurred.

semistructured interview A structured interview, combined with open-ended questions.

sensory questions Questions asked by a researcher to find out what a person has seen, heard, or experienced through his or her senses.

sign test A nonparametric inferential statistic used to compare two groups that are not independent.

simple random sample See **random sample.**

simulation Research in which an "artificial" situation is created and participants are told what activities they are to engage in.

single-subject design Design applied when the sample size is one; used to study the behavior change that an individual exhibits as a result of some intervention or treatment.

skewed distribution A nonsymmetrical distribution in which there are more extreme scores at one end of the distribution than the other.

snowball sample In qualitative research, a sample selected as the need arises during a study.

Solomon four-group design An experimental design that involves random assignment of subjects to each of four groups. Two groups are pretested, two are not, one of the pretested groups and one of the unpretested groups receive the experimental treatment, and all four groups are posttested.

split-half procedure A method of estimating the internal-consistency reliability of an instrument; it is obtained by giving an instrument once but scoring it twice—for each of two equivalent "half tests." These scores are then correlated.

spreads Measures of variability.

stability (of scores) The extent to which scores are reliable (consistent) over time.

stakeholders Those who have a vested interest in the outcomes of a study.

standard deviation (SD) The most stable measure of variability; it takes into account each and every score in a distribution.

standard error of the difference (SED) The standard deviation of a distribution of differences between sample means.

standard error of estimate An estimate of the size of the error to be expected in predicting a criterion score.

standard error of the mean (SEM) The standard deviation of sample means that indicates by how much the sample means can be expected to differ if other samples from the same population are used.

standard error of measurement (SEMeas) An estimate of the size of the error that one can expect in an individual's score.

standard error of a statistic The standard deviation of the sampling distribution of a statistic.

standard score A derived score that expresses how far a given raw score is from the mean, in terms of standard deviation units.

static-group comparison design A weak experimental design that involves at least two nonequivalent groups; one receives a treatment and both are posttested.

static-group pretest-posttest design The same as the static-group comparison design, except that both groups are pretested.

statistic A numerical index describing a characteristic of a sample.

statistical equating See **statistical matching.**

statistical matching A means of equating groups using statistical prediction.

statistical regression threat See **regression threat.**

statistically significant The conclusion that results are unlikely to have occurred due to sampling error or "chance"; an observed correlation or difference probably exists in the population.

stratified random sampling The process of selecting a sample in such a way that identified subgroups in the population are represented in the sample in the same proportion as they exist in the population.

structured interview A formal type of interview, in which the researcher asks, in order, a set of predetermined questions.

subject characteristics threat The possibility that characteristics of the subjects in a study may account for observed relationships, thereby producing a threat to internal validity.

subjects Individuals whose participation in a study is limited to providing information.

survey study/research An attempt to obtain data from members of a population (or a sample) to determine the current status of that population with respect to one or more variables.

systematic sampling A selection procedure in which all sample elements are determined after the selection of the first element, since each element on a selected list is separated from the first element by a multiple of the selection interval. Example: every tenth element may be selected.

T **score** A standard score derived from a *z* score by multiplying the *z* score by 10 and adding 50.

t-**test for correlated means** A parametric test of statistical significance used to determine whether there is a statistically significant difference between the means of two matched, or nonindependent, samples. It is also used for pre-post comparisons.

t-**test for independent means** A parametric test of significance used to determine whether there is a statistically significant difference between the means of two independent samples.

t-**test for correlated proportions** A parametric test of statistical significance used to determine whether there is a statistically significant difference between two proportions based on the same sample or otherwise nonindependent groups.

t-**test for independent proportions** A parametric test of statistical significance used to determine whether there is a statistically significant difference between two independent proportions.

target population The population to which the researcher, ideally, would like to generalize results.

test of significance A statistical test used to determine whether or not the obtained results for a sample are likely to represent the population.

testing threat A threat to internal validity that refers to improved scores on a posttest that are a result of subjects having taken a pretest.

test-retest method A procedure for determining the extent to which scores from an instrument are reliable over time by correlating the scores from two administrations of the same instrument to the same individuals.

theme A means of organizing and interpreting data in a content analysis by grouping codes as the interpretation progresses.

theoretical sample In qualitative research, a sample that helps the researcher understand or formulate a concept or interpretation.

thick description In ethnography, the provision of great detail on the basic data/information.

threat to internal validity An alternative explanation for research results, that is, that an observed relationship is an artifact of another variable.

time-series design An experimental design involving one group that is repeatedly pretested, exposed to an experimental treatment, and repeatedly posttested.

treatment variable See **experimental variable.**

trend study A longitudinal design (in survey research) in which the same population (conceptually but not literally) is studied over time by taking different random samples.

triangulation Cross-checking of data using multiple data sources or multiple data-collection procedures.

triangulation mixed method design A study in which quantitative and qualitative data are collected simultaneously and used to validate and clarify findings.

two-tailed test (of statistical significance) Use of both tails of a sampling distribution of a statistic—when a nondirectional hypothesis is stated.

Type I error The rejection by the researcher of a null hypothesis that is actually true. Also called *alpha error.*

Type II error The failure of a researcher to reject a null hypothesis that is really false. Also called *beta error.*

typical sample In qualitative research, a sample judged to be representative of the population of interest.

unit of analysis The unit that is used in data analysis (individuals, objects, groups, classrooms, etc.).

unobtrusive measures Measures obtained without subjects being aware that they are being observed or measured, or by examining inanimate objects (such as school suspension lists) that can be used in order to obtain desired information.

validity The degree to which correct inferences can be made based on results from an instrument; depends not only on the instrument itself, but also on the instrumentation process and the characteristics of the group studied.

validity coefficient An index of the validity of scores; a special application of the correlation coefficient.

values questions See *opinion questions.*

variability The extent to which scores differ from one another.

variable A characteristic that can assume any one of several values, for example, cognitive ability, height, aptitude, teaching method.

variance (SD)² The square of the standard deviation; a measure of variability.

Wilk's lambda The numerical index calculated when carrying out MANOVA or MANCOVA.

z score The most basic standard score that expresses how far a score is from a mean in terms of standard deviation units.

Index